THE ROYAL HORTICULTURAL SOCIETY

# VEGETABLE & FRUIT GARDENING

MICHAEL POLLOCK  EDITOR-IN-CHIEF

LONDON, NEW YORK, MUNICH, MELBOURNE, DELHI

## CONTRIBUTORS

| | |
|---|---|
| Jim Arbury | Tree Fruits, Grape Vines |
| Guy Barter | Vegetables, Crops |
| John Edgeley | Soft Fruits |
| Jim England | Vegetables, General and Crops |
| Michael Pollock | Growing Fruit and Vegetables, Culinary Herbs |

Revised Edition, 2012

### DK LONDON
Project editor  Caroline Reed
Project art editor  Elaine Hewson
Senior editor  Helen Fewster
Senior art editor  Joanne Doran
Jacket designer  Nicola Powling
Production editor  Sean Daly
Production controller  Claire Pearson
Managing editor  Esther Ripley
Managing art editor  Alison Donovan
Art director  Peter Luff
Publisher  Mary Ling

### DK INDIA
Editors  Kanarindhana Kathirvel, Nidhilekha Mathur
Assistant editor  Neha Ruth Samuel
Senior art editor  Balwant Singh
Senior DTP designer  Pushpak Tyagi
Managing editor  Glenda Fernandes
Managing art editor  Navidita Thapa
CTS manager  Sunil Sharma

### ROYAL HORTICULTURAL SOCIETY
Publisher  Rae Spencer-Jones
Editor  Simon Maughan

First Edition, 2002
Senior editor  Annelise Evans
Project art editor  Murdo Culver
Photographer  Peter Anderson

First published in Great Britain in 2002
by Dorling Kindersley Limited, London.

This revised edition published in 2012,
in association with the Royal Horticultural Society, by
Dorling Kindersley Limited, 80 Strand, London WC2R 0RL
A Penguin Company

2 4 6 8 10 9 7 5 3 1

001 – 183558 – February 2012
Copyright © 2002, 2008, 2012
Dorling Kindersley Limited, London

A CIP catalogue record for this book
is available from the British Library
ISBN 978 1 4053 9442 0

Printed and bound by Hung Hing, China

To find out more about RHS membership, visit
our website www.rhs.org.uk or call 0845 062 1111

Discover more at
**www.dk.com**

# CONTENTS

## The gardening year

Throughout this book, the gardening year is assumed to consist of 12 seasons, or part-seasons. These correspond to calendar months, as shown below.

| | |
|---|---|
| early spring: March | early autumn: September |
| mid-spring: April | mid-autumn: October |
| late spring: May | late autumn: November |
| early summer: June | early winter: December |
| midsummer: July | midwinter: January |
| late summer: August | late winter: February |

### ☥ RHS Award of Garden Merit (AGM)

The AGM is intended as a guide for the gardener, indicating plants that are excellent for garden use, easy to grow, reliably healthy and reasonably resistant to pests and diseases, and with outstanding ornamental or productive qualities.

# INTRODUCTION

Growing your own vegetables, culinary herbs, and fruit brings a very special satisfaction to gardening. There are of course substantial savings to be made in turning a small investment on seed or plants into a regular supply of food for the table, whether you grow only a selection of choice seasonal crops, such as asparagus, or strive for self-sufficiency. For those concerned about additives in commercially produced food, there is the security of knowing exactly how your produce has been grown. The exceptional pleasure of kitchen gardening lies however in the subtlety and freshness of flavour of crops gathered straight from your garden – a flavour that has not been diminished by long transport, storage, or special packaging.

**Fruits of your labours**
*Enjoy the intensity and subtlety of flavour that is possible only with produce freshly picked from the plant.*

The decorative qualities of edible crops, whether grown in a dedicated plot or among conventional ornamental plants, are too little appreciated. Colourful blossom smothers fruit trees in spring, handsome foliage such as the ferny fronds of carrots or crinkly leaves of lettuces adorn the summer garden, and evergreen herbs and overwintering vegetables are enhanced by frost. Tree and soft fruits trained along walls and fences or over archways can be very attractive as well as productive.

## Learning from experience

It is not surprising then that interest in growing fruit and vegetables is on the increase. Generations of professional gardeners from private estates and amateur allotment holders have built up an impressive body of expertise and knowledge over the years. This volume sets out to continue the tradition by distilling that experience into an accessible format for the modern gardener.

The cultivation of food crops, more than any other form of gardening, demands commitment from the gardener. Knowledge of basic principles, thoughtful planning, good preparation, and, above all, time spent in regular care of growing crops, are crucial to success. Failure in any of this leads to disappointing results, and wasted time and money.

Those new to kitchen gardening would be wise to start on a modest scale, but to plan the garden so that the area given over to food crops can expand with your experience. There is no ideal size for a kitchen garden because it depends on many variable factors such as family demand, the garden site, and personal abilities and preferences. The good news is that no garden is too small: crops can be grown in all sorts of containers, including windowboxes.

## In harmony with nature

Most gardeners have a particular affinity with the natural environment and fully appreciate the good sense of maintaining a natural balance of living organisms within the garden and of conserving natural resources. Many take the opportunity to run their kitchen garden entirely on organic lines. It is not necessary to grow produce that is totally free of blemishes or to extract the maximum possible yield from every plant – as is the case with commercial cultivation. A reasonable level of pests and diseases can be tolerated in the garden, and

there are means of recycling organic waste and of using water wisely. This philosophy is followed throughout the book and you may be inspired to examine further aspects of gardening organically. Chemical treatments are available for those who wish to use them, but there is no doubt that the range is diminishing because of safety regulations and commercial considerations.

## Increasing choice

The wide range of fruit, vegetables, and culinary herbs described in this book reflects the modern gardener's interest in growing an increasing variety of crops. Most of the crops can be reliably grown outdoors in temperate climates, although some, such as peppers and peaches, produce better quality crops for a longer season under cover. The prospect of climate change, and the popularity of the conservatory, however, raise new possibilities; so tender fruits such as citrus and pineapples are covered – to fire the imagination.

**Potager garden, Tintinhull**
*Orderly lines of well-managed vegetables and flowers for cutting, abundant and full of promise, have their own special beauty.*

The introduction of new cultivars (garden varieties), often with improved quality or genetic resistance to a pest or disease, is a great boon to the kitchen gardener. To help you choose from the bewildering number of cultivars now available, each crop covered in the text includes a core list of recommended cultivars. Many have received the Award of Garden Merit after extensive trials by the Royal Horticultural Society. Your own experience will eventually be the best guide.

The comprehensive information in this text will provide a good grounding for you to develop your own style of kitchen gardening. Never forget the principles, keep abreast of new developments, and, above all, take time to enjoy your garden.

# GROWING VEGETABLES AND FRUIT

Plants grown for food differ from ornamentals in one key respect – that in harvesting their crops, full of goodness and nourishment, we continually take something from the plants and from the soil. It is critical, therefore, that we repay this debt with care – choosing the best site possible for our crops, understanding and nurturing the soil, recycling where we can (for example, by making garden compost), and tending the plants as they grow – protecting them from competition from weeds, attack by pests and diseases, and harsh conditions.

Growing fruits and vegetables can be demanding, and does require commitment, but brings with it an enormous amount of satisfaction – the excitement of planning what crop, and which cultivar, to grow and how to grow it; control over how the food we eat is produced; a sense of expectation and work and patience rewarded as crops in their turn come into season; and, of course, plentiful harvests.

# Climate and location

For most of us the choice of where we live is governed by considerations other than the ideal conditions for gardening. In many cases one has to make do with a challenging site, but a great deal can be achieved by careful planning, imaginative design, and choosing suitable crops and cultivars.

The characteristics of your location are even more significant for fruit and vegetables than for ornamental plants, because the range of plants is narrower, with less scope for selecting to suit the climate. It is essential to understand the basic needs for healthy plant growth: light, suitable temperature, water, air, and nutrients. Each is influenced to varying degrees by the conditions in the area, which we cannot change; but through respecting, maintaining, or improving the physical characteristics of a garden within such constraints, we can still help meet these needs.

### THE IMPORTANCE OF LIGHT

Direct sunshine provides the quantity and quality of light needed to maximize photosynthesis – the process by which plants use light to convert water and carbon dioxide into energy for plant activity. This is vital for healthy growth, producing bulk in leafy vegetable crops and sturdy development of flowers and fruits. The importance of sunshine can be seen in the weak, unproductive growth of plants that are shaded by buildings or hedges. Summer sunshine

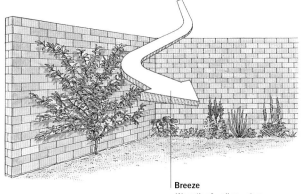

**Breeze**
*Warmth of wall counters cooling effects of any breeze*

**Warm spot**
*In a sheltered garden, a wall facing the sun absorbs heat during the day and then releases it again at night when the air temperature falls. It also concentrates the power of the sun by reflecting some warmth back immediately. Breezes will be deflected, but a solid wall is not suitable as a windbreak in an exposed position.*

ripens the shoots of woody fruit plants, improving flowering and consequent fruiting in the following season.

Average daily hours of sunshine vary from place to place, but in all areas the aim should be to ensure that any shade to the kitchen garden is kept to a minimum by avoiding, or removing wherever possible, any trees or other obstructions that create shade cover. Cane fruits, brassicas, and perennial vegetables will all tolerate moderate shade where a site is only partly in sun.

There are a few situations where it may be necessary to provide temporary artificial shade. Prolonged exposure to strong sun can cause scorch or, more often, wilting in newly transplanted crops; this is associated mainly with the sun's warmth, which is primarily of benefit to the gardener.

### THE EFFECTS OF TEMPERATURE

The way in which sunshine raises air temperature is almost entirely beneficial to the gardener. It encourages all stages of plant growth, from the sowing of vegetables or bud burst in woody fruit plants through to crop maturity. It raises the soil temperature, promoting seed germination and also enhancing root growth. Bright, warm days increase insect activity, essential for satisfactory pollination of fruiting crops. Areas that enjoy high levels of sunshine and resulting warm air usually have a relatively long local growing season. Growth starts early and finishes late, so cropping may be extended, especially in vegetable gardens.

The adverse effects of low temperatures are considerable. Cold air and soil lead to slower germination, growth, and bud burst; frost can be devastating. Tender vegetables, such as tomatoes or cucurbits, will be destroyed, and frost brings the threat of very serious damage to the blossom of fruit plants, resulting in loss of the crop.

The restrictions on fruit and vegetable growing in areas with a high risk of frost can be reduced by choosing hardier crops and cultivars. For instance, the brassica group of vegetables includes very hardy crops compared with the generally more tender pea and bean group, and among the fruit crops peaches are more tender than apples. There are lettuces bred to survive winter outdoors, and relatively late-flowering fruit plant cultivars are less likely to be damaged by spring frosts.

---

### WHAT IS A MICROCLIMATE?

Whatever the general climate of an area, variations due to topography, such as the sunny or shaded sides of a hill, will create differences within it, producing microclimates. The structures and plants around and in a garden create their own microclimates, making one garden, or even one area within a garden, markedly different from another. Levels of shade and shelter will almost certainly vary, some corners may be more prone to frost, and moisture levels are likely to differ across a site. It is important to be aware of these variations and use them to their best advantage when planning your fruit and vegetable garden, as plants that thrive in one area can do poorly in another.

- **Open areas** of the garden that face into the sun, particularly if they slope down towards it, warm up quickly in spring and are ideal for early crops.
- **Walls and buildings** can provide added warmth and protection for fruit trees if they face the sun, but can also create turbulence by blocking or funnelling winds.
- **Sheltering hedges** will provide a better microclimate for all crops, but the areas of the garden closest to them may be relatively dry and receive less light.
- **Low-lying areas** may be sheltered from wind, but are potential frost pockets and are also likely to have colder, wetter soil than higher areas in winter.

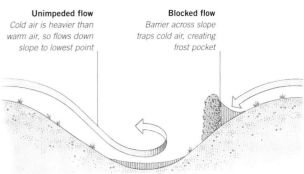

**Unimpeded flow**
*Cold air is heavier than warm air, so flows down slope to lowest point*

**Blocked flow**
*Barrier across slope traps cold air, creating frost pocket*

◀ **Winter freeze**
*Some crops, such as these Savoy and ornamental cabbages, are hardy enough to withstand even a freezing blanket of snow in winter.*

▲ **How frost pockets form**
*Cold air may accumulate in certain areas of the garden, making them prone to frost – these areas are known as frost pockets. They can occur in hollows in the ground or behind a barrier, such as a hedge; thinning the lower branches of hedging plants will improve the situation by allowing some cold air to flow through and away.*

Protection with glass or plastic is a well-tried method of growing fruit and vegetables in a frost-prone climate (*see pp.43–48*), and tender fruits may be nurtured in the shelter of a relatively warm wall (*see facing page*).

Frost does provide some benefits to gardeners. It helps in the shattering of clods on clay soils (*see pp.14–15*), and will also help to destroy or reduce overwintering pests and diseases.

Cold air accumulates in hollows, so be alert to the potential effects of frost pockets (*see above right*). Sometimes such reservoirs of cold air can be removed by opening up gaps in barriers, such as hedges, to allow air current to flow to a lower level. A slightly sloping garden site is therefore less likely to be prone to frost, provided that the air flow is not obstructed. Gardens in coastal areas are much less likely to be subject to frost, although this is inevitably at the expense of exposure to the damaging effects of high winds.

## LEVELS OF RAINFALL
Rainfall is a major influence on the success of fruit and vegetable gardening. Levels of rainfall across temperate regions are often highly variable, due to the effect of topographic features such as plains, hills, or mountains. A hillside facing the prevailing wind experiences relatively high rainfall, as the rising air cools, causing precipitation; the leeward side of the hill is its rain shadow, with

lower rainfall, as the falling air warms. In areas of low rainfall there is risk of drought, the effects ranging in severity from checked plant growth to crop loss. Leafy vegetables such as lettuces require a steady supply of water to develop into an edible product, and water is similarly essential for fruit to swell. Conservation of natural water resources is very important, and gardeners need to ensure that the soil holds moisture well and to reduce surface evaporation by the use of mulches (*see pp.41–42*).

A high-rainfall climate brings its own challenges: the greatest of these is the likelihood of waterlogged soil. Good soil drainage is important for kitchen gardens anywhere, but it is a prime consideration in such localities. Young vegetable plants are particularly vulnerable in saturated soils that are cold and airless: growth is inhibited, and vital nutrients, such as lime and nitrogen, may also become depleted.

High rainfall encourages some pests and diseases, such as slugs and snails and damping off (*see Plant Problems, pp.246–264*). Fruit crops are more prone to disease in areas of high rainfall and high humidity: trees suffer shoot, leaf, and fruit infections, and soft fruits, such as strawberries and raspberries, are affected by fruit soft rot and show root growth restriction. Fruit crop management in areas receiving more than 100cm (39in) of rainfall in an average year will be very demanding.

Chemical fungicides can be effective in controlling diseases, and if used as directed they should pose little risk to the environment or the gardener, but they can be less effective in high-rainfall areas. Where the gardener sensibly wishes to keep fungicide spraying to a minimum, it becomes essential to discourage diseases by excellent plant care. Some fruit and vegetable cultivars with natural resistance to disease are also available, but the general choice will inevitably be reduced in a high-rainfall climate.

## ALTITUDE AND EXPOSURE
Strong winds are predominantly a feature of exposed sites. Gardens at high altitudes will usually be more prone to strong winds, as will coastal sites, where salt deposits on leaves can be an additional problem. Strong winds can also be created where air is funnelled between buildings or natural features.

The most obvious effects of wind are physical damage and loss of stability; other adverse effects, less immediately apparent, include increased water loss and a reduction in the pollinating activity of flying insects.

Shelter, in the form of well-placed windbreaks (*see pp.12–13*), is necessary for the gardener to achieve success in cropping in these conditions. Fortunately of all the elements of natural climate, the effects of wind can perhaps most readily be modified.

# Shelter from wind

There is no doubt that the provision of shelter around a fruit and vegetable garden is vital to successful production. It has been shown to raise temperatures by up to 3°C (5°F), encouraging the opening and pollination of flowers and the ripening of wood and fruit. In any site, no matter how suitable the soil and climate, carefully selected shelter will increase yields. In some cases, shelter will be essential for any kind of success, and the earlier it is in place the better.

**Sheltered garden**
*The mature hedge that surrounds this garden affords the ideal protection from wind. Its semi-permeable nature has the effect of breaking up and slowing the wind without giving rise to damaging turbulence, and crops flourish in the settled conditions created.*

## THE EFFECTS OF WIND

Wind has both immediately apparent and unseen influences on crops. The most obvious effects result from high winds. Branches of fruit trees and bushes are broken, and trees on rootstocks that are shallow-rooting can be blown over in gales. There may be blossom damage in springtime, and loss of fruit as crops reach maturity. Physical damage to vegetables is most likely to be seen in taller crops, such as Brussels sprouts and broad beans, keeling over. Pea and bean supports may be loosened or destroyed, and high winds can damage or even destroy glass or plastic structures, such as tunnel cloches, used to protect crops like strawberries and many vegetables. More tender foliage, such as that of lettuces, beans, and cucurbits, may be damaged. Near to the sea, wind often also carries damaging salt deposits.

Apart from these clearly visible effects of wind, horticultural experiments have shown significant depression in the growth and cropping of fruits and vegetables on open sites. The most likely causes are higher water loss from plants and lower average air and soil temperatures. Winds increase water loss from plants, especially those newly planted out, because air moving over the leaves causes evaporation. This drying slows growth, as plants reduce activity to conserve moisture. The effect is heightened during hot, dry summer months and is aggravated by the drying effects of wind on the soil surface.

On exposed, flat or elevated sites, wind can erode very light or peaty soils. The pollinating activity of insects is likely to be reduced, and if pesticide sprays are used, their operation can be much less effective as they are blown off-target.

## PLANNING SHELTER

There is a wide range of potential benefits to be gained from shelter, both in gardens with some level of existing shelter within a developed urban setting, and in country gardens, but the advantages do need to be weighed against the possible disadvantages.

Establishing shelter incurs financial expense and physical effort. There is often a risk of creating a frost pocket by enclosing an area where very cold air can accumulate (*see p.11*). Shelter features can cause shade and impede the even distribution of rainfall. The enhanced temperature and relatively still air of the microclimate (*see p.10*) may create favourable conditions for plant pests and diseases. Where living plants are used to establish shelter, they may compete for moisture. In any situation, bear in mind all of these considerations at the planning stage.

Shelter is clearly most valuable in protecting crops from the prevailing wind, but there can be damage from cold winds from other directions, and the best practice is to establish shelter around all sides of the fruit and vegetable garden. A good windbreak will provide 10m (30ft) of protection on the leeward side for every 1m (3ft) of height, so a large garden will need some internal windbreaks if the perimeter shelter is not to be too high and cause possible shading problems.

**Action of wind**
*Solid windbreak barriers are actually counter-productive. Oncoming air is forced up over the barrier, then drawn down on the other side by the low pressure behind the barrier. Turbulence is created both on the leeward side and to a lesser extent on the windward side.*

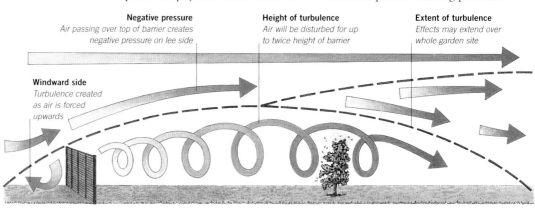

**Negative pressure**
*Air passing over top of barrier creates negative pressure on lee side*

**Height of turbulence**
*Air will be disturbed for up to twice height of barrier*

**Extent of turbulence**
*Effects may extend over whole garden site*

**Windward side**
*Turbulence created as air is forced upwards*

## PLANTS FOR SHELTER HEDGES

**Alder (*Alnus glutinosa*)** *Especially good on damp sites, and bears catkins in spring. Trim in autumn. Seed-raised and inexpensive.*
**Beech (*Fagus sylvatica*)** *Bears abundant small, attractive leaves. Tolerant of clipping; if done in late summer a large proportion of the crisp, dead leaves remain attached until spring. Seed-raised, so relatively inexpensive.*
**Hawthorn (*Crataegus monogyna*)** *Tolerates strong winds, but it is prone to fireblight disease and so not recommended for a fruit garden. Trim after flowering or in autumn.*
**Hazel (*Corylus avellana*)** *Multi-stemmed, with strong shoots, attractive catkins in spring if lightly trimmed, and yellow leaves in autumn.*

**Hornbeam (*Carpinus betulus*)** *Bears small leaves with saw-toothed margins. Like beech, it retains a large proportion of dead leaves until spring if clipped in late summer. Seed-raised and so relatively inexpensive.*
**Flowering currant (*Ribes sanguineum*)** *Makes a decorative hedge with pink flowers in spring if grown in full sun, and does well on most soils. Trim after flowering.*
**Roses (*Rosa*)** *Alba, Gallica, and sweet briar roses can be used in moderately exposed sites. Reduce some stems and remove a few of the oldest when dormant in winter.*
**Spiraea 'Arguta'** *Grows on most soils in full sun and bears dense clusters of white flowers in spring. Trim after flowering.*

*Spiraea 'Arguta'*

Avoid solid barriers, which can create turbulent eddies and cause damage on the leeward side. If gusting wind is filtered through a roughly 50 per cent penetrable shelter barrier there is little risk of this. Many hedges naturally give this sort of shelter; with artificial barriers, solid parts should be separated by their own width or slightly less.

### SHELTER HEDGES

Hedges will be the first choice for most gardeners, because they are attractive and have a natural association with fruit and vegetables. They require careful planning to ensure that they do not block sunlight and rainfall, and regular trimming to keep them tidy and within bounds. The garden needs to be large enough to allow for an uncropped area at least 2m (6ft) wide along the hedge, due to the moisture and nutrient needs of the hedging plants; in many sites this area can be used as access pathway.

Almost any woody ornamental plant can be trained as a hedge (*see box above*) and many evergreens are traditionally grown as excellent barriers. However, it is best to choose a deciduous subject for enclosing a kitchen garden, because it is more likely to filter the wind acceptably: native species will do well. A mix of shelter hedges provides a greater range of seasonal interest, and espalier- and cordon-trained apples and pears (*see pp.174–184*) make attractive shelter barriers within the garden.

Autumn planting allows trees or shrubs to establish over winter and grow well in the following spring. Set out plants at 60–90cm (24–36in) spacings, and plan to restrict shelter hedges to a maximum height of 2.5m (8ft). After planting, always add a mulch of rotted manure or compost (*see pp.41–42*) along the line.

### ARTIFICIAL BARRIERS

Shelter barriers made from fencing provide instant protection and require less annual maintenance than hedges. They do not encroach, and in many cases can more readily be moved, but initial outlay in cost and effort are generally greater than with planting a hedge, and the effect is less decorative. Artificial shelter screens are suitable for erection at the exposed boundaries of a garden or as internal dividers, and they should be no more than 2m (6ft) high. Make the fence with strong support posts, spaced at a distance equivalent to the screen height, and always attach the cladding to the windward side of the posts.

There are several purpose-made materials available, such as plastic net, or more durable and expensive plastic strap cladding; black is the least intrusive colour. Instant decorative cover can be achieved with post and wire fences planted with blackberries or rambler roses. Permeable wooden lath panels and willow hurdles are also suitable.

## Artificial shelter barriers

**Plastic strap cladding**
*This heavyweight windbreak is suitable for an exposed site. The initial cost is high, and it is not the most visually appealing solution, but it will stand up to strong winds and last for years. Relatively lightweight uprights must be closely spaced, as here.*

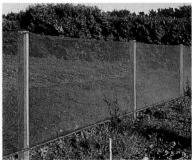

**Woven mesh fence**
*This lightweight plastic mesh makes an effective and relatively inexpensive windbreak. It can also be used to provide quick temporary shelter while hedging plants become established to provide a more permanent solution.*

# Soil types and structure

Just as we cannot alter features such as climatic conditions and aspect, so we have to accept the soil that comes with a garden or allotment. You may be fortunate enough to have a garden site with soil naturally quite suitable for producing excellent crops, or one that has been made so through a history of careful cultivation; the ideal soil would be a fertile, well-drained loam 45cm (18in) deep. Often, however, we have to contend with cold, heavy, poorly drained clay soil or light, sandy soil prone to rapid drying and loss of fertility. Luckily these less than ideal soils can almost always be improved; even where this cannot be done, at least some fruit and vegetables can be grown in raised beds (*see pp.32–34*) or in containers (*see pp.35–36*).

Soil supports and sustains plants, providing anchorage and a source of nutrients and water. It is highly variable according to location, even between sites in close proximity. Soils differ in their physical characteristics, their levels of organic matter, and their depth and condition. All soils are a mixture of weathered rock and rotted plant and animal remains or waste, naturally supporting myriad organisms, whose lifecycles make the soil into a living medium. It is organic matter and this soil fauna that give the surface layers their range of brown colouring.

### SOIL TEXTURE

The average gardener does not need to learn or understand soil science in depth, but it is necessary to be able to identify the essential type of the soil on which a kitchen garden is to be established. This is because the different soil types have different attributes, which affect plant growth and call for different ways of cultivating and maintaining the site. With a few specific preferences, most fruits and vegetables will grow reasonably well on a wide range of soils.

Soil texture is broadly classified into five main types: clay, silt, sand, chalk, and peat (*see chart below left*). The term loam is widely used to suggest fertility and a soil of all round excellence for growing, as in the recommendation to choose "a good medium loam". The term really needs qualification, for there is clay loam, silt loam, or sandy loam depending on the basic soil type; clay, silt, and sand describe soil textures based on the proportions of different-sized mineral particles found in them. Although the basic mineral content of soil is fixed by its origin, the structural nature is affected by the occurrence of stones or gravel and also by the addition of lime (*see pp.18–19*) and organic matter (*see pp.24–26*).

### SOIL FERTILITY AND STRUCTURE

The organic matter and fauna in the soil give it both its fertility and its structure; these two are closely linked.

One essential component of a fertile soil is humus. The term is usually taken to refer to the actual organic content of soil, but this is a simplification. Humus is a complex mix of compounds that derive from the decay of that organic matter to form a dark coloured, sticky substance. It has a crucial influence on the retention and release of nutrients, the formation of good soil structure, and the soil's ability to hold water.

Also essential to soil fertility are the wide range of living organisms that populate it, which we often take for granted. These include beneficial bacteria and fungi, and a range of microscopic worms and mites, besides the visible centipedes, earthworms, and beetles. All rely on organic matter, variously incorporated and applied annually in mulches, which they break down into humus.

## BASIC SOIL TYPES

*Clay*

Particles below 0.002mm in size are defined as clay. Clay soil is often described as heavy, and sometimes regarded as difficult, but it has very useful qualities. Clay naturally holds certain nutrients in chemical combination, so that they are not easily leached out and instead become available to plant roots gradually. It binds together better than sandy soil and is more water-retentive. Disadvantages are that it is relatively slow to warm and is susceptible to waterlogging in winter and baking in summer, problems reduced by adding bulky manures. Timing of cultivation requires care, but in many respects a clay soil is very desirable in the kitchen garden. Blackcurrants, plums, Brussels sprouts, and cabbages often do well on clay.

*Silt*

Particles between 0.002mm and 0.05mm in size are classified as silt. The silt soil is intermediate between clay and sandy soil, and has a smooth or silky texture. Silty soil is more retentive of nutrients and water than sandy soil, but it is liable to compaction, especially when it is dry. Plentiful organic matter will make this a good soil, especially for early sowings.

*Sandy*

Particles between 0.05mm and 2.0mm in size are sand; a sandy soil is commonly termed light. It does not hold together well, so is prone to erosion on exposed or sloping sites, and its ability to retain water and nutrients is poor because of its open nature. These properties can be corrected by the incorporation of generous amounts of bulky organic manures. Advantages are that it is relatively easy to cultivate and also early in warming, a trait useful for strawberries, salad crops, young root crops, and legumes.

*Chalky*

Chalky or limestone soil is abundant in some areas. It is invariably shallow and well drained, but the high lime content can pose problems, particularly in the cultivation of fruits. This kind of soil is moderately fertile, with organic matter being broken down quickly, and should be regularly dressed with acidic organic matter such as farmyard manure (*see pp.22–23*).

*Peat*

Peat soil is encountered on basically wetland sites where sedges and mosses naturally thrive. Where it is drained and dressed with fertilizer this type of soil can be made highly fertile, as it is both moisture-retentive and high in organic matter. Peat soils are usually acidic, and they can be prone to being blown away by wind when they are dry.

## Visual assessment of soil

**Clay soil**
*A clay soil is one containing more than 25 per cent clay particles. It is sticky after rainfall, sets into hard clods when dry, and is heavy to dig (see above left). Test the soil by handling it. When moist, a clay soil feels tacky, is shiny if smoothed, and can be formed into a ball that holds together (see above right).*

**Sandy and silt soils**
*Sandy soil has less than eight per cent clay and is mainly sand particles. It is very easy to dig (see above left), feels gritty when rubbed between the fingers, and does not hold together when squeezed (see above right). Silt soils are intermediate between clay and sand: they feel silky and show imprints when pressed, but do not form a cohesive ball.*

A soil must have good structure if plants are to thrive. Soil structure is measured by its tendency to form crumbs of mineral particles and organic matter held together by humus. Well-structured soil is easy to cultivate and has evenly distributed air spaces. This aeration allows plant roots to extend through the soil easily and facilitates movement of water and nutrients. It also has the effect of warming the soil and so promoting plant growth. Soil structure is influenced by the activities of soil organisms in creating humus and by the levels of organic matter present. Also important are the nutrients that the organisms need to form humus, and lime (*see pp.18–19*), which is vital to crumb formation.

Other factors helping the development of good soil structure include the action of frost and alternating wet and dry conditions. Ensure that the soil structure is not damaged by being cultivated in wet conditions or by excessive traffic over the dug surface. Walking or moving wheeled implements across the surface can compact soil at any time, but especially in wet conditions. Aeration can even be damaged by continual winter rain. This damage can be reduced by leaving a covering of organic matter (*see pp.41–42*) on the surface during winter, which can be dug in to maintain soil fertility, or by planting an overwintering green manure or crop cover (*see p.23*).

### SOIL PROFILE
The horizontal bands that can be seen when digging down into a soil make up the profile. The most easily identifiable profile in gardens is topsoil, subsoil, and the parent rock material below them. Topsoil is the layer of most activity, because this contains organic matter and organisms that live on it. The subsoil is usually paler in colour, and is formed from weathered rock. The depth of topsoil and subsoil through which roots can penetrate has great importance to the growth of plants. It is worth digging a small test hole on your site to ascertain the profile.

Fruit trees (*see pp.174–205*) do best where the total depth of well-drained, weathered soil is at least 60cm (24in); sweet cherries ideally need at least 90cm (3ft). Soft fruits (*see pp.211–233*) require a soil depth of at least 45cm (18in), except for strawberries, which can succeed in a depth of 38cm (15in), as can vegetable crops. These are general limits and are based on the success of crops grown commercially; what is of paramount importance is that water can drain freely through any depth of profile.

▲ **The gardener's friend**
*Among the most beneficial inhabitants of fertile soil, earthworms burrow extensively, improving soil aeration and pulling organic matter down from the surface and assisting in its breakdown by digesting it.*

▶ **Soil profile**
*Almost all soils are made up of distinct layers of topsoil, subsoil, and material weathered from the parent rock. The depth of all of these layers can vary depending on the soil's history.*

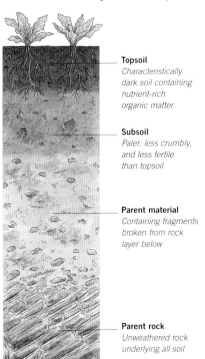

**Topsoil**
*Characteristically dark soil containing nutrient-rich organic matter*

**Subsoil**
*Paler, less crumbly, and less fertile than topsoil*

**Parent material**
*Containing fragments broken from rock layer below*

**Parent rock**
*Unweathered rock underlying all soil*

## DRAINAGE OF THE SOIL

Roots require air to grow and to absorb nutrients and water. Waterlogged soil becomes cold and airless. This prevents nutrient uptake and leads to plant roots becoming diseased or even dying.

There are clues that indicate a poorly drained garden site. The most obvious is evidence of persistent puddling after rain. Others are the presence of plants that thrive in wet conditions, such as sedges, rushes, or moss, and poor growth of perennial plants.

Poor drainage arises in several ways. It can occur if the topsoil is infertile through poor cultivation or lack of humus: careful cultivation and dressing with organic matter (*see pp.22–23*) will improve structure. The soil profile may naturally include an impervious layer known as a pan, which is often only 2.5–5cm (1–2in) thick. A pan can occur in the subsoil as a result of accumulated minerals, especially iron. Alternatively, there may be a barrier in the subsoil or the topsoil caused by compaction. Because free drainage is so important,

### A soil pan

*Digging an inspection pit to a depth of 90cm (3ft) should reveal the cause of any poor drainage. Here, the problem is a densely compacted layer or pan that has formed between the topsoil and the subsoil. This is preventing water from draining freely into the subsoil, and needs breaking up. Compaction like this can be avoided by minimizing traffic over the soil.*

**Topsoil**
*Open and crumbly soil can become temporarily waterlogged if drainage is impeded*

**Compacted layer**
*Dense, hard layer of compacted soil impedes flow of water*

**Subsoil**
*Once compaction is broken up, water should drain well through subsoil structure*

it is worth digging a narrow inspection pit on suspect sites to examine the soil profile. A natural hard pan is easily identified, as is compaction, which is often marked by a dark horizontal band (*see above*). Deep double digging (*see p.39*) will break up compacted layers, and a natural hard pan can be breached with a pickaxe. Other problems are more intractable: it may be that the garden lies in a hollow of natural drainage from surrounding land, or that the area has a naturally high water table. Both of these situations would be very difficult to remedy, and in such conditions it may be necessary to grow crops in raised beds (*see pp.32–34*) or in containers (*see pp.35–36*).

## Constructing drains

Where cultivation methods will not solve the problem, it can be worth installing a drainage system, but only the most difficult sites justify the expense and work. At their simplest, such a system consists of surface ditches (*see below*) leading into a soakaway – a large pit at a low point filled with rubble. Water will seep into the drains and be carried to the soakaway. The drains can be either left open or filled with gravel and topped with upturned turves. A more elaborate system is to lay a herringbone grid of buried pipes (*see right*).

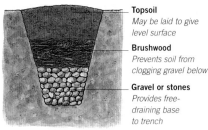

**Topsoil**
*May be laid to give level surface*

**Brushwood**
*Prevents soil from clogging gravel below*

**Gravel or stones**
*Provides free-draining base to trench*

### French drain

*This version of a land drain is simply a ditch with sloping sides, up to 90cm (3ft) deep, filled first with a layer of gravel or rubble, then brushwood, finally covered over with topsoil to give a level and natural surface.*

**Pipe trenches**
*Pipes should be at least 60cm (2ft) and up to 90cm (3ft) below ground level*

**Spacing pipes**
*Lines of plastic or clay pipes should be laid approximately 3.5m (11ft) apart*

**Joining pipes**
*Pipes are laid end to end – at junctions, pipe ends are roughly shaped to fit together, then covered by flat tiles to stop soil silting up inside*

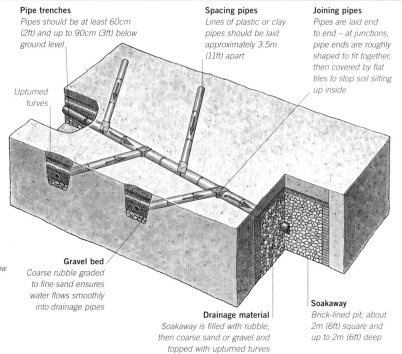

*Upturned turves*

**Gravel bed**
*Coarse rubble graded to fine sand ensures water flows smoothly into drainage pipes*

**Drainage material**
*Soakaway is filled with rubble, then coarse sand or gravel and topped with upturned turves*

**Soakaway**
*Brick-lined pit, about 2m (6ft) square and up to 2m (6ft) deep*

### Herringbone drainage system with soakaway

*A permanent system of 10–15cm (4–6in) diameter perforated plastic drain pipes can be laid, herringbone-fashion, across the site.*

*On a flat site, the pipes must be laid sloping down towards the soakaway; on a sloping site, they can be laid parallel to the surface.*

# Essential nutrients

All fruit and vegetable crops need a constant adequate supply of nutrients to sustain growth and yield a worthwhile harvest. Good nutrition is ensured by attention at the time of preparing the garden and then continual maintenance.

Soil nutrients come from several sources – weathering of minerals, the breakdown of organic matter, chemical reaction in the soil, and absorption from the atmosphere. The gardener can also influence nutrient levels by applying additional fertilizers and organic matter (*see pp.20–23*).

### MAJOR AND MINOR NUTRIENTS

The essential plant nutrients required in the greatest quantity are nitrogen, phosphorus, and potassium. Nitrogen is absorbed in quantity by plants to promote growth; leafy vegetables (*see pp.123–128*) use a great deal, as do blackcurrants, plums, and pears among the fruit crops (*see pp.146–237*). Phosphorus is necessary for chemical reactions within the plant and is vital for cell division and consequently the development of shoots and roots. Potassium is essential in plant metabolism, giving hardiness, steady growth, disease resistance, and colour and flavour in vegetables and fruit.

Magnesium, calcium, and sulphur also have essential roles, but are required in smaller amounts. Magnesium is a constituent of chlorophyll, needed to convert light into energy for growth, and has a role in the transport of phosphorus within plants. Calcium facilitates growth. Sulphur is a central constituent of the protein in living cells, and is usually in short supply.

There are also essential trace elements or micronutrients, required in much smaller quantities. The most important of these are iron, manganese, copper, molybdenum, boron, chlorine, and zinc.

### DETERMINING NUTRIENT LEVELS

Total absence of a nutrient from the soil is rare; low nutrient levels as a result of leaching by rainfall or flooding, or through depletion by successive crops over time are more common. Another significant cause of deficiency is reserves in the soil becoming unavailable due to

**Boron deficiency**
*Plants of the brassica family may occasionally be affected by boron deficiency in garden soil. The most common symptom is the appearance of hollow stems in the plants. This is most likely to be the result of either a naturally alkaline soil or excessive applications of lime, as a high pH causes boron to be locked up and so unavailable to plants.*

the effects of acidity (*see p.18*), excessive amounts of another nutrient, or poor root growth as a result of waterlogging (*see facing page*) or disease.

Measuring levels of nutrients such as nitrogen, phosphorus, and potassium in a garden soil is not easy – especially nitrogen because of its mobility. Proprietary kits are available, but, for accuracy, laboratory testing and professional analysis are best; this is inevitably less straightforward, and expensive. Once initial testing of the kitchen garden soil has taken place, annual testing thereafter is not necessary provided the soil is well maintained.

### LEVELS OF THE MAJOR NUTRIENTS

Nitrogen is used in quantity and is also highly prone to washing out in rain. Make regular supplementary dressings, but avoid excessive amounts, which can lead to rank growth and unfruitfulness; and also lead to the pollution of water courses. Follow directions on proprietary fertilizers (*see pp.20–21*).

Phosphorus is retained quite well, and sufficient levels are present in most soils, an exception being old, grazed pastures converted to garden. Supplements are probably needed only every two or three years in a well-maintained garden.

Potassium is usually held in clay soils by a chemical reaction, but is easily lost to leaching on sandy, free-draining and acidic soils. Dressings of potassium are needed annually in the kitchen garden; it should always be included in dressings that are applied prior to planting, in order to balance the effects of nitrogen.

### LEVELS OF MICRONUTRIENTS

Because plant growth requires very low levels of micronutrients, real deficiency symptoms are rarely seen. The effects of shortages most frequently occur on alkaline soils (*see p.18*), especially light soils affected by drought.

Plants on such soils frequently show symptoms of iron deficiency, such as severe yellowing of the growing tips, with the mature leaves also yellowed except around the small veins. Often seen in fruit crops, this is known as lime-induced chlorosis. Manganese deficiency also occurs on alkaline soils, causing yellowing of the older leaves, starting at the edges; on acid soils levels of manganese toxic to plants can occur. Boron deficiency may arise on light soils after heavy liming, and is often seen in hollow stems in brassicas; zinc deficiency can occur in similar conditions, stunting shoots and leaves. Molybdenum can be made unavailable on acid soils, causing damaged growing points and whiptail in cauliflowers, in which the leaf blade does not develop. Controlling the pH of the soil will help to prevent these problems (*see pp.18–19*).

# Lime and soil acidity

Lime is a vital soil ingredient in the kitchen garden because it affects the fertility of the soil in several ways. Lime is itself a source of calcium, an essential major element for healthy plant growth, and is also vital to the production of a good soil structure.

## THE EFFECTS OF LIME

The presence of lime governs the acidity of the soil: the more lime is present, the less acidic is the soil. This affects the micro-organisms that break down organic matter, which mostly cannot survive in a soil that is very acidic. Soil acidity is also important in the uptake of nutrients, because some of them, such as potassium compounds, become unavailable to plants in soils that are very acid, whilst others may accumulate to concentrations that are toxic to plants (*see p.17*). The incidence of some diseases is influenced by soil acidity; clubroot in cabbages thrives on acid soils and scab in potatoes on alkaline ones (*see* Plant Problems, *pp.246–264*).

Lime has a valuable beneficial effect on the structure of clay soils, because its presence initiates a chemical process that aggregates soil particles into stable crumbs, which are clusters of mineral and organic matter. A good crumb structure is important both for proper aeration of the soil and for effective water and nutrient retention (*see p.15*).

The level of lime also influences the living inhabitants of soil. The activity of earthworms and the micro-organisms, especially bacteria, that reduce bulky organic matter to a constituent of humus (*see p.14*), decreases as the acidity of the soil increases.

## KNOWING YOUR SOIL pH

To gain the maximum benefits of lime in soil and avoid the problems resulting from its absence or excess, it is necessary to understand firstly how to measure the acidity of the soil, and secondly how to adjust the level. The degree of acidity of a substance is measured on a graduated system known as the pH scale. At the middle of this scale, pH 7 represents the neutral condition: values lower than this, down to pH 0, indicate increasing acidity, and

values above it, up to pH 14, indicate increasing alkalinity. Garden soils usually have a pH of between 4.5 and 7.5, and most of the crops to be grown in a fruit and vegetable garden will do best on soils of around pH 6.5; this standard remains constant, and is the level for which you should aim in treating your soil; the pH level directly or indirectly affects everything else that you do.

There are accessible and inexpensive means for the gardener to determine the level of soil acidity and the need for lime. Simple pH measurement kits are available from good garden centres and mail-order retailers; their results are easy to read and sufficiently reliable. Use a kit in the first stages of planning, and rectify any imbalance before planting. It is also advisable to use them for checking every few seasons, as levels will change, and it may be necessary to make adjustments.

On a large site, take small samples from across the area, then mix them before testing a small quantity as a representative sample. Alternatively, carry out several tests at various points.

## EXTREME pH PROBLEMS

The acidity of the soil affects the availability of nutrients (*see p.17*), and modifying soil acidity by applying lime is an effective means of influencing nutrient availability. Some liming products can also be sources of the main nutrients; for example, ammonium nitrate formulated with lime contributes nitrogen, and dolomitic limestone also contains magnesium.

A soil with an excessively high lime content is just as unsatisfactory for fruit and vegetable growing as a soil with too little. In very alkaline conditions, most of the essential nutrients that are

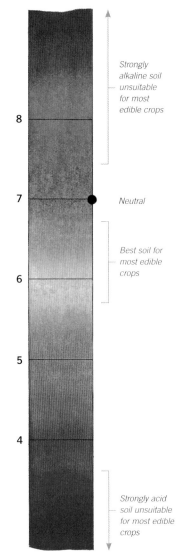

8

7    Neutral

6

5

4

*Strongly alkaline soil unsuitable for most edible crops*

*Best soil for most edible crops*

*Strongly acid soil unsuitable for most edible crops*

**pH scale and values**
*This section of the pH scale shows the range most likely to be found in garden situations. The best soil testing kits assess a suspension of soil in distilled water; the pH level is indicated by the colour of the suspension after mixing.*

| GUIDE TO LIME APPLICATION | | | |
|---|---|---|---|
| Original pH | Amount of ground limestone per sq m (sq yd) to adjust to pH 6.5 | | |
| | Sandy or gravelly soil | Medium loam soil | Peat or clay soil |
| 4.5 | 640g (1lb 3oz) | 920g (1lb 10oz) | 1150g (2lb 2oz) |
| 5.0 | 400g (12oz) | 650g (1lb 3oz) | 790g (1lb 7oz) |
| 5.5 | 225g (7oz) | 375g (11oz) | 470g (14oz) |
| 6.0 | 135g (4oz) | 190g (5oz) | 400g (12oz) |
| 6.5 | 0 | 0 | 0 |

## Liming the soil

**1** **Weigh out enough lime** to treat 1sq m (1sq yd) of your plot. Put it into a pot and mark the level, so that you can measure out the rest of the lime using the pot. Mark out your site into a square metre (square yard) grid.

**2** **Put the lime on** the blade of a shovel and scatter it gently and evenly over your marked-out square of soil. It is important that liming is done on a still day, so that the lime is not blown onto other areas of the garden, causing scorching of plants.

**3** **Work across the plot** treating each square of the grid in the same way. Rake over the surface to distribute the lime evenly and incorporate it into the soil, or dig it in to a depth of 15cm (6in).

required in only small quantities – trace elements such as iron, manganese, and copper – cannot be readily absorbed by the plant (*see p.17*). On overly lime-rich soil, apples and pears often show marked yellowing (chlorosis) between the leaf veins, due to iron or manganese having become unavailable, and similar chlorosis is found in some vegetables, for example beetroot.

### APPLYING LIME

It is much easier to reduce soil acidity than to raise it, so take care in deciding how to apply lime. Three forms of lime are generally available: quicklime, which is caustic and dangerous, hydrated lime, which is faster acting but can damage foliage, and crushed chalk or ground limestone, the least hazardous and usually the least expensive form of lime for garden use.

Rates of application to bring an acidic soil to pH 6.5 vary not only according to the existing pH value but also to the soil type: the chemistry of a clay soil makes it far more resistant to the effects of liming than a sandy soil. A general guide to application rates is shown in the table (*see left*). The pH of very acidic soil can be raised only

gradually, so regular pH checking is needed in the early development of the garden. Dressing requirements of more than 400g per sq m (12oz per sq yd) need to be applied over several seasons.

Whatever the quantity, best effects will be obtained where the application is made well before planting, ideally on two or more occasions in autumn and winter; this will allow the lime to initiate changes in the soil gradually and more effectively. Apply lime after incorporating animal manures, but not less than three or four weeks later, to avoid chemical reactions that will release ammonia and allow nitrogen to escape, and aim to work in the dressing to a depth of 15cm (6in).

### REDUCING ALKALINITY

Rainfall, continuous cultivation, and cropping will gradually increase soil acidity. Application of flowers of sulphur also has an effect, but this is slow, and dependent on relatively warm soil for bacterial activity. For general guidance, apply 270g per sq m (8oz per sq yd) on clay soils and half this quantity on sandy soils. Repeat pH testing and application as necessary; the process is only worth considering in extreme conditions.

### SAFETY TIPS

- **Store with care,** keeping lime or sulphur in a clearly labelled, closed container, securely placed out of reach of children.
- **Choose your time** and only ever apply lime or sulphur on a still day.
- **Cover your eyes** with protective goggles that offer protection around the sides and fit closely to the face.
- **Protect your skin** by wearing trousers, long sleeves, and close-fitting gloves.
- **Wear a simple cloth mask** over your mouth and nose, as lime is easily inhaled.
- **Be sensible:** the operation of liming is a perfectly safe practice if these simple precautions are followed.

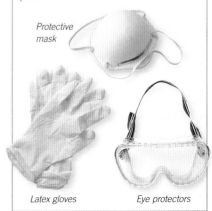

*Protective mask*

*Latex gloves*          *Eye protectors*

# Fertilizers and manures

Most previously cultivated garden sites have adequate levels of nutrients (*see p.17*), with the most likely exception of lime (*see pp.18–19*); old grassland converted to garden use is often low in phosphorus. Cropping makes heavy demands on soil, however, and a fruit and vegetable garden requires more feeding than an ornamental garden. As an insurance, incorporate fertilizers and manures (*detailed below and on p.22*) containing nitrogen, phosphorus, and potassium as a base dressing before planting. After good site preparation (*see pp.37–40*), maintain fertility by annual, light applications of fertilizer to areas dug over for cropping, and by top-dressing or surface application to growing crops.

## UNDERSTANDING TERMINOLOGY

The terms manure and fertilizer are commonly used interchangeably, but it is worth distinguishing them. Manure best describes bulky material that is derived directly from animal and plant wastes, while fertilizer is any material that provides more concentrated nutrients than bulky manure, and can be in powder, granular, or liquid forms.

Manure inevitably comes from organic sources; fertilizers may be from organic or inorganic sources. Organic substances are those derived from decomposed plant and animal remains and the waste products of animals; inorganic fertilizers are derived from non-living, carbon-free sources, including rock. Many gardeners, committed to the principles of organic growing, prefer to use organic products to the total or near exclusion of inorganic fertilizers, regarding their use as unacceptable for a variety of reasons. There is a view that organic derivatives are much less likely to pollute the environment, and that edible crops grown organically are more wholesome and of better flavour than those grown using other products.

## CHEMICAL CONSTITUENTS

The letters N, P, and K on fertilizer packaging are the chemical symbols standing for nitrogen, phosphorus, and potassium respectively.

Phosphorus and potassium are included in fertilizers as more stable or accessible chemical compounds: phosphorus as phosphate ($P_2O_5$) and potassium as potash ($K_2O$). The shorter chemical symbols are most used for convenience, but all the different descriptions are met with in general gardening parlance.

There is a recognized notation for the nutrient content of compounds, which is always printed on the fertilizer packaging. This gives the percentage content of each nutrient, always in the order N:P:K, so a compound fertilizer that is described as 20:10:10 will contain 20 per cent nitrogen, 10 per cent phosphate, and 10 per cent potash (*see also chart, below*).

## TYPES OF INORGANIC FERTILIZER

| Commonly available forms of fertilizer | Average nutrient content (per cent) | | | Approximate rate of application | Characteristics and uses |
|---|---|---|---|---|---|
| | Nitrogen | Phosphate | Potash | | |
| Sulphate of ammonia | 21 | 0 | 0 | 35–70g per sq m (1–2oz per sq yd) or 1½ times this for the higher-demand crops | Also called ammonium sulphate, this is a fast-acting, crystalline source of nitrogen, particularly suitable for top-dressing. Nitrogen is used in quantity, especially by cabbages, main-crop potatoes, celery, leeks, beetroot, pears, plums, blackcurrants, and rhubarb. |
| Sulphate of potash | 0 | 0 | 50 | 20–35g per sq m (½–1oz per sq yd) | Also called potassium sulphate. Potassium chloride has a higher potash content and is cheaper but can be toxic in excess, especially on tomatoes, gooseberries, and redcurrants. Potassium nitrate is expensive and used in liquid feeds. Potash is important for crop quality, balanced growth, and disease resistance. |
| Triple superphosphate | 0 | 47 | 0 | 35–70g per sq m (1–2oz per sq yd) | A concentrated form of phosphate, best added to a depth of 20cm (8in). Phosphate, vital for cell division and root growth, is relatively immobile and quite small annual dressings are needed. Farmyard manure and garden compost maintain suitable levels. Superphosphate is less concentrated, at about 18–21 per cent. |
| General compound | 7 | 7 | 7 | 135–210g per sq m (4–6oz per sq yd) | The widely available Growmore formulation is a general compound fertilizer suitable for the maintenance of nutrients in a well-prepared fruit and vegetable garden, ensuring adequate supplies of all three essential nutrients. |
| High-nitrogen compound | 20 | 10 | 10 | 35–70g per sq m (1–2oz per sq yd) | Artificial fertilizers that are incorporated as a base dressing at preparation time should be scattered evenly over the surface of the soil to avoid pockets of infertility: this is easiest to achieve with granulated formulations. This 20:10:10 compound is suitable for leafy crops. |

**Top-dressing crops**
*Weigh out fertilizer for 1sq m (1sq yd) and use a small container to judge the volume. Wearing protective gloves, tip out the fertilizer into one hand and scatter it evenly over the crop rooting area. Take care not to drop any onto the plants – it could scorch the foliage.*

## APPLYING FERTILIZERS

Wear gloves and take precautions against inhaling airborne particles when handling any kind of fertilizer or manure.

When applying base dressings before planting, ideally mark out the area in a grid; at least measure out one square to help you to estimate the area. Weigh out the appropriate quantity, mark its volume in a pot, and then use this to distribute. Incorporate the fertilizer down to a depth of 10cm (4in) by forking in or raking. This guidance applies to ground preparations for most planting or sowing. All fertilizers need moisture to be effective; wait until just before rainfall before applying it, or if this is not practicable, water in any dressings made to dry ground.

Liquid fertilizers may be applied by watering a solution along crop rows or around individual plants; always water onto moist soil for even distribution. Alternatively, liquids can be applied as foliar feeds through a watering can or sprayer. Cover the leaves thoroughly, and never apply foliar feeds in full sunshine, as the leaves may be scorched.

## INORGANIC FERTILIZERS

Inorganic fertilizers are often known as artificials. These fertilizers are usually fast-acting, and often more efficient than organics weight-for-weight, with quite consistent content. In most cases, however, they lack trace elements and have relatively short-term effects. Their beneficial effects are directed primarily at the plant, rather than the soil in which it grows.

Two types of inorganic fertilizer are available. Those formulated to supply mainly just one of the three principal nutrients of nitrogen, phosphate, or potash are referred to as straight

fertilizers. The average nutrient content is printed on the packaging (*see also chart, facing page*). Combinations of the elements are known as compound fertilizers. Straight fertilizers may be formulated as crystals, powder, or granules, while compounds are almost always sold in granular form, which is easier to apply. Inorganic fertilizers are also available in liquid form, suitable for watering in or using as a foliar feed to boost growth or supplement nutrition in developing crops.

Where straight inorganic fertilizers are used as base dressings, remember that both phosphorus and potassium take longer than nitrogen to become available to plants, and the ideal times for incorporation of these nutrients are autumn and spring respectively. These timings are not critical, however, and a base dressing of compound fertilizer can be applied when most convenient.

Inorganic fertilizers are suitable for nitrogen top-dressing around individual plants or along crop rows. Take care not to let the fertilizer touch the stems or leaves, which could be scorched. Work the top-dressing into the soil surface using a push hoe or a rake. The insurance dressings suggested in the chart (see *facing page*) are likely to be excessive on fertile soils. In the interests of economy and avoiding harm to the garden environment, always limit applications. Much can be learnt about your crops' annual requirements through careful observation.

## ORGANIC FERTILIZERS

In all situations concentrated organic fertilizers have a unique role, and their use in the kitchen garden can certainly be complementary to the use of inorganic fertilizers.

Processed organic fertilizers (*see chart, p.22*) are usually relatively expensive per unit of nutrient due to their manufacturing process, and weight-for-weight they contain less of the major nutrients than inorganic fertilizers. They have the advantage, however, of containing trace elements that are usually lacking in artificials, and are also useful for their slow release of nutrients as the substance decomposes in the soil. This release is governed by soil temperature, because the soil organisms involved need warmth for activity.

Soil of any texture also benefits from the presence of organic matter, which increases humus content and encourages worm activity, improving the soil structure and in turn its capacity to hold water and air, its temperature, and its drainage (*see pp.14–16*).

Seaweed meal, bone meal, hoof and horn, fish meal, and fish, blood, and bone meal are all widely available forms of concentrated organic fertilizer that have long been recommended for inclusion in base dressings.

For top-dressing growing crops, dried blood has excellent effects, and many organic growers also advocate the use of liquid feeds containing extracts of comfrey or seaweed, both of which are rich in minerals. Some animal carcass derivatives are likely to be withdrawn from sale because of associated risks to health, however remote these may be: take precautions when using to avoid any skin contact, accidental ingestion, or inhalation. Store these substances in sturdy, sealed containers, as they can attract vermin and flies.

**Raking in fertilizer**
*Measure out the fertilizer and scatter over the surface, here a seedbed. Draw a wide rake lightly and evenly over the surface so that the fertilizer is worked into the soil.*

## BULKY MANURES

Bulky organic manures contribute far more to good soil structure than any of the concentrated organic fertilizers. They are mainly used as a soil additive, but also have an important use as a surface mulch (*see pp.41–42*). Manures are often more difficult to find and transport, and are much more laborious to apply, but these challenges are well worth facing up to. Homemade garden compost has the advantages of being free and made on site (*see pp.24–26*).

The most commonly quoted form of bulky organic is farmyard manure. This term describes a variable mix of dung, urine, and some kind of litter, usually straw; the main constituent is cattle manure, but pig and poultry dung may be added. Nutrient levels are low and variable (*see chart, below*). Horse manure is often more readily available, and usually has a relatively high straw content and higher nutrient levels; it is excellent for improving soil structure.

Use only well-rotted farmyard or stable manure, in which the litter is already substantially broken down. Fresh manure is likely to generate ammonia as it breaks down, which can damage plants. If your supply has not been weathered outside, leave it in a covered stack in the garden for at least six months before use.

Spent mushroom compost is another possible source of bulky organic matter. It consists of straw well-composted with horse manure or a high-nitrogen fertilizer, together with the spawning layer, usually a mixture of peat and chalk or ground limestone. The nutrient value of mushroom compost is normally similar to that of farmyard manure.

In coastal areas it may be legal and practicable to collect seaweed; check with the relevant authorities before doing so. Seaweed is relatively rich in potassium, with 0.5 per cent nitrogen and one per cent potassium; it contains significant amounts of iron, magnesium, and manganese, too. To avoid subjecting young crops to unacceptable levels of common salt, leave seaweed out in heavy rain before incorporation. Seaweed is also excellent for mixing with farmyard manure in a stack to be rotted down. There are environmental reasons for considering the use of treated sewage sludge and municipal waste as bulky soil additives, but theoretically these substances can contain heavy metal contaminants and are best avoided in the domestic garden.

## APPLYING MANURES

Bulky organic manures are most often incorporated into soil during autumn or winter digging (*see pp.37–40*). For most crops, it is best to mix the manure evenly throughout the soil down to the depth of a spade blade (*see p.38*).

An alternative system is to overwinter the material as a deep layer spread over the surface of the soil and then dig in the residue during early spring. Much of a layer of manure overwintered this way will be pulled into the top layers of soil by the action of earthworms. This natural action does not allow for incorporation to much depth, but it is a suitable method for sandy soils. These

## TYPES OF ORGANIC FERTILIZER AND MANURE

| Fertilizer | Typical nutrient content (per cent) | | | Approximate rate of application | Characteristics and uses |
|---|---|---|---|---|---|
| | Nitrogen | Phosphate | Potash | | |
| Dried blood | 10–12 | 0 | 0 | 70g per sq m (2oz per sq yd) dry or in 1 litre (1¾pt) water | Dried blood has excellent effects on boosting growth when used as a top-dressing, and it may also be used as a base dressing. It can be applied either as a powder or as a liquid suspension. |
| Blood, fish, and bone meal | 3.5 | 8 | 5 | 135g per sq m (4oz per sq yd) | Use as a base dressing applied several weeks before planting or sowing, and as a top-dressing. |
| Hoof and horn | 7–15 | 1–10 | 0 | 135g per sq m (4oz per sq yd) | A slow-release fertilizer of varying nutrient levels, suitable for base dressing. Hoof and horn also raises the level of calcium in the soil. |
| Pelleted chicken manure | 2–5 | 1–4 | 1–2.5 | 135g per sq m (4oz per sq yd) | Pelleted chicken manure is often available. This processed form is easier to spread than bulky, unprocessed manures. Chicken manure has a higher nitrogen and phosphate content than farmyard manure. Use as a base dressing. |
| Rotted animal manures | 0.5 | 0.25 | 0.5 | 5kg per sq m (10lb per sq yd) | The most commonly available bulky organic manure. NPK content varies with methods of stock rearing, straw content, and time stored; horse manure usually has higher levels. Of special benefit in improving soil structure. |
| Spent mushroom compost | 0.7 | 0.3 | 0.3 | 5kg per sq m (10lb per sq yd) | A bulky organic material with physical properties that vary with age. Its main value is as a soil structure improver with low nutrient content. Because of its lime content, regular dressings of mushroom compost can raise the soil pH. |

**Neglected soil**
*Soil devoid of organic matter is likely to have poor structure. Water absorption can be a particular problem on poorly structured light soil, as shown here. Bulky manure improves absorption and retention on all soils.*

**Spreading manure**
*On light soil the structure can be protected from winter rain by spreading a 5–8cm (2–3in) layer of well-rotted manure over the surface. Much of the manure will be drawn into the soil by worms; dig or fork in the rest in spring.*

benefit from protection against severe weather during the winter, and are quite amenable to spring digging, when the residues can be turned in. Generally speaking, the more well-rotted bulky organic matter that can be worked into the fruit and vegetable garden soil at preparation time the better. Plan to add at least 5kg per sq m (10lb per sq yd).

## GREEN MANURES

Green manuring involves sowing a suitable fast-maturing crop, either broadcast or in very closely spaced rows, cutting it down while still young, and incorporating the bulky living plant material into the soil by digging. Here it will decay fast, quickly releasing its constituent nutrients and aiding the production of humus.

When a kitchen garden has been well established, with close attention to soil condition, there is no doubt at all that green manures are a useful means of improving and maintaining fertility. Well-managed green manuring practice is helpful in the production of humus and the maintenance of soil structure, although it is unlikely to be sufficient on its own.

Careful management, however, is crucial to the success of any green manuring. The choice of plants, the planning of their place in the cropping calendar, and their maturity at the time of incorporation into the soil are all important considerations. The soil type, as well as its existing state of fertility, will have a strong influence on the usefulness of green manuring. Green manuring is particularly relevant to the management of light-textured

soils, especially where the green manure can be left to grow over winter. It will help to stabilize the soil and also allow for the steady absorption of soluble nutrients that might otherwise be washed out in heavy winter rainfall.

Remember that in dry seasons green manures can actually deplete the soil of moisture reserves. Before digging in green manure plants, chop them to aid decomposition.

## PLANNING GREEN MANURES

Unless one is totally committed to this style of soil management, it is most sensible to see green manuring as a technique supplementary to the use of other types of organic manuring and fertilizer application, rather than a replacement for them. The system will

fit more easily into the plan of short-term vegetable crops than into the growing of perennial fruit crops.

The greatest nutrient contribution from green manuring is nitrogen. To gain the most benefit from this, plan for the shortest interval between incorporation and cropping. Usually the best time to dig in a green manure crop is as it nears flowering time; do not allow it to be in the ground so long that it becomes woody; this contributes less nitrogen and will temporarily take nitrogen from the soil on decomposition.

## GREEN MANURE CROPS

A suitable green manure crop needs to establish well from sowing and grow quickly to produce lush bulk. Suitable annuals for garden use are peas and annual lupins (*Lupinus*), both of which have root nodules capable of absorbing atmospheric nitrogen. Also suitable are rape (*Brassica napus*) and white mustard (*Sinapis alba*), both of which will grow rapidly and break down quickly to release nitrogen.

Of the perennial candidates, comfrey (*Symphytum officinale*) is well tried, as is borage (*Borago officinale*). Rye grass (*Lolium perenne*) is useful because of its searching root growth. The tops of all of the perennial green manures will need cutting down before digging; where tops have become very mature, consign them to the compost heap rather than digging them in.

## Digging in a green manure

**1** **Cut green manure** crops to the ground when they reach about 15–20cm (6–8in) in height and are still green and soft. Leave them to lie and wilt on the surface for a day or two.

**2** **Skim off** the wilted residue of the green manure plants into a trench as deep as a spade blade (spit) as single digging proceeds across the plot (*see p.38*).

# Making compost

Rotted plant refuse is a valuable source of organic matter for improving and maintaining the fertility of soil, and making garden compost from plant remains and kitchen waste has a place in even the smallest of gardens.

The practice also makes a positive contribution to recycling. When we compost household and garden waste materials we reduce the need for collection and dumping of refuse, and also avoid using wasteful and potentially polluting bonfires to dispose of plant remains. All of these factors are in the interests of our natural environment.

Composting is a practical alternative to the use of animal manures (*see p.22*), which may be difficult for the kitchen gardener to obtain. Garden compost is low in nutrients, but is a rich source of humus (*see p.14*). It has most of the advantages of other forms of bulky organic matter, without the possible disadvantages, such as difficulty of transportation or unacceptable odour.

Any heap of plant waste will gradually decay and reduce to yield a useful soil additive, but careful management of a compost heap will pay dividends. The aim is to produce a dark-coloured, friable material of even consistency that is agreeable to handle and not too wet. This is best achieved by what is called aerobic composting, which involves ensuring that air can get into the bulk of waste material, accelerating decay.

### COMPOST BINS

Place compost bins in a screened area, perhaps conveniently near the kitchen; they can be in shade. Depending on the productive garden size and the space available, plan for at least two bins side by side, each about 1–1.5m (3–5ft) square. The purpose of having more than one bin is to allow the rotting compost to be turned and moved from one bin to another. This exacting process is well worth the effort for aeration.

Bins need to be established either on a 20cm (8in) layer of thin, woody prunings laid on soil base, or with a floor of strong wire mesh laid over bricks. Both methods allow air to circulate at ground level. You can make your own bins (*see left*) with walls of strong, treated timber, builders' pallets, concrete blocks, or even straw bales. Ideally, construct the front walls with removable boards that slot in, allowing the height of the front to be raised as the bin is filled. A removable cover is essential to avoid the heap becoming too wet, but fit it so that some air circulation is possible over the surface of the compost.

Proprietary composting containers made from strong, rigid plastic are available, and these are suitable for use in the smaller garden.

### COMPOSTING MATERIALS

Any bulky matter of plant origin is suitable for composting. Nitrogen-rich material, in the form of leaves and nitrogen-rich additives such as animal manures, will accelerate decomposition. There must be a good balance of material in a heap in order to ensure the movement of air. Mixing in a proportion of semi-woody material helps this by preventing the heap from becoming compacted.

It is quite easy to ensure a supply of lush, leafy waste during the warm days of summer, but as the growing season

## Constructing a compost bin

**1** **Lay 2 uprights** on the ground. Nail planks to them using 2 nails each end. Start 8cm (3in) from the bottom and keep the planks 1cm (½in) apart. Make 2 sides in this way.

**2** **Stand the sides** up and tack 2 strips of wood across the tops to hold them the correct distance apart. Attach the planks for the back to the uprights, as for the sides.

**3** **Nail a plank** across the front of the bin at the bottom, so that it is in line with the bottom boards of the sides and back. Remove the stabilizing strips from the top of the bin.

**4** **Attach 2 battens** to the front uprights with nails, leaving a gap to allow planks to slide down between them. Nail a piece of wood in the bottom of this channel as a stop.

**5** **Try sliding each** of the planks for the front of the bin down between the battens to make sure that they fit correctly. If necessary, trim the ends to the correct length.

**6** **Paint the bin** with a water-based preservative, with particular attention to cut edges. Tie a strong nylon cord around the front posts to prevent the sides from bowing as the bin is filled.

draws to a close, the nature of material available for composting is relatively low in nitrogen. Temperatures also fall, slowing the composting process. At this time rotting can be encouraged by adding nitrogen in the form of a 5cm (2in) layer of animal manures, including litter from poultry or pets such as rabbits. Alternatively, add dried blood at a rate of 250g per sq m (8oz per sq yd) or a proprietary compost activator.

Lawn mowings, fallen leaves, and cleared plant debris from ornamental borders will all decay suitably, as will trimmings made from vegetables on harvesting and waste from fruit and vegetable preparation in the kitchen. Brassica leaves and stems can be added; the stems are best chopped up. Pea and bean plants, including the pulled roots, will compost. Unused root crops can be added, chopped into fragments, provided they are pest and disease free. Doubts are often raised about adding rhubarb leaves to compost, but this is quite acceptable. Blight-diseased potato haulms can be composted in a well-made heap that reaches a high temperature. Annual and perennial weeds are usually relatively high in nitrogen and the tops will compost well.

Hedge clippings and thin woody prunings will decompose if reduced to small fragments, and for this purpose it may be worth investing in a small shredding machine. Other less obvious materials can also be composted, as long as they are made from natural substances. Newspaper and card can be added if they are shredded first; even cotton and woollen items that have been cut up can be composted, although they will inevitably take a much longer time to break down than other waste.

## MATERIALS TO AVOID

Although the heat generated in a well-managed compost heap will destroy many plant pests and diseases (*see* Plant Problems, *pp.246–264*), exclude any material carrying persistent infections, such as clubroot in brassicas, black spot in roses, canker in apples, and white rot in onions. It is best not to add brassica roots, which may be diseased; similarly, potato tubers may perpetuate disease and can also be troublesome in re-sprouting.

Take care not to carry over weed populations in the form of seeds, roots, bulbs, corms, and fleshy parts that may survive composting. All the underground parts of grasses, docks, nettles, and oxalis, for example, should be excluded from compost; it is also best not to put in abundantly seeding annual weeds. Check that grass mowings and straw added to the heap have not recently been treated with selective (or hormone)

**Using a compost activator**
*Specially formulated compost activators that accelerate rotting are available, and are useful when leafy green material is scarce. Sulphate of ammonia is a good activator.*

weedkillers, for there is a small risk of contaminating the crops grown on ground to which these composted remains are added.

It is also important not to put plastics in a compost heap, nor any waste food products, such as meat, that might attract rats to it.

## MAKING THE HEAP

Build the compost heap up in layers of about 15cm (6in) depth, aiming to mix the type of material added where possible. It is best, if possible, to have a space beside the bins to store heaps of different materials until there is enough to make a proper layer, ensuring a good variety of material through the heap. Add chopped, moist straw to a similar depth over each layer to maintain aeration. Do not allow compacted layers of a single type of plant waste, such as lawn mowings, to lie in the heap, because they will form a slimy mass and create airless conditions that slow the rotting process.

The heap must not be allowed to become waterlogged, which will exclude air and lower the temperature. Keep it covered at all times to keep off rain and maintain warmth and internal moisture. Conversely, the heap should not be too dry, as this similarly slows decay; in warm summer weather you may need to water it.

**Layered material**
*Straw separates 15–23cm (6–9in) deep layers of preferably differently textured material*

**Rotting down**
*As compost rots, it will reduce in volume and sink down*

**Twin compost bin system**
*Fill the first bin with alternating layers of different types of organic material. Keep the heap covered with black plastic or carpet to keep it moist and warm. When the bin is full and partly rotted, turn the contents into the empty second bin and start refilling the first bin. Once the first load of compost is black and friable (above right), it can be removed and used. You can then turn the contents of the other bin (above left) into it, and repeat the process over again.*

Rotting waste generates heat through the activity of micro-organisms, and a well-made compost heap can reach around 70°C (158°F) within three or four weeks. It is most beneficial to turn the heap from time to time, ideally by forking rotting material out of a full bin into an empty one. Move less rotted material from the sides of the bin to the centre of the new load, where it will rot faster. Do this at least once per full loading and preferably more often.

The speed of decay is determined by the nature of the waste, but above all by the management of the heap. A heap that is carefully loaded, regularly turned, and has suitable additives can produce useable compost within six months, although it is wiser to plan for a year.

## ANAEROBIC COMPOSTING

It is not always possible or convenient to make compost in the ideal manner. There is still value in producing bulky organic manure simply by stacking plant waste to rot in the open or in plastic sacks, mixing types as much as possible as for a standard heap. This method allows less air to penetrate, and is known as anaerobic composting. Complete rotting takes much longer, at least one year and up to two years. Burying waste in a large trench and digging it up once it has rotted down is also suitable on a small scale.

## LEAF MOULD

Tree leaves collected in autumn can form compacted layers if not mixed with other materials before adding to a compost heap. They are best composted in a separate container of similar size to compost bins, but with mesh or netting sides. They rot slowly, taking at least a year to produce leaf mould. This has an excellent friable texture, and is very suitable for mulching and as an ingredient of potting composts. Oak and beech leaves in particular are a great bonus to a leaf mould mix.

**Forking out finished compost**
*Compost is ready for use when it has decayed to a crumbly, dark mass that has few large particles and runs easily through the hands. Use it for digging into beds or mulching.*

## WORM COMPOSTING

Worm composting is a relatively small-scale process, of particular use where space is limited or for dealing with kitchen waste. Dried samples of this small-scale nutrient-rich compost are especially suitable for adding to potting mixes. There are various sizes and styles of proprietary wormery; alternatively, a plastic bin, wooden box, or any large, rigid container can be adapted. The bin needs to have a lid and good drainage, and to be kept frost-free in a sheltered place. Suitable worms, known as muck or compost worms or brandlings, resemble small earthworms but are darker red. They can be found in rotting manure or plant waste, or be purchased from a specialist supplier. Managing the bin requires experience: only small quantities of kitchen waste should be added at a time. To harvest the waste, spread it on a plastic sheet and place wet newspaper over part of it: the worms will collect under the paper and can be returned to the bin.

## THE ROLE OF COMPOST

Any of these types of compost is beneficial: they all make an excellent mulch (*see pp.41–42*) for fruit canes, bushes, and trees, and for perennial vegetables and runner beans. Although a surprising amount of compost can be made in many gardens, it is likely that it will need to be supplemental to other means of improving the soil's organic content because of limited production.

## Making compost in a worm bin

Brandling worms will turn kitchen waste into fine worm casts in about ten weeks. Avoid onions and leeks, and citrus fruits, which can make the mix too acidic; crushed eggshells help counteract acidity. Meat and dairy products can attract flies and vermin if the bin is not securely lidded. Waste should be added in thin layers: compost worms can eat up to their own weight each day, but it is best to add at half this rate.

*Brandling worms*

**Covering**
*Layer of newspaper helps to keep bin moist and warm*

**Active layer**
*Worms thrive and work best in warm, dark conditions*

**Initial bedding**
*Dampened straw or shredded newspaper, or rotted manure*

**Drain tap**
*Excess liquid should be drained regularly to avoid flooding*

**Kitchen waste**
*Chop waste into small pieces and mix well*

**Composted material**
*Worms work upwards leaving casts below*

**Drainage material**
*Liquid drains through layer of boards or permeable membrane into gravel or crocks*

# Planning your garden

The content and layout of a garden is determined by many factors. Although practical considerations are paramount in growing fruit and vegetables, try to make the most of these plants as an extension of the ornamental qualities of a garden. They may not offer the same breadth of interest as ornamental plants, but they certainly have their attractions.

## CROPS IN THE GARDEN

Garden sites come in all aspects, shapes, and sizes. On the reasonable assumption that the majority of garden sites can be made suitable for fruit and vegetables, consideration of how they are to be laid out is to do with personal preference and the practical limitations of the site. Take some time to learn and think about the style of garden you want.

One of the most basic considerations in planning a garden is the structural form. Here, single specimens of fruit trees and bushes can be used to good effect; the structure of carefully trained trees will provide strong interest throughout the year. Bold architectural form is also found in perennial crops, such as tall artichokes and sweetcorn, and the dramatic leaves of rhubarb.

Climbing plants, such as peas, beans, squashes, and melons contribute height and structure from the supports needed to grow them. These may be woody poles, brushwood, or more ornate wooden or metal structures, and can make pleasing features themselves. The way in which plants are grown also has an effect: where fruit and vegetable plants are arranged in beds and straight rows, the geometric layouts can make a strong visual impact.

Once the form of a garden has been established, texture and colour can be considered. Many vegetable plants have striking leaves and stems. In the beet group, for example, are plants with corrugated, deeply coloured leaves, and chards with glowing coloured stems. Carrots have graceful, finely cut foliage, the leaves of brassicas are both bold in shape and glaucous, and lettuces mostly have a soft, crinkled texture. The great range of culinary herb plants includes many that could be grown as much for ornament as for usefulness. These include sage, with its felty leaves, ruffled parsley, and thymes, which contribute both aroma and flowers in addition to their carpeting foliage.

For most people, flowers and fruit are essential in any garden. Fruit trees, canes, and bushes produce beautiful blossom and brightly coloured fruits.

Taking all these considerations into account, there are three basic points to decide on at the outset. Do you wish to grow crops mixed with ornamental plants, or separately? If separately, should they be integrated within the overall garden design or in a separate plot? How large an area should be devoted to crops?

## BORDERS AND POTAGERS

There are two main possibilities for integrating fruit and vegetables in the ornamental garden. They can be grown within the mixture of plants in a herbaceous or mixed border, or they can be grown alongside ornamental features in formal beds, a system usually described as potager gardening.

Growing crops within the ornamental borders of a garden is particularly suitable where space is limited, or where only small supplies are wanted. There are disadvantages: the gaps left as annual vegetables are progressively harvested are not attractive, and it is

**Pretty potager**
*Even a small space can be planted with vegetables and herbs to create an attractive and functional potager plot. Here squares separated by box hedging allow for planned crop rotation, while crops of contrasting forms and colour are planted in simple patterns. As crops mature, the gaps will be filled with succeeding crops.*

more difficult to keep successional supplies going; raising plants in modules that can be transplanted to replace plants as they are harvested will alleviate these problems.

Fruit and vegetables grown with ornamentals require particularly close attention. Additional watering or feeding may be necessary, as it is very easy for them to be starved of nutrients or moisture by neighbouring plants, and intervention may be needed to prevent crowding by more vigorous species. It is also easier for pest and disease attacks to be overlooked, so extra vigilance is vital. For gardeners who wish to use garden chemicals on ornamentals but not on crops, mixing the two types will be impossible.

The potager is a more traditional approach for incorporating crops into your garden, with fruit and vegetables contained in formal beds. These are surrounded by permanent, trimmed edging of plants such as box (*Buxus*), lavender (*Lavandula*), or cotton lavender (*Santolina*). The crops within the beds are laid out in carefully planned proportions to maximize visual impact. A more relaxed variation is to use small island beds of a size and position to suit your particular garden. These could even be of a curved shape, making them suitable for an informal garden.

Another productive and potentially attractive way of including vegetables, herbs, and fruit in smaller gardens is by growing them in containers, such as tubs or pots, or even hanging baskets or windowboxes (*see pp.35–36*).

**Ornamental beds**
*In this kitchen garden, changes of level, decorative supports of woven willow, and close planting of colourful crops such as lettuce 'Red Oak Leaf', peas, red cabbage, and nasturtiums, create an exuberant display.*

**Temporary screen**
*A row of runner beans supported on canes provides a quick and colourful divide, whether between crops or between a kitchen garden and flowering plants. There are beans with red, white, or bicoloured flowers – try mixing cultivars to create a decorative effect.*

### THE KITCHEN GARDEN

The traditional approach to growing fruit and vegetables is to use a separate section of the garden. Making a special enclosed area will not only provide beneficial shelter (*see p.12*) but also create a "garden room" leading on from the ornamental areas, adding interest to the garden. An attractive entrance can be made with an archway of trained fruit, such as thornless blackberry, or a climbing vegetable, such as runner beans.

On a large garden plot the kitchen garden area can be enclosed with hedges or permeable fencing (*see p.13*). Hedging is attractive, but for small gardens the shade and the competition for water and nutrients from hedging plants makes fencing more advisable. Post-and-wire fences or trellis used to support ornamental climbers and ramblers or espalier- or cordon-trained apples, pear, gooseberries, or redcurrants

are also both attractive and productive options, as long as they are not exposed to severe winds.

### LOCATION AND SIZE

There are good reasons for siting a kitchen garden close to the house. Ease of access is especially desirable in wet or frosty weather, but there are likely to be frequent demands throughout the growing season if a wide range of produce is grown; this is particularly true for a herb garden. The shortest possible walk encourages both regular inspection of the wellbeing of crops and frequent use of compost bins (*see pp.24– 26*), and having the kitchen garden near the house may deter some animal pests.

The size of the area allocated to fruit and vegetables will depend on what you wish to grow, how much you wish to grow, and the overall size of the garden. It is not meaningful to make definite recommendations as to the size of a kitchen garden because of these variable factors, the most limiting of which is the area of ground available. Outlined below are the considerations that should be dealt with in planning your space.

There really must be room for some compost bins. You may wish to include a small glass or plastic-clad greenhouse and garden frames (*see pp.43–48*) in which to raise young plants, mature tender ones, or extend the cropping season by providing protection for an early start or late cropping. Such protection can increase the range and yields from a kitchen garden, and so will amply justify the time, effort, and garden space devoted to it.

Remember to allow for pathways, with a continuous one running around the perimeter of the kitchen garden and an internal network of paths dividing the growing areas into suitable permanent plots. Plan for widths of 60cm (24in), and remember the need for wheelbarrow access may require wider pathways of up to 90cm (36in).

Once any such features are allowed for, it is most realistic to think in terms of containing the range of what will be grown. If the available space and your enthusiasm are great enough, an area of 150 sq m (175 sq yd) will accommodate a good range of fruit and vegetables.

## USING SPACE EFFICIENTLY

It will be helpful in planning your garden to have some idea of the likely yield of individual crops. Estimates vary greatly, being dependent on many factors. The productivity of fruit plants varies with their age; vegetables may yield a small, succulent early harvest or a larger crop if harvested later, and different cultivars of the same crop can show considerable variation. On top of these factors, the time and length of the local growing season, the site, and the feeding and watering regime also all have considerable effects. Average yields (*see p.242*) are useful in planning

initial plantings, but, with so many variables affecting yield, these estimates always have to be refined through individual trial and error. In the long run, this is the only realistic means of planning the quantities to be grown.

In using the available space efficiently, take account of how long a crop will occupy the soil: a plot that produces a great deal if several fast-maturing crops are grown in succession will yield much less if one slow-growing crop occupies the ground all season. Intercropping is a practical way to increase output, in which rapidly maturing catch crops like lettuce and radish are planted between slower crops (*see p.70*). Also consider the alternative purchase price of what you grow. For instance, potatoes, Brussels sprouts, and cabbages not only take up a great deal of space for a long time, but are also fairly cheap to buy and so may not be worth growing in a small plot, whereas beans, lettuces, and peppers are relatively expensive and are frequently in great demand when they are in season. Rotation of crops is also a consideration at this point, because you will need to plan your groups of plants carefully (*see p.31*).

To some extent the freezing and storage qualities of crops are relevant to the quantities grown. Peas, calabrese,

raspberries, and blackcurrants freeze well, and apples, cabbages, onions, carrots, and potatoes can be dry stored (*see p.73*) well into the winter.

It is quite easy to overproduce fruit and vegetables; a little beetroot or radish, for example, goes a long way. You can avoid a glut by planning to make successional sowings (*see p.69*) of these, and of lettuces and French and runner beans. Some crops are demanding to grow successfully, so might not be a good choice for the less experienced; for example, cauliflowers require close attention to cultivation, and are then very likely to mature all together in greater quantity than can reasonably be used at one time.

## CROP SITES

Once you have chosen your crops and decided on the space you have available, you need to decide how they should be arranged within the allocated space.

The position of non-perennial crops should ideally be governed by rotation (*see p.31*). One consideration when planning crop sites is shade. Fruit and vegetable crops will not thrive in the dense shade of fences, hedges, or overhanging trees, but you should also ensure that there is a minimum of shading from one crop over another.

**Work and pleasure**
*In this kitchen garden ornamental alliums and marigolds* (Tagetes) *grow alongside crops of brassicas and beetroot. Some gardeners claim that additional flowering plants can attract more pollinating insects and improve the yields of fruiting crops; they certainly help to create an attractive setting.*

This can be achieved by planting fruit trees at the northerly end of the plot and low crops such as strawberries at the south. Very tall vegetables, such as sweetcorn, Jerusalem artichokes, or trained runner beans, are also best not arranged in east-to-west rows that will reduce the light available to shorter crops, but this is unlikely to be critical.

Take full advantage of relatively warm spots (*see* What is a microclimate?, *p.10*). Areas that slope towards the sun, and those backed by fences, or possibly walls facing the sun, are valuable for growing more tender plants such as outdoor tomatoes, melons, aubergines, and peppers, and also strawberries. Wherever possible, arrange rows to run north to south, so that sunlight is evenly distributed among the plants – but this is a bonus rather than an essential.

Another way of maximizing the sun is to use solid panels for part of the kitchen garden boundary or as internal dividers: if one side faces the sun, it will provide a warm surface against which a fan-trained peach or sweet cherry could

be supported. Position such panels carefully to minimize turbulence (*see p.12*) or shade. Cordons and espaliers or soft fruits trained on posts and wire make effective and attractive boundaries or dividers, while bush and cane fruits should be planted in blocks separate from those for tree fruits. Soft fruits, peaches, and cherries need protection from birds, and the same is true of peas and brassicas, especially when newly emerged or planted. The most effective solution is netting, usually in the form of a cage (*see p.51*), and you should allow for removing and replacing the netting where appropriate, and for working around the plants inside it.

## DESIGNING YOUR KITCHEN GARDEN

Settling down with a sheet of squared paper to plan the layout of a fruit and vegetable garden is a worthwhile contribution to good results.

Start by measuring the area, working from fixed points such as house corners for accuracy. Draw an outline plan with permanent features such as beds, trees,

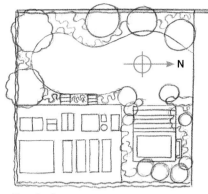

**Rough plan**
*Start by drawing a rough, relatively small-scale plan of the kitchen garden area within the whole site. This will give you an idea of the space you are going to devote to it and the impact that it will have on your garden.*

perennial vegetables, or compost bins: you can cut these out of paper so you can easily try them in different positions before reaching a decision. When the layout is set, you can plan planting of crops in detail: this last part is essential whether you have a kitchen garden, a potager, or informal island beds.

**Detailed plan**
*A larger-scale plan of the layout within the kitchen garden allows for proper calculation of how much you can expect to fit into each area. This is the time to adjust the design: decide just how important each element is and balance the plants' requirements of space, orientation, and shelter to find the best solution. Every plan involves compromises.*

**Compost bins**
*Allow for at least two bins, about 1.2m (4ft) wide*

**Cold frames**
*Useful for hardening off young crops and also for growing cucumbers and melons*

**Cordon-trained fruit**
*Cordon apples and espalier apples and pears can line boundary, while loganberries and blackberries can be trained over arches to make entrances into garden*

**Greenhouse**
*2 x 2.5m (6 x 8ft) greenhouse should be sufficient for most gardens: place water butts to collect run-off from roof as supplementary water supply*

**Fan-trained fruit**
*Allow 4m (12ft) between specimens for fan-trained trees*

**Rotation beds**
*Annual vegetables can be rotated in bed system, with temporary protection such as fleece or tunnel cloches when needed*

**Fruit cage**
*Must be big enough to allow access to all sides of fruit bushes – bushes will need to be 2m (6ft) apart for ease of management and optimum yield*

**Raspberry canes**
*You must be able to pick from both sides*

**Strawberry tunnel**
*Strawberries should be spaced at least 30cm (12in) in beds and can be protected by tunnel cloches*

**Climbing beans**
*Trained on cane wigwams*

**Dimensions:**
*17 x 12m (56 x 40ft)*

# Crop rotation

Generations of experience have shown that growth and yield can be reduced if crops are grown in the same ground year after year. Rotating crops in sequence is a long-established practice to prevent this. There are three main reasons for using rotation: to combat pests and diseases, to maintain soil fertility, and to keep the soil well cultivated.

## THE ADVANTAGES OF ROTATION

The greatest advantage in leaving a gap of at least three or four years before growing the same crop in a site again is in interrupting conditions that favour particular pests or diseases. Several fruit and vegetable problems (see pp.246–264), like eelworms in vegetables such as potatoes and tomatoes, foot and root rots in peas and beans, clubroot in brassicas, white rot in onions, and parsnip canker, are carried in the soil. Continually growing related or similar crops on the same site will only nurture the pests and pathogens.

Strawberries are highly susceptible to virus diseases, some of which are carried by eelworms; plant new stock where large populations of eelworms are less likely to have built up. It is also best to avoid replanting fruit bushes, canes, or trees on sites from which old ones have been removed. A condition known as replant

disease can cause reduced or even stunted growth. Nutrient exhaustion, virus transmission from eelworms, and fungal diseases may all be implicated.

A second reason for using rotation is to meet differing nutritional needs. Well-planned rotation can help to maintain fertility, taking account of the different preferences of crop groups. Legumes, especially broad beans, can extract nitrogen from the atmosphere (see p.95), while brassicas need plenty of nitrogen to produce edible leaves and flowerheads; therefore it makes sense to plant brassicas where legumes have recently grown. Root crops, which require low levels of nitrogen, can be grown after brassicas.

Alternating crops also sets up a regular pattern for maintaining ideal soil pH (see pp.18–19). Legumes benefit from ground dressed with organic matter, which lowers pH, while brassicas do best in soil with a higher pH, which discourages club root: alternating manuring and liming with these rotating crops ensures that the soil never becomes either too acid or too alkaline.

The third benefit of rotation is that it helps to control weeds and maintain good soil structure. This is where the third group is particularly beneficial: the cultivation of the soil for potatoes and other root vegetables helps to break up the ground and keep it open.

## THE LIMITATIONS OF ROTATION

There are practical problems in strictly following rotation. Crops in the groups may be required in different proportions, or their seasons may overlap. Close proximity of crops enables diseases or pests to spread readily to new areas; a few diseases, like clubroot and white rot, can remain viable in the soil for many years beyond a reasonable rotation period.

Rotation is an aid to pest and disease suppression, not a total prevention or cure. Some gardeners hold that in small areas it is better continually to grow one crop on the same ground, and then avoid it altogether for susceptible crops when infestation reaches an unacceptable level.

## PLANNING ROTATION

It is difficult to adhere strictly to a three plot rotation in a small garden, but the principles are sound and it is a practice to be aimed at. The plantings suggested here are reasonably flexible: as long as the main plant groups of legumes, brassicas, and potatoes and root crops are kept separate, the other crops that are included with them may be placed in one group or another to suit other planting considerations. The crucial rule is to have two complete cropping seasons without repeating a vegetable group if at all possible. Keeping a record of operations in the fruit and vegetable garden is always time well spent, and a diary of each year's planting is especially valuable for planning rotations.

**Rotation plan**
*This crop rotation plan suitable for kitchen gardens is based on dividing the vegetables that are grown into three groups. Some crops are grouped not with the plants to which they are most closely related, but with those that share their cultivation needs. Tomatoes, for example, are related to potatoes, but as they are not a root crop they would neither break up the soil nor benefit from the low levels of nitrogen left by brassicas, and so they are placed with the legumes instead.*

Beetroot; carrot; leek; lettuce; onion; parsnip; potato; spinach; spinach beet; Swiss chard; salsify; scorzonera
**Root vegetable group**

Broccoli; Brussels sprouts; cabbage; calabrese; Chinese broccoli; Chinese cabbage; kale; kohlrabi; land cress; mustard greens; seakale; swede; turnip; radish; texsel greens
**Brassica group**

Aubergine; beans: broad (fava), French; kidney; Lima; runner; celery; courgette; cucumber; marrow; okra; peas; pepper; sweet and chilli; pumpkin; squash; sweetcorn; sweet melon; tomato; tomatillo; watermelon
**Legume and fruit vegetable group**

# The bed system

Fruit and vegetables are best grown in open ground, either on the flat or in raised beds. In these situations the soil benefits from rainfall and weathering, and the plants have a free root run.

Although it is quite possible to mix edible crops with ornamental plantings (*see pp.27–28*), it is more usual to set aside a particular garden area specifically for fruit and vegetables. This area can be a wide, open plot, but an excellent alternative is to set out the vegetable garden as a series of narrow beds divided by pathways.

## THE TRADITIONAL VEGETABLE PATCH

A common arrangement for a kitchen garden is to have long rows of vegetables across the plot. A packet of lettuce seed, for example, will advise sowing in rows 30cm (12in) apart, and thinning seedlings to 20cm (8in).This is a perfectly good way to grow produce, including strawberries, allowing all of the ground to be used with maximum flexibility and large areas to be cultivated.

Growing crops, however, requires constant access for sowing, thinning, planting out, watering, top-dressing, pest and disease control, weeding, harvesting, and clearing. Where long rows cover the whole plot, each of these tasks brings the need to tread on the ground alongside the growing plants, and every visit results in compression of the soil.

**High raised beds**
*This version of raised beds is suitable for a wheelchair user, but it could provide moveable beds in a courtyard. There needs to be at least 15cm (6in) depth of growing medium.*

Compaction reduces the air in the soil, resulting in poor growth (*see pp.14–16*). Look at the rows of vegetables beside heavily trafficked pathways, and you will invariably find that they are less vigorous than the rest. The adverse effects of compaction can be avoided or reduced by taking care not to tread on wet soil and by walking on planks to spread the weight; narrow beds avoid the need to walk on cropped areas.

## USING BEDS

In a bed system, the kitchen garden is divided into semi-permanent or fixed beds. All the cultivation tasks can be carried out from the dividing pathways, without needing to step onto the soil.

**Large bed**
*Large beds like this one can be planted with several crops in longer rows, but have the disadvantage that the crops can be reached only by walking on the soil.*

**▲ Standard raised bed**
*The soil in raised beds remains uncompacted, providing better conditions for plant growth, in this case Swiss chard.*

**◄ Narrow flat bed**
*Narrow beds that are easily reached from the surrounding paths are particularly suitable for crops that are frequently harvested, such as these cut-and-come-again vegetables.*

This avoids soil compaction, and one important benefit is that harvesting and other jobs can be done soon after rain without risk of damaging soil structure. There is less need to dig beds once they are established and fertile, and what cultivation is necessary is greatly reduced because of the smaller cropped area. Another advantage of using beds is that, because bulky organic manures are concentrated on a smaller area, it is easier to build up high levels of fertility: this encourages better soil aeration and drainage, which in turn leads to stronger root growth.

The number of plants per square metre (or square yard) can generally be increased in a bed system, because there is no need for access along crop rows, so it is possible to grow the plants equidistant from each other. In a bed system, the lettuces of the example above might be arranged 20cm (8in) apart in all directions in staggered rows. This arrangement will allow the maximum root space for each plant in the smallest area, making the best use of the soil available and increasing the total yield of the area.

The close spacing of plants in beds has further indirect benefits. Irrigation using low-level distribution systems such as seep hoses (*see p.54*) will be more manageable, due to the smaller areas that are to be served.

Close spacing of plants in fixed beds also results in the smothering of annual weed growth, so there is usually less weeding to be done.

Using a bed system can also make crop rotation (*see p.31*) much easier, as each crop group can be allocated a bed and then planted in a different bed each year according to the rotation.

### PLANNING BED LAYOUTS

Beds may be rectangular, square, or even curved if that suits your garden best; the prime consideration is that they must allow the whole bed to be cultivated from the paths.

An ideal width is 1.2m (4ft); this can be increased to 1.5m (5ft) if this makes better use of available space, or reduced to 1m (3ft) if you have an area to be protected with glass or plastic cloches. Narrow strips are particularly suitable for strawberries, for ease of mulching and harvesting. The length of a bed is governed only by how far one has to walk to get around to the opposite side without treading on the bed, although it is of course possible to bridge the bed with a plank resting on raised edging. The orientation of the beds is not of vital importance, but running them from north to south generally ensures the most even distibution of sunlight.

The width of the paths between beds is also important: they will need to be at least 45cm (18in) wide in order to allow for easy access.

## Making a flat or semi-flat bed

**1** **Measure and mark out** the beds and paths to the dimensions you require (here, 1.2m/4ft beds with 45cm/ 18in paths), bearing in mind access and convenient use.

**2** **Rake the soil** from the path area over to the adjoining bed area, so that the beds are raised slightly above the surrounding paths. Incorporating organic matter into the growing area will also slightly raise the level to make a semi-flat bed.

**3** **Tread down** the paths to firm them and define the edge of the beds more clearly. The paths can simply be left as soil or given another surface covering (*see p.34*).

### TYPES OF BEDS

There are many terms that are used to describe beds, but for most purposes it is simplest to distinguish between flat or semi-flat beds and raised beds.

A flat or semi-flat bed is simply marked out from the surrounding garden and cultivated (*see above*). With repeated annual cultivation and the

addition of bulky organic dressings, the surface of such a bed will gradually become raised above the path level.

Raised beds are constructed by similarly marking out beds and then building sides up to 30cm (12in) high from timber, such as railway sleepers, or even bricks or cement blocks (*see below*). It is possible to dispense with the walls,

## Making a raised bed

**1** **Measure and mark out beds.** Edge with 15 x 2.5cm (6 x 1in) boards, sunk into a 5cm (2in) slit trench and supported by timber pegs driven into the ground every 1.2–1.5m (4–5ft).

**2** **Fill the bed** with good-quality topsoil that has been enriched with organic matter such as well-rotted manure (*see pp.22–23*) or garden compost (*see pp.24–26*).

**3** **Spread the soil** using a rake. Break up any lumps, aiming to achieve an even, firm texture and bring the surface roughly level with the top of the boards.

**4** **Level the soil** with the back of the rake to leave a smooth finish. Top up with more soil as necessary in later weeks when the filled bed settles and the level of the soil falls.

## Making a mulched path

Pathways between beds can be formed simply of trodden soil, but it is worth making a semi-permanent path, as shown here, to avoid unsightly and invasive weeds and to provide a firm, all-weather surface. Use preservative-treated 10 x 2.5cm (4 x 1in) planks as edging and make sure that they are proud of the bed surfaces. Once the base of the path has been constructed, it can be finished with any of a variety of surfacing materials (*see box below*), such as the bark chips shown here.

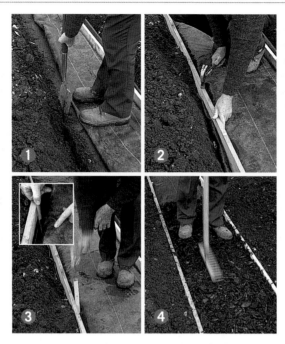

**1** Mark out a path 45–60cm (18–24in) wide. Cut a length of landscape fabric 15–20cm (6–8in) wider than the path. Level and tread down the path, then cut a 2.5cm (1in) slit trench along each edge.

**2** Fold the landscape fabric edge into the slit trench on one side, then lay the wood edging into the trench on top of it and knock down with a hammer until it is level. Repeat on the other edge, making sure that the fabric is taut.

**3** Using a sharp knife, cut crosses in opposing pairs in the landscape fabric close to the plank at 1.5–2m (5–6ft) intervals. Knock in a wooden peg through each cross, to at least 2.5cm (1in) below the top of the plank, to support the board.

**4** Pour in the mulch (here of bark chips). Rake it level and tamp down with the rake, so that the mulch surface is flush with the top of the boards and the supporting pegs are completely covered.

but in that case the base of the bed should be about 30cm (12in) wider than the finished top for stability; this shaping is most suitable for narrower beds, such as for strawberries. Making the top of any bed rounded rather than flat aids drainage and increases the surface cropping area.

### THE ADVANTAGES OF RAISED BEDS

Raised beds bring all the advantages of flat beds, but have improved drainage and warm up faster in spring. Making a raised bed higher along one side than the other, so that the surface slopes towards the direction of the sun, will warm the bed even more effectively and promote early plant growth.

Raised beds provide a means of gardening successfully on the most unpromising ground, such as where a site is naturally very badly drained (*see p.16*) or perhaps even concreted over.

Higher raised beds can also extend the pleasure of gardening to people who are less mobile; this is inevitably a more expensive undertaking, but certainly worthwhile. Higher beds can be made by constructing walls to a height of 60–90cm (24–36in). The base of the bed should be filled with rubble, which is then topped with 30–45cm (12–18in) of fertile soil.

### MAKING PATHS

At their simplest, the paths between beds can be maintained as soil areas from which weed growth is regularly skimmed off.

A mulched path is an alternative that requires more initial effort, but which should reduce maintenance in the longer term. The path should first be covered with a weed-suppressing landscape fabric, which is then topped with mulch of bark or gravel (*see above*) to make a hard-wearing and attractive garden feature.

Grass pathways are also a possibility, provided that a durable edging, for example rigid plastic or concrete blocks, is constructed around the beds; the grass surface must stand proud of the edging to allow for unobstructed mowing.

## Types of path surfacing

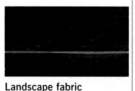

**Landscape fabric**
*Available by the roll and can be cut to measure; water-permeable.*

**Bark chips**
*Relatively inexpensive, blends well with surroundings, and soft to walk on.*

**Granite chips**
*Easily obtained and long-lasting; use with landscape fabric base.*

**Slate chips**
*An attractive option, available in blue or green hues, but relatively expensive.*

**Grit**
*Soft surface material that needs regular raking.*

**Turf**
*Fairly inexpensive and easy to establish, but requires regular maintenance.*

# Using containers

Not all gardens are suitable for growing crops in the open ground. The soil may have intractable drainage problems (*see p.16*), or contain persistent soil-borne pests or diseases, or just be paved or otherwise sealed over. In these situations many crops can be grown in containers.

This is a technique much used with flowering plants, allowing every area of a garden be fully exploited. Growing in containers has its benefits: crops can be grown immediately outside the kitchen door, especially herbs, or small containers moved to a prominent spot when most attractive, and containers can be filled with soil or compost of better structure than exists in the open garden site.

Container growing also makes demands. There will be expenditure on containers, although some can be made at home. With most containers large quantities of growing medium must be made up or purchased and transported. Above all, there is the need for constant attention to watering and feeding.

**Herbs on display**
*Many fruits and vegetables are as decorative as flowers, and in containers can make very attractive garden features. This range of herbs, including basil, chives, mint, parsley and thyme, make a bright and aromatic feature in a sunny corner.*

## CHOOSING CONTAINERS

There are various types of container to choose from: pots of all shapes and sizes made in earthenware, concrete, plastic, galvanized metal, or terracotta; wooden tubs, either specially made or adapted from barrels; or units temporarily built up from blocks, bricks, or timber. Even small containers like windowboxes and hanging baskets can be used, and there is scope for all sorts of ingenuity in adapting various used containers of all sizes for growing vegetables or fruit – even stacks of used tyres or sections of very wide drainpipe. Purpose-made growing bags come ready filled, or sacks made from thick, flexible plastic sheet can be filled with compost.

When choosing containers, make sure they will be large enough for the crop you intend to grow. The greater the volume of a container, the more likely it is that the growing conditions of open ground can be matched, and this is most important with regard to maintaining water supplies. Some specially made plastic containers for tree and bush fruits or most vegetable crops may be as much as 90cm (36in) wide and 60cm (24in) deep. Smaller versions for annual vegetables or strawberries should have a depth of at least 15cm (6in); the deeper they are, the better. A windowbox approximately 60cm (24in) long by 20cm (8in) wide and deep can hold a useful selection of salad vegetables or herbs, and a 40–45cm (16–18in) basket can hold herbs, strawberries, or a trailing tomato plant. Growing bags are usually 90cm (36in) long, 30cm (12in) wide and up to 15cm (6in) deep.

Whatever type of container is used, think carefully about its position. Avoid shade but at the same time aim to site containers away from full sun and wind exposure, where they are likely to dry out quickly. The largest sorts should be correctly placed before filling, because they can be very heavy to move after. Always raise containers on pot feet or shallow blocks about 5cm (2in) high to aid drainage. Make sure that pots for woody plants or tall crops on climbing supports will not become top-heavy when the crop is fully grown; they must be large and of heavy construction. Lightweight containers can be weighted with ballast in the bottom. Growing bags can be laid out on any firm base. Attach windowboxes and hanging baskets securely with strong brackets for safety, and place them conveniently for watering and to avoid troublesome drips.

## SUITABLE CROPS FOR CONTAINERS

Apple and pear trees raised on semi-dwarfing rootstocks (*see pp.174 and 181*) can be grown in large containers, as can many bush fruits; even blueberries can be grown in a lime-free growing compost. Strawberries can be grown in pots or tall planters with holes for several plants. Special care in watering, feeding, and pest and disease monitoring is necessary for these mostly long-term crops.

Almost any vegetable crop can be raised in containers. Successional sowing will keep supplies constant, and transplanting multi block-sown plants is recommended for all container-grown vegetables (*see pp.65*).There are tomatoes suitable for any of the types described, including hanging baskets; other fruiting vegetables and legumes

will also succeed. Salad crops are an excellent use of containers, and herbs lend themselves to growing in windowboxes or other small containers. Root vegetables are possibilities; these particularly benefit from transplanting as multiblock-sown plants. Perennial vegetables and brassicas are the least worthy of space in containers.

## PLANTING CONTAINERS

All containers must be well drained; waterlogging leads to crop failure. This can be ensured by the existence of several drainage holes in the base; if there is only one and more cannot be made, put plenty of broken pots in the bottom to provide a drainage layer.

Proprietary soilless or soil-based growing composts are best for filling the smallest of the containers, including windowboxes and hanging baskets. Soil-based products will give more stability and are likely to hold moisture better. Adding up to 20 per cent sand or grit by volume will aid drainage, add weight, and probably make the overall purchase less expensive. For the largest of rigid containers and plastic sacks, the best course is to resort to filling with fertile garden soil, specially prepared by mixing in well-rotted and shredded farmyard manure or garden compost and a good measure of grit.

**Scaling the heights**
*Peas and beans can be grown in containers, and the largest pots will accommodate brushwood or bamboo-cane wigwams or proprietary kinds of support.*

## Planting crops in a growing bag

Shake the growing bag to loosen the compost, and place it against a sunny wall to take advantage of the radiated warmth and shelter. Tall crops such as tomatoes will need support: use wires 30cm (12in) apart fixed to the wall, single canes, or proprietary supports as shown here. Cut holes in the bag – for tomatoes, three holes are sufficient – and plant the tomatoes through them. Sink a 8cm (3in) plastic pot in front of each plant to act as a watering reservoir. Tie in each plant to a support, using garden twine in a figure-of-eight; tie twice around the support and loosely around the stem to allow for growth. Water thoroughly to settle.

In addition, apply a compound fertilizer to the soil surface at 50g per sq m (1oz per sq yd) and work it in to a depth of 5–8cm (2–3in).

## WATERING AND FEEDING

Where porous materials are used, such as terracotta, it is helpful to line the sides with thin plastic sheet, which will effectively reduce water loss. Surface evaporation can be reduced by applying a mulch of well-rotted organic matter or even composted bark or stone chippings (*see below*). In all cases, watering crops in containers requires close attention to the plant and weather conditions, and the feel of the soil. Always water copiously and not in dribbles; in hot or windy weather this may be necessary twice a day or more. Never assume that natural rainfall has done the job for you.

Nutrients are also used up rapidly in free-standing containers. The roots will be restricted, and have to obtain all the necessary nutrients from a smaller

volume of soil than they would have naturally, so the soil needs to be enriched by regular feeding. Supplementary feeds (*see pp.20–23*) can be added as growth proceeds. This can be done by top-dressing with a dry compound fertilizer, but liquid fertilizers are most effective and convenient. For annual crops, it is best to start each season with fresh compost, but the growing medium in large, well-fed and watered containers can be left in place for more than one season. Compost in growing bags is ready mixed with fertilizer and will usually serve for one season's tomato, cucumber, or sweet pepper crop; after clearing, bags can be used in a second season for strawberries or salad crops.

The need for constant attention to crops grown in containers cannot be over-emphasized. Plants in containers are living in fundamentally stressful conditions, and it is all too easy for much enthusiastic investment to go to waste, because of a little neglect.

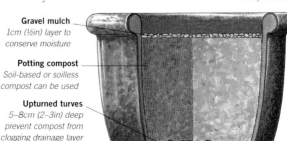

**Gravel mulch**
*1cm (½in) layer to conserve moisture*

**Potting compost**
*Soil-based or soilless compost can be used*

**Upturned turves**
*5–8cm (2–3in) deep prevent compost from clogging drainage layer*

**Drainage layer**
*Broken pots or stones*

**Pot feet**
*Hold base off ground so water drains through holes*

**Filling a container**
*A layer of porous ballast in the base, such as broken pots or stones, will help drainage. This should be 10cm (4in) deep in large containers and 2.5cm (1in) deep in the smallest. Cover this with upturned turf or twigs and leaves before adding growing medium to 2.5cm (1in) below the rim to allow for watering.*

# Soil preparation

The time and care that are invested in soil management will be repaid in the successful growth and productivity of fruit and vegetable crops. Seasonal weather is an inevitable challenge, but soil conditions can be governed to a large extent by improvement and good maintenance. Thorough preparation and continuing care serve to keep the soil free-draining yet suitably retentive of moisture, well aerated, and satisfactorily supplied with nutrients: characteristics that all encourage root growth and the supply of essential elements for healthy plant development (*see pp.14–17*).

Most vegetable crops are annuals or otherwise short-term crops, and basic soil preparation is th erefore a seasonal operation. Most fruit crops are perennials, and the considerations of soil preparation are occasional, but all the more important.

Garden soil that has been managed well for several years can be prepared shortly before planting, but previously uncultivated ground should be dug 12 months in advance, removing perennial weeds, breaking up any compaction, and improving soil fertility with the addition of lime and organic matter (*see pp.18–23*).

## DIGGING THE SOIL

Most gardeners find that the best soil preparation is digging. A prime reason for digging is that it provides immediate clearance of annual and perennial weed cover by burying or removing the upper layer, leaving a neat surface exposed to weathering. Digging can also break up compacted layers within the soil profile (*see p.15*), ensuring free drainage and allowing the roots of plants to explore to their maximum range. Turning the soil over allows rotted organic matter to be incorporated rapidly throughout the top layers – although do not underestimate the capacity of earthworms to do the same on undug sites – and at the same time exposes some soil-inhabiting insect pests to the attention of birds.

Certainly digging is laborious, but if it is tackled in limited sections, at the most suitable time, and using the best technique, it can in fact be a very satisfying activity.

**Forking sandy soil**
*Light, sandy soils may be prepared in spring with a fork. Spread a good layer, 5–8cm (2–3in) deep, of well-rotted manure or compost over the surface – preferably to overwinter, or at the time of cultivating. Keeping the fork as upright as possible, push it into the soil to its full depth and twist to turn over the soil, so that the manure is well worked in.*

Never attempt digging when the soil is saturated from heavy rain, as this risks compaction and damage to the existing structure. Most importantly, the task is made much harder because of the extra weight and stickiness of the turned-up soil, and it will be difficult to achieve a satisfying result.

## DEALING WITH DIFFERENT SOILS

Relatively heavy soils are best dug in the autumn or early winter. Turning over portions of topsoil exposes them to the beneficial effects of winter frost. Water in the soil freezes and expands, so that the soil clods are naturally shattered to provide the basis of good structure. Together with liming (*see pp.18–19*), this is the most effective way of handling soils of high clay content.

Light, sandy or silt soils are best dug in the spring a week or two before planting, because otherwise winter weathering may destroy what natural structure there is. With such soils it is a good plan to cover the surface with well-rotted organic matter in the autumn (*see p.22 and pp.41–42*).

Both types of soil can be dug with a spade, but the garden fork is an essential partner tool. It provides the best means of removing perennial weeds without breaking the roots before you dig, and of moving and spreading organic matter. It is just as suitable as the spade for digging light soils in spring.

## PREPARING TO DIG

Plan the digging in an orderly way. The best approach is to have or mark out a rectangular plot. Large plots can be divided into more conveniently sized segments by running a line down the middle: in this situation the ground is effectively dug as two plots side by side. Beds (*see pp.32–34*) are dug from end to end, following the same procedure as for a wide plot.

The length of a spade blade or fork prongs is 25–30cm (10–12in). This is referred to as the spit, and it is the most usual cultivated depth of soil. In some circumstances it is beneficial to cultivate to two spits depth, but this will really only be necessary on compacted soils when first preparing the kitchen garden, and only occasionally thereafter.

### DIGGING TIPS

- **Fix the principles** of the method in your mind at the outset, and work methodically and rhythmically.
- **Adopt a comfortable** and relaxed body posture when digging into and lifting soil; this will help you to work for longer periods without strain.
- **Keep your shoulders down** and use the weight of your body, not your arms, to drive the spade or fork into the soil.
- **Know your limits** and never attempt to do too much at one time.
- **Don't overload the spade** – it is quicker and less stressful to lift smaller amounts.
- **Keep the wall** of the digging trench vertical, so that the full spade's depth of soil is cultivated.
- **Use the best tools** you can afford; if you are tall, it may be worth seeking out long-handled tools for greater comfort when working.
- **Keep your tools** clean and sharp for ease of working.

## Single digging the soil

**1** **Mark out the plot** and dig out the first trench to a depth of one spit and a width of 30–40cm (12–15in). Place the spoil in a wheelbarrow to be taken to the other end of the plot, where it will be used to fill the last trench.

**2** **Scatter well-rotted manure** or compost over the base of the trench to a depth of 2.5–5cm (1–2in) and over the ground that is to be dug next.

**3** **Mark out the next area** to be dug. Insert the spade blade at right angles to the digging trench, nicking the soil

surface in order to mark out manageable portions that can be turned over neatly without overloading your spade.

**4** **Moving along the trench**, thrust the spade blade vertically into the soil to its full depth to loosen each section.

**5** **Press the handle downwards** while levering it back. Lean forwards and downwards and twist the spade blade to turn the portion of soil over into the trench. Take care to bend at the knees, and hold the shaft of the spade near the blade, to reduce the strain on your back.

**6** **At each progressive run** of digging across the plot, scatter some organic matter over the floor of the new trench, along the face of the turned-over soil, and on the ground to be dug next. Spreading it in this way results in a good mix through the top spit of soil.

**7** **Continue down the plot**, turning each trench into the previous one. Fill the last trench with the spoil from the first. Do not chop or beat the surface of the soil; leave it roughly dug so that weathering will break it down.

There are a number of systems of digging, but for general purposes soil preparation can be covered by two: single digging and double digging. Both procedures follow the same pattern of digging and suit most kitchen garden situations. For widely spaced fruit trees or row planting, the principles can be adapted to preparing either individual planting holes or trenches.

### SINGLE DIGGING THE SOIL

This is the most common annual treatment, in which the ground is cultivated to the depth of a single spit. The operation requires moving methodically backwards down the plot, digging trenches from right to left and left to right on alternate runs.

Take out a trench about 30–40cm (12–16in) wide to a spit depth across

the width of the plot. Remove the soil from this trench by wheelbarrow to the opposite end of the plot and deposit it in an even line outside the plot boundary. This transported soil will be used to fill in the last trench at the end of the dug site.

Digging proceeds by pitching soil into the first trench, which in turn creates a second trench (*see above*). If organic matter has previously been spread over the surface it will automatically be incorporated. Manure may also be added at the base of each trench or, much better, scattered in forkfuls over the full profile. Scattering in this way is generally a preferable system to burying manure at the bottom of the trench, because the matter will break down faster.

Skimmed-off grass and annual weeds can be buried (*see facing page, top*), but

perennial weeds are best removed manually, teasing out the underground runners of weeds like couch grass, ground elder, and nettles with a fork.

The operation is repeated down the plot, and the last trench is filled with the soil from the first. In the case of a large split plot, the second plot is dug in the opposite direction to the first, and the last trench will be adjacent to the first. This removes the need to transport the soil removed from the first trench; it can be deposited outside the plot boundary right next to where digging the first plot began.

### DOUBLE DIGGING THE SOIL

This is a system for first opening up a site and for occasional use thereafter if necessary. Double digging follows the same pattern as single digging, but the

ground is cultivated to two spits depth. The working trench is 60–75cm (24–30in) wide; this allows the base of a much more clearly defined succeeding trench to be forked to a second spit depth. Because the trench is wider, it is necessary to turn over two parallel furrows into the previous trench, instead of one (*see below*).

In all digging operations be sure not to bring the subsoil to the surface; this is most likely to be a problem when double digging a plot.

### THE NO-DIGGING SYSTEM

Some gardeners hold that digging is not essential and point to disadvantages in treating the soil in this way. The most obvious disadvantage of digging is that it is hard work – although the energy required can make it a healthy exercise. It is possible to damage soil structure by digging, and there may be disadvantages in disturbing the balance of beneficial soil-inhabiting organisms. Buried weed seeds are brought to the surface by the procedure, and digging is also likely to result in the soil losing moisture as it is exposed to the air.

Management of a no-digging system is based on minimum disturbance of the surface, which is regularly dressed with a thick mulch of rotted organic

matter (*see pp.41–42*). This needs to be applied well in advance of cropping, to allow for worms to pull the material down into the surface layers, improving soil structure and enhancing fertility.

On soils that have a good structure, the no-digging regime is a good way of dealing with the areas between crop rows or between widely spaced trees. It is vital initially to remove perennial

weeds like couch grass, nettle, and dock from a site that is to be managed without digging. This can be done by meticulous forking out of clumps of weed, or by laying a covering of sheet mulch over the infested area; this latter treatment will be successful only if left in place for many months (*see p.49*). The weedkiller glyphosate is also an effective treatment for

## Skimming weeds

**1** **If the ground** to be dug is covered with weeds, remove any established perennial weeds with a fork. You can then skim off the annual weeds and bury them.

**2** **Before you dig** each trench, use the spade to nick the soil into sections about the size of a spade blade, then slide the blade just under the surface of the soil and lift the weeds off.

**3** **Turn the skimmings** into the base of the previous trench, so that the weeds lie upside-down. Once they are covered by soil they will die down and enrich the soil.

## Double digging the soil

**1** **Mark out the plot;** with a large area, as here, divide the plot lengthways into 2 halves. At one end, dig out a trench 60–90cm (2–3ft) wide to the depth of a spit, as for single digging. Place all the removed soil in a long heap, next to the end of the adjoining section.

**2** **Cover the base** of the trench with a 5–8cm (2–3in) layer of well-rotted manure or compost. Fork it into the soil to another full spit depth, so that the manure is worked into the subsoil.

**3** **Mark out** a second trench to the same width. Dig the trench in 2 halves, or strips. Take out the soil from the strip furthest from the first trench,

placing it against the wall of the trench. This will keep the shape of the trenches clearly defined.

**4** **Fill the first trench** with the soil from the remaining strip to be dug. A new, second, trench has now been created. Repeat the process, working down the plot to the other end.

Fill the last trench of a half-plot with soil dug from the first trench of the second half-plot. Continue to the end, filling the final trench of the second half-plot with the soil that was placed off the plot at the very outset.

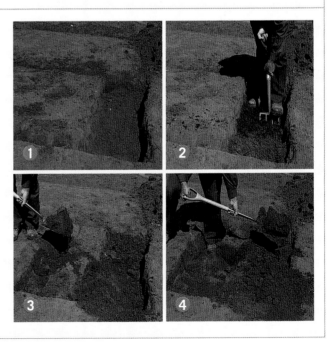

gardens that are not committed to organic principles.

Include the possibility of a no-digging policy when planning the kitchen garden (*see pp.27–30*), but do not regard it simply as an easier solution. It is crucial to pay close attention to soil preparation by this means. Incorrectly managed, it can result in a very weedy patch carrying poor crops.

### SURFACE PREPARATION

How the soil surface is prepared after digging and weathering is dependent on the cropping intention.

Where fruit plants and robust transplanted vegetable plants, such as brassicas (*see pp.78–81*) and leeks (*see p.93*), are to be grown, all that is necessary is to level the surface with a wide wooden rake. On light soils, the ground may also need to be firmed by gentle treading as levelling proceeds.

For seed-raised crops and the smaller vegetable transplants, it is necessary to prepare a tilth: a surface layer with a fine, crumbly structure. This is easiest on light, sandy and silt soils, where it can be achieved by cultivating the surface in different directions with a wide rake.

Stones and plant remains are most easily pulled off by holding the rake near to upright, whereas levelling and tilth-making are more readily achieved by holding the tool with its handle as

**Avoiding soil compaction**
*When preparing the surface of beds for planting or sowing, stand on planks laid across the bed to avoid compacting the soil. Mark the intervals for drills (here with canes), and line one of the planks up with these. Stand on the planks and draw out a straight drill along the plank edge with a hoe or cane.*

close as is comfortable to the ground. Heavy soils dug in autumn or early winter that have benefited from the action of frost and rain are effectively cultivated with a multi-tined cultivator, followed by raking – all in various directions. Treading with your feet is helpful on heavy soils for breaking down clods and on light soils for firming soft ground. Treading must never be done on wet soil, no matter what the soil texture: a suitable test is that the soil should not stick to boots – it should instead disintegrate quite easily when crushed in a hand grip.

The process of creating a tilth can include the incorporation of granular fertilizer dressing (*see pp.20–21*). When the top 5–8cm (2–3in) of surface is suitably friable, seed drills

can be drawn out or the area marked out with shallowly drawn drills for transplant lines (*see pp.66–67*).

In a no-digging situation, preparation beyond the surface mulching stage entails simply pulling aside remaining organic matter to expose the soil, with possibly the need for shallow hoeing off of any established annual weeds. This operation can be done either at spaced planting stations, as appropriate to fruit plants or well-spaced vegetable plants, or along marked out rows for smaller transplants or sowing seed. The vital mulch dressing will have improved the surface texture of the soil, and taking out planting holes and drawing drills will be no problem: in many instances it is perfectly suitable to plant through the mulch remnants.

## Preparing soil for planting and sowing

**Multi-tined cultivator**
*A three- or five-tined cultivator is an effective tool for preparing roughly dug ground. Draw the tines through the soil to break down large clods and loosen the surface.*

**Wooden rake**
*Use a wide wooden rake to level the surface and remove large stones. To achieve a good level, hold the rake low and guide it through one hand so that it glides through the surface.*

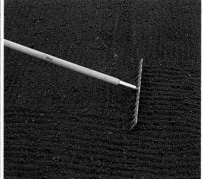

**Metal-headed rake**
*Use a metal rake with a head at least 30cm (12in) wide to create a fine tilth suitable for sowing. Rake the entire surface first in one direction, then at 90° to this.*

# Mulching

Mulching is the process of covering the soil surface with a layer of organic or inorganic material. It is one of the most useful gardening practices, which can bring significant improvements in cultivation of fruits and vegetables. The benefits of mulching cannot be overemphasized, and it is a technique not sufficiently appreciated and used.

Mulching should feature in the plans and maintenance of any size of kitchen garden; it will save labour and result in better quality and yield. There is a wide choice of methods, so mulches can be used by anyone, in any size of garden.

### THE BENEFITS OF MULCHING

All crops require continuous supplies of water, and mulching helps this in two ways. Any type of mulch provides a seal, reducing evaporation from the soil: this is particularly beneficial during warm or windy weather when large quantities of water are lost in this way. Organic mulches also help moisture retention by improving soil structure and fertility (*see pp.14–17*) as they are drawn down into the surface layer by earthworms. A mulch can also protect soil structure from being damaged by heavy rain.

Mulches can enhance or maintain soil temperature. A mulch reduces heat loss as air temperature falls: this can keep plant growth active and in many cases prevent physical damage to parts below ground, such as mature carrot roots. A clear plastic sheet mulch applied before sowing raises soil temperature, encouraging germination and early growth. Most other types of mulch keep the ground relatively cool during

### Straw mulch
*Mulching is useful to keep developing fruits clean of soil on surface or trailing plants such as strawberries, melons, marrows, and pumpkins (as here). Straw is particularly suitable for this.*

## Using organic mulches

▼ **Choose well-rotted manure**
*Farmyard and all other animal manures should be well weathered before use, to avoid the emission of ammonia, which can be damaging to plants. After a period of stacking, coarse-textured, strawy manure takes on a darker colour and becomes more friable.*

Fine, crumbly texture

Well-rotted manure

Straw still prominent

Fresh manure

▲ **Applying organic mulch**
*Apply well-rotted manure or garden compost to a depth of 2–3in (5–8cm) while the ground is still moist. Take care not to heap the mulch up around the stems of the plants (here runner beans), as this would encourage rot.*

summer: this reduces water loss and also maintains good conditions for the beneficial soil-inhabiting organisms.

These advantages apply to fruit plants as much as vegetables. Mulching around fruit trees and bushes can have a dramatic effect on growth, easily confirmed by leaving a plant or two untreated.

Covering the soil with a mulch of almost any sort will reduce germinating weeds by depriving them of light. Short-term coverings suppress annual weeds; to control perennial weeds, mulches such as heavy gauge black film plastic or thick carpet (*see p.49*) should be put in place for a long time, well in advance of cropping. If annual weeds do grow through mulches they are invariably weak-rooted and easily pulled out.

### ORGANIC MULCHES

Most bulky organic manures (*see pp.22–23*) can be used for mulching, providing they are well decomposed through weathering. Garden compost and leaf mould (*see pp.24–26*) are ideal, as well as spent mushroom compost. Shredded prunings, bark chips, and weathered sawdust are effective, but add supplementary dressings of nitrogen-rich fertilizer (*see pp.20–21*), for the soil may become deficient in this as the products are broken down. Cocoa shell is available for use as a mulch; it is relatively costly and its smell may attract animals. Straw is especially good around strawberries or over rhubarb beds. In coastal areas seaweed may be available, but check that gathering it is permitted. Organic mulches must be kept aerated

and free-draining: for this reason do not put thick layers of lawn mowings around plants as a mulch, because they become slimy and compacted. Some gardeners use old carpet and cardboard or newspapers for mulching. Each is effective, but unsightly.

## INORGANIC MULCHES

Film plastic is the most commonly used inorganic mulching material. Clear film plastic is most effective for raising soil temperatures, but because it lets light through it not only allows but also actually encourages weed growth. It is useful for warming and protecting a seedbed under preparation, and if carefully managed it can also be used as a floating mulch (see p.48) for the first few weeks after sowing.

Use black film plastic for longer-term cover. It suppresses weeds, conserves moisture, and is useful for keeping fruits and vegetables off the soil surface. Heavier grades of plastic sheet are less likely to tear and will last for more than one season, especially where made with a sunlight-inhibiting ingredient. Old fertilizer or compost sacks can be cut to form covers for use around trees.

Film plastics that are white or silver on one side and black on the other are very useful: with the black side downwards they reflect light up into the plants. These are more expensive, and probably most justified where crops are grown under protection. All-white plastic gives similar benefits.

Some heavy-gauge woven plastic sheets can be found, made for long-term mulching such as around fruit bushes and trees or for pathways, where they are an economic investment.

Decorative stone chips are possible candidates for some situations, especially around wall fruits. Such cover brings significant rise in soil temperature. Another less obvious form of mulching is provided by shallow hoeing of the soil surface (see p.72), which in effect produces a separate dust layer to aid moisture conservation.

## DISADVANTAGES OF MULCHING

Mulching has a few potential pitfalls. Organic kinds can encourage disease if layered heavily right up to the necks of plants. Fresh animal wastes can cause

**Landscape fabric mulches**
*Various brands of landscape fabric that are permeable to water and air are available for long-term mulching, or as a membrane on which loose mulching material can be laid.*

damage to plants through high levels of ammonia. More inert organic materials, like wood derivatives, can deplete the soil of nitrogen as they decompose. Some materials may be unsightly or troublesome by being scattered by foraging birds. All mulches provide refuge for slugs and some types similarly for snails and even small animal pests like voles. Most film plastics are impervious to rain or irrigation and may require watering lines (see p.54) laid beneath. None of these problems cannot be dealt with. The important thing is be aware of them and be watchful about methods of mulch application and of methods of pest control where appropriate.

## APPLYING MULCHES

Apply all mulches to soil that is neither very wet nor very dry: a mulch will only serve to exacerbate both these conditions. Spring application is valuable because the conservation of soil moisture encourages early growth and suppresses the first flushes of annual weeds. Mulch fruit plants immediately after planting, and put straw around strawberries just as young fruit trusses are enlarging. Mulch vegetable rows as soon as the plants are well established. Mulch in autumn to top up earlier applications as a soil improver or provide frost protection to root crops. Mulches of garden compost, leaf mould, or manure must be of friable texture. Apply to a depth of 2.5–8cm (1–3in). Straw and hay around robust plants may be twice as deep, allowing for settlement.

Fix all plastic sheet mulches as tightly as possible, and lay during a warm, sunny period, when the material will be flexible. The soil surface should be flat, so that water will not collect in puddles on the sheet. Push the edges of the sheet into the ground with a spade, making a deep slit in the soil beforehand. Ensure the sheet is removed as soon as its useful life is over, as it can shatter on degrading. Organic mulches are absorbed into the soil so do not need removing.

Mulching has a practical place for covering pathways, too, not only to control weed growth but also to give a safe, clean walking surface (see p.34).

▲ **Black plastic sheet mulch**
*Thin film plastic can be used as a mulch. Lay it as tightly as possible to stop wind lifting it or puddles forming on top.*

◄ **Perforated plastic**
*Perforated clear film plastic is available, or unperforated sheet can be punctured, to allow water to penetrate the soil while it is warmed under the plastic for use in early spring.*

# Protected cropping

Several factors govern the range and harvest period of fruits and vegetables that we can grow in the garden. Natural season and site are important, but the greatest influence is temperature.

Many popular fruit and vegetable crops either cannot survive low temperatures or struggle to grow satisfactorily. In cool climates, citrus and many other fruits can be grown outdoors in only a few areas. Potatoes, courgettes, and runner beans are among vegetable crops (*see pp.58–145*) that will not tolerate extremely low temperatures, and their natural season is therefore limited to frost-free periods.

## PROTECTING CROPS

The range of produce grown in the kitchen garden can be widened quite considerably by using various forms of protection: that is, raising the soil and air temperature above that of the surroundings by covering crops with some sort of protective layer. This differs from the practice of sheltering plants from wind (*see pp.12–13*), a procedure that itself helps to improve temperature in the vicinity of crops.

There are many ways of growing crops under cover. A greenhouse is probably the most ambitious and demanding possibility, but it provides

▲ **Early vegetables**
*Early crops of root vegetables – here broadcast-sown radishes – can be raised in greenhouse beds. A container of lettuces on the path makes maximum use of the floor area.*

◄ **Protection for fruit trees**
*Greenhouses give fruits such as peaches improved temperature, a controlled environment for watering and pollination, and some protection against birds.*

the greatest opportunity for growing variety over the longest possible period. Similar benefits can be obtained to some extent with garden frames and cloches of various sorts. Film plastic and spun fibre sheets are now widely available and are effective as protective ground covers, especially in vegetable production. Plant materials such as straw, hay, and fern fronds also make very useful insulating materials, and

well-rotted animal waste and plant remains can be used for covering root crops left in the plot over winter.

## GREENHOUSES

A greenhouse is invaluable for raising vegetables (*see pp.62–65*) such as brassicas, carrots, beetroot, onions, and lettuce. Crops can be started early, sown and established in modules in warmer air temperatures than those outside; they can be set out as sturdy plants when frost is less likely and soil temperature is rising (*see pp.70–71*). Quicker germination and better planning of succession are also possible, and establishing crops can be kept under close scrutiny. Module-raised plants are less dependent on high-quality tilth than those sown directly outdoors. Radishes, potatoes, lettuce, carrots, and turnips can be grown to maturity in a greenhouse.

Better-quality and earlier fruiting crops (*see pp.108–119*), such as tomatoes, sweet peppers, cucumbers, and melons can be grown in a greenhouse, in soil borders, large containers, or beds. Strawberries are suited to greenhouses and are commonly raised in growing bags. The largest greenhouses are suitable for tree fruits (*see pp.149–205*) such as peaches, apricots, and figs, and for vines (*see pp.227–233*).

**Tomato cordons in a greenhouse bed**
*Many half-hardy vegetables can be grown outdoors, but growing them in a greenhouse gives better results. Where soil-borne diseases build up, using growing bags is a solution.*

**Growing bags in a greenhouse**
*To extend the planting area, for crops such as these sweet melons, growing bags can be used in the greenhouse. Bags can also be placed on benching to grow cucumbers.*

## Greenhouse ventilation

Good ventilation is essential in a greenhouse. Warm air rises to the ridge of the greenhouse, and is dispersed by operating ridge ventilators. As a guide, the roof area that can be opened should be equal to 20 per cent of the floor area of the greenhouse. Side ventilators are needed to replenish the flow of air into the greenhouse; these should be plentiful, sited on both sides of the structure, and positioned as low as possible for maximum benefit. Hand operated ventilators are the least expensive option, but automatic controllers are available. Louvres provide effective side ventilation, and are opened or closed by means of a simple lever.

*Louvre vents*

*Top vents*

*Side vents*

A greenhouse is not essential. Seed-raised plants can be bought from garden centres to gain the seasonal advantages, and all the vegetable crops referred to as suitable for greenhouse cultivation can be grown outdoors, albeit with a more restricted season and often lower quality than is possible in the greenhouse.

At all costs do not underestimate the care and attention required to get good results: regular greenhouse maintenance will include ventilating, watering, and possibly shading, over and above the specific care of the crops grown.

### CHOOSING A GREENHOUSE

Glass is the best material for light transmission and heat retention, and it is the most durable cladding if carefully maintained, but it is relatively expensive, heavy, and fragile. Plastic requires less robust load-bearing structures than glass; units are therefore generally cheaper and easier to repair. Rigid plastic is available as acrylic or acrylic-coated polycarbonate sheet; sheets coated on both sides offer improved insulation. Although they are less durable than glass, these materials share many other properties.

Walk-in polytunnels are the cheapest greenhouse choice, in terms of covered surface and load-bearing structure. The flexible film plastic is stretched over regularly spaced tubular metal hoops and held in place by burying the edges along the sides of the structure. Film plastic containing an ultraviolet-light inhibitor gives up to three seasons' use.

Glass- or rigid-plastic-clad greenhouses come in many shapes and qualities: even polygonal shapes are available, and can make attractive garden features. They may be free-standing or abutted to a building as a lean-to structure, ideal for growing woody fruits, particularly vines. They may be made of wood, which needs the most maintenance, aluminium, or polyvinyl chloride plastic (PVC). Older or more traditional, glass-clad greenhouses may have brick wall supports up to half the side wall, or may be glass- or plastic-clad to ground level.

The larger the size that can be fitted in the better. A 2 x 2.5m (6 x 8ft) rigid-clad greenhouse is a very useful addition to a kitchen garden, and a polytunnel of 4.5 x 6m (14 x 20ft) is about the smallest practicable unit for the garden.

### EQUIPPING THE GREENHOUSE

For any greenhouse to be used to its fullest, supplementary heating is required. The higher the temperature desired, the more expensive it is to maintain. What is essential is to provide frost protection by keeping a minimum air temperature of 7°C (45°F) using an electric, oil-fired, or gas heat source. The supplier will usually advise on the size of heater needed to achieve this. Because film plastic does not retain heat as well as rigid plastics or glass, heating is much less worthwhile in a polytunnel. However, for propagating purposes it is feasible to build a small, enclosed frame or other unit within these structures. Heat loss from rigid-clad greenhouses can be reduced by fixing insulation during winter and early spring. Bubble-wrap products are particularly effective, and the light loss will not be crucial.

All greenhouses must have built-in systems for ventilation through air movement. In polytunnels it is most convenient to rely on air movement through the structure from large doors constructed at each end, operated by rolling up or down sheet covers strengthened with horizontal wooden battens. End-door ventilation is equally valuable for temperature control in glass and rigid-plastic clad structures, but here vents are also used (*see above*).

To avoid crop damage from overheating, an additional need is to provide shading facility to greenhouses. This can be a movable cover in the form of a roller blind; more economical,

### Extending the season
*While a polytunnel would not be an efficient choice for use as a heated greenhouse, it can extend the growing season considerably. Here a range of winter greens, including mizuna and pak choi, are being grown together with winter radish and beetroot.*

and suitable for all types of structure, is the application of a shading wash in early summer, removed in the autumn.

Be sure to have a continuous water supply connected to the greenhouse. Water-butt collection is a helpful supplement, but always limited at times of high demand.

Benching, preferably removable for convenience, is invaluable in a greenhouse. It is also worthwhile investing in a soil-warming cable to provide bottom-heat to germinating seed and developing plants; the ideal situation is to have this within a frame sitting on the benching. All heating equipment should be controlled by a thermostat for fuel economy, and the electrical installation should be made by a qualified person.

Most crops to be grown through to harvesting under protection need support, and this is best done by fixing wires and strings to the structural members of the greenhouse.

### USING COLD FRAMES

Garden frames have been used by fruit and vegetable gardeners for generations. The provision of frames is a possible alternative to a greenhouse for plant raising, especially where it is possible to fit a soil-warming cable.

Frames are important in acclimatizing or hardening off young plants raised under cover before planting out, encouraging sturdy growth with less chance of a growth check at planting out. Progressively more air is admitted to the frames every few days, until the young plants are completely exposed.

Another use of frames in the kitchen garden is for low-growing crops such as strawberries, courgettes, melons, and early root and salad crops. A minimum distance of 30cm (12in) between the soil surface and lid, or lights, is needed. With much taller lights, it is possible to grow cabbages and cauliflowers to maturity; tomatoes and cucumbers can be accommodated if bush cultivars are chosen, or the plants may be laid on the surface as the fruit ripens, in which case it is best to lay a plastic sheet mulch.

Site frames in an accessible position that is prone to neither wind nor shade. For raising young plants, frames may be stood on a hard surface area, but where

**Brick cold frame**
*The most durable cold frames have brick walls, which retain heat better than all-glass or plastic frames. If they are built onto the wall of a green-house, as here, they are very useful for hardening off plants.*

crops are to be grown to maturity under frame lights, ensure that there is a cultivated soil depth of at least 20cm (8in). Forming the beds with a slope further enhances early warming and crop maturity.

### TYPES OF COLD FRAME

Traditionally, frames are permanent structures made from low brick, block, or wooden walls covered by glass- or plastic-clad lights: redundant multi-paned window frames can be used. Glass is the most efficient cladding material, but rigid plastic and in some cases flexible film plastic are suitable alternatives. The most efficient frames have the rear wall higher than that at the front, in most cases with a fall of no more than 5cm (2in). This sheds rain and, when suitably orientated, captures the maximum sunlight. Custom-made aluminium or plastic frames (*see below*) are popular and effective: this type of unit is an expensive investment, but it is versatile and potentially long-lasting.

Frames are available in a range of sizes, and can also be made to fit the space available. The miniumum useful size is 120 x 60cm (4 x 2ft). Frames can be set out in any length of run that suits the need and location and they may be either single runs, or double runs each sloping from a central apex.

### MAINTAINING PLANTS IN FRAMES

Frames are relatively low in profile and likely to be nearly airtight when shut, so their management calls for close attention to ventilation. Lights require propping open as necessary with some wooden blocks or bricks. For maximum airing or to admit rainfall, the lights will need to be removed or at least tilted right back to expose all the cropped area; lights can be heavy and unwieldy, so take care when handling them. Taller frames are constructed so that the cladding sheets can be slid sideways in specially made grooves. Inadequate ventilation can lead to high humidity, in which plant disease may thrive or crops

**Aluminium and glass cold frame**
*This tall frame covers a crop of winter lettuces. It is excellent for light transmission, with the added benefit of a light-reflecting mulch. A low-level irrigation line takes care of watering.*

**Wooden cold frame**
*Frame covers or lights can be purpose-made, or redundant window frames can be used. Wood will require maintenance, and the struts reduce light transmission.*

may become overheated and their leaves scorched or simply flagged due to evaporation of available soil moisture. For the latter reason, frames may also need shading in hot sun: here a securely anchored covering of densely woven polypropylene netting is a good solution. Conversely, during winter and spring be prepared to add an insulating layer of thick plastic sheet mulch or old carpet over the lights to protect tender plants. Any snow covering serves as effective insulation, so do not remove it.

Be watchful for mice in frames, especially in cold periods. They can do considerable damage to young vegetable plants, particularly peas.

### INDIVIDUAL CLOCHES

Cloches (*see below*) are another long-established means of protecting and advancing edible crops. They are very useful for strawberries, and they can also be successfully used to grow early roots, lettuce, melons, and courgettes. Peas, beans, and potatoes can be effectively advanced before finishing in the open. Cloches provide good cover for plants being raised in outdoor seedbeds. They are an aid to warming the soil early before sowing, and at the other end of the season can be used in the ripening of onions and tomatoes. One novel use of barn cloches is to upend and place two together to form a more or less cylindrical unit, 60cm (2ft) tall, which is suitable for protecting crops such as tomatoes and sweet peppers.

**Tunnel and tent cloches**
*This kitchen garden is exploiting a range of crop protection methods, from large frames in the background to tunnel cloches over large crops and barn cloches over the smaller plants.*

The term cloche derives from the use of bell glasses, now also available in plastic, placed over individual plants to hasten maturity. There were variations in design with panes of glass in a metal frame, shaped rather like a lantern, which are again now also available in plastic. More usual are cloches consisting of panes of horticultural glass clamped together on a wire framework or simply held together with a patent clip. The simplest of these, the tent cloche, is made of two sheets of glass measuring 60 x 30cm (24 x 12in) held together by a central clip. More versatile is the barn cloche, constructed of four panes.

### CHOICE OF MATERIALS

Glass cloches have their disadvantages. They are prone to breakage because of the necessary pattern of regularly moving them within the garden. The glass requires cleaning every season to remove soil and particularly tenacious algal growth. Those of the barn type call for practice in assembling. Above all, glass cloches provide a potential safety hazard in the garden, especially to young children. Where they are to be used, a protective barrier of wire netting fixed to sturdy posts should be erected.

For economy, safety, and relative ease of handling, consider cloches made from materials other than glass, such as rigid plastic. These are widely on offer, in sheet form to match the tent or barn cloche pattern or as portable tunnel units made from corrugated plastic.

The main disadvantages are that these cladding materials usually transmit less light than glass and do not retain heat so well. Furthermore, they are light and more vulnerable to wind, so need securing with a line of strong cord fixed to two posts and held taut over each run of cloches. Whereas glass is durable when carefully handled, plastics are subject to degeneration through the action of sunlight, unless a light-inhibiting chemical is added to the material at the time of manufacture.

## Types of cloche

**Plastic bell cloches**
*Glass bell cloches are heavy enough to be simply stood on the soil; plastic bells need to be pegged down around the rim, but cost far less and sometimes have useful vents at the apex.*

**Glass barn cloche**
*Barn cloches have two sloping panes forming a roof and two more panes forming the sides at a steeper angle. Closing the ends with glass or sheets of plastic, as here, provides more protection.*

**Glass lantern cloche**
*Made from small pieces of glass held together on metal frames, these have the advantage of a lid that can be lifted and turned to allow ventilation without removing the cloche.*

**Corrugated PVC cloche**
*Used here to advance cauliflowers, these can be left open at the ends to allow ventilation. If greater protection is required, the ends can be closed by securing small sheets of plastic across them.*

## How to make a tunnel cloche

**1** **Use a former** made from a plank with coach bolts to make eyelets and 23cm (9in) legs in lengths of galvanized wire.

**2** **Bend the wires** into hoops about 60cm (2ft) wide. A second former, with the hoop shape outlined in nails driven into a thick sheet of wood, will be helpful for this.

**3** **Press the legs of the hoops** into the ground at intervals in a straight line. Drive wooden stakes into the ground at an angle of 45° beyond the last hoops. Secure one end of a roll of 150 gauge clear film plastic to the stake. Unwind the roll over the hoops as tightly as possible; this is easier if the roll is warm. Secure the other end to the second stake. Use polypropylene twine tied to the eyelets to hold the sheet taut.

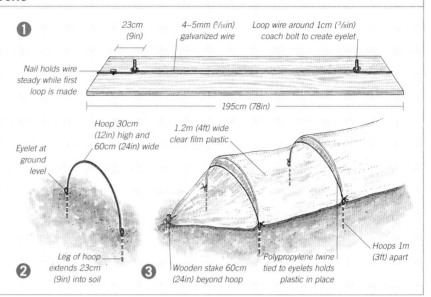

**1** 23cm (9in) · 4–5mm (³/₁₆in) galvanized wire · Loop wire around 1cm (³/₈in) coach bolt to create eyelet · Nail holds wire steady while first loop is made · 195cm (78in)

**2** Hoop 30cm (12in) high and 60cm (24in) wide · Eyelet at ground level · Leg of hoop extends 23cm (9in) into soil

**3** 1.2m (4ft) wide clear film plastic · Wooden stake 60cm (24in) beyond hoop · Polypropylene twine tied to eyelets holds plastic in place · Hoops 1m (3ft) apart

### CONTINUOUS TUNNEL CLOCHES

Film plastic is really too flimsy to make an effective cladding material for home-made rigid cloche frames; it is, however, very suitable for a system known as low continuous polytunnels or tunnel cloches, a different type of low-level protection that in many ways matches the glass or rigid-plastic cloche. This form of cloche is relatively inexpensive and easy to make, being constructed of film plastic stretched over galvanized wire hoops (*see above*). The plastic covering should last for two seasons.

Although the effects will not be quite as beneficial as with other cloche types, particularly glass, tunnel cloches can significantly advance crop maturity of strawberries, lettuce, runner and French beans, and numerous other vegetable crops, and are worth considering.

### USING CLOCHES

To get maximum use out of cloches, plan to grow crops in long, narrow strips. Even with tunnel cloches it is then possible to bring on one strip substantially, then move the cover over to a second strip. The second strip can then be advanced under cover, while the first crop matures in the open.

As with using cold frames, watering the covered crop is crucial. It is possible to benefit from rainfall by moving or opening the cloches, but for the best insurance lay inexpensive irrigation lines

(*see p.54*) along the crop rows. Consider using a plastic sheet mulch under cloches to conserve soil moisture; many crops can be planted through such cover (*see p.50*).

Choose a sheltered site wherever possible, but carefully fitted cloches can withstand quite strong winds. Glass cloches must be kept closely fitting, and the ends sealed with securely fixed panes of glass or plastic, and tunnel cloches must be constructed carefully so that the sheet is taut and the ends are tied or firmly buried in the soil.

### FLOATING MULCHES

Crops may also be protected with the use of fabricated ground covers, sometimes called floating mulches. This is a technique widely used by commercial growers, especially for advancing the bulking of early potatoes. The system is quite compatible with a vegetable garden laid out in 1.2m (4ft) wide beds (*see pp.32–34*).

Floating mulches are effective in raising soil temperature and protecting developing seedlings and young growing crops from wind and pounding rainfall, but only the thickest covers have any value as frost protection, and even then they do not match the benefits of frames or cloches. Another advantage is that some types of cover form a physical barrier to protect certain crops from crucial stages of damaging

pests such as aphids and carrot root fly (*see* Plant Problems, *pp.246–264*). Clear film plastic can be used to advance direct-sown vegetable crops, but perforated or woven film or spun fabric is much more likely to be successful. When using perforated plastic, choose lightweight, 150-gauge transparent film, with holes of about 10mm (¹/₂in) diameter distributed at around 200 holes per square metre (square yard). Film that has been UV treated is available, and this will last longer than untreated types. Plastic that is woven or manufactured with

**Access to tunnel cloches**
*To ventilate tunnel cloches push the film plastic up from ground level between the metal hoop and the retaining string. This also gives access for watering and harvesting.*

fine slits serves much the same purpose as the perforated types. An excellent alternative to perforated film plastic is horticultural fleece. This is a soft, lightweight material manufactured from spun and bonded acrylic fibres. It is usually white and is permeable to air and to some rainfall. It has better insulating properties than film plastic, and the heaviest grades will give protection from frost. The fleece is surprisingly strong in view of its softness, a characteristic that is particularly valuable in not causing chafing of the covered crops. If it is carefully handled, fleece can give service for at least two seasons.

Both film and fleece are suitable for encouraging the germination of seed crops, but perforated or slit film plastic is best for this purpose because, unlike fleece, it does not stick to the ground when it is wet. There are also fine woven mesh covers available, which are promoted particularly for their value in excluding insects.

### LAYING FLOATING MULCHES

Floating mulches need to be securely anchored to be effective and to prevent damage to the covered crops. The best means of doing this is to make a slit trench around the perimeter of the plot or bed by pushing the blade of a spade deeply into the ground. Bury

**Fine woven mesh**
*This fine-grade, insect-proof woven mesh is carefully laid to allow the lettuce plants beneath to develop with protection against insect pests.*

## Using floating mulches

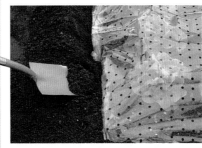

**Securing a long-term floating mulch**
*Open a slit trench all around the crop and push the edges of the floating mulch, here perforated plastic, into the trench until taut. Cover the edge with soil and tread to firm.*

**Securing a temporary mulch**
*The covering, here fleece, can be held down at the edges with bricks, large stones, or timber on a sheltered site.This makes it easier to use the mulch as a short-term covering.*

**Loosening horticultural fleece**
*Fleece covering can be used not only to advance a newly sown crop, but also to provide some protection against frost, as shown here on potatoes. In all cases the sheet must not be allowed to restrict growth; it is important to inspect the crop regularly and loosen the cover if necessary.*

the folded edge of the sheet by pushing it into the slit with a second insertion of the spade. Lay the film quite tightly, but be ready to ease it out of the ground as the crop develops, by pulling at the edges of the sheet and re-firming. Crops like carrot, lettuce, and beetroot can be sown in drills that remain slightly sunken when finished, so that whatever sheet mulch is used it is not in direct contact with the surface of the seeded lines.

Floating mulches can also be used to advance germinated crops in the spring, including early potatoes, and to provide some protection to crops going into autumn and winter to improve quality. With spring or autumn covering, use wider runs of material to allow for easement as the crops grow.

Remove any weed growth around the crop before laying, as this would rapidly develop. Be watchful, inspecting the crop regularly. Remember that coverings vary in the amount of rainfall that they allow through, so keep an eye on the covered crop and lift the floating mulch to water if necessary. Most important is to ensure that the developing crops are

not covered for too long, because almost all are likely to deteriorate if constricted. Film plastic should be removed from the site before it becomes brittle as a result of degradation by sunlight; if this happens it is liable to shatter.

### OTHER PROTECTION

Frost protection for figs and, in areas that are prone to severe ground frost, root vegetables can be provided by insulating them with layers of sacking, fleece, straw, or bracken as available. Whether the material is packed around the plants or layered on the ground, do not allow it to become saturated; this can be ensured by regularly loosening or turning it.

All of the protection methods described have a price in financial outlay and time commitment; it is not essential to introduce any of them into a new kitchen garden immediately. Think of protection as a desirable development, a means of extending the productive range, season, and quality of crops. These are areas to progress to once the principles of good basic fruit and vegetable production are mastered through a few seasons' experience.

# Weed control

Weeds are plants growing where they are not wanted. Usually they are native plants that grow successfully in the wild, but quite often they may be cultivated plants invading new areas.

Some weeds are not only attractive but may also have beneficial effects. Scarlet pimpernel (*Anagallis arvensis*) and wild pansy (*Viola tricolor*) bear attractive flowers, cow parsley (*Anthriscus sylvestris*) supports beneficial hoverflies, and red dead nettle (*Lamium purpureum*) attracts bees. It hardly needs saying that wild plants should be tolerated and indeed actively nurtured in appropriate places near the kitchen garden.

Crops will, however, be adversely affected by weed competition, and for most people a weed-free garden is more attractive than one left to its natural development. Weeds can be divided into two groups for the purposes of control: perennial weeds and annual weeds.

## HOW WEEDS AFFECT CROPS

By far the worst effects of weeds lie in competition. Weeds absorb water and nutrients from the soil, depriving crop plants and so restricting their growth. They compete for light, and vigorous weed growth can seriously shade young developing plants. They also compete for space, which may result in restricted or stunted growth of cultivated plants.

Weeds can also affect pest and disease incidence (*see* Plant Problems, pp.246–264). Some weeds may harbour pests such as eelworm and diseases such as clubroot of brassicas or rusts, these being found in weed plants closely related to cultivated crop species. Dense weed growth may become soaked by rain, reducing air movement and increasing humidity around plants, providing ideal conditions for diseases such as botrytis (*see p.252*), which affects the fruits of strawberries.

Heavy weed growth looks unsightly and can make harvesting more difficult; pulling vegetables that are surrounded by nettle growth can be painful. Another effect worth noting, although of very limited importance, is that some weeds may exude chemical substances at root level that have the effect of restricting the growth of non-related plants.

## Controlling weeds by light deprivation

**Using black film plastic**
*Annual and perennial weeds can be suppressed by covering the area with thick black film plastic buried at the edges. Cover for a whole season if possible.*

**Using old carpet**
*Any durable, light-excluding material can be used to control weeds. Even where some perennials are not killed, they are markedly weakened and much easier to fork out.*

### PERENNIAL WEEDS

Potentially most troublesome weeds are those perennials that increase primarily by vegetative means, such as spreading roots or runners or rooting stem tips, rather than by seed production. These weeds are of particular concern on uncropped sites where they have become well established; they are also potentially troublesome where they spring up among newly sown or planted fruit and vegetable crops and are then very difficult to eradicate without disturbing the crop. Notorious perennials are docks (*Rumex* species),

**Forking out perennial weeds**
*Established perennial weeds may have deep tap roots or spreading roots, like these nettles. Take care to loosen and tease out as much of the root as possible.*

dandelions (*Taraxacum officinale*), stinging nettle (*Urtica dioica*), creeping buttercup (*Ranunculus repens*), ground elder (*Aegopodium podagraria*), couch grass (*Agropyron repens*), brambles (*Rubus* species) and horse tail (*Equisetum* species).

A new site in which such weeds are well established can be daunting, but it is essential to clear out any of these inhabitants and destroy early any small colonies within already cultivated plots.

### MECHANICAL CONTROL

Non-woody perennials can be controlled by long-term covering with heavy-gauge black film plastic or other durable, light-excluding material such as old carpet. To be most effective it will need to be in place for at least a whole growing season, so forward planning is essential. Lift the cover occasionally and carefully dig out any struggling weeds.

The more usual method is to cultivate the ground with a spade or fork. Break open the ground to a spit depth, and shake or pick out by hand tuberous or woody roots or underground runners. This is best done on hot days, leaving weeds exposed for a while to be desiccated and killed; then dispose of them off-site. It is unlikely that one session will clear the land, because many of the weeds will regenerate from even the smallest fragment, so be prepared to repeat the task.

Using a mechanical rotary cultivator to chop up the existing ground cover is less advisable. It is effective only with many repeat operations, because underground weed parts are chopped into pieces, each of which will regenerate. Worst of all, it can destroy the soil structure and produce an impermeable soil pan (*see p.16*) at the depth of the spinning blades.

The persistence of perennial weeds varies. Ground elder, docks, dandelions, and creeping buttercup soon succumb to careful cultivation, but couch grass and stinging nettles require careful and repeated lifting. Worst of all are horse tails, which may be very deep-rooted and impossible to eradicate. The armed stems of brambles are formidable, but they can be successfully removed with methodical use of secateurs and a spade.

Bulbous perennials, such as a few *Oxalis* species or ramsons (*Allium ursinum*), call for meticulous lifting or constant removal of leaves to weaken the plant. Fortunately, these attractive weeds are less competitive than many, but in high density they can still smother other plants.

### USING WEEDKILLERS

Chemical weedkillers can be a great help in preparing new ground, in controlling persistent or deeply established perennial weeds, and where weeds invade from adjoining land. Their use is a matter of imposed as well as personal choice as the range is narrowed due to legal restrictions on manufacture.

There is no real risk to personal safety if the instructions are followed to the letter, but valued plants are vulnerable to drift or careless use of weedkiller. Important rules are: to keep a marked watering can or sprayer solely for weedkiller; choose the appropriate material; mix and apply it with great care, preferably on a still day – a dribble bar (*see p.53*) can be useful; and place physical barriers around any crop plants in the immediate area.

The chemical glyphosate is highly effective; it will be absorbed into actively growing plants. There are also chemicals specifically for perennial grasses and hormone weedkillers for persistent weeds like brambles and bindweed (*Convolvulus arvensis*). The latter can be painted on to aerial parts of plants. Inspect the shelves of a well-stocked garden centre and spend a while making a careful selection. Bear in mind that many perennial weeds are also prolific seeders, including dock and dandelion.

### ANNUAL WEEDS

Annual weeds complete their life cycle in one season; there may even be more than one life cycle per season. There are a few significant biennial weed plants, which make growth in one season and flower in the following one, and these may be regarded as annuals.

**Planting through a plastic sheet mulch**
*Avoid weeding by laying a sheet mulch (here landscape fabric) over the bed and secure at the sides by pushing into a slit trench. Cut crosses in the sheet and plant through them.*

By and large annuals are more readily controlled than perennials. The group includes chickweed (*Stellaria media*), groundsel (*Senecio vulgaris*), annual meadow grass (*Poa annua*), goosefoot (*Chenopodium album*), hairy bittercress (*Cardamine hirsuta*), speedwell (*Veronica* species) and annual nettle (*Urtica urens*). These weeds reproduce through the prolific production of seeds, making up a large part of the estimated 100,000 seeds in each square metre (square yard) of soil. Many seeds are lost to the predations of birds and soil-inhabiting creatures, while others fail to develop after germination. Cultivating will destroy many, but moves dormant seeds to conditions favourable to germination.

Destroy all flowering weeds before they have chance to set seed. Regular hoeing is the most effective means of controlling annuals, as severed parts do not regenerate. Hoe as soon as the crop rows can be identified, and repeat frequently. Work shallowly to avoid bringing more seeds to the surface and to minimize soil moisture loss. It is most important to hoe between crop rows.

Hand weeding is a quite satisfying pastime in the control of annual weeds. A flame gun can be used on pathways, but it is a specialist tool rather than an essential. A valuable technique for suppressing seeding weeds is the stale seedbed practice of allowing a flush of weeds to grow on a prepared bed, and then destroying them by shallow hoeing or with a flame gun before sowing.

### Spraying weeds with weedkiller

**1 Herbicides** such as those containing glyphosate are an effective aid for destroying perennial weeds. Take care not to use them on a windy day; the spray may drift onto valued plants and kill them.

**2 Over two weeks** the treated weeds progressively die back and are more readily removed. Glyphosate does not persist in the soil, so you can plant very soon after the weeds are cleared.

# Keeping your garden healthy

Neglected crops of fruit and vegetables may fail due to factors such as weather (*see pp.10–13*), nutrition (*see pp.14–17*), weeds (*see pp.49–50*), lack of water (*see pp.53–54*), and from pests and diseases (*see* Plant Problems, *pp.246–264*).

Animals, fungi, bacteria, viruses, and other organisms can destroy, disfigure, or debilitate crops, wasting the time, effort, money, and garden space devoted to them. It is vital to be aware of what problems may occur with each crop, and think ahead about how to combat them. Above all, inspect crops regularly and closely, so that you can deal with problems before they become serious.

## NATURAL STRATEGIES

Plants have remarkable mechanisms for repelling pests. Some produce chemicals that discourage feeding by their scent or taste. Some insects, such as the caterpillars (*see p.253*) of the cabbage white butterfly, can tolerate chemicals produced by brassicas and find a niche as specific

predators; other pests feed on a range of plants. Plants also emit scents that attract predators or parasites of their attackers. In nature, diversity in a plant community minimizes the effects of pests and diseases; in a kitchen garden, we tend to grow blocks of a single crop, advertising its existence and increasing the chances of attack. Keeping the area weed-free also reduces the habitat for beneficial predators and parasites.

## GROWING HEALTHY PLANTS

Weak or weed-choked crop plants will be more vulnerable to attack by disease, so prepare and maintain your garden well. Accumulated plant litter perpetuates diseases, as does infected wood, such as cankers (*see p.253*), left in fruit trees and bushes. Practice good garden hygiene.

Plant problems are encouraged by waterlogging and drought, so prepare and manage the soil well (*see pp.37–40*). Plants with unbalanced nutrient levels, especially where large amounts of

**Keeping equipment clean**
*Dirty equipment and containers can harbour diseases and minute pests. Clean your tools regularly and wash all containers between uses, scrubbing them out with a stiff brush and horticultural disinfectant.*

nitrogen-rich fertilizers (*see pp.20–21*) are applied, can be far more susceptible to aphid attack (*see p.251*) or botrytis disease (*see p.252*). Liquid conditioners, including those made from plant extracts such as comfrey or seaweed (*see p.21*) keep crops in good health and may stimulate the plants' natural defences.

Plants repeatedly grown on the same site are likely to suffer from a build-up of pests, such as potato cyst eelworm (*see p.260*) or onion white rot (*see p.258*). Rotation (*see p.31*) is therefore a good practice. A basic knowledge of life cycles assists in knowing how to prevent diseases from carrying over in the soil from season to season.

Buy only healthy stock. Clubroot of brassicas (*see p.254*) can easily be imported on purchased plants. Always look for certificated strawberries and other fruit plants. Remember also that there are degrees of resistance available in vegetable and fruit cultivars. We have apples resistant to scab (*see p.251*), carrots less prone to carrot fly (*see p.253*), and parsnips resistant to canker (*see p.258*).

## PROTECTIVE MECHANISMS

Plants can be effectively protected from birds (*see p.252*), rabbits (*see p.260*), and deer by netting or individual tree guards. Many insect pests can also be controlled by mechanical means: on a garden scale it is possible to remove

---

## Mechanical barriers and deterrents

**▲ Using a cage**
*Protect crops from birds with a cage of nylon netting, supported on metal or timber posts. You can make one yourself or buy a kit like this one, here protecting winter Savoy cabbages and Brussels sprouts.*

**▶ Netting on cabbages**
*Low-level netting can be fitted to home-made structures made from canes to exclude bird pests. Fine-mesh netting will also protect the crop from egg-laying insects, such as cabbage white butterflies.*

**▲ Bird scarers**
*A plastic bird of prey suspended on a line from a cane bobs and twists in the breeze to scare off birds. Bird scarers may need to be moved regularly to remain effective.*

## Natural allies in the garden

It is worth thinking of ways to encourage the activities of natural predators in and around the kitchen garden. This can be as simple as choosing to use hedges, which provide cover for hedgehogs, rather than fencing, or incorporating a pond for frogs and toads. Useful insects such as hoverflies need a range of flowering plants on which to feed. Reserve areas of uncultivated land on the margins of the kitchen garden for the food and cover of useful creatures

wherever it is practicable to do so. Bear in mind the wellbeing of friendly wildlife at all times, especially when applying any chemical treatments, which might harm them.

*Hoverfly*

*Hedgehog*

*Frog*

*Ladybird larva eating blackfly*

*Lacewing*

caterpillars (*see p.253*) or slugs and snails (*see p.262*) by hand, or to squeeze clusters of aphids on shoot tips. Cabbage root fly (*see p.253*) can be deterred by placing small mats or rings around the base of individual plants; carrot flies can be prevented from damaging carrots by surrounding the area with a low level protective barrier. Horticultural fleece (*see p.48*) can be used for the same purposes. Apples can be protected from winter moth caterpillar (*see p.264*) by fixing grease bands around tree trunks, and sticky traps impregnated with attractant chemicals are available to reduce infestations of codling moth (*see p.254*) or plum fruit moth (*see p.259*). Peach trees that are provided with winter covers are less susceptible to peach leaf curl disease (*see p.258*). It is also possible to avoid the effects of a pest by planting practices, for example by not sowing carrots until late spring, when carrot flies are less active.

### USING PREDATORS
Besides the natural predation by birds, small animals, and insects (*see above*), it is possible to introduce parasites or predators artificially. This is most effective under the protection of a greenhouse or conservatory, where the atmosphere can be controlled, and a successful example is the use of *Encarsia* wasps to parasitize the young stages of whitefly (*see p.264*). For outdoor use, parasitic nematodes are available for the treatment of slugs, vine weevil grubs, leatherjackets, and chafer grubs. All of these biological controls require careful understanding and management, but the range of such pest and disease control measures makes it clear that the choice is much wider than simply resorting to chemical sprays.

### CHEMICAL WEAPONS
It is possible to maintain an armoury of pesticides to eradicate or protect against pests and diseases. Because of increased regulation on the use of these substances, the range of treatments that is available has become much reduced, and the use of alternative control methods has now become essential.

It should be remembered that, unlike the commercial producer, the gardener usually has no need for maximum crop yield or unblemished produce. Many pest- or disease-induced defects can be cut out of harvested fruit and vegetables.

Chemical treatments are expensive in both purchase price and the time taken in applying them, and need to be applied at defined times for effectiveness. While quite safe for humans if applied strictly according to the instructions, chemical substances may have harmful effects on natural pest predators or other friendly insects like bees. Regard spraying and dusting as a last resort and other methods as the first line of attack or defence. The reasonable approach is to try to keep pests and diseases at an acceptably low level; attempting to eliminate them altogether is impractical and rarely vital.

**Biological controls**
*These pest controls take many forms, from predators to traps or parasites. Biological controls are released into the environment (usually in the greenhouse), or watered into the soil or compost as appropriate. Some must be applied at a particular time or temperature to be effective.*

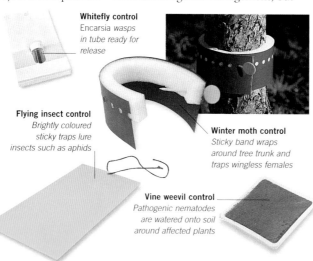

**Whitefly control**
Encarsia *wasps in tube ready for release*

**Flying insect control**
*Brightly coloured sticky traps lure insects such as aphids*

**Winter moth control**
*Sticky band wraps around tree trunk and traps wingless females*

**Vine weevil control**
*Pathogenic nematodes are watered onto soil around affected plants*

# Watering and irrigation

Good growth and yields depend on continuous adequate supplies of water. This is much influenced by the soil type and condition (*see pp.14–16*). Clay soils hold more water than sandy ones, because there are more spaces in the soil to hold it, but plants are able to extract water from sandy soils more easily, because the spaces are larger. The water-holding capacity of any soil is improved by the addition of organic matter (*see pp.22–23*), and water retention by the use of mulches (*see pp.41–42*).

The best source of water is rain, but due to seasonal fluctuations in rainfall and high temperatures in summer, soils often become dry during periods of crucial plant growth, and added water from stored sources or mains supply is needed. Many garden centres and stores stock a good choice of watering and irrigation equipment for this purpose.

### WATERING CROPS

Water thoroughly, so that the amount applied is absorbed down to a useful depth. This can be achieved by gentle and repeated applications of a fine, rain-like spray or continuous droplets applied around the base of plants. High-pressure or rapid, swamping applications lead to the water running off, resulting in waste and in erosion of

## Watering can attachments

An oval, flat rose with the face upwards produces a fine spray for watering seedlings or damping down foliage. Face downwards, it provides a fine drenching flow. A round, conical rose with the face downwards will give a drenching spray of greater volume for watering established plants or settling in robust transplants.

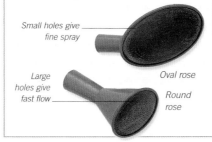

Small holes give fine spray

Large holes give fast flow

Oval rose

Round rose

**Dribble bar**
*A dribble bar attachment is very useful for watering crops or applying liquid feed. It provides an even, steady spray, ensuring good coverage of the crop.*

the soil around roots. As a very general guide to application rate, whether by watering can, spray gun, or sprinkler, aim at not less than 10 litres per square metre (2¼ gallons per square yard).

A good way of ensuring that water benefits the crop is to make mini-reservoirs around widely spaced plants or along planted rows such as peas and beans: pull the soil into shallow walls to form basins or troughs. Similarly useful are plastic pots – or cut-down plastic bottles – sunk up to their rims close to individual plants such as tomatoes.

### WATERING CANS

The most common way of watering is with a plastic or galvanized watering can. Models with a long spout are most useful, and they can be fitted with various interchangable roses, which are normally made of brass (*see above*). Round roses have large holes, ideal for settling in newly planted crops or heavy watering of established crops on a well-structured soil. Oval roses with smaller holes deliver a fine spray of water onto tender plants or newly sown areas.

Large droplets can be gently applied with a dribble bar fitted to the spout of the watering can (*see above*). This is most usually used for applying liquid feed, or weedkiller for which a separate, marked can and bar will be needed.

### SPRAY GUNS AND SPRINKLERS

A hand-held spray gun attached to a hose supply can provide the same distribution effects as a watering can. Spray guns may or may not have a solid lance (*see left*) to which the head is fitted. The flow and pattern of water can be adjusted by turning controls at the spray head, and with some models the flow can be locked on manually.

Low-level sprinklers, fed from a hose attachment, can also be used (*see far left*). Some models have heads that move under water pressure to distribute

▲ **Rotating sprinkler**
*Sprinklers are fixed to the end of a hose to water one area at a time. The simplest types have fixed heads: the rotating types often cover a slightly larger area, but their spray may be coarser.*

▶ **Hose attachment**
*A spray-gun attachment on a rigid lance fitted to the end of a hose allows you to reach crops without treading on beds. Because the lance can be manoevred between plants, water can be delivered more efficiently close to the soil.*

the flow, but for the kitchen garden the cheaper models made with a push-in spike are quite adequate.

Sprinklers have the advantage of watering unattended – but it is essential to check them frequently to ensure that the pressure and distribution of flow are not causing flooding. Even sprinkers with moving heads can distribute water unevenly, so do check regularly and move them when necessary.

## LOW-LEVEL IRRIGATION SYSTEMS

A range of low-level watering systems made from plastic or rubber are available. They are an excellent choice for effective distribution in the kitchen garden, ensuring that water is delivered close to the plants, in readily absorbed quantities and with a minimum of wastage.

The simplest form is a thin-walled plastic tube, which lays flat and is connected to a water supply. It emits thin arching sprays of water from pin holes 30–50cm (12–20in) apart (*see right*). Other useful types are seep hoses, which are small-diameter tubes. These may be made from heavy-gauge flexible plastic, and manufactured by stitching the edges in a continuous line: water seeps from the stitched seam to provide a band of water along a crop row. A variation on this is small-bore tubing of 1–2.5cm (½–1in) diameter formed from porous rubber, or sometimes plastic, from which water weeps in small droplets. Both of these flexible systems work with very low water pressure. They are prone to blockage over time, however, so regular maintenance is advisable; squeezing, rolling or otherwise flexing the pipe along its entire length and

**Drip hose used among strawberry plants**
*This irrigation system uses a perforated hose connected to a tap. The hose can be laid close to the crops, with the water dripping out directly near the roots, avoiding wasteful evaporation. The system can be controlled either manually or with a timer.*

then flushing it through with a strong flow of water should clear any build-up. Thick-walled rigid plastic pipe systems of 1–2.5cm (½–1in) diameter are available for rather more permanent placement, and these come with different distribution heads. Some have mini-sprinkler attachments at regular intervals. Others, called drip hoses, have short, flexible, drip lines of a smaller bore pierced into the feeder line, with each drip supported on a small plastic pin holder; metal or plastic trickle nozzles form another system, and both of these can deliver water right to the base of individual plants.

Check the output of all of these irrigation systems regularly, at each station where appropriate, to ensure that no plants are deprived because of blocked outlets; dig down with a trowel near plants to ensure that water has penetrated to a useful depth. Fit a timed switching device to the main supply line for maximum efficiency.

## USING WATER WISELY

Whatever watering and irrigation systems you use, remember that water is a valuable resource: use it effectively and economically. Priorities for irrigation are newly established plants and all fruits that are beginning to swell, such as strawberries, raspberries, peas, and beans, as well as leafy summer vegetables such as lettuce, and bulking potato tubers. Water at the start or end of a day; in the middle of the day, much will be wasted in evaporation. Collect rainwater wherever possible; water butts are soon emptied, but are worthwhile.

Household waste water, or grey water, usually contains residues that are best not used on edible crops, and should be reserved for watering woody ornamental plants. Keep an eye on the weather and the state of the soil, so that you can predict when plants are likely to be stressed due to inadequate water, and top up supplies before your crops show the obvious visual symptom, which is wilting.

**Seep hose**
*Hoses made from reconstituted rubber ooze water droplets along their entire length to provide a steady supply. Wind them among plants for even distribution.*

**Minisprinkler on hose**
*These small attachments can be strategically placed close to particular plants to direct the water to where it is most needed. They are available in a variety of spray patterns, watering to one or both sides of the hose.*

# Tools and equipment

A set of tools is necessary from the start in preparing and maintaining a kitchen garden. It is worth investing in the best-quality tools that you can afford; they will repay the expense and last a lifetime if they are properly used and cared for. A good-quality tool should be well-designed, strong, and, if appropriate, lightweight; such quality is guaranteed in well-known branded products.

Stainless steel is worth the expense, as it is both strong and durable, and handles of ashwood or aluminium are the best choice. When selecting new or second-hand tools make sure that the heads and handles are securely joined to the shafts. Test the weight of the tool and be sure that it feels comfortable to hold. Try out a range of sizes and designs to find a model that feels right for you.

## CHOOSING A RANGE OF TOOLS
A few basic tools are essential, especially a spade, fork, hoe, trowel, hand fork, and secateurs. There are many variations on all of these implements.

A lesser-known but recommended tool is the arrow-headed hand cultivator, which is very effective for breaking down roughly structured soil after digging or overwintering. It is also useful for loosening a

## Spades and forks

These are essential tools for digging, trenching, and skimming weeds (*see pp.37–40*) and for planting and moving soil. The handles of standard spades and forks are about 60cm (2ft) long, although longer ones are available to suit individual needs.

**▼ Choosing a spade**
*A standard digging spade has a 28 x 20cm (11 x 8in) blade; a border or lady's spade, with a blade usually of 23 x 15cm (9 x 6in), is lighter to use and is especially helpful for digging in confined spaces. There are other specialized spades for specific tasks.*

*Standard spade*     *Border spade*

*Handles may be of wood or metal*

*Narrow metal strips make digging more comfortable*

*Tines are usually square in section*

*Head of border fork is shorter and narrower*

*Digging fork*     *Border fork*

**▲ Choosing a fork**
*A standard fork has a head of four tines, or prongs, each 30cm (12in) long; there is also a border or lady's version, which is ideal for working between perennial plants.*

**▼ Handle grips for spades and forks**
*Handle grips may be shaped in one of several ways; a D- or Y-shaped grip is found to be comfortable by most gardeners.*

*T-shaped*     *Y-shaped*     *D-shaped*

## Rakes

Rakes are needed for making seedbeds, especially in levelling and preparing tilth. They are also useful for pulling off litter, tamping seed rows after sowing, and pressing out seed drills on soft ground.

*Metal prongs ideal for preparing a tilth*

**▶ Metal rake**
*Choose a metal rake with a head 30–38cm (12–15in) wide and prongs 6cm (2½in) long, spaced about 2.5cm (1in) apart. The handle should be about 1.5m (5ft) long.*

**▼ Wooden rake**
*Look for a head about 75cm (30in) wide, holding wooden peg teeth 8cm (3in) long, and fixed to a handle up to 2m (6ft) long, to allow for wide, sweeping strokes in various directions.*

*Wide head of wooden rake is best for clearing and levelling soil*

also useful for loosening a compacted surface between fruit plantings, and on paths. Also worth considering at an early stage is a spading or potato fork; this has flat tines, which come in various widths, and is particularly suitable for digging heavy-textured soils.

Other, more specialized tools can be added as the kitchen garden develops and as your preference and budget will allow: loppers and saws, for example, are really only needed in the cultivation of fruit trees. Tools such as dibbers and seed sowers make gardening tasks easier but are not essential.

## MAINTAINING YOUR TOOLS

Whatever tools you buy, it is vital to maintain them properly, keeping them clean, rust-free, and, where appropriate, properly sharpened. If you neglect this, the tools will be harder to use and less efficient, and will have a shorter life.

After using a tool, clean off all earth, plant matter, or other debris promptly. For stainless steel tools, this is all that is necessary for day-to-day maintenance. Tools made from carbon steel will rust if they are left damp, however, so these should also be wiped over with an oily rag after use. Always store tools in a dry place: never leave them outside.

All tools with cutting edges, such as secateurs and hoes, will need regular sharpening with an oilstone or steel to give the best possible performance.

If tools are not used over the winter, clean them very thoroughly and oil them well before putting them away.

## Cultivators and hoes

Cultivators are excellent tools for breaking down newly dug ground and working in top-dressings. The push hoe is used to slice off weeds with a push-pull action and must be kept sharp; conversely the draw hoe is used in a chopping motion, which entails walking forwards on the hoed ground. A draw hoe can also be used for marking out drills or earthing up crops. An onion hoe is most suitable for cultivating along vegetable rows and for thinning.

**Types of cultivating implements**
*A cultivator usually has 3 or 5 prongs; it is possible to buy models with interchangeable heads. A push hoe has a flat, oblong blade, while a draw hoe has a blade mounted at a right angle to the handle; an onion hoe is a smaller, hand-held version of the draw hoe.*

*Cultivator with interchangeable five-pronged head*

*Narrow three-pronged head*

*Swan-necked draw hoe*

*Push, Dutch, or scuffle hoe*

*Onion hoe*

## Planting tools

There are two essential tools for planting: the trowel and the hand fork. The trowel is ideal for making planting holes and firming soil around transplants, such as module-raised vegetables and strawberry plants. Forks are necessary for hand weeding and for loosening soil along rows and around plants.

**Trowels and hand forks**
*The trowel has a scoop-shaped, tapered blade about 15cm (6in) long, attached to a short, rounded handle. Forks have 3 or 4 prongs and a similar handle. There are long-handled versions of both tools available.*

*Lid can be rotated to adjust size of opening*

*Trowel*　　*Narrow trowel*　　*Fork*

**Seed sowers**
*These release one seed at a time, and so make it easier to make thin or spaced sowings. The outlet can be adjusted to suit small- to large-sized seeds.*

**Dibbers**
*Tray dibbers are pointed, pencil-like tools of wood, metal, or plastic, used to make planting holes or for pricking out seedlings at the propagating stage. Larger planting dibbers are used to sow bean seeds or to transplant vegetable plants in open ground.*

*Plastic tray dibber*　　*Metal tray dibber*　　*Steel-tipped planting dibber*

# Cutting tools

Secaters and loppers may be anvil or parrot-bill types. Anvil types have a single sharp blade that cuts against a flat anvil, and can cut thick wood; parrot-bill types act more like scissors, and make a cleaner cut without crushing. Saws are required for pruning large branches, and knives for a range of essential tasks.

## ▼ Pruning saws

*Folding saws are easily carried around, but a Grecian saw, with a curved blade and teeth set for use in a single pulling action, makes cutting easier and should be the first choice.*

## ▼ Secateurs

*Secateurs should be strong and able to cut woody stems up to 1.5cm (1/2 in) thick. Look for hardened steel blades with reasonably long handles and a comfortable grip, replaceable parts, and a simple safety catch.*

Look for comfortable cushioned grips

Blade folds into handle for safe carrying

Folding saw

Blade closes down onto flat anvil

*Anvil secateurs*

Grecian saw

Blade slices against bar

Curved handle gives an easier grip for more effective action

## ▼ Knives

*A good multi-purpose knife has a straight blade 9cm (3½in) long; a budding knife has a fine blade and relatively long handle to make precise cuts. Sharpen with an oilstone, then keep an edge with a diamond steel.*

*Parrot-bill secateurs*

Handles may be fixed, or telescopic for greater reach

## ◄ Loppers

*Loppers are suitable for reaching into fruit trees and bushes and exerting powerful leverage; they can be used on branches of up to about 4cm (1½in) diameter.*

*Budding knife*

*Pocket diamond steel*

# Watering and spraying

Watering cans will be essential for maintaining plants both under protection and outdoors, and they need to have detachable roses to deliver coarse or fine droplets. Long-necked watering cans are ideal, but there is a wide choice of other sturdy cans. It is vital to have separate and clearly labelled cans or sprayers for applying weedkillers, to avoid accidents.

Hand pump plunger

Garden pressure spray

Trigger on nozzle controls spray

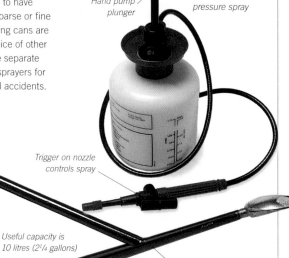

Useful capacity is 10 litres (2¼ gallons)

Long neck gives well-balanced can

*High-quality metal watering can*

# Measuring tools

Some measuring and marking tools are essential for spacing crops properly. A folding measure is easily portable, but you can make your own measuring stick by marking out a length of light timber at 15cm (6in) intervals. Marker line is used in sowing and planting outdoors, pegged taut at either end. Brightly coloured string is easily seen.

Home-made measuring rod

Marker line

Folding measuring stick

# VEGETABLES

The range of vegetables that can be grown in any garden is enormous, and there are many factors that may influence your choice. Certain basic principles and techniques – for example, sowing seed – are common to the majority of vegetable crops, involving skills that are easy and satisfying to master. In fact, for some gardeners the vegetable plot is the only area in which they practise raising and nurturing their plants from tiny seeds to maturity.

The crops in this section have been arranged in conventional groupings – the onion family, for example, or salad plants. The members of each group share a number of characteristics, such as soil preferences or vulnerability to certain problems, that make it convenient to grow them together. This also makes it easier to follow a crop rotation, vital for healthy plants and good harvests. Even within the groups, the wealth and variety of produce to be had – leaves, stems, and roots, flower buds, and fruits – will provide good food, fresh or from store, in every season.

# Vegetable seed

Most vegetables are grown from seed, of which there are two basic kinds. The first is open-pollinated seed, which, whether bought or home-saved, is produced naturally and derived from a mix of parent lines – although good open-pollinated seed from a reliable seed merchant will have been subject to careful selection of breeding material. The second is F1 hybrid seed, which is produced by crossing two inbred, stable parent lines; the resulting plants are more uniform and vigorous. This type can only be bought – seed saved from F1 hybrids will produce variable and often inferior plants – and is more expensive than open-pollinated seed. Both types may be bought untreated, or with various treatments to ease sowing or aid germination (*see chart, below*).

## SHOULD I BUY OR SAVE SEEDS?

Packeted vegetable seeds, widely available in great variety, are subject to legal requirements on "trueness" (where the offspring plant conforms to a described type) and viability – a guarantee, in practice, that a statutory minimum percentage of the seed will germinate and produce healthy seedlings with the expected characteristics of the named cultivar. The expertise and reputation of established seed merchants usually ensures good quality and reliability. Buying seed is convenient and packets usually carry helpful advice.

Many gardeners also like to save seed from the garden, to keep costs down and for the satisfaction involved in raising their own plants. There are two main problems, however, with amateur seed-saving: extracting and storing the seeds in such a way as to keep them viable, and maintaining trueness to type: any vegetables allowed to set seed in the open garden are likely to be cross-pollinated – fertilized by pollen from different cultivars – and their offspring will therefore show variation. An additional problem in cool climates is that it may be difficult to ripen home-saved seed sufficiently.

## HERITAGE SEED

Seed merchants are only allowed to sell vegetable cultivars that appear on approved official lists. These inevitably tend to feature only those cultivars that are commercially viable to produce, and so many older cultivars suitable for the amateur garden have disappeared from retailers' catalogues. Organizations have been set up to conserve such cultivars both for interest and to maintain the gene pool. Since they cannot legally sell the seed, they may operate as seed "libraries", where a joining fee enables the member to "borrow" seed. Contact details appear in gardening magazines. There are many fine traditional cultivars worth seeking out in this way.

## CHOOSING VEGETABLE SEED

Many factors may influence the type of seed that you buy. Organically raised seed may be of particular interest to you, for example. The various seed treatments available (*see chart, left*) can help in the control of particular pests and diseases. Pelleted seeds, being larger, are easier to handle and sow, and are easier to see, enabling more accurate spacing and thus reducing the need for thinning, which saves money.

The cultivars you choose will largely be determined by what will succeed in

## TYPES OF VEGETABLE SEEDS

*Natural (parsnip)*

**Natural/untreated seeds** have been saved, cleaned, and not coated in any way. They may be home-saved, conventionally produced for sale, organic, or heritage seeds. Organic seed is produced on land that has been certified as free from chemicals and added fertilizers.

*Coated (cauliflower)*

**Treated seeds** have been coated with fungicides or insecticides or soaked in hot water in order to produce disease-free seedlings, or, for ease of handling, pelleted in a clay coating which disintegrates in the soil. Chemical coatings will not rub off and are usually brightly coloured. Wear latex gloves when sowing these and wash your hands afterwards. They should be sown soon after purchase.

*Primed (carrot)*

**Primed or sprinter seeds** (usually of carrots and onions) have been specially treated to initiate germination and then dried again; they must be sown within two months of purchase. As the seed has already started to germinate, it is more reliable than conventional seed for use early in the season when soil conditions are not ideal.

*Multigerm (beetroot)*

**Multigerm seeds** (usually of beetroot and chard) consist of rough clusters of seeds, rather than individual ones, each of which may produce a clump of seedlings. These may be thinned or left to grow into a cluster of baby vegetables as in the multiblock sowing technique (*see p.65*). Monogerm preparations that produce only a single plant of these vegetables per seed are also available.

*Precision-treated seeds*

**Precision-treated seeds** are selected to have a high germination rate and vigour, and often graded so that all the seeds are of equal, larger size to produce better, more uniform plants. If treated with fungicide and insecticide, they may be brightly coloured to warn of the presence of chemicals. These seeds are expensive, so sow in plugs or modules to reduce the need for thinning and wastage.

*Chitted (sugar pea)*

**Chitted or pregerminated seeds** can sometimes be obtained by mail order; this is useful for seeds that the amateur finds difficult to germinate: cucumber and melon seeds, for example, which require high temperatures for germination. You can also help some seeds, such as peas or beans, to chit by soaking them for a short time (up to 24 hours); this speeds up germination when sown.

*Tape (spring onion)*

**Seed tapes** are available for a limited range of vegetables to enable evenly spaced sowings. These biodegradable paper tapes have seeds embedded at regular spacings and can simply be laid at the bottom of a seed drill (*see p.66*), enabling long rows of vegetables that will not need thinning to be sown very quickly and easily.

**Drying pea and bean pods**
*In damp conditions, it is a good idea to pull up whole stems (here beans), with their pods still attached, and hang them upside down by their roots in a dry, airy, frost-free place. When dry, crush the pods and shake out the seeds.*

## Preparing seeds from pulpy fruits

**1** **Scoop pulpy seeds** (here of sweet melon) from very ripe fruits with a spoon, and place in a household sieve. Rinse them in running water, making sure that all the pulp is removed; if left, it will hinder germination.

**2** **Spread the seeds** out on a layer of kitchen paper in a shallow container, and leave them to dry in a warm and airy place for at least a week. When they have dried out, store them in a cool, dry place for sowing in the following spring.

your region and by personal preference. If you have little practical experience, look for cultivars that have won awards from reputable organizations, such as the RHS Award of Garden Merit. Look around local gardens and allotments, or ask local gardeners, to discover cultivars that do particularly well in your area, or show good disease resistance. But be adventurous too: try out different cultivars to compare with your old favourites, and experiment with new introductions and novel plants such as differently coloured sweetcorn.

### BUYING VEGETABLE SEED
Seed can be purchased either from retail outlets such as garden centres or by mail order from seed merchants. The latter usually stock a wider range of cultivars. If using a seed merchant, send your order in early to secure your chosen

cultivars; otherwise unsuitable substitutions may be made. Well before sowing, read all of the information on the packets. Be particularly careful to sow at the recommended time, or you could face problems such as poor germination, or bolting of mature plants (*see also individual crops, pp.74–135*).

### HOW TO SAVE SEED
Choose only strong, healthy plants to save seed from. Remember that you cannot save seed from F1 hybrids, and that some crops, such as carrots, are biennial and will need to be over-wintered in order to flower in their

second year. Always allow the seeds, or the fruits that contain them, such as tomatoes and sweet melons (*above*), to ripen or mature fully before you collect them. Leave pea and French bean pods on the plants until they have dried and just split, and then extract the seeds; in damp weather, you can remove entire stems and dry them out under cover (*see above left*). With broad beans and runner beans, grow one type of cultivar only in one location to reduce the risk of cross-pollination, and select the best pods from which to collect the seeds.

### STORING VEGETABLE SEED
Seed loses viability and vigour with age, and this process is accelerated if seed is kept in moist, warm conditions. Some crops, such as parsley, carrots, and parsnips, are best sown fresh each year. Seed of peas, beans, and brassicas will last for several years if kept correctly.

Seed should be stored in a cool, dry, dark place, at 1–5°C (34–41°F) with even moisture and temperature levels. Sheds and kitchen drawers are not suitable. Unopened vacuum-packed seeds store best; reseal opened packets securely with sticky tape, or tape home-saved seeds into small paper packets. Keep packets in an airtight tin or jar, surrounded by silica gel to absorb any moisture. If you open a packet to sow only some of the seeds, do not let the rest get damp before resealing. Before sowing seed stored for more than a year, test its viability (*see left*).

## How to test seed for viability

When seed has been stored long-term, test its viability before sowing. Put 50 or 100 seeds on damp absorbent paper on a saucer, and keep it moist and in a warm, dark place. The seeds should germinate within 2–3 weeks, producing roots and first seed leaves. Count the seedlings and work out the percentage of germination.

Do not count seeds that have merely swollen; all seeds swell when wet, whether viable or not. Sixty per cent germination (30 out of 50 seeds, for example) is the minimum required for you to consider sowing that batch of seed, for when sown outside, the percentage will be lower. In the examples shown here, using cabbage seed, one set (*left*) shows 60% viability and the other (*right*) 100%. The growth of the seedlings on the right is also more even and vigorous, indicating that the seed will produce stronger, healthier seedlings.

*Low viability*

*High viability*

# Sowing seed under cover

There are several advantages in starting crops by sowing seed under cover, in a greenhouse or cold frame (*see pp.43–48*), or in the house. You can control the environment – temperature, compost moisture and air humidity, and nutrient supply – to provide optimum conditions for germination and for the seedlings to establish. Seed of frost-tender plants can be germinated in favourable conditions, and the seedlings grown on until all risk of frost outdoors is past. Starting off hardier crops such as lettuces, onions, and carrots in a cold greenhouse usually produces stronger plants and better crops than from a spring sowing outside. Seed can also be sown earlier for a longer cropping season. Even seed that will germinate outdoors in very low temperatures, like peas and broad beans, can benefit from being sown under cover, where the risk of seed and seedlings rotting in cold, wet soil is reduced.

If you have only a small garden, you may not have room for the outdoor seedbed that some crops, such as many brassicas, require. Young module-raised brassica plants suffer less transplant shock and resist some plant problems better than seedlings raised in and transplanted from open ground.

## TEMPERATURE REQUIREMENTS

Seed of many crops will germinate in an unheated greenhouse or cold frame, although extra warmth will speed up germination. However, seed of plants indigenous to warm climates – for example tomatoes, cucumbers, peppers, courgettes, sweetcorn, and aubergines – will only germinate at constant temperatures in the range, usually, of 15–24°C (59–75°F).

At this stage the soil temperature matters more than that of the air. The most energy-efficient way of raising soil temperature is to warm it from below; hence the expression bottom heat. Bottom heat can be provided by putting pots and trays on a bed of grit or sand containing soil-warming cables or on a heated blanket. The heating system may be built into the base of a specialized propagator (*see facing page*), the lid also helping to retain heat and moisture in the air.

Once seeds have germinated and the seedlings are growing they generally require lower temperatures. Many hardy crops can, once hardened off (*see p.65*) be planted directly outside, provided that conditions are favourable. Other crops need continued warmth; peppers and aubergines, for example, need to be kept at 21°C (70°F) until planting. This can be achieved by maintaining bottom heat, if convenient, but also by growing on the young plants in a warm room.

## SEED-RAISING SYSTEMS

Traditionally, most vegetable seed sown under cover is sown into pots or trays filled with seed compost. Once the seeds germinate and the seedlings need more room to develop, they are transplanted, spaced more widely apart, into larger trays or into their own small pots. This is known as pricking out.

The advantage of this system is that it minimizes the amount of space in a heated propagator needed at the first, critical period during which the seeds germinate – especially useful with slow germinators such as celery and parsley. It is also an easy way to sow fine seed. The disadvantage is that pricking out the delicate seedlings can cause root damage and a check to growth.

*Rigid modular insert*

*Standard seed tray*

*Flexible modular strip*

*Half seed tray*

*13mm module tray*

*20mm module tray*

*9cm (3in) pot*

*30mm module tray*

*13cm (5in) pot*

*13cm (5in) pan*

*37mm module tray*

*Treated paper tube pots*

### Types of containers
*A variety of containers may be used for sowing. Make sure that pots have holes at the base for drainage. Modular inserts and trays have a hole at the bottom of each cell. Tube pots are biodegradable, so can be planted without the need to disturb roots.*

To avoid this pricking-out stage, seed can be raised in modules – individual, self-contained cells within a tray – until ready for planting out. This modular method gives very good results. Each seedling can grow without competition, and is transplanted with its own well-established rootball, minimizing any check to growth. The disadvantages are that more compost is used, and that the trays take up more room in a propagator.

If propagator space is at a premium, you can sow seed into pots and trays and then prick out the seedlings into modules. This works particularly well for seed of tomatoes and peppers, which can be sown in small pots in a heated propagator and then transplanted into large-celled trays (*see p.64*).

### CONTAINERS
Any small pots can be used to sow seed; the shallow pots known as pans are also ideal for most crops. It is advisable to choose plastic over terracotta; plastic can be kept cleaner, and makes it easier to control soil moisture. If only a few plants are required, say 10–12, a 9cm (3¹/₂in) pot will suffice. If 30 or more, sow in 13cm (5in) pans, or in a tray. Large seed trays are known as standard or full trays; small ones as half trays.

**Seedlings in an unheated propagator**
*Propagators keep seeds warm and moist, and encourage them to germinate. Here, tomato and celery seedlings are developing well. Use the vent in the lid to control condensation.*

Some plants, for example sweetcorn, must be encouraged to form a long root from an early stage. For these, long, narrow pots known as tube pots are ideal. If made from treated paper they can be planted directly into the soil, as can compressed fibre pots.

Module trays are graded by the size and number of their individual cells. Those with 13mm cells produce small plug plants that will quickly need transplanting; they are ideal when soil conditions will soon be good for planting out. The large, 37mm cells are suitable for plants with large seeds that need time and space to develop before

transplanting. When ready, the young plants can be pushed out from below.

### PROPAGATORS
A propagator provides a warm and humid microclimate, aiding the rapid and successful germination of seeds.In its simplest form, a propagator can be a sheet of glass or clear plastic, or even plastic film or fleece, placed over a pot or tray of seeds until they germinate. To develop further, however, seedlings need more headroom; purpose-built propagators consist of a moulded plastic tray with a box-like, clear lid (*see left*), with vent holes to allow air to circulate.

Small unheated propagators are fine for windowsills. Large, heated ones are ideal for unheated greenhouses. The heating element should provide a minimum compost temperature of 15°C (59°F). An adjustable thermostat regulates how much heat is generated. In severe weather, cover propagators at night with bubble wrap.

### SEED AND POTTING COMPOSTS
Proprietary composts tend to be a more even product than home-made mixes; they will also be free of pests and diseases. It is important to use fresh composts every year; they undergo detrimental chemical changes in store.

---

## Broadcast sowing in a half seed tray

**1** **Fill the tray** past the rim with a special seed compost or a universal compost. Moisten it with water if dry. Tap the tray on a bench in order to settle the compost, and then remove any excess by drawing a piece of wood carefully across the surface.

**2** **Firm the compost** to remove air pockets using the base of another tray or a presser board, which can be easily made at home. With peat-based composts, only minimum firming is necessary, or you risk compaction. Water the compost lightly and leave it until any excess has drained off.

**3** **Carefully scatter the seeds** onto the surface of the compost, direct from the seed packet. The seeds should be sown evenly and not too thickly, to avoid overcrowded seedlings later.

**4** **Sieve a fine layer of compost** over the seeds, and lightly firm it down. Keep the compost moist, but not wet, to encourage successful germination.

## Broadcast sowing in pots

**1** For just a few plants, scatter the seeds (here cabbage) thinly and evenly in a 9cm (3¹/₂in) pot of moist seed compost. Sprinkle with a layer of compost equal to the seed depth, water, and label.

**2** When 2 seed leaves have developed, transplant the seedlings into individual modules of standard potting compost, discarding any that are damaged or diseased.

**Using vermiculite to cover seed**
*Vermiculite can be used instead of compost to cover some seed; it allows air to reach the seeds, while keeping them moist.*

Proprietary seed composts are usually soilless, consisting of a sieved bulky material such as peat or a peat substitute mixed with fine sand to ensure good drainage. Seed composts are low in nutrients, which germinating seeds do not need. Multi-purpose or home-mixed composts can be used, with added sand to open them up, but avoid products and ingredients that are high in nutrients.

For transplanting seedlings into larger containers, use a potting compost that contains a higher level of nutrients to help the young plants develop. Peat- and coir-based composts are widely available, lightweight, and convenient to use; coir and other peat-free composts need care with watering and feeding. Soil-based composts are more retentive of nutrients and easier to keep moist. If you are an organic grower, materials such as leaf mould and worm composts are good ingredients in potting mixes.

### THE IMPORTANCE OF HYGIENE

Conditions under cover – warmer, and with still, humid air – increase the risk of disease, and plants are most vulnerable at the seed and seedling stage. Composts, water, containers, propagators, and all other items used must be scrupulously clean to avoid contamination that might cause disease, especially damping off (*see also* Plant Problems, pp.246–264). Do not use rainwater from water butts.

### SOWING SEED IN POTS OR TRAYS

Large seeds to be sown in pots or seed trays can be pushed into the compost individually. Fine seed can be sown broadcast – scattered randomly – and then spaced out more evenly at the pricking out stage. To sow fine seeds in pots (*see above*) or trays (*see p.63*), shake them straight from the packet, or sprinkle pinches from between finger and thumb. Cover thinly with sifted compost, sand, or vermiculite (*see above right*), and lightly firm. The smaller the seeds, the lighter the covering should be. Water lightly; at this stage you could water in a copper-based fungicide to protect against damping off.

Place the container in a propagator, or cover with a sheet of glass or kitchen film. Remove covers as soon as germination occurs to avoid disease.

**Pricking out into modules**
*To avoid too much damage to the roots, as soon as the seed leaves are fully open (here celery), prick out the seedlings into modules or small pots. Gently ease out the seedlings from the compost using a dibber or pencil. Hold each seedling by its leaves, because the stems bruise very easily. Dibble a hole in each cell and drop in a seedling. Then use the tip of the tool to push and gently firm compost around it. Water and label.*

In the early stages, ensure the seedlings are kept warm and moist. It is helpful to stand seeded containers on water-absorbent matting, obtainable from garden stores. Avoid exposure to strong sun; a temporary covering of newspaper is a useful device. Plants on a windowsill will grow towards the light, so turn the container regularly. Check regularly for signs of disease, as this can rapidly spread. Once the seed leaves have fully developed, prick out the seedlings.

### PRICKING OUT SEEDLINGS

Always prick out seedlings promptly, or they will become crowded and grow weak and leggy. Water the seedlings, and fill the new container with moistened potting compost. Hold each seedling gently by a leaf; never touch the stalk or roots. Using a dibber or a pencil, lift out the seedlings in groups, and separate them carefully so as not to damage the delicate root hairs. Discard any unhealthy-looking seedlings.

Transplant them into fresh compost, either regularly spaced, 2.5–5cm (1–2in) apart, in a large seed tray, or one plant per module cell (*see left*), with the seed leaves just above the compost. To avoid scorching, keep the seedlings out of full sun for a couple of days. Grow the seedlings on and harden off (*see facing page*) ready for planting outside.

### PRICKING OUT INTO INDIVIDUAL POTS

This is ideal for frost-tender crops such as tomatoes and peppers that are to be grown on in the greenhouse before being planted out in warm conditions, because they have to be well spaced out

on the staging. Prick out each seedling into a 10cm (4in) pot. Place the pots close together initially, and then move them apart as the plants develop and their leaves begin to touch.

## SOWING DIRECTLY INTO MODULES

Large seeds are easy to sow individually in modules. Small seeds can be carefully pushed off a piece of board, glass, or paper, or lifted individually on a damp artist's paintbrush. Fill the cells with compost in the same way as described for pots and seed trays. Either sow one seed per module, just pushing it into the surface or, for seed of doubtful viability (for example old seed), sow three to a cell and thin to one strong seedling as soon as the seed leaves are fully developed.

Module trays sown with hardy crops can be placed in an unheated greenhouse or cold frame. Cover the trays with fleece, kitchen film, or glass to keep the seeds relatively warm and moist until they have germinated, especially if sowing early in the season when temperatures are low. When the seedlings start to emerge, uncover them, and grow them on in good light until large enough to plant out.

## MULTIBLOCK SOWING

This sowing technique (*see above right*), in which clusters of plants are grown rather than individual ones, is very useful if you have limited space. It produces a larger

### Multiblock sowing

**1** **Fill a module tray** with moist potting compost. Make a slight depression in each cell with your finger, and sow 3–5 seeds in it. One module tray could be used for a mixture of crops to avoid gluts. Cover the seeds with a 5mm (¼in) layer of grit, and water and label. Put the tray in a position with good light.

**2** **When the seedlings** have grown further and developed 1–2 true leaves, carefully plant out each group, without thinning, at an appropriate spacing for the vegetable (here turnips).

**3** **Allow the unthinned plants** to grow on to form a group of mature baby vegetables. This method enables you to grow many plants in a small space, and is especially suitable for root, bulb, and stem vegetables.

number of smaller, or baby, vegetables, and is suitable for turnips, beetroot, round carrots, spring and bulb onions, chives, leeks, and parsley. Multiblock seedlings should be raised in a greenhouse or a frame, where there is good overhead light that will reach all of the seedlings in the cluster, and be

planted out before they become leggy. It is important to give them enough space for the whole cluster to grow to maturity.

## FEEDING YOUNG PLANTS

If young plants have to be left in pots or modules for long periods because adverse weather conditions prevent planting out, give them a liquid feed (*see p.21*) to maintain health and vigour. As soon as the plant's roots fill the pot or module cell, pot up into larger containers of potting or multi-purpose compost, and feed regularly.

## HARDENING OFF

Young plants raised from seed under cover need to be gradually acclimatized to the outside temperature before they are permanently planted out. This is known as hardening off, and it should take at least 10–14 days. Put the plants in a cold frame, gradually increasing the ventilation each day until the plants are eventually completely uncovered. Leave them for a few days close together to protect each other; this helps them to establish when finally planted out singly. Less hardening off is needed if fleece or cloches are to be used (*see pp.46–48*).

### GROWING SALAD SEEDLINGS

You can grow mustard, rape, or cress (*see p.106*) in 2–3cm (¾–1¼in) of compost in small pots, punnets, or shallow pans. Scatter the seeds thickly on the surface and leave to germinate. Keep moist but not over-wet. This will produce a mass of seedlings ready to eat in 7–10 days. Cress must be sown three days before mustard or rape to obtain a mixture for salad. Alternatively, line a saucer, 13cm (5in) in diameter, with absorbent paper, add water to soak the paper, and drain off any excess before sowing the seeds thickly (*see below*). Cover with a plastic bag to retain moisture, and place on a windowsill, at a maximum temperature of 15°C (59°F).

*Scatter cress seeds thickly*          *Cress seedlings ready to eat*

# Sowing seed outdoors

Successful vegetable cropping from seed sown outdoors is dependent on a satisfactory seedbed and the care with which the sowing is carried out. The seed is usually sown in rows known as drills (*see below*). Most crops are sown where they will be harvested. Some, including leeks and cauliflowers, may be sown fairly closely spaced in a seedbed, and then transplanted (*see p.70*) when the plants are large enough. Seedbeds are less widely used since the advent of module trays (*see also pp.62–65*), which make it possible to raise sturdy plants under cover that transplant well after hardening off.

## WHEN TO SOW

The site where seed is to be sown must always be well prepared in advance. The soil should be moist enough for the seeds to take up water, and also sufficiently warm for the crop being sown (*see p.62 and individual crops, pp.74–135*). Few crops germinate at low soil temperatures, so do not be in a rush to sow before spring temperatures start to rise. The soil can be warmed with covers or cloches to advance sowing dates (*see pp.46–48*).

## PREPARING A SEEDBED

In the autumn before sowing, dig over the site of the seedbed thoroughly, incorporating organic matter (*see pp. 37–40*), and allow it to settle over winter, when frost will help break up clods. If the soil of the seedbed contains a high population of annual weed seeds, prepare it in advance: allow a flush of weeds to develop, then hoe these off or spray them with a contact weedkiller. This removes at a stroke large numbers of weeds that would otherwise compete with seedling crops, and is known as the stale seedbed technique.

Cultivate the ground with a three- or five-tined cultivator, and level it with a wooden rake. Apply a base dressing of fertilizer if appropriate (*see individual crops, pp.74–135*). For large areas of seedbed, if the soil is very lumpy or soft, carefully tread over the whole area evenly, but never do this when the soil is wet, or it will become compacted and airless. For small areas, stand off the bed and use the back of a rake head to tamp down lumps gently to break them up.

## PRODUCING A FINE TILTH

If the soil is dry, water it before working it. Rake the seedbed until the texture of the soil is quite crumbly and friable, with small particles – this is known as a fine tilth. Soils with a high organic matter content are usually easier to work than others. It is essential to use long sweeps of the rake and to pull and push the soil in different directions to ensure a level, even seedbed. Keep the rake handle low for the best results. The surface tilth should be deep enough to draw out a drill without going into undisturbed soil.

---

## Sowing seed in single drills

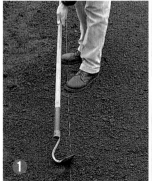

**1** **Stretch a marker line** of strong cord over the seedbed around canes marking the end of each drill line. Use the corner of a hoe to draw out an even drill along the line to the depth required for the seed. Stand on the line to keep it taut and straight.

**2** **If the seeds are large,** such as these parsnip seeds, sow 3 of them per station at the required interval, here every 15cm (6in), using a measuring stick to ensure the stations are regularly spaced.

**3** **For seeds in tape form,** which are supplied ready-spaced (here of spring onion), simply cut a length of tape to the length of the drill and lay it along the bottom.

**4** **For small seeds,** such as carrots, sow thinly along a drill. Rub the seeds between your fingers to scatter them evenly, or use a seed sower.

**5** **Cover the drill** promptly, by raking the soil back over it evenly, holding the rake at 90° to the drill. You can also use the back of the rake head.

## SINGLE DRILLS

Small seeds such as lettuce should be sown thinly in regularly spaced, single rows about 30cm (1ft) apart. Using a garden line and a draw or swan-necked hoe, pull out the drill (*see facing page*), making sure that the line is as tight as possible in order to get an even, straight depression. It is most important to achieve a uniform depth along the drill. Sow pelleted seeds shallowly at a depth of about twice their diameter, and keep the soil moist to aid germination.

Where a system of narrow beds is being used (*see pp.32–34*), drills can be made by drawing a hoe or stout cane along the edge of a straddling plank. Alternatively, it is possible to make drills by pressing a pre-measured length of timber into the tilth.

An adjustable marking tool (*see p.68*) can be useful, saving walking up and down. Draw out the first drill along a fixed line, then draw the tool down this drill to pull out subsequent ones.

## WIDE DRILLS

Wide drills are suitable for sowing peas (*see below*), and for broadcast sowing strips of early carrots, radishes, and cut-and-come-again seedling crops such as spinach, cress, and some types of lettuce. Such strips can be very close together, making good use of land, although they are less easily weeded than single rows. To make a wide drill, draw out a shallow trench 15–20cm (6–8in) wide using a line and a wide draw hoe (*see below*), or carefully shovel out the soil to the width of a narrow spade. Make sure that the depth of the drill is uniform.

## Sowing in wet or dry conditions

**Sowing in wet conditions**
*If the soil is wet, or very heavy and slow to drain, place a layer of sand in the base of the drill before sowing any seed. This will improve conditions for germination.*

**Sowing in dry conditions**
*If the soil is particularly dry, give the drill a good watering first, and then sow the seed immediately. Cover over with dry soil; do not water again until the seedlings emerge.*

### WET OR DRY CONDITIONS

You may not be able to wait for ideal weather conditions before sowing. It is possible to compensate for too much or too little soil moisture by adding sand or watering drills before sowing (*see above*). Use a fine-rosed can to water, always before, not after sowing, or the soil may become capped, or crusted.

### DEPTH OF SOWING

The depth at which you should sow seeds varies according to their size. Seedlings depend on their own reserves for nutrients in the first few days after germinating, until they pierce the soil surface and reach the light. Then they can start to make their own food. Large seeds have more reserves than small ones, and can therefore be sown more deeply. Very fine seed should be sown

### Hand-held seed sower

*This useful device is designed to release seeds gradually. It can be set for the flow of differently sized seed, from thin sowings of fine seed to space sowing of large seed, as here with pelleted seed.*

nearer the surface. Check the seed packet for recommended sowing depths (*see also individual crops, pp.74–135*).

### SOWING METHODS

When sowing, try to choose a still day; great care will be needed if it is windy, especially with light seeds like parsnips. Sowing seed evenly takes plenty of practice. For all the methods described, practise first by sowing seed into a piece of guttering about 90cm (3ft) long and adjusting the amounts until you achieve the correct density.

Seeds large enough to be handled individually can be station or space sown (*see p.69*) in drills at regular intervals. Use a measuring stick until you are practised and can judge the correct spacing. A hand-held plastic sower (*see above*) with adjustable settings will help. The sower must be shaken evenly and steadily as you go.

For small, fine seed, sowing direct from the packet works well with paper or rigid-plastic packets, if they have a clean-cut edge and a narrow opening. Shake evenly, holding the packet nearly horizontal to regulate the fall of seeds.

## Sowing in wide drills

**1 Draw out a drill** with the blade of a suitable hoe, flicking the soil to one side as you go. Make the drill as deep as required for the crop (here 5cm/2in).

**2 Sow pea seeds in 2 rows** along the drill. Here, they are sown at 5cm (2in) intervals in rows 10cm (4in) apart. Cover over gently, and protect from birds.

You can also sow small seeds from your palm. Hold a small quantity and move your hand horizontally and steadily over the prepared area, tapping it gently with your other hand so that seeds drop off. This is a very good means of broadcast sowing.

Another method is to put some seed in the palm of one hand and take a few between first finger and thumb of the other hand, rubbing them together to disperse the seed. The thinner the sowing required, the fewer seeds should be picked up at a time.

## COVERING SEED IN DRILLS
Once you have sown seed in drills, either use a rake to cover the seeds or shuffle your feet along the drill with your heels together. Gently rake the surface along the covered drill to ensure firmness. Never rake across the lines as this will disturb the seeds and could remove them from the drill. Cultivating carefully between drills with a cultivator will loosen any heavily compacted soil.

## SPACING OF PLANTS
Space is needed between rows of crops for air circulation, thinning, and for weeding. The spacing of crops sown directly outdoors, or planted out, is determined by the ultimate height and spread of the crop. Parsnips grow to about 30cm (12in) high, and butterhead lettuces up to 30cm (12in) wide, and therefore with both, the rows of plants

should be 30cm (12in) apart to allow in light to produce good crops. Peas may grow to 90cm (3ft), so allow 90cm (3ft) between rows. Carrot and radish rows can be as close as 10cm (4in) apart. Within the rows, thin root crops so that the vegetables will be just touching when mature.

To calculate the space required between rows of different crops, as a general rule of thumb you can add the recommended row spacing for each crop together and divide the total by two. For example, if growing parsnips and peas in rows next to each other at the spacings given above, add the row spacing for parsnips – 30cm (12in) – to the row spacing of peas – 90cm (3ft) – and halve it to give a between-row spacing of 60cm (2ft).

## THINNING SEEDLINGS
Thinning – removing surplus seedlings – is essential to obtain a satisfactory final spacing for each plant to grow to maturity. These distances vary with the crop. It should be carried out early, before competition for light and water occurs and the plants become drawn. Because thinning disturbs the roots of plants growing close by, and can attract pests, try to reduce the necessity for thinning by sowing seeds thinly or by station sowing (*see below*).

When the seedlings have reached the first true leaf stage, either pull or pinch out weaker seedlings (*see below*)

**Adjustable marking tool**
*These have adjustable tines that can be set at different spacings. Useful tools for marking out planting rows and stations, they can also be handy for marking out shallow seed drills.*

to leave the strongest and best. Pinching is better for carrots and onions because the soil is disturbed when the seedling is pulled out by its roots, and the foliage bruised, causing odours which attract carrot and onion flies which may then lay their eggs in the loosened soil. Remove all thinnings, to avoid the risk of disease and of attracting pests.

## STATION OR SPACE SOWING
This method is used to conserve seeds that are expensive, and to reduce the amount of thinning required later. Large seeds such as spinach may be sown 5cm (2in) apart and left to mature *in situ*. For marrows, sow two or three seeds per station 75cm (30in) apart. For crops like sweetcorn, which must be grown in a block rather than a row, mark out an area of a bed in a grid pattern, using a marking tool (*see above*). At each station where the rows cross, sow three seeds. These should later be thinned to one strong seedling.

## BROADCAST SOWING
Random broadcasting of seed is suitable for growing patches of radishes, early carrots, or turnips. It is also used for cut-and-come-again seedling crops, such as mustard and cress. Prepare the seedbed and scatter the seed evenly over the surface. Rake the seed into the surface. The method is easy but there can be a wide variation in size among the seedlings, and sowing in drills better allows for hoeing and weeding. Crops suitable for broadcasting can just as easily be sown in very closely spaced, wide drills (*see p.67*).

## How to thin seedlings

**Pulling**
*Once seedlings are large enough to handle, gently pull them out to leave single, strong specimens at the appropriate spacings.*

**Pinching out**
*With some crops it is best to thin by pinching seedlings off between thumb and forefinger at ground level, to avoid disturbing the soil.*

## SOWING LARGE SEEDS USING A DIBBER

This means of space sowing is ideal for crops with very large seeds, such as broad, French, and runner beans, sweetcorn, and marrows. First rake over the seedbed to ensure that the soil is loose. Then make a series of holes with a dibber (*see below right*). Drop one or more seeds into the bottom of each hole and cover with soil.

For beans, a single seed per hole is usual; for sweetcorn, three seeds; for marrows, two. Thin the seedlings (*see facing page*) to one per site when they are large enough. It is wise to sow some spares, to fill any gaps that may appear due to poor germination. You can cover the sites of marrow and sweetcorn seeds with jamjars – individual cloches – to keep the soil warm and moist to encourage germination.

## INTERSOWING

Intersowing involves sowing seed of two different vegetables in the same drill. One crop is quick to mature and therefore does not compete with the other, which is slow-growing or slow to germinate. Parsnips and radishes make a good combination for this method (*see above right*). The faster-growing radishes will show up the line of the drill long before the parsnips emerge, enabling earlier hoeing for weed control, and they are harvested before they represent competition to the slower crop.

## SUCCESSIONAL SOWINGS

To avoid harvesting gluts and to ensure continuity of supplies, especially of salad vegetables, sow just a few seeds at a time, following with a few more at regular intervals thereafter. This method is suitable for lettuces, radishes, turnips, beetroot, and salad onions. Sow the next batch when seedlings from the previous one have just come up; for example, sow a few lettuce seeds every 10–14 days for a succession of crops.

## CATCH CROPS

To save space, especially in a small garden, plan to grow fast-maturing crops such as radishes or spinach before or between other crops, such as tomatoes, sweetcorn, and winter brassicas.

---

## Intersowing parsnip and radish seed

**1** **Station sow the parsnip seeds,** 3 to a station, every 10cm (4in). Then sow radish seeds at 2.5cm (1in) intervals in-between the parsnip seeds. The radish seedlings will come up very quickly, indicating the line of the drill to guide early hoeing of any weeds.

**2** **Harvest the radishes when ready** so that they do not crowd the parsnip seedlings. Pinch out the parsnip seedlings to thin them when they have 4 leaves.

---

## RATES OF GERMINATION

The percentage of seed you sow that will actually germinate depends on a variety of factors, not all of which can be controlled by good gardening practice. Natural germination rate varies with crop groups: for example, brassicas generally have a germination rate of 90 per cent, whereas with leeks it is usually no more than 70 per cent. Large seeds are usually more viable than fine seeds, which are more prone to desiccation. In many cases, seed sown soon after harvest performs better than does stored seed. Parsnip and parsley seed is naturally very slow to germinate compared with that of radish and turnip. Dormancy of seed is affected by temperature – for instance, French bean germination is inhibited below 12°C (54°F) and lettuce above 25°C (77°F).

All these conditions may have an effect on how many plants you get compared with the amount of seed you sow, but given careful seed harvest and storage they are unlikely to affect greatly success in the garden provided they are understood. In practice, poor germination is more often due to something being amiss in the condition of the seedbed, such as moisture content, temperature, and air, or in the method of sowing. The ground rules for success: use quality seed and give careful attention to all aspects of sowing it.

## USING FLEECE FOR PROTECTION

Fleece or other sheet covers (*see p.48*), tucked into the soil or held down at the edges with bricks, can help to warm the soil before sowing. After sowing, it encourages early establishment, and keeps off birds and some insect pests. Remove it before the seedlings grow tall enough to be restricted.

**Station sowing large seed**
*Large seeds may be sown into individual holes made with a dibber. For broad beans, as here, make holes 5cm (2in) deep, 10cm (4in) apart in rows 15cm (6in) apart, and drop the seeds into them. Cover with soil, water, and label.*

# Planting out

Young vegetable plants that are raised under cover to be planted out, or raised in an outdoor seedbed and then transplanted to their final growing site, are known as transplants.

The main point to remember when transplanting is to cause as little damage to the young plant and its roots as possible; handle them carefully and no more than is necessary, and never allow roots to dry out. Water the young plants well in advance so that they are turgid – plump with water – on transplanting, to reduce the risk of wilting. Do not take transplants out of containers or lift them from seedbeds until the planting site is ready – forked over, with all weeds removed, and raked level.

## WHEN TO PLANT OUT CROPS

Young plants of some crops, like the sweet peppers shown opposite, are raised or bought in to be grown to maturity in pots, growing bags or soil beds in greenhouses (see pp.43–44), and these can be planted in their permanent homes as soon as their rootballs fill the container that they occupy.

If planting transplants raised under cover into beds outside, exactly when to plant out will be dictated by the development of the seedlings and the weather outside, since it affects the condition of the soil. Ideally, choose

**Plug seedlings**
*Transplants ordered by mail often now arrive in these transparent moulded plastic units. Each has its own self-contained rootball, or plug. The leafy tops are held up and protected from bruising by the plastic shell. Remove all packaging from them immediately on arrival, and pot up or plant out as soon as possible.*

a mild, dull day to plant out. Seedlings should be well-established, with four to six true leaves and a good root system. Do not allow them to become tall and drawn; if necessary, pot on the plants until conditions are right.

The soil should be moist but not sodden, and relatively warm – for many crops there should be no further danger of frost. The young plants must also be adequately hardened off (see p.65).

For specific planting times, refer to individual crop entries (see pp.74–135).

## BUYING IN TRANSPLANTS

Some crops, such as spring cabbages and hardy lettuces, are available as young plants in autumn, but the main time to buy transplants of vegetables is late spring. This is ideal if you do not have space to propagate crops yourself under cover, but beware of buying frost-tender plants such as tomatoes too early in the season if you do not have the facilities to protect the young plants until all danger of frost is past.

Young plants sold at garden centres are usually offered in large module cells, ready to be planted out with minimal root disturbance. Choose stocky, healthy plants; if possible, check for a good root system. Plant them as soon as possible; they will keep in a sheltered shady spot, if watered, for a few days. Brassicas are often sold bare-root in bundles, and these need planting, or heeling in (see below) immediately.

Smaller seedlings known as plug plants can be purchased from nurseries and by mail order (see above left). If you cannot plant these immediately on arrival, they will need potting up.

## HEELING IN PLANTS

If bad weather prevents you from planting bare-root plants straightaway, they should be heeled in temporarily in a spare corner. Make a shallow hole or trench, about 10cm (4in) deep, with a hoe, and lay the plants up against one side. Cover the plants up to their leaves in soil, firm, and water. Keep the plants watered until transplanting time.

## Transplanting seedlings from a seedbed

**1 Water the entire row** thoroughly to make the young plants (here cabbages) easy to lift without damage and to retain soil around the roots. Hold them by their leaves, not stems. Put them in a bucket with a little water to prevent wilting.

**2 Mark out planting stations** (here, 45cm/18in) in a prepared bed. Make a planting hole for each transplant and water each hole well. Hold the plant at the correct depth and firm by pushing the dibber sideways towards the roots.

**Planting out seedlings raised under cover**
*Young module-raised lettuces are here planted at equidistant spacing, following a grid marked out across the bed surface. Hold module-raised plants by the rootball, not the leaves.*

## Interplanting alliums with sweetcorn

**1** **In spring,** plant 3 rows of fast-growing alliums (here, cold-treated garlic cloves, shallot sets, and bunching onions) along a well-prepared bed covered with a black film plastic, laid down for weed control. Run a seep hose beneath it for irrigation. Use a dibber to punch holes through the plastic at the appropriate spacings to plant each bulb.

**2** **In early summer,** set out 3 rows of young sweetcorn plants in staggered rows between the alliums. Use a bulb planter or trowel to make holes in the film plastic large enough to accommodate the transplants' rootballs.

**3** **As summer progresses,** the alliums will mature. As it ripens, harvest each crop to leave more space for the maturing sweetcorn.

### TRANSPLANTING SEEDLINGS GROWN IN MODULES OR CONTAINERS

Before planting out (*see below right*), water plants well. Knock plants out of pots by tapping the rim on a hard surface until the rootball becomes free. Remove plants from modules either by squeezing the base of the cell gently, or by poking them up and out through the drainage hole with a dibber or similar. If necessary to avoid damage to roots, cut the modular cells off the plants.

Plant out carefully into prepared soil with the surface of the rootball just below the soil surface. Firm around the plant, remove any dead foliage, stake if necessary, water to settle the plants in, and label. If the sun is hot and strong, shade the young plants with sheets or cones of newspaper, or fleece draped lightly over them, and keep well watered. A moisture-conserving mulch (*see p.41*) can be applied around sturdy transplants such as brassicas and beans, but do not let it touch stems.

### TRANSPLANTING OUTDOORS

When seedlings raised in a drill or an seedbed outdoors reach a height of 10–13cm (4–5in), they are ready for transplanting. To minimize wilting after replanting, choose a dull, damp day, or transplant in the evening, and water the seedlings thoroughly before lifting. Loosen the soil around the seedlings with a trowel or small hand fork. Lift the plants and carefully tease them apart if necessary, trying to keep the roots intact (*see far left*). Select evenly sized plants, and discard any that are bent, damaged, weak, or showing signs of disease. Put the plants in a plastic bag to prevent them from drying out.

Do not delay replanting. Holding each plant by its leaves, make a hole deep enough for it to be planted to just below its first leaves. Set the plant in the hole, holding it upright while you fill and firm in gently around the roots. Water in and label the plants.

### SPACING

When raising transplants at home, keep the seed packets so that you have the information on spacing that they carry when you need it. Advice on crop spacings is also given in the A–Z listings of individual crops later in this section (*see pp.74–135*).

Distance between plants will also vary according to whether you are planting in a conventional row arrangement or using equidistant or block spacing, as for example in a system of 1.2m (4ft) wide beds (*see pp.32–34*) where there is no need to walk between rows of crops.

### INTERCROPPING

Provided that you get the timing right, you can plant transplants in the space between rows of maturing crops, ready to grow and fill the space left when those crops are harvested. This inter-cropping is an efficient use of space. You can also use the space between slow-growing transplants, such as brassicas, to sow catch crops (*see also p.69*) of fast-growing crops such as salads to harvest before the slower crops fill out the plot.

Transplants are also useful in potager or edible landscape gardening where vegetable plants are grown among established ornamental plants; they will grow away more successfully than plants raised from seed.

**Planting out**
*Here young sweet pepper transplants have been raised in 9cm (3½in) pots for planting out in a greenhouse bed. Water the plants thoroughly a little time before removing the pot. Take out a planting hole with a trowel and plant firmly with the top of the rootball just below the planting bed surface.*

# Routine care

All vegetables need attention as they grow to produce a good crop. However, you can do much to anticipate and prevent problems and extra work with good planning and preparation. A well-nurtured soil to which plenty of organic matter is added every year, for example, reduces the need for extra watering and feeding during the growing season. Regular, early attention to routine tasks such as weeding can lessen the incidence of some pest and disease problems. For all the topics mentioned below, specific advice on the requirements of individual crops are given on pp.74–135. *See also* Plant Problems (*pp.246–264*) for help with diagnosing and controlling specific pest and disease problems.

## PLANTS THAT NEED SUPPORT
Providing adequate supports for plants that need it, and checking ties regularly, can prevent unnecessary damage. Short, stout canes or stakes are needed for winter brassicas; tomatoes and other fruiting vegetables can be supported with individual canes or with canes and twine (*see p.109*). Peas generally require only light support; vigorous climbing beans (*see pp.96–97*) and cucurbits (*see p.115*) need rows or wigwams of canes or poles braced against each other, or more robust frames or nets.

## WATERING
How much and how often you need to water (*see also p.53–54*) will depend largely on weather conditions and also on the nature of your soil. The lighter the soil (*see p.14*), the less water it can hold, so plants in sandy soils need much more watering than those in heavy ones. A high organic content in the soil helps retain water. If crops are shaded for part of the day, this will also help reduce water loss. Bear in mind that the roots of nearby trees and shrubs, hedges or other tall crops will take water from a wide area around them.

A mulch (*see pp.41–42*), whether organic or inorganic, also conserves moisture. Hoe mulching (*see above, right*) is a traditional way of creating a loose surface layer that protects the lower levels of soil against evaporation.

**Hoe mulching**
*Lessen the need for watering by hoeing regularly to keep the top 1cm (½in) of soil loose, creating air spaces that reduce evaporation.*

**Providing supports**
*Make sure that supports are sturdy enough for the weight and number of plants they are to hold, and that the bases of poles and canes are firmly embedded in the soil.*

Propagation and transplanting are critical times for watering, but, once established, plants outdoors usually need no more than one good watering a week. Water heavily to ensure good penetration down to the roots. Frequent light sprinklings are wasteful and less effective. Leafy crops usually need more plentiful, regular watering than root crops. Other vegetables may need more water at critical stages of development; for example pod set in beans, and when tomato fruits are swelling.

Fleece-covered crops (*see p.48*) dry out more slowly, but plants growing in containers (*see p.35–36*) and under cover (*see p.43–48*) need more frequent watering than those in open ground. Use moisture-retentive composts, and mulch containers if possible to minimize evaporation. Water containers daily for best results. In hot weather, growing bags can need watering three times a day. Also, just as wind has a drying effect outdoors, over-ventilation can have a similar effect indoors. Damping down – sprinkling water on the greenhouse floor – increases air humidity and discourages some pests.

## FEEDING
If you have fertile soil to which you regularly add organic matter and general fertilizers when beds are prepared, plants are less likely to go short of essential nutrients (*see also p.17*). Supplementary feeding may be necessary on impoverished soil, however, or desirable to boost yields. As nitrogen is constantly washed out of the soil, it is the nutrient most likely to need replacing during the growing season, through the addition of organic manures or high-nitrogen fertilizers. Fast-acting liquid feeds can be useful. High-nitrogen feeds promote lush, leafy growth in crops such as spinach, but are not advisable for root crops. High-potash fertilizers, such as tomato feeds, are suitable for fruiting vegetables.

Deficiencies of the minor nutrients or trace elements are uncommon in well-managed soil, but can be caused by other cultural problems – drought, for example, can impede the availability of calcium to plants. Details of symptoms and remedies for the more common nutrient deficiencies can be found in Plant Problems (*see pp.246–264*).

## WEEDING
Good weed control, ideally by light, regular hoeing, lessens competition for water and nutrients, and also removes potential hosts for some garden pests and diseases. Both organic and inorganic mulches (*see pp.41–42*) are extremely effective means of suppressing weeds.

# Winter storage

Some vegetables will keep fresh in a refrigerator for up to a week; others freeze well. Preserving and pickling also provides out-of-season supplies. There are other storage methods, however, that can extend the season of availability of crops that are vulnerable to low temperatures, or where it is necessary to harvest all of a crop to clear the ground. For more detail on storage of individual crops, *see pp.74–135.*

### STORING IN SITU

Parsnips, swedes, and carrots can be left in the ground and lifted as required. However, roots can be difficult to lift when the ground is sodden or frozen, especially on heavy soil. Hard frosts will also damage turnips and beetroot. Beds can be prevented from freezing hard by covering them with a 15cm (6in) blanket of straw or bracken, held down with horticultural fleece or netting, once the temperature falls below 5°C (41°F). Remove the covering when the temperature rises to avoid encouraging new shoot growth, when the crop will start to deteriorate.

Pumpkins, marrows, and squashes can be left out on the ground after harvest, where in favourable weather conditions the sun will complete the hardening of the skins that is essential for good keeping properties. If the ground is wet, a plank or straw placed under the fruits will reduce the risk of rotting. Once the weather deteriorates, bring the crop under cover.

### BRINGING CROPS UNDER COVER

A cool but frost-free, dry place, such as a cellar or shed, is perfect for storing many crops after harvest. Some must not dry out if they are to stay in good condition for eating; others must be thoroughly dried, but in both cases good ventilation is essential. Slatted wooden shelves, trays, or racks are ideal, allowing good air circulation. Do not use plastic or cardboard boxes; they increase humidity and encourage rots.

Large, shallow, wooden boxes can be used to store lifted root crops, within layers of sand or peat substitute (*see right*). Potatoes left in the ground

are very vulnerable to pest damage; once mature, crops are also best lifted and stored. Potatoes exposed to light produce poisonous alkaloids, indicated by the greening of tubers, so must be stored in complete darkness. Paper sacks (*see below*) are ideal; plastic bags will encourage condensation and rots.

Onions, shallots, and garlic, once well ripened and dried, can be stored in single layers in stacked slatted boxes, or strung up in plaited ropes (*see below*), or hung in nets or even old nylon tights – anything that allows air to circulate freely around the bulbs. Whole plants of peppers can also be hung up for use as required, as can bean and pea plants to complete the ripening of drying crops. Alternatively, dry off the pods in slatted boxes before shelling and storing the beans or peas in jars.

While leafy, loose-headed cabbages do not store well, the densely hearted winter and red cabbages can either be hung in a net (*see below*) or stored

on wooden slatted racks. They keep best at an even temperature just above freezing.

Store only good-quality, undamaged produce. Check all stored crops regularly and remove any that show signs of disease or deterioration. In very cold conditions, cover with layers of sacking or newpaper for insulation.

### CLAMPING

If you do not have space under cover, this traditional outdoor storage method for root vegetables is effective, although rodent pests can be a problem. A clamp – basically, an insulated heap of roots – can be made against an outside wall or in an outbuilding or cellar. Make a 20cm (8in) base layer of light, sandy soil, or of sand. Stack the roots in a pile with sloping sides, with the largest roots at the base (maximum 60cm/2ft in height for carrots). Blanket the entire pile with a 20cm (8in) layer of straw, then a 15cm (6in) layer of soil.

---

## Storing vegetables over winter

**Storing potatoes**
*Keep only undamaged potatoes in a double-layered paper sack in a clean, dry place. Fold the top of the sack over loosely after access to exclude light.*

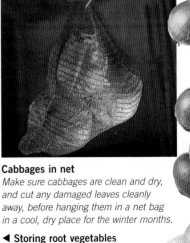

**Cabbages in net**
*Make sure cabbages are clean and dry, and cut any damaged leaves cleanly away, before hanging them in a net bag in a cool, dry place for the winter months.*

**◄ Storing root vegetables**
*Loosely pack root vegetables in a shallow wooden box, and cover with moist sand or peat substitute.*

**▶ Plaiting onions**
*To form a rope of onions, suspend one from a string hung from a beam or the ceiling, and then either use the long necks of the onions, or a second string, to secure successive bulbs above it, working from the bottom upwards.*

# Visual index of vegetables

**Use this index to locate details of individual vegetable crops.**

| | | | | |
|---|---|---|---|---|
| *Abelmoschus esculentus* p.112<br>**Okra** | *Allium cepa* p.92<br>**Onion** | *Allium cepa* p.94<br>Aggregatum Group<br>**Shallot** | *Allium cepa* p.94<br>**Spring onion** | *Allium fistulosum* p.94<br>**Welsh onion** |
| *Allium porrum* p.93<br>**Leek** | *Allium sativum* p.92<br>**Garlic** | *Amaranthus* species p.125<br>**Amaranth** | *Apium graveolens* p.121<br>var. *dulce*<br>**Celery** | *Apium graveolens* p.121<br>var. *dulce*<br>**Leaf celery** |
| *Apium graveolens* p.121<br>var. *rapaceum*<br>**Celeriac** | *Asparagus officinalis* p.133<br>**Asparagus** | *Barbarea verna* p.105<br>**Land, American cress** | *Beta vulgaris* subsp. p.128<br>*cicla* var. *flavescens*<br>**Chard, spinach beet** | *Beta vulgaris* p.85<br>subsp. *vulgaris*<br>**Beetroot** |
| *Brassica juncea* p.127<br>**Mustard greens** | *Brassica napus* p.88<br>Napobrassica Group<br>**Swede** | *Brassica oleracea* p.80<br>Acephala Group<br>**Kale, curly kale** | *Brassica oleracea* p.79<br>Botrytis Group<br>**Cauliflower** | *Brassica oleracea* p.78<br>Capitata Group<br>**Cabbage** |
| *Brassica oleracea* p.78<br>Gemmifera Group<br>**Brussels sprouts** | *Brassica oleracea* p.81<br>Gongylodes Group<br>**Kohlrabi** | *Brassica oleracea* p.79<br>Italica Group<br>**Calabrese** | *Brassica oleracea* p.81<br>Italica Group<br>**Sprouting broccoli** | *Brassica rapa* p.88<br>Rapifera Group<br>**Turnip, turnip top** |
| *Brassica rapa* p.126<br>var. *alboglabra*<br>**Chinese broccoli, Chinese kale** | *Brassica rapa* p.127<br>var. *chinensis*<br>**Pak choi** | *Brassica rapa* var. p.106<br>*nipposinica*<br>**Mizuna greens** | *Brassica rapa* var. p.126<br>*pekinensis*<br>**Chinese cabbage** | *Brassica rapa* var. p.104<br>*perviridis*<br>**Komatsuna** |
| *Capsicum annuum* p.111<br>**Sweet and chilli pepper** | *Cichorium endivia* p.104<br>**Endive** | *Cichorium* p.103<br>*intybus*<br>**Chicory** | *Cucumis melo* p.118<br>**Sweet melon** | *Cucumis sativus* p.117<br>**Cucumber and gherkin** |

*Cucurbita maxima, p.118*
*C. moschata, C. pepo*

**Pumpkin and winter squash**

*Cucurbita pepo p.117*

**Courgette, zucchini**

*Cucurbita pepo p.119*

**Vegetable marrow**

*Cynara cardunculus p.133*

**Cardoon**

*Cynara scolymus p.134*

**Globe artichoke**

*Daucus carota p.85*

**Carrot**

*Eruca vesicaria p.107*

**Rocket, erugala, rucola, roquette**

*Foeniculum vulgare var. azoricum*

**Florence fennel**

*Helianthus tuberosus p.135*

**Jerusalem artichoke**

*Ipomoea batatas p.88*

**Sweet potato**

*Lactuca sativa p.105*

**Lettuce**

*Lycopersicon esculentum p.113*

**Tomato**

*Mesembryanthemum p.104 crystallinum*

**Ice plant**

*Pastinaca sativa p.86*

**Parsnip**

*Petroselinum crispum p.86 var. tuberosum*

**Hamburg parsley**

*Phaseolus coccineus p.100*

**Runner bean**

*Phaseolus lunatus p.99*

**Lima, butter bean**

*Phaseolus vulgaris p.99*

**French, kidney bean**

*Physalis ixocarpa p.112*

**Tomatillo**

*Pisum sativum p.99*

**Pea**

*Portulaca oleracea p.107*

**Summer purslane**

*Raphanus sativa p.106*

**Radish**

*Rheum x hybridum p.135*

**Rhubarb**

*Scorzonera hispanica p.88*

**Scorzonera**

*Sinapis alba p.106*

**Mustard**

*Solanum melongena p.111*

**Aubergine, eggplant**

*Solanum tuberosum p.86*

**Potato**

*Spinacia oleracea p.128*

**Spinach**

*Tetragonia tetragonioides p.127*

**New Zealand spinach**

*Tragopogon porrifolius p.87*

**Salsify**

*Valerianella locusta p.103*

**Corn salad, lamb's lettuce**

*Vicia faba p.98*

**Broad, fava bean**

*Zea mays p.112*

**Sweetcorn**

## OTHER VEGETABLES

*Allium cepa* ..........................p.93
**Pickling onion**

*Allium cepa* Proliferum .......p.94
Group
**Tree, Egyptian onion**

*Allium fistulosum* ..................p.93
**Japanese bunching onion**

*Basella species* .......................p.125
**Ceylon, Malabar, vine spinach**

*Brassica campestris* subsp. ....p.126
*chinesis* var. *utilis*
**Flowering greens, choy sum**

*Brassica carinata* ...................p.81
**Texsel greens**

*Brassica napus* ....................p.106
subsp. *oleifera*
**Salad rape**

*Brassica rapa* .......................p.106
**Mibuna greens**

*Brassica rapa* subsp. ...........p.127
*perviridis*
**Spinach mustard**

*Bunias orientalis* ................p.107
**Turkish rocket**

*Citrullus lanatus* ................p.119
**Watermelon**

*Crambe maritima* ...............p.135
**Seakale**

*Cucurbita pepo* ..................p.117
**Summer squash**

*Diplotaxis* species .............p.107
**Wild rocket**

*Lepidium sativum* ..............p.106
**Cress**

*Lotus tetragonolobus* ............p.98
**Asparagus pea**

*Montia perfoliata* .............. p.107
**Winter purslane**

*Pisum sativum* ....................p.99
**Mangetout, Snow pea, Sugar, snap pea**

*Stachys affinis* ....................p.134
**Chinese artichoke**

*Vigna unguiculata* ..............p.100
subsp. *sesquipedalis*
**Asparagus, yard long bean**

# Growing brassicas

The botanical family Brassicaceae is the largest in the vegetable garden, including not only those members of the genus *Brassica* covered in these pages, sometimes called the Western brassicas – Brussels sprouts, cabbage, calabrese, cauliflower, kale, kohlrabi, sprouting broccoli, and texsel greens – but also leafy Oriental vegetables such as komatsuna and mizuna greens (*see* Salads, *pp.101–107*) and root crops such as swede and radish (*see pp.82–88*).

The brassicas in this section are cool-climate crops, many of them occupying growing space for a long time; for these, careful planning is needed as well as continued care. Many are attractive plants, several having striking cultivars – kales with vividly coloured leaf stems, for example, or the deep violet heads of the cauliflower 'Graffiti'.

A minimum crop rotation of three years (*see p.31*) is extremely important for brassicas, as they are very susceptible to the persistent soil-borne disease clubroot (*see box, facing page*). Serious pests such as cabbage root fly and caterpillars must also be controlled.

## SITE AND SOIL

Although brassicas tolerate partial shade, choose a sunny site if possible. Their tough leaves stand up well to wind, but some shelter and, usually, staking is necessary for tall-stemmed crops such as sprouting broccoli, Brussels sprouts, and some kales, to stop them being blown over. Cabbage and cauliflower plants are relatively stable. The best soil for most brassicas is fertile, well-drained yet moisture-retentive, and firm. Brassicas need to get a good roothold, especially those that must withstand winter weather, so incorporate plenty of organic matter into light, sandy soils (*see pp.22–23*). Prepare beds (*see p.66*) well in advance – for example, in the autumn prior to spring planting or sowing – to allow the ground to firm up again. Do not overwork the soil just before sowing or planting. Most brassicas sown or planted in spring and summer benefit from a base dressing of a general fertilizer (*see pp.20–21*). Do not add fertilizer when sowing or planting in autumn – it will encourage lush growth that will be vulnerable to frost damage. Instead, top-dress overwintered crops such as spring cabbage with fertilizer in spring.

Although brassicas grow well on neutral to slightly acid soil, a higher pH, of 6.8 or above, is desirable because it helps to discourage clubroot. If the pH of your soil is below this level, apply lime to raise it (*see also pp.18–19*). If you lime heavily, it is best not to follow brassicas with potatoes, because alkaline conditions favour potato scab.

## CONTINUITY OF CROPPING

Successional sowing (*see p.69*) is a simple means of extending supplies of spring cabbage, calabrese, and kohlrabi. Some brassicas are divided into distinct groups for planting and cropping at different times of year; there are specific groups of cabbages and cauliflowers, for example, for spring, summer, autumn, and winter, sown and planted in different seasons.

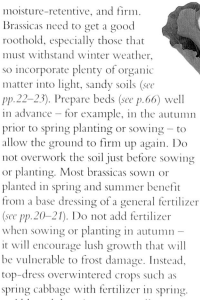

**Brassica transplants**
*These seedlings are both ready to be transplanted – they have four true leaves in addition to their seed leaves. Take care when handling the seedlings, especially if bare-root (left), rather than pushed out of a module cell (right). Roots can be easily damaged.*

Within each of these seasonal cropping periods there are cultivars that mature at slightly different times. F1 hybrids reach maturity simultaneously, ideal for the commercial grower but usually not for the gardener; open-pollinated cultivars (*see also p.60*) may be a better choice.

## SOWING SEED

Some brassicas are direct-sown where they are to crop in conventional drills. These include the leafier crops such as kale and texsel greens, often grown as cut-and-come-again plants. Calabrese and kohlrabi sown in summer should also always be sown direct, as they do not transplant well in warm weather. However, most brassicas, especially longer-term crops that need time to form substantial, dense heads, are usually raised either in seedbeds or in pots or module trays under cover. They are then transplanted into their final cropping positions, allowing the space meanwhile to be used for earlier crops such as peas or early potatoes.

Raising plants in modules not only saves space but also advances crops and helps to guard against clubroot: strong roots undisturbed on transplanting help the plant to grow away quickly. Sow directly into module trays, or sow in pots or trays and prick out into modules (*see p.64*). Harden off and plant out once seedlings are growing strongly, their roots filling their container.

Bare-root transplants are more straightforward to raise because they do not need protection or hardening

**Earthing up**
*On very light, sandy soils (left), draw a drill 10cm (4in) deep and plant into it. Once plants have grown clear of the soil surface, gradually fill in the drill. On heavy clay soils (right) where deep planting would risk water-logging, plant at soil level; then earth up as the plants grow.*

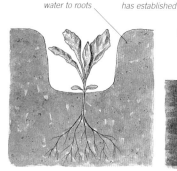

*Drill gives shelter from wind and directs water to roots*

*Soil mounded up by about 5cm (2in) once the plant has established*

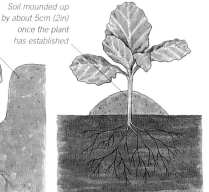

*Light sandy soil*

*Heavy clay soil*

**Planting through landscape fabric**
*Lay the sheet over the bed and secure the edges. Make holes at each planting station by cutting two cross slits about 2.5cm (1in) long with a garden knife. Use a large dibber to make holes, drop the seedlings in, and firm.*

**Putting collars around seedlings**
*Prevent cabbage root flies laying eggs at the bases of seedling stems by using collars made from 15cm (6in) squares of carpet underlay. Cut a slit into the centre of each square to fit the collar around the plant.*

seedbed. Protect them with horticultural netting or fleece (*see p.51*).

## ROUTINE CARE

Adequate water is crucial for good brassica crops. In dry spells, water seedlings and new transplants daily until well-established. Thereafter, water well once or twice a week if conditions are dry during the growing season. Plants overwintering rarely need extra water. One heavy watering, especially around 10–20 days before the crop is due to reach maturity, is more beneficial than several light ones. Mulching helps to conserve moisture and suppress weeds.

Garden hygiene (*see p.51*) and correct feeding appropriate to the individual crop (*see pp.78–81*) do much to help prevent diseases. Check plants regularly for signs of disease, removing any dead or dying leaves. Follow the advice below (*see box*) to reduce the risk of clubroot.

## HARVESTING AND STORING

Crops maturing in the warmer months are best harvested when ready and eaten fresh, but winter and spring crops will stand well in the garden, provided that they are protected from pigeons, especially in hard weather when other food is scarce. Many brassicas grow away again after harvest, even in cold weather, to produce useful secondary crops of sideshoots or leafy "tops".

off. Such plants are also often more robust, which can be an advantage. Once soil conditions in the seedbed are suitable for the crop, sow in drills (*see pp.66–67*), and transplant seedlings to the cropping site once it is vacant. Although the young plants must not be left too long to become drawn and leggy, there is less urgency in moving them to their cropping site compared to seedlings in modules, which soon become root-bound. Bare-root transplants take longer to grow away because of the greater planting check to growth, and require even more careful attention than module-raised plants until established.

## TRANSPLANTING SEEDLINGS

Transplanting is best carried out on a dull, ideally showery day; in warm summer weather, wait until the cool of the evening to minimize overheating and wilting. Brassicas can normally be planted to the same depth at which they were previously growing. Once both module-raised and bare-root plants have established, they may be earthed up (by drawing up a little soil around each plant's stem) to aid stability. On light soils, planting into a shallow drill aids establishment before earthing up in a similar fashion (*see facing page*). The drill provides some protection to young transplants and also helps retain water applied to the plants.

## PROTECTING YOUNG PLANTS

Place a collar of carpet underlay (*see above, right*) or cardboard around the base of brassica stems to deter cabbage root fly. This very serious pest lays its eggs around the base of the plants; the resulting maggots feed on the roots. A physical barrier prevents the females reaching the base of the stems and laying eggs there. For sturdy transplants, an alternative is to plant through landscape fabric (*see above, left*).

Pigeons love young brassicas, either newly planted out or growing in a

---

### CLUBROOT AND HOW TO AVOID IT

Clubroot is a slime-mould disease that causes brassica roots to develop gross swellings, which in turn decay to release disease spores into the soil. Infected plants become stunted, discoloured and wilted, eventually dying. The spores can remain active in the soil for up to 20 years, so it is essential to use every means possible in order to prevent infection.

- **Rotate crops** (*see p.31*). Continuous brassica cropping can lead to a buildup of clubroot in the soil.
- **Lime soil** if necessary (*see pp.18–19*).
- **Avoid importing clubroot** on bought-in plants by raising your own transplants.
- **Control weeds**. Some common weeds, such as shepherd's purse, belong to the brassica family and can harbour clubroot.
- **Clean hoes** and other tools to avoid bringing in disease from other garden areas.

If your soil is infected with clubroot, remember that it is young brassica plants that are most vulnerable.

- **Burn all affected material** after digging it up complete with roots; never compost it.
- **Start all plants off in modules,** in clean compost, and grow larger, sturdier transplants than usual; they will be less vulnerable than small seedlings. A larger planting hole filled with clean soil also helps transplants establish in safety.
- **Foliar feeding** (*see p.21*) can help young plants to establish quickly and well on infected sites.
- **Choose fast-growing crops** such as texsel greens. They may reach maturity before being affected.
- **Avoid using the green manures** fodder radish and mustard, which are brassicas.

# A-Z OF BRASSICAS

## Brussels sprouts

*Brassica oleracea* Gemmifera Group

| SEASON | SPRING | SUMMER | AUTUMN | WINTER |
|---|---|---|---|---|
| SOW | • • | | | • |
| TRANSPLANT | • | • • • | | |
| HARVEST | | | • • • • | • • • • |

These traditional winter vegetables can be picked fresh from late summer to mid-spring; the plants are strong and can survive severe winters. Most modern cultivars are F1 hybrids (*see p.60*), producing uniform plants and compact sprouts. Plants grown to full height can produce 60–70 sprouts each; weight depends on the size they are allowed to reach. The small buttons are excellent for freezing. There is also a small crop of leafy tops. Sprouts are suitable for intercropping (*see p.71*), for example with fast-growing salads.

■ **Site and soil** Brussels sprouts do well in firm, fertile soils, with plenty of organic matter incorporated well in advance. Lime if necessary (*see p.18*) to raise the soil pH to deter clubroot. Before sowing or planting, apply a base dressing of fertilizer (*see pp.20–23*), except on highly fertile soil – too much nitrogen produces loose, leafy sprouts.

■ **Sowing and planting** Sow under cover (*see p.62*) in late winter for an early crop in late summer and early autumn. For winter crops, sow from early to mid-spring, outdoors in a seedbed (*see p.67*) or under cover in modules (*see p.64*), and transplant to the cropping site in early to midsummer. Close planting (less than 60cm/2ft each way), for example on narrow beds (*see pp.32–33*), will produce smaller sprouts of uniform maturity, while wider spacing will yield larger sprouts to be picked in succession over a longer period. Sowing different cultivars to mature at varying times will ensure a long cropping period. Keep seedlings and new transplants well watered. Brassica collars (*see p.77*) will protect young plants against cabbage root fly.

| SOWING DEPTH | 2cm (¾in) |
|---|---|
| PLANT SPACING | 60cm (2ft) |
| ROW SPACING | 60cm (2ft) |

■ **Routine care** To produce small, evenly sized sprouts that will mature simultaneously, for example for freezing, pinch out the growing tips of the plants when the lower sprouts are 1cm (½in) in diameter. To encourage the sprouts to fill out, top-dress in midsummer with sulphate of ammonia at a rate of 25–50g per sq m (1–2oz per sq yd). Water after top-dressing. Once established, plants should grow away without further watering unless there is a period of severe drought. Overwintering plants need supporting with stakes, especially on light, sandy soils.

■ **Harvesting** Starting from the bottom of the plant, pick when the sprouts reach 2–3cm (¾–1¼in) in diameter for the sweetest taste; snap them off with a downward motion. At the same time, remove any yellow leaves and discard any loose or yellow sprouts. Whole stems or sticks of sprouts keep well standing in a little water in a bucket in a cool place. Later in the season, the leafy tops of the plants can also be picked as greens.

■ **Common problems** See p.77 for advice on protecting young plants against cabbage root fly (*see also p.253*) and birds (*see also p.252*). Caterpillars (*see p.253*), especially those of the cabbage white butterfly, can cause extensive crop damage. Flea beetle (*see p.255*) may be troublesome in dry weather and sheltered spots. Large colonies of mealy cabbage aphids (*see p.257*), can quickly establish, causing distorted foliage. Do not mistake them for whitefly (*see p.264*); although this can be a conspicuous pest, it rarely causes significant damage, although in mild winters whitefly can persist on brassicas to affect other young plants in spring. Other pests include cutworm (*see p.254*), leatherjackets (*see p.257*), and slugs and snails (*see p.262*).

In addition to clubroot (*see pp.76–77, p.254*), brassicas are susceptible to leaf diseases such as downy mildew (*see p.255*), and powdery mildew (*see p.260*). Bacterial leaf spot (*see p.256*) and white blister (*see p.264*) are becoming more widespread problems.

Plants grown well and fed correctly rarely suffer nutrient deficiencies. Hollow stems may indicate boron deficiency (*see p.252*). Poor seedling growth can be the result of molybdenum deficiency (*see p.257*).

■ **Recommended cultivars**
'Bosworth' ℣ – hybrid, tough cultivar, which stands well.
'Cronus' – hybrid, mid season variety, resistant to clubroot.
'Diablo' ℣ – hybrid, good flavour, crops early.
'Evesham Special' – old traditional cultivar.
'Maximus' ℣ – hybrid, autumn, medium-sized sprouts with good flavour.
'Red Bull' – small red sprouts, colour improves in cold weather.
'Revenge' ℣ – High-yielding, late-winter crop, hardy.

## Cabbage

*Brassica oleracea* Capitata Group

By growing cultivar groups that mature in different seasons, cabbages can be harvested and eaten fresh throughout the year. Spring cabbages are usually small, and may be either pointed or round-headed. Early summer cabbages are normally pointed or round, and late-summer or autumn ones rounded or oval, and more compact. The leaves of some spring

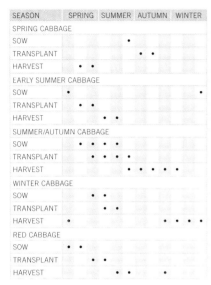

| SEASON | SPRING | SUMMER | AUTUMN | WINTER |
|---|---|---|---|---|
| **SPRING CABBAGE** | | | | |
| SOW | | • | | |
| TRANSPLANT | | | • • | |
| HARVEST | • • | | | |
| **EARLY SUMMER CABBAGE** | | | | |
| SOW | • | | | • |
| TRANSPLANT | • • | | | |
| HARVEST | | • • | | |
| **SUMMER/AUTUMN CABBAGE** | | | | |
| SOW | • • • • | | | |
| TRANSPLANT | • • • • | | | |
| HARVEST | | • • • • • | | |
| **WINTER CABBAGE** | | | | |
| SOW | • • | | | |
| TRANSPLANT | • • | | | |
| HARVEST | • | | • • • • | |
| **RED CABBAGE** | | | | |
| SOW | • • | | | |
| TRANSPLANT | • • | | | |
| HARVEST | | • • • | | |

and autumn cabbages may also be eaten as greens, before they form a heart. Winter cabbages include the Dutch white types, the January King purple-tinged types, and the crinkly-leaved Savoy types, as well as some hybrids between these. The Dutch whites are suitable for lifting and storing for later use, as are some of the red cabbages, of which there are both summer and autumn types. Yields vary according to the type of cabbage being grown (*see* Average crop yields, *p.242*).

■ **Site and soil**  Cabbages prefer fertile, well-drained, moisture-retentive, but firm soil (*see p.76*). Apply a base dressing of a general fertilizer (*see pp.20–21*) when sowing or planting in spring and summer. Lime soil if necessary to raise the pH to deter clubroot (*see also p.78*).

■ **Sowing and planting**  Sow either in a seedbed or in modules (*see p.76*) at the correct time of year for the type. To produce both spring greens and cabbages in the same bed, space the plants 10cm (4in) apart in rows 30cm (12in) apart. Use two out of each three for greens, and leave the third to heart up. Sow summer cabbages in succession for a continuous crop. The earliest transplants raised under cover should be hardened off carefully (*see p.65*), or they may be liable to bolt.

| SOWING DEPTH | 2cm (¾in) | | |
|---|---|---|---|
| **SPRING CABBAGE/SPRING GREENS** | | | |
| ROW SPACING | 30cm (12in) | | |
| PLANT SPACING | 25cm (10in) for hearted cabbages | | |
| | 15cm (6in) for greens | | |
| **EARLY SUMMER CABBAGE** | | | |
| PLANT SPACING | 38cm (15in) | | |
| ROW SPACING | 38cm (15in) | | |
| **SUMMER/AUTUMN CABBAGE** | | | |
| PLANT SPACING | 45cm (18in) | | |
| ROW SPACING | 45cm (18in) | | |
| **WINTER CABBAGE** | | | |
| PLANT SPACING | 45cm (18in) | | |
| ROW SPACING | 60cm (24in) | | |
| **RED CABBAGE** | | | |
| PLANT SPACING | 23–38cm (9–15in) | | |
| ROW SPACING | 45cm (18in) | | |

Covering them with fleece after planting out will reduce this risk and advance crops by 10–14 days. Winter cabbages should be sown in succession. Protect all seedlings and young transplants from cabbage root fly (*see p.77*).

■ **Routine care**  Practise good weed control. Keep young plants well watered if necessary until they are established, then water only in very dry weather. Earth up the stems of spring and winter cabbages during the winter, and remove dead leaves regularly. Top-dress with a high-nitrogen fertilizer or organic liquid feed before the leaves touch across the rows, except in the case of autumn-sown and planted crops; top-dress these in spring.

■ **Harvesting**  For greens, harvest young leaves as soon as they are large enough. Cut spring and summer hearting cabbages when the hearts are solid throughout. Stumps left in the ground may resprout to provide a small crop of greens, especially if a cross-cut is made across the surface of the cut stem. The hardier winter cabbages such as January King types can be left to stand in the ground for several months, to harvest as needed. Cut white or red cabbages for storing before there is any danger of hard frost, handling them carefully to avoid bruising. If stored in a net bag (*see p.73*), cabbages should keep for 6–8 weeks.

■ **Common problems**  As for Brussels sprouts.

■ **Recommended cultivars**

**Spring greens and spring cabbage**
'Dorado' ♀ – short stemmed, attractive dark blue-green, uniform, spring hearting cabbage.
'Duncan' ♀ – hybrid, hearted, attractive leaf, early cropping greens, also crops in summer.
'Durham Elf' ♀ – spring hearting cabbage.
'First Early Market 218' ♀ – fast-growing, well-filled heads, for greens or hearts.
'Myatts Offenham' ♀ – compact, short-stemmed, hearting cabbage.
'Pixie' ♀ – early hearting, also good for spring greens and successional or summer sowing.
'Pyramid' ♀ – old, dark-leaved cultivar, pointed heads; can also be grown for greens.

**Early summer cabbage**
'Derby Day' ♀ – old favourite, round-headed.
'Greyhound' ♀ – fast-growing, pointed heads.
'Hispi' ♀ – hybrid, old favourite, pointed head.
'Pyramid' ♀ – old-fashioned, dark-leaved, for overwintering or spring sowing.

**Summer/autumn cabbage**
'Kilaxy' – white cabbage, suitable for storing, resistant to clubroot.
'Stonehead' ♀ – hybrid, stands well.

**Winter cabbage**
'Celtic' ♀ – hybrid, reliable white/Savoy cross, hardy, stands well, heads do not split.
'Deadon' ♀ – vigorous, green purple heads.
'Famosa' ♀ – early maturing, good leaf colour.
'Tarvoy' ♀ – hybrid, very hardy, Savoy type, winter, spring.
'Wintessa' ♀ – reliable hybrid, stands well, dark, puckered leaves, very hardy.

**Red cabbage**
'Huzzaro' – strong, red storing cabbage.
'Red Flare' – Early sweet flavour, little core.

# Calabrese

*Brassica oleracea* Italica Group

| SEASON | SPRING | SUMMER | AUTUMN | WINTER |
|---|---|---|---|---|
| SOW | • • • • • • | | • | |
| TRANSPLANT | | | | • |
| HARVEST | • • | • • • • | | |

Also known as American, Italian, or green sprouting broccoli, calabrese is a fast-growing brassica that has become a very popular vegetable. Calabrese grows up to 60cm (2ft) tall, and produces bluish-green heads, up to 15cm (6in) in diameter and 110–225g (4–8oz) in weight, as well as further, smaller heads borne on sideshoots that appear after the main head has been cut. It can be sown in autumn for early crops, or in spring to crop in summer. Better heads are produced in cooler summers; in hot conditions the heads – immature flower buds – develop and run to seed quickly. Some cultivars resist this tendency better. Calabrese freezes well.

■ **Site and soil**  A fertile, well-drained, moisture-retentive, firm soil (*see p.76*) is best, but calabrese will grow well on less fertile soils than other brassicas, so a base dressing of fertilizer is not usually necessary. Lime the soil if necessary to raise the pH and thus deter clubroot (*see p.77*).

■ **Sowing and planting**  Early sowings can be made under cover, but calabrese does not transplant well in warm weather, resulting in premature production of tiny heads, so from mid-spring onwards it is best station-sown (*see p.68*) where it is to crop, and thinned to one plant per site. Closer spacing encourages smaller shoots. For a spring crop, when other fresh vegetables are scarce, sow under cover in modules in mid-autumn, and transplant in early winter to an unheated greenhouse or cold frame (*see pp.43–48*).

| SOWING DEPTH | 2cm (¾in), three seeds per station |
|---|---|
| SEED SPACING | 30cm (12in) |
| ROW SPACING | 45cm (18in) |

■ **Routine care**  Keep evenly moist throughout the growing season, watering at a rate of about 20 litres per sq m (4 gallons per sq yd) each week. After the main head has been harvested, apply a top-dressing of a nitrogenous fertilizer or organic liquid feed to encourage sideshoots to form.

■ **Harvesting**  Cut the central head while it is still firm, and before any flowers open. This stimulates the production of sideshoots.

■ **Common problems**  As for Brussels sprouts.

■ **Recommended cultivars**
'Fiesta' ♀ – hybrid, vigorous, heavy and prolonged cropping.
'Green Magic' ♀ – good crop, many sideshoots, fine quality.
'Kabuki' ♀ – compact, early, can be closely spaced for baby heads.
'Marathon' – Quick maturing, large deep heads, good for late and early sowings.
'Tendergreen' – small heads on edible stems, many sideshoots if central bud removed.

# Cauliflower

## Brassica oleracea Botrytis Group

| SEASON | SPRING | SUMMER | AUTUMN | WINTER |
|---|---|---|---|---|
| **EARLY SUMMER CAULIFLOWER** | | | | |
| SOW | | | ● | ● |
| TRANSPLANT | ● | | | |
| HARVEST | | ● | | |
| **SUMMER CAULIFLOWER** | | | | |
| SOW | ● ● | | | |
| TRANSPLANT | | ● ● | | |
| HARVEST | | | ● ● | |
| **AUTUMN CAULIFLOWER** | | | | |
| SOW | ● ● | | | |
| TRANSPLANT | | ● ● | | |
| HARVEST | | | ● ● ● | |
| **WINTER-HEADING CAULIFLOWER** | | | | |
| SOW | | ● | | |
| TRANSPLANT | | | ● | |
| HARVEST | ● | | | ● ● ● |
| **SPRING-HEADING CAULIFLOWER** | | | | |
| SOW | | | ● | |
| TRANSPLANT | | | ● | |
| HARVEST | ● ● ● | | | |
| **MINI CAULIFLOWER** | | | | |
| SOW | | ● ● ● | | |
| TRANSPLANT | | ● ● | | |
| HARVEST | | | ● ● ● ● | |

The typical cauliflower has a cream or white curd, or head, but there are also green- and purple-headed cultivars. Cauliflowers make large plants, and those that overwinter will occupy the ground for almost a year. They are quite difficult to grow because they need a lot of water, and this is not usually provided in sufficient quantity by summer rainfall. Cultivars maturing before midsummer are therefore the easiest to raise successfully. At a conventional wide spacing, only 5–6 cauliflowers can be grown in a 3m (10ft) row. Mini cauliflowers are produced by plants grown much closer together (up to 20 in a 3m/10ft row, taking 13–18 weeks to produce heads 4–8cm (1½–3in) in diameter.

■ **Site and soil**  To produce large, well-formed curds, cauliflowers need a fairly rich soil with plenty of nitrogen-rich fertilizer applied as a base dressing before planting (see p.76).

■ **Sowing and planting**  Sow early summer cauliflowers outdoors under cloches or in a cold frame (see pp.45–47) in mid-autumn, or in a heated greenhouse or propagator in midwinter (see p.63). Harden off seedlings and transplant in early spring, protecting with fleece (see p.65); this will advance early crops by 10–14 days. For summer types, sow in a seedbed in early and mid-spring or in modules in mid-spring, transplanting in early summer. Water in well if the weather is dry.

Autumn types should be sown in modules in mid- to late spring and transplanted in early summer, and kept well watered until established. Winter- and spring-heading cauliflowers are both sown in a seedbed in late spring, with no base dressing applied, and then transplanted in late summer. They need a sheltered site and protection from frost, which can damage the curds. All cauliflowers need to be planted firmly, and should be transplanted as young as possible since they suffer if their growth is checked. For mini cauliflowers, sow in succession, or sow several different cultivars, to ensure a prolonged harvesting season.

| SOWING DEPTH | 2cm (¾in) |
|---|---|
| **EARLY SUMMER CAULIFLOWER** | |
| ROW SPACING | 60cm (24in) |
| PLANT SPACING | 45cm (18in) |
| **SUMMER CAULIFLOWER** | |
| ROW SPACING | 60cm (24in) |
| PLANT SPACING | 45cm (18in) |
| **AUTUMN CAULIFLOWER** | |
| PLANT SPACING | 60cm (24in) |
| ROW SPACING | 60cm (24in) |
| **WINTER- AND SPRING-HEADING CAULIFLOWER** | |
| PLANT SPACING | 70cm (28in) |
| ROW SPACING | 70cm (28in) |
| **MINI CAULIFLOWER** | |
| SEED OR PLANT SPACING | 15cm (6in) |
| ROW SPACING | 15cm (6in) |

■ **Routine care**  It is essential to control weeds and keep the soil moist throughout the growing period, or small, deformed heads will form prematurely. In summer, snap and fold in leaves to protect the curd from strong sun. In winter, bunch and tie leaves together over the curd to protect it from frost. Top-dress (see p.76) spring-heading types in late winter or in early spring to stimulate new growth.

■ **Harvesting**  Harvest curds while they are still firm and dense; they are immature flower buds and will open up and deteriorate in time. Cut with enough leaf attached to protect the curd. Harvest mini cauliflowers promptly, as they readily deteriorate.

■ **Common problems**  As for Brussels sprouts (see p.78). Downy mildew (see p.255) is a particular problem with cauliflowers; they are also especially vulnerable to problems caused by nutrient deficiencies, such as whiptail (see Molybdenum deficiency, p.257). Boron deficiency (see p.252) may cause brown rings in the stalk. See also Frost damage, p.255.

■ **Recommended cultivars**
**Summer cauliflower**
'Avalanche' – closely plant for mini-heads.
'Beauty' ♀ – hybrid, show variety, long season, good for successional sowings.
'Nautilus' ♀ – hybrid, reliable and tolerant, wide sowing and harvesting period.
**Autumn cauliflower**
'Belot' ♀ – robust late-autumn cropping, high quality curds.
'Clapton' – fair quality heads for summer and autumn, resistant to clubroot.
'Graffiti' ♀ – deep violet.
'Kestel' ♀ – snow white, late summer–autumn.
'Skywalker' ♀ – high quality cauliflower, early, crops before 'Belot'.
**Winter-heading cauliflower**
'Deakin' ♀ – late autumn to winter, well protected heads.
'Medallion' – compact, robust, but only for mild regions.

'Triomphant' – mid- to late winter, but only for mild regions.
**Spring-heading cauliflower**
'Aalsmeer' ♀ – robust, very long-cropping.
'Galleon' ♀ – hybrid, mid-spring.
'Longships' – hybrid, late spring to early summer.
'Lundy' – hybrid, early to mid-spring from early summer sowing.
'Patriot' – good leaf protection, late spring.

# Kale

## Brassica oleracea Acephala Group

| SEASON | SPRING | SUMMER | AUTUMN | WINTER |
|---|---|---|---|---|
| SOW | ● ● | ● ● | | |
| TRANSPLANT | | ● ● | ● | |
| HARVEST | ● ● | | | ● ● ● |

Kale is the hardiest winter vegetable; fresh leaves and shoots can be harvested even in severe winters. As few as six plants picked regularly can provide 1.8–2.25kg (4–5lb) of greens over the season. Modern curly kale cultivars are sweeter and more tender than the older broad-leaved types, of which only the young shoots are eaten. Kale can grow to a height of 90cm (3ft), but the dwarf types reach only about 30cm (1ft), and are therefore more suitable for small gardens. All make ornamental plants for a winter garden. Some kales can be grown as a cut-and-come-again crop of salad leaves (see p.102).

■ **Site and soil**  Kale grown as a winter crop needs well-drained, rich soil that will not become waterlogged.

■ **Sowing and planting**  Sow either in a seedbed or in modules (see p.76). Transplant 6–8 weeks after sowing, planting them firmly. Dwarf cultivars may be spaced closer together than tall ones. If growing a seedling salad crop, cut the seedlings when they are 5–8cm (2–3in) tall, or thin them to 8–10cm (3–4in) apart and cut them when 15cm (6in) tall.

| SOWING DEPTH | 2cm (¾in) |
|---|---|
| PLANT SPACING | 60cm (24in) |
| ROW SPACING | 45cm (18in) |

■ **Routine care**  Control weeds, and water after planting if necessary until the plants are well established. Thereafter avoid overwatering, because this will produce lush, soft growth less able to survive the winter. If the crop shows sign of yellowing in early autumn, top-dress with a nitrogenous fertilizer or organic liquid feed (see pp.20–23) to maintain good colour. Remove any yellow leaves.

■ **Harvesting**  Harvest young leaves regularly from all plants to encourage more growth. Remove any flower shoots that appear. Continue to harvest until the plants go to seed, when they will become bitter.

■ **Common problems**  As for Brussels sprouts (see p.78). Whitefly (see p.264) can be a problem, because it infests the edible parts. However, leaf diseases do not normally occur if plants are harvested regularly, and clubroot is less of a problem than for other brassicas.

■ **Recommended cultivars**
'Black Tuscany' – very dark strap-like leaves, can be used as a cut-and-come-again crop.
'Redbor' ♀ – curly, dark purple.
'Red Russian' ♀ – purple green, frilly leaves.
'Reflex' ♀ – highly curled, sweet.
'Winterbor' ♀ – tall, tightly curled blue-green leaves.

# Kohlrabi

*Brassica oleracea* Gongylodes Group

| SEASON | SPRING | SUMMER | AUTUMN | WINTER |
|---|---|---|---|---|
| SOW | • • • • • • | | | |
| TRANSPLANT | • • | | | |
| HARVEST | • • • • • • • | | | |

This often underrated, tasty brassica has an unusual-looking swollen stem that is eaten like a turnip, or shredded for use in salads. There is a gap of 2.5–4cm (1–1½in) between the soil and the base of the swollen stem; you can obtain about 500g (1lb) from four plants, depending on how large the stems are allowed to grow. Young, tender leaves are also usable as greens. Green and purple cultivars are available. The green forms mature rapidly and are normally used for the main summer crop. The purple types are slower to mature and hardier, and more suitable for late harvests. Kohlrabi can also be grown as a catch crop (*see p.69*), because it is fast-growing.
■ **Site and soil** Kohlrabi needs less nitrogen than other brassicas, and will thrive in a rich, light, sandy soil, although it will also grow in heavy soil. It is essential to lime the soil if necessary to raise the pH and thus guard against clubroot (*see p.77*).
■ **Sowing and planting** Kohlrabi can be sown direct, or raised under cover for an early start up until around mid-spring; seedlings do not transplant well in warm weather. It is important to transplant the seedlings before they exceed 5cm (2in) in height, or they may bolt. Do not sow outside too early; plants sown when the temperature is below 10°C (50°F) also tend to bolt. Thin at an early stage to avoid unnecessary root disturbance to the plants that remain. Succession sow every two weeks for continuity.

| SOWING DEPTH | 2cm (¾in) |
|---|---|
| SEED SPACING | 23cm (9in), 3 seeds per station |
| ROW SPACING | 30cm (12in) |

■ **Routine care** It is essential to keep plants well watered throughout the growing period, in order to avoid a check in growth which will lead to unpalatable, woody flesh being produced. Control weeds promptly.
■ **Harvesting** When the stems are between golf- and tennis-ball size, usually 7–8 weeks after sowing for summer sowings or 12–16 weeks for winter ones, cut off at the root and trim off the outer leaves to 2cm (¾in), leaving the central leaves on the stem to help maintain its freshness. Newer cultivars grow rapidly, and can still be tender when larger. Eat summer crops as they become ready; after 1–2 weeks in hot weather the stems start to deteriorate. In mild areas, kohlrabi can

be left in the ground in winter, but in colder regions lift in autumn and store in boxes (*see p.73*).
■ **Common problems** As for Brussels sprouts (*p.78*). Some leaf damage can be tolerated as leaves are not edible. Clubroot can be severe.
■ **Recommended cultivars**
'Azur Star' – very attractive blue-purple stems, organic seed available.
'Kolibri' ♀ – large, robust, purple, tolerant.
'Korist' ♀ – ornamental, pale green, compact.
'Lanro' ♀ – sweet flavour, compact.
'Purple Delicacy' – large leaves for salads, purple bulb.

# Sprouting broccoli

*Brassica oleracea* Italica Group

| SEASON | SPRING | SUMMER | AUTUMN | WINTER |
|---|---|---|---|---|
| SOW | • • • • | | | • |
| TRANSPLANT | • • • • | | | |
| HARVEST | • | | • • • • • | • |

There are both purple and white forms of sprouting broccoli, the purple ones being much hardier and producing many more edible shoots. These crops are in the ground for a long time, taking up a lot of space, but give useful produce from late winter to late spring when other fresh garden vegetables are in short supply. Picked regularly, ten plants can yield 3kg (around 7lb) over the season. In good, rich soils, plants can grow to 90cm (3ft) across and up to 90cm (3ft) tall, and are liable to become top-heavy. Some new cultivars, such as 'Bordeaux', do not need a cold spell to produce a crop; these can be sown over a long period for harvest in the same season.
■ **Site and soil** This crop needs a fertile soil that is very well-drained in order to avoid winter waterlogging. It also needs shelter from wind to reduce rocking. Lime soil if necessary (*see p.18*) to raise the pH and deter clubroot.
■ **Sowing and planting** Sow traditional cultivars in spring, either in modules or in a seedbed (*see pp.66–68*), to transplant to their final site. Sow the newer cultivars such as 'Bordeaux' from late winter to midsummer and transplant a month after sowing.

| SOWING DEPTH | 2cm (¾in) |
|---|---|
| PLANT SPACING | 60cm (24in) |
| ROW SPACING | 60cm (24in) |

■ **Routine care** Keep weed-free, and water in dry spells until established. Thereafter, avoid overwatering, so that the plants become tough enough to withstand winter temperatures. Plants must be securely supported with stakes (*see p.72*) to avoid windrock. Earth up stems to increase stability.
■ **Harvesting** The new cultivars such as 'Bordeaux' should be ready to harvest 10–15 weeks after transplanting throughout summer and autumn. Traditional spring-sown broccoli becomes ready to pick from late winter. When the flowering shoots are about 15–20cm (6–8in) long, but before the flower buds open, snap off around 8–10cm (3–4in) of their length. New

sideshoots will be produced; harvest these as they are ready. Depending on the prevailing weather, you may be able to harvest for 6–8 weeks. As the weather warms up, the traditional winter cultivars deteriorate quickly.
■ **Common problems** As for Brussels sprouts (*see p.78*), although sprouting broccoli is not usually affected by leaf diseases. As with other winter brassicas, in mild years it may host whitefly to be carried over to affect other spring vegetables if not controlled. Pigeons will also be attracted to the crop in winter; you may need to net when it is nearing maturity.
■ **Recommended cultivars**
'Bordeaux' – crops in summer and autumn, does not need a period of cold.
'Claret' ♀ – attractive, dark purple.
'Late Purple Sprouting' ♀ – improved traditional cultivar.
'Red Spear' ♀ – productive over long period, fair colour, very hardy.
'White Eye' ♀ – white, early sprouting.
'White Star' ♀ – very fine, white sprouts.

# Texsel greens

*Brassica carinata*

| SEASON | SPRING | SUMMER | AUTUMN | WINTER |
|---|---|---|---|---|
| SOW | • • • • • • | | | |
| HARVEST | • • • • • • | | | |

This relatively new, fairly hardy brassica has been bred from Ethiopian mustard. Fast-growing, maturing in as little as seven weeks, it makes a useful catch crop. Texsel greens have shiny leaves, high in nutritional value and with a flavour slightly reminiscent of spinach. Young leaves are used for salads, and older plants for cooking. The flavour and texture is best in spring and autumn. When grown as a cut-and-come-again salad crop (*see p.102*), a 3m (10ft) row of texel greens yields 6–9kg (13–20lb) over the season, depending on the size of the leaves harvested. There are no named cultivars of texsel greens.
■ **Site and soil** As for all brassicas, texsel greens prefer a fertile, well-drained soil, but, because they crop so quickly, they often succeed even on clubroot-infected soils.
■ **Sowing and planting** Broadcast sow (*see p.66*) in succession every 2–3 weeks. Thin the seedlings to 2.5cm (1in) apart. If growing them as a seedling crop, there is no need to thin.

| SOWING DEPTH | 1cm (½in) |
|---|---|
| SEED SPACING | broadcast; thin to 2.5cm (1in) |
| ROW SPACING | 30cm (12in) |

■ **Routine care** Keep evenly moist for steady growth and to prevent bolting.
■ **Harvesting** For salad crops, harvest the shoots and leaves when young. Once they are mature, harvesting a few leaves from each plant rather than picking them all from one or two will keep plants cropping steadily.
■ **Common problems** As for Brussels sprouts (*see p.78*). Flea beetle (*see p.255*) may be a problem if the weather is dry during sowing.

# Growing root crops

This group of vegetables encompasses beetroots, carrots, parsnips and the very similar Hamburg parsley, potatoes, salsify, scorzonera, swedes, non-hardy sweet potatoes, and turnips, all of which produce edible crops below ground or at soil level. Potatoes and sweet potatoes have underground tubers whereas the others all have swollen roots. Salsify and scorzonera also have edible flowering shoots and buds (*see right*). Most store well and make useful winter vegetables.

Root crops are prone to several major soil-borne pests and diseases, and in some cases this influences methods of cultivation. Since root crops represent a wide range of species there are various cultural requirements to be considered, especially with regard to soil conditions. To obtain the best results with each crop it is important to think about its requirements with respect to the pH, texture, and fertility of the soil.

## SOIL pH
To grow a particular crop successfully, check the acidity level of your soil with a testing kit to ascertain whether liming will be necessary (*see pp.18–19*).

Potatoes do best on a slightly acid soil of pH 5–6; on soils that are rich in lime, the skin disease potato powdery scab (*see p.260*) will thrive to attack many cultivars.

Parsnips prefer slightly acid soils of pH 6.5. Beetroot, carrots, salsify, and scorzonera have a broader range of tolerance and will grow well on soils with a pH 6.5–7.5.

**Using fleece to advance crops**
*You can warm the soil and protect early crops from frost by covering the bed with a double layer of fleece (as here), or perforated plastic, as soon as the seedlings emerge or just after planting. Tuck the edges into a slit trench.*

**Edible buds**
*Shoots and flower buds of salsify may be cooked and eaten in the same way as asparagus. To obtain them, leave a few plants in the ground over winter so that they can produce flowering shoots the following spring. The buds should be picked just before opening, together with about 10cm (4in) of stem.*

Turnips and swedes grow thrive on slightly acid soil. However, like other members of the brassica family, they are vulnerable to the persistent soil-borne disease clubroot (*see p.254*), which is less prevalent on neutral to alkaline soil with a pH 7 or more.

## SOIL FERTILITY
It is important to take account of the nutrient requirements of each crop, which are various. Parsnips, salsify, scorzonera, swedes, and turnips have low nitrogen needs, and those of carrot and beetroot are very low. Potatoes and beet have high nitrogen requirements. All root crops do best on soils with a high content of organic matter, which is best incorporated into the soil six months or more prior to cropping. (*See also individual crops, pp.85–88.*)

## SOIL TEXTURE
Crops with long roots that grow down into the soil, such as carrots, parsnips, salsify, scorzonera, and some beetroot types, do best on light, sandy soils where the roots can penetrate easily, making vegetables of good shape and length. All of the root crops, however, can be grown on heavy soils, provided that they are well-drained, deeply cultivated, and free of stones.

## ROTATION
It is essential to rotate root crops (*see p.31*) in order to reduce infestation by pests and especially disease infections, to keep the soil nutrient levels suitably balanced, and to keep weeds in check. A minimum of a three-year rotation lessens the risk of a build-up of pests such as eelworm (*see p.255*) and diseases such as parsnip canker (*see p.258*).

Rotation helps to maintain fertility by permitting one crop to benefit from nutrient levels that were appropriate to the previous crop – a classical example is planning to grow nitrogen-hungry brassicas after nitrogen-fixing legumes. Following legumes with root crops, which need less nitrogen, can result in their developing excessive foliage growth at the expense of roots.

Rotation can also assist in controlling weeds. For example, in the cultivation of potatoes the ground is well dug and disturbed because the crop is earthed up regularly – a process that suppresses weed growth. The crop also has a good canopy of leaves to smother annual weeds. Subsequent crops benefit by resulting reduction in weed population, particularly because there is invariably no need for further deep cultivation that would bring even more weed seeds to the surface.

## SHORT- OR LONG-TERM CROPS?

If you have only limited growing space, short-term crops of beetroot, carrots, early potatoes, and turnips are helpful in allowing at least two crops per year to be obtained from the same piece of land. Clearing crops quickly in this way also reduces the likelihood of pests and diseases building up in the area. Harvest crops as soon as they are ready, to enjoy them at their best and to avoid any deterioration through splitting and development of pests and diseases.

Long-term crops such as parsnips and maincrop potatoes are suitable where space is not at a premium, but in order to ensure good quality they must not be subjected to a check in growth through lack of water. You should also be vigilant for signs of pests or disease and take appropriate action as soon as possible (*see also* Plant Problems, *pp.246–264*).

## SOWING

Root vegetables are grown from seed, with the exception of potatoes, which may be grown from tubers (*see below*). Root crops are best sown direct outdoors where they are to crop to minimize disturbance to their edible roots, but multiblock sowing (*see p.65*) is also possible. It is essential to produce a fine

tilth (*see p.66*) and a good depth of soil in the seedbed so that the roots can penetrate unhindered. Improve heavy soils by digging in plenty of well-rotted organic matter. Some root crops prefer soil that has not been freshly dug (*see individual crops, pp.85–88*).

In most cases, sowing is carried out from early spring (*see individual crops, pp.85–88*). Large seeds, such as those of parsnips, are best station sown (*see p.68*), whereas small seeds, such as those of carrots and turnips, should be sown thinly in single drills (*see p.66*) and thinned at the seedling stage (*see p.68*). Turnips and beetroot may be sown in successive batches (*see p.69*). Parsnips are suitable for intersowing with fast-maturing salad crops such as radishes (*see p.69*). Early carrots and turnips may be used as catch crops for intercropping (*see p.71*) between long-term crops.

## PLANTING TUBERS

Potatoes are normally raised by planting out small sprouted or "chitted" tubers referred to as seed potatoes (*see box, right*) direct in the ground. True potato seeds are unreliable, less convenient, and unsuitable for garden use.

Seed potatoes are usually planted in a deep drill or individual planting holes and earthed up as they grow. Planting

### Chitting seed potatoes

Seed potatoes are small tubers grown in areas of low virus infection, often obtained by mail order. "Chitting", or sprouting, aids early growth. As soon as tubers are obtained in midwinter, place them upright in trays, with the most eyes or dormant sprouts – at the "rose" end – uppermost, in a cool, frost-free, light place. They will send out healthy, short, green shoots or chits (*see below, right*), ideally 12mm (½in) long. Kept in a warm, dark place, chits will be pale, weak, and become too long (*see below, left*).

*Weak, pale chits*        *Strong, dark chits*

through black plastic sheet mulch (*see p.84*) dispenses with the need to earth up and also suppresses weeds.

### ADVANCING AND PROTECTING CROPS

To harvest very early roots, protect sown crops from the cold with fleece (*see facing page*), perforated plastic, or cloches (*see pp.46–48*). Cut the fleece about 30–40cm (12–16in) wider and longer than the plot. With a spade, make a slit trench, about half a spit deep, around the plot. Lay the fleece with a margin of at least 15cm (6in) on all sides. Push it into the slit trench with the spade and tread the edges to secure it. Remove it as soon as risk of frost is past and before it restricts growth.

### GROWING ROOT CROPS IN CONTAINERS

Where garden space is limited or there are persistent problems with pests or diseases, container growing is an alternative method of cultivating early beetroot, carrots, potatoes, and turnips.

Pots should be at least 25cm (10in) deep and wide, filled with a mixture of rotted compost or manure and good garden soil. Tubs, growing bags, and even windowboxes are other options. Always keep containers well watered.

### Planting seed potatoes in a drill

**1** **Draw out a drill** 8–15cm (3–6in) deep – sufficient to cover the chits with at least 2.5cm (1in) of soil. Press a tuber with chits uppermost into the soil every 30–38cm (12–15in) along the drill.

**2** **Push or pull the soil** back gently over the tubers with the back of a rake. Lightly rake over the soil surface to level it, and mark the drill. Fertilizer can be added along the drill before planting (*see p.87*).

## PROTECTING AGAINST CARROT FLY

Carrot fly (see p.253) can cause severe damage to some root crops, especially carrots and parsnips. The adult females fly low along the ground, especially in sheltered or shady sites, until they find a suitable crop of seedlings or plants; they lay their eggs in the soil, where larvae hatch out and bore into the roots.

There are no approved chemical treatments available to the amateur gardener, but some cultivars now have a degree of resistance to carrot fly. There are also several control strategies that can be put into action to avoid infestation by this troublesome pest.

Two generations of flies usually hatch out each season, and sowing times can be planned so as to avoid the worst periods of activity. The first hatching usually occurs in late spring, and the second in midsummer. To avoid the first wave, sow from late spring, in a stale seedbed (see p.66) or in a bed prepared well in advance in an open, sunny site. The second wave should then be less of a problem as the flies will not have already become established and begun to breed in your garden. Sometimes, a third hatching occurs in early autumn, so protect crops until winter.

Erecting low physical barriers (see box, below) can be a highly effective means of protecting carrots from attack.

Companion planting – planting possibly beneficial plant combinations – may also be successful in deterring the carrot fly. Sowing alternate rows of onions and carrots is frequently recommended to confuse both carrot fly and onion fly (see p.258), which locate their preferred crop by its odour.

The scent of thinnings attracts adult female flies, so sow seed as thinly as possible to avoid thinning altogether. Alternatively, thin the crop in the evening, nipping off the seedlings at ground level to avoid disturbing the soil. Firm down the soil again after thinning, and after lifting carrot crops.

Remove any infested crops as soon as possible off site. Storing or composting infested crops will assist in maintaining the life cycle of the carrot fly so it can return the following year.

## Planting potatoes under plastic sheet mulch

**1** **Lay a sheet** of black plastic on the bed. Plant tubers 15cm (6in) deep at usual spacings through slits cut in the sheet. Plant small tubers 30cm (12in) apart. Alternatively, cover a newly planted crop and cut slits as the new shoots push up. In either case, pull developing shoots through the slits.

**2** **To harvest tubers,** pull back the sheet and gather the new crop of tubers from the surface; a few will need digging out.

## HARVESTING AND STORING

To avoid encouraging carrot fly, harvest carrots and parsnips as soon as they are ready. If this pest is not a problem, the roots may be left in the ground until needed, as with beetroot, swedes, and turnips; cover with straw or bracken if frosts are expected (see p.73). Lift potatoes by early or mid-autumn; the later you leave them the greater the possible damage from slugs. Leave to dry outside for 2–3 hours before storing. Lift scorzonera and salsify as needed, and use fresh. Sweet potatoes will need to be cured (see p.88). Most root crops are suitable for storing (see p.73). Store only undamaged roots or tubers, which are least prone to rot.

## Using barriers to exclude carrot flies

To prevent carrot fly from attacking and devastating carrots and other susceptible crops, erect a barrier, at least 60cm (2ft) high, around the sown area before the seedlings appear. The females fly very low, so the barrier effectively stops them reaching the crop and laying their eggs. The barrier may be made from waxed cardboard stapled together at the corners (right), film or rigid plastics, or fine woven mesh netting (far right). Staple the netting or film plastic to wooden posts driven into the soil at the corners. Stretch strings between the four corner posts on which to staple the netting or film plastic. Insert canes at intervals along the sides to hold it in place. Ensure that the material is buried securely all along the base.

Waxed cardboard barrier

Fine woven mesh barrier

# A-Z OF ROOT CROPS

## Beetroot

*Beta vulgaris* subsp. *vulgaris*

| SEASON | SPRING | SUMMER | AUTUMN | WINTER |
|---|---|---|---|---|
| SOW | • • • • • | | | |
| HARVEST | | • • • • • | | |

Beetroot is easy to grow and the swollen roots can be harvested from early summer to autumn. It can be stored or pickled for use in salads or steamed as a sweet vegetable. It may be round, long, or oval in shape and comes in a range of outer colours, from purple or deep red to yellow or white. The inner flesh may be purple, red, yellow, white, or even red with white rings. All the colour forms are similar in flavour. Most beetroot types are short-term crops, suitable for catch cropping (*see p.69*), and they are easier to cook and are sweeter-tasting when harvested young; long-rooted types are slower-growing, but well-flavoured. The young leaves may be eaten like spinach.

Beetroot may also be grown in containers (*see p.83*). Early sowings may be prone to bolt and run to seed, but resistant cultivars are usually available. Mature beetroot normally yields 30 roots, each weighing 450g–1kg (1–2lb), per 3m (10ft) row.

■ **Site and soil** Beetroot needs an open, sunny site, with fertile, light, sandy soil, preferably one that has been manured in the previous season. Long-rooted cultivars need a good depth of soil. A pH of 6.5–7 is ideal.

■ **Sowing** For spring sowings under cover, use a bolt-resistant cultivar. Make successional sowings direct outdoors (*see p.69*) every two weeks in early and midsummer. Space sow seeds 5cm (2in) apart, then thin the seedlings for standard-sized beets. Leave unthinned for pickling beets about 5cm (2in) in diameter.

| SOWING DEPTH | 2.5cm (1in) |
|---|---|
| PLANT SPACING | Standard: 10cm (4in) |
| | Pickling: 5cm (2in) |
| ROW SPACING | Standard: 23–30cm (9–12in) |
| | Pickling: 15cm (6in) |

■ **Routine care** Protect early sowings from frosts, and seedlings from birds, with fleece (*see pp.82–83*) or cloches (*see p.46*). Keep the soil moist, and when the roots start to swell after about 8–9 weeks give the plants a good watering. In a dry spell, use 11 litres per sq m (2 gallons per sq yd) at intervals of 2–3 weeks. Too frequent or light watering leads to a lot of leafy growth and no roots. Light, sandy soils of high pH may be low in manganese and possibly boron (*see p.17*), so spray once or twice with a foliar, seaweed-based fertilizer (*see p.22*) that has a range of trace elements.

■ **Harvesting and storing** Start lifting roots once they are about 5cm (2in) in diameter; spring sowings will be ready in summer and summer ones in autumn. Lift the beets as they are needed; this thins out the crop, leaving other roots to achieve a larger size. Harvest by pulling up the beets and twisting off their tops about 2.5cm (1in) above the root. Roots can be overwintered *in situ* by covering them with a 15cm (6in) layer of straw or bracken.

■ **Common problems** Black bean aphid (*see p.252*), cutworm (*see p.254*), damping off (*p.254*), and fungal leaf spot (*p.257*) may all be troublesome, as well as occasional deficiencies of boron (*p.252*) and manganese (*see p.257*).

■ **Recommended cultivars**
'Red Ace' ♀ – good red, well-shaped hybrid.
'Boltardy' ♀ – round, red, bolt-resistant.
'Burpees Golden' – yellow root, good flavour; tops can be steamed like spinach.
'Cheltenham Green Top' ♀ – long, red root.
'Chioggia' – sweet and tender with striking red and white internal rings.
'Pablo' ♀ – hybrid, good texture, colour and flavour, fast-growing, resistant to bolting.

## Carrot

*Daucus carota*

| SEASON | SPRING | SUMMER | AUTUMN | WINTER |
|---|---|---|---|---|
| SOW | • • • • • | | • | • • |
| TRANSPLANT | • • | | | |
| HARVEST | | • • • • | • • • | • |

By successional sowings, it is possible to lift fresh roots of this popular vegetable from late spring through to early winter. The crop can also be stored so that it is available into late winter. Carrots are classified according to shape, maturity, and size, although root shape and also colour are influenced by soil type and growing conditions.

The earliest crops are obtained with Amsterdam-type cultivars: narrow, cylindrical, stump-ended roots with smooth skins and of small size, suitable for forcing. Nantes types are of similar shape, but broader and longer; they are suitable for early crops and forcing as Amsterdam types, but also for later crops. Chantenay cultivars are short, broad and more conical, and are suitable for maincrops for summer and autumn lifting. Berlicum types produce long, large roots which are suitable for winter use, as are the long-season, tapering Autumn King types, which produce the longest roots of all.

These types have been used as parents to breed new F1 hybrid cultivars with mixed characteristics and of high quality. Small, round-rooted, "baby" cultivars are also available and are suitable for container raising where garden space is restricted. All are available from garden centres and it is worth studying the packet information to choose cultivars for particular seasonal requirements.

■ **Site and soil** The preferred pH range is 6.5–7.5. Carrots do best on light soils, and a relatively dry site produces a sweeter flavour;

heavy soils can carry satisfactory crops if they are not waterlogged or compacted. All benefit from well-rotted organic matter incorporated in the previous season. A low-nitrogen base dressing should be added. Prepare a fine tilth several weeks in advance and destroy any germinated weeds just before sowing.

■ **Sowing** Precision-treated seeds (*see p.60*) give best results for early sowings; sow all seed thinly. For a spring crop, sow outdoors in mid-autumn or mid- to late winter under fleece, or in greenhouse beds. When thinning seedlings, pinch them out to avoid the stronger odour that results from pulling, which attracts carrot fly, or erect a barrier (*see p.84*). Early summer liftings can be obtained by sowing under protection in early spring or outdoors from mid-spring – as soon as the soil temperature rises to at least 7.5°C (45°F), naturally or with the aid of glass cloche or plastic film coverings – to midsummer. Round, Amsterdam, and Nantes types are all suitable for early sowings. Sowing seed in modules is another way to obtain early crops (*see pp.62–63*). Successional sowings outdoors in mid- and late spring of Chantenay and Berlicum types crop from late summer. Short-season crops are less prone to carrot fly attack; sowings made in early spring to early summer are likely to miss the most harmful hatches of the insect, although timings vary by latitude.

| SOWING DEPTH | 1–2cm (½–¾in) |
| --- | --- |
| SEED SPACING | sow thinly; thin to 10cm (4in) |
| ROW SPACING | 30cm (12in) in open garden |
| | 15cm (6in) under cover |

■ **Routine care** Keep weed-free by hand weeding until the leaf canopy suppresses any competition. Water in dry spells, but do not overwater carrots because this encourages leaf growth. Supplementary feeding should not be necessary on well-prepared sites.

■ **Harvesting and storing** Pull the first roots when 12–15mm (½–⅝in) thick, remembering that the roots will grow continuously as the seasonal temperature rises. On heavier soils, it is necessary to ease roots out of the ground with a fork. For winter use, roots can be left in the ground; cover with a secure layer of straw or bracken when frost approaches. Alternatively, roots can be lifted and stored (*see p.73*). Roots left in the ground for long periods are liable to sustain carrot fly damage.

■ **Common problems** Carrot fly (*see p.253*) is the most serious pest; aphids, especially root aphids (*see p.261*) can be troublesome. Downy and powdery mildews (*see p.255, p.260*) and violet root rot (*see p.263*) can cause problems.

■ **Recommended cultivars**
**Amsterdam type**
'Amsterdam Forcing 3' – sweet-flavoured, reliable for sowing at any time.
**Autumn King type**
'Autumn King 2' ♀ – good flavour, stores well.
'Flyaway' ♀ – sweet-tasting F1 hybrid, resistant to carrot fly.
'Kingston' ♀ – hybrid, tender, good size.

**Berlicum type**
'Berjo' ♀ – high-yielding cultivar, good colour; keeps all winter.
**Chantenay type**
'Chantenay Red Cored 2' – sweet-tasting maincrop, good for storing.
**Imperator type**
'Sugarsnax 54' – long roots, very sweet.
**Nantes type**
'Nairobi' ♀ – hybrid, stump roots, heavy yields.
'Nigel' – bright roots, good flavour and texture, stores well.
**Round type**
'Parmex' ♀ – raise under glass or outdoors.
**Heritage cultivars**
'Danvers' – Victorian, crops early summer to mid-autumn.
'James Scarlet' – good colour and flavour.
'New Red Intermediate' – good for exhibition and storage.
'St Valory' – maincrop, good for exhibition.

# Hamburg parsley

*Petroselinum crispum* var. *tuberosum*

| SEASON | SPRING | SUMMER | AUTUMN | WINTER |
| --- | --- | --- | --- | --- |
| SOW | | ● ● ● | | |
| HARVEST | ● ● | | ● ● ● ● ● ● |

Hamburg parsley has roots similar in taste and appearance to parsnips, although smaller. The plant has parsley-like leaves that remain green during severe winters, and can be used instead of more tender herb parsley (*see p.144*). Root yield is 3kg per 3m (6½lb per 10ft) row.

■ **Site and soil** As parsnip (*see below*).
■ **Sowing** Sow thinly in rows and thin seedlings when they have two true leaves.

| SOWING DEPTH | 2cm (¾in) |
| --- | --- |
| SEED SPACING | thin to 15–20cm (6–8in) |
| ROW SPACING | 30cm (12in) |

■ **Routine care** As for parsnip (*see below*).
■ **Harvesting and storing** As for parsnip (*see below*). Pick the leaves as required.
■ **Common problems** As for parsnip (*see below*).
■ **Recommended cultivar**
'Hamburg Parsley' – very strong flavour.

# Parsnip

*Pastinaca sativa*

| SEASON | SPRING | SUMMER | AUTUMN | WINTER |
| --- | --- | --- | --- | --- |
| SOW | ● ● | | | |
| HARVEST | ● ● | | ● ● ● ● ● ● |

This long-term root crop is valuable for its hardiness and distinct flavour. All types taste similar; the quicker the growth, the sweeter the taste. The roots can be 13–25cm (5–10in) long, and of various shapes – some long and narrow, some bulbous – depending on cultivar as well as soil and conditions. In shallow soils, a cultivar with a shorter root is best. Parsnips yield about 4kg per 3m (9lb per 10ft) row.

■ **Site and soil** For best results, parsnips need an open, sunny site, and a deep, light, sandy soil, although good crops can be obtained from heavy soils. The ideal pH is 6.5. Manure the soil in the previous season. Parsnips have a low nitrogen requirement.

■ **Sowing** Seed sown direct in mid- to late spring is more likely to germinate than seed sown earlier. Germination is slow.

Sow thinly or station sow with 2–4 seeds per station (*see p.68*). Use 10–15cm (4–6in) spacing for medium-sized roots up to 5cm (2in) in diameter and a wider spacing for later, stored roots. Parsnips can be intersown (*see p.69*) with radishes to mark the rows.

| SOWING DEPTH | 2cm (¾in) | |
| --- | --- | --- |
| SEED SPACING | Medium: 10–14cm (4–6in) | |
| | Large: 20cm (8in) | |
| ROW SPACING | 30cm (12in) | |

■ **Routine care** Control weeds. Water only in very dry conditions, at a rate of 11 litres per sq m (2 gallons per 10sq ft) every 2–3 weeks. If left too dry, the roots are liable to split after watering. Most late-sown seeds need watering to aid germination. Feeding is not usually needed, but if growth is poor, apply a liquid feed according to manufacturer's instructions.

■ **Harvesting and storing** Parsnips are ready for lifting from late summer but may be left in the soil until needed, although there may be a risk of carrot fly (*see p.84*). Alternatively, lift and store in sand in boxes (*see p.73*).

■ **Common problems** Apart from carrot fly (*see p.84 and p.253*), parsnip canker (*see p.258*) can be a major problem if resistant cultivars are not used. Powdery mildew (*see p.260*) can be a minor problem in dry weather as well as downy mildew in damp conditions (*see p.255*). Violet root rot (*see p.263*) and celery leaf miner (*see p.253*) can also affect parsnip.

■ **Recommended cultivars**
'Albion' – very heavy yield, white roots.
'Countess' ♀ – fine quality, pale yellow roots.
'Gladiator' ♀ – hybrid, sow early or late, very vigorous, canker-resistant, good in exhibition.
'Javelin' ♀ – long-rooted hybrid, good for exhibition.
'Tender and True' ♀ – long-rooted, canker-resistant, good for exhibition.

# Potato

*Solanum tuberosum*

| SEASON | SPRING | SUMMER | AUTUMN | WINTER |
| --- | --- | --- | --- | --- |
| PLANT | ● ● ● | | | |
| HARVEST | | ● ● ● ● ● | | |

The potato is a staple vegetable that stores well and may be eaten all year round. Tubers vary in size, colour, texture, and taste. Early types, often referred to as new potatoes, are small and are cooked whole for hot dishes and salads. Late-maturing types have large tubers that can be cooked in many ways.

## Planting out young leeks

**1** **In mid-spring** for early leeks, or early to midsummer for late leeks, lift seedlings (here 'Toledo') from the seedbed drill about eight weeks after sowing, when they are of about pencil thickness. Water the soil first if it is dry. Use a hand fork to loosen the soil beneath the roots, then gently pull the seedlings.

**2** **Select bundles** of about ten seedlings of equal thickness and trim with a sharp knife. Cut the roots to about 2.5cm (1in) and the leaves to 15–20cm (6–8in).

**3** **Draw out a drill** in the planting bed and make planting holes with a large dibber, here 15cm (6in) apart and deep. Place one seedling into each hole, so that the heart, or growing point, is at or only just below the soil surface.

**4** **Water the seedlings** well to settle their roots. It is not necessary to fill in the holes; this will occur naturally as the leeks grow.

Any thick-necked bulbs should be used fresh, as they will not store well. Lift carefully, so as not to bruise the bulbs, and place them in a single layer on a drying rack made from chicken wire (*see right*), sacking, netting, or inverted wooden slatted trays. This keeps them off the ground and allows plenty of air to flow around them. They will ripen best in full sun, but should be covered in rainy weather. Turn the bulbs regularly to achieve even ripening.

Bulbs should not be stored until the green parts and the papery skins are "rustling" dry. When fully dried, clean off any loose skins and plait the tops into ropes (*see p.73*) or hang the bulbs in bunches. Alternatively, trim off the tops and store in nets or in single layers in trays (*see p.73*). Do not store onions in the dark, as this encourages sprouting.

### BOLTING

Like some leafy salads, alliums are prone to premature flowering, or bolting. Sowing later can protect them from exposure to cold soil and waterlogging, which may check growth and initiate bolting. Use heat-treated sets and bolt-resistant cultivars to avoid this problem.

### COMMON PROBLEMS

Most crops in the onion family are susceptible to the same problems. To minimize the effects, grow some of the cultivars that have inbred resistance, and use preventative measures such as crop rotation (*see p.31*) and air circulation.

Onion white rot (*see p.258*) is a soil-borne disease and can stay in the soil for 20 years or more – if your onions have it, stop growing them and remove and destroy affected plants. A more expensive solution is to replace the affected soil with clean soil. Be careful not to spread the disease around on tools and footwear. Downy mildew (*see p.255*) appears when wet, humid conditions are causing soft growth, which increases the plants' susceptibility to infection. Onions should be kept as dry and hard as possible, so only water in very dry conditions. As soon as you see the tips of the leaves becoming grey and dying back, remove infected parts and burn them. Onion neck rot (*see p.258*) and fusarium, which rots the basal plates of the bulbs (*see p.256*), affect overwintered crops. Viruses (*see p.264*) are occasionally troublesome, especially with garlic, so always buy certified stock to get the best yields.

Onion fly (*see p.258*) is a particular problem in dry soils, and is active from late spring to late summer. When sowing seed at these times, use dressed seed, treat the drills, or cover the drills with fleece to keep out the flies until the crop has germinated. Be careful, however, as allium leaves will grow through the fleece fabric, and they can then be damaged when the fleece is removed. Onion thrips (*see p.258*) and stem and bulb eelworm (*see p.262*) can attack leeks, onions, and shallots.

**Drying shallots**
*Create a drying rack by attaching a piece of chicken wire to four short posts to raise the wire off the ground. Place the bulbs on top, where air can circulate around them.*

# A–Z OF THE ONION FAMILY

## Bulb onion

*Allium cepa*

| SEASON | SPRING | SUMMER | AUTUMN | WINTER |
|---|---|---|---|---|
| SOW/PLANT | • • | | • • • | • • |
| TRANSPLANT | • • | | | |
| HARVEST | | • • • • | | |

Bulb onions are either lifted at time of use or stored for winter use. Small bulbs are usually preferred. Most cultivars are yellow- or brown- skinned with white flesh, but there are also red-skinned ones, some of which have red-and-white striped layers inside. A long season of growth is needed, and the final size of the bulb is determined by spacing (*see pp.89–90*). For late-summer crops, size is also governed by how much leaf the plant has developed by early summer, when leaf growth stops and bulbs swell. A 3m (10ft) row will yield 60 small, 30 large, or 15 very large onions, or 1–3kg (2¼–6½lb). Onion sets are suitable for intercropping (*see p.71*).

■ **Site and soil** Bulb onions require an open, fertile, non-acid soil (*see p.89*). Good drainage is needed, especially for an overwintered crop. For late winter or spring sowings, use a cloche (*see p.46*) to warm the soil beforehand.

■ **Sowing and planting** Overwintered crops are more susceptible to disease, and therefore it is better to sow or plant in spring. For year-round supplies of onions, sow seed or plant sets twice a year, first in midwinter to mid-spring, and again in autumn. Treated seed is available that protects against fungal diseases. From late winter, sow seed in multiblocks (*see p.89*); as soon as conditions are warm and dry enough sow thinly outdoors in rows (*see p.67*), and thin the seedlings according to the desired size (*see p.89*). In autumn, sow seed of the hardy Japanese overwintering cultivars in a seedbed to which a moderate amount of nitrogenous fertilizer (*see p.72*) has been added. Plant sets (*see p.90*) from late winter to early spring, and heat-treated ones in mid-spring. Plant sets for overwintering from mid- to late autumn. Some seedlings may be lost during the winter, so you can afford to plant or sow a little more closely.

| SOWING DEPTH | 2cm (¾in) |
|---|---|
| PLANT/SET SPACING | 2.5–10cm (1–4in) as desired |
| ROW SPACING | 30cm (12in) |

■ **Routine care** Keep the crop well weeded, especially in the first month or so after sowing or planting. Water only until the plants are established; if spring-sown or planted onions are watered after midsummer, they take longer to mature and may keep less well. Check regularly for signs of disease. Top-dress overwintering crops in midwinter with a nitrogenous fertilizer (*see p.20 and p.72*), and thin in spring (*see p.89*).

■ **Harvesting and storing** Lift overwintered onions in early to midsummer. Harvest spring-sown or planted onions in late summer to early autumn and dry them (*see p.91*). Store some bulbs for winter use (*see pp.73 and 91*).

■ **Common problems** See *p.91* (for symptoms and controls, *see* Plant Problems, *pp.246–264*).

■ **Recommended cultivars**
**Heat-treated sets**
'Marshall's Showmaster' – mild, sweet flavour.
'Red Baron' ♀ – red onion, plant mid-spring.
**Untreated sets**
'Centurion' ♀ – widely available.
'Santero' – resistant to downy mildew, brown skin.
'Sturon' ♀ – sets also available.
**Seed**
'Bedfordshire Champion' – brown skin.
'Hylander' – resistant to downy mildew, vigorous.
**Overwintering**
'Senshyu Semi-globe Yellow' – Japanese cultivar.

## Garlic

*Allium sativum*

| SEASON | SPRING | SUMMER | AUTUMN | WINTER |
|---|---|---|---|---|
| PLANT | • | | • • | • • |
| HARVEST | | • • • • | | |

Garlic has a strong flavour and distinctive aroma, and is used extensively. A range of cultivars is available, some of which are virus- and nematode-free. Garlic also has medicinal properties and is often recommended for use in a healthy diet. Each bulb consists of a number of individual cloves, which are used in cooking. Even if the plants bolt, they will still produce reasonable bulbs.

To grow well, garlic requires a cold period of 1–2 months at 0–10°C (32–50°F), and is usually therefore planted in autumn or winter. Spring-planted garlic may not mature well, especially in a poor summer. Expect a yield of 17 bulbs per 3m (10ft) row. Garlic is also suitable for intercropping (*see p.71*).

■ **Site and soil** An open, sunny site and a well-drained, light, alkaline soil are best (*see p.89*); heavy soils should be lightened with horticultural sharp sand. Give the soil a good dressing of well-rotted organic matter. Avoid using fresh manure for the dressing.

■ **Planting** From autumn to early spring, split into cloves, ideally 1.5cm (½in) in diameter, and plant upright either outdoors or in modules, depending on the suitability of your soil (*see p.90*). Ensure that the basal plate is facing downwards. Planting 10cm (4in) deep on light soils gives the best yields.

| PLANTING DEPTH | 2.5–10cm (1–4in) |
|---|---|
| CLOVE SPACING | 18cm (7in) |
| ROW SPACING | 30cm (12in) |

■ **Routine care** Keep weed-free and moist throughout, to avoid any check in growth. Planting through a black plastic mulch (*see p.42*) keeps the plants warm as well as retaining moisture and suppressing weeds.
■ **Harvesting and storing** Lift autumn or winter-planted bulbs in late spring or early summer, as soon as the leaves start to yellow; if harvesting is delayed, bulbs may resprout, and rot more often in storage. Harvest spring-planted bulbs from midsummer to early autumn. Dry well (*see p.91*), taking care to avoid bruising them. Store in a dry place (*see p.73*) at 5–10°C (41–50°F); if stored correctly, bulbs keep for up to ten months.
■ **Common problems** As for bulb onions (*see p.91*); rust is often damaging. For symptoms and controls, *see* Plant Problems, *pp.246–264*.
■ **Recommended cultivars**
'Albigensian Wight' – soft neck, keeps well.
'Purple Moldovia' – purple bulbs with edible flowering spikes.
'Purple Wight' – early winter planting, early maturing, strong flavour, unsuited to storing.
'Solent Wight' ♀ – early winter planting, good flavour, purple bulbs, keeps well.

# Japanese bunching onion

*Allium fistulosum*

| SEASON | SPRING | SUMMER | AUTUMN | WINTER |
|---|---|---|---|---|
| SOW | • • • | • | • • | • |
| TRANSPLANT | • • • | | | |
| HARVEST | | | • • • | • • |

Japanese bunching onions are selections of Welsh onions (*see p.94*). They are perennial but best grown as annuals; forms vary from small salad onion types to large-leaved types like leeks. The clusters of stems, used in salads, are more pungent than spring onions. They will stand without winter protection in the open. Plants mature in two years, growing up to 60cm (2ft). A 3m (10ft) row yields 250–300 salad onions, or 40–50 large ones.
■ **Site and soil** Japanese bunching onions will tolerate less fertile soil conditions than most of the onion family (*see p.89*).
■ **Sowing and planting** For salad use, sow under cover (*see p.64*), from early autumn to late winter. Sow outside from mid-spring to midsummer; thin in stages to 8cm (3in) apart. For larger onions, at the outset sow 2–3 seeds per clump in holes 8cm (3in) apart. Healthy clumps can be divided.

| SOWING DEPTH | 2cm (¾in) |
|---|---|
| PLANT SPACING | 2.5cm (1in) for salad onions |
| | 8cm (3in) for large onions |
| ROW SPACING | 30cm (12in) |

■ **Routine care** Keep weed-free and moist.
■ **Harvesting** Seedling leaves may be picked after 10–14 weeks. In the second year, during autumn and winter, harvest the clusters by lifting the plant and splitting off the stems.
■ **Common problems** As for bulb onions (*see p.91*). Downy mildew, and rarely rust, may be particularly troublesome. For symptoms and controls, *see* Plant Problems, *pp.246–264*.
■ **Recommended cultivars**
'Ishikura' ♀ – strong in flavour in comparison with spring onions, and resistant to mildew.
'Shimonita' – tubular 'bulb-less' salad onions, mild flavour, strong-growing.

# Leek

*Allium porrum*

| SEASON | SPRING | SUMMER | AUTUMN | WINTER |
|---|---|---|---|---|
| SOW | • • | | | • • |
| TRANSPLANT | • • • • | • | | |
| HARVEST | • • | | • • • | • • • |

Leeks are a hardy winter crop, grown for their blanched white stem bases, or shanks (*see p.90*), which are harvested from late summer to the spring of the following year. Cultivars are available that mature early (in late summer and autumn), mid-season (in winter), or late (in spring). Earlies are generally tall, with long, white shanks and pale foliage. Later ones have darker foliage and shorter shanks. From a 3m (10ft) row expect 4–6kg (8½–13lb) of early leeks, or 3–5kg (6½–11lb) of late leeks.
■ **Site and soil** Leeks do best on a deep, rich soil of a neutral or slightly acid pH (*see p.89*), preferably a light sandy loam. Incorporate plenty of organic matter before sowing or planting. With a high-nitrogen base dressing (*see pp.20–23*), leeks produce a good fibrous root system, which improves soil structure and therefore contributes well in crop rotations.
■ **Sowing and planting** Sow in early to mid-spring in an outdoor seedbed (*see p.66*) at a minimum of 7°C (44°F). Alternatively, sow in modules in midwinter under cover (*see pp.62–63*) at a temperature of 10°C (50°F), and harden off (*see p.65*) before transplanting. To produce smaller leeks, sow in multiblocks (*see p.65*) without heat in late winter.

From mid-spring, when seedlings are 20cm (8in) tall, transplant them (*see pp.90–91*) into their final positions, using a dibber to make deep planting holes. Plant later leeks wider apart in rows, to allow them to grow larger. By carefully adjusting sowing times, you can crop the same cultivar earlier or later than the usual period, but quality may not be as good.

| SOWING DEPTH | 2.5cm (1in) |
|---|---|
| SEED SPACING | sow thinly |
| TRANSPLANTING DEPTH | 15cm (6in) |
| PLANT SPACING | 15–20cm (6–8in) |
| ROW SPACING | 30–38cm (12–15in) |

■ **Routine care** Keep seedbeds and transplanted seedlings free of weeds during the growing period. Once established, water only in very dry spells. Top-dress with a high-nitrogen fertilizer (*see pp.20–23*) in mid- to late summer, or in late winter for late crops. If the leeks have not been planted in deep holes (*see pp.90–91*) draw soil up around the stems as far as possible to aid the blanching process.
■ **Harvesting** Lift leeks as required from late summer onwards. In late spring, you can lift and heel them in until needed, if the same ground is intended for other planting. They will stand for some time at maturity, as long as they are disease-free.
■ **Common problems** Leeks are affected by all allium-related disorders (*see p.91*). *Fusarium* (*see p.256*) affects leek roots, so they are best raised in modules to give them a good start. Leek rust (*see p.257*), cutworms (*see p.254*), onion fly (*see p.258*), and onion thrips (*see p.258*) are also significant problems.
■ **Recommended cultivars**
'Carlton' ♀ – early hybrid, good colour.
'Longbow' ♀ – mid-autumn to early spring.
'Mammoth Blanch' ♀ – does not bolt if sown early, crops late summer to early autumn.
'Oarsman' ♀ – late hybrid, long straight shank.
'Toledo' ♀ – rust-resistant, crops early winter to late spring.

# Pickling onion

*Allium cepa*

| SEASON | SPRING | SUMMER | AUTUMN | WINTER |
|---|---|---|---|---|
| SOW | • • | | | |
| HARVEST | | | • | |

These are bulb onion selections (*see p.92*), grown to produce large quantities of very small, tender onions for pickling. Expect 1–1.5kg (2¼–3lb) from a 3m (10ft) row.
■ **Site and soil** They do best on a fertile, well-drained, alkaline soil, like other alliums (*see p.89*), but will tolerate poorer, drier soils.
■ **Sowing and planting** Sow outdoors *in situ* in early to mid-spring. The best density is about 30 plants per 30 sq cm (1 sq ft). Sow in 30cm (12in) rows, or in bands 23cm (9in) wide with 30cm (12in) between bands.

| SOWING DEPTH | 2.5cm (1in) |
|---|---|
| SEED SPACING | 5mm (¼in) |
| ROW SPACING | 30cm (12in) |

■ **Routine care** Thinning is not needed, since small bulbs are desired. Keep weed-free.
■ **Harvesting and storing** The onions are ready for harvesting when the foliage dies down, usually in late summer. Lift and dry as for bulb onions (*see p.92*) and store in a cool, dry place (*see p.73*) until ready to pickle.
■ **Common problems** The usual onion pests and diseases (*see p.91*) may be troublesome: *see* Plant Problems, *pp.246–264*.
■ **Recommended cultivars**
'Brown Pickling' – golden brown skin.
'Giant Zittau' – onions are medium-sized, larger than those of other cultivars.
'Paris Silver Skin' – pickles with white flesh.
'Purplette' – unusual, small purple bulbs for pickling.

# Shallot

*Allium cepa* Aggregatum Group

| SEASON | SPRING | SUMMER | AUTUMN | WINTER |
|---|---|---|---|---|
| SOW | • • | | | • |
| TRANSPLANT | • | | | |
| PLANT SETS | • • | | • • | • |
| HARVEST | | • • | | |

This easily grown allium has a distinct flavour, and can be used for both cooking and pickling. The most commonly grown types have firm bulbs and yellow or red skins. Shallots are usually planted as sets, and need a long growing season. Early in the season, offsets can be pulled off and used raw in salads. Types with long, narrow bulbs are available, as are cultivars that can be raised from seed to produce single shallots. A 3m (10ft) row produces 60–180 shallots. Shallots are suitable for intercropping (*see p.71*).

■ **Site and soil** A fertile, well-drained, non-acid soil is best (*see p.89*). For planting sets, the soil should be loose (*see p.90*).

■ **Sowing and planting** Sow seed outdoors (*see p.66*) in mid- to late spring, thinning to 2cm (¾in). Sow under cover (*see p.64*) from late winter and transplant in mid-spring, spacing seedlings 5cm (2in) apart. Plant sets (*see p.90*) in winter and early and mid-spring, as soon as soil is workable. Small sets are less likely to bolt than large ones.

| SOWING DEPTH | 2.5cm (1in) |
|---|---|
| SEED SPACING | 2cm (¾in) |
| PLANTING DEPTH (SETS) | so that just the tips are showing |
| PLANT SPACING (SETS) | 15–20cm (6–8in) |
| ROW SPACING | 30cm (12in) |

■ **Routine care** Keep weed-free. If conditions are dry, water in sets and seedlings to give them a quick start and a firm rooting.

■ **Harvesting and storing** Lift in mid- to late summer when the tops have died down and dry as for bulb onions. Cleaned shallots can be stored in trays or bags in a frost-free place (*see p.73*). If the stock is healthy, save some sets for next year – the best size for seed sets is 2cm (¾in) in diameter.

■ **Common problems** Shallots are prone to the usual onion problems (*see p.91*), especially downy mildew. For symptoms and controls, see Plant Problems, *pp.246–264*.

■ **Recommended cultivars**
'Golden Gourmet' – large, heavy-yielding.
'Pikant' ♀ – strong-flavoured, medium-sized shallot, stores well, good skin colour.
'Matador' ♀ – hybrid, heavy yield from seed, good size and colour.

# Spring onion

*Allium cepa*

| SEASON | SPRING | SUMMER | AUTUMN | WINTER |
|---|---|---|---|---|
| SOW | • • | • • • • | • | |
| HARVEST | • • | • • • | • | |

Spring or salad onions are immature bulb onions (*A. cepa; see p.92*) grown for their small, white shanks and tender, green stem and leaves. Often referred to as scallions, they are usually pulled when about 15cm (6in) tall and eaten raw in salads. Most commonly grown are the 'Lisbon' cultivars. Expect 250–300 per 3m (10ft) row. Spring onions are suitable for intercropping (*see p.71*).

■ **Site and soil** Prepare as for bulb onions (*see p.92*). Soil alkalinity of pH 6.8 or above is needed to achieve best results.

■ **Sowing and planting** For a continual summer harvest, sow *in situ* in single rows every two weeks from early spring. Higher yields could be obtained in closer rows, but the plants will be more susceptible to downy mildew (*see below*). Thinning is not usually required. For a spring supply the following year, sow in late summer and early autumn. The seedlings should make good growth before winter, otherwise frost may lift them out of the ground, especially on light soils.

| SOWING DEPTH | 1–2cm (½–¾in) |
|---|---|
| SEED SPACING | 1cm (½in) |
| ROW SPACING | 30cm (12in) |

■ **Routine care** Keep watered in dry weather to avoid any check in growth. Drought can cause the plants to become bulbous, especially 'Lisbon' types. In cold areas, protect winter crops with a cloche (*see p.46*).

■ **Harvesting** Pull and use as required after about two months.

■ **Common problems** Of the usual onion afflictions (*see p.91*), onion fly can be seriously troublesome, especially in dry weather, as well as onion white rot and downy mildew. For symptoms and controls, see Plant Problems, *pp.246–264*.

■ **Recommended cultivars**
**Spring-sown**
'Laser' ♀ – hybrid, non-bulbing.
'White Lisbon' ♀ – very susceptible to downy mildew, but an old favourite.
**Autumn-sown**
'Guardsman' – coated for mildew protection.
'Ramrod' ♀ – good winter-hardy cultivar.
'White Lisbon Winter Hardy' – very hardy.

# Tree or Egyptian onion

*Allium cepa* Proliferum Group

| SEASON | SPRING | SUMMER | AUTUMN | WINTER |
|---|---|---|---|---|
| PLANT | • • • | | • • • | |
| HARVEST | | • | | |

This perennial onion grows up to 1.2m (4ft) within two years of planting. It produces clusters of very small aerial bulbs instead of flowers. The bulblets sprout while still attached to the main plant, developing shoots and further clusters of bulblets to form a multi-layered plant. The stems eventually drop down to the ground under their own weight, where some of the bulblets take root and create new plants. Tree onions produce only low yields. The bulblets are harvested and used as a hot flavouring in cooking, and are also pickled. No named cultivars are offered.

■ **Site and soil** This allium needs a sunny situation in fertile, well-drained, alkaline soil.

■ **Sowing and planting** Plant single bulbs or clusters (*see p.90*), in spring and autumn.

| PLANTING DEPTH | with just the tip showing |
|---|---|
| PLANT SPACING | 25cm (10in) |
| ROW SPACING | 25cm (10in) |

■ **Routine care** The plants will reproduce readily (*see above*), so may need thinning out if they start to crowd one another.

■ **Harvesting** Pick the aerial bulblets as they ripen in late summer, before they start to grow.

■ **Common problems** This crop is prey to the same problems as all onions (*see p.91*), but more tolerant of pests.

# Welsh onion

*Allium fistulosum*

| SEASON | SPRING | SUMMER | AUTUMN | WINTER |
|---|---|---|---|---|
| SOW | • • • | • | | |
| HARVEST | • • • | • • • | • • • | • |

The Welsh onion, or ciboule, is a hollow-leaved, robust perennial that grows in clumps 30–45cm (12–18in) tall. The base of the stem is thickened, but does not form a bulb. It is useful as a year-round alternative to spring onions. The leaves, which stay green all year, and tiny bulbs are eaten cooked or raw, often in winter salads. In milder areas, it may be harvested for 2–3 years before division of the clump in spring or autumn (*see below*). In areas with severe winters, however, it is better to sow annually. Seed-raised plants are often hardier than those created by division.

■ **Site and soil** Welsh onions have the same requirements as bulb onions (*see p.92*).

■ **Sowing and planting** Sow seeds in spring or late summer, and thin to 20cm (8in) apart. For perennial plants, in spring lift the clump, divide it into several pieces, each with healthy leaves and root system, and replant the divisions 20cm (8in) apart.

| SOWING DEPTH | 2.5cm (1in) |
|---|---|
| SEED SPACING | sow thinly; thin to 20cm (8in) |
| ROW SPACING | 23cm (9in) |

■ **Routine care** Keep well weeded.

■ **Harvesting** Plants sown in spring should be big enough to start harvesting by autumn, and those sown in late summer by the following spring. Cut single leaves as required, or pull up part or all of the clump.

■ **Common problems** Prey to the same problems as all onions (*see p.91*), but more tolerant of pests.

■ **Recommended cultivars**
'Welsh Red' – native of Siberia, very hardy, retains foliage in winter.
'Welsh White' – native of Siberia, foliage dies down in winter.

# Growing legumes

The vegetable legumes include beans such as broad or fava, French or kidney (*see right*), Lima or butter, runner, and yard long or asparagus beans, as well as shelling and edible-pod peas. Although the young shoots may be used as green vegetables, legumes are mainly grown for their seeds and seedpods, which are eaten fresh or dried. All legumes are grown as annual crops. Some, such as broad beans and peas, are robust crops that resist frost and are well adapted to cool climates. Others, for example French and runner beans, are half-hardy and poorly adapted to cool weather; they thrive best in warm areas from late spring until the autumn frosts.

### NITROGEN "FIXING"

All the legume family (Leguminosae) have nitrogen-fixing root nodules (*see below*), and consequently they need much less nitrogenous fertilizer than many other vegetables. The process of absorbing nitrogen from the air takes energy from peas and beans, so that their yields are proportionately lower than those of other crops; therefore you will need to grow a reasonable number of plants in order to obtain sufficient pickings through the season. On the plus side, however, pea and bean crops are comparatively rich in protein.

Another benefit of nitrogen fixing in peas and beans is that their foliage makes a valuable addition to a compost heap.

**Nitrogen-fixing nodules**
*All legumes store, or fix, nitrogen with the help of* Rhizobium *bacteria that live in nodules on their roots. Root residues from legumes are rich in nitrogen and therefore they reduce the need for fertilizer.*

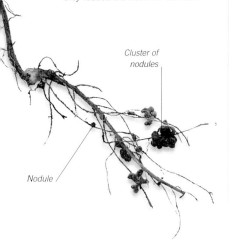

Cluster of nodules

Nodule

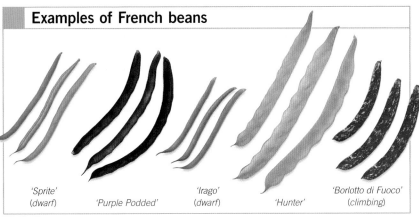

**Examples of French beans**

'Sprite'
(dwarf)     'Purple Podded'     'Irago'
(dwarf)     'Hunter'     'Borlotto di Fuoco'
(climbing)

### CHOOSING A SITE

Peas and beans are affected by similar pests and diseases (*see pp.98–100*), and should not be planted in the same soil every year. They are best grown in rotation (*see p.31*) as a group, usually preceding brassicas, which will benefit from the nitrogen residues in the soil. All legumes grow best in full sun, and the less hardy types demand a warm, sheltered position.

Although broad beans favour clay soil, other legumes perform best on lighter soil. A neutral to mildly alkaline soil (pH 6.5–7) is ideal, although mildly acid soils (not less than pH of 5.5) are usually acceptable. Peas and beans are generally hungry plants, demanding a rich soil. For best results, organic matter should be incorporated throughout the soil, but a traditional trench can be sufficient (*see below*). Adding some extra organic matter will also improve the drainage and soil structure, on heavy clay soils for example, and helps to retain soil moisture – which is very important at flowering time.

### THE NEED FOR LEGUME SUPPORTS

Many peas and beans are tall-growing and require some form of support. Without this, they will sprawl, or get flattened by rain. The benefits of using

**Preparing a bean trench**

**1** **Where organic matter** is not abundant or the soil is especially poor, a traditional bean trench will supply the nutrients legumes need. Mark out a line and excavate a trench 90cm (3ft) wide and 60cm (2ft) deep. Fork over the soil at the base to loosen it up.

**2** **Scatter organic matter**, such as compost or rotted manure, over the bottom of the trench and the dug-out soil. Replace the soil and apply some pelleted poultry manure at a rate of 2 handfuls per m (yd). Leave the soil to settle for at least 2 weeks before planting.

supports also include easier weeding, watering, and pest control, less weather damage, and more and better pods at harvest time. The disadvantages are the cost, effort, and inconvenience of installing the supports.

Common support methods (*see right*) include bamboo canes and twine, canes and netting, and bushy sticks (peasticks). All supports are most easily installed before they are actually needed, and this helps avoid damaging delicate stems when trying to raise fallen crops.

Dwarf cultivars of French and runner beans, peas, broad beans, and leafless peas can grow without supports, but a string along each side of the row is often helpful. Supports are also not required where climbing cultivars are made to branch by pinching out all the leading growth when the plant is 23cm (9in) tall, followed by further pinching to keep the plant bushy.

### SUPPORTS FOR BEANS

Climbing runner and French beans will twine around their supports as they grow. Double rows or strong wigwams of bamboo canes are ideal

## Types of pea and bean support

**Rows of canes**
*Pairs of canes 15–23cm (6–9in) apart tied together at the top form a good support for runner beans. Secure the top with another cane as a crossbar.*

**Canes and netting**
*For double rows of peas, suspend 30–60cm (12–24in) of chicken wire, or plastic pea and bean netting, from 1.2m (4ft) canes placed at 1.2m (4ft) intervals.*

**Peasticks**
*These are usually prunings of hazel or birch, inserted in the soil at 30cm (12in) intervals. As the crops grow, the sticks form a natural-looking support system.*

for these plants (*see below*). String or twine can be used instead of some of the canes. Train one plant up each string or cane. Mesh supported by tall posts is also suitable for runner beans.

Broad beans are not natural climbers and should be supported by means of strings running between stakes along the bean row. A stake positioned every 1.2m (4ft), with strings running from stake to stake, will hold up the heaviest broad bean crop.

### SUPPORTS FOR PEAS

Peas climb by means of tendrils. Better yields and easier picking come from supporting peas with netting, sticks, or canes and string. These supports should be put in place as soon as the seedlings emerge. Rustic peasticks (*see above*) are renewable forest products that make good pea supports. Insert the sticks so that a continuous "hedge" of twigs is formed. Wire or plastic netting that is supported by stakes is an effective alternative. Peas need a continuous run of netting, possibly with a string on each side to restrain the crop.

### SOWING THE CROPS

Pea and bean seeds are large and fairly expensive. Deep sowing – possibly using a dibber (*see p.69*) – is needed for legume seeds, but this often leads to seeds being placed at a wet, cold, and airless soil level. Wrinkled-seeded cultivars of peas as well as runner and French bean seeds are prone to rot in low soil temperatures. Such seeds have to be sown when the soil warms in mid-spring, or started under cover (*see pp.62–65*). The seeds are very attractive to mice, so sowing indoors, in a length of guttering (*see facing page*), or in containers under cloches also avoids that problem. To increase the chances

**Positioning legumes for optimum growth and yield**
*Many peas and beans are tall and need some support. Since they cast shade, a distance of at least half the full height of the crop should be left between them and adjacent crops. Here, runner beans are grown on wigwams of canes about 90cm (3ft) away from marrow plants.*

of success even further, soak the seed for up to 24 hours before sowing, or try pre-germinating the seeds in the same way as for germination testing (*see p.61*). Sow them when they have roots 5mm (¼in) long, spacing them carefully and evenly in the drill, and discarding any that have no roots.

## SOWING UNDER COVER

Sowing in module trays (*see p.65*) is an economical way of raising legumes under cover. Another option is to sow three seeds to a 5cm (2in) or 8cm (3in) pot. Biodegradable pots are suitable for broad beans, which have tap roots that can be easily damaged. Deep pots, such as tube pots (*see p.62*) and root trainers (*see p.108*), are ideal for the long tap roots of runner beans. You should transplant the seedlings outdoors (*see below, right*) as soon as the roots hold the compost together.

Alternatively, the soil can be warmed, and rain excluded, with cloches (*see p.46*) or some clear film plastic placed over the soil about four weeks before sowing. In warm, moist soil, seed germination is rapid. Cloche and fleece protection for seedlings against cold, wind, rain, and birds is also useful in early to mid-spring.

Peas and beans have a relatively short harvest period, but this can be extended by using successional sowing (*see p.69*). The plants grow faster in summer than in spring, so later sowings should be more frequently made than early ones.

---

### Sowing pea seeds in a length of guttering

**1** **Three-quarters fill** a length of plastic guttering with seed compost and sow the seeds 5cm (2in) apart in 2 staggered rows. Fill with more compost, water, and label. Keep in a bright place under cover at a minimum of 10°C (50°F).

**2** **Draw out** a shallow drill outdoors to the depth of the guttering, when the seedlings are 8cm (3in) tall. Slide the entire section of seedlings into the drill, firm well, and water.

---

An effective way of deciding when to sow is to use the size of the preceding seedlings as a rough guide (*see individual crops, pp.98–100*).

## ROUTINE CARE

Legumes are grown in wide rows, and so are vulnerable to weeds. Mulching (*see pp.41–42*) reduces the need for weeding and hoeing, and keeps the soil moist. Use black plastic sheet mulches or organic mulches, but take care not to cover plant stems with organic matter.

Watering legumes is unnecessary before flowering, unless the plants wilt, because it promotes foliage growth at the expense of flowers. However, plentiful watering during the flowering period greatly increases the intensity of flowering and setting of pods. At least 22 litres of water per sq m (4 gallons per sq yd) will be needed each week for a good crop.

## HARVESTING PEAS AND BEANS

Garden legumes are unsurpassable in flavour and texture as long as they are consumed very soon after picking. Picking them in the morning, while the pods are cool, and keeping them in the refrigerator help to prolong their shelf life. Because these days commercially frozen legumes, especially peas, taste nearly as good as home-grown ones, some gardeners prefer to concentrate on growing the less common cultivars (*see individual crops, pp.98–100*). To harvest dry peas and beans, treat the pods in the same way as for saving seed (*see below*).

## SAVING SEEDS

Some legumes are self-pollinated, and therefore their seed can be saved in the knowledge that there is very little risk of cross-pollination, and the resulting plants will be true to type. To save the seed of known self-pollinators, select some early pods and mark them with coloured wool. Let the crop mature, and gather the pods before they split and shed the seed. Alternatively, hang up immature pods to finish ripening. Dry the pods in a cool place (*see p.61*) and shell them; leave the seeds to dry out again, then store them in a dark, cool, dry place. Correctly stored, they should last for several years.

▲ **Transplanting climbing beans**
*With their support system already in place, plant out young plants that were sown under cover as soon as they are large enough. Position one plant next to each cane.*

◄ **Pinching out growing tips**
*When the plants reach the top of the canes, pinch out their growing tips in order to stimulate the production of sideshoots.*

# A–Z OF LEGUMES

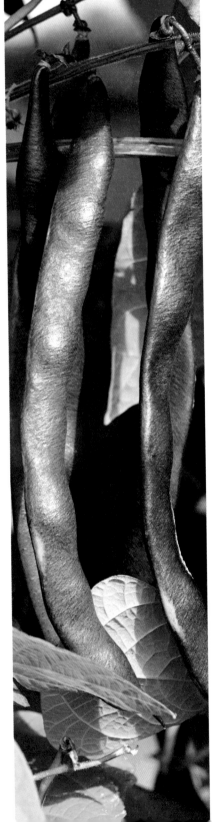

## Asparagus pea

*Lotus tetragonolobus*

| SEASON | SPRING | SUMMER | AUTUMN | WINTER |
|---|---|---|---|---|
| SOW | • • | | | |
| TRANSPLANT | • | | | |
| HARVEST | | • • • | | |

This annual is grown for its small, fluted pods. These have a fresh flavour, although they crop lightly and soon become stringy: average yield is 450g per 3m (1lb per 10ft) row. This pea has feathery foliage and red-brown flowers.

■ **Site and soil** Use an open site in full sun, with light but rich soil.

■ **Sowing and planting** Sow seed in mid-spring under cover (*see pp.96–97*), or in late spring outdoors, as for peas (*see facing page*).

| SOWING DEPTH | 4cm (1½in) deep in moist soils |
| | 5cm (2in) in dry soils |
| SEED SPACING | 25–30cm (10–12in) |
| ROW SPACING | 38cm (15in) apart |

■ **Routine care** No support needed, but sticks and canes keep it within bounds (*see p.96*).

■ **Harvesting** After two to three months, start picking immature pods, 2.5–5cm (1–2in) long, and continue regularly throughout summer.

■ **Common problems** As for pea. Pigeons strip off foliage in some areas, so you may need to provide protection. For symptoms and controls, *see* Plant Problems, *pp.246–264*.

## Broad bean

*Vicia faba*

| SEASON | SPRING | SUMMER | AUTUMN | WINTER |
|---|---|---|---|---|
| SOW | • • | | • • | • • |
| TRANSPLANT | • • | | | |
| HARVEST | | • • • • | | |

Broad, or fava, beans are delicious, easy to grow, and very hardy. Although these annuals are usually grown for the immature, green or white seeds or beans, young pods and even the shoot tips can be cooked and eaten. White seeds are reputed to be better flavoured than green ones. Traditional Longpod beans have eight seeds per pod, and Windsors, which have shorter, wider pods, have four large seeds per pod. Modern broad bean cultivars are intermediate in length between Longpods and Windsors, and have shorter stems and small, tender seeds. Broad bean yields average 3kg per 3m (6½lb per 10ft) row. Dwarf cultivars, because they grow only to about 60cm (2ft) – which is half the height of most broad bean cultivars – are especially suitable for growing in cloches, containers, and small gardens.

■ **Site and soil** Any moderately fertile, well-drained soil is suitable. Broad beans have a long tap root, so the soil should be deeply dug and

well-drained (*see pp.14–16*). The best yields are usually achieved on relatively heavy soils, but early crops do well on lighter soil if the plants are watered when in flower.

■ **Sowing and planting** Successional sowing in spring (*see p.69*) will give a constant crop from late spring to midsummer; sow the next batch when the preceding seedlings reach 8cm (3in). Dwarf cultivars are best for late harvests. You can sow outdoors in late winter if your soil is not waterlogged and the temperature is at least 5°C (41°F). In well-drained, sheltered gardens, autumn sowing is possible, although the crop may be lost in a severe winter. Alternatively, make autumn and winter sowings under cover, or winter ones indoors, transplanting in early to mid-spring.

| SOWING DEPTH | 8cm (3in) |
| SEED SPACING | 23cm (9in) |
| ROW SPACING | 45cm (18in) between single rows |
| | Double rows 23cm (9in) apart |
| | 60cm (24in) between rows |

■ **Routine care** Control weeds by hoeing, drawing a little soil around the base of the plants to support and protect them. Stake tall cultivars with stakes and string (*see p.96*). When the lowest blossom has set, pinch out the tops to promote earlier cropping and to remove any blackfly that may have appeared on the top shoots. Watering during flowering in dry spells greatly increases the crop.

■ **Harvesting** Crops mature in three to four months, although autumn- and winter-sown crops may take longer. Pick the pods regularly, before they have a chance to get too old – if the part of the seed that attaches it to the pod is brown or black, the pods are too old and the beans will probably be tough. The beans mature in succession, starting from the bottom of the haulm, and several pickings can therefore be taken from each crop.

■ **Common problems** Black bean aphid (*see p.252*) often sucks the plant sap, sometimes causing both leaves and stems to look soiled and stunted. Pea and bean weevil (*see p.258*) notches the leaves of young plants, but is not very harmful. Bean seed beetle (*see p.251*) and mice (*see p.257*) can damage the seeds. Chocolate spot (*see p.254*) is destructive in wet seasons, especially for overwintered crops. Rust (*see p.261*) may be a problem.

■ **Recommended cultivars**
'Aquadulce Claudia' ♥ – overwintering or early spring, Longpod, old favourite.
'Imperial Green Longpod' ♥ – disease- and weather-resistant. Suitable for exhibition.
'Jubilee Hysor' ♥ – Windsor, with excellent flavour and acceptable yield.
'Stereo' – Small pods, mild flavour, heavy crop.
'The Sutton' ♥ – dwarf, old favourite, ideal for containers and cloches. Small, tender beans.
'Witkiem Manita' ♥ – spring or autumn sowing. Fast-growing, long, high-quality pods.

# French bean

*Phaseolus vulgaris*

| SEASON | SPRING | SUMMER | AUTUMN | WINTER |
|---|---|---|---|---|
| SOW | • • | • • | | |
| TRANSPLANT | | • | | |
| HARVEST | | • • | • • • • • | |

Heavy cropping, trouble-free French or kidney beans picked fresh from the garden are a revelation in flavour. They ripen to "haricot beans" that may be dried and stored for winter use. Half-ripe beans are called "flageolets" and are shelled and eaten like peas. French beans have pods that are round or flattened in cross-section. Kenya beans, sold in supermarkets, are French beans. Although green beans are common, cultivars with yellow, purple, and red- or purple-flecked pods are available, too, making attractive and unusual plants for the ornamental vegetable garden.

Most French beans are dwarf and make a low, bushy annual plant. Climbing French beans, however, can be grown up supports in the same way as runner beans (*see p.96*). Alternatively, create a wigwam with four to eight 2.5m (8ft) canes and sow three seeds on the inside of each. Dwarf beans mature earlier than climbing ones and are especially valuable in cloches and frames; but climbing beans may yield more heavily and make better use of space in small gardens and greenhouses. The average yield of French beans is 4.5kg per 3m (10lb per 10ft) row.

French beans are self-pollinating, meaning that cultivars will come true to type from home-saved seeds.

■ **Site and soil** Both dwarf and climbing types are sensitive to frost and cannot be grown outside before early summer or after mid-autumn. Sheltered warm sites are best, but cloche or fleece protection (*see pp.46–48*) will help elsewhere. Light, fertile, and neutral soils are ideal, but any well-drained soil that has had organic matter added is suitable. French beans may be grown in pots, which can be started off in greenhouses to crop outdoors from early summer onwards.

■ **Sowing and planting** French beans require at least 12°C (54°F) to germinate. Sow under cover, one seed to a 8cm (3in) pot (*see p.64*), in mid-spring, and in cloches in late spring, or under cover at any time if your soil is cold and wet. Plant out the seedlings when they are 8cm (3in) tall. Pre-warming the soil with clear film plastic or cloches for several weeks prior to transplanting can be beneficial.

Leaving room for picking access and inserting supports if appropriate, plant 32–43 seeds per sq m (sq yd), evenly spacing them in single or double rows. The latter provides better yields, and, if they are the dwarf, bushy type, the plants will also suppress the weed growth between the rows.

From late spring to midsummer, sow in succession in open ground, as long as the soil is moist, every two weeks for a continuous supply until autumn.

| SOWING DEPTH | 5cm (2in) |
|---|---|
| SEED SPACING | 5–10cm (2–4in) single row |
| | 15cm (6in) double row |
| ROW SPACING | 45cm (18in) between single rows |
| | Double rows 23cm (9in) apart, |
| | 45cm (18in) between rows |

■ **Routine care** Mulching (*see pp.41–42 and p.72*) improves the growth of the plants and keeps their pods free from soiling. In the absence of mulch, drawing soil around the plant bases to a depth of 8–10cm (3–4in) helps to support them and suppress weeds. The numbers of pods and their texture can be improved by watering the soil to keep it moist, from flowering time onwards. Protect early and late crops with cloches.

■ **Harvesting and storing** Crops take two to three months to mature. Picking every two or three days encourages production of more beans and avoids any deterioration in quality that may occur once the seeds begin to swell. Pick in the early morning and store in the refrigerator to retain freshness. Unlike older cultivars, modern ones are free from strings on pods. Covering in mid-autumn with cloches prolongs the harvest for a few weeks.

■ **Common problems** Slugs (*see p.262*) and black bean aphid (*see p.252*) are the most common pests, but bean seed fly (*see p.252*), birds (*see p.252*), mice (*see p.257*), root aphid (*see p.261*), and red spider mite (*see p.261*) may occur. French beans may suffer from anthracnose (*see p.251*) and halo blight (*see p.256*), which are both serious, and increasingly rust (*see p.261*), but the most common disease is foot and root rot (*p.255*); avoid it by using a different site each year.

■ **Recommended cultivars**

**Climbing French bean**

'Borlotta Lingua di Fuoco' – red-flecked green pods, use fresh or dried.

'Hunter' ♀ – heavy crops of flat pods.

'Kingston Gold' ♀ – yellow, flat pods, ideal for ornamental wigwams, delicious flavour.

**Dwarf French bean**

'Allegria' ♀ – heavy, fine-quality crops.

'Safari' ♀ – pencil-sized pods, compact and reliable plants.

'Stanley' ♀ – tall plants, heavy crop over a long period.

# Lima bean

*Phaseolus lunatus*

| SEASON | SPRING | SUMMER | AUTUMN | WINTER |
|---|---|---|---|---|
| SOW | • • | | | |
| TRANSPLANT | | • | | |
| HARVEST | | | • • | |

Sold in supermarkets as butter beans, these tender annuals or short-lived perennials are grown as dwarf bushes or as climbers. The beans are either used green, in the same way as runner beans, or dried. The sprouted seeds, often called beansprouts, are also edible. Average yield is 560g per 3m (1¼lb per 10ft) row. There are no cultivars currently available.

■ **Site and soil** Lima beans need a well-drained, moderately fertile soil that warms up quickly in spring, and a site in full sun with protection from cold winds.

■ **Sowing and planting** Seeds need 18°C (64°F) to germinate, so it is best to sow in spring in a propagator (*see p.63*) and transplant in early summer when they are 10–15cm (4–6in) tall. Alternatively, pre-germinate them on damp absorbent paper (*see p.61*) before sowing *in situ* outdoors.

| SOWING DEPTH | 5cm (2in) |
|---|---|
| SEED SPACING | 15cm (6in) |
| ROW SPACING | Climbing beans: double rows |
| | 30cm (12in) apart, 1.5m (5ft) |
| | between rows |
| | Dwarf beans: as for French bean |

■ **Routine care** Grow as for runner bean (*see p.100*); they crop best in warm, sheltered sites, with fleece, cloche, or greenhouse protection. Minimum temperature needed is 20°C/68°F; reduce humidity and ventilate at flowering time to encourage pollination.

■ **Harvesting** When crops mature – in three to four months – pick regularly, two or three times per week, so pods do not become over-mature, which will suppress further flowering as the pods will be using up vital energy.

■ **Common problems** Lima beans usually suffer the same problems as French beans (*see left*). Greenhouse crops may also be prone to whitefly (*see p.264*).

# Pea

*Pisum sativum*

| SEASON | SPRING | SUMMER | AUTUMN | WINTER |
|---|---|---|---|---|
| SOW | • • • • | | • • | • • |
| TRANSPLANT | • • • | | | |
| HARVEST | | • • • • • | | |

Annual garden peas include robust early peas, tiny tasty petit pois, dwarf cultivars good for exposed, windy gardens, and tall cultivars that can be trained up supports to save space. The best-quality peas have wrinkled seeds, but are not as robust as round-seeded cultivars. Peas in which the whole pod is eaten include mangetout or snow peas, with thin pods, and sugar or snap peas, with thick fleshy pods. For ornamental kitchen gardens, cultivars that have coloured flowers and pods are attractive. Peas are easy to grow and, when picked fresh, their flavour is incomparably better than peas from shops. Modern developments include leafless and semi-leafless peas, where tendrils replace the normal foliage. These are self-supporting and much less vulnerable to bird damage. Modern peas have 2–3 pods at each flowering node, compared to the single pod of older peas. Such modern peas are dwarf in habit and more easily supported, and still yield as much as taller cultivars – an average yield being 3kg per 3m (6½lb per 10ft) row.

■ **Site and soil** Well-drained, neutral to alkaline soil that holds moisture is best. Good

soil structure is important and this can be achieved by adding organic matter (see pp.22–23). Open sunny situations are ideal.

■ **Sowing and planting** Late autumn and winter sowings of peas raised in troughs or pots are more likely to succeed, especially if covered by cloches, than seed sown direct into the soil, especially if it is cold and heavy – temperatures should be at least 5°C (41°F). Birds and mice may also eat seeds sown outdoors. Seeds may be sown in guttering to avoid this (see p.97). Peas sown after mid-spring may succumb to powdery mildew. In warm areas, autumn sowings may succeed, especially under cloches. Sow in succession, when the preceding seedlings are 5cm (2in) tall.

Peas can be sown in single drills or in double rows in a wide drill (see p.67) that are easy to hoe, or in beds with around 40 plants per sq m (yd) for optimum yield. However, beds are difficult to harvest and keep weed-free. An alternative is to sow in three drills, 13cm (5in) apart, with the seeds also spaced 13cm (5in) apart. Space each set of three rows at the same distance as the eventual height of the plants, as given on the packet. This way of sowing gives you a good crop of plants that are easy to harvest and hoe.

| SOWING DEPTH | 4cm (1½in) in moist soils |
| | 5cm (2in) in dry soils |
| SEED SPACING | 5cm (2in) in single or double rows |
| | 13cm (5in) in triple rows |
| ROW SPACING | Equal to plants' eventual height |

■ **Routine care** Many dwarf, especially leafless, cultivars support themselves, but better yields and easier picking come from using supports (see p.96). Regular hoeing and weeding are essential. Watering at flowering time, and again as the pods swell, greatly increases the crop, but irrigation before this time merely produces leaves, with little increase in harvest.

■ **Harvesting and storing** Unless sown in winter, early, dwarf cultivars mature in about 12 weeks, while higher-yielding main crop cultivars may take 14 weeks. Gather peas as soon as they are ready, to encourage the production of more pods. Pick peas shortly before they are needed, and once picked keep them cool, ideally in a refrigerator.

■ **Common problems** Pea moth (see p.258) gets into the pods spoiling the crop, and is hard to control. Occasionally pea aphid and pea thrips and pea seed beetle (see p.258) attack. Pea and bean weevil (see p.258) may eat the foliage. Using mouse traps and protecting seedbeds with fleece are the best counter-measures against, respectively, mice (see p.257) and birds (see p.252). Foot and root rot (see p.255) is troublesome where soil is wet and cold. Sowing indoors and transplanting peas is the best remedy, but later sowings are usually unaffected. Powdery mildew (see p.260) is the worst disease, but usually affects only late crops. Resistant cultivars are available. Pea leaf and pod spot (see p.258) is serious but uncommon.

■ **Recommended cultivars**
**Pea**
'Cavalier' ♀ – late. Long, mildew-resistant pods, mostly paired. Sweet, tender peas.
'Kelvedon Wonder' ♀ – early dwarf; also for later sowing. Heavy cropping, weather-resistant, old favourite. Small, tender peas.
'Greensage' ♀ – semi-leafless, needs little staking, limited bird damage, sweet flavour.
**Mangetout or snow pea**
'Oregon Sugar Pod' ♀ – tall. Tolerates poor soil and bad weather. Large, delicious pods.
**Sugar or snap pea**
'Cascadia' ♀ – medium height, heavy crop over a long period.

# Runner bean

*Phaseolus coccineus*

| SEASON | SPRING | SUMMER | AUTUMN | WINTER |
|---|---|---|---|---|
| SOW | • • • • | | | |
| TRANSPLANT | | • | | |
| HARVEST | | • • • • | | |

Runner beans are tender perennials, grown as annuals. Most are climbers growing up to 3m (10ft) tall. Dwarf cultivars, ideal for early crops in cloches and frames, are also available. Most have red flowers and red speckled seeds, but white-flowered, white-seeded cultivars are widely grown. Unusual beans include black-seeded ones and those with bicoloured flowers. The latter are valuable in ornamental kitchen gardens. Runner beans have a stronger flavour than French beans and give a heavier yield: 6kg per 3m (13lb per 10ft) row.

■ **Site and soil** Runner beans are sensitive to frost, and need warm, sheltered conditions where their insect pollinators will be most effective. Deep, fertile soil holding ample water is best. Preparing a trench filled with organic matter (see p.95) is a traditional way of ensuring this, although acceptable crops will result from ground prepared by normal digging methods (see pp.37–40).

■ **Sowing and planting** For successful germination, the soil temperature should be at least 12°C (54°F). Heavy, wet soils can be pre-warmed by covering them with clear film plastic or cloches for about four weeks before sowing. Alternatively, raise plants in deep pots (see p.62) indoors from mid-spring, planting out in early summer. Protect young plants with fleece or cloches to help them establish. The earliest crops come from dwarf cultivars grown under cloches or fleece, removing the covering at flowering time to allow pollination to take place. A midsummer sowing will prolong the harvest into autumn.

Sow runner beans in double rows using sturdy supports, such as 2.5m (8ft) long canes (see p.96), ideally with one plant per cane. If canes are in short supply, strings may replace alternate canes, or all of the canes may be replaced by nylon netting. Alternatively, use six to eight canes to make a wigwam and grow one plant up each cane. Dwarf cultivars need

no supports. Pinching out the tips of climbers stops them climbing, and they can be grown as bushes. Problems with failed pollination are less severe with pinched or dwarf crops.

| SOWING DEPTH | 5cm (2in) |
| SEED SPACING | 15cm (6in) |
| ROW SPACING | Climbing beans: double rows |
| | 60cm (2ft) apart, 1.5m (5ft) |
| | between rows |
| | Dwarf beans: as for French bean |

■ **Routine care** Twist young shoots around the canes to help them start to climb. Pinch out the growing tips (see p.97) when shoots reach the top of supports to stop them becoming top-heavy. Watering is vital in dry weather as soon as flower buds appear. During flowering, 5–9 litres per sq m (1–2 gallons per sq yd) every 3–4 days is needed. Sometimes pods fail to form despite plentiful flowering. Lack of soil moisture is the usual cause and abundant irrigation the remedy. Cold, windy weather may depress pollinator activity. Warm nights can lead to failure to set pods; the traditional remedy of spraying flowers with water is usually ineffective – but may cool flowers.

■ **Harvesting** Crops mature in about three months. Pick regularly, 2–3 times a week, to stop pods becoming over-mature, which will suppress further flowering. Similarly, remove any old pods. Saving seed (see p.97) is usually worthwhile, but if more than one cultivar is grown nearby the seedlings may not come true to type.

■ **Common problems** As for French beans (see p.99). Runner beans also suffer from poor setting (see p.259).

■ **Recommended cultivars**
'Hestia' – dwarf, bicoloured flowers, patio vegetable.
'Red Rum' ♀ – reliable, disease-resistant. Early maturing, tasty, tender beans.
'Starlight' – Good pollination even in hot dry periods, heavy crop.
'White Lady' ♀ – heavy crops of good flavour and quality.

# Yard long bean

*Vigna unguiculata* subsp. *sesquipedalis*

| SEASON | SPRING | SUMMER | AUTUMN | WINTER |
|---|---|---|---|---|
| SOW | • • | | | |
| TRANSPLANT | | • | | |
| HARVEST | | | • • | |

Yard long or asparagus beans are highly tender, tropical plants, up to 4m (12ft) long, with pods that can be a metre (yard) long in optimum conditions, where average yields are 560g per 3m (1¼lb per 10ft) row. In a warm site or under unheated glass or fleece, yard long beans can be grown in the same way as Lima beans (see p.99). They will not tolerate cold soils and chilly nights. Crops take 3–4 months to mature. Pick the pods when 30–45cm (12–18in) long, before they become woody. Seeds are not readily available in cool areas.

# Growing salad crops

The crops described here are mainly salad leaves, but radishes are included since they are grown primarily for use in salads. Apart from the traditional lettuce, salad leaves also include chicory, corn salad, endive, ice plant, komatsuna, land cress, mibuna and mizuna greens, mustard and cress, rocket, and summer and winter purslane. Salad crops are fast-growing – if sown in spring, radishes will mature in four weeks, and lettuces in 13 weeks. Salads can quickly become coarse and hot-flavoured, and run to seed, however. Sowing small batches in succession (*see p.69*) helps to overcome this problem. Using several cultivars, or crops that take different amounts of time to reach maturity, also helps avoid peaks and troughs in supply.

Leafy salads need little in the way of feeding; a light application of nitrogen fertilizer to the soil before sowing or transplanting should be sufficient.

## TEMPERATURE REQUIREMENTS

Leafy salad crops are quite sensitive to temperature, and this affects seed germination – they will not germinate if they are too cold, or even too hot. They grow best in a temperature range of around 10–20°C (50–68°F). Low temperatures of below 5°C (41°F) and slow growth rates can lead to a coarse flavour and texture, and may prevent crops such as lettuces from developing proper hearts. The use of cold frames, cloches, and fleece (*see pp.43–48*) alleviates this problem. Some salads, endive and chicory for example, flower prematurely, or bolt, if exposed to several weeks of low temperatures. These crops cannot be safely sown before midsummer unless bolt-resistant cultivars are used. Some crops will also bolt if exposed to high temperatures (*see above right*) as they mature.

## SOWING THE CROPS

Because of the sensitivity of leafy salads to temperature (*see above*), it is usually easier to achieve even germination, especially with early sowings, by sowing under cover (*see p.64*). If sown outdoors (*see p.68*), germination will depend on the warmth and moistness of the seedbed. Where soils do not

**Salad crops under a floating mulch**
*Horticultural fleece protects early crops from frosts and also deters flying insects and birds. Lay the fleece so that it floats lightly over the crops, and weigh it down at the sides. Check the crop regularly, and loosen if necessary.*

readily form a fine tilth, or if they form a cap after heavy rain so that seedlings cannot push through, raising leafy salads in modules under cover is preferable.

Sowing leafy salads in modules (*see p.65*) also saves space and time. Sow 2–3 seeds per cell, later thinning to the strongest seedling. Some lettuce cultivars need light to germinate; when germination rates are disappointing, try sowing on the surface in module trays, keeping the seeds moist by putting the tray in a clear plastic bag or propagator away from direct sun. For radishes, sow 4–5 seeds to a 8cm (3in) pot and plant out the entire clump of seedlings (*see below*), to avoid damaging the roots.

Outdoors, cover early sowings with fleece or cloches (*see pp.46–48*) to avoid problems with low temperatures. In

**Transplanting radish seedlings**
*For successional batches of small radishes, sprinkle a small quantity of seeds in 8cm (3in) pots indoors at two-weekly intervals. When the roots bind the compost, plant out the entire potful to grow on as a clump.*

**Bolting lettuces**
*Leafy salads, especially non-hearting types of lettuce, like these 'Revolution' cultivars, quickly bolt and run to seed in hot weather or if short of water. The leaves become bitter and fit only for the compost heap.*

summer, leafy salads germinate better if sown in light shade, such as provided by a fence or tree, and if protected from extremes of dryness and heat. In hot weather, over 25°C (77°F), lettuce seed may become dormant several hours after sowing. Avoid this by sowing in the afternoon so that the critical period falls in the cool of the night. Watering after sowing can also help.

## THINNING SEEDLINGS

Leafy salad crops grow quickly, making timely thinning difficult. There are two ways to alleviate this problem. Remove surplus seedlings (*see p.68*) as soon as they can be handled, in three stages: at the first stage, leave just a thumb's width between seedlings; at the second stage, leave half of the intended final spacing; finally, thin to the final spacing. You can use the thinnings in salads. Alternatively, try station sowing (*see p.68*), in which 3–5 seeds are sown together. Thin the seedlings to two strong-growing ones; later, when they have developed into young plants, choose the healthier, sturdier one and remove the other.

## TRANSPLANTING

For plants raised under cover, transplant to their outdoor positions before they become too large for the pot or module cell (*see p.70*). Bare-root transplants from an outdoor seedbed work well only as long as the seedlings are very small. When a newly sown row comes up and there are gaps, fill these in with surplus

seedlings thinned out from better populated parts of the row. Care must be taken with the tap roots of lettuces, endive, and chicory when transplanting. Radishes have delicate roots and should not be transplanted bare-root. Naturally, with transplanted seedlings there will be a check in growth, and these plants will mature later than the others. This can be an advantage, however, avoiding the problem of simultaneous maturation.

## INTERCROPPING AND CATCH CROPPING

Intercropping salad crops with longer-term vegetables (see pp.69 and 71) allows for a good return from a given space. A checkerboard planting pattern uses space best, but alternate rows are easier to manage. Lettuces and other leafy salads may be grown with Brussels sprouts and cauliflowers, for example, since they appreciate the same high-nitrogen soil conditions. Radishes and parsnips (see p.69) thrive on low levels of nitrogen. For details, see individual crops (pp.103–107).

Salads can also be used for a catch crop (see p.69). Grow early leafy salads in an area set aside for purple sprouting broccoli and leeks to be planted out in late summer, for example. At the other end of the season, peas, beans, and early potatoes harvested before midsummer leave space for a catch crop of endives, radicchio, corn salad, or winter radishes. Spaces in ornamental beds can also be used for catch crops of salads.

## Forcing and blanching chicory

**1** **In autumn,** lift chicon types (see p.103) and trim the leaves to 1cm (½in) from the roots. Position upright in a deep box on a layer of moist peat, or peat substitute. Cover with another 23cm (9in) of peat and firm this down. Put the box in a warm, dark place.

**2** **Several weeks later,** when they have grown to 15–20cm (6–8in) in length, remove the chicons from the box and cut them away from the roots.

## EXTENDING THE SEASON

Many salads, such as endive, chicory, corn salad, and rocket, can tolerate cold, and if protected (see pp.43–48) can be gathered from early autumn to winter. Chicory chicons may be forced either indoors (see above) or outdoors (see p.103) for harvest in winter. Winter radishes and cut-and-come-again leaves (see below) may be harvested in winter. In spring, overwintered lettuces, rocket, and land cress will be ready. If overwintering crops, make sure you choose suitable cultivars and sow at the correct time (see pp.103–107).

## CONTAINER GROWING

Salads can be grown in containers if garden space is limited. Large tubs are best for headed salads, but summer radishes, leafy crops, and cut-and-come-again leaves suit small pots or growing bags – ones that have already supported a cucumber or tomato crop are fine for salads, as their depleted nutrient levels are sufficient for salad crops. Careful watering will be required so as not to let the compost dry out.

## SAVING SEEDS

Lettuces are self-pollinating, so that home-saved seed will be true to type, especially if other plants are positioned more than 8m (25ft) away. The seed from rocket, which is a species and not a cultivar, will also come true.

## Growing cut-and-come-again salad crops

Most leafy salad crops can be grown to produce several flushes of young, tender leaves for eating. After one cut, the plants regrow to create another crop. Two or three harvests can be made from each sowing. This method is suitable for crops sown either in pots, modules, or a growing bag (see right) or outdoors in a seedbed. To cover the whole season, sow successionally (see p.69). Leafy vegetables other than salads can be treated in this way:

Amaranth (see p.125)    Kale (see p.80)
Swiss chard (see p.128)  Spinach (see p.128)
Leaf celery (see p.122)  Sorrel (see p.145)
Radish leaves (see p.106)

**1** **Plant seedlings** of non-hearting salads closely in a growing bag (here oriental greens, land cress, and lettuces). After 3–6 weeks, cut the leaves to 5cm (2in), leaving a stump with enough side-buds to regrow.

**2** **After two weeks,** the crops have already begun to regrow from the stumps. In another 1–2 weeks, a fresh crop of salad leaves may be harvested, and another one in a further 3–6 weeks.

# A–Z OF SALAD CROPS

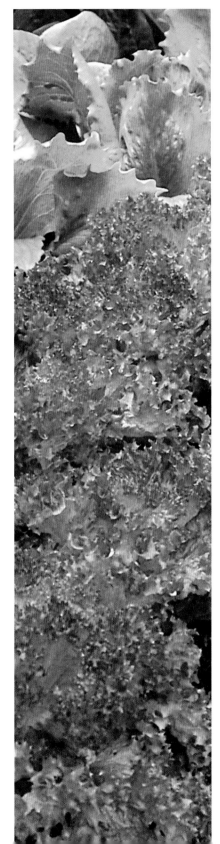

## Chicory

*Cichorium intybus*

| SEASON | SPRING | SUMMER | AUTUMN | WINTER |
|---|---|---|---|---|
| SOW | | • • • • • • • • | • | • |
| TRANSPLANT | | • | | |
| HARVEST | • | | • • • • • • • | |

Chicory is relatively cold- and drought-resistant, and makes a handsome plant in the ornamental vegetable garden. When eaten raw in salads, the taste of the leaves can be bitter, although sometimes such bitterness is welcome. Chicory can also be cooked. There are three types of chicory.

Witloof, or Belgian, chicory grows as a rosette of leaves forming a deep root, which when harvested and trimmed can be forced in a warm, dark place to produce white, compact, leafy buds, or chicons (*see p.102 and below*), with the bitterness blanched out.

Red chicory, also known as radicchio, and sugarloaf chicory both form hearts, like those of lettuces. The heart leaves are less bitter than the outer leaves, being naturally blanched or deprived of light. Red and sugarloaf chicory will normally yield 8–9 heads per 3m (10ft) row. A proportion of plants always fails to produce good hearts; older cultivars are especially vulnerable.

■ **Site and soil**  Chicory prefers an open, sunny site, but will tolerate light shade. It does well on poor soils and needs little fertilizer, making it suitable for organic gardens.

■ **Sowing and planting**  Sow Witloof chicory, in late spring and early summer for forcing (*see below*) in autumn. Sow red and sugarloaf chicories from mid-spring to late summer. Spring sowings may bolt (*see p.101*) due to cold and even bolt-resistant cultivars are safest raised in modules in warm conditions, then planted out beneath fleece or cloches. To grow red and sugarloaf chicories as cut-and-come-again crops (*see p.102*), sow indoors in late winter, spring, and autumn, or sow outdoors from early summer to late summer.

| SOWING DEPTH | 1cm (½in) |
|---|---|
| PLANT SPACING | 23cm (9in) for Witloof type |
| | 30cm (1ft) for red, sugarloaf types |
| ROW SPACING | 30cm (1ft) |

■ **Routine care**  Witloof chicory produces chicons from roots that are 3.5–5cm (1½–2in) in diameter. To force these *in situ* outdoors, cut off the leaves in early autumn, leaving a 5cm (2in) stub. Draw soil over the plants into a 15cm (6in) ridge. The chicons will form under the soil, especially if cloches (*see p.46*) are used to provide extra warmth and rain protection. However, better results are often achieved by forcing indoors (*see p.102*) at a temperature of 10–18°C (50–64°F). Although soil or a similar covering used to be required for well-shaped, compact

chicons, modern cultivars (*see below*) need only darkness, such as that provided by an inverted bucket. It is a good idea to keep a stock of roots for forcing in boxes of moist soil or sand until they are needed. Some kinds of red chicory may also be forced to produce small chicons.

Red and sugarloaf chicories need watering in dry spells and feeding with a nitrogen-rich fertilizer if growth flags. For late supplies dig up some of the plants and replant them in an unheated greenhouse. Alternatively, protect them with straw or a tunnel cloche (*see p.46*).

■ **Harvesting**  Blanched chicons of Witloof chicory will be ready for eating about a month after being covered for forcing. The heads of red and sugarloaf chicory should be gathered after 2–3 months, when they are fully formed and firm. Unlike those of lettuces, the heads are long-lasting (2–8 weeks, depending on the weather) and can be stored in a cool place until needed. After harvesting, the resulting stumps will often sprout another crop of usable leaves, about 2–6 weeks later.

■ **Common problems**  Slugs (*see p.262*), aphids (*see p.251*), lettuce root aphid (*see p.257*), and caterpillars can damage chicory foliage and roots. Tip burn (*see p.263*) is a physiological disorder associated with lack of calcium, and especially troublesome on very dry, light soils.

■ **Recommended cultivars**
'Palla Rossa'– red chicory, an old favourite.
'Pain de Sucre' – sugarloaf, hearted.
'Rossa Di Verona' – red chicory, traditional cultivar, good flavour, variable heads.
'Witloof' – good for forcing.
'Zoom' – Witloof chicory, for forcing.

## Corn salad

*Valerianella locusta*

| SEASON | SPRING | SUMMER | AUTUMN | WINTER |
|---|---|---|---|---|
| SOW/PLANT | • • | • • • • | | |
| TRANSPLANT | | • • | | |
| HARVEST | • • | • • • | • • • | • • • |

Corn salad provides tasty salad leaves in rosettes with a mild, earthy flavour in autumn and winter when lettuce crops have gone over. It can be useful in summer salads as well. If sown before midsummer, however, it is liable to run quickly to seed. It is used in supermarket salad packs, often called lamb's lettuce or mache. There are two types: a large-leaved form and a smaller, darker-leaved form. Corn salad matures in 4–12 weeks, and yields 18–20 plants per 3m (10ft) row.

■ **Site and soil**  Any moderately fertile soil in a sunny, open position is suitable. For autumn and winter crops, protection with cloches, cold frames, or even a fleece tunnel cloche (*see pp.46–48*) improves quality and reliability.

■ **Sowing and planting**  Either sow in moist soil where the plants are to grow, or raise

seedlings in module trays for planting out as soon as they can be handled (*see p.101*). Corn salad may also be grown as a cut-and-come-again crop (*see p.102*).

| SOWING DEPTH | 1cm (½in) |
| PLANT SPACING | 10cm (4in) |
| ROW SPACING | 15cm (6in) |

■ **Routine care** Thin seedlings (*see p.101*), and use the thinnings for salads. Watering in dry spells is sometimes helpful, but top-dressings of fertilizer are unnecessary.

■ **Harvesting** After 4–12 weeks, harvest by picking choice leaves or cutting the head from the lower part of the plant, which may resprout for further harvests.

■ **Common problems** Aphids, slugs, and snails are occasionally troublesome. For symptoms and controls, see Plant Problems, *p.251 and p.262*.

■ **Recommended cultivars**
'Cavallo' ♥ – small-leaved, neat growth.
'Large Leafed English' – large-leaved.
'Verte de Cambrai' – small-leaved, vigorous.
'Vit' – modern, small-leaved, earthy flavour.

# Endive

*Cichorium endivia*

| SEASON | SPRING | SUMMER | AUTUMN | WINTER |
|---|---|---|---|---|
| SOW | • • | • • • | | |
| TRANSPLANT | | • • | | |
| HARVEST | | • | • • • • | • |

Endive is similar to lettuce, although it has a bitter taste, and grows as a rosette. The leaves may be curled (frisée type) or broad-leaved (Batavian type). The former are extremely attractive in gardens or salads, but the hardier broad-leaved endive is more reliable for late crops. The bitterness can be reduced by excluding light to whiten or blanch the leaves (*see below*), making a refreshing late-summer or early-winter salad or cooked vegetable, although sometimes unblanched bitterness is appreciated in salads.

Endives can withstand light frosts, and therefore remain usable into the autumn. They mature over a period of 12 weeks, and will require an additional two weeks to be blanched. Plants should yield 9–10 heads per 3m (10ft) row.

■ **Site and soil** Endives prefer an open, sunny site and fertile, moisture-retentive soil, with only low levels of nitrogen. Light shade is tolerable for midsummer crops.

■ **Sowing and planting** Either sow in module trays under cover in spring (*see p.64*) for transplanting in early to midsummer, or sow direct outdoors in early summer. Early crops may be liable to bolt (*see p.101*), but bolt-resistant cultivars are available. Endives may also be grown as a cut-and-come-again crop (*see p.102*) under protection from spring to late summer.

| SOWING DEPTH | 1cm (½in) |
| PLANT SPACING | 23cm (9in) |
| ROW SPACING | 30–35cm (12–14in) |

■ **Routine care** Using cloches or unheated greenhouse protection (*see pp.43–48*) will extend the harvest period into winter. Early sowings may bolt (*see p.101*) if exposed to excess cold, of less than 5°C (15°F) for several days early in life. Using bolt-resistant cultivars (*see below*) and cloches or fleece coverings (*see p.101*) can help to counter this problem.

■ **Harvesting** When the heads reach full size, usually three months after sowing, blanch each one by covering the entire plant for about ten days (or 20 days in cold weather), with an inverted, lightproof container such as a bucket, or by laying an inverted dinner plate over the central area. Rots can be damaging at this stage; covering the heads with a cloche can help to dry them out. Alternatively, use twine to tie the head into a tight bunch in order to exclude light from the inner leaves. Use the heads as soon as they are blanched, since greenness and bitterness will soon return when they are exposed to light again.

■ **Common problems** Slugs (*see p.262*), aphids (*see p.251*), lettuce root aphid (*see p.257*), and caterpillars can damage foliage and roots. Tip burn (*see p.263*), associated with a lack of calcium, occurs mainly on dry, light soils.

■ **Recommended cultivars**
'Grobo' – broad-leaved, bolt-resistant.
'Moss Curled' – curled type, old favourite, summer and autumn crops.
'Pancalieri' ♥ – curled, bolt-resistant.
'Wallone' – traditional, reliable, good flavour.

# Ice plant

*Mesembryanthemum crystallinum*

| SEASON | SPRING | SUMMER | AUTUMN | WINTER |
|---|---|---|---|---|
| SOW | • | | | |
| TRANSPLANT | | • | | |
| HARVEST | | • • • • | • | |

These trailing tender perennials have unusual, swollen, succulent leaves. The leaves and young stems have a tangy flavour when eaten raw in salads or cooked in the same way as spinach. The plants mature in 4–12 weeks, yielding a 4.5kg (10lb) crop per 3m (10ft) row. Named cultivars are not offered.

■ **Site and soil** Well-drained, fertile, moisture-retentive soil and a sunny site are best.

■ **Sowing and planting** Sow under cover in module trays (*see p.64*), planting out when frost no longer threatens in early summer. New plants may be raised later from soft-tip cuttings, taken from non-flowering shoots and rooted in well-drained compost, for summer supplies. Ice plant may also be grown as a cut-and-come-again crop (*see p.102*).

| SOWING DEPTH | 2cm (¾in) |
| SEED SPACING | 15cm (6in) |
| ROW SPACING | 30cm (1ft) |

■ **Routine care** Thin seedlings (*see p.68*), and use the thinnings for salads. Watering in dry spells is sometimes helpful, but top-dressings of fertilizer are unnecessary.

■ **Harvesting** Pick tender young leaves and stems as soon as they are large enough. Regular harvesting encourages production of tender regrowth. Pickings will stay fresh for several days in a refrigerator.

■ **Common problems** Slugs are the only real problem. For symptoms and controls, *see* Plant Problems, *p.262*.

# Komatsuna

*Brassica rapa* var. *perviridis*

| SEASON | SPRING | SUMMER | AUTUMN | WINTER |
|---|---|---|---|---|
| SOW | | • • | | |
| TRANSPLANT | | | • | |
| HARVEST | | | • • | • • • • |

Komatsuna, or mustard spinach, is a diverse group of leafy brassicas with glossy green foliage that may be eaten raw in autumn and winter salads or cooked in the same way as spinach. They will grow into large, robust plants if left to mature fully, but can be harvested earlier, as small plants, if desired. This affects how they are grown (*see below*). The plants mature in 4–12 weeks, and yield 6–9 heads per 3m (10ft) row. Named cultivars are seldom offered.

■ **Site and soil** Open, sunny sites and fertile soils are best, but light shade is acceptable for midsummer crops.

■ **Sowing and planting** Sow outdoors in mid- to late summer or in module trays (*see p.64*) in late summer for transplanting. Thin the seedlings (*see p.101*) to 10cm (4in) if you desire only small plants, and 45cm (18in) for large ones. Komatsuna may also be grown as a cut-and-come-again crop (*see p.102*).

| SOWING DEPTH | 1cm (½in) |
| SEED SPACING | 2.5cm (1in) |
| ROW SPACING | 23cm (9in) for small plants |
| | 45cm (18in) for large plants |

■ **Routine care** Komatsuna will tolerate temperatures as low as −12°C (10°F), and is fairly drought-tolerant, so little attention is required, but a few plants may be lifted and grown under cover for a winter crop in case of extreme temperatures.

■ **Harvesting** Pick choice leaves as soon as they are ready. Regrowth will occur, giving a prolonged harvest period.

■ **Common problems** Flea beetle (*see p.255*) and slugs (*see p.262*) may cause minor damage. Cabbage root fly (*see p.253*), which can be very destructive, is best avoided by growing under fleece or insect-proof mesh (*see p.48*). As a member of the brassica family, this crop might also be affected by a range of problems. These include birds, boron deficiency, bolting, caterpillars, clubroot, cutworm, damping off, downy mildew, frost damage, leaf spot, mealy cabbage aphid, leatherjackets, molybdenum deficiency, whitefly, and white blister. Grow in the brassica part of the rotation (*see p.31*) to avoid clubroot

and other soil-borne brassica problems. For symptoms and controls, *see* Plant Problems, *pp.246–264.*

# Land cress

*Barbarea verna*

| SEASON | SPRING | SUMMER | AUTUMN | WINTER |
|---|---|---|---|---|
| SOW | • • • • • | | | |
| TRANSPLANT | | | • • | |
| HARVEST | • | | • • • • • • • | |

Land, American, or upland cress resembles watercress, with glossy green leaves and a strong, peppery flavour, but it may be grown on dry land. Land cress is robust, making it a useful winter salad. Plants mature in 4–12 weeks, and yield 18–20 heads per 3m (10ft) row. Named cultivars are not offered.

■ **Site and soil** Any moderately fertile but very moisture-retentive soil, preferably in a sheltered and slightly shaded position, is suitable for growing land cress.

■ **Sowing and planting** Either sow in moist soil outdoors where the plants are to grow in mid-spring to early summer, or raise seedlings in module trays (*see p.101*) in mid- to late summer for planting out as soon as seedlings can be handled. Land cress may be grown as a cut-and-come-again crop (*see p.102*).

| SOWING DEPTH | 1cm (½in) |
|---|---|
| PLANT SPACING | 15cm (6in) |
| ROW SPACING | 20cm (8in) |

■ **Routine care** Thin out the seedlings (*see p.101*); use the thinnings in salads. Generous watering in dry spells is vital to avoid coarse texture and fiery flavour, but top-dressing with fertilizer is unnecessary. For autumn and winter crops, protection with cloches, cold frames, or even a fleece tunnel cloche (*see pp.46–48*) improves quality and reliability.

■ **Harvesting** Harvest by picking choice leaves, leaving the lower part of the plant to resprout for further harvests.

■ **Common problems** There are few problems but aphids (*see p.251*), flea beetle on seedlings (*see p.255*), and slugs and snails (*see p.262*) may occasionally be troublesome.

# Lettuce

*Lactuca sativa*

| SEASON | SPRING | SUMMER | AUTUMN | WINTER |
|---|---|---|---|---|
| SOW | • • • • • • • | | | • • |
| TRANSPLANT | • • • | | | |
| HARVEST | • • • • • • • | | | |

There are two types of lettuce: those that form hearts or heads, and those that do not. Large, heart-forming lettuces include the cabbage-like butterheads, the crinkled crispheads, and the cos types. Iceberg lettuces are crispheads that develop for another two weeks, forming extremely dense heads. They need large amounts of water and fertilizer, and are much more demanding than other lettuces. Mini-lettuces are small-hearted cultivars that are well-suited to home gardens. Non-hearting lettuces include the Salad Bowl type and stem lettuces. Leaves of Salad Bowl lettuces can be repeatedly harvested, but are less tasty than mini-lettuces. Stem lettuces are seldom grown today, but yield leaves and a succulent stem that can be eaten like celery. Lettuces tend to mature in a rush, leading to gluts, and frequent sowings of small batches of seed are recommended to ensure an even supply. Packets of mixed cultivars are available; these contain reliable cultivars and are an inexpensive way of growing a variety of lettuces and so staggering the harvest.

Unheated cloches, cold frames, and even fleece (*see pp.43–45*) can be used to extend the harvest period for this hardy annual, although heated greenhouses are essential if you want to have a winter crop.

From a spring sowing, mini-lettuces will mature in 8–10 weeks, butterheads in 10–12 weeks, crispheads and cos in 12–13 weeks, and icebergs in 14 weeks. Mini-lettuces yield 18–20 heads per 3m (10ft) row, butterheads 9–12 heads, cos 9–12 heads, and crispheads and iceberg 8–9 heads.

■ **Site and soil** Open, sunny sites are best, but light shade is acceptable for midsummer crops. Fertile, moisture-retentive soils are needed for best-quality lettuces.

■ **Sowing and planting** Lettuces intended for an early-summer harvest can be sown under cover (*see p.101*) from winter to early spring, and planted out in spring. Lettuces for a summer harvest can be sown outdoors where they are to crop, from early spring onwards, in a continuous trickle. Thin the resulting seedlings (*see p.101*) to the required spacing, using the thinnings in salad leaves. Alternatively, to save time when thinning and to economize on seed, opt for station sowing the seed (*see p.101*).

Hardy cultivars can be sown outdoors in late winter, or in mild areas in early autumn, to crop in the spring. Protecting the crop with cloches and cold frames (*see pp.45–47*) will advance the harvest by about three weeks, greatly improve the quality, and make success more likely if the weather is frosty or very wet. Fleece covering (*see p.101*) advances harvest by about two weeks.

Lettuce seedlings resent root disturbance when transplanted and may soon wilt, especially in summer. Although they can be raised in seed trays or open ground and transplanted as bare-root plants, you will achieve better results by sowing them in module trays (*see p.101*), and transplanting as soon as they can be handled, before they have six leaves. Position the base of the leaves just above soil level. The depth of the seedling is crucial – too deep and it may rot off, too shallow and it will produce a poorly shaped lettuce. Water generously until the transplants are well-established.

Leafy lettuces, such as Salad Bowl types, may also be grown as a cut-and-come-again crop (*see p.102*).

| SOWING DEPTH | 1cm (½in) |
|---|---|
| MINI-LETTUCE | |
| PLANT SPACING | 15cm (6in) |
| ROW SPACING | 23cm (9in) |
| BUTTERHEAD | |
| PLANT SPACING | 25cm (10in) |
| ROW SPACING | 30cm (12in) |
| OTHER TYPES | |
| PLANT SPACING | 35cm (14in) |
| ROW SPACING | 38cm (15in) |

■ **Routine care** Water in dry spells, especially in the two weeks before the hearts reach full maturity. Feeding is not usually necessary on reasonably fertile soils but, if growth is particularly slow, top-dress occasionally with a nitrogen-rich fertilizer (*see p.20*) at the manufacturer's recommended rate.

■ **Harvesting** Begin to gather leaves from leafy lettuces, and thinnings from hearting lettuces, as soon as they are usable. When cutting leafy lettuces, leave 2.5cm (1in) of the stem to resprout for later harvests. Cut hearting lettuces as soon as the hearts are mature, in order to prevent rotting and bolting (*see p.101*). Solid, sound hearts may be stored in a refrigerator for several days. Butterhead and non-hearting types of lettuce run to seed much faster than crispheads or cos lettuce.

■ **Common problems** Cutworms (*see p.254*) may eat the roots. Slugs and snails (*see p.262*), and aphids (*see p.251*) can damage foliage. Fungal rots, or botrytis (*see p.252*), and downy mildew (*see p.255*) occur in wet weather, especially in autumn. Mildew and rotting leaves can usually be cut out at harvest, leaving sound heads. Lettuce root aphid (*see p.257*) is very damaging in some districts, but resistant cultivars are available. There may be occasional damage to roots from leatherjackets (*see p.257*) and wireworms (*see p.264*). Virus diseases can be avoided by using good-quality seed, eliminating aphids, and avoiding repeated cropping on the same piece of ground. Tip burn (*see p.263*) is a physiological disorder associated with lack of calcium, and can be especially troublesome on dry, light soils.

■ **Recommended cultivars**

**Mini-lettuce**
'Little Gem' ♀ – mini-cos, good texture and flavour, fast-growing, root aphid-resistant.
'Little Leprechaun' ♀ – red 'Little Gem' type.
'Pandero' ♀ – mini-cos, pretty, red, tasty.
'Pinokkio' ♀ – 'Little Gem' type, fast-growing.
'Tom Thumb' – mini-butterhead, sweet flavour, very hardy, ideal for earliest crops.

**Butterhead**
'Arctic King' – very hardy, for overwintering.
'Clarion' ♀ – vigorous, fairly disease-resistant.
'Diana' ♀ – large leafy heads, melting texture.

**Cos**
'Lobjoit's Green Cos' ♀ – hardy, reliable, suits spring and autumn (for early crops) sowing.
'Winter Density' – small cos, autumn and spring sown.

**Crisphead and iceberg**
'Lakeland' ♀ – crisphead, root aphid-resistant.

'Robinson' ♀ – iceberg, robust, resists root aphid and downy mildew.
'Webbs Wonderful' - crisphead, old favourite, sprawling.
**Leafy**
'Black Seeded Simpson' – leafy Batavian type with good flavour.
'Cocarde' ♀ – heavy cropper, neat plants.
'Lollo Rossa' ♀ – a favourite for its colour.
'Mottistone' – leafy Batavian type, red leaves.
'Red Salad Bowl' ♀ – reliable repeat-cropper.
'Salad Bowl' ♀ – good for repeat crops.

# Mibuna greens and Mizuna greens

*Brassica rapa* and *Brassica rapa* var. *nipposinica*

| SEASON | SPRING | SUMMER | AUTUMN | WINTER |
|---|---|---|---|---|
| SOW | • • | • • • | | |
| TRANSPLANT | | • | | |
| HARVEST | | • | • • • | • |

Mibuna and mizuna greens are types of Japanese brassica with rosettes of attractive, glossy green or red foliage and a succulent stem that can either be eaten raw in salads or cooked in the same way as spinach. The leaves have a mild mustard flavour, even when they are mature, and are good for winter harvests and container cultivation. Mibuna greens have a stronger flavour and strap-like leaves, but are less hardy; mizuna greens have feathery leaves.

You can grow mibuna or mizuna greens as small plants that will yield several harvests of young salad leaves. Pick the leaves when they are large enough and as required. Alternatively, leave them to mature into large plants, which are better cooked. Plants will mature in 4–12 weeks, and yield 6–9 heads per 3m (10ft) row. Named cultivars are seldom offered.
■ **Site and soil** Open, sunny sites and fertile soils are preferred.
■ **Sowing and planting** Sow in late summer and early autumn under cover (*see p.101*), *in situ* in early and midsummer, or indoors in mid- to late spring. Thin (*see p.101*) to 10cm (4in) apart for small plants and 45cm (18in) for large ones. These greens may be grown as a cut-and-come-again crop (*see p.102*).

| SOWING DEPTH | 1cm (½in) |
|---|---|
| PLANT SPACING | 10cm (4in) for small plants |
| | 45cm (18in) for large plants |
| ROW SPACING | 23cm (9in) |

■ **Routine care** Water in dry spells to keep the soil moist.
■ **Harvesting** For salads, pick choice young leaves as soon as they are ready. Regrowth will occur 2–8 weeks later (depending on the weather) for a prolonged harvest. Cut large plants when mature.
■ **Common problems** In common with other crops from the brassica family, these greens are prey to a range of problems, as for komatsuna

(*see p.104*). For symptoms and controls, *see* Plant Problems, *pp.246–264*.

# Mustard and cress

*Sinapis alba* and *Lepidium sativum*

| SEASON | SPRING | SUMMER | AUTUMN | WINTER |
|---|---|---|---|---|
| SOW | • • • | • • • | • • • | • • • |
| HARVEST | • • • | • • • | • • • | • • • |

Mustard and cress are tasty, fast-growing salad crops that are especially valuable between mid-autumn and mid-spring. Mustard seeds germinate in 4–5 days, and the seedlings can be cut after 8–12 days. Cress takes about two days longer to germinate than mustard, and can be cut after 10–14 days. Named cultivars of mustard and cress are seldom offered. Mustard is often replaced by rape (*Brassica napus* subsp. *oleifera*), which has a stronger flavour. Plain-leaved cress is usually sold; this grows better in winter than curled cress.
■ **Site and soil** Warm (10–16°C/50–60°F), well-lit windowsills, greenhouses, and conservatories and, in the summer, cloches or cold frames (*see pp.45–47*) are best for growing mustard and cress. Trays or pots filled with old potting or growing-bag compost provide ideal conditions. Outdoor crops need shelter and light shade, and they risk contamination from splashed soil.
■ **Sowing and planting** Seeds must be fresh to germinate quickly and evenly. Outdoor sowings should only be made between late spring and late summer. Mustard should be sown two days after cress where mixed crops are wanted. Crops can also be raised on a thick layer of moist kitchen towel (*see p.65*). Scatter the seeds lightly over a fine level surface, gently press them in, lightly water them with tepid water and cover with a damp cloth or a tile until germination has taken place. Mustard and cress may also be grown as a cut-and-come-again crop (*see p.102*).

| SOWING DEPTH | on the surface |
|---|---|
| SEED SPACING | almost touching |
| ROW SPACING | almost touching |

■ **Routine care** Keep soil or other growing medium moist.
■ **Harvesting** Cut at the base of the stems with scissors when the seedlings are 4–5cm (1½–2in) tall and the seed leaves or cotyledons are fully developed and green.
■ **Common problems** Damping off (*see p.254*), where seedling growth is slow or uneven, can ruin the salads. Keeping them warmer and using better-quality seeds can help. Grey mould (*Botrytis cinerea, p.252*) can also be a problem in overly damp conditions.
■ **Recommended cultivars**
**Mustard**
'White' – true mustard, stronger flavour than salad rape.
**Salad rape**
'Broad-leaved Essex' – mild-flavoured alternative to true mustard.

**Cress**
'Extra Double Curled' – curled leaves.
'Plain' – smooth leaves with stronger flavour; said to grow well in winter.
'Polycress' – especially fast-growing.

# Radish

*Raphanus sativa*

| SEASON | SPRING | SUMMER | AUTUMN | WINTER |
|---|---|---|---|---|
| SOW | • • • | • • • | • • | • • |
| TRANSPLANT | • | | | |
| HARVEST | | • • • | • • • | • • |

There are two main types of this fast-growing, crunchy, slightly hot root vegetable, which is used mainly as a salad ingredient. Summer radishes are small, round, cylindrical, or pointed, and are used when no larger than a walnut. Winter radishes are larger, and turnip-like. Summer radishes usually have red, pink, or white skins, but winter radishes may also have black, purple, yellow, or green skins; all usually have white flesh. Small roots are used raw as a salad ingredient, while the larger roots can also be used raw, or can be cooked in the same way as turnips or swedes. Oriental mooli radishes are grown in the same way as winter radishes. Summer radish plants take 2–8 weeks to mature, yielding a crop of 100–120 radishes per 3m (10ft) row. They can also be grown as a catch crop. In the summer months, maturation rates are more rapid. Winter radish matures in 8–10 weeks, with a yield of ten roots per 3m (10ft) row.

Seedling leaves can be used as cut-and-come-again salads (*see p.102*), while immature seed pods of older plants are also edible.
■ **Site and soil** Open, sunny sites are best, but light shade is acceptable for midsummer crops. Fertile, moisture-retentive soils are needed for good-quality summer radishes, but winter radishes are more tolerant.
■ **Sowing and planting** Radishes grow very quickly, soon maturing and becoming fibrous and inedible, so that fortnightly successional sowings are necessary for continuous cropping. Some small-leaved cultivars have been specially bred for early cropping; sow these directly into module trays (*see p.64*) or small pots, in mid- to late winter for planting out in mid-spring. Make follow-on sowings of normal cultivars in early spring under cloches, cold frames, or even fleece tunnel cloches (*see pp.46–47*). Subsequent sowings of summer radishes should be made outdoors.

One sowing of winter radish in mid- to late summer provides for autumn harvest and winter storage. Plant out stored roots to flower the following year and provide edible pods. Earlier sowing of winter types results in bolting (*see p.101*), unless bolt-resistant cultivars can be found. Thin seedlings (*see p.101*) of summer types to 2.5cm (1in) apart (double this for early covered crops), and winter types to 15–23cm

(6–9in) apart. Keep the crops well watered, but do not overwater them – excessive moisture can encourage leaf production at the expense of root growth.

| SOWING DEPTH | 1cm (½in) |
|---|---|
| PLANT SPACING | 1cm (½in) for summer radish |
| | 23cm (9in) for winter radish |
| ROW SPACING | 15cm (6in) for summer radish |
| | 30cm (12in) for winter radish |

■ **Routine care** Adding organic matter before sowing (*see p.68*) will help maintain soil moisture as well as providing adequate nutrients. Water to keep the soil moist; in dry spells, this may mean watering every week. Radishes may also be used for intersowing with parsnips (*see p.69*).

■ **Harvesting and storing** Use summer radishes as soon as the roots are large enough and before they become "woolly". Winter radishes may be left in the ground until they are needed, and may then reach the same size as turnips or swedes. They may be damaged by frost, however; to avoid this, lift in autumn and store in the same way as other root crops (*see p.73*).

To produce edible pods, leave some roots to sprout and flower, and gather the pods while they are still green and crisp, before they get stringy. Radish leaves can also furnish useful greens in the same manner as turnip tops (*see p.88*).

■ **Common problems** Flea beetle (*see p.255*), slugs and snails (*see p.262*) may cause minor damage. Cabbage root fly (*see p.253*) can be very destructive, and is best avoided by growing radishes beneath a fleece or insect-proof fine woven mesh (*see p.101*), which also promotes speedy growth and excellent quality. Grow winter radishes in the brassica part of a rotation (*see p.31*) to avoid clubroot (*see p.254*) and other soil-borne brassica problems.

■ **Recommended cultivars**
**Summer radish**
'Cherry Belle' ♀ – fast-growing.
'French Breakfast 3' ♀ – good-quality roots.
'Scarlet Globe' ♀ – reliable old favourite.
'Short Top Forcing' ♀ – Very fast-growing, small foliage, ideal in cold frames and cloches.
**Winter radish**
'Black Spanish Round' – very hardy, old favourite, ideal for cold gardens.
'Mantanghong' – red, hardy.
'Minowase' – white-skinned, long, Japanese-type with delicate flavour.
'Munchen Bier' – good for edible pods.

# Rocket

*Eruca vesicaria*

| SEASON | SPRING | SUMMER | AUTUMN | WINTER |
|---|---|---|---|---|
| SOW | • • | • • • • | • • | |
| HARVEST | • • | • • • • • | • • • | • |

Rocket or salad rocket is a tangy member of the cabbage family, whose young leaves add a "roast chicken" flavour to salads. It is a common ingredient of supermarket salad packs, where it may be called erugala, rucola, or roquette. Wild (*Diplotaxis* species) and Turkish rocket (*Bunias orientalis*) are almost identical with subtly different, more aromatic, but equally delicious, flavours. They may also be cooked like spinach. The plants mature in 4–12 weeks, and yield the equivalent of 9–10 bunches per 3m (10ft) row. Named cultivars are not offered.

■ **Site and soil** Any moderately fertile but moisture-retentive soil, preferably in a sheltered and slightly shaded position, is suitable. Protect autumn and winter crops with cloches, cold frames, or even a fleece tunnel cloche (*see pp.45–47*).

■ **Sowing and planting** Like radishes, rocket soon runs to seed, and repeated sowings are necessary for a constant supply of edible leaves. Sow where the plants are to grow when seedlings from the previous sowing have produced a couple of true leaves, anything from 4–21 days, depending on the weather. Early and late sowings should be made under cover (*see p.101*). Rocket may also be grown as a cut-and-come-again crop (*see p.102*).

| SOWING DEPTH | 1cm (½in) |
|---|---|
| PLANT SPACING | 15cm (6in) |
| ROW SPACING | 15cm (6in) |

■ **Routine care** Thin out the seedlings (*see p.101*) and use the thinnings in salads. Generous watering in dry spells is essential.

■ **Harvesting** Harvest rocket leaves as soon as they are usable. Frequent cutting will promote tender new growth.

■ **Common problems** Flea beetle, slugs, and snails may cause minor damage. For symptoms and controls, *see* Plant Problems, *p.255 and p.262*.

# Summer purslane

*Portulaca oleracea*

| SEASON | SPRING | SUMMER | AUTUMN | WINTER |
|---|---|---|---|---|
| SOW | | • • • | | |
| HARVEST | | • • | • • • | |

There are green- and yellow-leaved forms of this half-hardy, succulent, low-growing plant. The leaves and stems are either eaten raw or lightly cooked or steamed. The green forms are more vigorous, but are less striking in decorative mixed salads than the yellow form. Both forms of summer purslane have a relatively mild flavour and crunchy texture. Plants mature in 4–12 weeks, and produce the equivalent of 20–24 bunches per 3m (10ft) row. Named cultivars are not offered.

■ **Site and soil** Well-drained soil and a sunny, sheltered site are preferred.

■ **Sowing and planting** Sow successionally, sowing a new batch of seed when seedlings from the previous sowing have produced a couple of true leaves, for a constant supply of edible leaves. Early sowings should be made under cover (*see p.101*). Summer purslane may also be grown as a cut-and-come-again crop (*see p.102*).

| SOWING DEPTH | 1cm (½in) |
|---|---|
| PLANT SPACING | 15cm (6in) |
| ROW SPACING | 15cm (6in) |

■ **Routine care** Thin out the seedlings when large enough (*see p.101*) and use the thinnings in salads. Generous watering in dry spells is essential to maintain healthy growth.

■ **Harvesting** Pick the tender young leaves and stems as soon as they are large enough. Regular gathering encourages the production of fresh tender new growth, as long as some leaves are left on the plant after harvesting. Remove any seedheads that develop.

■ **Common problems** Slugs and snails may occasionally be troublesome. For symptoms and controls, *see* Plant Problems, *p.262*.

# Winter purslane

*Montia perfoliata*

| SEASON | SPRING | SUMMER | AUTUMN | WINTER |
|---|---|---|---|---|
| SOW | • • | • • • | | |
| TRANSPLANT | | • | | |
| HARVEST | | • | • • • • | • |

This half-hardy plant, also known as miner's lettuce or claytonia, has pale, succulent leaves that may be used, together with tender stems and flowers, in salads. Winter purslane thrives in poor soils and dry conditions, and frequently self seeds. It is easily controlled, however, and unlikely to become a nuisance. Plants mature over a period of about 12 weeks, and yield the equivalent of 20–24 bunches per 3m (10ft) row. Named cultivars are not offered.

■ **Site and soil** Choose a well-drained, sunny site, and moderately fertile soil.

■ **Sowing and planting** Sow in moist soil where the plants are to grow, or raise seedlings indoors in modules (*see p.64*) for planting out when all risk of frost has passed. Winter purslane may also be grown as a cut-and-come-again crop (*see p.102*).

| SOWING DEPTH | 1cm (½in) |
|---|---|
| PLANT SPACING | 15cm (6in) |
| ROW SPACING | 23cm (9in) |

■ **Routine care** Thin seedlings (*see p.101*), using the thinnings for salads. Regular watering or top-dressing with fertilizer are unnecessary.

■ **Harvesting** When the plants are mature, pick leaves, stems, and flowers, leaving the lower part of the plant in the ground. More leaves will be produced, giving several more harvests. Resprouting of new leaves may take from 2–6 weeks.

■ **Common problems** Aphids, slugs, and snails may occasionally be troublesome. For symptoms and controls, *see* Plant Problems, *p.251 and p.262*.

# Growing fruiting vegetables

Plants in this group of vegetables, which are grown for their "fruits", range from perhaps the most popular kitchen-garden crop – tomatoes, vine or bush types – to more exotic crops such as okra and tomatillo. Others that are well worth trying are aubergines, sweet and chilli peppers, and sweetcorn.

Fruiting vegetables are all half-hardy, and need a long, hot summer in order for the fruits to ripen fully. For this reason, they need to be sown quite early in the season, at a time when many temperate regions are still too cold for them. This means that it is essential in the early stages to provide some form of protection, such as cloches or fleece (see pp.46–48), if the plants are to produce a successful crop.

## SITE AND SOIL
Well-drained, light soils that warm up quickly in the spring are best for this group of vegetables. Sowing and harvesting may need to be delayed where the soil is predominantly clay and consequently slow to warm. Adding organic matter (see pp.37–40) will improve the structure of the soil, speeding up both the drainage and warming of the ground. Fruiting vegetables can be very deep-rooting, and shallow, waterlogged, or compacted soils

will limit their growth. Try to exploit any warm microclimates in your garden, for example, by planting crops next to a sunny wall (see right), in a sheltered corner, or in a raised bed.

You can also help nature along by pre-warming the soil with a clear plastic sheet mulch (see p.42) or a cloche covering from mid-spring, so that you can sow or plant out fruiting vegetables earlier in the season and give them as much time as possible for growth.

## SOWING UNDER COVER
Many crops in this group, especially aubergines, okra, peppers, and tomatillo, have small seeds that produce tiny, slow-growing seedlings needing an early start in a greenhouse, a cold frame, or even a windowsill from an early spring sowing. The majority of fruiting vegetables bear fruits over several weeks, eliminating the need for successional sowing.

Sow the seeds thinly in pots of multi-purpose compost, adding sufficient vermiculite or sieved compost to cover the seeds (see p.64). Warm conditions, with a minimum temperature of 16°C (60°F), are needed for successful germination, and this is best provided by a heated propagator (see p.63).

When seedlings emerge, transfer the pots to better-lit conditions, such as a greenhouse or a sunny windowsill in the house. The seedlings will still require warmth of at least 18°C (64°F) during

**Using a microclimate**
*When growing tender crops, such as this aubergine, outdoors in a temperate climate plant them against a sheltered, sunny wall. The wall absorbs heat and radiates it back onto the plant at night, raising the local temperature.*

the daytime, and 16°C (60°F) minimum at night. Make sure that any windowsill you are using for seedlings does not become cooler than this temperature at any time during the night. Some crops, especially aubergine and okra, benefit from a polythene or fleece tent to raise humidity; simply hang this over a wire hoop or short canes pushed into the soil at the edge of the pot.

When the seedlings are large enough to handle, prick them out (see p.64) into individual 8cm (3in) pots, large module trays, tube pots, or biodegradeable pots (see p.62). The latter are best for plants that resent root disturbance. Feed the seedlings with a balanced liquid fertilizer (see pp.22–23) if growth appears pale, and especially if the lower leaves start to turn yellow.

A limited range of aubergines, cucumbers, peppers, and tomatoes are offered as grafted plants, where individual cultivars have been grafted onto disease-resistant rootstocks. These plants are vigorous and can be grown where soil-borne problems occur. Seed of rootstocks is available, but the process is beyond the scope of most home gardeners.

## SOWING OUTDOORS
Sweetcorn has much larger seeds that grow quickly, and therefore they can be

**Planting sweetcorn in a block**
*Sweetcorn relies on the wind for pollination, so plant out seedlings in a block of several short, staggered rows to increase the chances of successful pollination occurring.*

*Sides of each cell are grooved to train roots*

**Root trainers**
*These containers snap together to form long cells – useful for plants that require deep rooting space, such as sweetcorn. They can be opened out easily to remove and transplant the seedling plug without disturbing the roots. Root trainers can be reused many times.*

station sown (*see p.66*) outdoors in milder areas from mid–spring. For early crops, and in colder districts, raise sweetcorn seedlings under cover in tube pots (*see p.62*) or biodegradable pots, at least 9cm (3½in) in diameter. These will hold the long roots of sweetcorn seedlings in their entirety, and there will be no danger of damaging them at transplanting, which could result in the plant becoming stunted.

For later crops or to extend the growing season, sweetcorn can be sown in succession (*see p.69*). Alternatively, you can grow a selection of cultivars that crop at different times.

## PLANTING OUT

The young plants should be ready for transplanting into their final positions, either outdoors or in a greenhouse, when the roots have fully filled the pot, but before they become overcrowded, usually after about 18 weeks. Harden young plants off (*see p.65*) before planting outdoors, by placing them in either a cold frame or beneath a double layer of fleece for at least a week; in these situations, temperature and humidity levels fall midway between those of the

seedling pot and those of the final site. Careful planting is essential to avoid a check in growth, which would curtail the period of cropping and the number of fruits produced. Covering with fleece (*see p.101*) after planting, for two weeks, provides extra warmth and humidity when the plants are at their most delicate. You can transplant plants that are not yet at flowering stage, in order

◀ **Sheet mulch**
*To minimize weed growth around your crop (here sweetcorn) and help conserve moisture, lay a black plastic sheet mulch on the bed and plant through it.*

▲ **Removing tomato sideshoots**
*When growing vine tomatoes, pinch out with your finger and thumb any sideshoots that appear in the angles between the main stem and any of the leaf stems.*

to free some space in the greenhouse if desired, but cropping will take place earlier if you wait until they are at flowering stage before planting out.

## PLANTING SWEETCORN IN BLOCKS

Plant out sweetcorn seedlings that have been grown under cover in tube pots when the plants are 8cm (3in) tall. Because they are wind-pollinated, it is best to plant them in blocks of at least 12 plants, no closer than 34cm (14in) apart, in a series of short rows (*see facing page*), rather than in single rows. This gives the plants a much better chance of being pollinated successfully, which is necessary for the production of cobs.

## MULCHING

Fruiting vegetables grow slowly and can easily be smothered by weeds. Plastic sheet and organic mulches (*see above and pp.41–42*) will prevent this happening, and are especially valuable inside cloches and cold frames where weeding may be difficult. Before planting, laying a sheet of black plastic, or clear plastic over black, can warm the soil as well as suppressing weeds. You can plant through slits cut in the plastic sheet mulch (*see p.77*). Mulching prevents evaporation.

The floppy habit of bush tomatoes leads to fruits lying on the ground, where they are prone to slugs and other problems. Mulching with straw or black plastic keeps the fruits clean and free from slug damage or rots.

## Providing support for fruiting crops

Because of the weight of their fruits, some fruiting vegetables, such as tomatoes and peppers, need supporting. Bamboo canes and twine are often adequate, but for very heavy crops you may need stronger supports such as sawn-timber stakes. The taller the crop, the more substantial the support system should be (*see below*).

**Supporting short crops**
*When lower-growing crops such as peppers (shown here) begin to form fruits, place 3–5 bamboo canes around each plant and tie in the stems with figure-of-eight loops of twine.*

**Supporting tall crops**
*Taller-growing crops like vine tomatoes are best trained up single bamboo canes tied into a greenhouse structure for stability. Tie the plants to the canes as they grow.*

### CONTAINER GROWING

Most fruiting vegetables, excluding sweetcorn, grow well in pots of at least 25cm (10in) in diameter, or three plants to a growing bag. The best position for a container is against a warm, sunny wall near the house, where the extra heat and light speed cropping and boost flavour.

Tomatoes are especially suitable for growing in containers, and the bigger the container, the easier they are to manage. Large pots, 35cm (14in) in diameter, filled with compost from used growing bags, are suitable without being unwieldy. Growing-bag compost is specially formulated to suit tomatoes. Unfortunately, growing bags contain only a small volume of compost, which rapidly dries out. Avoid this problem by growing only two plants per bag rather than three, or by planting in a pot with an open base, filled with similar compost, on the surface of a growing bag, to increase the volume of compost available and to ease watering.

Some bush tomatoes are extremely compact, growing no larger than 23cm (9in) in both height and spread; where space in the garden is short, these may be grown in hanging baskets.

### COMMON PROBLEMS

Peppers, including chillis, tomatoes, and occasionally aubergines, suffer blackish, sunken patches at the flower or blossom end of their fruits when calcium supply is insufficient. Inadequate or irregular water is often the cause. Better watering usually prevents blossom end rot (for controls, *see p.252*).

### ROUTINE CARE

The compact size of bush tomatoes allows them to be covered throughout their growing period with cloches, cold frames, or fleece (*see pp.45–48*). Cloches and cold frames exclude rain, preventing diseases that flourish in the humid environment of the foliage. Fleece is less effective at reducing disease, but is less likely to overheat in hot weather.

Fruiting vegetables need fertile soil in order to produce a succession of fruits. Before planting them, apply a general fertilizer (*see pp.20–21*) at a rate of 35–70g per sq m (1–2oz per sq yd). Alternatively, use 50–100g per sq m (1½–3oz per sq yd) of an organic food such as dried poultry manure with a 5 per cent nitrogen content (*see pp.22–23*); use double this amount for sweetcorn.

Water well in dry spells, at a rate of 20 litres per sq m (4 gallons per sq yd). Adequate water supplies are especially necessary during the flowering period, and as fruits swell.

For tall crops, like vine tomatoes, pinch out sideshoots (*see p.109*) to concentrate the plant's energy into fruiting. Tall crops may need staking. For bushy peppers and aubergines, pinch out the growing tip to encourage the production of sideshoots.

Only remove leaves if they turn yellow or become diseased; otherwise cropping may be reduced. An exception to this rule is tomatoes (*see p.113*).

If using containers, do not allow pots to dry out. Add a controlled-release fertilizer before planting or apply a balanced liquid fertilizer weekly if growth slows (*see pp.20–21*).

### HARVESTING

Most fruiting vegetables are ready for harvest in late summer. Regular picking encourages continuous fruit production. Sever the fruits, with a piece of stalk, using a sharp knife or secateurs. Harvest can usually be prolonged into the autumn by using a protective fleece layer, held clear of the plants by hoops of wire inserted into the soil (*see p.47*).

The fruits of most fruiting vegetables change colour when they are ripe, but it is more difficult to tell when the cobs of sweetcorn are ready for harvesting, so you will need to test them first. The cobs should also be broken off by hand rather than cut (*see below*).

### SEED SAVING

Saving seeds of fruiting vegetables such as sweetcorn and peppers, which cross-pollinate readily, or F1 hybrids, where progeny seldom come true to type, is not worth attempting. It is, however, worth trying with the pulpy seeds of ripe tomatoes (*see p.61*).

## Harvesting cobs of sweetcorn

With sweetcorn, it is quite difficult to tell when the cobs are ripe and therefore ready for harvesting. Because of this, cobs are often left on the plant for too long and are overripe when eventually picked.

To ensure that you pick cobs when they are at their most tender, test for ripeness as soon as the tassels turn brown in late summer. Peel back a little of the husk, and insert a thumbnail or fingernail into one of the kernels (*see far left*). If the juice that comes out is milky, the cob is ripe; if the juice is clear, the cob is not yet ripe.

Pick a ripe cob by pulling it sharply downwards with one hand – supporting the rest of the plant with the other – until the cob snaps off (*see left*). Only pick cobs just before they are required; once they are harvested, the sweet flavour is rapidly lost.

*Testing for ripeness*          *Picking a ripe cob*

# A–Z OF FRUITING VEGETABLES

## Aubergine

*Solanum melongena*

| SEASON | SPRING | SUMMER | AUTUMN | WINTER |
|---|---|---|---|---|
| SOW | • • | | | |
| TRANSPLANT | | • • | | |
| HARVEST | | • • | • • | |

Aubergines, also known as eggplants or brinjal, are very attractive, slightly spiny plants of tropical origin, and are therefore usually grown under cover in temperate regions. Yellow-, black-, white-, red-, or purple-fruited cultivars are available, but for the kitchen it is best to grow F1 hybrid black-fruited cultivars. Aubergines yield 3–4.5kg (6½–10lb) per 3m (10ft) row in cloches or frames; for outdoor crops, the yield will be lower. They may be grown in containers on a sunny patio.

■ **Site and soil** Outdoors, only the sunniest, most sheltered sites are suitable. Elsewhere, cloches or cold frames are essential for providing the extra warmth and especially the humidity aubergines need. Soil should be fertile, well-drained, and moisture-retentive, as well as warming quickly in spring (*see p.108*).

■ **Sowing and planting** Sow seed indoors at 21–30°C (70–86°F). The optimum growing temperatures after germination are 16°C (60°F) at night, 18°C (64°F) by day. Prick out into pots (*see p.108*) when they are about 5cm (2in) tall. Biodegradable pots are best. Plant out (*see p.109*) when the first flowers appear.

| SOWING DEPTH | sow thinly, with light covering |
|---|---|
| PLANT SPACING | 60–75cm (24–30in) |
| ROW SPACING | 75–90cm (30–36in) |

■ **Routine care** Pinch out the growing tip when the plants are about 20cm (8in) tall, and again later if necessary, to encourage bushy plants, which are easier to support (*see p.109*). Small, but numerous fruits result, unless fruits are thinned to one per stem. Water regularly to keep the soil moist. To increase humidity and warmth, grow the plants beneath a tent of fleece within the greenhouse. When the fruits begin to set, feed with a high-potash fertilizer or organic tomato feed every 10–12 days. (*See also* Mulching, *p.109*).

■ **Harvesting** Gather fruits when they develop their full colour, but before they become over-ripe and pithy. Cut the stem 2.5cm (1in) above the calyx – the joint of the stem and the fruit.

■ **Common problems** Aphids (*see p.251*), red spider mite (*see p.261*), and whitefly (*p.264*) are common in cloches and cold frames, but biological controls (*see p.52*) are very effective against these pests. *Botrytis* (*see p.252*) may rot fruits in cool or wet weather; speedy removal of diseased material reduces the risk. Soil-borne diseases, especially verticillium wilt (*see p.263*), are avoided by growing on a fresh site or in growing bags every year.

■ **Recommended cultivars**
'Black Enorma' – compact and prolific hybrid, suited to patio growing.
'Bonica' ♀ – large dark fruits, tall, vigorous.
'Giotto' – large dark fruits, resistant to verticillium wilt.
'Moneymaker' – outdoors in warm areas, or in cold frame or cloche, tasty purple fruits.
'Snowy' – small white fruits, good for patio.

## Chilli and sweet pepper

*Capsicum annuum* Longum Group and *C. annuum* Grossum Group

| SEASON | SPRING | SUMMER | AUTUMN | WINTER |
|---|---|---|---|---|
| SOW | • • | | | |
| TRANSPLANT | | • • | | |
| HARVEST | | • • | • • | |

Home-grown sweet peppers have excellent colour, texture, and flavour, including shapes and colours not usually available in shops. Chilli peppers are equally varied and have a hot taste, contained mainly in the seeds and veins, which is essential for certain cuisines; some forms are intended for ornament, with coloured foliage. Modern F1 hybrids are robust enough to crop reliably in cool seasons and gardens. Peppers are ideal for container and patio cultivation; they yield 2.75–4.5kg (6–10lb) per 3m (10ft) row in cloches or frames; outdoors, the yield will be lower.

■ **Site and soil** Any fertile, moisture-retentive soil suits peppers if it drains well and warms quickly in spring. Light soils are best; pre-warm heavy soils with cloches or clear plastic film. Outdoors, a sunny, sheltered site is vital; otherwise cover with cloches or cold frames.

■ **Sowing and planting** Sow indoors (*see p.108*) at 18–21°C (65–70°F). Optimum growing temperatures for seedlings are 16°C (60°F) at night, 18°C (64°F) by day. Prick out then plant out into borders, pots, or growing bags after hardening off (*see pp.108–109*).

| SOWING DEPTH | sow thinly, with light covering |
|---|---|
| PLANT SPACING | 38–45cm (15–18in) |
| ROW SPACING | 60–75cm (24–36in) |

■ **Routine care** Provide support for the plants as they develop (*see p.109*) or their stems can break under the weight of the crop. If growth is weak, remove the first flowers and feed with balanced liquid fertilizer weekly (*see p.110*). Pinching out the growing tip is not needed on peppers, and delays cropping. (*See* Mulching, *p.109, and* Routine Care, *p.110*.)

■ **Harvesting and storing** Pick the first fruits when they are green and the skin is smooth and glossy, to encourage further cropping. Later fruits can be picked green or allowed to ripen to yellow, orange, or red. Red peppers have a sweeter, richer

flavour. Allowing fruits to ripen, however, reduces cropping by about a quarter. Chilli peppers may be gathered green or allowed to ripen, and dried or pickled for winter storage. Some ripen yellow or even white. Black, purple, and violet chillis ripen to red or purplish-black, depending on cultivar. Fruits of both types will remain in good condition on the plant until frosted.

■ **Common problems** Aphids (*see p.251*), red spider mite (*see p.261*), and whitefly (*see p.264*) are common in cloches and cold frames, but biological controls (*see p.52*) are very effective. *Botrytis* (*see p.252*) rots fruits in cool or wet weather; speedy removal of diseased material reduces damage. To avoid soil-borne diseases, especially verticillium wilt (*see p.263*), grow on a fresh site or in growing bags every year.

■ **Recommended cultivars**

**Sweet pepper**

'Ariane' ♀ – orange fruits, fast-growing, heavy crop, attractive in salads.

'Bellboy' ♀ – hybrid, traditional, red ripe fruits.

'Gypsy' ♀ – old favourite, pale green, long, pointed fruits ripen bright red, heavy crop.

'Mavras' ♀ – black fruits.

'Redskin' ♀ – compact hybrid, small green fruits ripen to red, heavy cropper, good for patios or cloches.

**Chilli pepper**

'Apache' – red, round, hot fruits, compact size.

'Habanero' – very hot, small orange fruits.

'Hungarian Wax' – long-pointed, light green, mild and sweet, getting hotter as it matures.

'Jalapeno' – hot, tapering green fruits ripen red.

'Tabasco' – long, thin green fruits maturing to red, very hot.

# Okra

*Abelmoschus esculentus*

| SEASON | SPRING | SUMMER | AUTUMN | WINTER |
|---|---|---|---|---|
| SOW | ● ● | | | |
| TRANSPLANT | | ● ● | | |
| HARVEST | | | ● ● ● | |

Okra is a half-hardy annual related to cotton. Its immature parts have a unique glutinous texture, essential for some cuisines, and are used as a green vegetable. The dried pods can also be used as flavouring. Okra yields 1.5kg (3¼lb) per 3m (10ft) row in cloches or frames; for outdoor crops, the yield will be lower.

■ **Site and soil** A fertile, well-drained soil, under cold frames or cloches, in a sunny, sheltered site, is essential to provide the extra warmth and especially humidity needed. Even so, success is not guaranteed.

■ **Sowing and planting** The seeds are very hard, and a preliminary soaking in warm water for two hours will speed germination. Sow indoors (*see p.108*) at a minimum temperature of 16°C (60°F). The optimum growing temperatures for seedlings are 20–30°C (68–86°F). Prick out seedlings when they are large enough to handle (*see p.108*), and plant them out (*see p.109*) when they reach 8–10cm (3–4in) tall.

| SOWING DEPTH | sow thinly, with light covering |
|---|---|
| PLANT SPACING | 40–60cm (16–24in) |
| ROW SPACING | 60–75cm (24–30in) |

■ **Routine care** Pinch out strong growing tips to encourage bushiness. Provide support. (*See* Mulching, *p.109, and* Routine Care, *p.110*.)

■ **Harvesting** As soon as pods have formed, cut them off with a sharp knife. They quickly become stringy, so regular cutting is essential.

■ **Common problems** Aphids (*see p.251*), red spider mite (*see p.261*), and whitefly (*see p.264*) are common in cloches and cold frames, but biological controls (*see p.52*) are very effective. *Botrytis* (*see p.252*) rots fruits in cool or wet weather; speedy removal of diseased material reduces damage. To avoid soil-borne diseases, especially verticillium wilt (*see p.263*), grow on a fresh site or in growing bags every year.

■ **Recommended cultivars**

'Clemson's Stringless' – old favourite.

'Pure Luck' – vigorous, high yields.

# Sweetcorn

*Zea mays*

| SEASON | SPRING | SUMMER | AUTUMN | WINTER |
|---|---|---|---|---|
| SOW | ● ● | | | |
| TRANSPLANT | | ● ● | | |
| HARVEST | | | ● ● ● | |

Home-grown sweetcorn cobs cooked within minutes of harvest taste superb. The kernels are usually yellow, sometimes white or bicoloured. Improved forms are regularly introduced (older cultivars have poor growing characteristics and insipid flavour). Only one or two cobs are borne per plant; normal yields are 6–9 cobs per sq m (sq yd).

Uniquely for vegetables, sweetcorn (or maize) is a grass with long leaves, the base of which encloses the stem, and is pollinated by wind. Sweetcorn has architectural qualities that make it valuable in ornamental kitchen gardens. The male flowers at the top of the stem are called tassels. They shed pollen, carried on the wind to the "silk", which grows out of the cob containing rows of female flowers. The cob, or fruit, is enclosed in a sheath or husk of leafy bracts.

Supersweet corn has largely replaced the less sugary standard and sugar-enhanced varieties, and retains its very sweet flavour after picking. However, the less chewy, more tender Extra Tendersweet, which is almost as sweet, is widely grown. Synergistic corn, a new development, combines the best of both, but few cultivars are currently available. Baby corn is grown from special varieties, or regular sweetcorn closely spaced.

Nearby agricultural maize can cross-pollinate sweetcorn, leading to less tasty cobs. Purple and other coloured corn or maize can also pollinate sweetcorn, leading to less flavoursome, parti-coloured cobs.

■ **Site and soil** A warm, sunny, sheltered site with light, warm, rich soil is vital (*see p.108*). Cobs may not ripen in shade or windy sites.

■ **Sowing and planting** In cool areas, choose early cultivars, sow them in a greenhouse at 20–27°C (70–80°F), and plant out (*see p.108*) when about 8cm (3in) tall. Block planting (*see p.109*) will increase the chances of successful pollination, necessary for production of cobs. If sowing outdoors, a soil temperature of at least 10°C (50°F) is essential, occurring in late spring in milder areas. Help germination, and growth after planting, by pre-warming the soil with cloches or clear plastic (*see p.108*). Sow 2–3 seeds per station (*see p.108*), using the wider spacing (*see below*) where the soil is of poor quality. Thin to one strong seedling after germination. Seedlings grow best at temperatures of 20–30°C (68–86°F).

The harvest can be extended with a single sowing of early, mid-season, and late cultivars in mid-spring, providing up to three weeks of harvest. Alternatively, make three spring sowings of the same cultivar at fortnightly intervals. In cold areas, only early cultivars and sowings are likely to succeed.

| SOWING DEPTH | 2.5–4cm (1–1½in) |
|---|---|
| SEED/PLANT SPACING | 34–45cm (14–18in) |
| ROW SPACING | 45–60cm (18–24in) |

■ **Routine care** Watering is not required until flowering starts, when the soil should be kept moist, or at least be given one thorough soak. On windy sites, draw up soil around the bases of the plants to give stability, or give support (*see p.109*). (*See also* Routine Care, *p.110*.)

■ **Harvesting** Test for ripeness as soon as the tassels begin to dry up and turn brown, and if ready break off the cobs (*see p.110*).

■ **Common problems** The seeds attract mice (*see p.257*). Sweetcorn smut (*see p.263*) and frit flies (*see p.255*) attack occasionally but seldom cause heavy losses; crop rotation (*see p.31*) is the only control. Poor pollinating conditions may lead to gaps in the rows of ripe kernels. Birds (*see p.252*), squirrels (*see p.262*), and badgers (*see p.251*) may strip crops.

■ **Recommended cultivars**

'Earlybird' ♀ – early, high quality supersweet.

'Lark' – extra tender sweet, very sweet cobs.

'Ovation' ♀ – mid-season, supersweet yellow.

'Sundance' ♀ – normal sweetness, vigorous, suits cool areas.

'Swift' – extra tender sweet, easy to grow, heavy cropper.

# Tomatillo

*Physalis ixocarpa*

| SEASON | SPRING | SUMMER | AUTUMN | WINTER |
|---|---|---|---|---|
| SOW | ● ● | | | |
| TRANSPLANT | | ● ● | | |
| HARVEST | | | ● ● ● | |

The tomatillo, or Mexican husk tomato, is a frost-tender, sprawling plant, growing to about 1m (3ft). Its green fruits ripen to yellow, purple, or red, or may stay green. They are used in Mexican cuisine and for preserves. The berry is enclosed in a tight-fitting, papery calyx,

through which the ripening berry sometimes bursts. Tomatillos yield 1–2kg (2¼–4½lb) per plant. Named cultivars are seldom offered.

■ **Site and soil** As for peppers (*see p.111*).

■ **Sowing and planting** Sow seed in the greenhouse (*see p.108*) at a minimum of 16°C (60°F). Optimum growing temperatures for seedlings are 16°C (60°F) at night, 18°C (64°F) by day. Plant out in late spring and early summer into beds, pots, or growing bags after hardening off (*see p.109*).

| SOWING DEPTH | sow thinly, with light covering |
|---|---|
| PLANT SPACING | 45cm (18in) |
| ROW SPACING | 90cm (36in) |

■ **Routine care** Tomatillos seldom require feeding or watering. Use three canes and loops of twine to support them (*see p.109*). In frames and cloches, pinch out the growing tips to make the plants more compact.

■ **Harvesting** Many fruits fall before ripe and can be left to ripen on the ground. Full colour indicates ripeness, and green cultivars are ripe when the fruit breaks through the husk.

■ **Common problems** There are no significant problems with this crop.

# Tomato

*Lycopersicon esculentum*

| SEASON | SPRING | SUMMER | AUTUMN | WINTER |
|---|---|---|---|---|
| SOW | • • | | | |
| TRANSPLANT | | • • | | |
| HARVEST | | • • | • • | |

Tomatoes are short-lived, tender perennials grown as annuals. Seed suppliers cater for the great popularity of tomatoes by supplying many different types. Cultivars have been developed with fruits ranging from currant size, through cherry and plum tomatoes, to the grapefruit-sized beefsteak types. Shapes are spherical, oblong, elongated, or flattened globes, and colours include red, green, yellow, and purple. Another result of this popularity is that a fair range of different types may be bought as ready-grown plants in garden centres. There are two main types of tomato plant: vine (or indeterminate) tomatoes and bush (or determinate) tomatoes.

Vine tomatoes are usually grown with the central stem trained up a tall support (*see p.110*), with its sideshoots removed; these cordons will grow to several metres in frost-free conditions. The flowers and consequent fruits are borne on trusses that grow from the main stem. Vine tomatoes are easier to keep within bounds if grown in greenhouses, containers, or growing bags, although if in the latter they will need more attention (*see p.110*). Avoid greenhouse cultivars outdoors, since the fruits often need the protection and warmth under cover to ripen.

Bush tomatoes are much more compact plants with plenty of side branches, and are better for growing outdoors. Flowers appear on the end of each stem. After flowering, the stem ceases

to grow, but other stems arise, also bearing flowers, so that a short, bushy plant covered in flowers results. Bush cultivars crop very early and abundantly, and they are worth trying on greenhouse staging for the earliest crops. They can be time-consuming to harvest, their fruits tend to be less tasty, and the range of colours, shapes, and sizes is less than vine types.

There are also intermediate types, which have a habit between the fully bushy and the vine types. They usually require supporting, but removal of sideshoots is not carried out, the whole plant being loosely tied to the support. Many of the unusual Mediterranean and other less commonly grown cultivars have a semi-indeterminate habit, with some stems ending in flowers and others trailing without end. These unruly plants need careful judgement in curbing the straggling shoots and preserving the flowering ones.

Yields are very variable, with the most flavoursome cultivars and cherry tomatoes often cropping lightly, while heavy croppers are often dull in flavour. Vine tomatoes yield 1.8–4kg (4–9lb) per plant outdoors or 2.7–5kg (6–11lb) in an unheated greenhouse. Bush and semi-indeterminate tomatoes should yield 4kg (9lb) per plant outdoors.

■ **Site and soil** Any fertile, nutrient-rich, well-drained soil is suitable, if plenty of organic matter has been incorporated in the top 30cm (12in). If necessary, before planting add a general-purpose fertilizer at a rate of 105g per sq m (3oz per sq yd) or pelleted poultry manure at 150g per sq m (4oz per sq yd).

■ **Sowing and planting** Sow indoors no more than eight weeks before the last frost is expected. Plants sown earlier will be too large to plant out before the risk of frost has passed, and will need cloche or cold frame protection. Sow thinly in pots of multi-purpose compost, adding enough vermiculite or sieved compost to cover the seeds (*see p.108*). Alternatively, sow two seeds per pot, later selecting the strongest seedling. Warm conditions (15–30°C/59–86°F) are needed for germination, best provided by a heated propagator (*see p.63*). When seedlings emerge, transfer pots to better-lit conditions, such as a greenhouse or sunny windowsill.

After germination, seedlings should be grown at 21–27°C (70–81°F). When the seedlings can be handled, prick into individual 5–8cm (2–3in) pots, large modules or, better, biodegradable pots; feed with balanced liquid fertilizer after 2–3 weeks or if growth appears discoloured. Plant out after roots have filled the pot and the first flower buds appear.

| SOWING DEPTH | 2cm (¾in) |
|---|---|
| FINAL PLANT SPACING | vine: 38–45cm (15–18in) |
| | bush: 30–90cm (12–36in), depending on vigour |
| ROW SPACING | vine: 90cm (36in) single or staggered double rows |
| | bush: 90cm (36in) |

■ **Routine care** Cover bush tomatoes with fleece or cloches, and support if needed (*see p.109*). Support vine tomatoes, removing

sideshoots (*see p.109*). No more than 4–5 trusses can be relied upon to ripen outdoors before autumn frosts, so when enough trusses have set fruit, pinch out the terminal shoot, leaving two leaves above the final truss.

Water all types well in dry spells, especially container plants. Overfeeding or overwatering reduce flavour and may lead to disease. If the leaves become pale and are shed, weekly feeding with potassium-rich fertilizer, such as tomato feed, until foliage colour improves, boosts plant health and cropping. Mulch with organic matter or grow plants through black plastic (*see p.109*). Removing leaves below the lowest ripening truss helps air circulation and reduces disease; keep leaves higher up or fruits will not ripen or be poorly flavoured.

■ **Harvesting** Ideally allow fruits to ripen on the vine, and pick them when they have developed their full colour and flavour. At the end of the season either pick remaining green fruits and leave them in a warm place to ripen or pull up the entire vine and hang it upside down indoors. Cover bush types with cloches to finish ripening. Where vine types can be bent to ground level, similarly cover the vines.

■ **Common problems** Outdoor tomatoes share several diseases and soil pests with potatoes: blight (*see p.260*) can be serious and potato cyst eelworm (*see p.260*) and viruses (*see p.264*) also occur. Damp may cause foot and root rots (*see p.255*). Greenhouse tomatoes suffer mainly from whitefly (*see p.264*) and occasionally from aphids (*see p.251*), caterpillars (*see p.253*), and red spider mite (*see p.261*). In stagnant or damp conditions, botrytis will cause tomato ghost spot (*see p.263*) on fruits; high temperatures will exacerbate tomato blotchy ripening (*see p.263*). Magnesium deficiency is occasionally a problem (*see p.257*). To avoid soil-borne diseases, use containers or growing bags.

■ **Recommended cultivars**
**Bush tomato**
'Garden Pearl' – tumbling, small fruits, good for pots and hanging baskets.
'Red Alert' – early, heavy cropping, small sweet fruits.

**Cherry tomato**
'Gardener's Delight' ♀ – small, sweet fruits.
'Sungold' ♀ – heavy cropping, sweet, golden-orange fruit.
'Sweet Million' ♀ – heavy-cropping, sweet, very small fruits with thin skins, flavoursome.

**Plum tomato**
'Olivade' – heavy-cropping, brilliant texture, good flavour especially when cooked.

**Vine tomato**
'Alicante' ♀ – reliable, medium, tasty fruits.
'Black Russian' – beefsteak, purple-black fruits, semi-determinate, juicy, fine-flavour.
'Ferline' – hybrid, small beefsteak, resists blight.
'Golden Sunrise' ♀ – yellow fruits, extremely sweet, very heavy-cropping, old favourite.
'Outdoor Girl' ♀ – reliable, medium fruits.
'Tigerella' ♀ – striped fruits, very good flavour.
'Yellow Perfection' ♀ – yellow fruits, very sweet, heavy-cropping, old favourite.

# Growing cucurbits

Included in the cucurbit, or gourd, family (Cucurbitacae) are cucumbers, courgettes, melons, pumpkins, squashes, and marrows. These are all half-hardy annuals that make good potager plants where trained because the leaves and flowers are attractive as well as the fruits. The fruits are either eaten raw or cooked, or used in preserves. The young leaves and shoots are sometimes consumed as greens and the seeds as snacks, and even the flowers are occasionally eaten (*see individual crops, pp.117–119,* for details of which parts of any crop are edible). The closely related ornamental gourds may be harmful if eaten. If allowed to sprawl, marrows or squashes can take up quite a lot of space; training them vertically overcomes this problem.

## SOWING CUCURBIT CROPS

The large, flat seeds of cucurbits usually produce fast-growing seedlings, but germination requires soil temperatures of 13–30°C (55–86°F) and some of the crops are slow to mature. Seedlings need similar soil and air temperatures. Frost is fatal to leaves and stems, although ripe fruits may survive low temperatures. In cooler areas, therefore, it is best to sow all cucurbits under cover; in warmer areas, with long, hot summers, sowing fast-growing crops such as courgettes and ridge cucumbers directly outdoors usually produces stronger plants, since cucurbits resent root disturbance, but slow-maturing crops such as melons and squashes should still be sown under cover.

Sow in mid- to late spring in large modules or 8cm (3in) pots, preferably biodegradable ones (*see above*) so that there is no disturbance to the roots when planting out the seedlings later. Half-fill the pot or module with compost, and sow one or two seeds on their sides, rather than upright; this reduces soil resistance as the emerging seed leaves are raised clear of the soil, still encased in the seed coat. If necessary, thin out the weaker seedling after germination. When the remaining seedling reaches the top of the pot, fill in around it with more compost (*see above*) to produce a strong root system.

## Planting out seedlings in biodegradable pots

**1** **When seedlings sown** in biodegradable pots reach the top of the pot, fill in with more compost to earth up the stem and encourage strong roots.

**2** **About 2 weeks** after sowing, when the seedling has 3 or 4 true leaves and the roots are starting to show through the walls of the pot, it is ready for planting out.

**3** **Plant the seedling** in its pot after digging out holes at spacings appropriate for the crop; water the holes and pots thoroughly. Plant so the leaves sit just above the soil surface. Mound a little soil around the seedling stem to prevent water from collecting around it and encouraging rot. Water in to settle the soil, and label.

Outdoor sowings of fast-growing cucurbits can be made in late spring or in early summer in favourable areas, or earlier if the soil is pre-warmed with clear plastic or cloches (*see p.46*) for six weeks before sowing. Sow one to three seeds per station, on their sides; later, thin to the strongest seedling, if applicable. Protect newly sown areas with fleece (*see p.48*) for four weeks after sowing.

## SUCCESSIONAL SOWING

Because most cucurbit crops produce a succession of fruits, successional sowing (*see p.69*) is seldom required. The exceptions to this rule are courgettes and cucumbers, where an early spring sowing may need to be supplemented by an early summer sowing in order to produce later supplies.

## HARDENING OFF

Before planting out seedlings raised under cover, harden them off (*see p.65*) for two weeks in a cold frame, with gradually increasing ventilation, or under a double layer of fleece (*see p.48*).

## SITE AND SOIL

All cucurbits prefer a warm, sheltered site. Cucurbits were traditionally grown on ridges or mounds, often heavily enriched with organic matter. This helps particularly where soil is poor, shallow, and prone to waterlogging. Mounds and ridges require great labour to make and fill with organic matter, however, and are difficult to water adequately. Flat-topped beds, about 1m (3ft) wide and raised by about 15cm (6in), are just as successful, without the drawbacks. Another traditional practice was to prepare 30cm (12in) planting holes, refilled with soil enriched with organic matter. Equally good crops can be more conveniently grown on well-manured flat soil, especially if it is mulched after planting (*see p.72*).

Planting cucurbits on old compost heaps to utilize the residual fertility can be successful provided that the abundance of nutrients does not lead to leafy, non-flowering growth. The less vigorous cucurbits, such as cucumbers and courgettes, also grow well in pots of at least 25cm (10in) in

diameter, and in growing bags. Success, however, is dependent on plentiful and frequent watering and feeding (*see* Routine Care, *below*).

## PLANTING OUT

As soon as the seedlings have three or four true leaves, usually about two weeks after sowing, they are ready for planting out (*see facing page, and right*). Plant to the depth of the seed leaves; this buries some stem and allows more roots to form, which improves early growth. When conditions are dull and wet, however, shallower planting reduces the risk of disease. If in doubt, make a slight mound around the stem to prevent accumulation of water at the collar of the plant, which might cause rotting. The brittle roots and fragile area where the stem joins the roots means that each seedling needs very gentle handling, especially if it is being planted out as a bare-root seedling (*see p.70*).

Cucurbit seedlings benefit from extra warmth and protection after planting out, provided by either a cloche or fleece (*see pp.45–48*), especially if conditions are still chilly. On frosty nights, protect with hessian sacking or similar cloth.

**Planting out seedlings**
*As an alternative to growing seedlings in biodegradable pots (see facing page), sow seed in 8cm (3in) pots or modules and plant out with care when the seedlings have 3 or 4 true leaves. In a bed prepared with organic matter, plant at appropriate intervals – here 'Turks' Turban' squash seedlings are spaced 1m (3ft) apart. Use a hand trowel or a bulb planter to make the holes. Firm, water in, and label.*

## SUPPORTING CUCURBIT CROPS

The shoots of trailing or climbing cucurbits can be tied into twine, wires, trellis, or bamboo wigwams (*see below*) to save space and protect fruits from wet soil, slugs, disease and damage. However, they can ramble freely and crops are often heavier if this is allowed.

## ROUTINE CARE

Protect all early sowings and plantings, especially in cooler areas, with cold frames, cloches, or fleece (*see pp.45–48*). Melons and cucumbers will require protection throughout the year. In hot periods, ventilate cold frames and cloches sufficiently to prevent excessive temperatures. In greenhouses, use shading paint or netting in midsummer to protect plants from scorching.

Feeding will increase yields, although too much nitrogen should be avoided because it can lead to excessive leaf production at the expense of fruiting. Cucurbits need only small amounts of fertilizer; a suitable dressing is 75–100g per sq m (2–3oz per sq yd) of a general compound fertilizer, or 100–140g per sq m (3–4oz per sq yd) of an organic feed such as dried poultry manure with a 5 per cent nitrogen content (*see pp.20–23*). Halve these amounts for plants growing in fertile, recently manured soil. Regular feeding is vital for container crops.

Mulching (*see p.72*) helps to retain soil moisture, suppress weeds, and keep

## Supporting cucurbit crops

Some cucurbits have a climbing or trailing habit, and therefore need some form of support to prevent the fruits resting on the ground, where they will be susceptible to rotting, as well as the attentions of slugs and snails. Outdoor crops may be supported with bamboo canes and twine, either in a wigwam or row arrangement. A trellis would suit a sheltered spot and allow fruits to hang down. Greenhouse cordon crops can be twined around single strings hanging vertically from the roof. Individual fruits may also be supported with netting attached to the overall support network.

*Outdoor squashes on a fan trellis*

*Individual greenhouse melon supported by a net*

*Tying in outdoor cucumbers into cane wigwam*

*Greenhouse cucumber growing up vertical twine*

the fruits clean. Additionally, black plastic sheet mulches (*see p.42*) will help to warm the soil. Organic mulches feed the crops, but very rich ones, such as mushroom compost, can lead to more leafy growth than fruit.

Frequent, plentiful watering is essential, especially for crops grown under cover or in containers. Water after planting and sowing, during flowering and fruit swelling, and in dry spells. A low-level or drip-irrigation system (*see p.54*) can be indispensable. To grow very large fruits such as giant pumpkins as much as 11 litres (2 gallons) per week for each plant may be required, to which liquid fertilizer (*see pp.20–23*) should be added.

## WEED CONTROL

The spreading shoots and large leaves of mature cucurbits will suppress weeds by themselves. In the early stages, however, use organic or black plastic mulches (*see pp.41–42*). Alternatively, prepare the site in early spring and allow the weeds to germinate; before planting, remove them by shallow hoeing or with a contact herbicide. This is known as the stale seedbed technique. If left undisturbed, the soil will remain largely weed-free until the foliage spreads sufficiently to smother the weeds.

## POLLINATION

Pollination is an essential requirement for most cucurbits to set fruits, and separate male and female flowers are borne on the same plant. The only exception to this are greenhouse cucumbers (*see p.117*). Cucurbits are pollinated by insects, so fleece, frame, or cloche coverings should be opened at flowering time to allow insects access.

When there are too few pollinators, or they are insufficiently active, hand-pollination (*see above*) can be carried out by picking a male flower and pressing it lightly onto a female one so that the stigma, in the centre of the female flower, receives pollen from the stamens of the male. Small flowers, such as those of cucumbers and melons, which are easily damaged, are best shaken over the females. Male cucurbit flowers are fertile only for a short time; check that they are ready by brushing a finger over the male flower to detect

## Hand-pollinating cucurbit flowers

**1** **Help cucurbit plants to set fruit** by pollinating them by hand, rather than waiting for insects to do it. Pick a fully open male flower – one with no embryonic fruit at the base (*see below*) – and carefully pinch off all the petals to expose the stamens, which bear the powdery yellow pollen.

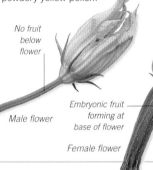

No fruit below flower

Male flower

Embryonic fruit forming at base of flower

Female flower

**2** **Insert the male flower** carefully into a female flower – one that has an embryonic fruit (*see left*) – so that the pollen is transferred from the male stamens onto the stigma of the female flower.

yellow, powdery pollen. Each fertile male flower has enough pollen for several females. Repeated pollination on consecutive sunny days is sometimes required for a good "set". Male flowers can predominate during short days early in the season, but the female flowers will prevail later on. Wider spacing between the plants, less shade, later planting, and potassium–rich liquid fertilizers (*see p.20*) can increase female flower numbers. Closer spacing

and early planting out will create a predominance of male flowers.

Cold temperatures cause incomplete pollination, where fruits swell only at the flower end, and shrivel at the other end. Cool weather can also lead to complete failure to set fruit, because pollination fails through lack of insects and impaired pollen germination and development. If pollination occurs but fruitlets fail to develop, the cause is often that there are more fruits than the plant can support. This will be resolved as the plant grows.

Fruitlets may be thinned to just one per stem, or even one per plant, where large fruits are wanted. This is especially necessary for melons. There is no need to thin cucumbers or courgettes.

## HARVESTING AND STORING

Frequent harvesting of immature courgettes, cucumbers, and melons is essential to prevent poor-quality, over-mature fruits forming. Cut the stalks cleanly with a sharp knife or secateurs. Fruits of marrows, pumpkins, and squashes are ready to harvest when they develop full colour and a hard skin, and ring hollow when tapped. The stem will also start to crack. Fruits for storage should be left to mature on the plants as long as possible. After cutting, cure them in a greenhouse or warm room at 27–32°C (81–90°F) for several days. Store at about 10°C (50°F), with fairly high humidity to prevent shrivelling.

**Protecting ripening fruits**
*If plants are grown unsupported outdoors, place a piece of wood or a brick underneath the ripening fruits (here, a marrow) to raise them off the soil. This will minimize any possibility of soiling or rotting.*

# A–Z OF CUCURBITS

## Courgette and summer squash

*Cucurbita pepo*

| SEASON | SPRING | SUMMER | AUTUMN | WINTER |
|---|---|---|---|---|
| SOW | • • • | • | | |
| TRANSPLANT | • | • | | |
| HARVEST | | • • | • • | |

Courgettes, or zucchini, differ from vegetable marrows (*see p.119*) only in that they produce fruits suitable for harvesting immediately after flowering, although if left they will eventually form marrows. Courgettes are seedless, since they are eaten when young and fresh, and have a firmer texture and a better taste than marrows. They are relatively robust and fast-growing, and grow easily outdoors. Some have a trailing habit. Summer squashes are treated in the same way as courgettes. The flowers, especially male ones, are considered a delicacy, stuffed or fried; the tendrils and shoot tips can also be steamed for eating. Courgettes and summer squashes yield 6–12 fruits per plant. They are not suitable for storing.

■ **Site and soil** Courgettes prefer an open, sunny position, and benefit from the addition of plenty of organic matter during soil preparation (*see p.114*), as well as dressing with a mulch (*see p.116*). Seeds need a minimum of 13°C (56°F) to germinate.

■ **Sowing and planting** For early crops, sow in a greenhouse in mid- to late spring (*see p.114*), and plant out under cloches or frames in late spring or outdoors in early summer (*see p.115*). Later crops can be direct sown, three seeds per station, outdoors in early summer (*see p.114*). Delay sowing, or planting out, for about two weeks in cooler districts.

| SOWING DEPTH | 2.5cm (1in) |
|---|---|
| PLANT SPACING | 90cm (36in) |
| ROW SPACING | 90cm (36in) |
| | 1.2m (4ft) for trailing cultivars |

■ **Routine care** Water regularly to keep the soil moist, especially during flowering. Feeding (*see p.115*) can help if growth appears too slow. Hand pollination (*see p.116*) is usually only required for plants grown in cloches and frames. Trailing types may be trained over canes or wires (*see p.115*). For early crops, use cloches or frames (*see p.115*).

■ **Harvesting** Gather the young fruits when they are about 10cm (4in) long, or when the remnants of the flowers fall off (*see p.116*). If left any longer, the swelling fruits will have less flavour and poor texture, and they will also divert the plant's energy away from the formation of new fruits.

■ **Common problems** Powdery mildew (*see p.260*) occurs in late summer. Cucumber mosaic virus (*see p.254*) is common, which results in poorly formed fruits, but disease-resistant cultivars

are available. Slugs and snails (*see p.262*) can be very destructive to young plants. Red spider mite (*see p.261*) and whitefly (*see p.264*) are especially damaging in cold frames. Foot and root rots (*see p.255*) affect the bases of the stems and are associated with overwatered plants and badly drained soil. Bean seed fly (*see p.252*) can occasionally damage outdoor sowings in early summer.

■ **Recommended cultivars**
**Courgette**
'Bambino' ♀ – early, small, dark green fruits, prolific over a long period.
'Defender' ♀ – dark green fruits, resistant to cucumber mosaic virus, high yields.
'Early Gem' ♀ – dark green fruits, prolific.
'Eight Ball' ♀ – round green fruits from compact plants.
'Jemmer' ♀ – compact, prolific, yellow fruits.
**Summer squash**
'Patty Pan' – scalloped, green and yellow fruits, ornamental, good flavour.
'Sunburst' – pretty, yellow, patty pan type, high yields over a long period.

## Cucumber and gherkin

*Cucumis sativus*

| SEASON | SPRING | SUMMER | AUTUMN | WINTER |
|---|---|---|---|---|
| SOW | • • • • | | | |
| TRANSPLANT | | • • • | | |
| HARVEST | | | • • • • | |

Home-grown cucumbers are worth the effort as they are far tastier than those in the shops. There are two basic types: greenhouse and outdoor cucumbers. Greenhouse types are more difficult to grow, but have long, smooth fruits. Some resilient greenhouse cultivars also grow well in cold frames. Outdoor types include ridge cucumbers and gherkins, which are short, rough-skinned, and hardier than greenhouse cucumbers, but equal in flavour. Japanese outdoor cucumbers are robust and approach greenhouse types in size and quality.

Cucumbers are climbing plants suitable for growing on wigwams, trellis, or wires (*see p.115*), or for trailing along the ground; better-quality fruits will be obtained by using supports, however, and the plants occupy less space. No cucumbers can tolerate frost. They normally yield about 15 fruits per plant.

Modern greenhouse cucumbers are all-female and do not require pollination to set fruit. For these plants, pollination can cause unshapely and bitter-tasting fruits, and should be avoided by growing them well apart from other cucurbits. Grown in cool conditions, however, male flowers (*see p.116*) occasionally arise, and these should be removed.

All outdoor cucumbers and gherkins, except all-female cultivars, need pollination by insects or by hand (see p.116), or no crop will result.

■ **Site and soil** For germination, cucumber seeds need a minimum temperature of 20°C (68°F); the optimum growing temperature is 28°C (82°F); in greenhouses, provide a minimum of 20°C (68°F) at night. Sheltered, warm, sunny conditions are therefore essential for outdoor cucumbers and gherkins, but black plastic mulches and fleece (see p.42) can help warm the soil. Plants benefit from the incorporation of organic matter during soil preparation, and mulching (see p.72) during the growing period. On heavy soils, it is better to grow cucumbers and gherkins on a flat-topped raised bed (see p.114) than a ridge. Cucumbers and gherkins will crop better when protected with cloches, cold frames, or even fleece (see p.48), in cold districts.

■ **Sowing and planting** Sow in a greenhouse (see p.114) in early to mid-spring, and from mid-spring outdoors. After hardening off (see p.114), plant out seedlings in late spring in cloches and cold frames, and in early summer outdoors; delay this by two weeks in cooler areas or for gherkins. Greenhouse cucumbers can be grown in growing bags.

Sowing direct (see p.114) is possible in early summer, especially if soil is pre-warmed with cloches or fleece, or in midsummer for gherkins. Sow three seeds per station, each seed 15cm (6in) apart. Where space is tight, seeds can be sown in a drill (see p.67), with the plants later trained up a mesh or trellis fence to make an attractive cucumber hedge.

| SOWING DEPTH | 2.5cm (1in) |
| --- | --- |
| PLANT SPACING | 45cm (18in) for drills |
| | 15cm (6in) at stations |
| ROW SPACING | 60–75cm (24–30in) |

■ **Routine care** For supports, use wigwams, trellis, twine, or wires (see p.115). Pinch out growing tips of climbers only when they reach the top of the support; plants allowed to trail on the ground crop better and use space more efficiently if growing tips are regularly removed to encourage bushy growth. In cold frames and cloches, train sideshoots to the corners and pinch out the tips again. Water plentifully (see p.116); never allow cucumbers to dry out. If growth slows and leaves become pale, use a balanced liquid fertilizer (see p.21) as directed by the manufacturer until leaves green up again. Alternatively, use an organic mulch (see p.41) to add nutrient, keep fruits clean, reduce water loss, and suppress weeds.

■ **Harvesting** Cucumbers and gherkins are best harvested before any yellowing begins, and after the sides become parallel. Avoid picking excessively young fruits, however, as they often taste bitter. Greenhouse cucumbers are usually ready from midsummer; gherkins a month later. Outdoor cutting can be done in late summer to mid-autumn, or the first frosts; and for gherkins, in late autumn.

■ **Common problems** Powdery mildew (see p.260) often occurs in late summer; good cultivation, especially watering and feeding,

helps prevent this. Cucumber mosaic virus (see p.254) is common and can cause poorly formed fruits; disease-resistant cultivars are sometimes available – remove all diseased plants. Slugs and snails (see p.262) can destroy young plants. Red spider mite (see p.261) and whitefly (see p.264) are very damaging in cold frames; biological controls are very effective in these situations. Foot and root rots (see p.255) affect stem bases and are associated with overwatered plants and badly drained soil. Bean seed fly (see p.252) can sometimes damage outdoor sowings in early summer. Fleece will exclude them. If male flowers are allowed to pollinate the plant, the fruits will be bitter and inedible (see p.252).

■ **Recommended cultivars**
**Greenhouse cucumber**
'Carmen' ♀ – hybrid, dark-ribbed, well-shaped fruits.
'Femspot' – hybrid, dark fruits, easy to grow.
'Green Fingers' – miniature fruits, crisp flesh, prolific.
'Improved Telegraph' – good frame type, not all-female, reliable, high yields, good flavour.
'King George' – large, old-fashioned fruits.
**Outdoor cucumber and gherkin**
'Burpless Tasty Green' – trailing, tender fruits.
'Bush Champion' ♀ – ridge type, good in containers, resistant to cucumber mosaic virus.
'Crystal Lemon' – lemon-shaped, yellowish, tasty fruits.
'Kyoto' – Japanese type, slender fruits.
'Marketmore' ♀ – ridge type, disease-resistant.
'Tokyo Slicer' – Japanese type, slender fruits.
'Venlo Pickling' – traditional pickling gherkin.

# Pumpkin and winter squash

*Cucurbita maxima, C. moschata, and C. pepo*

| SEASON | SPRING | SUMMER | AUTUMN | WINTER |
| --- | --- | --- | --- | --- |
| SOW | • • | • | | |
| TRANSPLANT | | • • | | |
| HARVEST | | | • • | |

Pumpkins and winter squashes are a valuable, highly ornamental winter vegetable. Most trail to form very large, rambling plants, but some bushy types also exist. Although mainly grown for storage, the immature fruits may be eaten in the same way as courgettes (see p.117). The seeds of some cultivars may be roasted to eat; the flowers, tendrils, and shoot tips are edible as for courgettes (see p.117). Normal yields are one large fruit or 4–6 small fruits per plant.

■ **Site and soil** An open, sunny site and fertile, well-drained soil are essential (see p.114). Seeds require a minimum of 13°C (56°F) to germinate, and the plants grow best at 18–21°C (65–70°F). Pumpkins and winter squashes can be unreliable in cooler areas.

■ **Sowing and planting** A long growing season is required and seed is best sown indoors (see p.114) in mid- to late spring for planting out in

late spring and early summer (see p.115). Alternatively, station sow outdoors in early summer (see p.114), ideally in soil pre-warmed with fleece or cloches (see pp.46–48).

| SOWING DEPTH | 2.5cm (1in) |
| --- | --- |
| PLANT SPACING | 90cm (3ft) bush cultivars |
| | 1.5m (5ft) trailing cultivars |
| ROW SPACING | 90cm (3ft) bush cultivars |
| | 1.5m (5ft) trailing cultivars |

■ **Routine care** Trailing types need less water and feeding than other cucurbits as they spread widely, rooting deeply as they go. Bushy plants need normal amounts (see p.115), and a mulch (see p.116) also helps retain moisture. To save space, you can use short canes to train shoots of trailing types into circles on the ground. Alternatively, grow them up a support (see p.115), making sure it is sufficiently sturdy to support large, heavy fruits. Support individual fruits with netting if necessary (see p.115). If very large fruits are desired, thin when they are still small fruitlets to only 2–3 per plant.

■ **Harvesting and storing** Gather fruits when they are fully coloured and have a hollow ring when tapped. Allow the skins to harden in the sun. For storing, use larger, more mature fruits. If carefully cured and stored (see p.116), they will keep for several months, sometimes even into early spring.

■ **Common problems** Powdery mildew (see p.260) is the only real threat. The crops might be affected by foot and root rots (see p.255), cucumber mosaic virus (see p.254), and slugs and snails may attack seedlings (see p.262).

■ **Recommended cultivars**
**Pumpkin**
'Atlantic Giant' – trailing, exhibition type, huge record-breaking fruits.
'Baby Bear' – trailing, miniature, orange fruits, stores well.
'Jack o' Lantern' – classic Halloween type.
'Rouge Vif D'Etamp' – trailing, flat shape, rich orange fruits, stores well.
'Triple Treat' – trailing, bright orange fruits, Halloween type, edible seeds.
**Winter squash**
'Crown Prince' – trailing, steely blue colour, nutty flavour.
'Harrier' ♀ – butternut, bell-shaped fruits with small seed cavity.
'Queensland Blue' – trailing, blue-green fruits, good flavour.
'Sweet Dumpling' – small, densely fleshed fruits, sweet, nutty.

# Sweet melon

*Cucumis melo*

| SEASON | SPRING | SUMMER | AUTUMN | WINTER |
| --- | --- | --- | --- | --- |
| SOW | • • • | | | |
| TRANSPLANT | | • | | |
| HARVEST | | • • | • • | |

Sweet melons are trailing, tender annuals from tropical regions that need plenty of warmth; in

temperate areas, they can only be grown successfully if protection is provided. There are three main types of sweet melon: cantaloupe, winter or casaba, and musk. Cantaloupe types have thick, rough, grooved skins, greyish green in colour. Winter melons have yellow, or yellow-and-green-striped, smooth skins, and include honeydew melons. Musk types are usually smaller than the other two types, and have smooth skins, often covered with a network of fine lines. Sweet melons yield 2–4 fruits per plant.

■ **Site and soil** For uninterrupted growth and good flavour, sweet melons need an especially sunny, warm, and sheltered site, and a rich soil with plenty of organic matter added to it (*see p.114*). A minimum temperature of 16°C (60°F) is required for seed to germinate, and the plants grow best at around 25°C (77°F). In cool, temperate areas, this means growing them in a greenhouse or a cold frame, or protecting them with fleece or cloches (*see pp.43–48*).

■ **Sowing and planting** In cool areas, sow in the greenhouse (*see p.114*) in mid-spring, and plant out in early summer. When planting, the rootball should only just be covered in soil, since deep planting encourages rotting. In warmer areas, station sow direct outdoors under cover in late spring (*see p.114*).

| SOWING DEPTH | 2.5cm (1in) |
|---|---|
| PLANT SPACING | 60–100cm (2–3ft) |
| ROW SPACING | 1m (3ft) |

■ **Routine care** Constant moisture is required, especially during the flowering period (*see p.116*). If growth flags, apply a liquid fertilizer weekly (*see p.21*). If growing in a greenhouse, train the stems up supports (*see p.115*). In a cold frame, train the shoots into the corners as they grow. After planting, "stop" the main stem by pinching out the leading shoot after two leaves have developed, resulting in two further shoots. Stop these after seven leaves have been produced, and stop the shoots resulting from this when they have five leaves. Subsequent shoots bear the crop.

The first fruits to set inhibit further fruit formation. To avoid this, keep cloches, cold frames, or fleece in place and closed until the plant is in full flower, then open up the protective covering to allow insects to gain access and to pollinate all the flowers simultaneously. Thin the fruits to two or four per plant when they are about 2.5cm (1in) in diameter. Stop any fruit-bearing shoots at 2–3 leaves beyond the fruit to concentrate the plant's energy into the fruits. Support individual greenhouse fruits with netting (*see p.115*).

■ **Harvesting and storing** When the stalk begins to crack and the fruit develops a sweet scent, cut the stem with a sharp knife or secateurs. Sweet melons may be stored successfully for several weeks in a refrigerator. Covering fruits with cloches or fleece as cool autumn nights approach will help speed the process of ripening.

■ **Common problems** Powdery mildew (*see p.260*), cucumber mosaic virus (*see p.254*), foot and root rots (*see p.255*), slugs and snails (*see p.262*), red spider mite (*see p.261*), whitefly (*see p.264*), aphids (*see p.251*), and bean seed fly (*see p.252*) may all be troublesome.

■ **Recommended cultivars**
'Blenheim Orange' – old favourite, netted fruits, yellow flesh.
'Castella' – striped fruits, grown outdoors under cloches or fleece, sweet amber flesh.
'Edonis' ♀ – Charentais cantaloupe, early, netted pale green skin, delicious orange flesh.
'Galia' – sweet, vigorous, resists mildew.
'Ogen' ♀ – cantaloupe, reliable, dark green striped skin, flavoursome green flesh.
'Sweetheart' ♀ – cantaloupe, vigorous, tasty yellow fruits, high yields, susceptible to mildew.

# Vegetable marrow

*Cucurbita pepo*

| SEASON | SPRING | SUMMER | AUTUMN | WINTER |
|---|---|---|---|---|
| SOW | • • • | | | |
| TRANSPLANT | • • | | | |
| HARVEST | | • • • • | | |

Vegetable marrows are easy-to-grow, bush or trailing annuals; the fruits are traditional summer and autumn vegetables that can also be stored for winter use. Marrows are usually elongated and striped, but plain-coloured and rounded types are also available. Vegetable marrows normally yield two large fruits, or six to eight small ones, per plant.

■ **Site and soil** Vegetable marrows prefer an open, sunny position and benefit from the addition of plenty of organic matter during soil preparation (*see p.114*). They also do well if grown through a mulch (*see p.116*). Seeds need a minimum soil temperature of 13°C (56°F) to germinate.

■ **Sowing and planting** For early crops, sow in the greenhouse in mid- to late spring (*see p.114*), and plant out either under cloches or in frames in late spring or outdoors in early summer (*see p.115*). Later crops can be direct sown, 2–3 seeds per station, outdoors in early summer (*see p.114*). Delay sowing, or planting out, for about two weeks in cooler districts.

| SOWING DEPTH | 2.5cm (1in) |
|---|---|
| PLANT SPACING | 90cm (3ft) |
| ROW SPACING | 90cm (3ft) bush types |
| | 1.2m (4ft) trailing types |

■ **Routine care** Constant moisture is required especially during the flowering period (*see p.116*). Liquid fertilizer (*see p.21*) can be beneficial if growth slows down, and also during swelling of fruits. If necessary, provide support (*see p.115*) for trailing types. (*See also Routine Care, pp.115–116.*)

■ **Harvesting and storing** For small summer marrows, regular harvesting, when they are at least 15cm (6in) long, encourages further fruiting and increases the yield. For winter storage, let the marrows develop to a full size and acquire a hard, resilient skin. For a perfect finish, turn them occasionally as they ripen in the sun and rest fruits on a piece of wood or brick rather than allow them to lie on the soil (*see p.116*). Vegetable marrows should be stored in a dry, cool, frost-free place (*see p.116*).

■ **Common problems** As they are so closely related, vegetable marrows suffer the same problems as courgettes (*see p.117*).

■ **Recommended cultivars**
'Badger Cross' ♀ – bush type, dark green fruits.
'Bush Baby' – compact bushy plants, smaller fruits.
'Green Bush' – traditional, large marrows.
'Long Green Trailing' – trailing type, long dark green fruits, traditional, high yields.
'Tiger Cross' ♀ – resistant to cucumber mosaic virus, bush type.
'Vegetable Spaghetti' – trailing type, flesh forms strands when cooked.

# Watermelon

*Citrullus lanatus*

| SEASON | SPRING | SUMMER | AUTUMN | WINTER |
|---|---|---|---|---|
| SOW | • | | | |
| TRANSPLANT | • • | | | |
| HARVEST | | | • • | |

Watermelons are spreading annual plants. Their stems can grow up to 4m (12ft) in length. The large fruits – up to 60cm (2ft) long – are oblong or rounded, cream or green in colour, striped or mottled, and are eaten raw. Watermelons need a long growing season and plenty of warmth in order to thrive. In cool, temperate regions, a cold frame can give adequate protection if sited in a very warm, sunny, sheltered position; otherwise, grow them in a greenhouse. New developments include small-fruited, quick-growing cultivars. Watermelons yield one or two fruits per plant.

■ **Site and soil** Watermelons require similar, conditions to sweet melons (*see above*), but optimum temperatures for growth are higher: 25–30°C (77–85°F).

■ **Sowing and planting** Sow indoors in mid-spring (*see p.114*), planting out in late spring to early summer (*see p.115*).

| SOWING DEPTH | 2.5cm (1in) |
|---|---|
| PLANT SPACING | 60–100cm (2–3ft) |
| ROW SPACING | 1m (3ft) |

■ **Routine care** Watermelons are vigorous and require the same watering, feeding, and training as sweet melons (*see above*).

■ **Harvesting** Gather when the stem dries, and the fruit changes colour, especially if there is a slight yellowing of the pale area that is resting on the ground (*see p.116*). Covering fruits with cloches or fleece as cool autumn nights approach will help speed ripening.

■ **Common problems** Watermelons suffer the same problems as sweet melons (*see above*).

■ **Recommended cultivars**
'Charleston Grey' – long-established, slow-growing, sprawling, oblong fruits.
'Sugar Baby' – small-fruited, compact, fast-maturing, juicy fruits.

# Growing stem vegetables

This group includes celeriac, celery, and Florence fennel, all of which have edible fleshy stems and decorative foliage. They are biennials usually grown as annuals, since most are unable to withstand anything other than light frosts. Celery and fennel are not the easiest crops to grow, but celeriac is much simpler. Celeriac and celery both make useful winter vegetables.

Celery types include modern self-blanching kinds, traditional trench celery, and leaf celery, which is grown for its tender young leaves instead of its stems. Self-blanching types are easier to grow, although the seed must be sown in heat in early spring and the plants will not be ready to plant out until mid- to late spring; ready-grown plants can be purchased by mail order if you cannot raise them yourself from seed. Celery cultivars with green, red, or pink stems (*see below*) are also available.

Celeriac and most celery are long-season crops, but leaf celery and fennel are quicker to mature. Leaf celery is very hardy and will last through to the following spring. Celery and fennel are prone to bolting and running to seed, especially if planted too early, but some bolt-resistant cultivars are now available.

### SITE AND SOIL
All stem vegetables need a fertile, well-drained, moisture-retentive soil, with plenty of organic matter incorporated

**Pink-stemmed celery**
*For an interesting salad, try growing one of the attractive pink- or red-stemmed trench celery cultivars (here 'Blush'). These are usually hardier than the white-stemmed types, and can therefore be used later in the season.*

into it, in an open site. For celery and celeriac, acid soils should be limed (*see pp.18–19*). Self-blanching celery can be grown either under cover or outside, but is susceptible to frost, and should be harvested by mid-autumn unless given some protection. Celery needs high levels of nitrogen, whereas celeriac and fennel prefer low levels.

### BLANCHING STEMS
Celery, in particular, needs to be blanched; that is, the plants should be deprived of light so that the stems remain white and more tender to eat. The traditional, laborious method of planting in a trench (hence the name trench celery) and then earthing up the stems is now seldom employed. Self-blanching celery plants should be planted closely in blocks (*see right*) so that their own foliage helps to restrict the availability of light to the stems of the plants in the middle.

The outer plants in a block of self-blanching celery, however, and all trench celery plants, are best blanched with collars (*see above*). In late summer, when the plants are 23–30cm (9–12in) tall, loosely wrap strips – 38cm (15in) long and as wide as the plant is tall – of lightproof paper or black plastic around the stems, and secure with two loops of garden twine. Black plastic must also be lined with paper to prevent the stems sweating, which could cause rotting. In windy areas, tie the twine around a cane to provide support. Leave one-third of the plant exposed

to allow it to keep growing, and also make sure that there is plenty of room for the stem to expand within required for show purposes, repeat the blanching process 2–3 weeks later. It may be necessary to take off the collars from time to time to check for slugs and snails, since they will flourish in the shelter of the protective sleeves.

### ROUTINE CARE
To produce tender, non-stringy stems, provide a constant supply of moisture throughout the growing season to swell the stems, but avoid waterlogging. Mulching (*see p.72*) will help to conserve moisture. Celeriac and celery can be protected from winter frost by a layer of straw or bracken placed around the plants. For feeding requirements, *see individual crops, pp.121–122*.

**Blanching stems**
*For all trench celery plants, and outer plants in a block of self-blanching types, loosely wrap a length of paper-lined black plastic around the stems when they are 23–30cm (9–12in) tall. Leave 8–10cm (3–4in) of overlap to allow for plant growth and secure with twine.*

**Planting in a block**
*For celery, especially the self-blanching types – here 'Victoria' (background) and 'Celebrity' (foreground) – block planting, with the plants positioned 25cm (10in) apart each way, aids the blanching process by excluding some light.*

# A–Z OF STEM VEGETABLES

## Celeriac

### *Apium graveolens* var. *rapaceum*

| MONTH | SPRING | SUMMER | AUTUMN | WINTER |
|-------|--------|--------|--------|--------|
| SOW | • • | | | |
| TRANSPLANT | | • • • | | |
| HARVEST | • • | | • • • | • • • |

Celeriac produces a knobbly, swollen "bulb" at the base of the stem, up to 13cm (5in) in diameter (*see illustration, p.34*); the bulb can be cooked or grated raw into winter salads. It is sometimes described as turnip-rooted celery, having a similar taste to celery. Celeriac is more hardy than self-blanching celery, being able to survive temperatures as low as –10°C (14°F) if protected by straw. It is a useful alternative to celery in the winter, because it is much hardier, and less prone to problems. Newer cultivars are being bred to produce smoother stems that are easier to peel. Celeriac yields ten heads, 225–400g (8–12oz) each, per 3m (10ft) row.

■ **Site and soil** Celeriac needs a rich soil with plenty of organic matter incorporated into it (*see p.120*). It prefers an open site, but will tolerate a limited amount of shade.

■ **Sowing and planting** For best results, celeriac needs a long, uninterrupted growing season. Sow seeds in early to mid-spring in a propagator at 15°C (59°F) either in modules or seed trays, or several seeds to a pot or module (*see pp.64–65*). When large enough to handle, prick out the seedlings into larger modules (*see p.64*), or thin to one per pot or module, and keep above 10°C (50°F). From mid-spring to early summer, harden the plants off (*see p.65*) before planting out in well-spaced rows or blocks (*see p.71*); they need plenty of light and air around them, and if planted too closely will produce poor roots. Better crops are usually achieved if planted out in late spring rather than early summer, so they can establish before the hot, dry weather.

| SOWING DEPTH | on surface |
|--------------|------------|
| PLANT SPACING | 30cm (12in) |
| ROW SPACING | 45cm (18in) |

■ **Routine care** Water well once or twice a week; in dry spells, use 22 litres per sq m (4½ gallons per sq yd) for each watering. Apply a mulch to retain moisture (*see p.72*). If the crop is slow-growing, or looks pale, top-dress with sulphate of ammonia (*see p.20*) at a rate of 35g per sq m (1oz per sq yd) in midsummer, remove any outer leaves that are splitting away from the stem and yellowing; this should produce stems that are less knobbly. If you are leaving the crop in the ground over winter, protect it against frost with a 15cm (6in) layer of bracken or straw tucked around the plants.

■ **Harvesting and storing** Celeriac takes six months to mature. Early cultivars can be harvested from early autumn and later ones up to mid-spring. The stems are ready when they reach 8–13cm (3–5in) in diameter. Lift the stem, trim off the roots, and wash it clean. Twist off the top, unless some of the leaves are to be used in soup. Celeriac is best left in the ground until needed and then used fresh. Where the winters are particularly severe, however, it can be stored. Dig the plant up in early winter, leaving the roots and central tuft of leaves untrimmed, and place it in a box of moist sand in a cool, dark place (*see p.73*).

■ **Common problems** As for celery (*see p.122*).

■ **Recommended cultivars**
'Alabaster' – smooth, round bulbs.
'Balder' – large, smooth bulbs, stores well.
'Giant Prague' – traditional celeriac for any site or soil.
'Monarch' ♥ – smooth bulbs, harvest autumn or early winter.
'Prinz' ♥ – early, smooth, large bulbs.

## Celery and leaf celery

### *Apium graveolens* var. *dulce*

| SEASON | SPRING | SUMMER | AUTUMN | WINTER |
|--------|--------|--------|--------|--------|
| **SELF-BLANCHING/GREEN CELERY** | | | | |
| SOW | • • | | | |
| TRANSPLANT | | • • • | | |
| HARVEST | | | • • • • | |
| **TRENCH CELERY** | | | | |
| SOW | • • | | | |
| TRANSPLANT | | • • | | |
| HARVEST | | | • • | |
| **LEAF CELERY** | | | | |
| SOW | • • | • | | |
| TRANSPLANT | • • • | | • | |
| HARVEST | • • | | • • • • | • • • |

Celery is grown for its fleshy, blanched stems, up to 25cm (10in) in length, which are eaten raw in salads or cooked as a vegetable or in soups. The inner stems gradually get smaller, but are more tender and better blanched than the outer ones. There are three main types: self-blanching and green celery; trench celery; and leaf, or cutting, celery.

Self-blanching celery cultivars have off-white stalks; these and green celery cultivars are easy to grow, but less hardy and slightly less flavoursome than trench types. Trench celery demands a lot of space in the garden and a fair amount of skill to blanch the stems successfully, whether this is done in the traditional way using trenches and earthing up or in the more modern way of planting on the flat and using collars (*see p.120*). There are white-, red-, and pink-stemmed cultivars (*see p.120*). Leaf celery is a small, very hardy plant, with fine stems and scented leaves,

that can be grown in containers. It is useful as a salad herb or flavouring. When working with celery, beware of celery rash; always keep your hands and arms covered for safety. Self-blanching, green, and trench celery yield 12 heads, 450g (1lb) each, per 3m (10ft) row. Leaf celery yields 15–20 heads per 3m (10ft) row.

■ **Site and soil**  Celery needs an open site and rich, moisture-retentive, well-drained soil with plenty of organic matter added to it (*see p.120*); it also needs a pH of 6.6–6.8, so you should add lime to acid soils (*see pp.18–19*). For trench celery, in autumn dig a trench 38–45cm (15–18in) wide and 30cm (12in) deep, working in plenty of organic matter. If growing the celery on the flat, fill in the trench to the top; if the celery is to be earthed up, fill to 8–10cm (3–4in) below the surface, leaving the rest of the soil at the side of the trench for earthing up later.

■ **Sowing and planting**  Always use treated seed in order to avoid seed-borne diseases (*see below*) that can spoil the crop. Celery seed may be slow to germinate (*see p.62*). For self-blanching celery, sow seed in pots or modules in a propagator (*see p.63*) in early to mid-spring at 15°C (59°F); sow on the surface, since the seed needs light to germinate, and keep it moist. Prick out the seedlings when they have one true leaf into larger modules (*see p.64*). Grow the seedlings at a minimum temperature of at least 10°C (50°F) to avoid bolting. When the plants have 4–6 true leaves, plant them out so that the crown of the plant is at soil level. They can withstand light frosts, but early crops should be protected with frames, cloches, or fleece (*see pp.45–48*). Space the plants about 25cm (10in) apart in a block (*see p.120*). Water in well.

Sow trench celery as for self-blanching celery. Harden off before transplanting in late spring to early summer in the prepared trench or on the flat in single rows, for ease of management; the exact plant spacing depends on the size of stick required. If you need to conserve space, you can use a double row, sited 60–75cm (24–30in) from the next crop.

For leaf celery, sow either in seed trays or pots (*see p.64*) as for self-blanching celery, or preferably as multiblocks (*see p.65*). You can also sow a few multiblocks in late summer to crop in a greenhouse in winter and spring.

| SOWING DEPTH | on surface, or very shallow |
|---|---|
| PLANT SPACING | self-blanching: 25cm (10in) |
| | trench: 30–45cm (12–18in) |
| | leaf: 13cm (5in) single plants |
| | 20cm (8in) multiblocks |
| ROW SPACING | self-blanching: 25cm (10in) |
| | trench: 30cm (12in) |
| | leaf: 30cm (12in) |

■ **Routine care**  Celery requires plenty of moisture, and must grow evenly without any checks to prevent stringiness. Water well once or twice a week; in dry spells, use 22 litres per sq m (4½ gallons per sq yd) per watering. Use a mulch to retain moisture (*see p.72*). When the plants are about half their final size, before

the leaves touch, top-dress with sulphate of ammonia (*see p.20*) at a rate of 50g per sq m (1½oz per sq yd), washing any excess off the foliage to avoid scorching. Repeat this, or give a liquid feed (*see p.21*), if the leaves yellow. Earth up trench celery planted in a trench. For trench celery planted on the flat, and for self-blanching celery plants on the outside of a block, wrap collars around the stems (*see p.120*). For leaf celery, remove yellow leaves.

■ **Harvesting and storing**  Celery takes 4–8 months to mature. From midsummer to the first frosts, test self-blanching celery for maturity before harvesting – take an inner stalk from a plant in the middle of the block and see if it will snap and not show any stringiness. It is vital to harvest before the stems deteriorate and the leaves yellow. Water the plants well before harvesting, or the stems will quickly wilt. Dig up the plant, trim off the outer side roots and any small stems; the stick can be stored whole in a refrigerator for up to a week. Break individual stems off the main stick as required, and wash and prepare them. If the individual stems are prepared before storing, the cut ends will turn brown. Trench celery is ready in late autumn and early winter; harvest in the same way as self-blanching celery. Wash the whole stick before storing. For leaf celery, regularly pick leaves from the edges of the plants as needed.

■ **Common problems**  Carrot fly (*see p.253*), celery leaf miner (*see p.253*), and slugs and snails (*see p.262*) may be troublesome pests. Diseases that may affect the crop include fungal leaf spots (*see p.257*), foot and root rots (*see p.255*), and violet root rot (*see p.263*).

■ **Recommended cultivars**
**Self-blanching/green celery**
'Granada' ♀ – hybrid, crisp, resistant to leaf blight.
'Lathom Galaxy' ♀ – strong ribbed stems.
'Loretta' ♀ – vigorous, easy to grow.
'Tango' ♀ – hybrid green type.
'Victoria' ♀ – hybrid with apple-green leaves.
**Trench celery**
'Blush' – attractive, pink stems.
'Giant Pink' – pink stems.
'Giant Red' – hardier than white types.
'Ideal' – finest show bench cultivar, with a pink basal tinge to the stems.
'Pascal' – giant, white stems.
'Solid White' – traditional, white stems, tasty.
**Leaf celery**
'Parcel' – leafy type for flavouring.

# Florence fennel

*Foeniculum vulgare* var. *azoricum*

| MONTH | SPRING | SUMMER | AUTUMN | WINTER |
|---|---|---|---|---|
| SOW | • • | • • | | |
| TRANSPLANT | • • | | | |
| HARVEST | | • • | • • • | |

Florence, or sweet, fennel produces very handsome, feathery foliage, and makes an extremely ornamental vegetable for the

garden. Succulent, aniseed-flavoured "bulbs", which can be either cooked or eaten raw, develop from the swollen bases of the leaf stalks. The leaves and stalks may also be eaten in salads. Plants are extremely prone to bolting, but bolt-resistant cultivars are available. Florence fennel will yield 1.4–2.25kg per 3m (3–5lb per 10ft) row.

■ **Site and soil**  Florence fennel prefers fertile, well-drained, sandy soil (*see p.120*) that has preferably been well manured for a previous crop (*see pp.22–23*).

■ **Sowing and planting**  For early crops, sow a quick-maturing cultivar in modules (*see p.62*) in early to mid-spring and plant out when the seedlings have no more than four true leaves, taking care not to disturb the young roots. Cover the seedlings with fleece, cloches, or cold frames (*see pp.45–48*). Even with these precautions, there is still a risk that the crop may bolt. For direct sowings, sow a few seeds at a time, at weekly intervals, after the longest day in midsummer; bolt-resistant cultivars may be sown earlier.

The seed needs a minimum of 15°C (59°F) in order to germinate. Sow 3–4 seeds per station at 30cm (12in) intervals, and thin to a single, strong-growing seedling when they are large enough to handle. The depth of sowing is critical for success; if the seeds are sown too shallowly the resulting plants are liable to rock in the wind, and they may even twist and break off.

| SOWING DEPTH | 2.5cm (1in) |
|---|---|
| PLANT SPACING | 30cm (12in) |
| ROW SPACING | 30cm (12in) |

■ **Routine care**  Florence fennel needs plenty of moisture throughout the growing period, so mulch (*see p.72*) to help conserve moisture. Feeding is not usually required. If plants start to rock, lightly earth up the stems. When the stems begin to swell, earth up to half-way over the bulb to make it whiter and sweeter.

■ **Harvesting**  Florence fennel takes at least three months to mature. When the bulbs have reached a good size, harvest them by cutting at ground level to leave a stump, which will resprout to produce shoots suitable for use in salads. If any bulbs start to elongate, showing that they are running to seed, harvest them quickly or they will be too tough to use.

■ **Common problems**  Rhizoctonia, causing plants to rot off either as seedlings or mature bulbs, can be a problem. Practise good crop rotation (*see p.31*) and avoid growing lettuce or radish crops on the same ground.

■ **Recommended cultivars**
'Romanesco' – large bulbs, with high resistance to bolting.
'Rudy' – quick-maturing hybrid, white bulbs.
'Selma' – bolt-resistant, very good for braising and as a salad ingredient.
'Victorio' ♀ – vigorous, very reliable for later sowings.
'Zefa Fino' ♀ – bolt-resistant, solid bulbs, with good colour.
'Zefa Tardo' – solid bulbs, late-maturing.

# Growing leafy vegetables

Leafy vegetables are grown for their tasty and sometimes decorative leaves, which, unlike those of salad crops (*see pp.101–107*), are usually cooked before eating. They tend to be frost-sensitive, or, even if they tolerate frost, grow slowly in cold weather; so they are often grown as annuals, especially in temperate regions. Some are also quite ornamental – Swiss chards and pak choi have coloured stems and leaf veins that contrast vividly with the green foliage. All yield abundantly and are easy to grow. They fall into two broad groups: spinaches and chards, and oriental brassicas. For western brassicas, such as cabbage and texsel greens, *see pp.76–81*; for salad leaves, *see pp.101–107*.

The spinach and chards group includes amaranths, spinach, Ceylon spinach, New Zealand spinach, Swiss chard, and spinach beet. Some, such as Ceylon spinach, are tropical or subtropical in origin and require high temperatures to grow well; others, like spinach and Swiss chard, are cool-season crops that can withstand some degree of frost. They are therefore very useful crops for overwintering, to provide fresh leafy vegetables early in the "hungry gap", the period from late winter to mid-spring when not many vegetables are available.

Oriental brassicas include Chinese broccoli, Chinese cabbage, flowering greens, mustard greens, spinach mustard, and pak choi. They are adapted to hot climates with high rainfall and adequate soil moisture, and respond to the colder weather and dry summers of more temperate climates by bolting (*see above*) or developing very strong flavours. This limits them to sowing after midsummer for late-summer and autumn cropping, unless bolt-resistant cultivars are used. However, some are sufficiently hardy to survive the winter and provide crops in the spring. Although usually grown for their young leaves, flowering shoots of oriental brassicas can also be used in salads to add a touch of spiciness.

## SITE AND SOIL

Both spinach and oriental brassicas need very fertile soil that is neutral to slightly alkaline in pH (*see p.18*), with very moist

**Bolting crops**
*In summer, or earlier in a greenhouse, oriental brassicas (here mustard greens 'Braising Mix') may bolt, or run to seed, if they are exposed to excessive cold early in their development, especially in periods of lengthening days. They will also bolt if exposed to excessive warmth or kept too dry. The flowerheads, however, are edible and tasty, and the seeds may be saved unless they derive from a hybrid cultivar.*

soil; this is best ensured by liberal applications of organic matter when preparing the soil. Freedom from any traces of clubroot (*see p.254*) is also vital for oriental brassicas. Swiss chard and spinach beet, and New Zealand spinach can be grown on relatively dry soils.

## SOWING AND PLANTING

Leafy vegetables are best raised from seed sown direct outdoors. If sowing under cover, however, do not sow in trays or pots, since transplanting the bare-root seedlings of leafy vegetables

**Cut-and-come-again leaves**
*Some leafy vegetables, such as this Swiss chard, make good cut-and-come-again crops. When the seedlings are 10–15cm (4–6in) tall, cut them 2.5cm (1in) above ground level.*

promotes bolting. Plants sown directly in modules (*see p.65*) can be safely transplanted. Leafy vegetables are fast-growing crops, taking 6–12 weeks from sowing to harvest (*see individual crops, pp.125–128*), and they can soon become overmature and unpalatable. It is a good idea, therefore, to make regular successional sowings (*see p.69*); Swiss chard and spinach beet can be picked over a long period, however, and oriental brassicas may bolt if sown early.

## SEEDLING CROPS

Diseases, pests, and bolting can be avoided by growing greens (meaning the foliage of leafy vegetables, rather than spring greens which refers to unhearted spring cabbage, *see p.78*) for use as seedlings or as cut-and-come-again crops (*see left and p.102*). Seed packets containing mixes of different leafy vegetables are sold for this very purpose, as an economical alternative to buying several packets. If densely sown, in rows only 10–15cm (4–6in) apart, to obtain one seedling every 1cm (½in), surprisingly large crops of seedling leaves can be taken from small areas – equivalent to 9–12 lettuce heads per 3m (10ft) row. If, when harvesting the first crop, you leave intact the heart leaves in the centres, the seedlings will resprout vigorously to yield another crop. Several harvests of leaves can be taken from late

sowings, but early sowings containing oriental brassicas bolt so readily that only one crop is usually possible. The tender leaves are suitable for eating raw in salads or for very light cooking.

Prevent damage from foliage pests by protecting the seedlings with fleece or fine woven mesh (see p.48), and also control slugs and snails (see p.262). Dead leaves and garden debris can make subsequent harvests unattractive, so a thorough clean-up after each harvest is essential. Weed control (see below) must also be scrupulous, to avoid weed leaves being gathered with the edible leaves.

## MAXIMIZING YOUR CROPS

Leafy vegetables are quick-growing and their leaves can be gathered while the plants are still small. They are therefore useful for growing as catch crops (see p.69) and for intercropping (see p.71). Spinach, mustard greens, Swiss chard and spinach beet all tolerate light shade, and will fit neatly between tall, widely spaced crops such as sweetcorn.

## OVERWINTERED CROPS

Spinach and spinach beet sown in late summer will grow all winter to provide fresh greens in mid-spring. Sown in late summer (spinach beet) or early autumn (spinach) in open ground, they can be gathered from mid-spring to early summer. Alternatively, sow in modules (see p.65) and plant out into greenhouses or under cloches (see p.48). In both

cases, protect from slugs and snails, and birds. The leaves may be harvested even if they do not fully mature.

## CONTAINER GROWING

Leafy vegetables, especially seedling crops, because they are fast-growing and shallow-rooted, are suitable for growing in containers (see above), using multipurpose compost or spent growing bags. These materials are sterile and therefore free of weeds and diseases, ideal where clubroot is present and to minimize weeding. If using a spent growing bag, clean out any old roots and water the growing bag thoroughly to wash out any residues from the previous crop. By growing them in containers, fresh vegetables can be raised on balconies, near the back door, or in greenhouses in winter. The quality of the crops grown in

containers is, however, dependent on correct and regular watering and feeding (see below).

## ROUTINE CARE

The best way to control weeds with leafy vegetables is to give them a weed-free start, using a stale seedbed (see p.66). Remove any further weeds by hoeing between the rows as necessary.

Apply a base fertilizer before sowing (see individual crops, pp.125–128), unless the soil has been enriched with organic matter. For cut-and-come-again leaves, apply a compound fertilizer at a rate of 35g per sq m (1oz per sq yd) or pelleted poultry manure at 50g per sq m (1½oz per sq yd). Some crops may require another top-dressing of nitrogenous fertilizer (see individual crops, pp.125–128).

Water frequently to keep the top 20cm (8in) of soil moist. Lack of water, even if brief, can lead to slow growth, loss of texture, peppery flavours, and bolting in all crops. If keeping your containers well watered is difficult in spells of hot weather, or at holiday times, move them into a shaded area to avoid damage to the plants.

## HARVESTING

Once mature, the leaves quickly coarsen in texture and flavour, and the stems become fibrous, so commence picking or cutting the leaves and shoots as soon as they reach the desired size, and continue until the plants flower (see left). They are best harvested in the cool of the morning or evening, and stored in a refrigerator, to avoid wilting. If an entire plant is cut at an early stage as a cut-and-come-again crop, leaving a stump, it should provide another crop.

**Harvesting amaranths**
*Gather young shoots and leaves, cutting them with a sharp knife, when the plants are about 25cm (10in) tall. Keep harvesting until the plants produce flowers and growth ceases.*

**Harvesting spinach**
*You can start to pick the outer leaves about 6–10 weeks after sowing. Alternatively, use a sharp knife to sever the whole plant 2.5cm (1in) above ground level; it will then resprout.*

# A–Z OF LEAFY VEGETABLES

## Amaranth

*Amaranthus* species

| MONTH | SPRING | SUMMER | AUTUMN | WINTER |
|---|---|---|---|---|
| SOW | • • | | | |
| TRANSPLANT | | • | | |
| HARVEST | | • • • • • | | |

Amaranths, which are also known as African or Indian spinach, are rapidly growing annuals, typically reaching 60cm (2ft) tall, whose leaves can be used in salads or cooked in the same way as spinach. They have a sharp, spinach-like flavour. *Amaranthus cruentus* is the most commonly grown cultivar, and has light green, oval leaves. *A. caudatus*, widely grown as an ornamental plant, has bright red, tassel-like flowers and pale green leaves. *A. tricolor*, or Chinese spinach, has greenish-white flowers and green, yellow, or red leaves. Although they are not frost-hardy, amaranths grow well in temperate summers and are not fussy about soil or site; however, they will appreciate a very sunny, sheltered position. Amaranths yield 7.25kg per 3m (16lb per 10ft) row.

■ **Site and soil** Amaranths prefer a moderately deep, fertile, well-drained, acid to neutral soil, in a sunny, sheltered position. If necessary, apply a base dressing as for spinach (*see p.128*) before sowing.

■ **Sowing and planting** When the soil is warm enough in late spring, sow thinly *in situ*. Protect the sowing with fleece or cloches (*see pp.46–48*). Thin as soon as the seedlings can be handled (*see p.68*), and remove alternate plants when they are large enough to harvest. Alternatively, sow seed singly in modules (*see p.65*) indoors in mid-spring.

| SOWING DEPTH | 2cm (¾in) |
|---|---|
| SEED SPACING | sow thinly; thin to 8cm (3in) |
| PLANT SPACING | 15cm (6in) |
| ROW SPACING | 30cm (12in) |

■ **Routine care** Water and top-dress as for spinach (*see p.128*). Pinch out the growing tip when 20cm (8in) tall to promote bushiness.

■ **Harvesting** Amaranths mature in 10–12 weeks. Start to gather young shoots and leaves when the plants are 25cm (10in) tall (*see p.124*). Continue to harvest until the plants flower and growth ceases. Amaranths often set abundant seed, which is worth saving (*see p.61*), although the seedlings may not come true.

■ **Common problems** Powdery mildew and aphids occasionally occur. For symptoms and controls, *see* Plant Problems, *p.260 and p.251*.

■ **Recommended cultivars**
'Calalo' – green leaves with violet veins.
'Indian Spinach' – bold green leaves.
'Red Amaranth' – green leaves with red herringbone patterns.

## Ceylon or Malabar spinach

*Basella* species

| MONTH | SPRING | SUMMER | AUTUMN | WINTER |
|---|---|---|---|---|
| SOW | • • | | | |
| TRANSPLANT | | • • | | |
| HARVEST | | • • • • | | |

Also known as Malabar nightshade, vine spinach, or basella, these plants are very popular leafy greens in the tropics, and are used in a similar way to spinach. They are green- (*Basella alba*) or red-leaved (*B. rubra*), trailing perennials, usually grown as annuals. They are useful for ornamental kitchen gardens, especially if grown as climbers. Ceylon spinach yields 3kg per 3m (6½lb per 10ft) row. Named cultivars are not available.

■ **Site and soil** A fertile, well-drained, but moisture-retentive soil with a good organic matter content (*see p.123*) and a pH of 6–7.5 (*see p.18*) in a sunny, sheltered site is best. Ceylon spinach needs temperatures of 25–30°C (77–86°F) to thrive. If necessary, apply a base dressing as for spinach (*see p.128*), before planting out the seedlings.

■ **Sowing and planting** Sow seed under cover singly in modules or small pots (*see pp.64–65*). Plant out when the seedlings can be handled by the leaves, usually after four weeks; protect them with fleece or cloches (*see p.48*) in adverse weather. Later crops may be raised from stem cuttings, that are 10–15cm (4–6in) long, rooted in small pots and transplanted as for seedlings (*see above*).

| SOWING DEPTH | 2.5cm (1in) |
|---|---|
| PLANT SPACING | 10–15cm (4–6in) |
| ROW SPACING | 30cm (12in) |

■ **Routine care** Weed thoroughly, and apply organic mulches (*see p.72*). Top-dress with a nitrogen-rich fertilizer (*see pp.20–23*), and water regularly to keep the soil moist. Train plants up vertical netting supports to save space, or across netting stretched horizontally just above the level of the crop when it begins to need support – 30–45cm (12–18in) above the ground – to keep the leaves off the ground and therefore clean. Pinch out the growing tips when shoots are about 30cm (12in) long, and remove any flowers to keep plants bushy and producing young foliage.

■ **Harvesting** Ceylon spinach usually reaches maturity in 10–12 weeks. Gather the fresh young sideshoots when they are 15cm (6in) long. Frequent picking will encourage more shoots to be produced. The seed is worth saving (*see p.61*), but remember that it may not always come true.

■ **Common problems** This crop is usually trouble-free.

# Chinese broccoli

*Brassica rapa var. alboglabra*

| MONTH | SPRING | SUMMER | AUTUMN | WINTER |
|---|---|---|---|---|
| SOW | • • • • | | | |
| TRANSPLANT | | • | | |
| HARVEST | | • • | • • • | |

Chinese broccoli, or Chinese kale, is an oriental brassica (*see p.123*) with succulent, pleasant-tasting, leafy, flowering shoots reminiscent in flavour of purple-sprouting broccoli or calabrese sideshoots, but more tangy. The shoots of Chinese broccoli are green, with white or yellow flowers. The plants are similar to hybrid calabrese, and hybrids have also been developed between the two. Chinese broccoli is tolerant of hot weather, and slightly frost-resistant. It yields 9–12 bunches per 3m (10ft) row.

■ **Site and soil** A deep, fertile, moisture-retentive soil with plenty of organic matter (*see p.123*) in a sheltered, sunny site is best. If necessary, apply a base dressing as for spinach (*see p.128*) before sowing or planting out.

■ **Sowing and planting** Sow in summer *in situ* and thin (*see p.68*) to the final spacing, or raise seedlings in spring singly in module trays (*see p.65*) and transplant as soon as they can be handled, usually after 5–7 weeks, or as soon as the rootball can be handled without breaking up; modules, composts, and growing conditions will all influence this timing. To avoid bolting (*see p.123*), if sowing before midsummer, use bolt-resistant cultivars.

| SOWING DEPTH | 2cm (¾in) |
|---|---|
| PLANT SPACING | 30cm (12in) |
| ROW SPACING | 30cm (12in) |

■ **Routine care** Water regularly, thoroughly wetting the top 20cm (8in) of soil. Feeding is not usually necessary.

■ **Harvesting** Chinese broccoli takes about 10 weeks to mature. Cut the mature shoots just before the flowers open, starting with the central one and moving onto the sideshoots. Peel the stems, and use the tender inner flesh. They will not be as large as calabrese shoots.

■ **Common problems** Oriental brassicas are prone to many of the problems suffered by western brassicas, especially cabbage root fly and clubroot. Other pests may include flea beetle, caterpillars, whitefly, mealy cabbage aphid, birds (especially pigeons), cutworm, leatherjackets, and, to a lesser extent, slugs and snails. Diseases may include white blister, powdery and downy mildew, and sometimes bacterial leaf spot. Occasionally boron or molybdenum deficiency may also affect the crop. For symptoms and controls, *see* Plant Problems, *pp.246–264*.

■ **Recommended cultivars**
'Green Lance' – vigorous hybrid, bearing white flowers.
'Kailaan White Flowered' – thick, tasty stem.
'Tendergreen' – derived from a cross between Chinese broccoli and calabrese; intermediate size and flavour, and yellow flowers.

# Chinese cabbage

*Brassica rapa var. pekinensis*

| MONTH | SPRING | SUMMER | AUTUMN | WINTER |
|---|---|---|---|---|
| SOW | • • • • | • | | |
| TRANSPLANT | | • • | • | |
| HARVEST | | • • | • • • | |

Chinese cabbage, or Chinese leaves, is an oriental brassica (*see p.123*) with dense heads and a crisp, mild cabbage flavour, suitable for light cooking or salads. Flowering shoots are extremely palatable. The head may be barrel-shaped or elongated; the leaves are usually pale green, with white veins and broad, flat ribs. They are very fast-growing, and ideal for use as catch crops (*see p.69*) sown in late summer. Non-hearting cultivars, known as loose-headed cabbage, have darker leaves and a stronger cabbage flavour; the attractive crops are grown in the same way. Chinese cabbage normally yields 9–12 heads per 3m (10ft) row.

■ **Site and soil** A deep, fertile, moisture-retentive soil, with plenty of organic matter added, in a sheltered, sunny site is best (*see p.123*). Feed as for spinach (*see p.128*), but double the rate of application if the soil is not very fertile and top-dress with nitrogenous fertilizer (*see p.20*) if growth appears to slow. Early and late sowings will benefit from cloche or fleece protection (*see pp.46–48*).

■ **Sowing and planting** Late summer sowings will not usually bolt and may be station sown *in situ* (*see p.68*), but spring sowings are risky because the lengthening days exacerbate the inclination to bolt due to cold. Sowing seed at temperatures of 20–25°C (68–77°F) and growing seedlings at 18–25°C (64–77°F) will prevent bolting even when sowing in spring, although 10–13°C (50–55°F) is usually adequate for bolt-resistant cultivars and later sowings. For spring sowings, therefore, raise seedlings of bolt-resistant cultivars singly in module trays (*see p.65*), in heated conditions, and transplant as soon as they can be handled.

| SOWING DEPTH | 2cm (¾in) |
|---|---|
| PLANT SPACING | 30cm (12in) |
| ROW SPACING | 45cm (18in) |

■ **Routine care** The roots are shallow, so water little and often, never letting the soil dry out fully. Wet the top 20cm (8in) of soil, adding a nitrogen-rich fertilizer (*see pp.20–23*) before watering if growth slows down. Protect spring-sown crops after planting with fleece or cloches if cold weather threatens.

■ **Harvesting and storing** Chinese cabbage matures in 9–10 weeks. Cut the heads just above soil level when they feel solid. They can be used fresh, or stored in a refrigerator for six weeks or more. Harvest the leaves of plants that have bolted as loose greens. If a 2.5cm (1in) stump is left when cutting the head, it will resprout to produce more leaves after 2–4 weeks, and may be harvested again several times. Late-sown seedlings are useful as cut-and-come-again crops (*see p.123*) that can be harvested after about two weeks.

■ **Common problems** As for Chinese broccoli (*see left*); except for resistant cultivars, it is very susceptible to clubroot (*see p.77 and p.254*).

■ **Recommended cultivars**
'Apex' – barrel-shaped, slow bolting.
'Green Rocket' – long, thin, mild heads.
'Tah Tsai' – leafy, non-hearting cabbage, bolts readily, good for cut-and-come-again crops.
'Wa Wa Sai' – sweet flavour, quick growing.
'Wong Bok' – traditional, barrel-shaped.
'Yuki' ♀ – dense, vigorous, barrel-shaped.

# Flowering greens

*Brassica campestris subsp. chinensis var. utilis*

| MONTH | SPRING | SUMMER | AUTUMN | WINTER |
|---|---|---|---|---|
| SOW | • • • | • | | |
| TRANSPLANT | | • • | • | |
| HARVEST | | • • | • • • | |

Also known as Chinese flowering cabbage or choy sum, these oriental brassicas (*see p.123*) are flowering versions of pak choi (*see p.127*), and are used like Chinese broccoli (*see left*). They have a tender, red or green, leafy stalk bearing unopened flowers, and possess a mild, peppery, cabbage flavour that needs light cooking. They are best grown in late summer for harvesting in autumn, as earlier sowings will bolt (*see p.123*). Bolted stems are usable, but only for a brief period. The flowering shoots will become overmature quickly in hot summer weather. Flowering greens normally yield 9–12 bunches per 3m (10ft) row.

■ **Site and soil** A deep, fertile, moisture-retentive soil, with plenty of organic matter added, in a sheltered, sunny site is best (*see p.123*). If necessary, apply a base dressing as for spinach (*see p.128*), for both normal and cut-and-come-again crops, before sowing.

■ **Sowing and planting** Late summer sowings will not usually bolt and may be station sown *in situ* (*see p.68*), but early sowings are risky because the lengthening days exacerbate the tendency to bolt due to cold. Sowing seed at 20–25°C (68–77°F) and then growing on the seedlings at 18–25°C (64–77°F) prevents bolting even when sowing in spring, although 10–13°C (50–55°F) is usually adequate for bolt-resistant cultivars and later sowings. For spring and early-summer sowings, therefore, raise seedlings of bolt-resistant cultivars singly in module trays (*see p.65*), in warmth, and transplant as soon as they can be handled.

| SOWING DEPTH | 2cm (¾in) |
|---|---|
| PLANT SPACING | 15cm (6in) |
| ROW SPACING | 45cm (18in) |

■ **Routine care** The roots of flowering greens are quite shallow, and should therefore be watered little and often, never letting the soil dry out fully. Wet the top 20cm (8in) of soil, adding a nitrogen-rich fertilizer (*see pp.20–23*) before watering if growth appears to slow. If cold weather threatens, protect spring-sown crops after planting with fleece or cloches.

■ **Harvesting** Flowering greens take about ten weeks to mature. Flowering stems should be cut then, but outer leaves may be picked earlier. Pick while the stalk is tender and the flower buds are closed. Storage is not possible, and they are best used fresh. Regrowth from stumps can be used for greens (see p.123), and these make good cut-and-come-again crops.

■ **Common problems** As for Chinese broccoli (see facing page).

■ **Recommended cultivars**
'Hon Tsai Tai' – purple flower stalks and midribs, green foliage.
'Purple' – very attractive purple foliage.

# Mustard greens and spinach mustard

*Brassica juncea* and *B. rapa subsp. perviridis*

| MONTH | SPRING | SUMMER | AUTUMN | WINTER |
|---|---|---|---|---|
| SOW | | • • • • | • | |
| TRANSPLANT | | | • • | |
| HARVEST | | | • • • • • | |

Mustard greens (*Brassica juncea*) are a varied group of oriental brassicas (see p.123) with a tangy, peppery, cabbage flavour that becomes more fiery as they run to seed. The flowering shoots can be extremely hot, but the leaves may be lightly cooked or used in salads. Leaves may be green, red, or purple, with smooth or blistered surfaces and straight or jagged edges. Rich in vitamins and minerals, mustard greens are nutritionally among the most valuable of vegetables. Spinach mustard (*Brassica rapa subsp. perviridis*) is similar, but more closely related to Chinese cabbage (see p.126). Mustard greens and spinach mustard yield 1.5kg per sq m (3¼lb per sq yd).

■ **Site and soil** A deep, fertile, moisture-retentive soil, with plenty of organic matter added, in a sheltered, sunny site is best (see p.123). If necessary, apply a base dressing as for spinach (see p.128) before sowing.

■ **Sowing and planting** Late summer sowings will not usually bolt and may be station sown *in situ* (see p.68). Early sowings are risky since lengthening days exacerbate the inclination to bolt due to cold. Sowing seed at 20–25°C (68–77°F) and growing seedlings at 18–25°C (64–77°F) will prevent bolting even if sowing in spring, although 10–13°C (50–55°F) is usually adequate for bolt-resistant cultivars and later sowings. For early sowings, therefore, raise seedlings of bolt-resistant cultivars singly in module trays (see p.65), in heated conditions, in late spring and early summer; transplant as soon as they can be handled.

| SOWING DEPTH | 1cm (½in) |
|---|---|
| PLANT SPACING | 15–30cm (6–12in) |
| ROW SPACING | 45cm (18in) |

■ **Routine care** The roots are shallow, and should therefore be watered little and often, never letting the soil dry out fully. Wet the top 20cm (8in) of soil, adding a nitrogen-rich fertilizer (see pp.20–23) before watering if growth slows down. Protect spring-sown crops after planting if cold weather threatens.

■ **Harvesting** Mustard greens and spinach mustard take 6–8 weeks to mature, after which you can cut selected leaves as required. The plants will stand in good condition for several weeks, allowing a prolonged harvest, and regrowth from cut stumps will yield further harvests. They may also be used as cut-and-come-again seedling crops (see p.123), usually ready after about two weeks. The seed is worth saving (see p.61).

■ **Common problems** As for Chinese broccoli (see facing page).

■ **Recommended cultivars**
'Green in Snow' – dark green, jagged leaves.
'Red Giant' – crinkly Savoy-like, red leaves.
'Sheurifong Improved' – bolt-resistant.

# New Zealand spinach

*Tetragonia tetragonioides*

| MONTH | SPRING | SUMMER | AUTUMN | WINTER |
|---|---|---|---|---|
| SOW | • • | • | | |
| TRANSPLANT | • | | | |
| HARVEST | | • • • • • | | |

New Zealand spinach is a trailing, half-hardy perennial usually grown as an annual. It has spiky, triangular leaves, about 5cm (2in) long, and trails for up to 1.2m (4ft), sometimes reaching heights of 60cm (2ft). Its young shoots and leaves are used like spinach (see p.128). It is slow to bolt, grows quickly, and is fairly tasty. It is an attractive groundcover plant, needing little care, and is suitable for containers, hanging baskets, or the ornamental kitchen garden. It yields 6kg per 3m (13lb per 10ft) row. Named cultivars are not offered.

■ **Site and soil** Sunny, sheltered sites are best. Although fertile, moisture-retentive soil (see p.123) is ideal, New Zealand spinach can survive on much less water than spinach, Swiss chard, or spinach beet, and requires no fertilizer on fertile ground of good organic matter content. If necessary, however, apply a base dressing as for spinach (see p.128), before sowing or planting out.

■ **Sowing and planting** Soak the elongated, woody fruits, containing seeds, for 24 hours before sowing, to break down the hard seed coats and speed up germination. Sow singly in module trays (see p.65) in mid-spring and transplant as soon as they can be handled, or station sow (see p.68) outdoors after risk of frost has past, in late spring or early summer.

| SOWING DEPTH | 2.5cm (1in) |
|---|---|
| PLANT SPACING | 45cm (18in) |
| ROW SPACING | 45cm (18in) |

■ **Routine care** Keep weed-free, and water only in the driest spells.

■ **Harvesting and storing** Shoots and leaves are usually ready to pick about six weeks after sowing, depending on conditions; those from spring sowings may take longer. It is best used fresh, but may also be frozen. Regular picking promotes fresh growth. Young plants may be cut near ground level; the stumps will regrow (see p.124). The seed is worth saving (see p.61).

■ **Common problems** This crop is usually trouble-free, but may suffer from downy mildew (see p.255) and from birds eating the seedlings (see p.252).

# Pak choi

*Brassica rapa* var. *chinensis*

| MONTH | SPRING | SUMMER | AUTUMN | WINTER |
|---|---|---|---|---|
| SOW | • • • | • | | |
| TRANSPLANT | | • • | | |
| HARVEST | | • • | • • • | |

Pak choi, or celery mustard, is an oriental brassica (see p.123) with a handsome head of paddle-shaped leaves with wide midribs. Light cooking will preserve its refreshing, delicate texture and flavour; it can also be eaten raw in salads. Flowering shoots are very palatable. Like Chinese cabbages, it is an excellent crop for late summer, including catch crops (see p.69), but will bolt (see p.123) if exposed to cold and long days. Pak choi grows speedily in early autumn, and with protection (see pp.46–48) can be harvested until late autumn. It yields 9–12 heads per 3m (10ft) row.

■ **Site and soil** A deep, fertile, moisture-retentive soil, with plenty of organic matter added, in a sheltered, sunny site is best (see p.123). If necessary, apply a base dressing as for spinach (see p.128) before sowing or planting.

■ **Sowing and planting** Late summer sowings will not usually bolt and may be station sown *in situ* (see p.68), but early sowings are risky because the lengthening days exacerbate the inclination to bolt due to cold. Sowing at 20–25°C (68–77°F) and growing seedlings at 18–25°C (64–77°F) will prevent bolting even when sowing in spring, although 10–13°C (50–55°F) is usually adequate for bolt-resistant cultivars and later sowings. For early sowings, therefore, raise seedlings of bolt-resistant cultivars singly in module trays (see p.65), in heated conditions, in mid- to late spring and transplant as soon as they can be handled.

| SOWING DEPTH | 2cm (¾in) |
|---|---|
| PLANT SPACING | 10cm (4in) |
| ROW SPACING | 45cm (18in) |

■ **Routine care** The roots are shallow, and should therefore be watered little and often, never letting the soil dry out fully. Wet the top 20cm (8in) of soil, adding a nitrogen-rich fertilizer (see pp.20–23) before watering if growth slows. Protect spring-sown crops with fleece or cloches if cold weather threatens.

■ **Harvesting** Pak choi takes about ten weeks to mature. Pick leaves whenever needed from the seedling stage onwards; or wait for the tight, plump heads of mature plants to form after around ten weeks. Use the leaves while they are fresh; they wilt quickly if stored. Like Chinese cabbage, the stumps will repeatedly resprout (*see p.124*), providing several pickings of useful greens over 2–6 weeks. Pak choi is also useful for cut-and-come-again crops (*see p.123*), ready to harvest in about two weeks.

■ **Common problems** As for Chinese broccoli (*see p.126*).

■ **Recommended cultivars**
'Cantong Dwarf' – compact, thick-stemmed.
'Joi Choi' – relatively bolt-resistant.
'Purple Choi Sum' – tasty flowering stalks and leaves.
'Tatsoi' – traditional, flattened rosette, tasty.

# Spinach

*Spinacia oleracea*

| MONTH | SPRING | SUMMER | AUTUMN | WINTER |
|---|---|---|---|---|
| SOW | • • • • • • • | | • • | |
| TRANSPLANT | • | | | |
| HARVEST | • • • • • • • • | | | |

True spinach is a reasonably hardy annual, with leaves that are flat, wrinkled (like Savoy cabbage), or semi-wrinkled. The leaves have a very distinctive texture and flavour, and may be cooked or eaten raw in salads – in fact, spinach is often harvested as a cut-and-come-again crop (*see p.123*), or used as a catch crop (*see p.69*). The seeds may be prickly or round.

Traditionally, spinach cultivars were divided into summer and winter types; this distinction no longer applies, however, as many modern cultivars are dual-purpose. Spinach is not the easiest crop to grow, but for taste there is no real substitute. It normally yields around 6kg per 3m (13lb per 10ft) row.

Oriental spinach is a new form of the same species as true spinach. It differs from true spinach in having darker leaves and very long stalks. It is fast-growing, and best suited to late-summer and autumn production. Seed is less commonly sold than ordinary spinach, but named cultivars are available.

■ **Site and soil** Any fertile, moisture-holding soil (*see p.123*) is suitable. Unless the soil is enriched with organic matter, apply a base dressing of compound fertilizer at a rate of 100g per sq m (3oz per sq yd) or pelleted poultry manure at 135g per sq m (4oz per sq yd). Sunny or, in summer, partially shaded sites are best. For cut-and-come-again crops, use compound fertilizer at a rate of 35g per sq m (1oz per sq yd) or pelleted poultry manure at 50g per sq m (1½oz per sq yd).

■ **Sowing and planting** Sow thinly *in situ* in succession every three weeks (*see p.69*) from midwinter to early autumn. Thin (*see p.68*) the seedlings first to 8cm (3in) as soon as they can be handled, and then remove alternate plants when they are big enough to use. Alternatively, you can station sow (*see p.68*). Alternatively, in midwinter raise seedlings singly in modules (*see p.65*) and transplant as soon as they can be handled. Wide drills (*see p.67*) are best for cut-and-come-again crops.

Late sowings will overwinter for harvest in spring. Overwintered crops need exact timing if they are not to bolt before spring or be too small to survive the winter. If neighbouring gardeners cannot advise on local conditions and practice, try fortnightly sowings during late summer and early autumn, each one 1–2m (3–6ft) in length. In subsequent years, fewer sowings will be required. Alternatively, make your best guess and, if wrong, replace with module-raised plants sown in late winter indoors (*see p.65*).

| SOWING DEPTH | 2cm (¾in) |
|---|---|
| SEED SPACING | sow thinly; thin to 8cm (3in) |
| PLANT SPACING | 15cm (6in) |
| ROW SPACING | 30cm (12in) |

■ **Routine care** Water freely to avoid bolting. Top-dress with a nitrogen-rich fertilizer (*see pp.20–23*) if growth appears to slow down.

■ **Harvesting and storing** Spinach takes 10–12 weeks to mature. Cut individual leaves of mature plants as required, or sever the whole plant about 2.5cm (1in) above ground level, leaving it to resprout for further harvests (*see p.124*). The shoots and leaves may be frozen. Spinach also makes an easy cut-and-come-again seedling crop (*see p.123*), ready to harvest after about two weeks.

■ **Common problems** Downy mildew (*see p.255*) can be damaging, but resistant cultivars are available, and allowing 50 per cent more space between plants also helps. Birds (*see p.252*) are partial to spinach seedlings; netting (*see p.52*) is the remedy.

■ **Recommended cultivars**
'Emilia' ♀ – robust, disease resistant, slightly crinkled leaves.
'Giant Winter' ('Gigante d'Inverno') – hardy, sow in autumn or early spring.
'Reddy' – red leaf veins and stems, disease resistant.
'Palco' ♀ – mildew-resistant, slow to bolt.
'Tetona' ♀ – reliable, upright habit.

# Swiss chard and spinach beet

*Beta vulgaris* subsp. *cicla* var. *flavescens*

| MONTH | SPRING | SUMMER | AUTUMN | WINTER |
|---|---|---|---|---|
| SOW | • • • • • | | | |
| TRANSPLANT | • | | | |
| HARVEST | • • • • • • • • | | | |

Swiss chard and spinach beet are botanically similar to beetroot (*see p.85*), but have edible leaves and insignificant roots. Their foliage is used as an alternative to spinach. Although less flavoursome and a little more peppery than spinach, these leaves are much easier to grow, more winter-hardy, and much less susceptible to bolting. Swiss chard leaves have prominent midribs which may be cooked separately as an alternative to seakale (*see p.135*). Spinach beet is grown exclusively for its leaves. Swiss chard and spinach beet make useful cut-and-come-again crops (*see p.123*), ready to harvest after about two weeks. Their bold leaves, which often have brightly coloured – pink, red, yellow, or green – veins and stems, are highly valued as an ornamental vegetable, and they are also suitable for growing in containers (*see p.124*). Swiss chard and spinach beet normally yield 6kg per 3m (13lb per 10ft) row.

■ **Site and soil** A sunny, sheltered site with fertile, well-drained, moisture-retentive soil (*see p.123*), with added organic matter, is best. The pH should be neutral to slightly alkaline, so acid soils may need liming (*see pp.18–19*). Unless the soil has been enriched with plenty of organic matter, apply a base dressing of compound fertilizer at a rate of 210g per sq m (6oz per sq yd) or pelleted poultry manure at 270g per sq m (8oz per sq yd).

■ **Sowing and planting** Swiss chard and spinach beet are raised from multigerm seeds (*see p.60*), which are each actually a cluster of seeds. Sow thinly, thinning (*see p.68*) to 10cm (4in) apart when the plants can be handled; then remove alternate plants when they are large enough to use. Mid- to late-summer sowings, for harvest in the spring when few other vegetable crops are available, are the most useful, but spring and early-summer sowings will provide supplies until the plants bolt in mid- to late autumn.

| SOWING DEPTH | 2.5cm (1in) |
|---|---|
| SEED SPACING | sow thinly; thin to 10cm (4in) |
| PLANT SPACING | 20cm (8in) |
| ROW SPACING | 45cm (18in) |

■ **Routine care** Water in dry spells. Top-dress with a nitrogen-rich fertilizer (*see pp.20–21*) if growth appears to slow down.

■ **Harvesting** Swiss chard and spinach beet usually take 8–10 weeks to mature, but late-summer sowings will mature throughout the winter for harvest in spring. Pick tender, young, blemish-free leaves as soon as they are large enough, and continue to pick regularly to promote fresh, new growth of new tender leaves. Mature plants may be left to stand until the leaves are needed, but they become more coarse and unappetizing, and vulnerable to weather and pest damage, until they bolt.

■ **Common problems** Fungal leaf spot can disfigure older leaves, but the young, tender foliage is seldom affected. For symptoms and controls, see Plant Problems, *p.256*.

■ **Recommended cultivars**
'Bright Lights' ♀ – very brightly coloured stems, in hues of pink, red, orange, violet, gold, and green, all on one plant.
'Perpetual Spinach' ♀ – very hardy, drought-resistant, succulent, green leaves; less prone to bolting on dry soils.
'Rhubarb Chard' ♀ – bold scarlet stems and ribs and purple-green foliage; wide midribs.
Swiss chard – large, crinkly, green leaves, edible white midribs, sometimes called silver or seakale beet.

# Growing perennial vegetables

Perennial vegetables can make unusual, attractive, and interesting additions to the vegetable garden. They are long-term crops that die right down to ground level each autumn and resprout the following year, just like ornamental herbaceous perennials. The perennial group encompasses asparagus, cardoons, Chinese artichokes, globe artichokes, Jerusalem artichokes, rhubarb – which is normally eaten as a dessert – and seakale. The edible parts of perennial vegetables range from the young leaves, shoots, stems, and the flower buds to underground tubers. Asparagus is widely popular for its delicious young shoots, known as spears, and is best suited to continuous long-term production on a reasonably large scale.

This group of vegetables tends to need less intensive care than other groups, because they are hardy and more robust. Most may be grown and harvested for 3–4 years, while asparagus is more long-lived, cropping for 15–20 years. Once they cease to be productive they may be propagated or rejuvenated by the methods described below, so bear in mind that they will semi-permanently occupy a lot of space, which may be a drawback if you have only a small garden.

## ORNAMENTAL CROPS

Apart from the benefit of their edible produce, these plants often have foliage, flowers, or architectural forms that would make them worth growing for their ornamental value alone. The stems of rhubarb glow bright pink or scarlet; globe artichokes and cardoons have narrow, serrated, silver leaves and large, thistle-like flowerheads; and asparagus and seakale both possess delicate, ferny foliage. Such features can liven up what might otherwise be a rather dull vegetable patch.

These crops can be used for their decorative qualities in a potager (*see p.27*) or as special feature plants in herbaceous or mixed borders. On the practical side, Jerusalem artichokes provide height at the back of a border, and may even be used as a windbreak to protect other, more vulnerable plants from the elements.

## SITE AND SOIL

Before you plant perennial vegetables you will need to think very carefully about where to site them, since these long-term crops could prevent light reaching other, fast-maturing plants. As with most vegetables, an open, sunny site is best, with a deep, rich soil that has free drainage but good moisture retention. The ground must be very well prepared before planting; dig over the entire plot thoroughly (*see pp.37–40*) and incorporate a good deal of organic matter (*see pp.22–23*). After planting, add a good layer of organic mulch (*see pp.41–42*) around the base of the stems to retain moisture and suppress weeds.

## ROUTINE CARE

Because perennial vegetables are long-term crops, routine care involves regular weeding to remove competition for water and soil nutrients, keeping the plants healthy and strong by removing old foliage, and mulching annually with organic matter (*see below*). The crops will also need regular watering and feeding, and some may require support in order to crop well (for individual crop needs, *see pp.133–135*).

## PROPAGATION

Unlike most other groups of vegetables, which are usually grown from seed, perennial vegetables are usually cropped for several years until they reach full maturity, and then they are propagated by cuttings or division to produce new, vigorous, healthy plants. Perennial vegetables can also be increased from bought or home-saved seed (*see p.61*), but this method is much slower and the results are more variable.

The propagation method used (*see pp.130–131*) depends on the crop. Dividing rootstocks is suitable for both rhubarb and asparagus – although seed raising is preferable for the latter. Divide offsets to propagate globe artichokes and cardoons; replant healthy tubers for Chinese and Jerusalem artichokes; and take root cuttings for seakale.

## Mulching perennial vegetables

**1** **In mid- to late autumn,** cut off the dead stems at the base, and pick off any dead or dying foliage (here of globe artichoke 'Purple Globe').

**2** **Clear away any debris,** and fork over the soil to loosen it. This aerates the soil and also enables moisture to pass through any old mulch and into the soil.

**3** **Cover the soil around the plant** with a 5–8cm (2–3in) layer of well-rotted manure or compost, extending to about 45cm (18in) from the base of the plants. Use a plank to define a neat edge.

## DIVISION OF ROOTSTOCKS

The rootstock, or crown, of a perennial consists of the part of a mature plant at ground level from which both the stems and roots grow. This may be lifted when the plant is dormant in late winter, or just as the buds begin to break in early spring, and divided into several, smaller pieces, each with buds and roots of their own, which are then replanted to form new, complete plants. For this procedure to be successful, you need healthy rootstocks or the divisions may not grow or crop very well. Weak or unhealthy rootstocks should be discarded. It is best to take the divisions from around the edges of the rootstock, discarding the old, woody central part. This method works well for asparagus and rhubarb when the plants are at least 3–4 years old (see right).

For asparagus, carefully lift the entire rootstock with a fork, and shake off any excess soil. Separate it into two or more sections, or "sets", using your hands or a sharp knife. With rhubarb, use a spade either to cut through the crown while it is still in the ground, lifting the sections individually, or to dig around and lift the entire rootstock before cutting it into sections, each of which should have at least one healthy bud.

Tease out the roots, and cut away any old ones that are damaged or diseased with a sharp knife, to prevent rot from

| | |
|---|---|

## Dividing mature rootstocks

Asparagus and rhubarb may be propagated by dividing their mature rootstocks into sections, or "sets", each with a healthy bud and roots, that will grow into a new plant. This is best done in late winter or early spring. With asparagus (right), lift the rootstock and prise it apart with your thumbs; if necessary, use a sharp knife to complete the job. With rhubarb (below), use a spade to cut through the rootstock. Replant the sections to grow on.

**1** **Gently uncover the top** of the rhubarb rootstock to expose the buds. Look for a side section with at least 1 healthy bud. With a spade, chop down through the rootstock to separate the section.

**2** **The new section** may be divided further; each set must have 1 good bud and be as large as a small melon. Replant the sets with the bud just above the soil surface.

setting in later. Take care not to damage the buds or roots, and never allow the roots to dry out before replanting.

For asparagus, dig a trench 30cm (12in) wide and 20cm (8in) deep. Work in well-rotted manure and top up with 5cm (2in) of soil. Then make a 10cm (4in) ridge along the centre. Plant the

### Dividing tubers
*Before planting, in spring, Jerusalem artichoke tubers that are larger than a hen's egg should be cut into sections, at the joints, with a sharp knife. Each section should have a number of healthy buds, which should be uppermost when planted.*

*Cut tubers at joints*

divisions 30cm (12in) apart on top of the ridge, carefully spreading the roots so that they sit evenly on the soil below. Cover with soil to leave just the bud tips visible. Mulch the divisions with 5cm (2in) of manure to keep them moist; the resulting plants can be harvested two years later.

For rhubarb, plant the divisions in holes with the main bud just above the surface; planting too deeply, especially in heavy soil, can cause rotting of the rootstock around the bud. Firm in the soil around the rootstock, but leave it loose on top to allow the rain to penetrate. Mulch (see p.129), leaving a space just around the rootstock to allow the shoots to be produced and to discourage slugs and snails from reaching the buds.

## DIVISION OF OFFSETS

Offsets are tiny plantlets produced naturally by the parent plant at the side of the rootstock. These may be detached and replanted to form new plants. Offsets can be taken from established plants that

**Dividing globe artichoke offsets**
*In spring, choose a healthy sideshoot with 2–3 leaves. Using a sharp knife, cut down into the rootstock of the parent plant to separate the offset. Take care to preserve any roots, and trim off old stems to just above the leaves.*

were produced in the same way, so they will all be true to type. This method of propagation is suitable for cardoons and globe artichokes. It is best carried out in the spring when the new shoots are actively growing. Wait until the young shoots around the edge of the plant have started rooting into the soil, as this makes establishment of the new plant much quicker and easier.

In spring, select from the outside of a mature plant a young, healthy shoot with 2–3 leaves (*see facing page*). Scrape away the soil with a trowel so that you can see the roots and the point where the offset is attached to the parent plant. Using a clean, sharp knife, cut the offset away from the parent plant, together with a piece of root and if possible any new roots just starting on the offset. Fill in the hole at the side of the parent plant and leave it to grow. Trim off the old stalks around the base of the offset to avoid rotting. Remove all but one of the leaves to reduce unwanted moisture loss through the process of transpiration – the evaporation of water from the leaves once it has carried nutrients from the roots.

To replant, space the offsets 60cm (24in) apart in rows 75cm (30in) apart. Place each offset in a planting hole, fill in around it with soil, and carefully firm it in. The offset should be planted deeply and firmly enough to remain upright.

Do not bury the growing point, or it will rot, wither, and die. Water in and cover with fleece (*see p.48*) to keep the offset moist, warm, and protected from desiccating winds.

## DIVISION OF TUBERS

Chinese and Jerusalem artichokes are normally raised from tubers that are simply replanted. Because the tubers of Jerusalem artichokes grow much larger than those of Chinese artichokes, however, they may require dividing into smaller sections (*see facing page*) before replanting (*see p.135*).

## ROOT CUTTINGS

The best way to propagate seakale is to use root cuttings, sometimes known as thongs, taken from established plants (*see below*), although thongs may also be obtained through mail order.

Select a healthy plant that is three or more years old and mark its position. In late autumn to early winter, when the leaves have died down, check that the rootstock is free from rot and lift it out of the ground with a fork or spade, taking care not to damage any of the roots. Select a number of roots of about pencil thickness around the side of the rootstock and cut them from the parent plant. When making the cuttings, it is important to remember which is the top

of each root cutting, so make a straight cut at the top – that is, the end that was nearer the rootstock – and an angled cut at the bottom.

Tie the cuttings carefully together in bundles of 5–6, with their straight ends aligned. Stand the bundles, angled ends downwards, in a box of moist sand in a cool, frost-free shed. The cuttings in the box should be covered just enough to leave the tips sticking out and to keep the roots moist. Store until early spring when buds start to develop at the top of the cuttings (*see below*).

The cuttings are ready for planting just as the buds begin to break; if they are allowed to develop too far, the cutting will use up too much of the energy needed for producing roots after planting. It is important to select the most suitable cuttings, and to remove all but the strongest bud from the top of each one (*see below*), as this will increase the chances of producing robust, healthy new plants.

Using a dibber, plant out the cuttings 38cm (15in) apart in a well-prepared bed so that the buds are 2.5cm (1in) below the surface of the soil. As the plants develop, remove any flowering shoots so that all the energy possible is channelled into root production. It is also a good idea to apply a mulch (*see p.129*) in order to conserve as much moisture as possible.

## Taking root cuttings of seakale

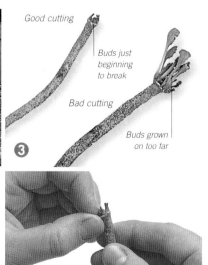

*Good cutting*

*Buds just beginning to break*

*Bad cutting*

*Buds grown on too far*

**1** **Lift a healthy three-year-old plant**, in late autumn to early winter, and clean off any soil. Choose roots that are pencil-thick, and separate them by making a straight cut where they join the crown and an angled cut at the other end.

**2** **Cut the severed roots** into sections about 8–15cm (3–6in) long, using a straight cut at the top and an angled one

at the bottom, as before. Tie into bundles of 5–6 with twine, matching up the straight ends. Place the bundles, angled ends down, in a box of sharp sand, and cover.

**3** **Lift the cuttings in spring** when the buds are starting to break.

**4** **Rub off all the weaker buds** with thumb and forefinger, leaving only the strongest, before planting the cuttings out.

## OBTAINING AN EARLY HARVEST

Some perennial vegetables, such as rhubarb and seakale, may be induced to crop earlier than they normally would by a process known as forcing. The purpose is to bring the plant back into production earlier than would occur naturally. This also makes for sweeter-tasting and more tender crops. You need to use plants that have been in the ground for at least two seasons; if forced too early, the plants suffer and only recover slowly when they are left to grow on. Either force them outdoors where they are growing, or dig them up and force them under cover; if you do the latter, the plants will have to be discarded after forcing because the energy of the roots will have been exhausted.

## FORCING OUTDOORS

Seakale is best forced outdoors. Between late autumn and midwinter, when the crowns have died back, clear away the old leaves, which may be rotting, and cover the crown with 8cm (3in) of dry leaves, straw, or bracken to help raise the temperature. Then exclude all light from the crown by covering it up. For this you could use a traditional forcing jar (*see above*) with a removable lid, which can be opened up so that you can check on progress. Alternatively,

**Using a forcing jar to produce an early crop**
*Crops such as seakale and rhubarb may be forced for early cropping. Place a forcing jar, or upturned pot, over the emerging stems to exclude light. Remove the cover once the leaves reach the top to reveal blanched stems.*

use an upturned box, bucket, or large flowerpot; cover the drainage hole with a stone to keep out the light. The cover needs to be at least 38cm (15in) high, and the stems will be ready to harvest in 2–3 months. To speed up the process, pack a thick layer of fresh horse manure around the cover; the heat generated by the composting manure will warm up the crown. When the stems are 10–20cm (4–8in) long, cut them with a piece of root attached.

With rhubarb, plants require a period of cold, which varies according to the cultivar, to break dormancy before they are ready to force (*see p.135*). When this point has been reached, in midwinter, cover as for seakale; you do not need to pack the cover with manure. Shoots are produced 2–3 weeks earlier than normal, and they are softer, more tender, and pinkish in colour. Leave the stems to grow as tall as the height of the cover before harvesting them (*see above*).

## FORCING UNDER COVER

In autumn, after the first frosts, either dig up the crowns to be forced, or lift and expose them to frost to break dormancy. Trim the roots, and plant into compost in large pots or boxes, at least 30cm (12in) deep. The tips should be just covered. Place a lid or some newspaper over each box to exclude the light; keep the compost moist. If stored in a cool room or greenhouse at 15–21°C (59–70°F) for seakale and for rhubarb 7–15°C (49–59°F), they will be ready for harvest in a few weeks.

## HARVESTING

Lift tubers of Chinese or Jerusalem artichokes with a fork (*see far left*), and cut globe artichokes just before they open (*see left*). For details of harvesting other perennial crops, *see pp.133–135*. These vegetables are best eaten fresh.

**Harvesting Chinese artichokes**
*When the foliage has begun to yellow, the tubers are ready to harvest. Lift the plant with a fork, taking care not to damage any of the tubers. Remove all tubers by the end of the season since this plant can become invasive.*

**Harvesting globe artichokes**
*When the largest head on the plant is plump and its scales are green, soft and just about to open out, cut off the head with a sharp knife. Allow any other heads to grow on to the same size before harvesting them.*

# A–Z OF PERENNIAL VEGETABLES

## Asparagus

*Asparagus officinalis*

| SEASON | SPRING | SUMMER | AUTUMN | WINTER |
|---|---|---|---|---|
| SOW/PLANT | • | | | • |
| TRANSPLANT | | • | | |
| HARVEST | • • | | | |

Asparagus is grown for its delicately flavoured young shoots, or spears. Most modern plants are all-male F1 cultivars which are much more vigorous than older, open-pollinated cultivars, and have the advantage of not producing seed which can germinate haphazardly in the surrounding beds. Female cultivars do not reproduce true to type and are of poorer vigour. Once established, plants should crop for 15–20 years, yielding 9–12 spears per crown.

■ **Site and soil**  Asparagus needs a soil with good drainage and a pH of 6.3–7.5 to thrive; it can be grown in heavy soils in traditional raised beds (*see pp.32–33*) or in light, sandy soils on the flat. Avoid frost pockets because the spears are tender and may be damaged by late frosts; asparagus also needs some shelter from winds (*see pp.12–13*). Always use fresh ground to avoid disease problems building up from previous asparagus crops. Dig the soil deeply, or even double dig it (*see p.39*), adding plenty of organic matter.

■ **Sowing and planting**  Asparagus can be raised from seed, or young plants can be purchased. Asparagus seed is best sown singly into modules (*see p.65*) and transplanted in early summer, at spacings shown below. The seedlings often find it difficult to establish in hot, dry weather. Alternatively, sow in an open seedbed (*see p.66*) in early spring. Thin to 15cm (6in) apart (*see p.68*).

To save time, most asparagus is planted, rather than sown. One-year-old crowns planted in early spring establish best: you can divide your own rootstocks (*see p.130*), but there is much to be said for buying in crowns of a good stock. If dividing your own stock, the parent should be a healthy plant that is at least 3–4 years old, preferably an F1 hybrid, all-male cultivar. A male plant would have produced no female flowers or berries on the fern during the previous summer. Make sure to remove seedlings if they occur.

The crowns can be planted in single rows on raised beds, but double rows are best in flat beds. To plant a row, dig a trench 30cm (12in) wide and 20cm (8in) deep. Work in well-rotted manure to the base, cover with 5cm (2in) soil, then make a 10cm (4in) high ridge along the centre of the trench. Place the crowns on the ridge, 30cm (12in) apart. Spread the roots evenly and fill in with soil so that the bud tips are just visible. Mulch the crowns with 5cm (2in) of well-rotted manure to keep them moist. Leave 45cm (18in) between double rows and stagger the plants. Allow for paths 90cm (3ft) in width between the beds.

| SOWING DEPTH | 2.5cm (1in) |
|---|---|
| PLANT SPACING | 15cm (6in) |
| ROW SPACING | 30cm (12in) |

■ **Routine care**  Keep asparagus beds free of weeds and mulched (*see p.129*) to avoid soil compaction and bent spears and to retain moisture. Top-dress with a general fertilizer (*see pp.20–23*) in early spring and repeat when cutting has finished. Be careful not to overfeed because excess nitrogen makes for soft fern growth and can reduce yields.

Support the ferny top-growth with canes and twine to avoid it breaking off in the wind and damaging the crown. Remove any seedlings as they occur and any female plants to avoid seedlings in future years. When the foliage has died and yellowed in autumn, cut it down to 2.5cm (1in) above the ground.

■ **Harvesting**  Normally asparagus spears are not harvested until the plants have been in the ground for two years, to allow for good crops in future years. In the third year, harvest from mid-spring for six weeks, and in subsequent years for eight weeks. Use an asparagus knife – which has a forked blade for cutting spears singly – and carefully cut the spears 2.5cm (1in) below the soil when they are 13–18cm (5–7in) tall. To avoid wastage, you will need to harvest every 2–3 days in warm weather or every 5–7 days in cold weather.

■ **Common problems**  The main pests to affect the crop are slugs and snails (*see p.262*), which can be very damaging to young spears, and the asparagus beetle (*see p.251*). Diseases to look out for are violet root rot (*see p.263*), foot and root rots (*see p.255*), and fusarium wilt (*see p.256*).

■ **Recommended cultivars**
'Backlim' ♀ – an all-male hybrid with a good yield of fat, juicy spears with purple tips.
'Gijnlim' ♀ – all-male hybrid; early, high yield.
'Jersey Knight' – hybrid, robust, reliable.

## Cardoon

*Cynara cardunculus*

| SEASON | SPRING | SUMMER | AUTUMN | WINTER |
|---|---|---|---|---|
| SOW | • • | | | |
| TRANSPLANT | | • • | | |
| HARVEST | | | • • • | |

Although similar to globe artichokes in appearance, cardoons are grown for their stalks and thick midribs, which are blanched just before harvesting. Their architectural leaves make an attractive feature in a herbaceous border or the vegetable garden. They are frost-hardy and need a lot of space, and are generally replaced every 3–4 years. New plants can be raised from collected seed. Expect to harvest

up to ten stems from an established plant. No named cultivars are available.

■ **Site and soil**  Cardoons need a deep, rich soil and moist conditions with plenty of organic matter applied before planting. In temperate climates, they also need full sun.

■ **Sowing**  Sow the seed in modules (see p.65) in early to mid-spring and leave it to germinate at 10–15°C (50–59°F). If using home-collected seed, do not try to separate the seed plumes; simply spread them out on the compost surface and thin the resulting seedlings (see p.68). Harden off (see p.65) the young plants when they are 25cm (10in) tall and transplant into trenches 45cm (18in) wide, to allow room for earthing up.

Once you have some plants, you can increase your stock by taking offsets (see pp.130–131). Offsets are all true to type, so if you select the best of your seed-raised plants you will have good stock for life.

| SOWING DEPTH | 2.5cm (1in) |
| PLANT SPACING | 38cm (15in) |
| ROW SPACING | 1.2m (4ft) |

■ **Routine care**  When the plants are 30cm (12in) tall, stake with 60cm (2ft) slender stakes or canes and keep well watered throughout the growing season. The plants are ready to blanch in late summer or early autumn. Gather the leaves together at the top of each plant, tie with soft string, wind brown paper around the stems from base to top, and pack soil around the plants to keep out the light.

■ **Harvesting**  About eight weeks after blanching, dig the plants up and remove the wrappings. Prepare the stems for the table by trimming the lower end neatly and removing the upper leaves.

■ **Common problems**  Slugs and snails (see p.262) are the main problem, but black bean aphid (see p.252) can also attack the leaves and stem tips. Root aphid (see p.251) can be a problem with sown plants. Artichoke bud rot (see p.251) causes rotting of the heads in wet weather, but there is no remedy. Cold, wet winters may rot the plants.

# Chinese artichoke

*Stachys affinis*

| SEASON | SPRING | SUMMER | AUTUMN | WINTER |
|---|---|---|---|---|
| PLANT | ● | | | |
| HARVEST | | | ● | ● ● |

The tubers of Chinese artichokes are 5cm (2in) long and 2cm (¾in) wide with small ridges that make them difficult to clean. They are, however, delicious: when cooked straight from the ground, the translucent flesh has a nutty flavour. The plants sprawl a bit like mint, but reach a height of only 45cm (18in). They should yield 20–30 tubers per plant. No named cultivars are available.

■ **Site and soil**  These plants need an open, sunny site and do best on rich, light soils; the

heavier the soil, the more difficult the tubers are to clean. Chinese artichokes also require plenty of moisture; the best soil is one that has been improved for a previous crop with plenty of organic matter.

■ **Planting**  New plants must be raised from tubers, which can be bought from reputable suppliers, or taken from your own stock. Plant direct in early spring, as soon as conditions permit, or sprout the tubers indoors in late winter. To do this, settle the tubers in a seed tray of moist compost, then plant out as soon as the sprouts appear. Carefully place the tubers upright in the drills, then cover over.

| PLANTING DEPTH | 4–8cm (1½–3in) |
| TUBER SPACING | 15–30cm (6–12in) |
| ROW SPACING | 45cm (18in) |

■ **Routine care**  Keep the bed free from weeds and the plants well watered, especially in mid- to late summer. When the plants are 30cm (12in) tall, earth up round the stems to a depth of about 8cm (3in). If the top-growth becomes very straggly, cut some of it back and before the leaves form a full canopy, mulch, and apply a high-potash liquid feed (see pp.20–21). Remove the flowers as they appear, to encourage tuber production.

■ **Harvesting**  Begin harvesting tubers when the foliage dies back. The tubers shrivel very quickly, so leave them in the soil until you need them. It is easier to lift tubers in frosty weather if the soil has been protected with straw, bracken, or fleece (see p.48).

■ **Common problems**  Slugs and snails (see p.262) may attack young plants. Root aphid (see p.261) may sometimes infest the soil.

# Globe artichoke

*Cynara scolymus*

| SEASON | SPRING | SUMMER | AUTUMN | WINTER |
|---|---|---|---|---|
| SOW/PLANT | ● ● | | | ● |
| TRANSPLANT | | ● | | |
| HARVEST | | ● ● | ● | |

The globe artichoke is a very decorative plant, with silvery foliage and large, thistle-like green or purple flowerheads. It grows 60–90cm (2–3ft) tall, with a mature spread of 90cm (3ft). Each plant has a few flower stalks with several small flower buds below the large terminal bud. The sepals of the flower bud, and the base of larger buds, are edible. The plants will crop for 3–4 years.

■ **Site and soil**  This crop requires shelter from winds, and sun, but must not be shaded by trees. If there are tree roots nearby, beware of honey fungus (see p.256), which can spread to the woody parts of globe artichokes. Avoid planting in frosty sites, since losses are likely in severe winters (see p.11). Globe artichokes need a rich, well-drained soil that is not too light, because they cannot tolerate soil drying out in summer. You will need to prepare the site well (see pp.37–40) and incorporate plenty

of organic matter into the soil to improve moisture retention.

■ **Sowing and planting**  Globe artichokes are usually raised from offsets planted in spring so that the offspring are true to type. Select a healthy parent plant and take offsets (see pp.130–131), preferably with roots. Plant the offsets in rows, just deep enough to stay upright. Water after planting to settle the soil, then cover with fleece to keep the offsets moist, warm, and protected from desiccating winds. Aim to replant one-third of the plot each year for regular cropping.

If you cannot obtain offsets, sow seed (see pp.62–65) indoors in late winter at 15°C (59°F). Prick out seedlings into 10cm (4in) pots and grow on until you have good-sized plants to transplant in early summer. Seed can also be station-sown (see p.68) outdoors in early spring and the seedlings thinned. This method gives rather small plants by autumn which may not survive the winter in cool regions. When plants grown from seed are well-established, select the ones that produce good artichokes for eating and use offsets from these to grow more plants (see above).

| PLANTING DEPTH | 5cm (2in) |
| PLANT SPACING | 75cm (30in) |
| ROW SPACING | 90cm (3ft) |

■ **Routine care**  Mulch (see p.129) the crop to control weeds and keep the soil moist. Plants in their first season will produce only a single head; remove it promptly to allow the plants to gain vigour. In their second season, if large heads are required, reduce the number of stems to three per plant and and apply a high-potash liquid feed (see pp.20–21). Globe artichokes are most vulnerable in their first year. In cold areas, earth up round the plants and cover with 15cm (6in) straw or bracken over winter; add fleece (see p.48) in severe weather. In warm areas, cover with double fleece in frosty spells.

■ **Harvesting**  The smaller artichoke flowers can be removed (see p.132) when they reach 4cm (1½in) in diameter, to encourage the terminal bud to grow to a good size. These small buds can be eaten, but they are not as tasty as mature ones. Artichokes are ready for harvesting usually in late spring or early summer, when the heads are plump and the scales still soft and green and just about to open. If there are no secondary heads left, snap the stem off at the base; if there are secondary heads on the stem, cut off the terminal bud together with a short length of stem. This stimulates secondary shoots which may yield a second crop; encourage this by top-dressing with a general fertilizer and watering (see p.72).

■ **Common problems**  As for cardoon.

■ **Recommended cultivars**
'Green Globe' – the most widely available and easy to grow. Delicious and tender.
'Purple Globe' – similar to 'Green Globe'.
'Romanesco' – tight purple heads produced later in the season than 'Green Globe' but with a superior flavour.

# Jerusalem artichoke

*Helianthus tuberosus*

| SEASON | SPRING | SUMMER | AUTUMN | WINTER |
|---|---|---|---|---|
| PLANT | • • • | | | • |
| HARVEST | | | • • | • |

This hardy relative of the sunflower is grown for its tubers, which are usually cooked but occasionally eaten raw. The plants can grow 3m (10ft) or more in height, and may be used as a screen or windbreak if planted 30cm (12in) apart in rows 2–3 deep; allow 90cm (3ft) between the rows. They are very vigorous, and should yield 10–12 tubers per plant.

■ **Site and soil** Jerusalem artichokes will grow on a wide range of soils, including heavy ones, in either sunny or shady positions.

■ **Planting** Plant tubers, either bought from a greengrocer or saved from your own stock, that are no bigger than a hen's egg, dividing them if necessary (*see pp.130–131*). Check first that they are showing no signs of disease.

| PLANTING DEPTH | 10–15cm (4–6in) |
|---|---|
| TUBER SPACING | 30cm (12in) |
| ROW SPACING | 30cm (12in) |

■ **Routine care** Earth up the stems to stabilize them when they are 30cm (12in) tall, by drawing soil up to a depth of 15cm (6in). In midsummer, remove the flowerheads and cut back the stems to 1.5–2m (5–6ft) so the plants' energy is concentrated into the tubers. Keep the plants moist to get better-shaped tubers, and provide supports (*see p.72*). When the leaves begin to yellow in autumn, cut back the stems to 8cm (3in) above ground level. Lay them over the plant to keep the soil warm and ease lifting of the tubers in frosty weather.

■ **Harvesting** Harvest the tubers as required (*see p.132*), making sure to remove every one, however small, by the end of the season, since any part left could grow and become invasive.

■ **Common problems** Sclerotinia, a fungal rot (*see p.262*), may damage stems up to 30cm (12in) above soil level. Slugs and snails (*see p.262*) attack both tubers and foliage. Root aphid (*see p.261*) is a less common problem.

■ **Recommended cultivars**
'Dwarf Sunray' – crisp and tender, no need to peel.
'Fuseau' – long, smooth-skinned tubers.

# Rhubarb

*Rheum x hybridum*, syn. *R. cultorum*

| SEASON | SPRING | SUMMER | AUTUMN | WINTER |
|---|---|---|---|---|
| SOW/PLANT | • • | | • • | • • • |
| TRANSPLANT | | • | | |
| HARVEST | | • • • • • | | |

Rhubarb is an attractive hardy perennial with pink, red, and greenish leafstalks that are used as a

dessert, often in pies and crumbles. It needs a cold period to break its dormancy (*see below*), and is suitable for forcing (*see p.132*). When forcing is finished, do not harvest from the same crown; leave it to replenish its energy for the rest of the season. Plants should yield 4.5–13.5kg per 3m (10–30lb per 10ft) row. The flavour varies in sweetness depending on the age of the stems.

■ **Site and soil** Choose an open site with moist but free-draining soil, since rhubarb does not like to be waterlogged in winter; avoid frost pockets as the stems are susceptible to frost.

■ **Sowing and planting** Rhubarb does not always come true from seed, so to obtain the best results it is advisable to divide rootstocks into "sets" (*see p.130*) and replant these. This may be done at any time from mid-autumn to early spring. If seed is used, it is best sown in modules (*see p.65*) in late winter and planted out in late spring, or sown thinly in a seedbed (*see p.66*) and thinned to 15cm (6in) apart (*see p.68*). Plant sets a minimum of 75cm (30in) apart; the ideal is 90cm (3ft).

| SOWING DEPTH | 2.5cm (1in) |
|---|---|
| SEED SPACING | sow thinly; thin to 15cm (6in) |
| PLANT SPACING | 75–90cm (30–36in) |
| ROW SPACING | 30cm (12in) |

■ **Routine care** Rhubarb must be kept free of weeds. Apply a mulch (*see p.129*) to hold in moisture, but do not bury the crown as it will rot. Prevent neighbouring crowns smothering each other by removing yellowing leaves. Top-dress with sulphate ammonia in summer to feed the crown. Water regularly to keep it moist and actively growing until autumn.

Each rhubarb cultivar requires a certain number of "cold units" before it will start to grow. In commercial production these cold units are calculated by daily monitoring of the temperature of the soil and air, but this is not practicable in the home vegetable garden. Instead, when the top-growth has died back in autumn, simply remove the dead leaves to expose the crowns to frost.

■ **Harvesting** Do not harvest in the first year, as this will reduce vigour. In the second year, lightly pull up some of the stems. Take around one-third to a half of the stems each time, and leave some to keep the plant in active growth. If stripped completely, it will take longer to recover. Take hold of the stalk to be pulled, which should be at least 23–30cm (9–12in) long, and push your thumb between the stalk and the next one, easing it out of ground to avoid snapping off or pulling out another stalk which is not ready. Do not pull too late in the season, as the leaves have to feed the crown buds for the following year. Harvest forced stems as soon as they are ready (*see p.132*).

■ **Common problems** Aphids (*see p.251*), slugs and snails (*see p.262*), crown rot (*see p.254*), honey fungus (*see p.256*), fungal leaf spots (*see p.257*), and viruses (*see p.264*) may cause problems.

■ **Recommended cultivars**
'Bakers All Season' – crops all year round if there is no frost.

'Cawood Delight' – keeps its texture well when cooked and has a brilliant red stain.
'Early Champagne' – early type, grown from seeds and sets, with a sweeter flavour than other varieties.
'Victoria' – late type, heavy-yielding, grown from seed and sets.

# Seakale

*Crambe maritima*

| SEASON | SPRING | SUMMER | AUTUMN | WINTER |
|---|---|---|---|---|
| SOW/PLANT | • • | | | |
| TRANSPLANT | | • | | |
| HARVEST | • • • | | | |

Seakale is a very hardy perennial vegetable grown for its uniquely flavoured stems, which are eaten raw. The young flowerheads and very young leaves can also be eaten raw, and the leaf midribs cooked. An established plant can be 90cm (3ft) in diameter with stems up to 60cm (2ft) tall. Each plant yields 8–10 stems. Seakale is usually propagated from root cuttings or "thongs" (*see p.131*).

■ **Site and soil** Seakale needs an open, sunny site and a deep, rich, sandy soil, with a pH of 7 (*see p.18*); lighten heavy soils by adding grit or sand. It is closely related to brassicas, so occasionally suffers from clubroot (*see p.254*).

■ **Sowing and planting** Plant thongs (*see p.131*) in early spring. Raising plants from seed is an alternative if you cannot obtain thongs. Scrape the corky coverings from the seeds with your nails; if not removed, these will inhibit germination.

Sow thinly in seed trays from late winter (*see p.64*) at 7–10°C (45–50°F) and prick out seedlings into 10cm (4in) pots (*see p.64*). Plant out the seedlings in early summer (*see pp.70–71*) when they are 8–10cm (3–4in) tall. Alternatively, sow thinly in drills (*see pp.66–67*) in spring, and thin out the seedlings (*see p.68*) later.

| PLANTING DEPTH | 2.5cm (1in) |
|---|---|
| SEED SPACING | sow thinly; thin to 15cm (6in) |
| PLANT SPACING | 38cm (15in) |
| ROW SPACING | 38cm (15in) |

■ **Routine care** Remove any flowering shoots to concentrate energy into the stems. In spring, mulch (*see p.129*) with well-rotted manure, or top-dress with low-nitrogen fertilizer or liquid feed. When the plants die back in autumn, follow the procedure for forcing outdoors (*see p.132*) to blanch the stems.

■ **Harvesting** Cut the forced stems when they are ready (*see p.132*). Stop cutting in late spring to allow the plant to regenerate.

■ **Common problems** Flea beetle (*see p.255*) may attack seedlings. Clubroot (*see p.254*) can be a problem, so use a long rotation (*see p.31*) and avoid planting after brassicas.

■ **Recommended cultivars**
'Seakale Angers' – the most vigorous cultivar, with good flavour as long as it is properly blanched and forced.

# CULINARY HERBS

Just as fresh-picked herbs in the kitchen add zest and colour to dishes, so herb plants have decorative qualities that enhance both the ornamental and kitchen garden. Many are attractive, with the bonus of flowers and aromatic foliage. Statuesque, feathery herbs such as dill and fennel deserve a place in any border; sun-loving, creeping herbs such as thymes are ideal for softening the edges of paths and paving. Pots spilling over with mints, sweet marjoram and tender basil clustered by the kitchen door give a cottage-garden feel to any plot, but herbs have a place in formal design too. A neatly trimmed bay tree in a decorative container would make a perfect focal point in a pattern of beds neatly edged with parsley or rows of chives.

Herbs, among the easiest edible plants to grow and to propagate, can be available to pick fresh, with a flavour beyond compare, all year round. They bring with them a rich tradition of varied use in the home that is fascinating to explore.

# Growing culinary herbs

In general use, the word "herb" refers to a range of annual, biennial, perennial, and shrubby plants that are grown for culinary or medicinal use. Culinary herbs are sometimes called pot herbs. The word also has a more specific botanical usage, where it means any non-woody plant; strictly, a plant without persistent above-ground parts, most commonly a perennial.

## GROWING CULINARY HERBS

Almost all the plants that we grow in a culinary herb garden (see pp.141–145 for those covered here) produce aromatic oils in their leaves, stems, and in some cases in their seeds. This group of herbs includes basil, marjoram, mint, sage, and thyme, which are all members of the nettle family, the Lamiaceae. Chervil, coriander, dill, fennel, and parsley, other popular herbs, are umbellifers belonging to the Apiaceae,

as do carrots and parsnips, and produce attractive flat heads of small flowers. All of these are not only useful as culinary herbs, but also decorative: there are many with attractive leaf and flower variations. A few herbs, including sweet Cicely and horseradish, are valued for the culinary use of their roots.

One advantage of growing herbs is that they are much less demanding than most vegetable crops. Although the annual herbs need raising from seed each year, most are easy and need no additional heat. Growing culinary herbs is made even easier by the wide availability of seed and plants now on offer. Establish just a few herbs to begin with, choosing the plants that are most frequently used, for example basil, chives, fennel, mint, parsley, and thyme. Experiment with other kinds of herbs and their cultivars as the garden and your experience develop.

## WHERE TO GROW HERBS

Herbs are usually required in limited quantity, and kitchen needs can easily be met by a few plants in a small plot in the open ground or in containers.

A herb plot need not take up much space in the garden. Select a site that receives plenty of sunshine, because most culinary herbs originate in warm climates. Ensure that the site is well-drained, and avoid areas where there has been heavy dressing of organic matter, since rich soil is likely to promote the growth of lush foliage, which may be less intense in flavour than if plants are grown in poorer conditions.

Provide shelter (see pp.12–13) from wind around the herb plot: this will create a warmer microclimate and raise soil temperature. Herbs such as lavender and rosemary can be grown as low protective hedges to create this shelter. Plant herbs in close proximity to the

---

## Planting a herb trough

**1** **Half-fill** a 15cm (6in) deep trough with compost. Plant annual herbs (here parsley) raised from seed. Lift and divide perennial herbs and plant the best piece.

**2** **Confine a plant** with spreading roots, such as mint, by potting it first in a small plastic pot. Sit the pot in the trough so the rim is level with that of the trough.

**3** **Before planting chives** in the trough, trim the leaves back to about 15cm (6in) to promote fresh growth. Cut back any straggly top-growth on other herbs.

**4** **Take care** to leave enough space between plants to allow them to grow for some time. Fill in with compost to within 2.5cm (1in) of the rim; firm well.

**5** **Position** the planted trough in a well-lit place indoors, such as a kitchen windowsill, and keep it well watered. Harvest the herbs as required.

kitchen door if at all possible, because the shortest walk encourages the most frequent use, especially in poor weather.

## GROWING HERBS IN CONTAINERS

It is also possible to grow a few herbs in a windowbox (*see facing page*) or a large pot or growing bag on any paved area. A particular advantage of container growing is that the plants may be taken under cover to avoid frost damage or to keep up their growth through winter.

Choose a large container with a diameter of at least 30cm (12in) for herb growing. Terracotta or ceramic pots are more stable and attractive than plastic, and strawberry pots planted with herbs make fine garden features.

It is essential for container growing (*see pp.35–36*) to ensure that enough water is available at all times, but avoid waterlogging, especially for herbs. Make the compost as light-textured as possible by adding 20 per cent grit by volume to garden soil or a proprietary soilless compost, and ensure that the container has plenty of drainage holes.

## HERBS AS DECORATIVE PLANTINGS

The ornamental qualities of herbs – from the neat flowerheads of chives and the variegated leaves of some sages to the shapes of trained bay trees and the graceful leaves of fennel – mean that many can be included in decorative borders. Large herbs, especially those that do not need so much sun, such as angelica (*Angelica archangelica*), chervil, and lovage, mix well in informal woodland or hedgerow plantings. Formal schemes can be created by planting herbs in patterns such as the traditional knot gardens. Thyme is especially suitable, similarly chamomile (*Chamaemelum nobile*), marjoram, and sage: all of these have golden foliage forms, and sage and thyme have other colourful cultivars. A popular scheme is to plant a herb garden in the shape of a cartwheel, with each section planted with a single species. Quite small areas between paving stones can be similarly planted, perhaps to brighten up a utility area close to the house.

## PREPARING A HERB GARDEN

Making a herb garden in the open ground requires the same preparation

**Confining mint**
*Mint will spread invasively in the open ground: planting it in a pot sunk into the ground keeps it within bounds. Some gardeners also claim that the distinctive flavours of different mints merge if the roots mix, and pots prevent this.*

as a kitchen garden, including clearing weeds (*see pp.49–50*) and ensuring free drainage (*see p.16*) and suitable levels of lime (*see pp.18–19*). Do not, however, incorporate organic matter. On heavier soils, dig in gravel to improve aeration and drainage. Plant herbs in spring, and keep young plants well watered in the time immediately after planting (*see pp.70–71 for more on planting out*).

The majority of perennial herbs can be bought container-grown. To plant these out, first water the container well. Dig the planting hole a little larger than the pot, and fork over the soil at the bottom to encourage rooting. Each herb should be planted to the same depth as it was in the pot, and firmed in well. Plants that spread by invasive underground parts – in particular

horseradish and mint – should be grown within a barrier, such as a large plant pot or bottomless bucket sunk into the ground, and often replanted.

It is worth considering laying down landscape fabric over the area to be planted and covering it with medium-sized stone chippings (*see p.34*), which serve both to anchor and conceal the fabric. Pull back the chippings at the planting stations and make cross-cuts in the fabric: plant the herbs firmly through the cuts before replacing the stone chip mulch. This method will suppress weed growth, maintain a suitable soil temperature in summer and winter, and also conserve soil moisture.

It is important to ensure that the soil is thoroughly watered before covering it, and from time to time check that the soil remains adequately moist – it may be worth laying irrigation hoses (*see pp.54*) under the fabric at the outset.

## ROUTINE CARE

Keep herb plants productive by regular trimming: if not trimmed, some will become straggly, unattractive, and woody, producing fewer new shoots suitable for culinary use. Inspect herb plants regularly, and deal with weeds (*see pp.49–50*) and pests or diseases (*see pp.51–52*) as necessary.

Keep an eye on those plants that may become troublesome weeds through self-seeding, for example borage and fennel (*see p.143*). Self-seeding can be reduced or prevented by removing the flowerheads

**Pinching out bushy herbs**
*Bay, rosemary, and (as here) sage can be kept compact by frequent trimming of new growth. Pinch out between thumb and forefinger the top 2 or 3 leaves at the growing tips.*

**Cutting herbs for drying**
*Regular harvesting throughout the growing season keeps herbs compact and productive. Choose unblemished stems about 15cm (6in) long and dry them for winter use.*

before they set seed. Periodic renewal by propagation (*see below*) will keep the herbs vigorous and productive.

### PROPAGATING HERBS
Most of the culinary herb plants can be propagated at home. Many herbs, especially those grown as annuals, can be raised from seed (*see individual crops, pp.142–145*). Shrubby herbs such as rosemary can be propagated by cuttings; those with creeping roots, like mint by root cuttings; and others, such as sweet Cicely, by division (*see below*). Some of these methods require practice.

You will also need a protected area (*see pp.43–48*) in which to start off both cuttings and seed-raised herbs (*see pp.60–65*). If only small numbers of perennial herbs are needed, it may be worth simply buying container-grown plants, widely available in reputable nurseries or garden centres.

### MAINTAINING SUPPLIES
Steady supplies of herbs can be kept up through the growing season by ensuring that the plants do not suffer excessive drought and by trimming the plants regularly (*see p.139*). Fresh supplies of many annual herbs can be extended by making successional sowings later in the growing season (*see p.69*), or by dividing perennial plants late in the season and potting up some divisions to take indoors over winter.

Outdoors, the main growing season of some herbs, such as parsley, can be extended by covering the plants with cloches (*see p.46*) for protection before the weather deteriorates.

Cutting and preserving herbs ensures continuing supplies through the winter, although with some loss of the original intensity of aroma or flavour. Air drying in a warm, dark cupboard, by hanging herbs in bunches or laying them out on trays, is well tried, and the slow process preserves quality of flavour better than rapid microwave drying.

Freezing is possible in many cases: either freeze in sealed plastic bags or fill compartments of an ice-cube tray with chopped herbs and top up with water before freezing it. The ice cubes can be added to food during cooking or the herbs used after thawing the ice cubes in a kitchen sieve. Herbs can also be used to make flavoured oil or vinegar: steep for a couple of weeks in a warm place, shaking regularly, then strain off the liquid into a clean bottle.

### WIDENING YOUR RANGE
Almost all of the herbs mentioned here are included in the following list of those that are most commonly grown. The potential choice is much wider, however, and there are many other plants not necessarily thought of as herbs that nonetheless have interesting culinary uses.

Some ornamental garden plants rate equally as culinary or medicinal herbs, including marigold (*Calendula officinalis*) used for the yellow colour of its petals, which brighten rice and soups; lavender (*Lavandula angustifolia*), the flowers of which may be added to jams; bergamot (*Monarda didyma*), used for the orange flavour of its leaves in teas and the flowers in salads; and cotton lavender (*Santolina chamaecyparissus*), which has anti-inflammatory properties.

---

## How to propagate culinary herbs

▶ **Growing from seed**
*Tender annual herbs, like these young purple-leaved and green-leaved basils, are best raised from seed sown in modules and started under cover. Plant them out in early summer, either into beds or into containers.*

▼ **Taking softwood cuttings**
*Trim the base of each piece (here of lemon balm) to just below a leaf joint to create a 8–10cm (3–4in) cutting. Remove all leaves below the top 2 or 3 Insert the cuttings into a mix of equal parts peat substitute or peat and grit or perlite.*

*Softwood cuttings are taken from tips of new shoots*

▲ **Dividing shrubby perennial herbs**
*Lift a vigorous, mature plant (here thyme) in late summer. Shake off as much loose soil as possible and remove any dead or damaged parts. Using clean, sharp secateurs, divide the plant into smaller pieces, each with strong roots and top-growth; replant immediately.*

◀ **Taking root or rhizome cuttings**
*Divide roots (here mint) into 4–8cm (1½–3in) sections with at least one growth bud. Make a straight cut at the top end and an angled cut at the other. Insert vertically, angled end down, in cuttings compost, to root in 3–4 weeks.*

# Visual index of culinary herbs

## Use this index to locate details of individual herb crops.

| *Allium schoenoprasum* p.142 | *Anethum graveolens* p.143 | *Anthriscus cerefolium* p.142 | *Armoracia rusticana* p.143 |
|---|---|---|---|
| Chives | Dill | Chervil | Horseradish |

| *Artemisia dracunculus* p.145 | *Coriandrum sativum* p.143 | *Cymbopogon citratus* p.143 | *Foeniculum vulgare* p.143 |
|---|---|---|---|
| Tarragon | Coriander | Lemon grass | Fennel |

| *Laurus nobilis* p.142 | *Levisticum officinale* p.144 | *Melissa officinalis* p.143 | |
|---|---|---|---|
| Bay | Lovage | Lemon balm | |

| *Mentha* species p.144 | *Myrrhis odorata* p.145 | *Ocimum basilicum* p.142 | *Origanum* species p.144 |
|---|---|---|---|
| | Sweet Cicely | Basil | |
| | *Petroselinum crispum* p.144 | *Rosmarinus officinalis* p.144 | |
| Mint | Parsley | Rosemary | Marjoram, oregano |

| *Salvia officinalis* p.145 | *Satureja* species p.145 | *Thymus* species p.145 | **OTHER HERBS** |
|---|---|---|---|
| Sage | Savory | Thyme | |

**OTHER HERBS**

*Allium tuberosum*..........................p.143
**Chinese, garlic chives**

*Chenopodium bonus-henricus*............p.143
**Good King Henry**

*Helianthus annuus*........................p.145
**Sunflower**

*Rumex* species..............................p.145
**Sorrel**

# A-Z OF CULINARY HERBS

## Basil

*Ocimum basilicum*

This is a strongly aromatic herb with leaves producing a clove-like flavour commonly used in culinary dishes, especially with tomatoes. Common or sweet basil has oval, bright green leaves and whorls of small, white flowers from summer. It originates in tropical Asia, so should be grown as a tender annual, and belongs to the Lamiaceae family, along with mint and sage (*see pp.144–145*).
■ **Cultivation** Grow in a sheltered, reliably warm position in full sun: basil often does best in a greenhouse or indoors on a sunny windowsill. Sow seed under cover (*see pp.62–65*) in early to mid-spring, and harden off young potted-on plants for setting out 30cm (1ft) apart when risk of frost is past. Supplies can be maintained into winter from midsummer sowings grown on in containers and kept in full light indoors. Pinch out the growing tips continually as the plants develop (*see p.139*) to promote a bushy habit.
■ **Harvesting and storage** Basil cannot be frozen or dried; leaves can be stored in oil.
■ **Forms and cultivars** There are many forms including bush, compact, and low-growing kinds, and a wide range of leaf forms and aromas, such as 'Cinnamon'. Those with coloured leaves, such as 'Purple Ruffles', are decorative, but are less intensely flavoured.

## Bay

*Laurus nobilis*

The tough, aromatic leaves of bay are used variously in cooking, in particular as a basic ingredient of bouquet garni. Bay originates from the Mediterranean region. It is a small, tender, evergreen tree or shrub, naturally growing to at least 5m (15ft) tall. Cream flowers are borne in clusters in spring.
■ **Cultivation** Bay is unreliably hardy: the leaves are susceptible to cold winds, although plants with aerial parts severely damaged by cold may produce new basal growth. Grow bay in a large container (*see pp.35–36*) to allow it to be brought under cover during cold weather, and restrict its size by trimming with secateurs into decorative shapes such as cones, pyramids, or as standard mop-heads. Position containers in a sunny place sheltered from strong winds to avoid scorching the leaves. Propagation from ripe heel cuttings, layers, or seed is not easy: it may be best to buy a well-grown plant. Grow bay in a fertile, loam-based compost, and water and feed container-grown plants regularly.
■ **Harvesting and storage** Bay leaves are best used fresh, but can be dried (*see p.140*).

■ **Forms and cultivars** There are leaf shape and colour variants, but do not confuse sweet bay – also called bay tree, bay laurel, or true laurel – with cherry laurel (*Prunus laurocerasus*) or the Portuguese laurel (*P. lusitanica*), both of which are inedible and often used in hedging.

## Chervil

*Anthriscus cerefolium*

Chervil is used in cooking, particularly as an ingredient of *fines herbes*, for its delicate aniseed flavour. A hardy annual growing up to 60cm (2ft), it is decorative, but its tendency to self-seed prolifically can become a nuisance. The leaves have some resemblance to parsley (*see p.144*), to which chervil is related.
■ **Cultivation** This herb does best in partial shade in light, but moisture-retentive and relatively rich, soil: it tends to bolt and run to seed in full sun and dry soil. Sow chervil direct (*see pp.66–69*) in early to mid-spring; plants can also be successfully raised in modules (*see p.62*). Germination may take three weeks, and established seedlings should be thinned to 15cm (6in) apart.

A repeat sowing in late summer will provide plants for use over the autumn and winter; although chervil will survive outdoors over this period, better quality is maintained where plants are kept under cover (*see pp.43–48*). Water thoroughly in dry spells, and remove some of the flowerheads, leaving only a proportion of them to self-seed.
■ **Harvesting and storage** Chervil grows quite fast, and young leaves can be harvested only nine weeks after sowing. Pick young outer leaves for the best flavour, especially for use as a salad garnish or in egg dishes. Chervil leaves are better frozen than dried (*see p.140*).

## Chives

*Allium schoenoprasum*

Chives are grown for their distinctive flavour when finely chopped as a garnish for a wide range of prepared dishes, especially salads. A hardy perennial member of the onion family, they have the general appearance of salad onions, but are clump-forming, usually up to 25cm (10in) tall. They bear attractive mauve flowerheads in summer, which may also be used as a salad garnish but more importantly make the plants very decorative additions to the garden.
■ **Cultivation** Choose a situation in full sun and keep the plants well watered. Sow seed in plugs or larger modules (*see pp.62–65*) at 18°C (64°F) in early or mid-spring, and plant out in groups of three at 23cm (9in) stations. Lift and divide clumps (*see p.140*) in the autumn every three

years, or re-sow or transplant self-sown plants. Chives die back during winter. Early leaf production can be encouraged by covering with a cloche in spring, or potted clumps can also be kept in growth in a greenhouse (*see pp.43–48*).

■ **Harvesting** Remove the flowers and harvest regularly for a supply of young leaves, cutting the leaves close to ground level. Chives are best used fresh.

■ **Forms and cultivars** There are many cultivars available, including 'Black Isle Blush' ♀ and 'Pink Perfection' ♀.

# Chinese chives

*Allium tuberosum*

The leaves of Chinese, or garlic, chives are cut as for other chives (*see above*), but they can be blanched for a milder flavour. The plant has a rhizomatous stem, flat, garlic-flavoured leaves up to 50cm (20in) tall, and white flowers.

■ **Cultivation** As for chive (*see above*). Blanch leaves by placing an upturned container over young developing shoots to exclude light.

■ **Harvesting** As for chives (*see above*). Harvest blanched leaves after 4–6 weeks once they are pale and yellowed.

# Coriander

*Coriandrum sativum*

Grown for the curry flavour of its lower, lobed leaves and seeds, used especially in oriental dishes, coriander is also sometimes used like a cut-and-come-again salad (*see p.102*). A hardy annual relative of parsley (*see p.144*), it grows up to 45cm (18in) tall in the flowering phase, with heads of small white flowers.

■ **Cultivation** Grow in well-drained soil, but keep seedlings moist or they may bolt. Plants grown for leaves can be grown in partial shade; for seeds, choose a sunny site. Sow in succession from early spring to late summer *in situ* (*see pp.66–69*) in rows 30cm (12in) apart, and thin to 15cm (6in) stations. Leaves for winter use can be obtained from autumn sowings kept under cover (*see pp.43–48*), but remember that the plants can produce an unpleasant odour in enclosed spaces.

■ **Harvesting and storage** Pick leaves when young and use fresh or frozen (*see p.140*). Seeds can be gathered when ripe and stored.

# Dill

*Anethum graveolens*

Dill is grown for the mild, distinctive flavour of its leaves, used in a range of dishes from soups to salads. Seeds are added to pickling vinegars. It is a decorative annual, up to 1.2m (4ft), with flat heads of yellow flowers, much resembling fennel, to which it is related.

■ **Cultivation** Dill does best in moist, fertile

soil, otherwise plants bolt early in hot weather. Do not grow dill near fennel, since the plants will hybridize, losing their distinctive flavours. Sow seed *in situ* (*see pp.66–69*), because dill is not amenable to being transplanted. Make successional sowings from spring through to midsummer in rows 60cm (2ft) apart, and thin the plants to 15cm (6in) stations.

■ **Harvesting and storage** Pick young leaves before flowering; they can be dried, but are best fresh. Harvest seeds as they turn brown.

# Fennel

*Foeniculum vulgare*

Fennel provides aniseed-flavoured foliage for chopping and stems for peeling, as well as seeds, to use as a flavouring for salads and meat and fish dishes. A hardy perennial with attractive, fine, feathery, green or bronze foliage on stems up to 1.5m (5ft) tall, and bearing flat-headed clusters of yellow flowers, fennel is a particularly decorative plant. Do not confuse this herb with Florence fennel, *Foeniculum vulgare* var. *azoricum*, which is an annual vegetable grown for its swollen, aniseed-flavoured leaf-stem bases (*see p.122*).

■ **Cultivation** Choose a site with well-drained soil in full sun. Do not grow it near dill, since the plants hybridize. Sow seed *in situ* outdoors after the risk of frost has passed, thinning to 45–60cm (18–24in) apart. Plants may also be raised from indoor sowings potted up into modules, or by dividing clumps (*see p.140*) in the spring. To ensure a regular supply of young leaves, remove developing flowerheads and cut the plants back during the season to a height of 30cm (12in). Fennel self-seeds freely on many sites and can become a nuisance.

■ **Harvesting and storage** Pick leaves and stems throughout the growing season. Unripe seeds can be used fresh, ripe seeds dried.

■ **Forms and cultivars** The attractive bronze-leaved 'Purpureum' is slightly hardier than the species.

# Good King Henry

*Chenopodium bonus-henricus*

Cultivated for its asparagus-flavoured shoots and young leaves, which add interest to salads, Good King Henry is a herbaceous perennial, growing up to 75cm (30in) tall.

■ **Cultivation** Best-quality shoots, or spears, are produced on moist, fertile sites, and Good King Henry does well in relatively shady positions. Sow seed during spring under cover (*see pp.62–65*) or *in situ* (*see pp.66–69*), for planting out or thinning to 38cm (15in) stations. Established plants can also be propagated by division in spring (*see p.140*).

■ **Harvesting** Spears can be harvested for eating fresh from the second year by severing them just below the soil surface.

# Horseradish

*Armoracia rusticana*

The white-fleshed and pungent roots of horseradish are used to make a hot-flavoured sauce traditionally served with roast beef, and also in coleslaw. It is a hardy perennial, closely related to the brassicas (*see pp.76–81*) with basal, bright green leaves. The roots are strong, fleshy or woody, and branching. They establish tenaciously, and it can become an invasive weed if not carefully controlled. Horseradish has a long history as a medicinal and culinary herb and its widespread use has resulted in its natural establishment in uncultivated areas.

■ **Cultivation** Plant in rich, well-drained soil in sun or partial shade. Horseradish can be raised from seed, but the best propagation method is to drop 15cm (6in) root cuttings in spring into dibbled holes spaced 60cm (2ft) apart. Horseradish will grow whichever way up the root pieces are put in the ground.

■ **Harvesting and storage** Lift the plant to harvest its roots in autumn. To ensure that horseradish does not spread within the garden, carefully lift all plants, not just the ones wanted for harvest, and store the roots in bundles in moist sand, replanting them in spring when new shoots appear on them.

# Lemon balm

*Melissa officinalis*

Grown for its lemon-scented leaves, which are used in a range of dishes and tea infusions, lemon balm is a hardy perennial that can grow up to 1.5m (5ft) in suitable conditions.

■ **Cultivation** Lemon balm is quite vigorous; it will grow in a range of soil types and is tolerant of drought. Propagate by sowing seed *in situ* in spring (*see pp.66–69*), by taking softwood cuttings (*see p.140*) in spring, or by dividing clumps in the spring or autumn (*see p.140*).

■ **Harvesting and storage** Lemon balm should be regularly cut back (*see p.139*) in order to maintain leaves with a strong aroma and prevent the plant from becoming straggly. The leaves can be dried.

■ **Forms and cultivars** A yellow-leaved type is available. Do not confuse lemon balm with lemon verbena (*Aloysia triphylla*) which is an attractive, half-hardy shrub that in its natural surroundings can reach a height of 3m (10ft).

# Lemon grass

*Cymbopogon citratus*

A strongly lemon-scented, tender perennial grass, this is used extensively as a grated or chopped food flavouring in Asian cuisine. Lemon grass produces strong, often cane-like stems, and is capable of reaching over 1.5m (5ft) in favourable conditions. The leaves are blue-green in colour and the flowers are attractive,

although these are not often produced in cultivation. All parts of the plant are lemon-scented.

■ **Cultivation** Lemon grass originates in warm temperate regions, and needs a moderately humid atmosphere and a minimum temperature of 55°F (13°C). In most regions, this means growing it in large containers of fertile, moisture-retaining compost in a greenhouse or similarly protected environment (*see pp.43–48*). Propagate by division or from seed (*see p.140*). Bought stems with a little root left on them may root if potted up and stood on a heated propagating tray.

■ **Harvesting and storage** Cut stems at ground level at any time and use the lower 8–10cm (3–4in) of the stems.

# Lovage

*Levisticum officinale*

Lovage leaves and shoots are celery- or yeast-flavoured; they are added to salads and used to flavour soups and stock, savoury or sweet dishes, cold drinks, and herb teas. Blanched shoots can be eaten as a vegetable, and the roots are edible as a cooked vegetable or used raw in salads. An elegant, hardy, herbaceous perennial, widely naturalized, lovage is capable of growing to the considerable height of at least 2m (6ft); its placement therefore requires thought. The leaves are divided, and clusters of pale green to yellow flowers are borne in flat heads in midsummer.

■ **Cultivation** Grow in sun or partial shade in rich, deep, moist soil. Propagate by seed sown *in situ* (*see pp.66–69*) in late summer or collect self-sown plants. Clumps can be divided in spring (*see p.140*).

■ **Harvesting and storage** Young shoots are blanched by earthing up rather like trench celery (*see pp.120–121*) as they develop in spring. Leaves are best picked before flowering.

# Marjoram

*Origanum* species

Two sorts of marjoram are grown for their distinctively flavoured leaves: pot marjoram or oregano (*Origanum vulgare*) is usually used dried, while sweet marjoram (*Origanum majorana*) has a more delicate flavour and is used fresh. Pot marjoram is a bushy, hardy perennial growing up to 60cm (2ft) high, and bears small mauve flowers in summer. Sweet marjoram, although shrubby, is grown as a half-hardy annual and is less decorative, with insignificant white to pink flowers.

■ **Cultivation** These herbs do best on fertile soil in a sunny position. For a winter supply, the plants can be lifted, potted, and taken into a well-lit position under cover (*see pp.43–48*). Both types also can be grown as container plants (*see pp.138–139*) either outside or under cover. Propagate pot marjoram from softwood

cuttings or by division (*see p.140*) and keep the plants trimmed, cutting dead stems hard back. Sweet marjoram is raised from spring-sown seed under cover (*see pp.62–65*). Germination is erratic, over several weeks. Established plants should be set out at 15–20cm (6–8in) stations.

■ **Harvesting and storage** Pick leaves just before the flower buds open and use fresh, frozen, or dried (*see p.140*).

■ **Forms and cultivars** There are numerous forms, many making attractive garden plants because of their leaf or flower colours.

# Mint

*Mentha* species

The culinary use of mint is long established: leaves are chopped to use in sauces, added to salads and drinks, cooked with vegetables, or used whole as garnishes. The mints comprise a large group of creeping perennials, with many and varied forms, all characterized by highly aromatic foliage and pinkish flowers.

■ **Cultivation** Mints have an invasive habit and they can be troublesome weeds if allowed to become old and woody or established among other plants or in pathways. It is possible to restrict its growth by planting it in a sunken container (*see p.139*) or within some other form of physical barrier. Extended supplies can be obtained by potting up roots in the autumn and bringing them indoors.

Propagate by division in spring or autumn, taking rooted shoots or planting 5cm (2in) long pieces of rhizome horizontally so they lie 5cm (2in) deep and 25cm (10in) apart. Replant every three or four years. Mint is prone to mint rust (*see p.257*), which can be devastating. Where infection occurs, dig up and burn the plants as soon as it appears, and replant fresh stock on a new site.

■ **Harvesting and storage** Pick leaves throughout the growing season and use them fresh. For storage, freezing is more successful than drying (*see p.140*).

■ **Forms and cultivars** Commonly grown mints include spearmint (*Mentha spicata*) and apple mint (*Mentha suaveolens*); Bowles' mint (*Mentha villosa* var. *alopecuroides*) is particularly aromatic and resistant to rust. There are many other kinds that are attractive for their range of aromas, leaf forms, and variegation.

# Parsley

*Petroselinum crispum*

Parsley foliage is used chopped as a flavouring and a garnish in a wide range of hot and cold dishes. It is a biennial herb, which is generally hardy, but is usually grown as an annual. Most selections grow up to 30cm (12in) in the leafy first-year stage, though some flat-leafed forms may exceed 60cm (2ft), according to growing conditions and site. Flat heads of

small, yellow flowers are borne in the second season, and the plants will self-seed in favourable places.

■ **Cultivation** Parsley does best on fertile, moisture-retentive soil, and is tolerant of partly shaded or sunny sites. The main production period is from early summer through to autumn. The most reliable method of raising early plants is to sow in plugs or larger modules under cover (*see pp.62–65*). Parsley is slow to germinate and may take several weeks to appear. Set out hardened-off plants with the minimum of root disturbance at 23cm (9in) stations. Plants develop quite slowly and the soil must be kept moist.

Successional sowings can be made outdoors (*see pp.66–69*) in drills 1cm (½in) deep in rows 45cm (18in) apart. Thin the seedlings to 23cm (9in) spacings. This system works well for sowings made from summer onwards. Be sure that the seed is sown into moist soil.

Remove flowerheads to prolong the useful life of the plants. Parsley foliage dies back in late autumn on the majority of sites; supplies can be prolonged by covering the plants with a cloche (*see p.46*) or by container growing (*see pp.138–139*) in a greenhouse or similarly protected situation (*see pp.43–48*).

■ **Harvesting and storage** Cut single leaves or bunches low down on the stems with scissors. Parsley leaves can be frozen (*see p.140*) for out-of-season use.

■ **Forms and cultivars** There are two main sorts. Plain-leaved cultivars of the French and Italian types are the easiest to establish and grow, and are more strongly flavoured than the decorative cut and curled leafed types, of which there are many cultivars. Selections range from pale to dark green in colour.

# Rosemary

*Rosmarinus officinalis*

The highly aromatic leaves of rosemary are a traditional flavouring for cooked meats. An evergreen shrub related to mint and sage, it has short, needle-like leaves densely packed on long branches, and pale blue, sometimes white flowers borne especially in the summer but at other times throughout the year in mild sites. Rosemary is vulnerable to low temperatures, especially when young, or in exposed areas; some selections are less hardy than others.

■ **Cultivation** Rosemary bushes are attractive as specimens in the shrub border or as low, semi-formal hedges. One or more plants can be grown in a large container (*see pp.138–139*) and kept trimmed with secateurs; in this form, the plants can be brought under cover during winter in cooler areas. Rosemary can be propagated from seed, but softwood cuttings (*see p.140*), as well as cuttings taken from semi-ripened shoots, root easily and the plants establish well on suitable sites. Keep young plants pinched to maintain a bushy habit (*see p.139*), and aim to prune regularly and moderately.

■ **Harvesting and storage** Pick leaves and flowering shoots in spring and early summer and use them fresh, frozen, or dried (*see p.140*). Leaves can be picked for use fresh all year, but will be tougher when picked late in the year.

■ **Forms and cultivars** There are spreading and upright forms. The shrub may grow up to 1m (3ft) high but can be contained by hard pruning, which it tolerates well.

# Sage

*Salvia officinalis*

Sage leaves are used in meat stuffings, and can also be added to salads. A shrubby perennial, sage grows up to 60cm (2ft) tall, with tough, grey-green, highly aromatic leaves, and bears spikes of attractive blue flowers in summer.

■ **Cultivation** Sage grows best in full sun on well-drained, light soils. It can be propagated by seed sown indoors (*see pp.62–65*) in spring or by softwood cuttings in summer or more mature shoots with a "heel", a small piece of the previous year's wood at the base, in early autumn (*see p.140*). Plants establish best from setting out in spring, spaced 45–60cm (18–24in) apart. Pruning after flowering helps maintain shape and encourage new growth, but aim to renew plants every three or four years.

■ **Harvesting and storage** Leaves can be picked for use fresh or dried (*see p.140*) for winter use. It is best to pick leaves before flowering if drying them for storage.

■ **Forms and cultivars** The numerous cultivars with coloured and variegated leaves are excellent border plants, but generally less hardy than the common sage.

# Savory

*Satureja species*

There are two types of this strongly flavoured herb, often used like sage but especially added to cooked broad beans, salads, and soups. Winter savory (*Satureja montana*) is a quite hardy, shrubby perennial,which grows to 50cm (20in), with small, grey-green leaves. Summer savory (*Satureja hortensis*) is a smaller annual with softer, less intensely flavoured leaves. Both bear whorls of white to pink or purple flowers in summer.

■ **Cultivation** Both types of savory thrive on light, well-drained soil in a sunny position and can also be grown in containers to overwinter under cover (*see pp.43–48*). Propagate winter savory by seed sown in spring, by division in spring, or by taking softwood cuttings in summer or heel cuttings in early autumn (*see p.140*). Summer savory should be raised from seed in spring. The plants will grow to approximately 30cm (12in), and should be cut back after flowering in order to encourage new growth.

■ **Harvesting** Pick the leaves during the growing season and use fresh.

# Sorrel

*Rumex species*

The young leaves of sorrel are added to soups, sauces, soft cheeses, and egg dishes for their fresh, tart flavour. The buckler-leaf or French sorrel (*Rumex scutatus*) is slightly less acidic and more frequently grown than the common sorrel (*Rumex acetosa*). Both are hardy perennials; common sorrel is upright with long, leathery leaves, while buckler-leaf sorrel is low-growing and has shorter, shield-shaped leaves.

■ **Cultivation** Both species grow well in moist soil in sun or partial shade. Site them with care: buckler-leaf sorrel can be invasive, and both can be hard to eradicate once they have become established. Propagate sorrel by sowing seed outdoors (*see pp.66–69*) in mid-spring or by dividing the plants (*see p.140*) in spring or autumn.

■ **Harvesting** Pick the leaves before flowering in summer and use fresh; remove the flowers as they appear to prevent bolting.

# Sunflower

*Helianthus annuus*

This tender annual is widely grown for its seeds, which are eaten fresh or roasted or used in baking. With its height of 3m (10ft) or more and cheerful, large yellow flowers, the sunflower is a versatile plant, filling the role of a herb, a food crop, and an ornamental plant.

■ **Cultivation** Grow in well-drained soil in full sun. Propagate by sowing seed outdoors (*see pp.66–69*) in spring; sow direct or in modules to minimize root disturbance.

■ **Harvesting and storage** Pick flowerheads as the petals fade in late summer or early autumn and pick out the chaff from between the seeds. The seeds should readily come free when the flowerhead is flexed and firmly stroked.

# Sweet Cicely

*Myrrhis odorata*

The leaves and seeds of sweet Cicely are sweetly aromatic, with an aniseed flavour, and are used in salads and fruit dishes. The thick taproot is edible as a cooked vegetable. A hardy, herbaceous perennial, it requires space to accommodate its large stature, as it grows up to 1.5m (5ft) tall. It is a handsome plant over a long season, especially for a woodland garden, and has fern-like foliage and bears flat heads of white flowers in summer.

■ **Cultivation** Sweet Cicely should be grown in rich, moist soil in sun or partial shade. Raise it from seed sown outdoors in the autumn (*see pp.66–69*), or by division or root cuttings (*see p.140*). Self-seeding is common, and the plant can become a weed, so remove the seedheads before maturity. Sweet Cicely responds well to periodic cutting down during the growing season by producing a new flush of growth.

■ **Harvesting and storage** Pick leaves throughout the growing season and use fresh or frozen (*see p.140*). Pick unripe seeds for use fresh. Lift the roots in autumn and use fresh.

# Tarragon

*Artemisia dracunculus*

The leaves of tarragon are strongly aromatic and are chopped for use in salads, and in fish and chicken dishes, particularly as a flavouring for sauces. It is one of the large group of wormwoods, which belong to the daisy family, and is a herbaceous perennial available in two forms. French tarragon (*Artemisia dracunculus*) grows to 75cm (30in) and is variably hardy compared to the more robust Russian tarragon (*Artemisia dracunculus dracunculoides*), which is not so well-flavoured when young and grows about twice as tall. Both have narrow, glossy leaves.

■ **Cultivation** The tarragons succeed on fertile, well-drained soil, especially in a sheltered, sunny site. French tarragon does not reliably set seed in cool summers but spreads by rhizomes that may be divided in spring, or softwood cuttings can be taken (*see p.140*) in midsummer. Russian tarragon is propagated by sowing seed under cover in spring (*see p.140*).

■ **Harvesting and storage** Harvest leaves or whole stems throughout the growing season for use fresh, frozen, or dried (*see p.140*).

# Thyme

*Thymus species*

Thyme is a popular culinary herb, used in a wide range of dishes. An ornamental, low-growing perennial or subshrub, it has small leaves and bears tubular, two-lipped flowers in shades of pink or purple.

■ **Cultivation** Thymes prefer well-drained, sunny sites. *Thymus vulgaris* and several other culinary thymes are hardy, while others are half-hardy. All can be grown indoors in pots for steady winter supplies. Propagate every two or three years to avoid straggly plants, by sowing outdoors (*see pp.66–69*) in late spring or early summer, or by dividing clumps and using the parts furthest from the centre (*see p.140*). Thymes tolerate hard trimming after flowering (*see p.139*) to maintain a good flush of growth and to contain their size.

■ **Harvesting and storage** Pick sprigs during the growing season and use fresh, frozen, or dried (*see p.140*).

■ **Forms and cultivars** *Thymus vulgaris* is most commonly grown for the kitchen; it develops a semi-shrubby habit up to 30cm (12in) tall and gives a strong flavour. Also noteworthy are *Thymus pulegioides* and the lemon-scented *Thymus x citriodorus*.

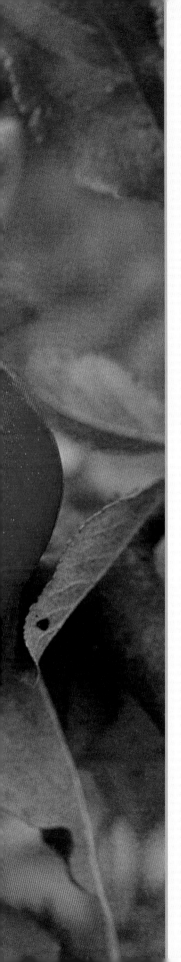

# FRUIT

In recent times, the work of researchers, plant breeders, and specialist growers has encouraged gardeners to innovate in fruit cultivation, to adopt new techniques and develop old ones – growing traditionally large trees such as apples and pears in patio pots, for example, or pushing back the boundaries of hardiness with tender crops such as citrus. Despite the undoubted value of modern techniques, fruit growing still appeals to the senses in ways that bring us closer to nature – the beauty of the plants both in fruit and in blossom, the buzz of pollinating insects about their work, the sun's warmth ripening the crops, the scents and flavours of fresh-picked produce.

One of the pleasures – and sometimes problems – of fruit growing is the fact that many wild creatures are as attracted to fruits as we are. These visitors remind us that to be fruitful, in every sense of the word, a garden must be full of all forms of life. A balanced approach must be sought that protects crops from pests while encouraging "garden friends" to help control problems.

# Visual index of fruit

**Use this index to locate details of individual fruit crops.**

*Actinidia deliciosa* p.235
**Kiwi fruit, Chinese gooseberry**

*Ananas comosus* p.236
**Pineapple**

*Citrus* species p.234
**Citrus**

*Corylus avellana* p.203 and *C. maxima*
**Cobnut and filbert**

*Cydonia oblonga* p.200
**Quince**

*Ficus carica* p.197
**Fig**

*Fragaria* x *ananassa* p.211
**Strawberry**

*Juglans regia* p.204
**Walnut**

*Malus domestica* p.174
**Apple**

*Mespilus germanica* p.201
**Medlar**

*Morus* species p.202
**Mulberry**

*Olea europaea* p.236
**Olive**

*Opuntia ficus-indica* p.237
**Prickly pear**

*Passiflora* species p.235
**Passion fruit**

*Prunus armeniaca* p.196
**Apricot**

*Prunus avium,* p.189, p.191 *P. cerasus*
**Sweet and acid cherry**

*Prunus domestica,* p.185 *P. insititia*
**Plum and damson**

*Prunus dulcis* p.205
**Almond**

*Prunus persica* p.193
**Peach and nectarine**

*Pyrus communis* p.181 var. *sativa*
**Pear**

*Ribes nigrum* p.223
**Blackcurrant**

*Ribes rubrum* p.221
**Redcurrant**

*Ribes rubrum* p.221
**Whitecurrant**

*Ribes uva-crispa* p.219
**Gooseberry**

*Rubus fruticosus* p.215 and *Rubus* hybrids
**Blackberry and hybrid berries**

*Rubus idaeus* p.215
**Raspberry**

*Vaccinium corymbosum* p.225
**Blueberry**

*Vaccinium macrocarpon* p.226
**Cranberry**

*Vitis vinifera,* p.227 *V. labrusca*
**Grape vine**

# GROWING TREE FRUITS
# Planning

Tree fruits are those that naturally grow as trees, including apples, pears, plums, cherries, peaches, nectarines, apricots, figs, quince, medlars, and mulberries. As well as producing their fresh, succulent fruits, these trees often have spectacular spring blossom. The shape and size of the tree is affected by the rootstock (*see p.153*) and cultivar being grown, and the way in which it is pruned. Many may be trained to grow in the restricted but ornamental forms of cordons, espaliers, and fans, all of which take up less space than the bush form. Included among the tree fruits are several nuts: cobnuts, filberts, and almonds are all suitable for an average-sized garden. Walnuts reach a great height; consider them only for very large gardens.

### USING TREE FRUITS IN THE GARDEN
By choosing cultivars carefully and restricting their size, you can grow quite a range of tree fruits in a small space. For instance, a useful quantity of fruit can be gained from ten apple cordons, five pear cordons, three plum pyramids, and a cherry fan. Spacings depend on rootstocks chosen. Yields vary widely according to cultivar, soil, climate, and site (*see individual crops, pp.174–205*).

If growing a number of trees, plant them in rows north to south to reduce shading, with the largest trees to the north. Grow the same fruits together to aid pollination and management. To save space, or for decorative effect, fruit can be trained on fences, walls, arches, and pergolas. The choice of cultivar depends on preference, although mid- and late-season apples and pears can be stored, whereas earlier ripening cultivars must be used soon after picking. For a limited space, use high-quality dessert cultivars – they can also be cooked.

### CHOOSING A SITE
For healthy growth, flowering, and pollination (*see pp.156–157*), and ripening of fruit and wood, grow tree fruits on a warm, sunny site, sheltered

**Forms of young fruit trees**
*In the first growing season after grafting, a fruit tree will form a main vertical stem, and sometimes a few short side branches. A tree with a single stem is a maiden whip. If it has side branches after one year, it is a feathered maiden. A two-year-old feathered tree should have several well-placed branches.*

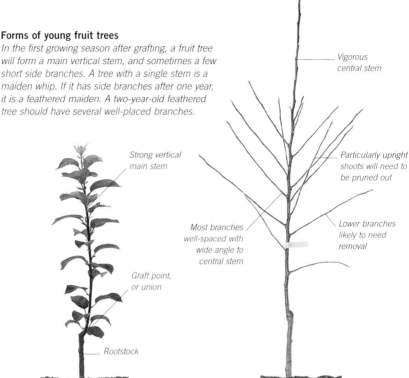

Strong vertical main stem

Graft point, or union

Rootstock

*Maiden whip*

Vigorous central stem

Particularly upright shoots will need to be pruned out

Most branches well-spaced with wide angle to central stem

Lower branches likely to need removal

*Feathered maiden*

from strong winds. Spring frosts at flowering can be devastating, so choose a site on a gentle slope so the cold air will flow away from the trees. South-, south-west-, or west-facing slopes are preferable. Avoid frost pockets (*see p.11*) or, if this is not possible, protect the trees (*see individual crops, pp.174–205*).

Altitudes below 120m (400ft) provide best growing conditions, because winds increase with altitude and temperature decreases by about 1°C (1.8°F) per 100m (330ft). Tree fruits can be grown at higher altitudes in a sunny, sheltered position with, if necessary, windbreaks (*see pp.12–13*). At altitudes above 120m (400ft), and in cool and wet areas, exploit the favourable microclimates provided by south-, south-west-, or west-facing walls and fences.

### SUITABLE SOILS
Soil requirements vary for different tree fruits, including nuts (*see individual crops, pp.174–205*). A well-drained soil,

preferably 60cm (2ft) or more deep, is desirable, although thinner soils are tolerated by most tree fruits. On thinner soils, trees will be stressed from water shortage and less stable in wind. The ideal soil is a deep, medium loam and, for most tree fruits, a slightly acid to neutral pH (*see p.18*). Tree fruits are long-term crops, so the more you improve the soil before planting (*see pp.37–40*), the better start they have.

### SOIL WATER LEVELS
Tree fruits have searching roots that need a constant supply of water and nutrients, so both light and heavy soils (*see pp.14–15*) should be thoroughly cultivated prior to planting. Working in plenty of organic matter, such as well-rotted manure or compost, will improve the drainage on heavy soils and the moisture-retention on light soils.

The surface drainage of heavy clay soils can be improved by working in a 2.5–5cm (1–2in) layer of coarse grit to the top 15cm (6in) of soil, but this is

laborious. All improvements must be done over the entire planting area – if only the planting hole is treated in this way, it may create a sump in which moisture from the surrounding soil collects. If waterlogging is severe, the installation of a drainage system may be necessary (*see p.16*) or you could resort to growing fruit trees in containers.

All types of soil will need watering at some time, but free-draining, shallow soils with 30cm (12in) or less of topsoil, especially in dry areas, require more frequent irrigation (*see p.160*).

After planting, an annual mulch (*see p.161*) around the trees in late winter or in early spring will continue to improve the soil's moisture-holding capacity.

### THE IMPORTANCE OF SOIL pH
If the soil pH differs very much from pH 6.5, which tree fruits prefer, it will need to be corrected. The pH of acidic soils can be increased by adding lime (*see pp.18–19*), and the pH of alkaline soils can be lowered by digging in sulphur. It is best to apply a little and repeat a few months later if needed. Check the pH every few years. If soils have reverted to their former pH, you will need to apply either sulphur or lime to the surface, a little at a time, and rake and water it in.

### TYPES OF TREE TO BUY
Trees establish best if planted in their final positions when young; a more mature tree will usually be overtaken by a younger sapling within a few years. Choose one- or two-year-old trees for most tree forms (*see p.152*). or fan- and espalier-trained trees, part-trained trees, about three years old, are best.

If possible, buy a feathered maiden (*see p.149*), which has a main stem with a number of side branches. These are particularly good for training as bush, spindlebush, pyramid, and cordon trees. Maiden whips (*see p.149*) can be trained into all forms, but take a year longer than feathered maidens. Some cultivars, such as 'Blenheim Orange' apples and the plum 'Count Althann's Gage', do not branch easily in the first year, and so are available only as whips.

Trees are available as either bare-root or container-grown. Bare-root trees are lifted and sold with the roots wrapped, but bare of soil, and there is usually a

much better selection of these. They must be planted between late autumn and early spring. Container-grown trees can be planted all year, but need more attention to watering if they are planted in spring and summer (*see above*).

Reputable garden centres and mail-order nurseries are good sources of fruit trees. In a garden centre the range may not be so wide, but you can inspect the plant before buying. For mail-order plants, you need to order in good time, since trees are despatched from late autumn, and be prepared to unpack and check over the trees when they arrive.

---

### Good and bad rootballs

When buying a container-grown fruit tree, don't be afraid to knock off the pot and inspect the rootball thoroughly. If the plant is in good planting condition, you should be able to see larger, anchoring roots growing out of the centre and holding together the compost without forming a thick mat. Finer, pale, feeding roots should also be visible. Avoid plants with roots that do not appear to be established in their pot, where the soil falls away from the rootball. At the other extreme, avoid pot-bound specimens with matted roots growing around the sides of the rootball and even out of the top or base of the pot. These roots are unlikely to spread and establish well when planted.

**Good rootball**
*Some healthy, fibrous roots visible, holding compost together*

**Pot-bound rootball**
*Roots coiling around outside of rootball, forming thick, matted layer*

---

### HEELING IN
Trees should be planted only when the soil is not frozen or waterlogged. If the conditions are unfavourable or you are not ready to plant, the trees will need protecting. The aerial part of the tree is frost-hardy, but the roots must not be exposed to frost or allowed to dry out. Find a suitable area of ground to heel in bare-root trees and keep their roots moist. If you cannot heel them in the ground, cover the roots with moist compost or straw, and store in a cool but frost-free place, such as a shed or greenhouse. Insulate pots of container-grown trees in severe cold weather.

◀ **Heeling in tree fruit saplings**
*Dig a trench deep enough to cover the roots. Place the trees (here feathered maiden pears) at an angle along one side of the trench so they do not touch. Fill in the trench with soil to cover the roots; firm gently.*

▶ **Small orchard**
*A productive orchard can be created in a small spa[ce] if planned with care. Here small forms such as apple cordons have been used [to] obtain a variety of cultivar[s] in a cottage garden.*

# Tree fruit forms

Fruit trees can be trained to grow in a range of different forms. Combined with different rootstocks (*see facing page*), which influence their final size, they can be trained to suit a variety of situations, for both large and small gardens, and for growing in containers.

Before choosing a form for your trees, consider the space available, the type of fruits to be grown, the site, and the amount of fruit required. Tree forms can be divided into unrestricted forms, which are generally pruned in winter, or spring in the case of stone fruits, and restricted forms, which are generally pruned in summer. Restricted forms tend to be earlier into cropping and are more productive per area than the unrestricted forms. In less climatically favourable areas, for later ripening cultivars, or for fruits that require warm conditions to crop reliably – such as peaches, nectarines, apricots, sweet cherries, late dessert plums, and figs – the fruits benefit from being grown in a restricted form against a south-, south-west-, or west-facing wall or fence. Training against a wall is also a good method in high rainfall areas, giving improved ripening of shoots and buds.

Apples and pears are the most versatile of the tree fruits, with a great range of forms possible, including the elaborate restricted forms that were traditionally used in walled kitchen gardens. Other fruits cannot be trained into such a range of forms, usually due to their fruiting habit or vigour, but there is still a selection suitable for training against walls or freestanding post-and-wire supports. For pruning details on each form, *see pp.166–173.*

---

## Common tree fruit forms

### Bush

*The bush is an unrestricted, open-centred tree with a clear stem of 75cm (30in) before the branches start. All tree fruits can be trained as bush trees, and the final size of the tree will depend upon the type of fruit and the rootstock onto which it is grafted (see facing page). This form is most suitable for fruits that grow well in the open, such as apples, pears, plums, and quinces. Standards and half-standards are trained as for bush trees, but are grown on more vigorous rootstocks and have a longer clear stem – 1.35m (4½ft) for a half-standard and 2m (6ft) for a standard; they are suitable only for large gardens.*

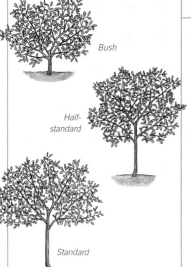

Bush

Half-standard

Standard

### Cordon

*These are restricted forms trained as a single stem, or several stems (a multiple cordon), and suitable for apples, pears, and some plums. The stems can be trained at a 45-degree, oblique angle, horizontally, or vertically, and are closely spaced, so many trees can be grown in a small area. Summer pruning is needed to control their vigour and encourage cropping close to the stem. Cordons are useful on walls or fences, but also flourish on post-and-wire structures or over arches. One of the most productive forms, and easy for a beginner, they come into cropping early in their lives.*

Cordon

Multiple cordon

### Centre-leader trees

*These take two forms: the pyramid and the spindlebush. Each has a central stem and is cone-shaped, with branches starting at 60cm (2ft) from the ground. The slightly neater pyramid is used for many fruits; the spindlebush only for apples and pears. Centre-leader trees are restricted forms, that come into cropping early in the life of the tree. There is good light distribution to all parts, and they cast less shade than a bush tree. They are usually small, from 2m (6ft) to 2.4m (8ft) tall, depending on the rootstock. The spindlebush is best for more vigorous cultivars.*

Pyramid

Spindlebush

### Espalier

*Most suitable for apples and pears, espaliers consist of a central stem with horizontal arms about 45cm (18in) apart. They can be grown on freestanding posts and wires or a wall or fence. Although productive, they take longer to reach maturity than cordons. A highly ornamental restricted form, espaliers are an attractive way of dividing a garden.*

### Fan

*In this restricted form, the branches radiate out on either side of the low, central stem and are attached to wires. Fans can be trained on freestanding posts and wires or a fence and can be used for almost all fruits. They are particularly useful for peaches, nectarines, apricots, and figs, which benefit from the shelter of a wall or fence.*

# Rootstocks

Almost all tree fruits are propagated by grafting, in which the scion – a bud or shoot – from one tree is joined onto the rootstock – or root system – of another tree to produce one plant. Therefore the rootstock of the tree is different from the fruiting part of the tree. This method of propagating fruit trees has been practised since ancient times and current techniques are little different from those carried out by the Romans and ancient Greeks.

There are a number of advantages to be gained from propagating a fruit tree in this way. Fruits grown from seed do not usually come true, and the majority of seedlings are inferior to the parent. Trees grown from seed also take many years before flowering and fruiting – seven to ten years for apples – and have first to go through a juvenile phase. Most tree fruits do not root easily from cuttings, so grafting is a more reliable method of reproducing a particular cultivar. Trees on their own roots have differing and unpredictable amounts of vigour, and tend to be very vigorous, maturing into large trees that are unsuitable for many garden situations.

Rootstocks are usually classified by the effect they have on vigour, and they help to determine the final size of the tree, although they may also confer other qualities, such as disease resistance, onto the whole plant.

## PROPAGATING ROOTSTOCK MATERIAL
Rootstocks can be propagated by a variety of techniques, but the most common is the stool bed method. This

**The rootstock grafting point**
*The point at which the rootstock and scion join should be visible on all grafted fruit trees as a bump near the base of the stem. This point should never be buried, since the scion may root, negating the effect of the rootstock.*

involves cutting down the rootstocks to ground level in late winter. They will produce a number of shoots during the growing season and these are earthed up gradually as they grow. The earthing up encourages the shoots to develop new roots at their bases. Each rooted shoot can then be severed during the following winter and planted out in rows in a nursery bed ready for grafting. This method is mainly used by professional growers to produce large numbers of rootstocks, but can be undertaken by the enthusiastic amateur. For information on grafting methods, *see pp.154–155.*

## THE QUALITIES OF ROOTSTOCKS
The general trend in fruit growing has been towards producing smaller, more manageable trees and, to this end, research stations have concentrated on selecting and breeding more dwarfing rootstocks. This benefits commercial and garden growers, since small trees on dwarfing rootstocks come into fruit bearing earlier in their life and are generally more productive. There is a greater choice of rootstocks available for apples than for other fruits. It has proved difficult to find suitable dwarfing rootstocks for plums and cherries.

When buying a tree you need to find out what rootstock it is grafted onto and the eventual size that can be expected. This can only be a general guide since mature tree heights vary according to soil, site, and cultivar. Some rootstocks are more suitable for training different forms (*see individual crops, pp.174–205 for specific guidelines; see also the table below*).

| ROOTSTOCKS FOR TRAINING APPLE TREE FORMS | |
|---|---|
| Apple form | Rootstock |
| Pyramid and spindlebush | M27, M9, M26, or MM106 |
| Cordon | M27, M9, or M26 |
| Espalier | M26, MM106, or M111 |
| Fan | M26, MM106, or M111, depending on size required and soil |

## How rootstocks affect tree size

The following chart gives an indication of the way in which different rootstocks can affect the mature size of a tree (here apple). There are a great many rootstocks available commercially worldwide, selected according to local soil conditions, climate, pest and disease resistance, and other such factors.

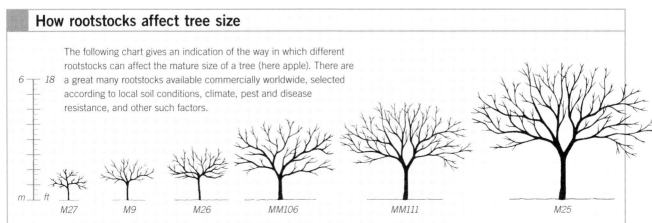

M27     M9     M26     MM106     MM111     M25

# Grafting tree fruits

Grafting is a term that covers a number of methods of joining a rootstock – or root system – and a scion – or a bud or shoot – both of which have been selected for desirable characteristics. It is a fairly challenging method of propagation, requiring attention to detail, strict hygiene, and fast working, so that the plant material does not dry out during the process.

However, for the keen fruit gardener, grafting can be a very satisfying way of producing new trees, and it is particularly useful when you wish to propagate a tree not easily obtained from a nursery, such as an unknown garden cultivar or a seedling that you have raised. Most fruit trees can be propagated by grafting. Exceptions include cobnuts, which are easily propagated from suckers and make medium-sized trees on their own roots.

Grafting involves making a matching cut on both scion and rootstock – different methods involve different cuts – and placing the cambium layer of each together. The cambium is the tissue between the bark and the pithy centre of a stem, and it is capable of producing new stem cells. Because this tissue is delicate, once exposed by cutting it is vulnerable to bacteria and fungi. Keep grafting knives (*see p.57*) sterile and sharp to avoid infections. A tree from which you are propagating should be disease-free and growing well if good offspring are to be produced.

## CHOOSING A GRAFTING METHOD

The two simplest methods of grafting, with the highest success rates, are chip-budding and whip-and-tongue grafting. For both methods, rootstocks are needed. You can grow these yourself (*see p.153*), or buy them from a specialist nursery. If you are using several, plant them out in the dormant season 45cm (18in) apart in rows 1m (3ft) apart.

Chip-budding (*see box, below*) is usually carried out in mid- to late summer, and can be done the summer after the rootstocks have been planted. Whip-and-tongue grafting (*see box, facing page*) takes place in late winter to early spring, and can be done the year after the rootstocks have been planted.

## AFTERCARE OF GRAFTED TREES

After grafting, ensure the graft does not dry out, and remove the tape once callus tissue has formed. As chip-budded shoots grow out, the new growth may need staking, especially on pears and plums. Once whip-and-tongue grafts have united, choose one shoot from the scion and tie it to a cane during the growing season. Remove any other shoots on the scion or on the rootstock when they are 8–10cm (3–4in) long.

For both methods, the resulting maiden trees can be lifted and planted out in the following dormant season.

## Chip-budding a tree fruit

**1** **Collect scions** (here of the apple 'Laxton's Superb') for budding in mid- to late summer. Choose well-ripened shoots of the current season's growth from the sunny side of the tree canopy, and cut lengths of 25cm (10in) or more.

**2** **Remove the leaves** from the ripened part of the scion, or budstick, using a clean, sharp grafting knife. Leave 4mm (⅛in) long leaf stalks (petioles), but pick off any small sub-leaves (stipules).

**3** **Prepare buds** from the scion at the site of the rootstock so that no time is lost between taking the bud and grafting it to the stock, minimizing the risk of it drying out. To remove a bud, first make a cut about 2cm (¾in) below a bud. The cut, known as a toe cut, should be about 3mm (⅛in) deep, and angled downwards at about 20°.

**4** **Make a second** cut 3.5cm (1½in) above the first. Slice behind the bud and down to meet the first cut. Remove the bud chip (*see inset*), holding it by the bud so that you do not touch the cambium layer, which might infect it with bacteria or natural oil from your hand and so impair bonding of the graft tissues. Work quickly to minimize any moisture loss.

**5** **Choose a smooth section** of the stock (here MM106) at 15–30cm (6–12in) above ground level. Make a toe cut just above a node or joint at the same angle and depth as that on the bud.

**6** **Hold the bud** against the rootstock to judge where to start the second cut, then slice out a sliver of bark above the toe cut to match that on the bud (*see inset*).

**7** **Position the bud** so that its base sits on the lip of the rootstock cut. Check there is good contact between the cambium layers of the scion and stock on at least 1 side. Move the bud to line up with the stock cambium on 1 side only, if necessary.

**8** **Bind the bud** firmly to the rootstock by wrapping the entire area with 2.5cm (1in) wide plastic grafting tape. Make sure that the graft is completely covered so that it cannot dry out.

**9** **Secure the binding** with a knot. Leave the tape in place for 4–6 weeks until a callus has formed around the bud, then cut the knot and unwrap the tape.

**10** **In early spring** of the following year, cut off the rootstock just above the bud, using a sloping cut. The bud should then grow out and become a strong shoot.

## Whip-and-tongue grafting a tree fruit

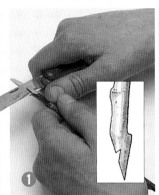

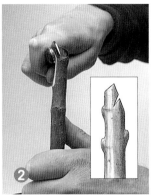

**1 Collect scions** for grafting in midwinter. Cut some strong, hardwood shoots of the previous season's growth, about 23cm (9in) long, and keep them in a dry plastic bag in a refrigerator. Prepare the graft in early spring when the rootstock is coming into growth. Choose a healthy bud on the scion, and remove a sliver of wood 3cm (1¼in) long on the opposite side of the stem, with the bud half-way down the cut. Then create a tongue (*see inset*) by cutting into the exposed wood to a depth of 1cm (½in).

**2 Cut back the rootstock** to 15–30cm (6–12in) from the ground, making a gently sloping cut just above a smooth area of stem. On the high side of the sloping cut, remove a sliver on the stock to match that on the scion, and create a matching tongue (*see inset*).

**3 Gently fit the tongue** of the scion into that on the stock (*see inset*). If the scion is narrower than the stock, make sure the edges align on at least 1 side, and that the cambium layers fit snugly together.

**4 Bind the scion and stock** together firmly using 2.5cm (1in) wide grafting tape. On thin rootstocks the tape may cover the cut on the top of the rootstock, otherwise paint all exposed surfaces with grafting wax to prevent moisture loss. After 6–8 weeks, the graft should have callused and the tape can be carefully removed.

# Pollination

Almost all of the fruit trees need to be pollinated to produce fruits. Figs are the main exception, producing fruit in cool climates without fertilization taking place. Pollination involves the transfer of pollen from the anthers (one of the male parts of the flower) to the stigmas (one of the female parts of the flower). Then, under favourable conditions, fertilization will take place. It is vital to understand the pollination needs of the cultivars you wish to grow to ensure a good fruit crop.

## HOW POLLINATION OCCURS

Flower structure and the method of pollination can vary. Most fruit trees have flowers that contain both the female parts – stigma, style, and ovary – and male parts – anther and filament, known collectively as the stamen. Within this group, some are self-fertile, that is, the flowers can be pollinated with the tree's own pollen. Often, however, pollen is not released at the same time as the stigmas are receptive, so pollen needs to be transferred from one tree to another.

Completely self-fertile tree fruits include most peaches and apricots, some plums and cherries, and a very few apples. Self-fertile cultivars usually crop more reliably if grown with a pollinator. No pears are truly self-fertile, but some bear seedless (parthenocarpic) fruits if not pollinated.

Some trees, even if their flowers have male and female parts, still need to be cross-pollinated. This involves a transfer of pollen from the flowers of one cultivar to those of a different cultivar of the same fruit that happens to be flowering at the same time. Most apple cultivars require cross-pollination with another cultivar to set a good crop.

Some fruit trees have separate male and female flowers on the same plant – these are known as monoecious plants. They include many of the nuts. Many of these are self-fertile trees, but they crop better if cross-pollinated, since the male and female flowers do not always open at the same time on the same tree.

A few fruit species have male and female flowers on separate plants – these are known as dioecious plants.

## The structure of a flower

This is an apple flower containing male and female reproductive parts. Most tree fruit flowers conform to this structure. Once a flower is pollinated, by insects or by wind, and fertilized, the seeds develop in the ovary, contained within the receptacle, and a fruit starts to form. This occurs in different ways. Apples and pears, for example, are formed of the expanded receptacle of the flower, whereas the flesh of apricots and peaches is formed of the swollen ovary wall.

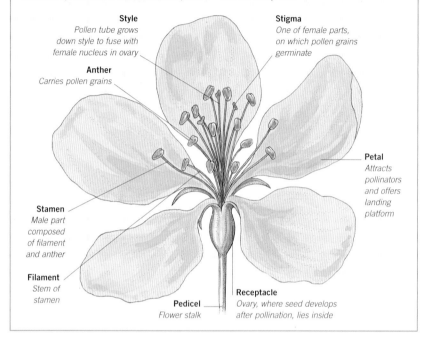

**Style**
*Pollen tube grows down style to fuse with female nucleus in ovary*

**Stigma**
*One of female parts, on which pollen grains germinate*

**Anther**
*Carries pollen grains*

**Petal**
*Attracts pollinators and offers landing platform*

**Stamen**
*Male part composed of filament and anther*

**Filament**
*Stem of stamen*

**Pedicel**
*Flower stalk*

**Receptacle**
*Ovary, where seed develops after pollination, lies inside*

They include kiwi fruits. This means that, for pollination to occur, both male and female plants must be grown.

## POLLINATION COMPATIBILITY

For cultivation, tree fruit cultivars are grouped into those that flower at about the same time (*see individual crops, pp.174–205*). Most cultivars that flower at the same time are compatible with one another, although there are some exceptions, including some apples, pears, and a number of sweet cherries.

Most cultivars are diploids (with two sets of chromosomes) or, in a very few cases, tetraploids (with four sets of chromosomes); diploids and tetraploids will pollinate each other. The triploid cultivars, such as those found in some apples and pears, have three sets of chromosomes and are ineffective pollinators, needing to be grown with two other diploid cultivars that will pollinate one another and the triploid. Some cultivars, particularly of pears,

are male-sterile, producing little or no pollen, so are ineffective as pollinators.

## CONDITIONS FOR POLLINATION

Flower pollination and the subsequent fertilization occur only if the conditions at flowering time are favourable. Pollination takes place in various ways. Many fruits, including apples, pears, and plums, are insect-pollinated, by such pollinators as bumblebees, solitary bees, and honey bees. These insects are necessary for self-fertile plants as well as self-infertile ones to transfer pollen from one flower to another.

Wind-pollinated plants include cobnuts and filberts, and walnuts, all of which are monoecious. The male catkins on these plants produce lots of pollen to ensure successful pollination.

For pollination by both insects and wind, the site is very important, since wind speeds and temperatures can vary over a short distance. A sunny, sheltered site can be several degrees

warmer than another site just a few metres away. Insect-pollinated plants need conditions that are warm and calm enough for pollinating insects to fly. Wind-pollinated plants need a fair degree of shelter, too. Conditions may be suitable for pollination on only a few occasions during the blossoming of early-flowering fruits such as peaches, apricots, plums, and pears. Fortunately, under favourable conditions, adequate pollination can take place in just a few days. Once pollination has taken place, fertilization will occur only if the air temperatures are warm enough for pollen tube growth to take place.

To improve chances of pollination, it may be necessary to provide an extra windbreak or hedges (*see pp.12–13*). It is an advantage if honey bees are kept nearby, and it is possible to increase the numbers of wild pollinating insects, including solitary bees and bumblebees. This can involve leaving part of the garden with longer grass, and leaving hedge bottoms unweeded.

For solitary bees it is also possible to obtain bee nesting boxes. Providing nectar-rich plants throughout the year will maintain a good insect population. These include numerous native and traditional flowering plants. Plant species, rather than cultivars, tend to be more successful, and soft fruits, including redcurrants and cane fruits, also attract insects.

## AVOIDING FROST DAMAGE

One of the greatest barriers to achieving pollination, fertilization, and subsequent crops of fruit is frost. Most fruit trees are fully winter-hardy, but the developing

**Windbreak**
*Deciduous trees make good windbreaks for tree fruits, filtering the wind, but providing enough shelter to protect the blossom. The windbreak should be over 2.5m (8ft) away so that it does not compete for moisture and nutrients. This windbreak is Italian alder (Alnus cordata), which leafs out early and tolerates dry conditions.*

buds, flowers, and fruitlets are very susceptible to frosts. Frost damage occurs at different temperatures, depending on the stage of development of the buds, flowers, and fruitlets (*see box, below left*). Temperatures at which this damage occurs differs with the fruit type and cultivar, some being much more resistant than others.

Fortunately, in a garden situation, some frost protection can be provided. When planting, try to avoid frost pockets (*see p.11*). Trees grown against walls or fences are the most easily protected. On nights when frost is forecast, a cover of double layers of horticultural fleece, shade netting, or hessian (or similar) can be rolled down to cover the tree. Support the cover with bamboo canes (or taut wires) so that it does not touch the tree. Secure this against the wind. Roll up the cover during the day to allow access by pollinating insects.

## HAND POLLINATION

Fruit trees that flower in early spring, such as peaches, apricots, and fruits grown under glass, benefit from hand pollination since there are few insects around at this time of year. Pollinate on warm days, preferably around midday when the pollen is being shed freely. It shows as bright yellow grains and collects on the finger when touched. You may need to repeat the process on a number of occasions because different flowers open at different times.

**Hand pollinating blossom**
*The best tool for this task is a rabbit's tail tied to a cane, but you can use a fine paintbrush. Simply brush each blossom on the tree gently, one after the other, to spread the pollen from flower to flower.*

---

### FROST DAMAGE TO APPLES

This table shows the temperatures at which frost damage occurs at various stages of growth in apple trees. It illustrates the general point that the later the stage of development, the more susceptible the tree.

| Stage of development | Temperature where damage occurs |
|---|---|
| Green cluster of buds | –3.5°C (26°F) |
| Pink (closed) bud | –3.0°C (27°F) |
| Full (open) bloom | –2.0°C (28°F) |
| Petal fall | –2.5°C (27°F) |
| Fruitlets forming | –1.0°C (30°F) |

---

### POOR POLLINATION

If trees flower well but do not bear fruit, poor pollination is likely to be the cause. Sometimes unpollinated flowers produce fruitlets, which will develop for a while and then drop off; this is particularly common with cherries and plums. There are several reasons for poor pollination:
- the absence of a suitable pollinating cultivar nearby
- unfavourable conditions for pollinating insects to fly, for example cool, wet, or windy weather
- frost at, or following, flowering time.

# Planting tree fruits

For the future development of the tree, it is important to plant correctly. For closely planted trees, prepare the entire area (see pp.149–150), ensuring that it is free of perennial weeds (see pp.49–50). It is best to do this at least two weeks before planting to allow it to settle. This is particularly crucial on soils that need improving, such as heavy clay or thin, sandy soils. For widely spaced trees, each planting hole can be prepared separately. Do this just before planting since, if a planting hole is left open for a while, it can fill with water or dry out, depending on the weather, or the sides become too solid for roots to penetrate.

Planting both bare-root and container-grown tree fruits is best done when the trees are dormant between late autumn and early spring. Planting trees in late autumn is preferable if the soil is still warm because this allows some root growth before the winter. If the soil is frozen or waterlogged, however, delay planting until conditions improve (see p.150). Bare-root trees must be planted while dormant, while container-grown trees can in fact be planted all year round if necessary. If they are planted during spring and summer, they will need more attention to watering and may get off to a slower start.

### STAKING FREESTANDING TREES

All freestanding trees require staking, at least initially. The stake supports the tree until the roots have developed enough to anchor it. For trees on semi-vigorous and vigorous rootstocks, the stake can be removed after one or two years, but trees on dwarfing and semi-dwarfing rootstocks need a permanent stake.

A softwood, or, less often, a chestnut stake that has been pressure-treated or has been soaked with wood preservative should last for at least five years. Wear gloves when handling newly treated stakes. The length of stake and its angle depends on the type of tree you are

## Planting a bare-root tree

**1** **Dig a hole** wide enough to spread out the roots and deep enough so that the tree will be at the same depth as it was in the nursery. Check the depth with a spade or cane across the hole – the nursery soil mark is darker than the trunk above. If the planting area has not been prepared, add well-rotted manure or compost to the soil you have removed, plus a slow-release fertilizer, such as bonemeal.

**2** **Remove the tree** and drive a sturdy stake about 60cm (2ft) into the soil.

**3** **Place the tree** in the hole and refill the hole with soil a spadeful at a time, raising and lowering the tree as you fill so the soil settles around the roots.

**4** **Firm down the soil** in the hole with your foot half-way through filling and again when you have finished, but avoid over-firming or stamping.

**5** **Attach the tree** to the stake with a tie (here a belt tie). Loop the tie around the tree and through the buffer, then fasten it and nail it to the stake.

**6** **Mulch around the stem** of the tree with a 5–8cm (2–3in) layer of well-rotted compost or manure in a 45cm (18in) band around the tree, but do not let it touch the trunk.

planting. Upright stakes should be driven in before planting, angled ones afterwards. Angled stakes are very useful for container-grown trees since they can be inserted clear of the rootball.

Pyramid and spindlebush trees on dwarfing and semi-dwarfing rootstocks will need permanent upright stakes 2.5m (8ft) long that are driven 60cm (2ft) into the ground. Bush, standard, and half-standard trees require short stakes, either about 1.2m (4ft) long and inserted vertically with 60cm (2ft) of the stake below ground, or 1.5m (5ft) long, driven at a 45° angle into the soil.

## CHOOSING TREE TIES
A tie should form a buffer between the stake and the tree – ideally with a gap of about 8cm (3in) – and should be easily adjustable or removable to allow for the growth of the stem.

There are three main types of tree tie available. A belt tie comes with a buffer, through which the end of the tie is threaded. Use a short nail to secure the tie to the stake so it does not slip down. Check regularly that the tie does not constrict the trunk. Soft plastic tubing is widely used commercially. It is tied in a figure-of-eight knot, with the knot against the stake and fixed to it with a nail. These ties stretch so do not constrict readily, and are particularly useful where a number of ties are required. A chain-lock tie comes in the form of a plastic chain in different grades. Fasten the tie around the stake then cross back through to form a buffer, fastening it on the tree. Check and adjust regularly since these ties can soon become constricting.

## PLANTING FREESTANDING TREES
The same basic method of planting can be followed for freestanding bare-root (*see facing page*) or container-grown trees. Water them well before planting. With container-grown trees, dig a hole a little larger than the rootball; you do not need to shake the rootball as you firm it. If container-grown trees are pot-bound, any thick, thong-like roots should be cut back and the other roots teased out to encourage them to spread.

When planting, always make sure that the graft union is well clear of the soil. This is to prevent the scion rooting: if

## Planting cordons against a fence

**1** **Fix 3 horizontal wires** to the fence at 60cm (2ft) intervals, starting at 60cm (2ft) from the ground. Tie bamboo canes to the wires so that they are 75cm (30in) apart and angled at 45°.

**2** **Dig out a semi-circular hole** at the base of each cane 15–23cm (6–9in) from the fence. Place the tree in the hole at an oblique angle. Ensure the graft union is above soil level and that the scion is uppermost, growing away from the cane; this discourages the scion from rooting. Fill in and firm the soil.

**3** **Tie the stem** of the tree to the cane at intervals, using soft twine in a figure-of-eight knot.

the graft union is buried, the scion itself may root, and so the tree will in effect be growing on its own roots, negating the effect of the rootstock (*see p.153*).

If using a proprietary slow-release fertilizer to mix with the soil from the hole, always apply it in accordance with the manufacturer's instructions. On clay soils, fork gently around the edge of the hole after planting to break up any compacted or smeared soil.

## PLANTING TREES TO BE TRAINED
For trees to be trained as cordons, fans, and espaliers, whether they are against freestanding posts and wires or fixed to a wall or fence, supporting wires should be fixed in position before planting (*see p.162*). For all tree forms planted against a wall or fence (*see above*), plant the tree 15–23cm (6–9in) from the fence so that the roots can benefit from rainwater out of the shadow of the wall or fence. With bare-root specimens, spread out the roots and cut back those growing towards the wall or fence. Those planted by freestanding posts and wires can be planted just in front of the wires. Where a row of cordons is being planted, it

is often easier to take out a trench rather than single holes. The trench size depends on the size of the trees' root systems, but a trench 60cm (2ft) wide and 45cm (18in) deep is generally adequate.

## MULCHING A NEWLY PLANTED TREE
The mulch that you apply after planting conserves moisture and improves the organic matter content. If it is allowed to touch the tree stem, it could lead to diseases such as collar rot, canker (*see p.253*), or scion rotting. On very fertile soils, an alternative to organic matter is a sheet mulch of black film plastic or landscape fabric. To put this in place, cut a square of the sheet at least 30cm (1ft) larger on each side than the area of ground to be covered – so to cover an area of 120 x 120cm (4 x 4ft), cut a 150 x 150cm (5 x 5ft) piece of sheet. Cut a slit to the centre of the square from half-way along one side, to allow the sheet to fit around the tree. Place it around the trunk and secure by pushing the edges into slit trenches. Check the sheet is tight to the soil, and firm in.

# General care

Once you have planted your fruit trees, they need as close to ideal conditions as possible to grow well and produce good crops. This involves carrying out various routine tasks to meet their needs for water and nutrients, and making regular checks to ensure that the fruits develop without overcrowding and that they are not attacked by pests or diseases.

## TIMING OF WATERING

The demands for water vary according to the tree's stage of growth and to the rainfall in a growing season. The most critical times for watering are after planting in the spring, and from early summer, as the fruitlets are developing, until they are ripe. From midsummer, water is also needed for the production of fruit buds for the following year. If the tree suffers drought stress at this time it may fail to flower the following year and so become biennial bearing. When this happens, a tree fruits heavily in alternate years, bearing little or no fruit in the years in-between.

Additional water applied as irrigation is required during prolonged dry spells, particularly on shallow and light soils. Even in a generally wet year there may be dry periods when irrigation is helpful. Water loss from plants and soil is greatest in early to midsummer when trees are in active growth, temperatures are highest, and sunshine hours greatest, but aim to water

**Sprinkler watering among fruit trees**
*These apple spindlebushes planted in rows are being watered by mini-sprinklers attached to hoses. The sprinklers can be adjusted so that the spray covers the soil between the trees.*

## Thinning blossom and fruitlets

**Blossom thinning**
*On trees prone to biennial bearing, about a week or 10 days after flowering remove alternate blossom clusters. Use scissors or pinch out each blossom at the stem, leaving the leaves below undamaged.*

**Thinning fruitlets**
*Remove misshapen, damaged, or poorly positioned fruits first to leave large, healthy, well-shaped fruits. On plums (shown here), thin the fruitlets by picking to leave a single fruitlet every 5–8cm (2–3in).*

trees all through early summer and early autumn if there is a lack of water. Apply 5cm (2in) of water over the rooting area every two weeks – about 50 litres/sq m (11 gallons/sq yd). The rooting area extends to the perimeter of the tree canopy.

## WATERING METHODS

Apply water economically and reduce water loss wherever possible. Ideally, irrigate at night when evaporation and consequent wastage is at its lowest. Surface mulches over the rooting area (*see facing page*) can be very effective in reducing water loss.

Drip irrigation from purpose-made hoses is a good method, particularly if trees are grown in rows or trained on walls or fences. There are several types available (*see p.54*), some of which leak along their length, while others have drippers at intervals and give out water at a controlled rate. Drip irrigation operates at low pressures, so pipes and outlets need to lie close to the trees.

Where trees are more widely spaced, low-level sprinklers are useful because the spray can be adjusted to fit the tree spacing. Both systems can be set up to work at intervals using timers if needed.

If you water manually using a watering can or hose, water thoroughly every two weeks rather than little and often.

## BLOSSOM AND FRUIT THINNING

In favourable conditions, fruit trees set more fruit than is ideal. Overcropping results in small, low-quality fruit, poor growth, and stress on the tree. This sometimes causes biennial bearing since the tree is unable to produce flower buds for the next year. In extreme cases overcropping can cause the tree to die.

To counteract biennial bearing where this is known to be a problem, thin the blossoms (*see above*), either removing alternate clusters, or removing most in a cluster. Blossom removal is also needed on all fruit trees in the first growing season after planting.

Fruit thinning should be done as a routine task in early to midsummer to leave the fruits at the optimum spacing (*see individual crops, pp.174–205*). The earlier the thinning, the better the increase in fruit size, since thinning when cell division is still taking place in the early stages of fruit formation has the greatest effect. Many trees drop some fruit naturally – this is known as June drop – but further thinning is usually required (*see above*). It is the

amount and spacing of the fruit left on the tree that matters, not how many fruits you remove. Depending on how many fruits set in a season, you may not need to thin; in heavy cropping years, you will need to remove several times the number left on the tree.

## FEEDING TREE FRUITS

All plants need a supply of nutrients (*see p.17*) to grow and fruit well. Fruits vary in their nutrient needs (*see individual crops, pp.174–205*). Some, such as stone fruits, pears, and culinary apples, require more nitrogen than others for growth, while most fruit trees have a fairly high demand for potassium – vital in fruit bud and fruit development.

Magnesium is often important since some fruits – especially vines, apples, peaches, and raspberries – are prone to magnesium deficiency (*see p.257*), particularly on thin, free-draining soils.

The major nutrients can be applied as inorganic or organic fertilizer and as mulches (*see below*), although the latter provide limited feed value. To correct magnesium deficiency, use magnesium sulphate, also sold as Epsom salts. You can apply this direct to the soil or, for a more rapid response, in solution to leaves at a rate of 20g/litre (½oz/pint). Adding a proprietary wetting agent improves the effectiveness of spraying. To avoid leaf scorch, do not spray in bright, sunny conditions.

## MULCHING AND WEED CONTROL

There are two basic types of mulch: organic and inorganic (*see pp.41–42*). Organic mulches are useful on most soils to maintain a good level of organic matter in the soil, helping to keep the soil free-draining and improving its moisture and nutrient retention. A thick layer will also help with weed control. Inorganic mulches are excellent for weed control, although they may lead to a depletion of organic matter in the soil in the long term. On thin, dry soils, inorganic sheet mulches work best with drip irrigation (*see p.54*) beneath them.

Growth and cropping suffer if there is strong competition for water and nutrients. Weeds and grass compete if they are too close to a fruit tree, as do ornamental plants and vegetables.

Trees on dwarfing rootstocks are particularly susceptible to competition. Mulching is one of the best ways of weed control; for other methods, *see pp.49–50*.

Trees on semi-vigorous rootstocks can be grown in grass, but they need a weed-free area of 60cm–1m (2–3ft) and, for the first four years, an annual mulch 5–8cm (2–3in) deep to a radius of about 45cm (18in). Trees on dwarfing and semi-dwarfing rootstocks grow best in clear ground. A surface mulch of organic matter is beneficial. Those grown against supports should have a weed-free strip of 60cm (2ft) along the fence or wall or on either side of freestanding posts and wires.

## PROTECTING YOUR CROPS AGAINST DEER AND RABBITS

Deer and rabbits can kill or damage young trees by girdling the tree: this is when a ring of bark is eaten around the tree, killing it by preventing moisture and nutrients from travelling up and down the trunk. Deer also eat young shoots. If deer and rabbits are present, the ideal solution is to fence off the whole garden to exclude them.

To be rabbit-proof, wire fencing of a 2.5cm (1in) mesh needs to be buried vertically 30cm (12in) deep with 30cm (12in) laid horizontally to form an L-shape underground. It should extend above ground by 90–120cm (3–4ft). If

this is not possible, a guard around each tree is effective. There are several types: a plastic or galvanized metal mesh guard is best as it allows air circulation. Close-fitting, wrap-around plastic guards are available, but are less satisfactory since they produce damp conditions around the stem, which can encourage canker infection, and they may cut into and restrict the stem. After four or five years, the stem and bark become thick enough to be of no interest to rabbits.

To protect against deer, taller wire fencing is needed, of 2m (6ft) or over. Where deer are a problem and the area cannot be fenced, half-standard or standard trees are the only types suitable for growing because the branches will be above deer browsing height.

## PROTECTION AGAINST BIRDS

As tree fruits ripen, they need to be protected against birds (*see also p.252*). Trees on dwarfing rootstocks and those grown against a support can have a net draped over them, with a cane structure to keep it off the fruits. For an area of fruit trees, a fruit cage can be made, up to 2–2.2m (6–7ft) high, with a structure of wooden posts, and draped netting, or a proprietary cage obtained. Apples, pears, and plums are susceptible to bullfinches attacking fruit buds, so need protection in winter and early spring.

**Mulching and rabbit protection**
*Each spring, spread a layer of mulch around each tree. Use well-rotted manure, compost, or bark chippings about 5–8cm (2–3in) deep and extending around the tree as far as the canopy. Here, a plastic mesh rabbit guard attached to the stake keeps the mulch away from the trunk. If the mulch should lie against the trunk, it may create damp conditions, increasing the risk of disease infection and of the scion rooting.*

# Pruning and training principles

Pruning is the cutting away of growth to keep a plant healthy, and influence its shape, size, flowering, and fruiting. Training encourages a plant to grow in a specific shape and direction, often so it is more productive. When a fruit tree is young, it needs formative pruning to create a healthy branch framework of the shape needed to carry crops in the future. When mature, it needs routine pruning so that it bears regular crops of good fruit of a good size. At all stages, pruning is not as complex as it may at first seem. It is crucial to understand the basic principles to get the best possible crop from your tree. Bush and pyramid forms need pruning but little training. Spindlebushes require more pruning and training than the bush and pyramid, but not as much as the restricted forms. Cordons, espaliers, and fans need both pruning and training.

## SUPPORTS FOR DIFFERENT TREE FORMS

Freestanding forms require staking (*see pp.158–159*). Restricted tree forms need to be trained onto horizontal wires. The wires can be attached to a wall or

fence or between freestanding posts. The support framework and wires need to be erected before planting so that you can start training the newly planted tree at once. Use galvanized wire for the supports. For fan-trained trees the wires should be 14 gauge, or 1.2mm (¹⁄₁₆in) in diameter, and spaced 15cm (6in) apart horizontally; for espaliers use 12-gauge, or 2.5mm (⅛in) in diameter, wires that are spaced 45cm (18in) apart; and for cordons, which are about 2m (6ft) tall, you need three 12-gauge wires spaced 60cm (2ft) apart.

There are a number of ways of fixing wires to fences or walls. Space the fixings about 2m (6ft) apart along the fence or wall. They need to be held 4–10cm (1½–4in) away from the

**Attaching support wires**
*To fix horizontal wires to a brick or stone wall, use eye bolts secured to the wall with expanding bolts. Insert the expanding bolt into a drilled hole and then screw it in to trigger the outer casing to expand to fit the hole tightly. Fix the wires to straining bolts slotted through the eye bolts.*

*Eye bolt in casing*

*Bolt casing*

*Eye bolt*

surface to allow air to circulate. A useful method for walls is to use expansion bolts screwed into the wall and straining bolts fixed through these. Alternatively, screw 10–15cm (4–6in) vine eyes into plugs in the wall or directly into a wooden fence. Fit straining bolts to the vine eyes at one end to adjust the wire tension. Always take care when straining wires: use safety goggles as eye protection, and avoid overstraining the wires since this may cause them to snap.

If a number of closely spaced wires are needed for fan-trained trees, wires can be stapled directly to wooden posts or fixed to wooden battens in walls. Since there are more wires used, straining bolts should not be needed.

## MAKING A FREESTANDING SUPPORT

Support frameworks can be of timber or metal posts and must be substantial to withstand the strain put on them by mature trees. The height depends on the tree form chosen and is commonly 2–2.2m (6–7ft). Space posts up to 4m (12ft) apart; the spacing between the posts needs to be at least half the width of the mature tree. At either end, strengthen the post by using a diagonal strut at 45 degrees, and fix it firmly two-thirds of the way up the stake.

If you are using timber posts as uprights, ensure that they have been treated with preservative and are at least 8cm (3in) in diameter. The bases should be sunk at least 45–60cm (18–24in) into the ground or into metal post supports. Galvanized angle iron is ideal for metal uprights; these need to be sunk to a similar depth.

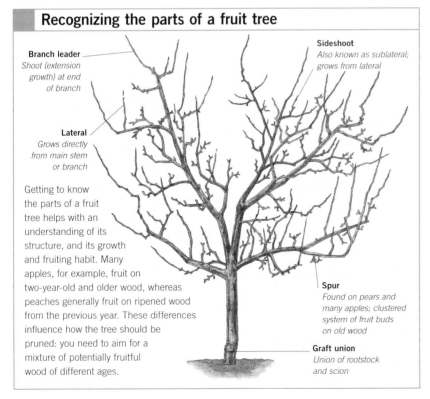

## Recognizing the parts of a fruit tree

**Branch leader**
*Shoot (extension growth) at end of branch*

**Sideshoot**
*Also known as sublateral; grows from lateral*

**Lateral**
*Grows directly from main stem or branch*

Getting to know the parts of a fruit tree helps with an understanding of its structure, and its growth and fruiting habit. Many apples, for example, fruit on two-year-old and older wood, whereas peaches generally fruit on ripened wood from the previous year. These differences influence how the tree should be pruned: you need to aim for a mixture of potentially fruitful wood of different ages.

**Spur**
*Found on pears and many apples; clustered system of fruit buds on old wood*

**Graft union**
*Union of rootstock and scion*

## Making a good pruning cut

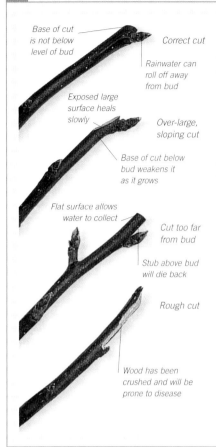

Base of cut is not below level of bud

Correct cut

Rainwater can roll off away from bud

Exposed large surface heals slowly

Over-large, sloping cut

Base of cut below bud weakens it as it grows

Flat surface allows water to collect

Cut too far from bud

Stub above bud will die back

Rough cut

Wood has been crushed and will be prone to disease

When pruning, it is important to make cuts correctly to avoid damaging or impairing growth or introducing disease. The cut needs to be in the appropriate place in relation to a healthy bud or to the branch, and it should be clean to promote swift healing. Always use clean, sharp cutting tools.

#### ◀ Good and bad pruning cuts
*A correct cut is made just above a bud, sloping at a gentle angle away from it. This allows the bud to grow away strongly to form a new shoot. Cutting too close to, or too far from, the bud allows disease to enter the wound.*

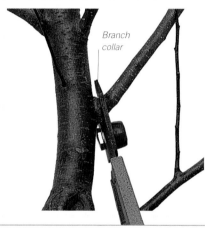

Branch collar

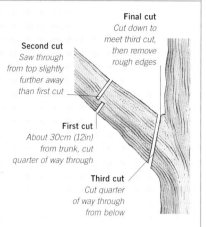

Final cut
*Cut down to meet third cut, then remove rough edges*

Second cut
*Saw through from top slightly further away than first cut*

First cut
*About 30cm (12in) from trunk, cut quarter of way through*

Third cut
*Cut quarter of way through from below*

#### ▲ Removing a large branch
*When removing a big branch, it is vital to cut it away in sections to prevent the wood splitting or tearing under its own weight. Leave the branch collar intact to aid healing.*

#### ◀ Branch collar
*When removing a branch at the point of origin, look for a slight ridge at the base of the branch, known as the collar. Cutting back to this allows the wound to heal naturally. If the branch is cut flush with the stem, it will wound the framework of the tree. Leaving a larger snag beyond the collar causes dieback and often a cavity.*

For metal or timber posts, fix the wires to a straining bolt through one end post, thread them through holes drilled in intermediate posts, and fix them to the other end post.

### CHECKING TREE SUPPORTS
Permanent ties on freestanding trees on dwarfing or semi-dwarfing rootstocks, or on restricted forms, should hold the tree in position without constricting it, and provide a buffer against the stake or wire. Neither stake nor wire should rub against the tree in case it damages the bark, providing an easy entry point for disease. Check all ties and stakes in spring and during the growing season, adjusting or replacing them as needed.

### PRUNING TOOLS
Your tools should be kept clean and sharp to make the best pruning cuts. You need secateurs for basic pruning of shoots, loppers for larger growth, and a pruning saw for larger branches (*see also*

*p.57*). Pruning saws are either straight-bladed or have a curved blade – called a Grecian blade – and are much easier to use in a tight space than other saws.

### AIMS OF PRUNING
Basically, pruning is carried out to keep the structure of the tree strong and open, allowing light penetration and air circulation. This promotes the growth and ripening of new shoots and fruits, and helps to reduce pests and diseases.

Pruning also aims to remove dead, diseased, and damaged wood to protect the health of the tree. Any dead and damaged or broken wood may attract disease, and wood that already has become diseased may infect the rest of the tree. The most common diseases affecting apple and pear branches are apple and pear canker (*see p.253*). Any affected branches should be cut back to healthy material, but if the infection has affected only one-third or less of the branch circumference, and the branch is

essential to the structure, it is possible to treat it by cutting away the canker back to healthy tissue with a sharp knife; disinfect the knife after use.

Stone fruits are often affected by bacterial canker (*see p.253*). Affected branches should always be removed by cutting them back, either to the point of origin of the branch or to a suitable side branch at least 30cm (12in) below the infection.

Any crowded and crossing branches should be removed to maintain the open shape of the tree. If these branches start to rub against each other, they may chafe the bark, causing wounds through which disease may enter.

Selective pruning produces a supply of new wood to replace the old wood that has been removed. It also controls the height and spread of the tree, and maintains it in the required form and of satisfactory vigour. Vigour is also greatly affected by training (*see p.164*). Finally, pruning aims to promote the

## Removing crossing, broken, and diseased wood

▲ **Diseased branch**
*This tree has canker, which will affect the entire branch above the infection. Remove the branch back to its point of origin to prevent the canker from spreading into the tree.*

▲ **Crossing branches**
*Where two branches are crossing, choose the one that is best placed – that is, growing outwards away from the centre of the tree – and remove the other by cutting it back to the base where it joins the main framework.*

▶ **Broken branch**
*A branch may be broken by chafing with another branch, by its own weight, or by high winds. Whether it snaps off or is still attached, the wound is vulnerable, and so the branch needs to be removed back to the branch collar.*

formation of fruit buds (*see p.164*), taking account of the tree's fruiting habit.

To achieve a balance between growth and cropping, it is vital to understand how trees respond to different pruning intensities. Pruning too hard results in vigorous growth and light crops of large, poor-quality fruits, which do not store well. Underpruning or lack of pruning results in poor growth and large crops of small, poor-quality fruits that are mainly borne at the top of the tree. Any fruit lower down will tend to suffer more from pests and diseases. Underpruning or neglect can also lead to biennial bearing (*see p.160; see also* Pruning to a bud, *facing page*).

### AIMS OF TRAINING

Horizontal growth tends to be less vigorous but more productive than upright growth, with more fruit buds, and so more fruit, being produced on horizontal branches. Much of the training of fruit trees is intended to maximize horizontal and low-angled growth, and several trained forms, such as the espalier, have been developed with this in mind. On the spindlebush

(*see pp.169–170*), branches are tied down for the same reason. Training, along with pruning in many cases, also aims to make the management of the tree easier, with fruits more exposed to sunlight and accessible for picking.

### WHEN TO PRUNE?

Pruning times vary according to the form and the type of fruit being grown (*see individual crops, pp.174–205*). In general, apples and pears are pruned in summer or winter, according to the tree form being grown, whereas stone fruits should be pruned only in spring or summer, when risk of infection from silver leaf and bacterial canker is lowest. Pruning in winter or early spring promotes new, vegetative growth, while summer pruning restricts growth.

### RECOGNIZING FRUIT BUDS

There are two types of bud found on a fruit tree: fruit buds and vegetative buds. Vegetative buds, also known as growth buds, produce non-fruiting growth. Fruit buds, or flower buds, are larger than vegetative buds because they contain embryonic flowers.

**Different types of buds**
*This pear shoot clearly shows one-year-old vegetative buds, and two- and three-year-old fruit buds. The age of the wood can be seen by the growth from the previous pruning cuts as well as by the sizes of the various buds.*

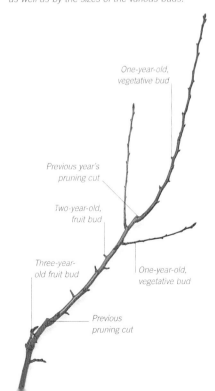

*One-year-old, vegetative bud*

*Previous year's pruning cut*

*Two-year-old, fruit bud*

*Three-year-old fruit bud*

*One-year-old, vegetative bud*

*Previous pruning cut*

A good supply of fruit buds is crucial to the fruiting of any tree, so that the tree has enough to produce good crops. On the other hand, if the tree has too many fruit buds, the resulting crop may be too heavy and will strain the tree physically, possibly breaking branches. An overly abundant crop will also divert energy from the development of fruit buds for the following year.

Fruit buds of apples and pears contain a vegetative bud as well as a flower; the vegetative bud produces a shoot from directly behind the flower, known as a bourse shoot. Due to their natural habit and careful pruning, some apples and pears develop short, woody fruit bud systems, or fruiting spurs.

*Prunus* species (plums, acid and sweet cherries, peaches, nectarines, apricots, and almonds) have separate fruit and vegetative buds. These are found either as single, separate buds or, more often, as double or triple buds, with both fruit and vegetative buds grouped together. The fruit buds tend to be plumper and rounder, while the vegetative buds are more pointed in shape.

## PRUNING TO A BUD

In general, always prune to a vegetative bud. For apples and pears, if this is not possible, you can prune to a fruit bud since there is a vegetative bud behind it. For stone fruits, it is simpler to look for a double or triple bud since you can be more certain of having distinguished a vegetative bud from a fruit bud.

The fruit buds on young shoots are generally of better quality and will produce better fruit than those on old wood. One-year-old shoots often do not produce fruit buds to fruit the following year, although this depends on the fruiting habit of the tree. Those that do fruit on wood produced the previous year include tip-bearing apples (*see p.175*) and pears (*see p.182*), as well as peaches (*see pp.193–195*) and acid cherries (*see pp.191–192*).

On trees that bear fruit mainly on two-year-old or older wood, such as spur-bearing apples and pears, and plums, it is still important to retain many one-year-old shoots when pruning since these will bear fruit in the future and so you will ensure a good supply of fruiting wood.

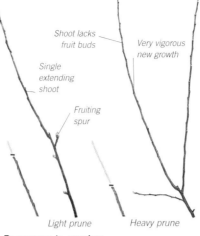

Shoot lacks fruit buds

Very vigorous new growth

Single extending shoot

Fruiting spur

Light prune

Heavy prune

### Responses to pruning
*In the shoot on the left, light pruning has produced some extension growth and fruiting spurs on the two-year-old wood. In the example on the right, harder pruning has resulted in vigorous, branching growth, but no more fruit buds.*

## DEGREES OF PRUNING

One-year-old shoots respond differently to varying levels of pruning. Unpruned, they produce some growth at the tip – extension growth – and fruit buds, but do not branch much. Light pruning results in a little extension growth, some branching, and fruit buds. Moderate pruning causes more extension growth, strong branching, and some fruit buds. Hard pruning produces vigorous growth, little branching, and no fruit buds. If you decide to remove a one-year-old shoot, remove it at the base without leaving a stub, otherwise the stub will produce strong, new growth.

In general, the harder you prune, the more vigorous is the resulting growth because the tree is trying to restore the balance between the root system and the aerial parts of the tree. Growth is needed for replacement wood and new fruit buds, but not too much; you need to decide the type of growth you want before choosing how hard to prune.

## PRUNING AFTERCARE

Many fruit trees used to be treated routinely with a wound paint to seal wounds after pruning. This is now recommended only in certain cases. On apples and pears, do not seal the cuts since this tends to slow the callusing of the wound. For stone fruits with cuts over 1cm (½in), seal each wound with a proprietary wound paint immediately after pruning. This helps stop infection from silver leaf or bacterial canker, both of which may enter through the newly exposed wood of pruning cuts.

## Spur thinning

The many apple and pear cultivars that bear their fruits on knobbly fruiting spurs will need spur thinning from time to time, when the spurs become congested. Overcrowding of fruit buds on the spurs prevents fruits from developing to their full size and the spurs may be more disease-prone if they touch. To thin an overcrowded spur system, use secateurs to remove any old, weak, or very congested spurs altogether. Thin out the growth on the remaining spur systems until only strong spurs bearing plenty of fruit buds remain.

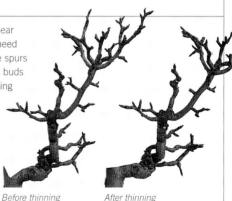

Before thinning

After thinning

# Pruning different tree forms

To create the tree form that you would like, whether it is a freestanding tree such as a bush or pyramid, or a restricted form, such as a cordon or fan, it is necessary to start the appropriate pruning and training soon after planting the tree. Formative pruning is first needed to produce a tree of the desired shape. This pruning is fairly severe to produce strong growth and a good branch framework that can carry future crops. As the tree matures, the pruning becomes lighter to encourage cropping rather than growth. The early years are crucial, for a lack of careful formative pruning can result in a mature tree that is difficult to manage.

This section lays down the principles for pruning all the basic shapes of fruit trees at the formative and mature stages. Most pruning is undertaken in the winter while the tree is dormant.

Any differences in timing, and pruning and training techniques, are covered in individual crop entries (*see pp.174–205*).

## FORMATIVE PRUNING OF A BUSH, HALF-STANDARD, AND STANDARD TREE

For trees grown in the open, the most common form is the open-centre tree. This can be a bush, a dwarf bush, a half-standard, or a standard (*see p.152*). The pruning is similar for all of these forms, the difference being the height of the stem before the branches start.

The bush form is suitable for trees on all but the most vigorous rootstocks. Prune apples and pears immediately after planting in the dormant season and prune stone fruits in mid-spring.

In the first year the pruning depends on the type of maiden (one-year-old) tree obtained. A maiden whip, which is a single stem with no branches, will

take a year longer to develop than a feathered maiden, which has a single stem with a number of side branches arising from it, allowing quicker formation of the basic bush shape (*see box, below*). During the growing season, little is needed in the way of additional formative pruning; simply remove any badly placed, unwanted shoots. The aim of formative pruning is to build and extend the basic branch framework of the bush. A maiden whip should start fruiting in the fourth summer, and a feathered maiden in the third.

To train a standard or half-standard, you will need to grow on the main vertical stem for a season or two to reach the desired stem height of 1.35m (4½ft) for a half-standard, and 2m (6ft) for a standard. Retain the sideshoots until the main stem is the correct height, then train as for a bush.

## Formative pruning of a bush

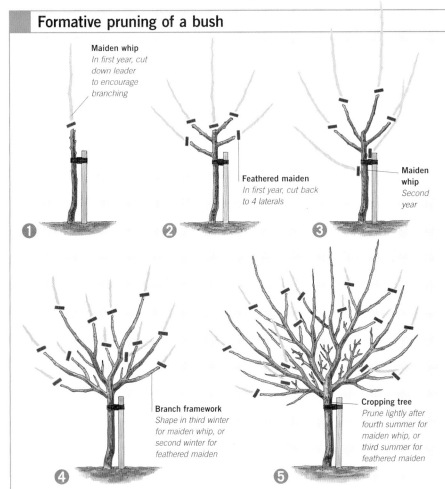

**Maiden whip**
*In first year, cut down leader to encourage branching*

**Feathered maiden**
*In first year, cut back to 4 laterals*

**Maiden whip**
*Second year*

**Branch framework**
*Shape in third winter for maiden whip, or second winter for feathered maiden*

**Cropping tree**
*Prune lightly after fourth summer for maiden whip, or third summer for feathered maiden*

**1** **Starting with a maiden whip,** prune to a bud at about 75cm (30in) from ground level. Ensure there are at least 4 consecutive plump buds beneath it.

**2** **Starting with a feathered maiden,** choose a wide-angled lateral at about 75cm (30in) from ground level with 3 or 4 well-spaced laterals (feathers) directly below it. Remove the central stem above your chosen lateral. Shorten the 3 or 4 laterals below the cut, by about two-thirds of their length, to buds facing in the required direction – an upward-facing bud if the shoot is near to horizontal, and an outward bud if the shoot is near to vertical. Sideways-facing buds can also be chosen. Remove any low laterals not needed for the basic framework.

If a feathered tree has only 1 or 2 sideshoots, remove them and then treat the tree as for a maiden whip.

**3** **In the second winter** for a maiden whip, between 3 and 6 strong shoots should have been produced. Select the best 3 or 4 to form the primary branches. The top 1 or 2 shoots are often nearly vertical so it is better to cut these back to a lower shoot that forms a wide angle to the stem – this wide angle will make the branch stronger. Shorten each selected branch by about two-thirds

## PRUNING AND TRAINING AN ESTABLISHED BUSH

After the fourth year, annual pruning becomes lighter. There are several ways to treat the mature tree according to the fruit type and its fruiting habit. Fruit trees can be broadly divided into three groups for pruning purposes, based on the age of wood on which they fruit. Most apples and pears fruit on spurs borne on older wood; they require spur pruning once they are mature to encourage new spurs to form year by year and keep trees productive.

Tip-bearing apples and pears, as well as peaches, nectarines, and acid cherries, fruit on growth made the previous year. Apples and pears, as the name implies, fruit just at the tips of the new growth. All need renewal pruning to encourage a steady supply of new wood, while maintaining a strong framework.

Plums, sweet cherries, and apricots fruit at the base of the previous year's wood as well as on older wood, and do not respond well to annual pruning once mature; however, regulative pruning (*see below*) will sometimes be required to keep a balanced canopy.

Winter pruning stimulates growth – the harder the pruning, the stronger the growth. The aim is to achieve a balance between cropping and growth. A young tree making strong growth is pruned lightly, while a tree producing weak, drooping growth is pruned hard, until its vigour improves (*see box, below*). For spur bearers, the amount of pruning depends on the vigour of the tree.

Renewal pruning, for tip-bearing apples and pears, and for stone fruits, is lighter than spur pruning, focusing on keeping an open tree shape, and making new fruiting shoots (*see box, below*).

As the tree becomes older, whatever its fruiting habit, it is necessary to carry

out regulative pruning. Remove any crossing, crowding, dead, and diseased branches (*see p.164*). Keep the centre open but not bare of fruiting wood, removing any large branches, but leaving fruiting spurs and laterals. If the tree is becoming too large, reduce its height and spread by cutting back to a lower placed branch or replacement branch that is growing in the required direction, which should be at least one-third of the diameter of the piece being removed. On spur bearers, thin out spur systems as they become overcrowded (*see p.165*).

For more detail on pruning specific fruits, *see individual crops, pp.174–205*.

### OVERVIGOROUS BUSH TREES

Summer pruning is not usually carried out on bush trees, but it can be effective in controlling overvigorous trees, since pruning when the tree is in leaf restricts growth. Prune well-ripened laterals longer than 30cm (12in), cutting them

to a bud facing in the required direction. Remove any shoots that are below the desired framework back to the stem.

**4 By the third winter** for a maiden whip, or the second for a feathered maiden, the branch framework will be well-developed. Pruning should be lighter at this stage. Shorten each branch leader by one-third to a suitably placed bud. Select 1 or 2 further shoots per branch to form secondary branches, and shorten these by one-third. Any other shoots can be either shortened to about 4 buds to form spurs, or removed if they are badly placed. Remove shoots growing into the centre and cut back to the stem any shoots below the framework junction.

**5 By the fourth summer** – or the third for a feathered maiden – the tree will probably have started cropping, and so lighter pruning is required during the following winter. The framework will still need to be extended, however. To do this, select a further leader from each branch and secondary branch and shorten by about one-third of its new growth. Leave shoots of 23cm (9in) or less unpruned if there is space, and shorten longer shoots to 4–6 buds to continue spur formation. Remove any badly placed shoots altogether.

## Pruning an established bush

Prune laterals to encourage spurs to form

**◄ Spur pruning**
*Shorten each branch leader by one-third of the previous year's growth to a bud facing in the required direction. This should produce branching and new spurs along the leader. If the leader is very vigorous, do not prune it, or at most, lightly tip prune it. Leave laterals under 15cm (6in) unpruned, and remove those over 30cm (12in). Prune the remaining laterals to about 6 buds.*

**Renewal pruning ▶**
*Remove unproductive or crowded branches. On apple and pear tip bearers, tip prune the branch leaders, without removing too many fruit buds. Leave laterals less than 30cm (12in) long unpruned, and shorten other laterals to produce more shoots, or remove them altogether. Remove low-growing shoots.*

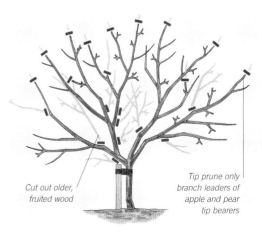

Cut out older, fruited wood

Tip prune only branch leaders of apple and pear tip bearers

to a bud at about 15cm (6in). This will encourage fruit bud formation on the remaining shoots and allow better light penetration and air circulation through the tree. Start pruning in late summer as shoots ripen, and continue into early autumn as the remaining laterals lengthen and become woody.

A vigorous tree pruned in this way will require minimal subsequent winter pruning which would only stimulate growth. If necessary remove branches to keep the centre of the tree open.

### RENOVATING A NEGLECTED BUSH
A regularly pruned tree is easier to manage and it will maintain a balance between cropping and growth, producing regular crops with fruit of a good size. A tree neglected for several years is likely to suffer from a lack of light and air circulation, leading to weak growth; there will be few fruits in the lower part of the tree, and a build-up of pests and diseases. There may also be a number of very tall branches, taking the best fruit out of easy reach.

Before attempting renovation, weigh up whether it is really worthwhile. If the tree is very diseased, with cankered and dead branches, it may not be worth keeping. If it is very large it may be too difficult to restore and require the help of a tree surgeon. If a fruit tree is dominating the garden or is heavily shaded by nearby trees and buildings, it might be easier to remove it and replace it with a number of trees on dwarfing rootstocks, which would be easier to manage and more productive. You may just wish to leave the tree untouched as a feature of the garden but, if it is generally sound with a good original framework, renovation should be possible.

There are two types of neglected tree – the overvigorous, large, and crowded one, and the starved, stunted tree – and two different approaches to pruning are required. For large, overvigorous trees, thin the canopy over a couple of years (*see below*). Do not remove more than one-third of branches in one year. If needed, delay pruning of some until the third year, when you can remove more

water shoots (strong, upright shoots with few buds) that will have arisen and more crossing branches. In the third year, you may start routine pruning.

Starved and stunted trees usually have a mass of weak fruiting spurs and little or no young growth. The cropping and fruit quality is usually poor. To improve matters, thin out all of the spurs by about a half and remove any dead or diseased branches. This will stimulate some growth to replace worn-out branches and create new spurs and new, healthy fruit buds.

### FEEDING A NEGLECTED BUSH
The soil surrounding a neglected tree may be depleted of nutrients. This will compound the problems of poor growth, poor leaf quality, and weak fruit buds. Such trees will need feeding annually after renovation; use a balanced feed containing trace elements at a rate of 70g/sq m (2oz/sq yd). After three or four years, change to a fertilizer generally recommended for the crop (*see individual crops, pp.174–205*).

## Renovation pruning a large neglected bush

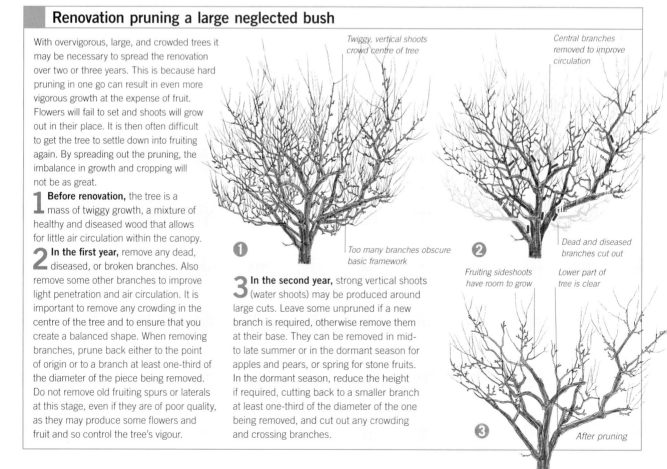

With overvigorous, large, and crowded trees it may be necessary to spread the renovation over two or three years. This is because hard pruning in one go can result in even more vigorous growth at the expense of fruit. Flowers will fail to set and shoots will grow out in their place. It is then often difficult to get the tree to settle down into fruiting again. By spreading out the pruning, the imbalance in growth and cropping will not be as great.

**1** **Before renovation,** the tree is a mass of twiggy growth, a mixture of healthy and diseased wood that allows for little air circulation within the canopy.

**2** **In the first year,** remove any dead, diseased, or broken branches. Also remove some other branches to improve light penetration and air circulation. It is important to remove any crowding in the centre of the tree and to ensure that you create a balanced shape. When removing branches, prune back either to the point of origin or to a branch at least one-third of the diameter of the piece being removed. Do not remove old fruiting spurs or laterals at this stage, even if they are of poor quality, as they may produce some flowers and fruit and so control the tree's vigour.

**3** **In the second year,** strong vertical shoots (water shoots) may be produced around large cuts. Leave some unpruned if a new branch is required, otherwise remove them at their base. They can be removed in mid- to late summer or in the dormant season for apples and pears, or spring for stone fruits. In the dormant season, reduce the height if required, cutting back to a smaller branch at least one-third of the diameter of the one being removed, and cut out any crowding and crossing branches.

*Twiggy, vertical shoots crowd centre of tree*

*Too many branches obscure basic framework*

❶

*Central branches removed to improve circulation*

*Dead and diseased branches cut out*

❷

*Fruiting sideshoots have room to grow*

*Lower part of tree is clear*

❸

*After pruning*

## Formative pruning of a spindlebush

**1** **In the first winter,** starting with a feathered maiden tree, choose 4 evenly spaced laterals about 60cm (2ft) from the base. Remove any laterals below the chosen 4; leave any shorter laterals above these. Prune the leader to a bud at about 10cm (4in) above the topmost lateral. Do not prune the laterals if they appear strong, but if they are growing weakly, prune each to a downward-facing bud.

**2** **In the first summer,** if the laterals are making vigorous growth, tie them down to about 20° from horizontal in late summer; otherwise leave them to grow naturally.

**3** **From the second summer,** tie down any new laterals arising from the main stem or existing branches if they are not already growing at a low angle. Remove at their bases any strong vertical shoots that are spoiling the overall shape of the tree.

**4** **In the fourth winter,** if any of the upper branches start to grow too wide, spoiling the tree's conical shape, prune them back to a weak, low-angled lateral. Also, shorten lower branches if they are competing with nearby trees. Remove or thin congested branches or shoots to keep light and air circulating.

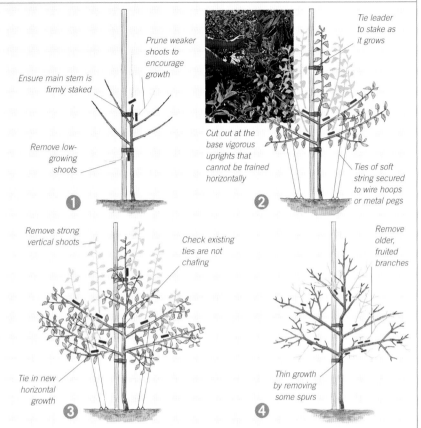

**①** Ensure main stem is firmly staked / Prune weaker shoots to encourage growth / Remove low-growing shoots

**②** Cut out at the base vigorous uprights that cannot be trained horizontally / Tie leader to stake as it grows / Ties of soft string secured to wire hoops or metal pegs

**③** Remove strong vertical shoots / Check existing ties are not chafing / Tie in new horizontal growth

**④** Remove older, fruited branches / Thin growth by removing some spurs

## FORMATIVE PRUNING OF A SPINDLEBUSH

The spindlebush is a conical form with a central leader and staggered tiers of productive, almost horizontal branches. This form, which needs a permanent, tall stake (*see p.159*), is suitable for pears and apples. For formative pruning of a feathered maiden, see above. If you are starting with a maiden whip, prune it to a bud at 75cm (30in) in the first winter. The following summer, tie in the leader to the stake and, if needed, tie down the laterals that have developed (*see p.170*) to train them about 20° above horizontal. From then on, treat as for a newly planted feathered maiden.

In the first two or three winters, prune the leader by one-third of its new growth – less if it is very vigorous, more if it is not. Cut it to above a bud, on the opposite side to the previous winter's cut, to form an upright central leader and to promote laterals below. Remove any shoots below the lowest tier and any upright, poorly placed shoots. If it

is growing well, the tree should start to bear fruit in the second summer (or the third summer for a maiden whip). Thin the fruit (*see p.160*) to avoid the tree being overloaded. By the third summer, the tree should be cropping and reach its full height of 2–2.2m (6–7ft). Continue tying down branches as necessary and removing any strong vertical shoots as before.

### PRUNING AN ESTABLISHED SPINDLEBUSH

By the fourth winter, the tree should have developed its mature cone shape, with a wide tier of lower branches and shorter upper branches. From now on, the aim of pruning is to keep the cone shape so that light reaches all parts.

Prune an established spindlebush on a renewal basis in winter to give a supply of young wood that will maintain the tree's vigour and replace older branches. The branches in the upper part of the tree are not permanent. After three or four years, cut out a proportion as they

**Pruning an established spindlebush**
*In winter, prune out older growths. Cut out the old stems back to the main central leader, using a cut at a 45-degree angle to the trunk – a Dutch cut. This leaves a stub (see inset) of about 2.5cm (1in) to stimulate a new shoot to grow from the dormant bud beneath it.*

become too long and make the tree's shape unbalanced. Treat fruiting laterals from the lower branches in the same way. If the laterals are crowded, remove them entirely or leave an angled stub to encourage a new replacement lateral. In winter or late summer, remove strong shoots that are competing with the leader, and any growing vertically from the branches. In late summer or spring, continue tying down new shoots.

Do not allow the leader to become too tall (over 2.2m/7ft) or dominant. If necessary, replace a dominant leader by cutting back to a weaker lateral and tying this up in its place. If the leader is crooked, it is an advantage: non-vertical growth tends to be less vigorous.

## TYING DOWN SPINDLEBUSH BRANCHES

There are several ways to tie down the branches so that they grow horizontally. Use strong but fairly soft string, such as three-ply twine. Avoid tying the string tightly around the branch – use a loop instead. Tie lower branches to pegs in the ground or to a nail low down on the stake. Upper branches can be tied down to the lower branches. Remove the strings once the branches have set in position, usually after a few weeks.

An alternative for one-year-old branches is to lower them by attaching a weight to a clothes peg or a loop of wire at the end of the string.

## FORMATIVE PRUNING OF A PYRAMID AND DWARF PYRAMID

The pyramid form, which requires a permanent stake (*see p.159*), consists of a central leader with branches radiating from it to form a cone shape. Economical with space, its shape allows the sun to reach fruits on the upper and lower parts of the tree. It is particularly popular for plums because the pruning can be carried out in the spring and summer, but it is also good for apples,

pears, sweet and acid cherries, peaches, and apricots. The method shown here is for plums, sweet cherries, and apricots. Pruning differs slightly for the other fruits due to their fruiting habits (*see individual crops, pp.174–184, 191–195*). A dwarf pyramid is trained as for a pyramid, but is on a more dwarfing rootstock, available for apples and pears.

Formative pruning aims to establish the basic tree shape and a spreading, outward habit. If possible, start with a well-feathered maiden (*see box, below*). If you are starting with an unfeathered maiden, prune to a bud at about 90cm (3ft) and follow the instructions for a feathered maiden from the next spring.

## PRUNING AN ESTABLISHED PYRAMID

It is important to maintain the pyramid shape of the tree. Any vigorous vertical shoots will become dominant and shade the more horizontal, fruiting branches and so should be removed in summer.

---

## Pruning a pyramid

**1** **In early to mid-spring** following planting, cut back to a bud at 10–20cm (4–8in) above the topmost feather. Remove any feathers below about 45cm (18in) from the ground. Cut the remaining feathers to a bud at about half their length. For strong feathers choose a downward-facing bud, and for weak feathers an upward-facing bud.

**2** **In the first summer,** tie in the central leader to the stake. In mid- to late summer, when the young shoots have stopped growing, prune the current season's growth of branch leaders back to above a downward-facing bud at about 20cm (8in). Cut back laterals growing from the branches to about 15cm (6in), preferably to a downward-facing bud. Repeat until established.

**3** **In early to mid-spring** of the following years until the tree is established, cut back the central leader by two-thirds of the previous summer's growth to a bud on the opposite side to the previous year's pruning.

**4** **Once the full height** has been reached (this depends on the tree and its rootstock), towards the end of each summer when growth has stopped, prune any shoots at the top of the pyramid to about 2.5cm (1in). At the same time, prune the current season's growth on branch leaders to about 20cm (8in) to a downward-facing bud. Cut back laterals arising from the branches to about 15cm (6in), also to a downward-facing bud.

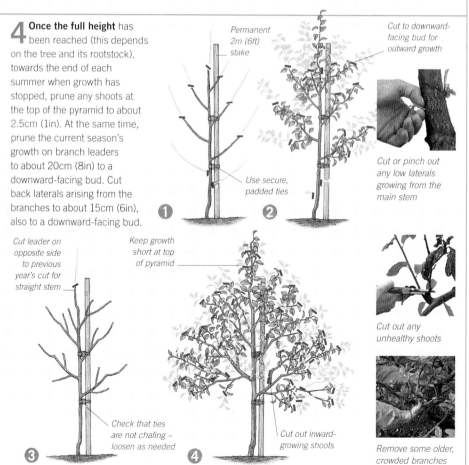

Permanent 2m (6ft) stake

Use secure, padded ties

❶

Cut to downward-facing bud for outward growth

Cut or pinch out any low laterals growing from the main stem

❷

Cut leader on opposite side to previous year's cut for straight stem

Check that ties are not chafing – loosen as needed

❸

Keep growth short at top of pyramid

Cut out inward-growing shoots

❹

Cut out any unhealthy shoots

Remove some older, crowded branches

## Summer pruning of restricted tree fruit forms

Summer pruning, also known as the modified Lorette system, is undertaken on the restricted forms – cordons, espaliers, and fans – for apples and pears. It restricts growth, maintaining the tree's shape, and encourages the formation of fruiting spurs. Timing is important. Pruning needs to be carried out as the growth slows down in late summer, and may need to be done gradually over a few weeks. At this time the shoots start to form terminal buds and the stems are becoming woody. The exact timing varies with each season and between different areas. It is earlier in warm, dry, sunny conditions, and later in cool, wet areas and seasons. If pruning is carried out at the correct time, some of the remaining buds will become fruit buds – these are produced from late summer to early autumn. If summer pruning is carried out too early, weak leafy growth will be produced at the expense of fruit buds. If this happens, cut the weak new growth back to one leaf in early to mid-autumn.

**1** **First look for** any of the current season's laterals that are more than 23cm (9in) long. If the lateral is growing from another lateral or spur, cut it back to 1 leaf or about 2.5cm (1in) above the basal cluster – the basal cluster is the small group of leaves where the new season's growth starts.

**2** **If the lateral** is growing directly from a main branch, cut it back to 3 leaves or 5–8cm (2–3in) above the basal cluster.

**3** **Leave unpruned** until early autumn any shoots that are not well ripened or that are less than 23cm (9in) long. After pruning (*see the right side of this 'Ashmead's Kernel' apple fan*), the form of the tree will be restored, allowing the light to reach the developing fruits and ripen the remaining wood for the next year.

As the tree matures, you may need to remove or shorten branches that start to spoil its shape. Do this in mid-spring, cutting back to the point of origin or a suitable branch at least one-third of the diameter of the piece being removed.

### FORMATIVE PRUNING OF AN OBLIQUE CORDON
The oblique cordon consists of a single stem trained at an angle, with fruiting branches and spurs. It is very productive and the quickest form to fruit, usually producing some fruit in the second summer, and is suitable for apples, pears, and plums. It is also possible to grow apples and pears as vertical or multiple cordons (*for details, see p.176 and p.182*).

The best tree to obtain for training is a feathered maiden or a two-year-old part-trained cordon. Otherwise, start with a maiden whip. For instructions on planting, *see p.159*. If you are starting with a feathered maiden or part-trained cordon of apple or pear, *see p.172*.

If you are starting with a maiden whip, lightly cut back the tip of the leader to an upward-facing bud to promote sideshoots, then prune as for a feathered maiden from the following winter. In the first spring for a feathered maiden (or second for a whip), remove any blossom to prevent the tree fruiting too early and allow it to establish well. After the initial winter pruning, no further pruning in winter is needed until the tree is well established. For variations for plum cordons, *see p.186*.

### PRUNING AN ESTABLISHED OBLIQUE CORDON
Summer pruning is needed annually to restrict new growth, while winter pruning is needed from time to time to thin any crowding and congestion (*see p.172*). For pruning established plum cordons, *see p.186*.

### FORMATIVE PRUNING OF AN ESPALIER
An espalier is a symmetrical form with pairs of branches extending horizontally at about 45cm (18in) intervals from a central, vertical trunk. This form is good for apples, pears, and mulberries.

Start with a maiden whip and, during the first winter, prune the stem at 45cm (18in) from the ground where there are four healthy buds below. This height should roughly correspond with the level of the first wire (*see p.162*). Insert a vertical cane to the height of the top wire, and tie the stem to it. Fix two short canes to the wires at 45° on either side. From the first summer on, or if you have bought a part-trained espalier, follow the instructions on p.172. An espalier should start to bear a few fruits from the second summer.

### PRUNING AN ESTABLISHED ESPALIER
When the tree has enough tiers to reach the top of the wires, remove the leader in summer after you have started to train the final tier. This allows you to keep it as an insurance until the shoots have been trained in on either side, and allows them to develop at a wider angle to the stem. Over the next few years, continue to train in the leaders of the tiers of the branches until they have reached the required length, leaving the extension growth unpruned. Prune the rest of the laterals and any new shoots on the basic summer pruning system (*see box, above*).

As the espalier matures, it may be necessary to carry out some spur thinning in winter (*see p.165*). Full cropping will not be reached until all the tiers of the espalier are formed.

# Pruning an oblique cordon

**1** **Following planting,** prune back any laterals longer than 10cm (4in) to 3 buds. Leave the leader and any shorter laterals unpruned.

**2** **From the first summer onwards,** the main pruning takes place in the summer, following the basic summer pruning for restricted forms (*see p.171*). Tie the leader into the cane as it develops during the summer, leaving it unpruned.

**3** **Each summer,** follow the basic summer pruning guidelines, tying in the leader to the cane until it has reached the required length – this is usually about 2m (6ft) from the ground, which is the height of the top wire. If space allows, lower the cordon to 35–40° to provide a greater length and so a greater crop. When the leader has reached its final length, prune it back and treat subsequent growth as for other laterals.

**4** **Winter pruning** may be necessary after a few years. Thin out and reduce crowded spur systems (*see also p.165*) over a period of several years since winter pruning stimulates growth.

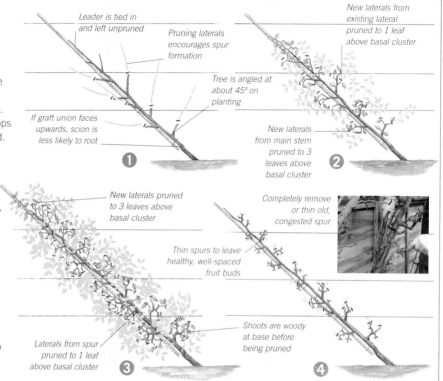

Leader is tied in and left unpruned

Pruning laterals encourages spur formation

Tree is angled at about 45° on planting

If graft union faces upwards, scion is less likely to root

**①**

New laterals from existing lateral pruned to 1 leaf above basal cluster

New laterals from main stem pruned to 3 leaves above basal cluster

**②**

New laterals pruned to 3 leaves above basal cluster

Laterals from spur pruned to 1 leaf above basal cluster

**③**

Completely remove or thin old, congested spur

Thin spurs to leave healthy, well-spaced fruit buds

Shoots are woody at base before being pruned

**④**

# Pruning an espalier

**1** **In the first summer,** select 3 strong shoots and, as they develop, tie one to each cane. Remove any others. In early autumn, lower the shoots and canes on either side so that they are horizontal, and tie them to the wires.

**2** **In the second winter,** look for 4 healthy buds at the level of the second wire, and prune the leader just above the topmost of these. Fix a cane to the wires on either side at 45°, ready for the next tier. Repeat each winter until all the tiers are formed.

**3** **In the second summer,** tie in 2 shoots to produce the next tier, and tie the central leader to the vertical cane. Prune any sideshoots on the first tier or main stem on the basic summer pruning system (*see p.171*) in late summer when the shoots are mature. In the autumn, the shoots trained at 45° can be lowered to the horizontal. Repeat this process of training in and lowering the arms each summer until all the tiers are formed, pruning the existing arms on the basic summer pruning system.

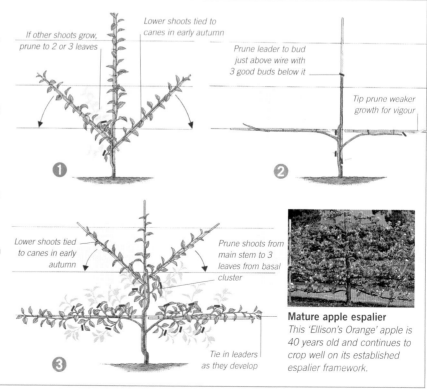

If other shoots grow, prune to 2 or 3 leaves

Lower shoots tied to canes in early autumn

**①**

Prune leader to bud just above wire with 3 good buds below it

Tip prune weaker growth for vigour

**②**

Lower shoots tied to canes in early autumn

Prune shoots from main stem to 3 leaves from basal cluster

Tie in leaders as they develop

**③**

**Mature apple espalier**
*This 'Ellison's Orange' apple is 40 years old and continues to crop well on its established espalier framework.*

## Formative pruning of a fan

**1** **Starting with a maiden whip,** prune in winter to a bud at 38–45cm (15–18in) with 3 or more consecutive healthy buds beneath it. Fix two canes to the wires, one on either side, at 45°. In the growing season, train in a shoot on either side, fixing it to the cane. Once these are growing well, remove any other shoots. Often the topmost shoot needs to be removed as it is near vertical.

**2** **Starting with a feathered maiden,** cut the tree back in winter to 2 sideshoots at 38–45cm (15–18in). Shorten these by two-thirds to an upward-facing bud. In the growing season, treat the tree as a second-year maiden whip.

**3** **In the second year** for the maiden whip, prune back the 2 shoots by about two-thirds of their length to an upward-facing bud in winter. During the growing season, train in the new growth, attaching it to the cane. Choose 2 equally spaced shoots on the upper side and 1 on the lower side of each branch and tie these to canes fixed to the wires.

**4** **In the third year** for the maiden whip (second year for a feathered maiden), cut back the 4 shoots on each side by one-third of their length to an upward-facing bud. During the growing season, tie in leaders from each branch to the canes. Select more shoots from each branch to extend the framework as space allows. Rub out shoots growing inwards.

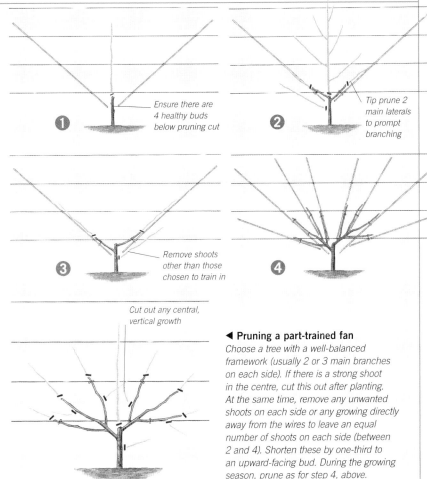

**①** *Ensure there are 4 healthy buds below pruning cut*

**②** *Tip prune 2 main laterals to prompt branching*

**③** *Remove shoots other than those chosen to train in*

**④**

*Cut out any central, vertical growth*

◄ **Pruning a part-trained fan**
*Choose a tree with a well-balanced framework (usually 2 or 3 main branches on each side). If there is a strong shoot in the centre, cut this out after planting. At the same time, remove any unwanted shoots on each side or any growing directly away from the wires to leave an equal number of shoots on each side (between 2 and 4). Shorten these by one-third to an upward-facing bud. During the growing season, prune as for step 4, above.*

## FORMATIVE PRUNING OF A FAN

A fan tree has a short vertical stem and two main arms that bear a network of permanent ribs and sideshoots spread out evenly on each side. There is no central leader as this vertical growth would tend to dominate the rest of the tree. This form is suitable for all tree fruits including almonds, although the timing and details of pruning will vary according to the specific fruit (*see individual crops, pp.174–199*). Basic formative pruning, essential for a well-balanced framework, is the same for all.

Fans can be developed from a maiden whip, feathered maiden, or from a part-trained fan obtained from a nursery. In all cases, follow the instructions given above. When choosing a feathered maiden, make sure it has two suitably placed shoots opposite one another to form the first two branches of the fan.

## PRUNING AN ESTABLISHED FAN

From the fourth year onwards for a maiden whip, or from the third if pruning a feathered tree, you should aim to extend the branch framework while keeping a strong, balanced shape. How you should treat individual shoots varies according to the fruit type being trained (*see individual crops, pp.174–199*).

## RENOVATION OF FANS, ESPALIERS, AND CORDONS

If the basic summer pruning (*see p.171*) of restricted forms is neglected for only a few years, trees can soon lose their shape, developing branches that are unbalanced and detract from the vigour of fruiting branches. Renovation may not be worthwhile if the form is lost, except in the case of figs (*see p.199*). If the tree is healthy and the original shape still clear, it can be restored.

Renovation will take one or two years, depending on how overgrown the tree is. In the winter, for apples and pears, or spring for stone fruits, cut back any branches not needed for the framework to the point of origin or to a spur near the base. Cut back all the growth at the top of the tree to bring it down to the level it should be. Thin any congested spurs (*see p.165*). If there is a lot to do, spread the pruning over two years to avoid producing too much vigorous growth; remove every other unwanted branch in the first year and the rest in the second. If the top tier of an espalier has become dominant, remove it and then train a new tier in its place (*see formative pruning, pp.171–172*). In the summer after pruning, start to prune new shoots as for routine summer pruning (*see p.171*) and continue in subsequent years to restrict growth.

# TREE FRUIT CROPS

## Apple

Apples (*Malus domestica*) are the most versatile of the tree fruits. A wide range of dessert and culinary cultivars ripens in different seasons, offering fruit from midsummer to mid-spring, provided that they are correctly stored.

Apples originated in Central Asia, and so are adapted to cold winters and can be grown in the open in most areas. There are cultivars suited to most sites and soils. A sunny, sheltered site is best, with shelter if needed (*see pp.12–13*). Planting in a frost pocket (*see p.11*) should be avoided. Most apples tolerate a range of soils if they are well-drained with a pH of about 6.5. Poorly drained and shallow soils, and soils of unsuitable pH (*see p.18*) can be improved.

### CHOOSING A TREE FORM
Apples can be grown in a diverse range of tree forms on a wide choice of rootstocks. Some forms are more suited to one of the two types of fruiting habit (*see facing page*) and this might influence your choice of apple cultivar. Suitable freestanding forms are the standard, half-standard, bush, spindlebush, and pyramid. The bush suits both tip and spur bearers, whereas a spur bearer is the best choice for the spindlebush and pyramid forms. The latter both need permanent staking (*see pp.158–159*).

Apples also thrive in the restricted cordon, espalier, and fan forms, all grown on a wire framework either with freestanding posts and wires or against a wall or fence (*see p.162*). Because fruits

**Classic apple**
*There is a great range of apple cultivars to choose from, including old favourites such as this crisp 'Cox's Orange Pippin', widely grown since the mid-nineteenth century.*

are borne on spurs along the stems of cordons, espaliers, and fans, a spur bearer is again the best choice for these forms. Cultivars for espaliers may be available part-trained (usually with two tiers), which saves two years of pruning and training. However, the choice of rootstocks and cultivars is limited, and part-trained trees are more expensive than maidens. Part-trained fans are available, but it is more likely that you will have to buy a maiden tree.

Standard and half-standard trees are suitable only for larger gardens and orchards. They make tall trees, which are more difficult to prune and pick. For most sites, a bush is a better choice. The spindlebush is a useful form for small gardens and container growing. The pyramid and dwarf pyramid forms are also ideal for the small garden, casting less shade than a bush tree, and producing well-coloured fruits.

Of the restricted forms, the cordon allows a range of cultivars to be grown, even where space is limited. Espaliers and fans are both decorative and suitable for the average garden. Some apple cultivars are sold as Ballerina trees. These are genetically bred to have compact, columnar growth (*see p.177*) so they can grow in small spaces.

### CHOOSING A ROOTSTOCK
The rootstock you choose, combined with the tree form, will have a decisive effect on the final size of the apple tree. It is essential to choose one that is appropriate for the space you have available and the amount of fruit you wish to grow (*see chart below, and p.153*).

The very dwarfing rootstock M27 is ideal for vigorous cultivars, particularly triploids (*see p.156*). It is less suitable for very weak cultivars, such as 'Sunset'. Horizontal cordons (*see p.176*) need to be on an M27 rootstock. Trees on M27 need good soil, no competition from weeds or other plants, and permanent support (*see pp.158–159 and p.162*).

### SPACINGS FOR APPLE TREE FORMS AND ROOTSTOCKS

| Type of rootstock and vigour | Standard | Half-standard | Bush | Spindlebush | Pyramid | Cordon | Espalier | Fan |
|---|---|---|---|---|---|---|---|---|
| M27 very dwarfing | – | – | 1.2–1.8m | 1.5–1.8m | 1.2–1.5m | 75cm | – | – |
| M9 dwarfing | – | – | 1.8–3m | 1.8–2.1m | 1.5–1.8m | 75cm | – | – |
| M26 semi-dwarfing | – | – | 2.4–3.6m | 1.8–2.25m | 1.8–2.1m | 75cm | 3.0–3.6m | 3–3.6m |
| MM106 semi-vigorous | – | 3.6–5.5m | 3.6–5.5m | 2.4–3.0m | 2.1–2.4m | – | 3.6–4.5m | 3.6–4.5m |
| MM111 semi-vigorous | 4.5–6.5m | 4.5–6.5m | 4.5–6.5m | – | – | – | 4.5–5.5m | 4.5–5.5m |
| M25 vigorous | 6–9m | 6–9m | – | – | – | – | – | – |

Trees on the dwarfing rootstock M9 also need permanent support and must have no competition from weeds or other plants. M9 is a good choice for spindlebushes, pyramids, and cordons on good soil, and for vigorous cultivars.

M26 is a semi-dwarfing rootstock, reliable for most conditions. It is ideal for bushes, spindlebushes, in the ground or in a container, as well as for dwarf pyramids, cordons, and small espaliers up to three tiers. Freestanding trees on M26 need staking for one or two years.

The semi-vigorous MM106 is widely used, especially for bush trees, espaliers, and fans. Freestanding trees on MM106 need staking for a year or two. Ballerina trees are sold on MM106 rootstocks. Slightly more vigorous than MM106, MM111 is useful for half-standards, bush trees, and espaliers, particularly on poorer soils. M25 is very vigorous and so is best in orchards or large gardens for standards grown in grass. Trees on this rootstock are large even on poorer soils, and slow to start fruiting.

## POLLINATION

Apples flower in mid- to late spring, depending on the season and cultivar. This is not early compared with other tree fruits, but they are vulnerable to damage by late spring frosts. In frost-prone areas, choose late-flowering cultivars (*see chart, p.180*) or those with some resistance to frost (*see chart, p.179*).

Almost all apples are, to some extent, self-infertile and so will not set a good crop with their own pollen. They crop more consistently when pollinated by compatible cultivars. Exceptions are 'Crawley Beauty', which is self-fertile and will fruit despite flowering after all other common cultivars, and a self-fertile clone of 'Cox's Orange Pippin'.

Most apples are diploid (*see p.156*), and need another pollinator to set a good crop. Some are triploid (*see p.156*) and must be planted with at least two compatible diploid cultivars to ensure successful pollination.

Apple cultivars are grouped according to the time at which they flower. For good pollination, choose cultivars from the same group if possible (*see p.180*), although those from adjacent groups will also serve as pollinators. Some cultivars are cross-infertile, generally because they are closely related, such as 'Cox's Orange Pippin' with 'Kidd's Orange Red', 'Holstein', or 'Suntan'; and 'Mutsu' with 'Golden Delicious'.

Sports (natural mutations) of cultivars, such as colour sports, russet sports and the self-fertile clone of 'Cox's Orange Pippin', usually flower at the same time as the cultivar from which they originated. Trees grown close by in neighbouring gardens and ornamental *Malus* trees can act as pollinators if they flower at a suitable time.

## PLANTING

The best time to plant apples is in the dormant season (*see pp.158–159*). Prepare the stakes and wires (*see p.162*) required for the form you have chosen before planting. Bare-root plants will usually establish well. You can also plant container-grown apples, but before you buy, check that they are not pot-bound.

## PRUNING AND TRAINING

The fruiting habit of the cultivar (*see below*) dictates which pruning methods are needed for the mature tree. It is important to prune correctly in order to avoid removing the following year's fruit buds. If pruning an unknown cultivar, you can identify its fruiting habit by looking at where the fruit buds (*see p.164*) arise. Partial tip bearers may demand a combination of pruning methods to obtain the best crop. Most pruning is carried out in winter while the tree is dormant. Summer pruning is done on restricted forms.

Some forms, such as standards, half-standards and bush trees, may be pruned as described on pp.166–168. Some details of pruning a mature apple bush will depend on the fruiting habit of the tree (*see right*). The pruning of spindlebush apples (*see pp.169–170*) is carried out in the dormant season to promote vigour, and in the summer to restrict growth.

## Fruiting habits of apples

Apples fall into two groups according to their cropping habit:

**Spur bearers:** 'Arthur Turner', 'Ashmead's Kernel', 'Beauty of Bath', 'Charles Ross', 'Cox's Orange Pippin', 'Edward VII', 'Ellison's Orange', 'Howgate Wonder', 'James Grieve', 'Lane's Prince Albert', 'Lord Derby', 'Reverend W. Wilks', 'Ribston Pippin', 'Sunset'

**Tip and partial tip bearers:** 'Bramley's Seedling', 'Cornish Gilliflower', 'Discovery', 'Irish Peach', 'Kerry Pippin', 'Worcester Pearmain'

**Tip bearer**
*Tip bearers bear fruits at the tip of each shoot. Partial tip bearers produce some spurs as well as fruit buds at the shoot tips. Both types of tip bearer are best grown as bush trees.*

**Spur bearer**
*Spur-bearing apples bear their blossoms and fruits on sideshoots, or spurs, along the main branches. This habit is more convenient for all forms, but is especially useful for pyramids, cordons, and espaliers.*

For pruning of apple oblique cordons and espaliers, *see pp.171–172*. For formative pruning of a fan, *see p.173*. Once a fan is established, shoots that are not needed to extend the framework are pruned using the summer pruning system (*see p.171*).

## PRUNING AN APPLE PYRAMID AND DWARF PYRAMID

Once the basic framework is formed, pyramids are summer pruned to control vigour and maintain a compact shape. A dwarf pyramid, grafted on a dwarfing rootstock, is pruned similarly. Pruning apple pyramids differs slightly from the basic pruning method (*see pp.170–171*) and in the timing, with additional formative pruning being done in the winter while the tree is dormant. If possible, start with a feathered maiden.

In the first winter, shorten the main stem to a bud at 60cm (2ft). Shorten any sideshoots over 15cm (6in) long to a bud at 13cm (5in), and remove any that are less than 45cm (18in) from the ground. In the first summer, tie the developing leader to the stake. In the second winter, shorten the leader to 20–25cm (8–10in) of the previous season's growth, to a bud facing in the opposite direction to that chosen in the first winter. Shorten branch leaders and laterals to 15–20cm (6–8in) to a downward- or outward-facing bud.

From the second summer, start summer pruning (*see p.171*), but prune branch leaders to 5–6 leaves above a basal cluster and a downward-facing bud. In subsequent winters, shorten the central leader to 20–25cm (8–10in) of the previous season's growth until the full height of 2–2.2m (6–7ft) is reached. On a mature tree, pruning is done in the summer. You may need to do some winter spur thinning (*see p.165*) or remove branches that spoil the shape.

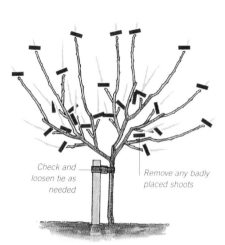

*Check and loosen tie as needed*

*Remove any badly placed shoots*

**Pruning an established bush (spur bearer)**
*In winter, shorten the branch leaders by a quarter to one-third of the season's growth. Prune the sideshoots to 4–6 buds. This pruning should stimulate formation of fruiting spurs from the sideshoots.*

## PRUNING A HORIZONTAL APPLE CORDON

The horizontal cordon is trained into a single wire suspended 45cm (18in) from the ground and secured to posts, so that the tree forms a low barrier, hence the name "stepover". For a continuous boundary, trees are usually spaced 1.5–2m (5–6ft) apart, with support posts that are 3–4m (10–12ft) apart.

To start training, select a very young, weak maiden whip that is flexible enough to bend over. Plant the whip next to a support post, or a stout cane if it is in-between posts, and tie the tree to it. In the spring after planting, carefully bend the tree until it is horizontal, and tie it into the wire at several points. From the first summer, when the tree should have developed several sideshoots, prune as for an

**Pruning an established bush (tip bearer)**
*In winter, cut out some of the older branches that have fruited for several years to make space for younger ones. Cut the branch to where it meets an outward-facing young shoot or back to the trunk to stimulate a dormant bud.*

oblique cordon (*see pp.171–172*). During the summer leave the leader unpruned and prune any other shoots on the summer pruning system (*see p.171*). Tie the leader extension growth to the wire in early autumn. Repeat this until the leader has reached the required length, then treat it as any other shoot when following the summer pruning system.

## PRUNING A VERTICAL APPLE CORDON

This form, sometimes also called a minarette, can consist of one, two, or several stems (three is not advisable as the central stem tends to become dominant). To obtain a single-stemmed cordon, plant a maiden tree next to a vertical stake that is 2.5m (8ft) long and has been driven 60cm (2ft) into the ground. Prune the tree as for an oblique cordon (*see pp.171–172*), except that the leader should be pruned by one-third of the new growth each year until it reaches its mature height of 2–2.5m (6–8ft). This pruning method stimulates the production of laterals and fruiting spurs.

For a multiple cordon with two stems, plant a maiden whip against wires as for an oblique cordon (*see p.159*), but place it vertically. Prune to about 45cm (18in) from the ground in winter.

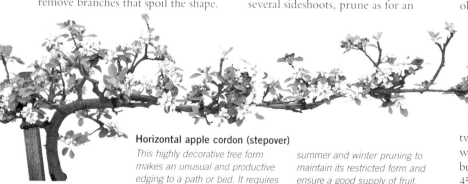

**Horizontal apple cordon (stepover)**
*This highly decorative tree form makes an unusual and productive edging to a path or bed. It requires summer and winter pruning to maintain its restricted form and ensure a good supply of fruit.*

In the first summer, train one shoot on each side at about 45°, then lower these to the horizontal in autumn. In the second winter, prune both branches to about 40cm (16in). In the second summer, tie the leaders of both branches to vertical canes and start to train both leaders as for a single vertical cordon.

For a multiple cordon with more than two stems, in the second summer choose two shoots at the end of each branch. Train one of each pair of shoots upright, and one at 45°. In the following autumn, lower the shoots from 45° to the horizontal, and proceed as for a two-stemmed cordon.

### TRAINING A CORDON OVER AN ARCH
This is an ornamental and effective way of training a cordon. At first it is trained as a vertical cordon, with the stem going up the side of the arch. Once the cordon reaches the curve, it is trained as an oblique cordon. Summer pruning restricts it and maintains its shape.

### PRUNING A BALLERINA TREE
If any sideshoots are produced on the Ballerina, use the summer pruning system (*see p.171*). Once the required height of 2–2.5m (6–8ft) has been reached, remove the leader. Thin out the spurs (*see p.165*) in winter.

### FEEDING
Apples usually benefit from an annual application of potassium and nitrogen. Apply sulphate of potash in late winter at 35g/sq m (1oz/sq yd). Top-dress with nitrogen at the same rate in early spring, using calcium ammonium nitrate on acid soils or sulphate of ammonia on alkaline soils. For trees in grass, and for culinary apples, you will need to increase the rate of nitrogen; if the leaves are pale rather than mid- or dark green, double the application. As an alternative to straight fertilizer, a compound of 1:1:2 N:P:K can be used at 70g/sq m (2oz/sq yd).

Every third year, apply phosphorus in the form of super phosphate at 70g/sq m (2oz/sq yd) in late winter. Sprinkle the fertilizers over the tree's rooting area; that is, to just beyond the branch canopy. You will need to moderate these quantities if a mulch such as well-rotted manure or compost is used, or if the trees are growing vigorously.

On thin soils and in regions with high rainfall, apples can suffer from magnesium deficiency – which appears as a yellowing between the leaf veins in early summer. Correct by spraying magnesium sulphate (*see p.161*), giving two further sprays at 14-day intervals. If this problem occurs regularly, apply magnesium sulphate to the soil at 70g/sq m (2oz/sq yd) in mid-spring.

### MULCHING
Apply an organic mulch to young trees for the first three or four years, and then annually for trees on dwarfing rootstocks on thin soils. Apply in spring while the soil is moist, at a depth of 5–8cm (2–3in) over a radius of 45cm (18in), keeping it clear of the stem (*see p.161*). For closely planted trees on dwarfing rootstocks, mulch the area with a 2.5–5cm (1–2in) layer of a light organic material, such as chipped bark or straw. On fertile soils with a high organic matter content, sheet mulches (*see p.42*) are a useful alternative to organic ones. Like organic mulches, they should cover a 45cm (18in) radius.

### WATERING
Apples grow best in a moist, freely drained soil. Newly planted and closely planted trees, and restricted forms grown on dwarfing rootstocks can quickly become short of moisture in drought conditions. Water in prolonged dry periods in spring and summer and also while the fruits are swelling in midsummer. Water can be supplied in several ways (*see pp.53–54*). For rows of trees, such as cordons, drip irrigation hoses are particularly efficient.

### FRUIT THINNING
Given favourable conditions at their flowering time, most apple trees set a lot of fruit, but a heavy crop of small, poor-quality fruits can lead to biennial bearing with the tree unable to produce fruit buds for the following year. Most apple cultivars shed some of their fruitlets in early summer. However, if there is a heavy set, most require further thinning, particularly young trees that are still extending their framework.

Start thinning (*see p.160*) in early to midsummer with the earliest ripening cultivars. The earlier the thinning, the greater is the increase in fruit size. Remove the king fruit – this is the central fruit of a cluster; it tends to be misshapen and have a short stalk.

Vigorous trees are likely to bear more fruit than weakly growing ones. Use the following as a general guide. Thin

**Ballerina apples**
*A Ballerina tree is bred to grow in a vertical, columnar shape with compact, fruiting spurs and few long sideshoots. It requires little summer pruning. Four dessert cultivars are available: 'Bolero', 'Polka', 'Waltz', and 'Flamenco'. There is also one culinary cultivar: 'Charlotte'.*

dessert apples to one or two fruits every 10–15cm (4–6in), and culinary apples to one fruit every 15–23cm (6–9in). Dwarf trees growing on M27 and M9 rootstocks should usually be thinned to one fruit per cluster.

## HARVESTING APPLES
Apple yields vary according to the form in which trees are grown, the cultivar, rootstock, and growing conditions. For an apple bush tree, you may expect an average of 27–55kg (60–120lb) per tree, for an apple spindlebush or pyramid 13.5–22.5kg (30–50lb), for a single cordon 2.25–4.5kg (5–10lb), for an espalier 13.5–18kg (30–40lb), and for a fan 5.5–13.5kg (12–30lb).

Early and some second early dessert apples can be eaten straight from the tree, but most mid- and late-season ones benefit from storage before they are eaten. Correct timing for mid- and late-season apples is important. Pick too early and they will not have developed their full flavour and may shrivel in

**Supporting fruit-laden branches**
*Where branches are particularly heavily laden, tie string around the centre of the branch and secure the other end to a temporary cane through the middle of the tree or to the trunk.*

store. Pick too late, and they will not store well. The time of ripening varies with season and site, and is partly affected by the rootstock. Pick apples only when they are ready (*see facing page*), and avoid bruising them. You will need

to pick several times; the well-coloured apples on the sunniest side of the tree first and those towards the centre last. Some signs that fruits are ripe are that they may change colour, or there may be some first windfalls, or the pips turn from white to straw-coloured to brown – although some early apples are eaten before the pips turn brown. Harvest apples carefully. Line a bucket with soft paper, straw, or hay, or use a special picking bucket (*see below*).

## STORING APPLES
Storage conditions are important, but need not be sophisticated. Apples require a cool, dark, frost-free, and rodent-proof place with some humidity. There should be some air circulation: too much can cause shrivelling, while too little can deprive apples of oxygen. An ideal temperature is 2.5–4.5°C (36–38°F); make sure it does not exceed 7°C (45°F). Cellars, sheds, and unused garages are suitable, unless the apples could be tainted by chemical fumes, such as those of paint. Lofts and attics are usually unsuitable due to temperature fluctuations.

Store undamaged fruit with stalks (*see left*), keeping cultivars apart because they ripen at different rates. Remove rotting and overripe fruits regularly.

## COMMON PROBLEMS
Apples suffer from a range of pests, diseases, and disorders, but some cultivars have good resistance to the more common problems. Pests that may affect apples include codling moth (*see p.254*), apple sawfly (*see p.251*), aphids (*see p.251*), in particular rosy apple aphid (*see p.261*) and woolly aphid (*see p.264*), apple sucker (*see p.251*), birds (*see p.252*), capsid bug (*see p.253*), caterpillars (*see p.253*), especially winter moth caterpillars (*see p.264*), and red spider mite (*see p.261*). Frost can cause damage (*see p.255*). Apples may also be affected by the following diseases and disorders: canker (*see p.253*), apple scab (*p.251*), apple powdery mildew (*see p.251*), brown rot (*see p.252*), blossom wilt (*see p.252*), fireblight (*see p.255*), iron deficiency (*see p.256*), replant disease (*p.261*), and bitter pit (*see p.252*).

## Harvesting and storing apples

**1 To test** whether an apple is ripe, lift it in the palm of the hand and give it a slight twist (never pull it as this can bruise it). If it is ripe it should part easily from the spur. If the stalk and spur are broken, it is not ready.

**2 Place the apples** as you pick them into a padded picking bucket, taking care not to drop them or cause bruising in any other way.

**3 To store apples,** use either moulded liners used by grocers (*far right*, with 'Pixie' apples) or a plastic or wooden crate with slats (*right*, with 'Blenheim Orange' apples). Ensure that the container is clean and the apples are not touching – rots spread quickly from one to another if the fruits touch.

**Lined fruit bucket**
*Soft liner chute can be unfastened to empty fruits through base*

## RECOMMENDED APPLE CULTIVARS

| Cultivar (T) *Triploid* | Pollination group | Picking time | Storage time (months) | Characteristics |
|---|---|---|---|---|
| **Dessert apples** | | | | |
| 'Delbarestivale' ('Delcorf') ♀ | 3 | Late summer | – | Crisp, juicy and heavy cropping. |
| 'Discovery' ♀ | 3 | Late summer | – | Good flavour, crisp, juicy, and sweet. Fairly compact, with some scab and mildew resistance. Partial tip bearer. |
| 'Laxton's Epicure' ♀ | 3 | Late summer | – | Aromatic flavour. Hardy, may overcrop, prone to canker. Spur bearer. |
| 'Scrumptious' ♀ | 3 | Late summer | – | Crisp with aromatic flavour. Reliable and a partial tip bearer. |
| 'Egremont Russet' ♀ | 2 | Early autumn | 3 | Excellent, nutty, russet flavour. Reliable. Spur bearer. |
| 'Ellison's Orange' ♀ | 4 | Early autumn | 1 | Aniseed flavour. Hardy, reliable. Good scab resistance, canker prone, can be biennial if not thinned. Some frost resistance. Spur bearer. |
| 'Greensleeves' ♀ | 3 | Early autumn | 1 | Crisp, juicy, good flavour. Heavy crops, reliable. Spur bearer. |
| 'Laxton's Fortune' ♀ | 3 | Early autumn | 1 | Excellent flavour, crisp, aromatic. Good scab resistance, but canker prone, can be biennial if fruit not thinned. Spur bearer. |
| 'Lord Lambourne' ♀ | 2 | Early autumn | 1–2 | Sweet flavour. Hardy, reliable, some scab resistance. Partial tip bearer. |
| 'Sunset' ♀ | 3 | Early autumn | 3 | Excellent, Cox-like flavour. Compact, reliable. Spur bearer. |
| 'Worcester Pearmain' ♀ | 3 | Early autumn | 1 | Sweet, chewy, good flavour. Hardy, reliable cropping, mildew-resistant, but prone to scab. Tip bearer. |
| 'Cox's Orange Pippin' ♀ | 3 | Early–mid-autumn | 3–4 | Excellent, juicy, aromatic. Prone to scab, canker, and mildew. Not suitable for cooler areas. Choose the self-fertile clone. Spur bearer. |
| 'Idared' ♀ | 2 | Early–mid-autumn | 6–7 | Firm, crisp, juicy, with fair flavour. Moderate vigour. Spur bearer. |
| 'Kidd's Orange Red' ♀ | 3 | Early–mid-autumn | 3–4 | Excellent, rich, aromatic flavour. Reliable, hardy, needs thinning to maintain good fruit size. Spur bearer. |
| 'Ashmead's Kernel' ♀ | 4 | Mid-autumn | 4–5 | Excellent, firm, aromatic, russet flavour. Light to moderate cropping, flowers prone to frost damage. Spur bearer. |
| 'Falstaff' ♀ | 3 | Mid-autumn | 3–4 | Sweet, crisp, juicy. Hardy, reliable crops. Some frost resistance. Spur bearer. |
| 'Jonagold' ♀ (T) | 3 | Mid-autumn | 4–5 | Good flavour, juicy. Reliable cropping, fairly vigorous. Spur bearer. |
| 'Orleans Reinette' | 4 | Mid-autumn | 3–4 | Nutty flavour. Vigorous. Fruits shrivel easily in storage. Spur bearer. |
| 'Pixie' ♀ | 4 | Mid-autumn | 5–6 | Juicy, aromatic. Heavy crops, reliable. Some frost resistance. Spur bearer. |
| 'Winston' ♀ | 4 | Mid-autumn | 4–6 | Firm, good flavour. Fairly vigorous, reliable. Spur bearer. |
| **Culinary (cooking) apples** | | | | |
| 'Emneth Early' ♀ | 3 | Midsummer | – | Good flavour, breaks down in cooking. Compact, heavy cropping, needs thinning to prevent biennial bearing. Spur bearer. |
| 'Grenadier' ♀ | 3 | Late summer | 1 | Sharp flavour. Reliable, hardy, some scab and frost resistance. Spur bearer. |
| 'Golden Noble' ♀ | 4 | Early autumn | 2–3 | Excellent flavour, breaks down in cooking. Reliable, quite vigorous. Partial tip bearer. |
| 'Blenheim Orange' ♀ (T) | 3 | Mid-autumn | 3–4 | Excellent dual-purpose, rich flavour, stays in slices when cooked. Very vigorous, best on dwarfing rootstock, can be biennial. Partial tip bearer. |
| 'Bramley's Seedling' ♀ (T) | 3 | Mid-autumn | 4–5 | Excellent, acid flavour. Very vigorous, best on dwarfing and semi-dwarfing rootstock. Blossom susceptible to frost. Partial tip bearer. |
| 'Dummellor's Seedling' ♀ | 4 | Mid-autumn | 4–6 | Good, acid flavour, breaks down in cooking. Fairly hardy. Spur bearer. |
| 'Howgate Wonder' | 4 | Mid-autumn | 4–6 | Fair flavour. Good and reliable cropping, hardy, large fruits. Spur bearer. |
| 'Lane's Prince Albert' ♀ | 3 | Mid-autumn | 4–6 | Acid, stays intact. Hardy, reliable, susceptible to mildew. Spur bearer. |
| 'Edward VII' ♀ | 2 | Mid–late-autumn | 5–7 | Good, acid flavour. Reliable, some scab and frost resistance. Spur bearer. |

## APPLE POLLINATION GROUPS

(B) *Biennial bearer*
(T) *Triploid*

### Group 1: very early
'Gravenstein' (T)
'Lord Suffield'
'Manks Codlin' (B)
'Stark Earliest' ('Scarlet Pimpernel')
'Vista-bella' (B)

### Group 2: early
'Adams's Pearmain' (B)
'Alkmene' ♀
'Baker's Delicious'
'Beauty of Bath'
'Ben's Red' (B)
'Bismarck' (B)
'Bolero' ('Tuscan')
'Cheddar Cross'
'Christmas Pearmain' (B)
'Devonshire Quarrenden' (B)
'Egremont Russet' ♀
'George Cave'
'George Neal' ♀
'Golden Spire'
'Idared' ♀
'Irish Peach'
'Kerry Pippin'
'Keswick Codling' (B)
'Lord Lambourne' ♀
'Margil'
'McIntosh Red'
'Michaelmas Red'
'Norfolk Beauty'
'Owen Thomas'
'Reverend W. Wilks' (B)
'Ribston Pippin' ♀ (T)
'Ross Nonpareil'
'Saint Edmund's Pippin' ♀
'Striped Beefing'
'Warner's King' ♀ (T)
'White Transparent'

### Group 3: mid-season
'Acme'
'Alexander'
'Allington Pippin'
'Arthur Turner' ♀
'Barnack Orange'
'Baumann's Reinette' (B)

'Belle de Boskoop' ♀ (T)
'Belle de Pontoise'
'Blenheim Orange' ♀ (TB)
'Bountiful'
'Bramley's Seedling' ♀ (T)
'Brownlees Russet'
'Charles Ross' ♀
'Cobra'
'Cox's Orange Pippin'
'Delbarestivale' ('Delcorf')
'Discovery' ♀
'Duchess's Favourite'
'Elstar' ♀
'Emneth Early' ♀ (B)
'Exeter Cross'
'Falstaff' ♀
'Fiesta' ♀
'Gavin'
'Granny Smith'
'Greensleeves' ♀
'Grenadier' ♀
'Holstein' (T)
'James Grieve' ♀
'Jerseymac'
'John Standish'
'Jonagold' ♀ (T)
'Jonathan'
'Jupiter' ♀ (T)
'Katja' ('Katy')
'Kidd's Orange Red' ♀
'King of Tompkins County' (T)
'King Russet' ♀
'Lane's Prince Albert' ♀
'Langley Pippin'
'Laxton's Epicure' ♀
'Laxton's Fortune' ♀ (B)
'Limelight'
'Loddington' ('Stone's')
'Lord Grosvenor'
'Lord Hindlip'
'Malling Kent'
'Mère de Ménage'
'Meridian'
'Merton Knave'
'Merton Russet'
'Merton Worcester'
'Miller's Seedling' (B)
'Mutsu' ('Crispin') (T)
'Norfolk Royal'
'Peasgood's Nonsuch' ♀

'Polka' (Trajan) (B)
'Queen'
'Red Devil'
'Red Victoria' (B)
'Redsleeves'
'Reinette du Canada' (T)
'Rival' (B)
'Rosemary Russet' ♀
'Rubinette'
'Saint Cecilia'
'Scotch Dumpling'
'Scrumptious' ♀
'Spartan'
'Stirling Castle'
'Sturmer Pippin'
'S.T. Wright'
'Sunset' ♀
'Taunton Cross'
'Tom Putt'
'Tydeman's Early Worcester'
'Wagener' (B)
'Waltz' ('Telamon')
'Wealthy'
'Winter Gem'
'Worcester Pearmain' ♀
'Wyken Pippin'

### Group 4: mid-season
'Annie Elizabeth'
'Ashmead's Kernel' ♀
'Autumn Pearmain'
'Barnack Beauty'
'Cellini'
'Chivers Delight'
'Claygate Pearmain' ♀
'Cornish Aromatic'
'Cornish Gilliflower'
'Cox's Pomona'
'D'Arcy Spice'
'Delicious'
'Duke of Devonshire'
'Dummellor's Seedling' ♀
'Ellison's Orange' ♀
'Encore'
'Gala'
'George Carpenter'
'Gladstone' (B)
'Gloster '69'
'Golden Delicious' ♀
'Golden Noble' ♀

'Hawthornden'
'Herring's Pippin'
'Howgate Wonder'
'Ingrid Marie'
'Jester'
'Joybells'
'King's Acre Pippin'
'Lady Henniker'
'Lady Sudeley'
'Laxton's Superb' (B)
'Lord Burghley'
'Lord Derby'
'Mannington's Pearmain'
'Monarch' (B)
'Newtown Pippin' (B)
'Orleans Reinette'
'Pixie' ♀
'Roundway Magnum Bonum'
'Saturn'
'Sir John Thornycroft'
'Sweet Society'
'Tydeman's Late Orange'
'Winston' ♀
'Woolbrook Russet'

### Group 5: late
'Coronation' (B)
'Gascoyne's Scarlet' (T)
'Heusgen's Golden Reinette'
'King of the Pippins' ♀ (B)
'Mother' ♀ ('American Mother')
'Newton Wonder' ♀
'Reinette Rouge Etoilée'
'Royal Jubilee'
'Suntan' ♀ (T)
'William Crump'
'Woolbrook Pippin' (B)

### Group 6: late
'Bess Pool'
'Court Pendu Plat'
'Edward VII' ♀
'Laxton's Royalty'

### Group 7: very late
'Crawley Beauty'

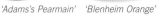

'Adams's Pearmain'  'Blenheim Orange'  'Lane's Prince Albert'  'Malling Kent'  'Winter Gem'  'Claygate Pearmain'  'Pixie'

# Pear

Fully ripe pears (cultivars of *Pyrus communis*) are possibly the most delicious of tree fruits. They need more warmth and sunlight than apples to fruit well; they also flower early so are more at risk from late spring frosts. Pears therefore need a warm, sheltered site. A warm, south-, southwest-, or west-facing wall or fence is of benefit in less favourable conditions, and for late-ripening cultivars. You may also need extra windbreaks (*see pp.12–13*).

Pears will tolerate a range of soils providing they are well-drained, fairly moisture-retentive, and of reasonable depth – about 45–60cm (18–24in). The ideal pH is 6.5. They do not grow well in thin, calcareous soils, such as those over chalk, because the lack of moisture and the high pH cause lime-induced chlorosis (*see p.254*). On these, and other thin soils, incorporate plenty of organic matter before planting.

## CHOOSING A TREE FORM

Pears can be trained in a wide range of forms (*see p.152*): as half-standards, bushes, spindlebushes, pyramids, cordons, espaliers, and fans. Generally, half-standards are not a good choice: they form large trees that are difficult to protect to ensure reliable cropping, and are often too big for the average garden. The few tip bearers (*see p.175*), including 'Jargonelle' and 'Joséphine de Malines', are best grown as bush trees. The restricted forms are particularly successful for pears because they readily form fruiting spurs and benefit from the shelter of a warm wall or fence.

## CHOOSING A ROOTSTOCK

Pears are usually grafted onto quince rootstocks; these are more dwarfing and earlier into cropping than pear

**Pear espalier**
*Restricted forms, such as this espalier of 'Doyenné du Comice', are particularly suitable for growing pears in the warm, sheltered locations that they need to thrive. Highly trained forms such as this also make the tree more decorative.*

rootstocks, although some promising pear stocks that have a more dwarfing effect are currently being developed.

Quince C rootstock is semi-dwarfing and trees grown on it are early to come into bearing. It is good for fertile soils and is particularly useful for cordons and for more vigorous cultivars. Trees grafted on Quince C will require permanent support.

Quince A is a good rootstock for all conditions and is slightly more vigorous than Quince C. Trees on Quince A will normally need staking for the first two years only. BA29 is similar to, but a little more vigorous than, Quince A. The chart below details how the rootstocks affect spacing for different tree forms.

Not all pear cultivars are compatible with quince rootstocks; they need to be double grafted or double budded using a cultivar compatible with both the quince and pear cultivar as a bridge, or interstock, between the two. It involves whip-and-tongue grafting or chip-budding (*see pp.154–155*) the interstock

cultivar onto the quince stock in one year and grafting or budding the chosen pear cultivar as a scion onto the inter-stock in the next year. This will already have been done on nursery-raised trees.

## POLLINATION

Pears flower in early to mid-spring and so are at risk of frost damage at this time. Avoid planting in a frost pocket (*see p.11*), but, if this is not possible, choose late-flowering cultivars (*see chart, p.184*) and be prepared to protect the trees at flowering time. Use fleece, shade netting, or hessian when frosts are forecast, either rolling the protective cover down over a restricted tree form (*see also p.157*) or draping it carefully over a freestanding tree.

All pears need pollen from a second cultivar to produce a satisfactory crop. Most pears are diploid but some are triploid (*see p.156*); a triploid requires a diploid to pollinate it and a second diploid to pollinate the first one. Pear cultivars are grouped

## SPACINGS FOR PEAR TREE FORMS AND ROOTSTOCKS

| Type of rootstock and vigour | Half-standard | Bush | Spindlebush | Pyramid | Cordon | Espalier | Fan |
|---|---|---|---|---|---|---|---|
| Quince C semi-dwarfing | – | 2.4–3.6m | 1.8–2.25m | 1.5–1.8m | 75cm | 3–3.6m | 3–3.6m |
| Quince A semi-vigorous | 3.6–5.5m | 3.6–5.5m | 2.25–3m | – | 75cm | 3.6–4.5m | 3.6–4.5m |
| BA29 semi-vigorous | 3.6–5.5m | 3.6–5.5m | 2.4–3m | – | 75cm | 3.6–4.5m | 3.6–4.5m |

according to the time at which they flower (*see chart, p.184*). To ensure good pollination, choose cultivars from the same group, if possible. Cultivars from adjacent groups will however also provide some cross-pollination.

Some cultivars, including 'Beurré Bedford', 'Bristol Cross', and 'Marguérite Marrillat', produce little viable pollen, so are ineffective pollinators. 'Conference' is not self-fertile, but may produce seedless (parthenocarpic) fruits without being pollinated. (*See also box, right.*)

## PLANTING

Before planting, prepare the stakes and wires (*see p.162*) for the form you have chosen. Plant (*see pp.158–159*) in the dormant season because pears start into growth in early spring or even late winter. Bare-root plants usually establish well. Container-grown plants grow away well if they are not pot-bound.

## PRUNING AND TRAINING

Most pears are pruned as spur bearers, but the few cultivars that are tip bearers require a modified pruning technique. Pears can be pruned harder than apples if needed without producing excessive growth – except for very vigorous cultivars such as 'Pitmaston Duchess'.

### Pruning a pear pyramid

*In late summer, prune back the sideshoots to reveal the branch leaders and maintain the basic pyramid shape of the tree (here 'Conference').*

*Select sideshoots over 23cm (9in) long and cut to 1 leaf above a basal cluster if they are growing from an existing spur, or 3 leaves above a basal cluster if they are growing from the main stem.*

*Cut branch leaders back to a downward- or an outward-facing bud 5–6 leaves above the basal cluster (see right).*

---

### INCOMPATIBILITY OF PEAR CULTIVARS

There are three recognized incompatibility groups for pears. Cultivars in these groups are all self- and cross-infertile, so will not pollinate themselves or each other.

**Incompatibility group 1**
*'Fondante d'Automne', 'Louise Bonne of Jersey', 'Précoce de Trévoux', 'Seckel', 'Williams' Bon Chrétien'*

**Incompatibility group 2**
*'Beurré d'Amanlis', 'Conference'*

**Incompatibility group 3**
*'Doyenné du Comice', 'Onward'*

---

Pear espaliers are pruned in the usual way (*see pp.171–172*), but other forms require different degrees of pruning.

## PRUNING A HALF-STANDARD OR BUSH PEAR TREE

For formative and established pruning of pear half-standards and bushes, *see pp.166–167*. Pears tend to be upright in habit so if branch leaders start to crowd the centre, you should replace them by pruning each to an outward-facing lateral. Remove the stakes of trees on semi-vigorous rootstocks after two or three years of pruning. On a mature tree, in winter, thin spur systems (*see p.165*), and, from time to time, thin out crossing branches (*see p.164*) by cutting back to a suitable replacement branch.

## PRUNING A PEAR SPINDLEBUSH

For formative and established pruning, *see pp.169–170*. The only modification for pears is that branches should be tied down to 20–30° above the horizontal, not any lower, otherwise fruiting suffers. Pears produce better fruit on compact spurs, which are less subject to wind damage and bruising from other branches. Shorten laterals not required for the framework to four to six buds in winter to encourage more spurs to grow.

## PRUNING A PEAR PYRAMID AND DWARF PYRAMID

Pruning a pear pyramid is done in the same way as for apples (*see pp.175–176*), using the basic system (*see pp.170–171*) with a few adaptations of technique and timing. Once established, the pyramids are maintained by routine summer pruning (*see p.171 and below left*).

## PRUNING A PEAR CORDON

For formative and established pruning, *see pp.171–172*. In summer, follow the summer pruning system (*see p.171*). Pears can also be trained as vertical cordons and over arches in the same way as for apples (*see pp.176–177*). However, they cannot be trained as horizontal cordons, since there are no suitable dwarfing rootstocks for pears.

## PRUNING A PEAR FAN

For formative pruning, *see p.173*. For pruning and training an established pear fan in winter, *see facing page*. For summer pruning, *see p.171*.

## FEEDING AND MULCHING

Under most conditions pears benefit from an annual application of potassium and nitrogen and an application of phosphorus every three years. Follow the guidelines given under apples for feeding and mulching (*see p.177*), although pears may require an additional nitrogen fertilizer.

## WATERING

Pears benefit from plenty of moisture during the growing season and do not tolerate dry conditions well. Water during dry periods in summer. This can be done by several methods (*see pp.53–54*), including drip hoses, which are ideal for rows of trees.

## FRUIT THINNING

Pear fruits should be thinned out (*see p.160*) to gain good-sized fruits and to reduce the risk of branches breaking or the tree becoming overstressed. Thin in early to midsummer, starting with the earliest ripening cultivars; the earlier the thinning, the greater is the increase in fruit size. As a general guide, thin the fruits on vigorous trees to two fruits per cluster 10–15cm (4–6in) apart. For compact forms such as cordons, thin to one fruit per cluster 10–15cm (4–6in) apart. It may be necessary to support heavily laden branches (*see p.178*).

## HARVESTING PEARS

Pear yields will vary according to the season and site, the form of the tree, the cultivar, and the rootstock. In general, the more vigorous the tree, the heavier is the crop. For a pear bush, you can expect an average yield per tree of 18–45.5kg (40–100lb), for a spindlebush or pyramid 9–18kg (20–40lb), for a single cordon 1.75–3.5kg (4–8lb), for an espalier 9–13.5kg (20–30lb), and for a fan 5.5–13.5kg (12–30lb).

It is particularly important with pears to take care in picking and storing the fruit to prolong the season of use. Pears need to be picked while they are still firm, before they are fully ripe. When it is time to pick there should be a slight colour change, to a lighter green in most cases. Test late cultivars by lifting the fruit in the palm of the hand and giving it a slight twist. If it is ready it should part easily from the spur. Early and mid-season pears may shrivel in storage if picked too early or become rotten at the core if left on the tree for too long. To test an early or mid-season pear for readiness, bite into the pear; if it is hard but sweet it is ready, if it is hard but starchy it is not yet ready.

## STORING PEARS

Early and mid-season pears require storing for one to three weeks before they are ready to eat. Some late-season pears can be stored until mid-spring in relatively simple conditions.

Store pears in a cool, dark, rodent-proof place with some humidity. An ideal temperature is 0–4.5°C (32–40°F); do not allow the temperature to exceed 7°C (45°F). There should be some air circulation, but not too much as this can cause shrivelling in storage. Cellars, sheds, and garages can be suitable; lofts and attics are usually unsuitable due to fluctuations in temperature and dry air. Store undamaged fruits in shallow trays with the fruits separated – rot spreads quickly if fruits touch. Check regularly to remove rotting fruits.

## COMMON PROBLEMS

Pears suffer from fewer troublesome pests and diseases than apples, but may be affected by: birds, bullfinches in particular damage fruit buds (*see p.252*), squirrels (*p.262*), codling moth (*p.254*), pear midge (*see p.259*), pear and cherry slugworm (*p.259*), pear leaf blister mite (*see p.259*), caterpillars including winter moth (*see p.264*), and aphids (*see p.251*) including pear bedstraw aphid. The latter is a whitish-grey, sap-sucking insect that infests pears in late spring and early summer, causing the leaves at the shoot tips to become yellowish-green and curl up. Use a plant oil wash in midwinter to control overwintering eggs; if aphids are seen in spring, spray with deltamethrin after petal fall.

Pears can also be affected by the following diseases and disorders: canker (*see p.253*), pear scab (*see p.251*), pear rust (*see p.261*), brown rot (*see p.253*), blossom wilt (*see p.252*), fireblight (*see p.255*), replant diseases (*see p.261*),and especially on light, sandy soils, boron deficiency (*see p.252*).

## Pruning an established pear fan

**1** **While the fan is dormant** in winter, thin out the complex and overcrowded growth to maintain the balanced shape of the fan and encourage even fruiting the following year. At this time of year, it is easier to see the basic framework of the fan.

**2** **Cut back** overly long shoots to a strong, outward-facing spur.

**3** **Prune spurs** that have too many branches to a point with only 1-2 branches. This simplifies the spur so that it produces fewer flowers and fruits, but of better quality, and allows light and air circulation.

**4** **Take out any wood** showing signs of canker, or that is bare or dead-looking. Remove the affected section back to a spur or shoot showing healthy buds. If the shoots are more than about 1cm (¼in) thick, use a pruning saw for a smooth cut.

## RECOMMENDED PEAR CULTIVARS

| Cultivar (T) Triploid | Pollination group | Picking time | Storage time (months) | Characteristics |
|---|---|---|---|---|
| **Dessert plums** | | | | |
| 'Beth' ♀ | | Late summer–early autumn | – | Small, juicy, sweet flavour. Hardy and reliable, early into cropping. |
| 'Williams' Bon Chrétien' ♀ | 3 | Late summer–early autumn | – | Sweet, strong musk flavour. Fairly hardy, but scab-prone. Will not pollinate 'Fondante d'Automne' or 'Louise Bonne of Jersey' and vice versa. |
| 'Buerré Hardy' ♀ | 3 | Early autumn | 1 | Medium to large fruits, tender, juicy flesh. Vigorous upright growth, fairly slow into bearing, but hardy with some scab resistance. |
| 'Buerré Superfin' | 3 | Early autumn | 1 | Sweet, rich flavour. Fairly reliable, moderate cropping. |
| 'Concorde' ♀ | 4 | Early autumn | 1–2 | Juicy, good flavour. Compact, reliable, and early into bearing. |
| 'Conference' ♀ | 3 | Early autumn | 1 | Juicy, sweet, and good flavour. Regular, reliable, and heavy cropping. |
| 'Fondante d'Automne' | 3 | Early autumn | – | Juicy, melting flesh. Moderate vigour and cropping. Will not pollinate 'Williams' Bon Chrétien' or 'Louise Bonne of Jersey' and vice versa. |
| 'Gorham' | 4 | Early autumn | – | Juicy, musk flavour. Fairly reliable, moderate cropping. |
| 'Louise Bonne of Jersey' | 2 | Early autumn | 1 | Small to medium fruits of melting flesh, good flavour. Reliable and hardy. Will not pollinate 'Williams' Bon Chrétien' or 'Fondante d'Automne' and vice versa. |
| 'Merton Pride' (T) | 3 | Early autumn | – | Very juicy, fine-textured, and good flavour. Vigorous-growing and only moderate cropping. |
| 'Onward' ♀ | 4 | Early autumn | – | Juicy, melting flesh of good flavour. Hardy and reliable. Unsuitable as a pollinator for 'Doyenné du Comice' and vice versa. |
| 'Emile d'Heyst' | 2 | Early–mid-autumn | 1–2 | Melting flesh, good flavour. Hardy and reliable. |
| 'Doyenné du Comice' ♀ | 4 | Mid-autumn | 1–2 | Juicy and melting with excellent flavour. Fairly vigorous, needs a sunny situation to crop well, susceptible to scab. |
| 'Glou Morceau' | 4 | Mid-autumn | 3–4 | Fine, smooth flesh, good flavour. Needs a warm situation to crop well. |
| 'Joséphine de Malines' ♀ | 3 | Mid-autumn | 3–4 | Small fruits, with melting, good flavour. Moderate to weak growth, some scab resistance. Tip bearer. |
| **Culinary (cooking) pears** | | | | |
| 'Catillac' ♀ (T) | 4 | Mid-autumn | 5–6 | Large, hard, slightly gritty flesh, turns pink in cooking, good flavour. Fairly vigorous, reliable, and hardy, suitable only for very slow cooking. |

## PEAR POLLINATION GROUPS

(MS) *Male sterile and ineffective as a pollinator*
(T) *Triploid*

**Group 1: very early**
'Brockworth Park'
'Précoce de Trévoux'

**Group 2: early**
'Baronne de Mello'
'Beurré Alexandre Lucas' (T)
'Beurré d'Amanlis' (T)
'Beurré Clairgeau'
'Beurré Six'
'Doyenné d'Eté'

'Duchesse d'Angoulême'
'Easter Beurré'
'Emile d'Heyst'
'Invincible'
'Louise Bonne of Jersey'
'Marguérite Marillat' (MS)
'Packham's Triumph'
'Passe Crasanne'
'Seckel'
'Uvedale's St Germain' (T)
'Vicar of Winkfield' (T)

**Group 3: mid-season**
'Belle Julie'
'Bergamotte d'Automne'

'Bergamotte Esperen'
'Beurré Dumont'
'Beurré Hardy' ♀
'Beurré Superfin'
'Black Worcester'
'Concorde' ♀
'Conference' ♀
'Docteur Jules Guyot'
'Doyenné Boussoch '(T)
'Doyenné George Boucher'
'Durondeau'
'Fertility'
'Fondante d'Automne'
'Hessle'
'Jargonelle' (T)

'Joséphine de Malines' ♀ (T)
'Le Lectier'
'Merton Pride' (T)
'Olivier de Serres'
'Roosevelt'
'Souvenir du Congrés'
'Thompson's'
'Triomphe de Vienne'
'Williams' Bon Chrétien' ♀

**Group 4: late**
'Beth' ♀
'Beurré Bedford' (MS)
'Beurré Mortillet'
'Bristol Cross' (MS)

'Catillac' ♀ (T)
'Clapp's Favourite'
'Doyenné du Comice' ♀
'Glou Morceau'
'Gorham'
'Improved Fertility'
'Laxton's Foremost'
'Marie Louise'
'Nouveau Poiteau'
'Onward' ♀
'Pitmaston Duchess' ♀ (T)
'Santa Claus'
'Winter Nelis'

# Plum

Plums form a group of stone fruits, which includes gages, and damsons, and bullaces (*Prunus insititia*), and cherry plums or myrobalans (*Prunus cerasifera*). They originate mainly from northern Asia and from southern Russia. Plums (cultivars of *Prunus domestica*) and gages are the most widely grown; all have similar cultivation needs.

A warm, sunny, sheltered site is best for plums; improve upon the available shelter if necessary (*see pp.12–13*). They flower early so, if possible, avoid planting in a frost pocket (*see p.11*). Plums can be grown as freestanding trees in the open in sheltered areas, or trained as cordons or fans against a warm south-, southwest-, or west-facing wall or fence in less favourable areas. Plums tolerate a range of soils provided that they are well-drained, but prefer a heavy clay loam at least 60cm (2ft) deep with a pH of 6–6.5.

**Ripe damsons**
*The damson is a less commonly grown form of plum. It is too tart to be eaten raw, but when cooked, makes delicious jams, fruit cheeses, and sauces. The older cultivars have the most intense flavours, but modern cultivars produce larger fruits. Damsons thrive on alkaline soils.*

## CHOOSING A TREE FORM

There are several tree forms in which plums can be grown, but not as great a range as for apples and pears. Of the freestanding forms, the pyramid is the best choice since it is economical with space, easily managed with summer pruning, and the low-angled branches are less subject to branch breakage than those of bush trees. The bush form is also suitable for plums, but the half-standard and standard forms are not so satisfactory since such large trees are unsuitable for the average-sized garden.

Of the trained forms, the fan is the most successful. It is particularly suitable for growing well-flavoured plums and gages, which can benefit from the improved microclimate of a warm wall or fence, and in less favourable areas.

Usually a good range of cultivars may be bought as part-trained fans. You could also use a maiden tree.

Plums are less suitable for training as cordons than are apples and pears, due to the lack of a suitably dwarfing rootstock. However some of the more compact cultivars, including 'Blue Tit', 'Czar', 'Early Laxton', and 'Opal', can be grown as cordons on Pixy rootstocks (*see chart, below*).

## CHOOSING A ROOTSTOCK

A relatively limited range of rootstocks is available for plums, with no truly dwarfing rootstock. Pixy, which is semi-dwarfing, is a good rootstock for garden cultivation; trees come into cropping fairly early in their life, and

seldom produce suckers. It is suited to bushes, pyramids, fans, and for less vigorous cultivars grown as cordons. On a Pixy rootstock, a plum pyramid will reach 2–2.2m (6–7ft) in height, and fans will reach a minimum height of 2m (6ft). Ferlenain is a semi-dwarfing rootstock of similar vigour to Pixy, but with fruit of better size. It is prone to suckering.

St Julien A is semi-vigorous. It is a reliable rootstock and is suitable for half-standard, bush, pyramid, and fan forms. On St Julien A, a pyramid reaches 2.2–2.7m (7–9ft) high, and a fan reaches a minimum of 2.2m (7ft). Brompton is a vigorous rootstock. It can be used for standard and half-standard trees, but these are generally too large for most garden situations.

## POLLINATION

Plums usually flower in early to mid-spring and so are at risk of damage from frosts at this time. In areas prone to spring frosts, choose late-flowering cultivars (*see chart, p.188*) and be prepared to use some frost protection (*see p.157*); this is easiest to do on wall- or fence-trained trees.

A large number of plums are self-fertile, so if you wish to grow only one tree, choose one of these. All cultivars

## SPACINGS FOR PLUM TREE FORMS AND ROOTSTOCKS

| Type of rootstock and vigour | Standard | Half-standard | Bush | Pyramid | Cordon | Fan |
|---|---|---|---|---|---|---|
| Pixy semi-dwarfing | – | – | 2.4–3.6m | 2.4–3m | 75cm–1m | 3.6–4.5m |
| Ferlenain semi-dwarfing | – | – | 2.4–3.6m | 2.4–3m | 75cm–1m | 3.6–4.5m |
| St Julien A semi-vigorous | – | 3.6–4.5m | 3.6–4.5m | 3–3.6m | – | 4.5–5.5m |
| Brompton vigorous | 5.5–6.5m | 5.5–6.5m | – | – | – | – |

benefit from cross-pollination. Plum cultivars are grouped according to the time at which they flower (*see chart, p.188*). In order to be sure of good pollination, choose cultivars from the same group, if possible, although those from adjacent groups will give some cross-pollination. A few cultivars are not compatible with each other (*see box, below*).

### PLANTING
Plant plum trees during the dormant season (*see pp.158–159*) before they start into growth in late winter or early spring. Bare-root plants usually establish better than do container-grown ones, although the latter will grow well as long as they are not pot-bound. Prepare before planting the stakes and wires (*see p.162*) required for the tree form that you have chosen.

### PRUNING AND TRAINING
Pruning is usually carried out in spring or summer. Never prune stone fruits in the dormant season, or in mid- or late autumn. Pruning cuts at these times expose the plant to the risk of infection by silver leaf (*see p.262*) and bacterial canker (*see p.253*). To guard against these potentially serious problems, take care to observe good hygiene when pruning and use wound paint on all large cuts immediately. Plums fruit on a mixture of one- and two-year-old wood and older shoots. Plum pyramids may be

**Pruning an established plum fan in spring**
*As the fan matures, you will need to thin out crowded spur systems (here on 'Reine-Claude Vraie'), either before flowering or at petal fall. Cut back each old spur to a strong bud.*

pruned in the standard way (*see p.170*), but other forms have more particular pruning requirements.

### PRUNING A STANDARD, HALF-STANDARD, OR BUSH PLUM
Formative pruning of standard, half-standard, and bush trees is as described on pp.166–167. The main distinction, as with other stone fruits, is that formative pruning is carried out in mid-spring.

After formative pruning, little regular pruning should be carried out, because pruning cuts can lead to infection from disease. As the branches become more crowded, some thinning out may be necessary, but not too much since a plum tolerates a more crowded head than apples or pears. Do this in spring after flowering, removing dead and broken, and weak and spindly branches back to their point of origin or to a suitable replacement.

### PRUNING AN OBLIQUE PLUM CORDON
The pruning method for plum cordons differs slightly from that employed for apples and pears. If possible, start with a feathered maiden tree. In the mid-spring following planting, shorten any sideshoots back to about three buds. Shorten the leader, beyond the topmost feather, by about half. If you are starting with an unfeathered maiden, you should also shorten the leader by about half. The following summer, tie in the leader

to the cane. Pinch out sideshoots at six leaves of the new growth, usually in midsummer, and any regrowth later in the season, to just one leaf. In late summer, further shorten the sideshoots that were pinched back to six leaves, by cutting them down to three leaves in order to encourage the formation of compact, fruiting spurs.

In mid-spring of the second year, shorten the leader by about one-third of its new growth to a bud. Repeat this until the cordon has reached the top of the wires. If space allows, you can then lower the leader to about 35° and allow it to grow further. Once at its final length, treat the leader as any other lateral, pinching it back and pruning it further in summer.

### PRUNING A PLUM FAN
For formative pruning, follow the standard method (*see p.173*). From the second summer for a maiden tree, or the first summer if a part-trained tree is being grown, regular summer pruning will also be needed to produce compact fruiting spurs. In early summer, thin out to 10cm (4in) apart any shoots that are not required to extend the framework, or those growing from spurs on the framework; at the same time, pinch these shoots back to six leaves. If there is any regrowth on these shoots, pinch it out to one leaf. After picking, shorten to three leaves the laterals previously pinched to six leaves in order to maintain the compact spurs.

Prune an established fan in spring, either after the buds break and before flowering, or when the petals fall, to take out unhealthy material. Cut out any dead, diseased, or damaged shoots, as well as any badly placed shoots that are growing towards the support or the centre of the fan, and thin out spurs (*see above, left*). In the summer, prune and train the fan to keep its shape well defined (*see above, facing page*).

### FEEDING AND MULCHING
Plums need a steady supply of nutrients for healthy growth. In late winter apply sulphate of potash at 20g/sq m (½oz/sq yd). In early spring, apply a nitrogen fertilizer, such as sulphate of ammonia, at 70g/sq m (2oz/sq yd). Every third year, in late winter, top-dress with

### INCOMPATIBILITY OF PLUM CULTIVARS

There are three recognized incompatibility groups for plums. Cultivars in these groups are all self- and cross-infertile, so will not pollinate themselves or each other.
**Incompatibility group 1**
'Allgrove's Superb', 'Coe's Golden Drop', 'Crimson Drop', 'Jefferson'
**Incompatibility group 2**
'Cambridge Gage', 'President', Reine-Claude group*
**Incompatibility group 3**
'Blue Rock', 'Rivers's Early Prolific'
*This group includes several similar cultivars (such as 'Reine-Claude Vraie'). They are seedlings or sports of each other and have the same pollination incompatibility.

## Pruning an established plum fan in summer

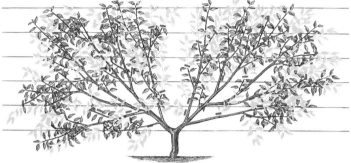

**1** **In early summer**, tie healthy laterals into the support wires to fill in gaps in the fan shape. Use garden twine tied in a loose figure-of-eight knot to avoid chafing.

**2** **Pinch back sideshoots** that are not going to be part of the framework to 6 leaves. If the shoots have more than 9–10 leaves, you may have to cut them with secateurs because they will be getting woody. After fruiting in late summer, shorten these pruned shoots again to 3 leaves.

**3** **Look for any unhealthy** or badly placed shoots and cut them out at the base. Here an unproductive shoot bare of leaves is pruned back to a junction with a healthier shoot.

**Established plum fan after summer pruning**
*In addition to routine summer pruning as outlined above, keep shoots at the top of the fan pinched back to 3 leaves, and cut them again to 1 leaf after fruiting. This allows the tree to direct its energies into ripening fruit.*

superphosphate at 70g/sq m (2oz/sq yd). Alternatively, apply a compound fertilizer (*see p.20*) annually in late winter at 70g/sq yd (2oz/sq m). Plums also benefit from an annual organic mulch, (*see p.161*) in early spring.

### WATERING

Plums need more watering than apples. Water especially during prolonged dry periods in spring and summer (*see p.160*). In early to midsummer, keep plums watered as the fruit is swelling and continue until harvesting if dry conditions persist. Irrigation can be supplied to plums by several methods (*see pp.53–54*); for rows of trees, drip hoses are particularly efficient.

### FRUIT THINNING

It is particularly important to thin the fruitlets on plums – if any overladen branches break, the trees can be badly affected by silver leaf or bacterial canker. Begin thinning in early summer when the first fruitlets fall naturally (*see p.160*). You may also need to support heavily laden branches by tying them temporarily to a central stake or sturdy cane (*see also p.178*).

### HARVESTING AND STORING PLUMS

Plum yields differ according to the form in which they are grown, the cultivar and rootstock, and the growing conditions. For a plum bush, you might expect an average yield of 13.5–27kg (30–60lb) per tree, for a pyramid about 13.5–22.5kg (30–50lb), for an oblique cordon 3.5–6.75kg (8–15lb), and for a plum fan 6.75–11.25kg (15–25lb).

Plums develop their best flavour if left to ripen on the tree. If they feel soft when gently squeezed, they are ripe. A tree will generally need picking over several times. Fruit to be used for preserving may be picked slightly early. Plums can be stored in a refrigerator for a short while before use.

### COMMON PROBLEMS

Plums are subject to a number of pests and diseases: silver leaf (*see p.262*), bacterial canker (*see p.253*), brown rot (*see p.253*), caterpillars (*see p.253*), including winter moth caterpillars (*see p.264*), frost damage (*see p.255*), several species of aphid (*see p.251*), including the plum leaf-curling aphid (*see p.259*), plum fruit moth (*see p.259*), red spider mite (*see p.261*), and birds (*see p.252*).

**Using a plum or codling moth trap**
*Proprietary traps come as flat packs, easily assembled. A small pheromone capsule in the trap attracts male moths, which stick fast to the glue on the base. This may reduce the number of females laying fertilized eggs, and therefore of caterpillars eating the plums or apples.*

## RECOMMENDED PLUM CULTIVARS

| Cultivar | Compatibility group | Picking time | Characteristics |
|---|---|---|---|
| **Dessert plums** | | | |
| 'Early Laxton' ♀ | B | Mid–late summer | Yellow fruits, red flushed, sweet flavour. Small tree. |
| 'Sanctus Hubertus' ♀ | B | Mid–late summer | Blue fruits with yellow flesh and rich flavour. Reliable. |
| 'Blue Tit' ♀ | C | Late summer | Blue, juicy fruits, not very sweet. Compact and reliable. |
| 'Imperial Gage' ♀ | C | Late summer | Greenish-yellow, juicy, sweet fruits. Reliable. |
| 'Mallard' ♀ | A | Late summer | A good flavoured and reliable red plum of medium size. |
| 'Opal' ♀ | C | Late summer | Orange-red fruits with fairly sweet flavour. Very reliable. |
| 'Oullins Gage' ♀ | C | Late summer | Greenish-yellow, fairly sweet fruits. Reliable gage-type. |
| 'Cambridge Gage' ♀ | B | Late summer–early autumn | Green, rich, sweet fruits. Most reliable of the gages. |
| 'Jefferson' ♀ | A | Late summer–early autumn | Yellow-green, juicy sweet fruits with fibrous flesh. |
| 'Reeves' ♀ | A | Late summer–early autumn | Red, large fruits. Needs good pollination to fruit well. |
| 'Victoria' ♀ | C | Late summer–early autumn | Orange-red, juicy fruits. The best dual-purpose plum. Cooks well. |
| 'Coe's Golden Drop' | A | Early autumn | Yellow, sweet, rich flavour. Fan train for full ripening. |
| 'Laxton's Delight' ♀ | B | Early autumn | Large, yellow, juicy, and sweet fruits. |
| **Culinary (cooking) plums** | | | |
| 'Rivers's Early Prolific' | B | Mid–late summer | Blue fruits, rich but sharp. Makes a neat pyramid. |
| 'Czar' ♀ | C | Late summer | Blue fruits, improved with cooking. Reliable, compact. |
| 'Marjorie's Seedling' ♀ | C | Early–mid-autumn | Blue fruits, juicy, but not sweet. Heavy cropping. |
| **Damsons** | | | |
| 'Farleigh Damson' ♀ | C | Early autumn | Blue-black, rich, true damson flavour. Compact habit. |
| 'Merryweather Damson' | C | Early autumn | Blue fruit, larger than other damsons. |
| 'Prune Damson' ♀ | C | Early–mid-autumn | Blue-black, long, oval fruits. Vigorous but neat habit. |

## PLUM POLLINATION GROUPS

| Flowering group | Compatibility group | | | |
|---|---|---|---|---|
| | A: self-infertile | B: partly self-infertile | C: self-fertile | Unclassified |
| Group 1 (very early) | 'Jefferson' ♀, 'Mallard' ♀ | 'Angelina Burdett', 'Blue Rock', 'Utility' | 'Monarch' | |
| Group 2 (early) | 'Black Diamond', 'Coe's Golden Drop', 'Edwards' ♀, 'President', 'Valor' ♀ | 'Ariel', 'Avalon', 'Curlew', 'Edda' | 'Brandy Gage', 'Guthrie's Late Green', 'Imperial Gage' ♀, 'Reine-Claude de Brahy', 'Warwickshire Drooper' | |
| Group 3 (mid-season) | 'Allgrove's Superb', 'Bryanston Gage', 'Reeves' ♀, 'Washington' | 'Belgian Purple', 'Cox's Emperor', 'Early Laxton' ♀, 'Goldfinch', 'Laxton's Delight' ♀, 'Merton Gem', 'Reine-Claude Violette', 'Rivers's Early Prolific', 'Sanctus Hubertus' ♀ | 'Bonne de Bry', 'Bountiful', 'Czar' ♀, 'Golden Transparent', 'Herman', 'Jubilaeum', 'Laxton's Cropper', 'Laxton's Gage', 'Merryweather Damson', 'Opal' ♀, 'Pershore' ♀, 'Purple Pershore', 'Severn Cross', 'Victoria' ♀ | 'Swan' |
| Group 4 (mid-season) | 'Count Althann's Gage', 'Kirke's', 'Wyedale' | 'Cambridge Gage' ♀, 'Stint' | 'Early Transparent Gage', 'Farleigh Damson' ♀, 'Giant Prune', 'Ontario', 'Oullins Gage' ♀ | |
| Group 5 (late) | 'Excalibur', 'Laxton's Delicious', 'Reine Claude-Vraie' ('Old Greengage'), 'Pond's Seedling', 'White Magnum Bonum' | | 'Belle de Louvain', 'Blue Tit' ♀, 'Marjorie's Seedling' ♀, 'Prune Damson' ♀ | |

# Sweet and duke cherry

The sweet cherry is a cultivated form of the wild cherry (gean or mazzard), *Prunus avium*. The duke cherry is thought to be a hybrid of *P. avium* and *P. cerasus* (acid cherry), and is cultivated in the same way as the sweet cherry.

Cherries flower fairly early (usually in mid-spring), so are at risk from spring frosts and poor pollinating conditions at flowering time. A warm, sheltered site is best, and training a cherry against a wall or fence that faces south-, southwest-, or west is advantageous, particularly so in less favourable areas; this also helps fruits to ripen well. Avoid planting in a frost pocket (*see p.11*). Cherries tolerate a fairly wide range of soils. Good drainage is important and soils should be at least 60cm (2ft), preferably 90cm (3ft), deep with a pH of 6.5–6.7. Shallow and waterlogged soils are not suitable and need improving, by deep cultivation (*see p.39*) or drainage (*see pp.15–16*), if cherries are to be grown.

## TREE FORMS AND ROOTSTOCKS
Cherries are naturally vigorous and produce large trees. They can be grown as bush or pyramid trees or as fans. Generally the fan form is the most suitable because it controls the cherry's vigorous nature and can be most easily protected against frost and birds.

There are few rootstocks available for cherries. Colt is semi vigorous and most suitable for fan-trained trees. On a Colt rootstock, a fan requires a space 5–5.5m (15–18ft) wide and 2.5m (8ft) high. Gisela 5 is a quite new semi-dwarfing rootstock and is an improvement on Colt, producing smaller trees which are more easily netted against birds. On Gisela 5 space bush trees 2.7m (9ft) apart and pyramids 2.5m (8ft) apart. Fans need a space 3.6m (12ft) wide and 2m (6ft) high.

## POLLINATION
Be prepared to protect trees at flowering time if frosts threaten (*see right*). Sweet cherry pollination is complex, and by far the best choice for garden cultivation are cultivars that are self-fertile (particularly if there is space for only one tree). Other cultivars are not only self-infertile, they

**Cherry in blossom**
*Sweet cherries (here 'Stella') need warm, sheltered conditions when flowering to achieve pollination and a good set of fruit.*

are also incompatible with some others that flower at the same time. Sweet cherry cultivars are grouped by the time at which they flower (*see chart, p.190*). A cultivar will be pollinated by another from the same pollination group or adjacent groups, provided that they are not in the same incompatibility group.

## PLANTING
Plant cherries in the dormant season (*see pp.158–159*). Dig in plenty of well-rotted organic matter beforehand. Bare-root plants usually establish better than container-grown ones, although the latter should grow well if they are not pot-bound. Prepare the stakes and wires (*see p.162*) for the form you have chosen before planting.

## PRUNING AND TRAINING
Sweet cherries fruit on one- and two-year-old wood and on spurs of older wood. Never prune in the dormant season due to the risk of infection from silver leaf (*see p.262*) or bacterial canker (*see p.253*). For pruning a young bush, *see pp.166–167*; of an established bush, *see p.186*, and of a pyramid, *see p.170*.

## PRUNING A SWEET CHERRY FAN
As well as carrying out the basic formative pruning for a fan (*see p.173*), you should follow the guidelines for plums (*see pp.186–187*) regarding formative summer pruning and pruning of an established fan. A cherry fan will quickly fill its space, and it

---

## Protecting cherry blossom from frost

**1 To protect the blossoms** and fruits of a trained fan (here 'Stella') from frost, cover it with a "tent" of fine netting overnight. Drape the netting over a crossbar of 25 x 25mm (1 x 1in) timber wired onto the support wire above the fan. Use 3 canes as struts to hold the netting clear of the plant.

**2 Weigh down** the edge of the netting by wrapping the end around 2 or 3 bamboo canes. Secure with thin garden wire by feeding the end of the wire in and out of the net as if stitching with a needle.

**3 Uncover the fan** during the day to allow access by pollinating insects. Hold the rolled-up netting at the top of the plant by securing it to the crossbar with twine or, as here, with small tree ties.

is important to shorten the new growth produced each year by about half to stimulate the production of sideshoots and spurs, otherwise bare wood can develop.

## FEEDING AND MULCHING

Sweet cherries are naturally vigorous with fairly high nutrient needs. In late winter, apply a compound fertilizer (*see p.21*) at 110g/sq m (4oz/sq yd) over the rooting area. For mulching, *see p.161*.

## WATERING AND PROTECTION

Cherries grow best in a moist but freely drained soil. They benefit from an even supply of water in the growing season, which may demand extra watering in dry periods (*see p.160*), especially on shallow soils. Irrigation can be supplied by several methods (*see pp.53–54*).

Fruit splitting is one of the main causes of fruit loss. It can occur through alternate dry and wet soils as the fruits are swelling. The most common cause, particularly as the fruit reaches maturity, is rain or overhead irrigation falling on the fruit. Once the fruits begin to ripen, the skins stop growing and any absorbed moisture will swell the flesh and split the skins. So, once the cherries form but before they ripen, protect them with a raincover (*see above*). Use a similar method to protect blossom from frost and fruits from birds (*see p.192*).

**Erecting a raincover**
*To protect the ripening fruits, place a length of clear plastic, 2.5m (8ft) wide, over the top of the plant (here 'Stella'). Hold it in place with vertical guy ropes of thin cord tied to pegs. To attach the cord to the plastic, wrap a golf ball or cane ball in the plastic at the edge and knot the end of the cord around it (see inset). This prevents the plastic from tearing. Do not cover the sides to avoid scorching the fruits or creating excessively humid conditions.*

## HARVESTING AND STORING

An average yield for a sweet cherry bush might be 13.5–45.5kg (30–100lb), for a pyramid 13.5–27kg (30–60lb), and for a fan 5.5–15.75kg (12–35lb). Pick cherries when they are fully ripe. Once harvested (*see below*), they are best eaten within a few days. Alternatively, they can be stored if cleaned and frozen as soon as they are picked.

## COMMON PROBLEMS

Birds (*see p.252*) are a serious pest and eat fruits and buds. Other problems include aphids (*p.251*), fruit fly (*p.256*), winter moth caterpillars (*p.264*), pear and cherry slugworm (*p.259*), bacterial canker (*p.253*), blossom wilt (*p.252*), brown rot (*p.253*), frost damage (*p.255*), silver leaf (*p.262*), scorch (*p.262*), and magnesium deficiency (*p.257*).

### RECOMMENDED SWEET CHERRY CULTIVARS

| Cultivar | Compatibility | Picking time | Fruit colour |
|---|---|---|---|
| 'Lapins' | Self-fertile | Late summer | Black |
| 'May Duke' | Partly self-fertile | Midsummer | Dark red |
| 'Merchant' ♀ | Self-infertile | Midsummer | Black |
| 'Stella' ♀ | Self-fertile | Midsummer | Dark red |
| 'Summer Sun' ♀ | Self-infertile | Midsummer | Dark red |
| 'Sunburst' | Self-fertile | Midsummer | Black |

**Harvesting cherries**
*When the cherries (here of 'Stella') are ripe, cut the stalks with scissors or secateurs. Take care to hold the stalk to avoid the fruit falling and bruising. A tree will usually need picking over 2 or 3 times as the fruit ripens.*

### SWEET CHERRY POLLINATION GROUPS

Many sweet cherries are incompatible with one another. Those in this table can be pollinated by cultivars in the same group or an adjacent group unless otherwise mentioned.

| Pollination group | Self-infertile | Self-fertile |
|---|---|---|
| Group 1 | 'Early Rivers' | |
| Group 2 | 'Mermat' (incompatible with 'Waterloo'), 'Merton Glory', 'Noir de Guben' | |
| Group 3 | 'Roundel Heart', 'Van', 'Vega'; 'Elton Heart' and 'Governor Wood' are incompatible with each other and 'Amber Heart', 'Inga', 'Merchant' ♀ | 'Starkrimson' |
| Group 4 | 'Amber Heart' (incompatible with 'Governor Wood' and 'Elton Heart'), 'Bigarreau Napoléon', 'Kordia' (incompatible with Governor Wood and vice versa) 'Hertford' ♀ , 'Penny', 'Regina' (incompatible with 'Van' and vice versa), 'Summer Sun', 'Summit' | 'Celeste', 'Lapins', 'Stella' ♀, 'Sunburst', 'Sweetheart' |
| Group 5 | 'Bigarreau Gaucher' (incompatible with 'Bradbourne Black'), 'Florence' | |
| Group 6 | 'Bradbourne Black' (incompatible with 'Bigarreau Gaucher') | |

# Acid cherry

Acid (or sour) cherries are derived from *Prunus cerasus*. The fruits are generally too acid to eat raw, but are full of flavour and cook and preserve well. Being less vigorous than sweet cherries, acid cherries are well suited to gardens. They also have different pruning needs.

In general, acid cherries crop reliably. They are however susceptible to frost at flowering, although less so than sweet cherries, and do not need full sun. Fan-trained trees can be grown against a north-facing wall or fence, making them very useful for cooler positions. They tolerate a range of soils as long as they are well-drained and moisture-retentive, with a pH of 6.5–6.7. The soil needs to be at least 45cm (18in) deep; shallow soils or waterlogged soils will need improving, by deep cultivation (*see p.39*) or drainage (*see pp.15–16*).

## TREE FORMS AND ROOTSTOCKS

Acid cherries bear most of their fruit on wood made the previous year. Because of this, they need to be grown as tree forms which are maintained by replacement pruning. These forms are the bush, pyramid, and fan. The pyramid casts less shade than the bush, and is easier to net against birds. Bushes need spacing 3.5–5m (11–15ft) apart and pyramids 3–3.5m (10–11ft). Fans need a space 3.5–5m (11–15ft) wide and 2–2.2m (6–7ft) high. Acid cherries are not large trees, so the semi-vigorous rootstock Colt is suitable for all forms.

**'Morello' cherry**
*This acid cherry has been trained on wires as a fan and still fruits well after 20 years. A fan makes a highly attractive structural form in the garden, allows the fruits to ripen well, and gives easy access to the tree at harvest time.*

## POLLINATION

Acid cherries generally flower in mid- to late spring. Be prepared to protect trees at flowering time if frosts threaten (*see p.189*). They are self-fertile, so there is no problem with pollination and, in most cases, only one tree is required to provide a satisfactory crop.

## PLANTING

Plant cherry trees during the dormant season (*see pp.158–159*) before they start into growth. Dig in plenty of well-rotted organic matter before planting, especially on shallow soils, to improve moisture-retentiveness. Bare-root plants usually establish better than container-grown ones, although the latter should grow well as long as they are not pot-bound. Prepare the

stakes and wires (*see p.162*) required for the tree form you have chosen before planting.

## PRUNING AND TRAINING

As for other stone fruits, acid cherries are susceptible to silver leaf (*see p.262*) and bacterial canker (*see p.253*) if pruned in winter. To avoid these problems, always prune in early spring and summer. Since the tree fruits on the previous season's wood, pruning aims to remove some fruited wood and promote new, vigorous wood, while maintaining the structure of the tree.

## PRUNING AN ACID CHERRY BUSH

Formative pruning of a bush is undertaken in early to mid-spring (*see pp.166–167*). After the first four or five

---

## Pruning an established acid cherry fan in early summer

Thin the new shoots along the ribs of the fan (here a 'Morello') to 5–10cm (2–4in) apart. Aim to keep shoots near the base of those that are bearing this ear's fruits. The shoots you retain will form the fruiting wood for next year. Tie these new shoots into the supports. Shorten to two leaves any shoots growing directly outwards from the fan. This thinning allows the fruits and new shoots to ripen well without being crowded.

*Thinning new shoots*

**Established fan framework**
*After pruning, the fan should be balanced and free of crowded, crossing shoots. For each shoot*

*that is bearing fruit, there should be 1 or 2 new shoots that will replace it in the next season.*

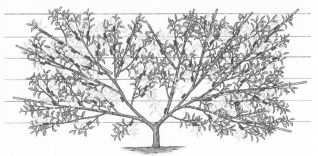

years, prune it after fruiting, as for the cropping tree (*see* Renewal pruning, *p.167*), in late summer to early autumn. Cut out a quarter of the older wood to young shoots to stimulate production of more new wood. As the tree matures, it will be necessary to take sections of three- and four-year-old wood back to young shoots. If the tree is unpruned or pruned lightly, it will eventually crop only around the edge.

### PRUNING AN ACID CHERRY PYRAMID

Starting with a feathered maiden in early to mid-spring, cut the leader to 10cm (4in) above the topmost feather or sideshoot. Remove any feathers below 45cm (18in). Shorten remaining sideshoots by half to a downward-facing bud. In the first summer, tie the leader to the stake. In the second spring, shorten the leader by half of the new growth to a bud on the opposite side to the previous pruning cut. Shorten other one-year-old shoots by half. Tie the leader to the stake in the summer. In the third spring, prune the leader by half, but leave laterals unpruned; repeat the process with the leader until it gains its full height of 2–2.5m (6–8ft). No pruning is needed in the third summer.

From the fourth summer, prune after picking. Remove some sections of older wood, cutting back to young shoots and maintaining the pyramid shape. As the tree matures, you may need to cut back

**Protecting the fruits from birds**
*In midsummer, erect a fine net over wall-trained trees. Use 2.5m (8ft) canes as struts over which to drape the net. Insert them 60cm (2ft) clear of the base and tie at the top with twine. The net should not touch the fruits.*

## Pruning an established fan after fruiting

In late summer, after fruiting, thin out the fan (here 'Morello') and train in shoots that will fruit next year. Cut back shoots that have fruited this season to leave a replacement shoot of new growth, which will fruit next year. Then cut out any badly placed shoots, including any that are growing outwards from the fan or towards the wall or fence. Also remove shoots that have grown beyond the boundaries of the fan, cutting back to a lower-placed shoot. Tie in the remaining shoots to the supports with twine in a figure-of-eight knot.

*Removing fruited wood*

*Established fan before pruning*

*Established fan after pruning*

some three- and four-year-old wood to replacement shoots. Once the tree is at its full height, cut back shoots at the top to two buds in late summer.

### PRUNING AN ACID CHERRY FAN

After formative pruning (*see p.173*) and once the fan framework is established, thin shoots (*see p.191*) in late spring to early summer, and remove fruited wood in late summer (*see above*). As the fan becomes older, remove three- and four-year-old sections of the framework back to young replacement shoots. If this replacement pruning is not carried out, the fan will fruit only at the periphery.

### ROUTINE CARE

To produce strong replacement shoots, acid cherries need more nitrogen than many other fruits. In late winter, apply sulphate of potash at 35g/sq m (1oz/sq yd) over the rooting area. In the early spring, apply 70g/sq m (2oz/sq yd) of sulphate of ammonia. Every third year in late winter, apply 70g/sq m (2oz/sq yd) of superphosphate. Mulch to help keep soil fertile and moist (*see p.161*).

Water during dry periods in spring and summer; this is especially

important on shallow soils. Irrigation can be applied in several ways (*see pp.53–54*). Drip hoses are useful as they allow for regular, even application of water. If the soil dries out and then becomes wet, fruits may split as they ripen. Protect them with a raincover (*see p.190*).

### HARVESTING ACID CHERRIES

An average acid cherry bush or pyramid may yield 13.5–18kg (30–40lb) of fruit, and a fan 5.5–15.75kg (12–35lb). Harvest fruits when they are fully ripe, cutting them off by the stalks. You may need to pick over a tree twice.

### COMMON PROBLEMS

Acid cherries suffer the same problems as sweet cherries (*see p.190*). Protect ripening fruits against birds (*see left*).

### RECOMMENDED CULTIVARS

**'Morello'** ♀ *Self-fertile cultivar; harvest the fruits in late summer and in early autumn; this is a very old cultivar of excellent flavour.*
**'Nabella'** *Self-fertile; harvest the fruits in late summer; this is a more recently introduced cultivar.*

# Peach and nectarine

Peaches (*Prunus persica*) and nectarines (*P. persica* var. *nectarina*) originate from China. They have similar cultivation needs, so throughout this text all details on peaches apply also to nectarines. The trees are fully winter-hardy but flower early – usually in early spring or even late winter – and so the blossom is at risk from frost damage and poor conditions. However, it is possible to grow peaches successfully in a warm, sheltered site, preferably trained against a wall or fence that is facing south, southwest, or west. Provide extra shelter (*see pp.12–13*) if needed. For cultivation outside, it is important to choose the cultivars that will ripen in mid- to late summer (*see chart, p.195*); later-ripening cultivars will not do well outside in most areas. Both early- and late cultivars can be grown successfully under glass.

There are two types of peaches: the conventional cultivars, which grow fairly vigorously and naturally produce a medium-sized tree, and genetically dwarf compact peaches, which are sometimes known as patio peaches.

Conventional peach and nectarine cultivars will grow in a range of soils as long as they are well-drained, moisture-retentive, and at least 45cm (18in) deep, with a pH of about 6.5. Thin soils over chalk are not suitable unless improved with plenty of organic matter (*see p.22*).

Compact cultivars are most successful grown in containers in a warm situation such as a sheltered patio. They flower early, but are susceptible to peach leaf curl (*see p.258*). However they can be brought under cover – into an unheated greenhouse, a porch, or a polytunnel – over winter and while flowering to overcome these problems.

## TREE FORMS AND ROOTSTOCKS

The type of peach cultivar you choose will dictate the tree form in which it can be grown. The conventional peach cultivars can be grown as bushes, pyramids, and fans, but the fan-trained tree is the only form that is generally successful outdoors in cool climates, and is also the best method for growing peaches under glass. Fan-trained trees need a space of 3.5–5m (11–15ft) wide, and 2–2.5m (6–8ft) high. Bushes and

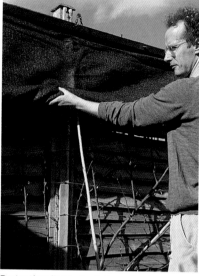

**Protecting flower buds from frost**
*Wall-trained trees (here 'Hale's Early') need protection in early spring from frosts: cover them with fleece or shade netting from just before bud break to protect the buds. When the flowers open, roll up the fleece during the day to allow access by pollinating insects.*

pyramids may produce fruit outdoors in particularly favourable locations. There are few rootstocks for conventional peach cultivars. The most common is the semi-vigorous St Julien A. Peaches can also be raised as seedlings to obtain ungrafted trees (*see p.195*).

Compact peaches produce extremely short-jointed, neat growth and so are suitable only for growing as bush trees.

## POLLINATION

Peaches and nectarine cultivars are self-fertile, so it is possible to obtain a crop from just one tree. They are pollinated by insects, but since they flower very early there are often few pollinating insects around. Hand pollination is usually necessary, using a soft brush or a rabbit's tail (*see p.157*).

Since both the flowers and fruitlets are very vulnerable to frost damage, be prepared to protect them against frost (*see above*) on nights when it is forecast. Alternatively, a plastic raincover in place to avoid peach leaf curl (*see p.195*) gives 1–2°C (2–3.5°F) of frost protection and will improve the ambient temperatures, which will also be an aid to pollination.

## PLANTING

Plant (*see pp.158–159*) in the dormant season, preferably in late autumn, since peaches start to grow in early spring. Bare-root plants usually establish well. Container-grown plants grow away well as long as they are not pot-bound. Before planting, prepare stakes and wires (*see p.162*) for the form you have chosen. For planting in a pot, use a loam-based compost. Start a young tree in a 15–20cm (6–8in) diameter pot.

## PRUNING AND TRAINING

Peaches fruit on young wood formed in the previous season, as do acid cherries, and so they also require replacement pruning to produce a supply of new wood each year. When you are pruning to produce a new shoot, it is important to prune to a growth bud, rather than a fruit bud, so you need to recognize the two types (*see below*). If necessary, prune to a triple bud and remove the two side fruit buds. As for all stone fruits, prune peaches in spring and summer to avoid infection from silver leaf (*see p.262*) and bacterial canker (*see p.253*).

For conventional peach and nectarine cultivars, prune the bush and pyramid forms as you would for acid cherries (*see pp.191–192*). Compact cultivars grow slowly and need little or no pruning, apart from the removal of dead or diseased wood when necessary.

## PRUNING A PEACH OR NECTARINE FAN

Formative pruning of a peach fan is undertaken following the basic method (*see p.173*), with some extra pruning in early summer (*see overleaf*). Peaches usually grow quite vigorously at first,

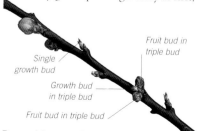

Single growth bud

Fruit bud in triple bud

Growth bud in triple bud

Fruit bud in triple bud

**Recognizing peach buds**
*Peaches, as well as other Prunus tree fruits, have separate fruit and growth buds, but some are found together as double and triple buds. The growth buds can be distinguished because they are pointed, while fruit buds are round.*

so it is vital to train shoots early on into position. Remove all vertical or near-vertical shoots in the centre as these will tend to dominate at the expense of the rest of the fan. In the third summer, a few fruits appear along the ribs of the fan, but the first real crop will be in the fourth summer.

On an established peach fan, routine pruning is in spring (*see box, below*) and summer, after fruiting. The aim is to choose a replacement shoot for each fruiting shoot and then to train it in alongside the fruiting shoot – a shoot higher up is also kept as a reserve. Keep the replacement shoots tied in flat so that plenty of light reaches the fan and also because they are difficult to bend flat later in the summer when growth becomes woodier. Other shoots can be

kept pinched to one leaf to feed the fruits. Tie in any shoots required to extend the framework if it has not yet reached its full size. If shoots outgrow the available space, pinch them back.

After picking in midsummer to late autumn, cut back the fruiting laterals to the replacement shoots unless there is room to extend the lateral. Cut out any dead or diseased wood to a healthy shoot. If a rib has developed a lot of bare wood, cut the section back to a replacement shoot. If replacement pruning is not carried out, the tree will eventually fruit only around the edges.

### ROUTINE CARE

Peaches require annual feeding to produce large, good-quality fruits and replacement shoots and fruit buds for

the next year's crop. In late winter, apply a general compound fertilizer (*see p.20*) at 100g/sq m (3oz/sq yd) over the rooting area – beneath the canopy of the tree or along the length of a fan-trained tree. Wall-trained trees benefit from an additional liquid feed with a high-potash fertilizer, such as tomato fertilizer, at about 5 litres (1 gallon) per tree every 10–14 days from fruitlet stage until the fruits are full size. All forms grow better with a mulch (*see p.161*).

Peaches, especially wall-trained trees, need plenty of moisture in the growing season. Do not allow them to become dry, since this can cause checks to growth and the problem of split stone (*see p.262*). The most effective method for wall- and fence-trained trees is to use drip irrigation (*see pp.53–54*).

---

## Pruning a peach or nectarine fan

**1** **Starting with a feathered maiden,** choose a strong lateral on either side at 25–30cm (10–12in) from soil level to form the main arms. In early spring, prune each one to about 38cm (15in) and an upward-facing bud, and tie them to canes attached to the wires. Remove the leader above these laterals; cut back any shoots below. In summer, select shoots to tie in to form the framework – 2 on the top of each arm and 1 below. Pinch back all other shoots to 1 leaf. The next spring, prune main shoots by a quarter of the last year's growth.

**2** **In early summer,** keep tying in shoots as they grow. Remove any growing into the support and below the 2 main arms; cut those growing outwards to 2 leaves.

**3** **In early summer** of the following year, thin laterals arising from the framework branches to 10–15cm (4–6in) apart. Remove any shoots growing directly towards the wall;

stop laterals growing straight out and any other surplus shoots at 2 leaves. Tie in the retained laterals to fruit the next year.

**4** **On an established fan** in spring, choose a replacement shoot near the base of each fruiting shoot, and a second reserve one further up the lateral; tie them in. Pinch out all other shoots at 1 leaf.

*Cane at about 40° to wires*

*Prune low shoots to 1 bud*

**❶**

*Fix canes to wires, then tie in new shoots*

*Remove vertical shoots* **❷**

*Cutting outward-growing shoot to 2 leaves*

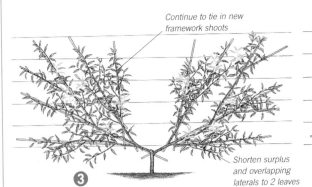

*Continue to tie in new framework shoots*

*Shorten surplus and overlapping laterals to 2 leaves* **❸**

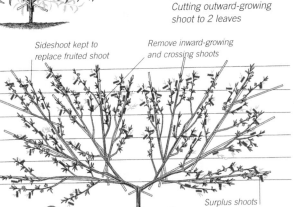

*Sideshoot kept to replace fruited shoot*

*Remove inward-growing and crossing shoots*

*Surplus shoots pinched to 1 leaf* **❹**

Feed container-grown, compact peach cultivars with a liquid feed or slow-release fertilizer during the growing season. Top-dress annually with fresh potting compost and repot into a larger container every other year. Once a tree has reached the maximum suitable pot size – 40cm (16in) diameter – repot it into the same pot, removing and replacing any loose compost and cutting away pot-bound roots.

## FRUIT THINNING

Fruit thinning is important to obtain good-sized peaches (*see right*) and avoid overstressing the tree. Thin nectarines to about 15cm (6in) apart.

## HARVESTING AND STORING PEACHES AND NECTARINES

Peaches are variable in their fruiting, but in favourable conditions a peach or nectarine bush may yield an average of 13.5–27kg (30–60lb) and a peach or nectarine fan 5.5–11.25kg (12–25lb).

Harvest peaches when they are ripe or almost ripe. To test for ripeness, cup the fruit in one hand and gently press near the stalk with the fingertips. If the flesh is soft, it is ready and the fruit should part easily from the tree. Place the fruits in containers lined with soft material so that they are not touching each other. Some will be ready to eat immediately, while some will require a day or two to ripen fully.

**Thinning peach fruits**
*Thin in 2 stages. First, when the fruitlets are about the size of a hazelnut, thin to single fruits 10cm (4in) apart, removing misshapen fruits and those next to the wall or in other places where they have no room to swell. When the fruits are the size of walnuts, thin to 20–25cm (8–10in) apart.*

*After thinning, healthy fruits have room to grow*

## RAISING PEACHES FROM SEED

Peaches are one of the few fruits that can be grown successfully from seed. The seedlings do not grow true from seed, but they are usually similar or inferior to the peach from which it is raised – and only occasionally better. Seedlings generally take about four or five years to bear fruit.

To be sure of success, select several stones. Clean them and leave them in the sun to dry for a few days. The stones require a period of cold before germination can take place, so store them over the winter in a mixture of 50:50 sharp sand and peat in a 25cm (10in) pot. Plunge the pot in soil in a shady part of the garden, cover it with a fine wire mesh to deter rodents, and keep the sand and peat mixture moist. Protect the stones against hard frosts with a layer of straw or similar material.

In late winter, sow the stones singly in 14cm (5½in) pots of a loam-based compost. Place on a sunny windowsill or, ideally, on a propagating bench

with bottom heat of 15–20°C (59–68°F). As each seedling grows, tie it into a vertical cane. In late spring, once risk of frost is past, place the pots outside, preferably plunged in soil. The next winter, plant out the best seedling in its permanent position. It is best not to keep it in a container unless you want to grow it in one permanently. A seedling tree can be trained in the same forms as a grafted tree (*see p.193*).

## COMMON PROBLEMS

Peaches are affected by a variety of problems. The most troublesome disease is peach leaf curl (*see p.258*). Other problems include aphids (*see p.251*), red spider mite (*see p.261*), particularly with wall- and fence-trained trees and those cultivated under glass, brown scale (*see p.253*), bacterial canker (*see p.253*), silver leaf (*see p.262*), brown rot (*see p.253*), replant disease (*see p.261*), split stone (*see p.262*), and squirrels (*see p.262*).

**Raincover for a wall-trained peach**
*Use a raincover from early winter to late spring to keep buds dry, avoid peach leaf curl, and give frost protection. Make a wooden frame with clear plastic sheeting to cover the fan, leaving the ends and base open for air circulation.*

| RECOMMENDED PEACH AND NECTARINE CULTIVARS | | |
|---|---|---|
| Cultivar | Picking time | Characteristics |
| **Peaches** | | |
| 'Avalon Pride' | Late summer | Reliable with some resistance to peach leaf curl. Large fruits with a red flush and yellow flesh. |
| 'Peregrine' ♀ | Late summer | Light green and crimson, white-fleshed fruit. |
| 'Rochester' ♀ | Late summer | Very reliable; large, juicy, fibrous, gold fruits. |
| **Nectarines** | | |
| 'Early Rivers' ♀ | Midsummer | Richly flavoured, juicy, pale yellow flesh. |
| 'Humboldt' | Late summer | Orange and crimson fruit. Best under glass. |
| 'Lord Napier' ♀ | Late summer | Pale yellow and crimson, juicy fruits. |
| **Compact peach cultivars** | | |
| 'Garden Anny' | Midsummer | Pale yellow, juicy fruits with excellent flavour. |
| 'Garden Lady' | Midsummer | Yellow fruits with red flush; juicy flesh. |
| **Compact nectarine cultivars** | | |
| 'Nectarella' | Late summer | Orange fruits flushed red, with juicy flesh. |

# Apricot

Apricots (*Prunus armeniaca*) originate from China and Central Asia. They are fully winter-hardy but flower early – generally in early to mid-spring, but sometimes in late winter – so cropping in the open is often unreliable. Apricots will grow on a range of soils providing they are well-drained, fairly moisture-retentive, and at least 45cm (18in) deep with a pH of 6.5–7.5. On light, sandy soils (*see p.22*), add plenty of organic matter to improve moisture-retention.

## TREE FORMS AND ROOTSTOCKS

Apricots can be grown as bushes or pyramids in favourable, warm, sheltered positions. A pyramid is also suitable for growing in a container, which can be moved under cover for protection. Due to early flowering, the most practical tree form is as a fan against a warm south-, southwest-, or west-facing wall or fence. Fan-trained trees need a space 3.5–5m (11–15ft) wide and 2–2.5m (6–8ft) high. The most often used rootstocks are St Julien A and Torinel; both are semi-dwarfing.

## POLLINATION

Apricots are self-fertile and so just one tree is required for fruits. The blossom is pollinated by insects, but the flowers open at a time when there are often few pollinating insects around. Hand pollination is generally necessary (*see p.157*). The flowers and fruitlets are very vulnerable to frost damage: be prepared to protect against frost on nights when it is forecast (*see above, right*).

## PLANTING

Plant (*see pp.158–159*) in the dormant season, preferably in autumn, as apricots may start to grow away in late winter. Bare-root plants usually establish well. Container-grown plants also grow away well if not pot-bound. Before planting, prepare the stakes and wires (*see p.162*) for the form you have chosen.

## PRUNING AND TRAINING

Apricots fruit on one- and two-year-old wood, and on older fruiting spurs. As for all stone fruits, prune in spring and summer to avoid infection from silver leaf (*see p.262*) and bacterial

**Growing an apricot under cover**
*In colder areas, apricots crop most reliably under glass. The fan form is decorative as well as practical: the buds and ripening fruits receive plenty of light and warmth.*

canker (*see p.253*). For formative pruning of a bush, *see pp.166–167*; for established pruning, *see Plum, p.186*. For pruning of an apricot pyramid, *see p.170*.

## PRUNING AN APRICOT FAN

Carry out formative pruning for the basic framework (*see p.173*) in late winter or early spring as the tree starts early into growth. In addition, follow the guidelines for plums (*see pp.186–187*) for formative summer pruning and pruning an established fan.

## ROUTINE CARE

In late winter, apply sulphate of potash at 35g/sq m (1oz/sq yd) over the rooting area (to just beyond the extent of the branches). In early spring, apply calcium ammonium nitrate at 20g/sq m (½oz/sq yd). Every third year, apply super phosphate at 70g/sq m (2oz/sq yd) in late winter. Apply a mulch (*see p.161*) after the fertilizer in spring. Give extra water in dry periods in spring and summer. For wall-trained apricots, drip irrigation (*see pp.53–54*) is very useful.

## FRUIT THINNING

Apricots seldom set enough fruit to need thinning. However, if a heavy crop is set, thin (*see p.160*) in late spring or early summer, when fruits are the size of hazelnuts, to 5–8cm (2–3in) apart.

**Frost protection for a wall-trained apricot**
*Cover the tree with fleece or netting just before the buds break to protect them from frost. When the flowers open, roll up the covering in the day to allow access by insects.*

## HARVESTING AND STORING

Harvest apricots when they are fully ripe and soft; they should part easily from the spur. Use them as soon as possible after picking, storing them briefly if necessary in a cool place.

## COMMON PROBLEMS

Apricots suffer from a few pests and diseases, including brown scale (*see p.253*), dieback (*see p.254*), silver leaf (*see p.262*), and bacterial canker (*see p.253*). Birds (*see p.252*) can attack the ripening fruit, and so netting may be necessary (*see p.192*).

---

### RECOMMENDED CULTIVARS

The available cultivars are generally similar in reliability. The following are in order of season of ripening.

**'New Large Early'** *Midsummer. Pale yellow fruits with juicy, orange flesh.*

**'Alfred'** *Mid–late summer. Rich-flavoured orange flesh. Some resistance to dieback.*

**'Early Moorpark'** *Mid–late summer. Juicy, fine-textured, orange flesh.*

**'Flavorcot'** *Late summer. A promising new cultivar, possibly more reliable than established cultivars. Orange fruits.*

**'Moorpark'** ♀ *Late summer–early autumn. Old cultivar with orange, red-flushed fruits.*

FIG **197**

# Fig

Figs (*Ficus carica*) have long been grown in the Mediterranean region, where there are warm, sunny conditions, low rainfall, and few frosts. These are the garden conditions in which figs grow best. If it is to fruit well in cooler areas, it is essential to grow a tree in a warm, sunny position. A fig can be fan-trained against a south-, southwest-, or west-facing wall or fence; a house wall is ideal for providing some extra warmth all year. Figs can thrive in containers. In very favourable, sheltered areas, it is possible to grow a fig as a freestanding half-standard or bush.

Figs can be grown on a range of soils providing they are well-drained. Light and shallow soils, including thin soils over chalk, are suitable; very fertile soils tend to induce too much growth.

## CHOOSING A TREE FORM

The best form for growing a fig outside is a fan-trained tree. Each tree needs a space about 3.5m (11ft) wide and 2–2.5m (6–8ft) high. Grow it as a bush in a very sheltered spot or in a pot. You can choose the height of stem before the branches start – a convenient stem height is generally 60–90cm (2–3ft) in open ground. In containers, figs can be grown as a multi-stemmed bushes (*see p.199*) or as standards with a clear stem of 60–90cm (2–3ft).

Figs are grown on their own roots and propagated from hardwood cuttings (*see p.199*). Unfortunately, there are no rootstocks to control their vigour, and they grow very vigorously on fertile soils where there is plenty of rainfall.

## POLLINATION

The fig cultivars that are cultivated in cool temperate regions develop parthenocarpic fruits – that is, seedless fruits produced without fertilization. Therefore no pollination is necessary. Figs are unusual among tree fruits because the flower is enclosed within what becomes the fruit and so is never visible; the fig simply grows in size.

## PLANTING AND ROOT RESTRICTION

Figs are available as container-grown plants. Choose a young plant that is not pot-bound – take it out of the pot and inspect it before buying. Plant in late spring when the danger of severe frost has passed; if you have bought it before then, keep it in a cool but frost-free place, such as greenhouse or porch, until planting time.

When planting a fig in open ground it is a good idea to restrict the root run; this keeps the tree compact and enables it to fruit well rather than putting all its energies into producing new growth. The size of the rooting area will determine the ultimate size of tree.

For a fan-trained tree 2–2.5m (6–8ft) tall and 3.5m (11ft) wide, a rooting volume of about 0.15 cubic metres (5 cubic feet) is needed. This can be provided by making an open-bottomed box with paving slabs, bricks, or heavy-duty hard plastic sunk into the soil (*see below*). For a freestanding tree, make the open-bottomed box with four sides instead of three. Other ways to provide root restriction include planting a fig in a narrow border between a wall and a concrete path, or planting it in a hole set in a paved area.

Growing figs in containers will automatically provide root restriction. Generally, containers of 30–40cm (12–16in) in diameter are most suitable; a larger pot can be used, but will be too heavy to lift. Ensure good drainage by filling the base of the pot with crocks. Use a loam-based potting compost.

## PRUNING AND TRAINING

Although figs fruit freely in a warm climate, in cooler areas only one crop per year is produced. Figs develop in the axils of the leaves of the young shoots and, provided that they are not subjected to frost, overwinter as embryo figs about the size of peas. These fig embryos ripen in midsummer to early autumn of the following year (*see p.198*). Occasionally, or when grown under glass, a second crop will develop in one season and ripen from early to mid-autumn.

---

### Constructing a planting pit

**1** **For a fan, construct a pit** about 45cm (18in) deep against a wall and line it with three 60 x 60cm (24 x 24in) paving slabs. The tops of the slabs should stand proud of the surface by at least 5cm (2in) so that roots cannot not stray along the soil surface. Fill the bottom 15–20cm (6–8in) with large crocks or rubble to provide good drainage and to discourage any large roots from growing through.

**2** **Fill the pit with soil** enriched with compost, or with loam-based potting compost plus a slow- or controlled-release fertilizer, leaving a watering rim of 2.5cm (1in). Plant a young fig (here 'Brown Turkey') in the centre, leaning it towards the training wires; fill with more compost.

**3** **Firm in the plant** and cut back the stem to a bud facing to one side 45cm (18in) from the ground. Water and label.

However, if this second crop does not ripen, remove it in late autumn.

Prune figs twice a year. In early to mid-spring, after the danger of frost has passed, cut them back to regulate the shape. In summer, pinch out the shoot tips (*see right*); this encourages the formation of a new supply of embryo figs for the next year, and allows light to reach ripening fruits.

*Embryo figs for next year's crop develop in leaf axils*

*This year's secondary fruit*

*Overwintered fruit now ripening*

*Pinch soft shoot firmly with fingertips*

### Development of fig fruits
*Figs at 3 stages of development are visible on this shoot. At the base is a ripening fruit that has overwintered from last year. Above it are 2 figs formed this spring that may ripen in favourable conditions. Near the tip are embryo figs that may overwinter and ripen next year.*

### Summer pruning
*In order to produce compact, short-jointed shoots with plenty of embryo figs, pinch or cut out the tips of the shoots when they have formed 5 leaves in early summer. This allows time for the shoots that grow out to ripen and produce embryo figs in the autumn.*

## PRUNING A HALF-STANDARD FIG OR A FIG BUSH
Formative pruning of a half-standard or bush is similar to that for other tree fruits (*see pp.166–167*), with the pruning being done in early spring. For spring pruning of an established bush, see box, below; it may not be necessary to remove large, bare branches every year, but just as needed. In early summer each year, pinch or cut out the growing tips of all the shoots once they have five leaves (*see above, right*). For pruning a container-grown fig, *see facing page.*

## PRUNING A FIG FAN
Formative training and pruning of a fan is as for other tree fruits (*see p.173*), and is done in early spring after the worst of the frosts. If the tree has two or more

sideshoots, choose two well-placed shoots and prune them back by only one-third of their length to an upward-facing bud, and remove the rest.

For pruning an established fan in spring, *see box, below.* In midsummer, continue to tie in the developing shoots to the wires so that they are exposed to the full sun and ripen well.

## RENOVATING A NEGLECTED FIG
If a fig tree has been neglected for a number of years, most of the fruit will be borne on young shoots around the edge of the tree, with bare sections in

the centre. For a neglected bush tree, remove a proportion of the older, bare branches in mid-spring back to a stub of about 5cm (2in). If there are quite a few old branches to remove, spread the pruning over two or three years to avoid stimulating excessive new growth in the fig. As new shoots grow, select the strongest and best-placed for a balanced tree, and prune out the others.

For a fan-trained tree, also prune in mid-spring. Start by removing branches growing directly out from the wall or fence, cutting back to their point of

## Pruning an established fig tree in spring

**1** **Take out about a quarter** of the oldest and most congested stems, cutting them to a stub of 5–8cm (2–3in) at the base to encourage new, vigorous growth. Use a pruning saw for a clean cut.

**2** **In late spring**, before bud break, look for any badly placed shoots that are growing into or away from the fence, or, as here, are crossing other branches. Remove them and tie in the remaining new shoots.

### Pruning an established fig bush
*In mid-spring, cut back branches that have become long and bare to a stub of about 5cm (2in) to stimulate new shoots from the base. Remove frost-damaged growth and shoots that are crowded and crossing the centre.*

*Balanced, open, crown after pruning*

*Keep base of trunk clear*

*FIG* **199**

origin. Thin out crowded branches by cutting back to a stub of about 5cm (2in). Again, if there is a large number of branches to remove, spread the pruning over two or three years.

With both forms, remove any suckers (vigorous shoots) arising from the base. These will spoil the shape of the tree, taking strength from the other shoots.

## ROUTINE CARE

In early spring each year, apply a top-dressing of a high-potash (1:1:2 NPK) compound fertilizer (*see pp.20–21*) at a rate of about 70g/sq m (2oz/sq yd). During the summer, feed the fig with a high-potash liquid fertilizer, such as a tomato feed.

Figs require regular watering during the spring and summer because the root restriction, and the required good drainage, increases the risk of the roots drying out.

## CARE OF FIGS IN CONTAINERS

Feed trees in containers every week during spring and summer with a liquid feed. Alternate between a high-potash fertilizer, such as a tomato feed, and a more balanced feed. Water all year as required and do not allow the compost to dry out completely.

Every two years, the fig is likely to need repotting in the dormant season. Remove the tree carefully from its pot, knock off any loose compost, and cut away with secateurs any thick, thong-like roots. Repot with some fresh loam-based potting compost into the same container or into a slightly larger one.

## WINTER PROTECTION

Cropping laterals and their embryo figs will survive only light frosts. In areas that are prone to winter frosts, protect the figs by covering the plant in late autumn with a thick layer of bracken, straw, or conifer branches, secured with mesh netting (*see above, right*). Remove the protection in spring once the danger of frost has passed, but before the buds break.

Trees in containers can be moved to a frost-free place, such as a shed or garage. If they have to be left outside, plunge the pot in the ground and cover the branches in the same way as figs growing in the ground. Remove

**Pruning a container-grown fig**
*As an alternative to the bush with a short stem, a fig in a container can be grown with several stems. Cut a two- or three-year-old fig to soil level, then select up to 10 good shoots that grow from the base. Remove 3 or 4 stems each year to keep a new supply of shoots. Summer prune by pinching shoots to 5 leaves.*

the protection in mid-spring after the risk of severe frosts has passed.

## PROPAGATION

Figs can be propagated by hardwood cuttings in autumn. Take cuttings at least 30cm (12in) long from the ripe, current season's growth, and trim off the leaves and any soft growth from the tip to make woody cuttings of about 23cm (9in) long, each with a straight cut at the base and an angled cut above a bud at the top. Insert the cuttings in a trench 15cm (6in) deep, spacing them 10–15cm (4–6in) apart. They should root within several months; leave them to develop to the end of the following growing season and then transplant to their final positions.

**Protecting figs from frost**
*Use dried bracken, straw, or conifer branches to protect a trained fig. Pack behind the stems with a thin layer of bracken, then work in bundles of bracken among the branches so that the stems are covered by a layer at least 5cm (2in) thick. Secure with a 15cm (6in) mesh net pinned to the support with wire staples.*

## HARVESTING FIGS

Fig yields vary very widely according to the tree size and growing conditions. Harvest figs when they are fully ripe and soft. When ready to pick, they hang downwards and splits appear in the skin, especially at the stalk end. A drop of nectar may exude from the eye of the fig. Pick fruit by holding the stalk and breaking it away from the shoot. Figs are best eaten soon after picking.

## COMMON PROBLEMS

The following pests and diseases may affect figs: brown scale (*see p.253*), and red spider mite (*see p.261*), particularly under glass or in a warm situation outside, birds (*see p.252*), and coral spot (*see p.254*).

| RECOMMENDED FIG CULTIVARS | | |
|---|---|---|
| Cultivar | Picking time | Characteristics |
| 'White Marseilles' | Early | Large, yellowish-green fruits. Can be grown outside. |
| 'Brown Turkey' ♀ | Mid-season | Brown fruits, sweet, dark red flesh. Excellent outside. |
| 'Brunswick' | Mid-season | Greenish-brown large fruits. Can be grown outside. |
| 'Rouge de Bordeaux' | Mid-season | Small purple fruits with sweet, dark red flesh. Good for containers in a warm site outside or under glass. |
| 'White Ischia' | Mid-season | Pale green, rich-flavoured fruits. Best in containers. |
| 'Bourjassotte Grise' | Late | Blue fruits with rich, brown flesh. Suitable for containers, but needs protection to ripen. |

# Quince

The true quince (*Cydonia oblonga*) is a relative of the pear, and originated in central to southwestern Asia. It is often confused with the shrubby ornamental *Chaenomeles* species, which are also edible. Those are thorny shrubs, whereas the true quince is a thornless, medium-sized tree. Quinces make ornamental and productive trees, with an attractive habit and large, dog-rose-like flowers. The fruit is never soft enough to eat raw when grown in cool countries, and is used for cooking and preserving.

Quinces need a warm, sheltered site since the flowers are susceptible to frost, and warm conditions are needed for the fruit to ripen properly. Provide extra shelter if necessary (*see pp.12–13*). They tolerate a range of soils, but grow best in a deep, moisture-retentive soil. The trees grow well beside streams or ponds, but not in soil prone to waterlogging.

## TREE FORMS AND ROOTSTOCKS

The most suitable forms for quinces are the half-standard and bush tree. Restricted forms are not suitable.

Quinces can be established on their own roots but are often grown on the quince rootstocks Quince A and C. Quince A is semi-vigorous, producing a half-standard tree 3.5–4.5m (11–15ft) in height and spread. Quince C is semi-dwarfing and will produce a bush tree 3–3.5m (10–11ft) in height and spread.

## POLLINATION

Quinces are self-fertile and are insect-pollinated, so only one tree needs to be grown to produce a crop.

## PLANTING

Plant (*see pp.158–159*) in the dormant season. Bare-root plants usually establish well, as do container-grown plants if they are not pot-bound. It is worth obtaining a two-year-old bush tree with the first branches already formed. Stake quinces for the first two years.

## PRUNING A QUINCE HALF-STANDARD OR A BUSH TREE

Quinces fruit mostly on the tips of the shoots made the previous year, and produce few fruiting spurs. Prune in the dormant season between late autumn

---

## Pruning an established quince tree

*Before pruning*

*After pruning*

Before pruning (*see far left*), the quince displays typical, haphazard growth, with shoots growing in any direction, creating a crowded canopy. Winter pruning is needed to thin out the canopy and to improve light penetration and air circulation.

Remove no more than a quarter of the oldest branches by cutting them back to the point of origin, or to a shoot that is one-third of the diameter of the branch being removed. Cut off crowded branches (*see above*), very vigorous shoots, and branches showing little growth.

The canopy after pruning (*see bottom left*) is more open, with a neater outline and plenty of fruit-bearing laterals.

---

and early spring. Formative pruning is undertaken as on pp.166–167; this pruning is vital as quinces have a rather irregular growth habit and need a good basic framework. For the cropping tree, prune every winter (*see above*). This pruning is generally fairly light, but make sure you remove any vigorous shoots that may spoil the tree shape.

## ROUTINE CARE

Quinces benefit from regular feeding. In late winter, apply sulphate of potash at 20g/sq m (½oz/sq yd) over the rooting area, and sulphate of ammonia at 35–70g/sq m (1–2oz/sq yd) in early spring. Every third year, apply super phosphate at 70g/sq m (2oz/sq yd).

For the first four years after planting, and every year for trees on dry soils, mulch well (*see p.161*). Give extra water during dry spells in spring and summer.

## HARVESTING AND STORING

Quince yields are very variable. Harvest the fruits when they are fully ripe, golden-coloured, and aromatic, usually in mid- to late autumn before there are

---

any air frosts. Store undamaged fruits in a cool, dark, frost-free place on shallow trays so the fruits do not touch. They are highly aromatic so avoid storing them with apples or pears, otherwise the apples and pears may taste of quince.

## COMMON PROBLEMS

Although quinces are troubled by some of the same pests as apples and pears, these are seldom significant. They might however suffer from a few diseases: quince leaf blight (*see p.260*), brown rot (*see p.253*), fireblight (*see p.255*), and powdery mildew (*see p.260*).

### RECOMMENDED CULTIVARS

**'Champion'** *Produces good crop of large, rounded fruits.*

**'Meech's Prolific'** *Pear-shaped fruits of very good flavour.*

**'Portugal' (syn. 'Lusitanica')** *Vigorous and less hardy than the other cultivars, but has the best-flavoured fruits.*

**'Vranja Nenodovic'** ♀ *Pear-shaped, aromatic fruits of very good flavour. Comes early into cropping.*

# Medlar

The medlar (*Mespilus germanica*) is an attractive ornamental, as well as fruiting, tree. It is related to the hawthorn and to the quince. A deciduous native of southeastern Europe and central Asia, it has been naturalized throughout much of Europe. Its spreading habit makes it a graceful addition to the garden, while it also has large, leathery leaves that have good autumn colour, and simple, white rose-like flowers in mid- to late spring.

The fruits can be used after picking for making a pleasantly flavoured jelly. Alternatively, they can be eaten raw if left until they reach the point of decomposing in the process known as "bletting" (*see below*).

Medlars thrive in a warm, sheltered site in sun or partial shade and are tolerant of a range of soils provided that they are well-drained.

## TREE FORMS AND ROOTSTOCKS

Due to the spreading habit of the medlar, the standard and half-standard are the only suitable tree forms. Space each tree about 5–6m (15–20ft) from surrounding plants to allow it to fulfil its natural habit without restriction.

Medlars can be grafted on quince or hawthorn rootstocks. Quince rootstocks are generally the better choice, offering greater stability. Of these rootstocks, the semi-vigorous Quince A and BA29 are most suitable. These will produce a standard or half-standard tree 4–6m (12–20ft) in height and spread.

## POLLINATION

Medlars are self-fertile and pollinated by insects, so only one tree needs to be grown to produce a crop.

## PLANTING

Plant in the dormant season (*see pp. 158–159*). Bare-root plants usually establish well. Container-grown plants also grow away well if they are not pot-bound. If possible, obtain a part-trained standard or half-standard tree and tie it in to a low stake at planting. If you are starting with a maiden tree, plant it next to a tall stake – with about 2m (6ft) out of the ground for a standard and 1.5m (5ft) for a half-standard – and tie it in to the stake to ensure a straight stem.

**Ripening fruits of the medlar tree ready to harvest**
*The brown, distinctive medlar fruits are about 2.5–5cm (1–2in) across when ready to pick. They should be left on the tree into autumn to* *develop their flavour until they are fully mature. They will then part easily from the spur when lifted gently in the hand.*

## PRUNING A MEDLAR STANDARD OR HALF-STANDARD TREE

With a ready-trained standard or half-standard, for the first three or four years after planting, prune the branch leaders by about one-third of the previous summer's growth to an outward-facing bud. Leave any short shoots unpruned and remove any poorly placed or crowded branches in winter if needed. For a maiden tree, grow on the main stem, tying it in, until it reaches the required height. Remove low branches and train the remaining ones as above. On a mature tree, winter prune only to keep an open framework, removing any crowded, diseased, or dead branches.

## ROUTINE CARE

In late winter each year, apply a general compound fertilizer (*see p.20*) at about 70g/sq m (2oz/sq yd) over the rooting area. Mulch (*see p.161*) with organic matter, such as well-rotted manure, compost, or bark, for the first three or four years. Water well in dry periods in spring and summer for the first three or four years; after that medlars should be able to grow well without irrigation.

## HARVESTING AND STORING

Pick medlars in mid-autumn (*see above*) in dry conditions, and dip the stalks in a strong salt solution to prevent them rotting. Store them eye downwards and not touching, on trays in a cool, dark, frost-free place. Bletting, when the flesh softens and turns brown, will take two to three weeks. The medlars will then be ready to eat.

## COMMON PROBLEMS

Medlars are rarely troubled significantly by pests or diseases. They may be affected by fungal leaf spot caused by *Diplocarpon mespili* and Monilinia blight caused by the fungus *Monilinia mespili*.

---

### RECOMMENDED CULTIVARS

**'Dutch'** *Spreading habit and fairly large fruits.*
**'Nottingham'** *More upright habit than 'Dutch'. Fruits fairly small with best flavour.*
**'Royal'** *Fairly upright habit. Medium-sized fruits.*

# Mulberry

The mulberry species most frequently cultivated for fruit is the black mulberry (*Morus nigra*). Native to western Asia and grown throughout Europe, it is a long-lived and decorative tree. The white mulberry (*Morus alba*) is used to feed silk worms, but has inferior fruit.

Mulberries grow best in sheltered, warm sites. They are tolerant of a range of soils, provided that they are well-drained with a pH of 5.5–7, but prefer a fertile, moisture-retentive soil.

## TREE FORMS AND ROOTSTOCKS

Mulberries in the open are best grown as standard or half-standard trees. They are fairly slow-growing, taking five years or so to start cropping. Eventually they make substantial trees, needing 5–10m (15–30ft) for their natural shape to develop, and so are suitable only for very large gardens. In cool areas, they benefit from training as an espalier on a warm south-, southwest-, or west-facing wall, where they need a space 4.5m (15ft) wide and 2.5m (8ft) high.

Mulberries are usually grown on their own roots or grafted onto seedling rootstocks. There are no dwarfing rootstocks available.

## POLLINATION

Mulberries are self-fertile. They flower relatively late, so tend to escape the effects of the worst of the frosts.

## PLANTING

Plant (*see pp.158–159*) in the dormant season. Bare-root plants usually establish well. Container-grown plants also grow away well if they are not pot-bound. For a standard or half-standard tree, try to buy a part-trained tree to obtain a well-formed tree more quickly.

## PRUNING A MULBERRY STANDARD OR HALF-STANDARD TREE

Prune mulberries when they are fully dormant: cutting in the growing season results in bleeding from the wounds. In the winter after planting, remove any shoots that spoil the shape, and any on the stem below the framework branches. Repeat in early to midwinter each year, removing any poorly placed

**Mature mulberry tree and fruit**
*Once established, the mulberry soon develops a gnarled appearance and somewhat irregular shape. As long as the branches are well-spaced, this adds to its decorative value in the garden. Pick fruits (see inset) when they have turned black and are fully ripe.*

shoots for a good framework. Once the tree is established, little pruning is needed; simply remove any crossing, crowding, dead, or broken branches.

## PRUNING A MULBERRY ESPALIER

Formative pruning of an espalier is undertaken (*see pp.171–172*) in early to midwinter. Once the tree is established, prune lateral shoots arising from the stem and branches of the espalier in late summer, when the growth has slowed down, shortening them to three or four leaves to produce fruiting spurs.

## ROUTINE CARE

In late winter each year apply a general compound fertilizer (*see p.20*) at 70g/sq m (2oz/sq yd) over the rooting area. Apply a mulch of organic matter such as well-rotted manure, compost, or bark in spring (*see p.161*). Give extra water during dry periods in the spring and summer for the first three or four years after planting; after that mulberries should grow well without irrigation.

The branches of mature trees may become brittle. If necessary, provide support by driving a forked stake into the ground and resting the branch on cushioned sacking in the fork.

## HARVESTING MULBERRIES

Mulberry yields are very variable. The fruits mature over a few weeks in mid- to late summer, and are almost black when ripe, parting easily from the spur. For preserving, use slightly underripe fruits. Take care when harvesting as the juice stains clothes easily. For large trees spread a cloth beneath the tree to catch fruits, then gently shake the branches.

## COMMON PROBLEMS

Mulberries are seldom troubled by pests and diseases. However, birds (*see p.252*) will take the fruits, and trees may be affected by mulberry canker (*see p.258*).

### RECOMMENDED CULTIVARS

Choose from these named clonal selections rather than unnamed seedlings.
**'Chelsea'** *An old variety with juicy, rich fruits.*
**'Large Black'** *A good-fruited clone.*

# Cobnut and filbert

These two forms of hazelnut are similar in appearance and there also are hybrids between the two. The cobnut (*Corylus avellana*) has a short husk with the nut protruding, while the filbert (*Corylus maxima*) has a long husk, which covers the nut. Cobnuts and filberts grow best in full sun or light shade; they will grow, but not crop well, in heavy shade.

Choose a sheltered site, avoiding frost pockets (*see p.11*). The trees are tolerant of a range of soils provided that they are well-drained and have a pH of 6.7–7.5. Light sandy soils are preferable, since on very fertile soils the trees tend to produce too much growth.

### TREE FORMS AND ROOTSTOCKS

The most suitable tree form is an open-centred bush grown on a leg of 30–45cm (12–18in). Space bushes about 4.5m (15ft) apart. Due to this wide spacing, and the fact that more than one tree is needed for pollination (*see below*), these trees are not suitable for a small garden. Cobnuts and filberts are grown on their own roots.

### POLLINATION

Cobnuts and filberts are monoecious, that is they have separate male and female flowers on the same tree (*see below*). The flowers are fairly hardy but appear early, often in late winter to early spring, so may be affected by frost.

Although cobnuts and filberts are self-fertile, pollen is not always produced

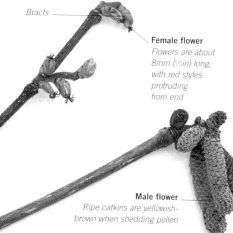

Bracts

**Female flower**
*Flowers are about 8mm (⅓in) long, with red styles protruding from end*

**Male flower**
*Ripe catkins are yellowish-brown when shedding pollen*

**Successful pollination**
*Flowers are wind-pollinated; pollen drifts from catkins to female flowers, so it helps to plant a group of trees in square formation.*

when the female flowers are receptive, so you need to grow more than one cultivar for good wind pollination.

### PLANTING

Plant (*see pp.158–159*) in the dormant season. Bare-root plants usually establish well. Container-grown plants also grow away well if they are not pot-bound. If possible, obtain a part-trained bush. In a very sheltered situation, staking may not be needed; otherwise secure to a short stake for the first two or three years.

### PRUNING A COBNUT OR FILBERT BUSH

Formative pruning (*see pp.166–167*) is done in the winter following planting. With cobnuts and filberts, about eight branches can be retained. Once the tree is established, prune twice a year.

Summer pruning (*see above*) is known as "brutting". In the spring, when the pollen is being shed (the movement aids pollination), shorten branch leaders by about half to an outward-facing bud. Shorten strong laterals brutted (*see above*) the previous summer to three or four buds, or remove them if they are very vigorous. Leave weak laterals unpruned. If the tree becomes too tall – above 3–3.5m (10–11ft) – cut the leader back to a lower replacement lateral. Remove any branches crowding the centre.

As the tree matures, remove overlong side branches, cutting back to a stub of about 2.5cm (1in); the branch will regrow from this. Remove any suckers at the base in the growing season.

**Brutted cobnut shoots**
*In late summer, stop strong laterals 30cm (12in) or more in length half-way along by snapping them without completely breaking them off, and leave them hanging down. This encourages fruit buds to form and reduces vigour.*

### ROUTINE CARE

In late winter each year, apply a general compound fertilizer (*see p.20*) at 70g/sq m (2oz/sq yd). For the first 3–4 years, mulch in spring (*see p.161*) and water during dry spells in spring and summer.

### HARVESTING AND STORING COBNUTS AND FILBERTS

Yields are very variable for cobnuts and filberts. Harvest in early autumn when husks start to turn yellow, but before they start to drop. Nuts harvested too early do not store well and those left too long may be eaten by squirrels and mice. Dry the nuts in the sun, and remove the husks when dry. Store in a cool, rodent-proof place in containers that allow some air circulation, such as slatted trays or suspended net bags.

### COMMON PROBLEMS

Nut weevil (*see p.258*) and powdery mildew (*see p.260*) may be troublesome. Squirrels (*see p.262*) are a serious pest.

---

### RECOMMENDED CULTIVARS

**Cobnuts**
'Cosford Cob' *Sweet nuts with a thin shell. Reliable and a good pollinator.*
'Pearson's Prolific' *Round nut of good flavour. A compact tree producing a lot of catkins, and a good pollinator.*
**Filberts**
'Butler' *Heavy cropping with large nuts.*
'Kentish Cob' *Very good flavour and fine-textured nuts. Hardy and reliable.*
'Gunslebert' *Heavy cropping with medium-sized nuts of strong flavour.*

# Walnut

The species cultivated for its edible nuts is the Persian or English walnut (*Juglans regia*), native to Iran, Central Asia, and China. The North American black walnut (*Juglans nigra*) is more vigorous and the nuts are of poorer quality.

Walnuts make very handsome, but substantial trees of 18–20m (60–70ft) in height and spread. Slow-growing at first, they reach 10m (30ft) in the first 20 years. Although there are some more compact cultivars available, they still are suitable only for very large gardens.

Walnut trees are fully winter-hardy, but the early growth is susceptible to spring frosts. A warm, sheltered site is best, avoiding frost pockets (*see p.11*). They grow best in deep, well-drained, moisture-retentive soil with a pH of 6.5 to 7, and will tolerate some alkalinity.

## TREE FORMS AND ROOTSTOCKS
Grow walnut cultivars as centre-leader standards. They are usually grown on a seedling rootstock of *J. regia* or *J. nigra*. Plant only grafted, named cultivars since seedlings take a long time to come into bearing and usually offer inferior nuts.

## POLLINATION
Walnuts are monoecious – with male and female flowers on the same tree – and pollinated by wind. Most cultivars are self-fertile, but the male flowers often open before the females, so good crops are assured if there is at least one other cultivar growing no more than

**Harvesting walnuts**
*For storing, gather the nuts when their hulls crack to release the nuts from the shell (as here), and they start to fall. For pickling, harvest before the shell and hull harden.*

80m (280ft) away for cross-pollination. Spring frosts may damage flowers and young shoots, causing poor cropping.

## PLANTING
Plant (*see pp.158–159*) in late autumn or winter. Choose young, 3–4-year-old plants part-trained as standards. Avoid pot-bound specimens as walnuts have a long taproot. Tie into a short stake 45–60cm (18–24in) above ground. It

is essential to site a walnut 12–18m (40–60ft) in a large garden, well away from other plantings. Walnuts secrete chemicals into the soil that may inhibit growth of some plants, so it is best not to grow plants in their rooting area.

## PRUNING AND TRAINING A WALNUT CENTRE-LEADER STANDARD
Prune walnuts as little as possible as they bleed sap easily. Mid-autumn, when risk of bleeding is least, is best. For formative pruning, *see box, below*. A mature tree needs minimal pruning: remove crossing or broken branches.

## ROUTINE CARE
On poor soil, broadcast a balanced compound feed (*see p.20*) at 70g/sq m (2oz/sq yd) in early spring beneath the canopy area. After planting and for the first 3–4 years, mulch (*see p.161*) and water in dry conditions.

## HARVESTING AND STORING
Walnut yields are erratic. Harvest in autumn (*see left*). To store nuts, clean the shells before they discolour – wear gloves as the sap stains easily – and dry, preferably in sun. Store in a slatted box in cool, airy conditions such as a shed.

## COMMON PROBLEMS
Walnuts are fairly problem-free, apart from walnut blotch (*see p.264*) and walnut leaf blight (*see p.264*). Birds (*see p.252*) of the crow family and squirrels (*see p.262*) will take the nuts.

## Formative pruning

The centre-leader tree shape is basically pyramidal, although due to the walnut's spreading habit, it will become rounder with age. The aim in formative pruning is to promote a central, vertical leader from which all the main framework branches will grow. First, remove any competing leaders and vertical shoots that might spoil the shape. Then remove all laterals on the lower third of the stem to leave several wide-angled branches that start to form the crown of the tree. Continue in subsequent years to remove vertical shoots and maintain the crown.

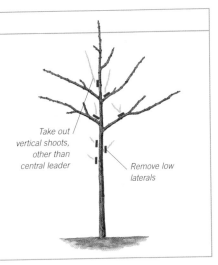

Take out vertical shoots, other than central leader

Remove low laterals

## RECOMMENDED CULTIVARS

**'Broadview'** *Relatively compact and early into bearing after only four or five years; has resistance to walnut leaf blight.*

**'Buccaneer'** *Round nuts, good for pickling. Vigorous, but early into bearing.*

**'Franquette'** *Reliable with good-quality, thin-shelled nuts, but is slow into bearing and makes a large tree.*

**'Lara'** *Heavy cropping and of moderate vigour.*

**'Mayette'** *Produces good-quality nuts, but is slow into bearing and makes a large mature tree.*

**'Parisienne'** *Produces good-quality nuts, but is vigorous and slow into bearing.*

# Almond

The sweet almond (*Prunus dulcis*), which is cultivated for its edible nuts, is closely related to the peach and nectarine (*see pp.193–195*). It originated in central Asia and the eastern Mediterranean. Bitter almonds and many almond seedlings have a high concentration of hydrocyanic acid in their nuts, and so are grown only as ornamental trees.

Almonds have very similar cultivation requirements to peaches. They need a favourable spring and warm, sunny conditions throughout summer and early autumn to produce and ripen good crops. Because they flower in early spring – often even earlier than peaches – they are vulnerable to frost damage in spring. Consequently they do not crop reliably in a cool climate. However, in a sheltered position, they are well worth growing for their ornamental value, with the bonus of nut crops in some years.

Choose a sunny spot sheltered from cold winds (*see pp.12–13*), and avoid frost pockets (*see p.11*). Almonds can be grown on a range of soils provided that they are well-drained, ideally with a pH of approximately 6.5.

## TREE FORMS AND ROOTSTOCKS

The two most successful forms for growing almonds are the bush and the fan. Both forms also have excellent ornamental value in the garden, and the fan is particularly useful in a less favourable situation, where the tree can be trained against a warm, south-, southwest-, or west-facing wall or fence. Space bushes 4.5–6m (15–20ft) apart. A fan requires a space 3.5–4.5m (11–15ft) wide and 2–2.5m (6–8ft) high when mature.

**Maturing almonds**
*Almond trees look very similar to peach trees, but need particularly warm conditions to set and ripen their crop reliably. Unlike peaches, the crop does not need thinning.*

Almonds can be grown on St Julien A rootstock, which will produce a medium-sized tree. Seedling peach or almond rootstocks can also be used, but tend to produce a larger tree.

## POLLINATION

Almond cultivars are either self-fertile or partly self-fertile and crop better if they are cross-pollinated. They flower in early spring when pollinating insects are not always active, so it may be necessary to hand pollinate them using a soft brush or a rabbit's tail (*see p.157*).

## PLANTING

Plant (*see pp.158–159*) in the dormant season, preferably in late autumn, since almonds come into growth early. Bare-root plants usually establish well. Container-grown plants also grow away well if not pot-bound. Before planting, prepare the stakes and wires (*see p.162*) for the form you have chosen.

## PRUNING AND TRAINING

Almonds fruit on young wood made the previous season in the same way as peaches and nectarines, and so will need replacement pruning to produce a supply of new wood each year. Prune them in spring and summer to avoid infection from silver leaf (*see p.262*) and bacterial canker (*see p.253*).

For formative pruning of an almond bush, *see pp.166–167*. For established pruning, follow the method for acid cherries (*see pp.191–192*). For formative pruning of a fan, *see p.173*. To prune an established almond fan, follow the method for peaches (*see pp.193–194*).

## ROUTINE CARE

Follow the guidelines under peaches (*see pp.194–195*).

## HARVESTING AND STORING

Almonds start cropping after three or four years, although their yields are unpredictable. When they are ready to harvest, the hulls will crack open and they will fall to the ground. When this starts to happen, pick the remainder and clean them (*see below*). Store them in cool, airy conditions such as in a rodent-proof shed or garage.

## COMMON PROBLEMS

Almonds suffer from similar problems to peaches and nectarines (*see p.195*).

**Cleaning almond fruits**
*Remove the almonds by peeling away the soft husks. Clean them, and dry thoroughly, preferably in the sun, before placing them in a slatted tray or box for storing.*

---

### RECOMMENDED CULTIVARS

In cool climates, the range of cultivars available is quite small.

**'Ingrid'** *Strong-flavoured nuts.*
**'Macrocarpa'** *Not self-fertile, large fruit. Some resistance to peach leaf curl.*
**'Mandaline'** *Self-fertile, pink flowered.*

# GROWING SOFT FRUITS

# Planning

Soft fruits include cane fruits, such as raspberries, blackberries, and hybrid berries; bush fruits, for example red-, white-, and blackcurrants, gooseberries, blueberries and cranberries; and strawberries, which are herbaceous perennials. Of these, strawberries bear fruit the soonest after planting, in just under a year. Most cane fruits crop from the second year after planting; autumn-fruiting raspberries may crop in the same year. For bush fruits, speed of cropping depends on the age of the plant and its fruiting habit. Black-currants and blueberries bear fruit on the current or last season's wood, so may fruit within a year of planting.

**Potted strawberries**
*With their dainty flowers, pendent scarlet fruits, and shapely foliage, strawberries (here 'Gorella') look particularly attractive in pots. They* appreciate the free drainage and the fruits remain free of soil splash and slug damage, although they need extra watering.

## SOFT FRUITS IN THE GARDEN

Soft fruits are highly rewarding. Not only are they at their most flavoursome when eaten straight from the plant, but they are also the most versatile of all the fruits in terms of how they are grown in the garden. They can be positioned in a separate area, possibly in a netted cage to fend off the birds (*see p.209*). An area of 10 x 20m (30 x 70ft) would yield enough fruit for a family of four.

Alternatively they can be mixed with other plants in the ornamental garden to exploit their attractive features: some strawberry cultivars have white and pink flowers, or variegated leaves, while blackberries and hybrid berries have a long, slender habit that makes them ideal for climbing up a fence or archway. This informal

approach may also have the benefit of companion planting, since the mix of plants attracts a wider range of beneficial insects.

Growing soft fruits in containers increases opportunities in the garden and, with greenhouse protection, can extend the season from the usual outdoor span of early summer to mid-autumn to mid-spring to early winter. Suitable containers include hanging baskets, patio pots, and growing bags.

## GOOD SOIL FOR SOFT FRUITS

For details about different soil types, *see p.14*. The ideal soil for soft fruits is

a fertile, well-drained loam about 45cm (18in) deep. Heavy soils require careful management to create a warmer soil with improved drainage. Blackcurrants and blackberries are more tolerant than other soft fruits of wet sites, but still prefer good drainage. Sandy soils will need improvement to increase retention of moisture and nutrients. The addition of organic matter, in the form of garden compost, farmyard manure, or green manures, has the potential to improve most soils. For details on preparing your soil, *see pp.37–40 and p.208*.

## SOIL-BORNE PROBLEMS

Replant diseases (*see also p.261*) may occur when replanting fruit beds, particularly in a mature garden. Caused by soil-borne fungi, the symptoms are stunted growth of successive plantings of the same plant group. Replacing the topsoil overcomes the problem, but it is expensive and hard work. Choosing a vigorous cultivar and planting into a black plastic sheet mulch (*see p.208*) will help mitigate the disease's effects.

Avoid planting strawberries after strawberries or potatoes for at least five years to minimize the possibility

**Hanging garden**
*Make use of hanging baskets to grow strawberries (here 'Viva Rosa'). Plant about 4 or 5 to a 40cm (16in) basket in potting compost, and add water-retaining gel and slow-release fertilizer granules to help the plants thrive.*

of verticillium wilt (*see p.263*), which is also a soil-borne disease. Soil drench formulations containing beneficial micro-organisms are available to redress the balance and revive a "sick soil". Growing soft fruit in containers (*see p.208*) avoids all of these problems.

### NUTRITION AND pH LEVELS

The levels of nutrients in the soil and its acidity or alkalinity affect the growth and productivity of soft fruits. It is worth testing your soil nutrient and pH levels before planting (*see p.17 and p.18*) and monitoring these levels at intervals to avoid under- or overfeeding, both of which can adversely affect crops.

Strawberry crop sites may need to be sampled annually, whereas the woody, longer-living cane and bush fruits may need sampling every three years if the soil was prepared well before planting. Periods of heavy rain and overwet soil conditions, especially when plants are dormant, cause particular nutrients, like nitrogen, to leach out of the soil.

Most soft fruits perform best at a slightly acidic pH 6.2–6.7. Blueberries are an exception, preferring the more acidic pH 4–5.5. An alkaline soil above pH 7 causes manganese and iron to be unavailable to plants and a resulting chlorosis of the leaves will show (*see p.254*). This is especially visible in raspberries, and dieback of sideshoots on cane and bush fruits is another symptom. An acidic soil will cause some minor nutrients to be too readily available at levels toxic to most plants.

### CHOOSING A SITE

A garden fence or wall that faces south-east, south, or south-west provides the warmest and sunniest aspect for soft fruits. The sun ripens growth, especially cane- and bush-fruit wood, encourages healthy flower buds, and gives ripe, flavoursome fruits. Hybrid berries and blackberries tolerate partial shade.

Frost is particularly damaging to soft fruits when they are in blossom as the low temperatures can kill the flowers, causing the loss of the crop. If it is not possible to avoid planting in a frost pocket (*see p.11*), choose more frost-tolerant crops, or later-flowering cultivars. Cane fruits flower later than bush fruits and many strawberries, so

are less susceptible to loss of fruit due to frost. For methods of protecting crops from frost, *see p.209*.

### PROVIDING SHELTER

Soft fruits need shelter (*see pp.12–13*) to prevent strong winds from damaging new growth, flowers, and fruits. Shelter will also increase the local temperature slightly, encouraging pollinating and other beneficial insects, and providing a more favourable environment that leads to less disease, and improved ripening of fruit and stems.

Artificial windbreaks of plastic mesh may be preferred to hedges or used as a temporary measure on the leeward side of a young natural windbreak while it is stilling growing to maturity.

### ALTITUDE AND RAINFALL

Soft fruits can be grown at altitudes of up to 180m (600ft), although they will need sufficient shelter from the stronger winds at such heights. At high altitudes, the temperatures are generally lower and the growing season shorter; bear this in mind when choosing cultivars.

Water is essential for plant growth, including the swelling of the fruit as it ripens, but excessive rainfall – 900mm (36in) or over per year – will cause

nutrients to be lost from the soil and plants, diseases such as botrytis (*see p.252*) to proliferate, and some physical damage, which could also be the entry point for disease infections.

If you live in an area of high rainfall, you may decide to plant soft fruits in a greenhouse or polytunnel, which must be provided with shade and adequate ventilation in summer and winter. Chemical fungicides control diseases encouraged by wet. Some cultivars have some resistance to botrytis diseases.

### PLANNING THE LAYOUT

Once you have found a suitable site for soft fruit, plan the positioning of the plants. This will help you to judge how many plants you can fit in, and ensure that taller plants will not shade others (*see pp.29–30*). A square or rectangular plot will be easier to net against birds. Strawberries are best planted in a bed or area of their own for three or four years before replacing. They can also be included with vegetables so that they can be replanted regularly along with the vegetable rotation. Select cultivars that fruit in succession to extend the season and avoid a glut. Of the soft fruits, only blueberries need another cultivar as a pollinator.

**Wall fruit**
*All the cane fruits and most bush fruits, such as these delicious redcurrants 'Jonkheer van Tets', can be trained against a wall or fence. This is an economical use of space in the garden, ensures that the fruits receive as much sun as possible to ripen them. Plants grown in this way are also easier to net against birds, as well as to harvest.*

# Planting soft fruits

To ensure sound establishment, a good crop of fruits, and maintain healthy plants, it is important to prepare the soil properly before planting (*see pp.37–40*). Growing soft fruits in containers can provide fruit in the short term if long-term soil preparation is needed.

## PREPARING THE SOIL

When you are planting an area with soft fruits, prepare the whole patch rather than individual planting holes. Unless you are following the "no-dig" system (*see p.39*), start by digging over the area, removing any perennial weeds.

Incorporate organic matter before planting to provide a good medium in which the roots can establish. Add additional fertilizer as an insurance to top up nutrient levels. New gardens may need up to one barrowload of organic matter per 3sq m (3sq yd), 35g/sq m (1oz/sq yd) of sulphate of potash, and 15g/sq m (½oz/sq yd) of superphosphate.

There are a number of ways in which to improve less-than-perfect soils (*see pp.22–26*). On heavy soils, mounding the soil up to 20cm (8in) for planting can improve drainage and soil warming and reduce the root rots caused by fungus like *Phytophthora* (*see p.259*). On shallow soils, mounding will improve the local soil depth.

**Planting a bare-root plant**
*In winter, when the plant is dormant, prepare a planting hole large enough to accommodate the roots. Use a cane across the hole to check that the planting level will match the nursery soil mark on the stem once it is firmed in. Hold the plant at this level while you fill in with soil.*

---

**1** **Using a black plastic sheet mulch** will help to warm the soil and suppress weeds. Rake a 10cm (4in) deep bed to a mounded surface. Cut a piece of plastic about 30cm (12in) wider than the bed. With a spade, push the edges of the plastic into a slit trench around the bed.

**2** **Mark out** the planting holes at the correct spacing. Use a garden knife to cut cross-slits at each planting site.

**3** **Dig a hole** large enough to take the rootball. Place the plant (here a bush gooseberry) in the hole, checking that it is at the same depth as it was in its pot. Fill in with soil and firm it in well. Water the plant thoroughly through the planting slits.

---

If you are planting in a raised bed, add bulky organic matter and, in a heavy soil, plenty of grit. To prepare growing bags, plump them up, cut out the number of holes required, and water them if they are dry. For containers, use a mixture of peat-based compost or peat substitute and soil-based compost. Mix coarse bark and grit into the lower levels of large containers to increase drainage. Adding a slow-release fertilizer will provide optimum nutrition.

## CHOOSING AND PLANTING SOFT FRUITS

Start with vigorous, healthy plants from a reliable source. Many soft fruits have certification schemes in which the fruits have been inspected and certified as free of pests and diseases. Plants are supplied with bare roots or in containers. Bare-root plants are usually less costly but can be planted only when dormant – from late autumn to early spring. Autumn is preferable, if the soil is still warm, to promote root establishment. Bare-root strawberry plants (runners) can be planted all the year round (*see p.212*), as can container-grown plants.

It is best to plant bare-root plants as soon as you buy or receive them. If this is not possible, store them with the roots in moist peat or peat substitute in a plastic bag on a concrete floor in an unheated building, or heel them in the garden by digging a shallow trench, placing the roots in the trench, and covering with well-firmed soil. Before planting, soak the roots in water for two hours. Adding a biostimulant, such as seaweed extract, will give faster and improved root growth. As you plant, shake the soil progressively around the roots to avoid any air holes. Firm in each plant carefully, water it thoroughly and then mulch with organic matter.

Container-grown soft fruits should grow away well even in the summer, provided they do not dry out. Rootballs in peat-based composts dry out more than the surrounding soil; to counteract this, plant them slightly deeper to cover the rootball, and apply a mulch. For planting in containers, *see p.36*.

Plant most soft fruits at the depth of their nursery soil mark – plant cane fruits and blackcurrants more deeply.

# General care

Although good soil preparation is the basis for healthy, sound soft fruit plants, a simple programme of routine care will ensure that your plants remain at their optimum health.

## WATERING

Watering is essential to the wellbeing of soft fruits, especially at planting and as fruits swell. Avoid overwatering mature fruit plants, which causes the fruit to rot more readily as it ripens, and reduces the taste and sweetness. It can also result in poor root activity and nutrient loss from the soil.

## FEEDING

The organic matter incorporated before planting needs to be topped up annually with mulches (*see pp.41–42*), usually in early to mid-spring when the soil temperature has started to rise. Hay, which has been shown to break down more readily and release more nutrients than straw, is particularly beneficial.

Green manures (*see p.23*), such as grazing rye, white clover, vetch, and mustard, can be sown around newly planted soft fruit in late summer to avoid creating too much competition. Their flowers will attract beneficial insects, both pollinators and predators, but cut them before they set seed.

Apply any additional dressings of fertilizers (*see pp.20–23*) needed to maintain soil fertility sparingly in order to avoid wastage and pollution of water courses. Use nitrogen and potassium annually in spring or early summer, and phosphorus occasionally in spring. Soil analysis (*see p.17*) is advisable to monitor the soil pH and potassium and phosphorus levels. Growing bags will require liquid feeds after four weeks of growth. To other containers, add a slow-release fertilizer in spring, according to the instructions on the packaging.

## WEED CONTROL

Remove perennial weeds as soon as they become apparent; if left, they will compete with soft fruits for moisture, nutrients, and light, and, since they can prevent air movement around the plant canopy, they may cause damp-related

▲ **Protection from birds**
*Fruit cages for bird protection are available in kit form or you could make a system of sturdy stakes wired together and drape netting over them. Secure the netting to the soil with pegs.*

◀ **Protection from rain**
*A simple raincover, such as plastic sheeting, will protect ripe fruit (here blackberry 'Loch Ness') from being ruined and can extend the fruiting period from late summer into autumn.*

diseases to arise. Annual weeds also compete with the crop for nutrients and water. Although some species may attract beneficial insects and serve as green manure, they should be left only where organic growing systems are carefully managed – and none should be allowed to set seed.

## FROST PROTECTION

To protect flowers and young fruits against frost damage, you may be able to cover soft fruit bushes with hessian or fleece. Since they are low-growing, strawberries can be covered with fleece or cloches, with the addition of some newspaper if the frost is severe. Move container-grown fruits under cover.

## SOFT FRUIT PROBLEMS

If proper care is taken over preparation of the site, over planting, training and pruning, and routine care, the incidence of pests and diseases will be reduced. Overfeeding with nitrogen will cause soft growth that attracts sucking insects such as aphids (*see p.251*).

If problems do occur, choose an appropriate method of control – either chemical methods or exploiting natural predators with use of biological controls (*see p.52*). Always follow the supplier's instructions with care.

Soft fruits are particularly prone to attack from birds, which are attracted by the colour and smell of ripening

and over-ripe fruit, and eat soft fruit as a source of water as well as food. The most effective way to protect ripening fruit is in a fruit cage. This may also be needed in winter when birds such as bullfinches eat the following year's fruit buds, especially of gooseberries.

Fruit cages can be bought in kit form in all shapes and sizes. For the most basic cage, you can erect corner posts and put flower pots or plastic bottles over the tops of the posts to support the netting. A fine woven mesh will keep out insect pests (and any beneficial insects), but roll the netting up at the sides at flowering time so pollinators can enter. Remove the netting when the plants are not at risk from birds.

Netting draped over plants is less expensive than a fruit cage, but needs to be removed to give access to pick the fruit and, unless it is very well-secured, birds will find their way in. Noisy bird scarers can be effective, but may irritate you and the neighbours. A line that hums in a slight wind can be strung across the garden, emitting sound that disturbs birds, but other animals, including pets, will also be affected. Container-grown soft fruits can be brought under cover for protection as their fruits ripen.

For other problems that may be likely to affect soft fruits, *see individual crops, pp.211–226*.

## PRUNING SOFT FRUITS

Soft fruits require dead, diseased, and damaged growth to be removed to maintain health and vigour. Pruning at planting reduces the need for water until the roots are established. Pruning also encourages productivity. Crown thinning of strawberries (*see p.213*) and spur pruning (*see below*) of gooseberries improve air circulation as well as flower quality and fruit size by regulating the numbers of flower buds. Fruit size is an important consideration when exhibiting soft fruits at shows.

Pruning is also vital for creating and maintaining the shape of woody soft fruits. On a basic level, the removal of crowded and crossing branches ensures that the plant has a balanced shape. Replacement pruning to produce new growth can also break the lifecycle of some diseases, like American gooseberry mildew (*see p.251*) on gooseberries and blackcurrants, and coral spot (*see p.254*) on red- and whitecurrants. Some bush fruits, such as gooseberries and red- and whitecurrants, may also be pruned and trained into cordon or fan shapes to make use of a wall or fence, for ease of fruit picking and management, and for a more decorative effect.

Since cane fruits (except autumn-fruiting raspberries) produce their fruits on the previous year's wood, they need annual pruning to remove the fruited wood. Strawberries also need routine pruning in the form of removal of their runners as they appear (*see below*).

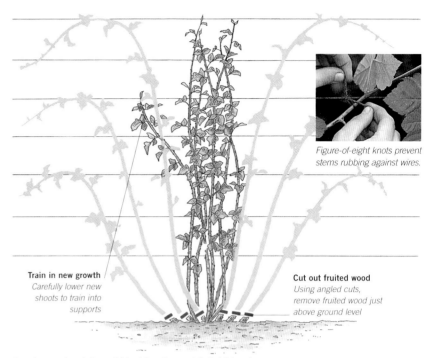

**Train in new growth**
*Carefully lower new shoots to train into supports*

*Figure-of-eight knots prevent stems rubbing against wires.*

**Cut out fruited wood**
*Using angled cuts, remove fruited wood just above ground level*

### Pruning and training of blackberries and hybrid berries
*This basic method shows how the new season's shoots are trained in vertically at the centre of the plant. Once the previous season's shoots have fruited, they can be cut out. The new season's shoots can be lowered and tied in to the support wires as replacements when growth restarts in spring. There are several other ways of training cane fruits (see p.216).*

## TRAINING AND SUPPORT SYSTEMS

Training goes hand in hand with pruning. It is needed to form the basic shape of woody soft fruit plants, and, for those grown against supports – such as cane fruits, and fan- and cordon-trained bush fruits – it is the means of maintaining the plant shape.

### Pruning strawberries
*Rooted runners affect the size and quality of fruit on the parent plant by competing for water, light, and nutrients. Remove the runners before they have rooted by cutting or pinching them out close to the parent plant.*

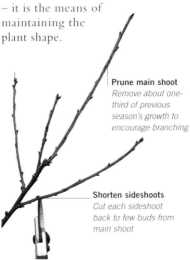

**Prune main shoot**
*Remove about one-third of previous season's growth to encourage branching*

**Shorten sideshoots**
*Cut each sideshoot back to few buds from main shoot*

### Spur pruning bush fruits
*When forming a permanent framework of fruiting branches on a red- or whitecurrant or gooseberry bush, aim to produce a system of short, fruiting spurs on the main shoot by reducing long sideshoots in winter.*

Cane fruits are traditionally trained on a freestanding post-and-wire support system to avoid breakage of the canes and to keep fruit off the soil. There are several ways of erecting the posts and horizontal galvanized wires according to preference and the number of plants being grown (*see p.216*). Wires can also be attached to fences and walls using vine eyes. Allow up to 10cm (4in) between the wires and the supporting structure so that air can circulate.

The use of wooden trellis, pergolas, and arches will show off cane fruits to good effect in the ornamental garden. Planting cane fruits by a single post and training them around it will use less space, but demands careful training to keep the canes within bounds.

Bush fruits, such as blackcurrants and blueberries, are usually grown as stooled plants, meaning that new stems grow from below ground to maintain vigour. These need no training. Gooseberries, redcurrants, and whitecurrants are generally trained as a bush form on a short stem, or leg, to reduce vigour. Where they are trained as fans or cordons, they require a system of wire supports on posts or against a fence.

# SOFT FRUIT CROPS
## Strawberry

Strawberries are renowned for their succulent and sweetly flavoursome fruits. They can be enjoyed for up to ten months of the year, from early spring to early winter, by planting a variety of cultivars and judicious use of containers and protective covers.

The cultivated strawberry, *Fragaria x ananassa* (pineapple strawberry), is the result of a cross between the Chilean strawberry *Fragaria chiloensis* and the North American meadow strawberry *Fragaria virginiana* (first reported in 1766). Breeders have since created a vast range of more productive, better tasting, and larger-fruited cultivars. Strawberries are commonly grown in temperate regions as a hardy herbaceous perennial that may crop for up to four years. In warmer regions, they are often grown as annuals where they produce very high yields of quality fruit over an extended season.

Cultivars are grouped according to their season of fruiting. "Summer bearers" produce flower buds in the short days of late summer and early autumn; "perpetual" (remontant) types

**Pretty and productive**
*The pink-flowered strawberries, such as 'Viva Rosa', shown here, add interest to the fruit garden. They can also be used to great effect to edge ornamental borders, and when grown in patio pots and hanging baskets.*

usually form flower buds in the longer days of summer. Alpine strawberries (*see p.214*) are a selection of the wild strawberry *Fragaria vesca* subsp. *alpina*. They make an attractive ornamental edging for the border, and the fruits, although small, are fragrant and sweet.

Strawberry plants are inexpensive, compact, and versatile. Planting them direct into garden soil, either in flat or raised beds, allows unrestricted root growth, which benefits perennial crops. Strawberry beds usually last for three or four years with the plants in good health and cropping well before they need replanting. Strawberry plants can also be incorporated with the vegetable rotation and replanted annually. Raised beds can improve drainage on heavy soils, increase rooting depth on stony ground, and, if covered with a sheet mulch (*see box, right*), can be used to extend the growing season.

Another way of extending the season is to grow strawberries in containers, such as hanging baskets, windowboxes, tubs, and growing bags. As well as being free of soil-borne problems, container plants can be raised up off the ground for easier maintenance and picking, placed under cover to protect them from the weather, and moved around the garden as you wish.

With their pretty flowers, sometimes variegated foliage, and red and white fruits, strawberries are too versatile to be confined to the fruit patch. Try pink- and white-flowered cultivars with trailing Artic raspberries for a productive and colourful container.

### WHICH SHEET MULCH?

- **Plastic sheet mulches** control annual, and most perennial, weeds and allow early soil preparation for planting. All plastic mulches need to be laid as tight to the soil as possible throughout the life of the crop to avoid surface puddles forming and encouraging rotten fruit. Laying the sheet in warm weather helps to keep it tight.
- **Black plastic** warms the soil, helping to bring forward cropping, but may become too hot in summer and cook the fruits.
- **Coloured plastics** generally stay cool by transmitting heat into the soil and can bring forward cropping by up to four days.
- **White plastic** and other reflective plastics keep soil cooler so delay the start of fruiting, but increase light levels in the crop's canopy, helping photosynthesis and fruit ripening. Research has shown that aphid numbers and consequent virus infections have been considerably reduced where reflective mulches have been used.

**Hanging strawberry planter**
*Suspended from a firm support, a standard growing bag can be used as a hanging planter for strawberries. Place the growing bag in a sunny location outdoors, or keep it under cover to obtain early fruits.*

## Planting strawberries in a flat bed

**1 Mark out a planting row** with a garden line in well-prepared and levelled ground. Measure out planting holes for each strawberry plant at 30–38cm (12–15in) intervals.

**2 Plant a runner** at each of the marked points. Avoid constricting or bending the roots, trimming any over-long roots to no less than 10cm (4in) if necessary.

**3 Ensure that the crown** of each plant is level with the surface. Fill in the hole and firm in with your fingers. Test whether the plant is sufficiently firm by gently pulling at a leaf.

**4 Water the row** of runners thoroughly to settle the soil around the roots. After planting, keep all the plants well watered, especially while they are starting to produce new leaves.

### PREPARING STRAWBERRY BEDS

Strawberries thrive in a free-draining, fertile loam, so prepare the soil well before planting (see p.208). Develop good soil structure for root growth and free drainage, discouraging soil-borne diseases that thrive in waterlogged conditions. For the best growth and fruit flavours, avoid planting in shade. Mix in plenty of well-rotted organic matter – to a spit's depth on clay and sandy soils. Dig out perennial weeds or treat them with a systemic chemical weedkiller well before planting, when they are in active growth.

When growing strawberries through a sheet mulch on a raised bed, keep the plastic taut so that it is effective in warming the soil. Prepare the soil underneath to a fine tilth to ensure a snug fit, and mound it so that water will run off the plastic. Plastic mulches conserve existing moisture in the soil, but the plants will soon fill the planting holes and prevent the penetration of sufficient water to the roots. They will need additional watering during hot, dry weather and when the fruits are swelling, so you will need to install a watering system. This could be through plant pots sunk through the plastic into the raised bed or via a low-pressure watering system underneath the plastic.

### PLANTING

Traditionally bare-rooted strawberry runners are planted in beds. Buy in new plants from a certified source for successful crops.

Late-summer plantings of summer bearers establish well and fruit in the following year; autumn and spring plantings should have their first flush of flowers removed so the plants crop well in their second year. Perpetuals are best planted in autumn or spring. Cold-stored runners, frozen at –2°C (28°F) after lifting from nurseries, are available for planting out from late spring to midsummer. If watered with a fine spray until established, they should crop well in 60 days. They revert to the usual season of fruiting in the second year. When planting bare-rooted runners

**Planting through a sheet mulch**
*To plant through a plastic sheet mulch, spread the sheeting tautly over a mounded bed that is 10–20cm (4–6in) deep and 1.2m (4ft) wide. Cut cross-slits in 2 rows at 30–38cm (12–15in) staggered intervals. Plant each strawberry at least as deep as it was in its pot. Firm; water.*

in flat beds, first rake over the bed, then plant as shown above. Alternatively, plant in a raised bed through a sheet mulch (see left). It is easier in both cases to insert plants with a special planting fork, using the fork to straighten out the roots in the soil. Ensure that the crown is at soil level with its top uncovered so that it does not rot.

In containers, use a loam-based potting compost or add water-retentive granules to a soilless compost to reduce the need for watering. Installing an automatic low-pressure watering system or a reservoir and wick system can also help, but beware of overwatering.

### ROUTINE CARE

Keep plants well watered after planting until they produce new leaves; during dry spells and as the fruit is ripening to improve crop yields; and in early autumn for summer bearers to ensure a healthy supply of flower buds for the following year. Once the fruits have formed, avoid watering plants overhead, especially late in the day, in case the damp encourages botrytis (see p.252) and slugs (see p.262) on the fruits.

Fruiting plants often need liquid feed through the watering system. Using tomato feeds with a high potash content during the growing season will markedly improve flower quality and the flavour and colour of the fruit. Those in growing bags will need a balanced

liquid feed after four weeks of growth and until flowering. From then to the end of harvest use a tomato feed, then revert to the balanced feed.

The use of sheet mulches and of containers will keep plants neat, giving good flower and fruit quality. Where the runners that arise naturally from strawberry plants root, they compete for water, nutrients, and light. Unless they are needed for propagation (*see p.214*), remove them as they appear (*see p.210*).

In early spring, tidy plants to make way for new leaves (*see right*). Crown numbers will increase as the plants get older and may need to be thinned out at the same time (*see right*).

### PROTECTING THE CROP

Protective coverings can be used to extend the fruiting period and protect ripening fruit from the weather and birds. Covering outdoor plants in the early spring with a tunnel cloche (*see pp.46–47*), at least 45cm (18in) wide and 30cm (12in) high, or a fleece (*see p.48*) will encourage flowering and hence fruiting about seven days earlier.

The fleece can be laid over the plants or, for added frost protection, raised on wire hoops. Lift the covering during the day at flowering to allow access by pollinating insects. Similar protection in early autumn will shield late fruit from the effects of rain and cold.

## Tidying and thinning strawberry plants

**1** **Tidy up** strawberry plants in early spring. Retaining the leaves over the winter affords some protection from cold weather, and the increase in light and air to the plant after tidying encourages healthy new growth. Pinch out or cut off all dead, damaged, or diseased leaves and old runners and fruits to eliminate any pests and diseases. The healthier the remaining leaves, the better the development of new leaves, flower buds, and roots.

**2** **Thin out crown numbers** as the plants get older. A crown is formed by a cluster of leaves arising from a growing point at the base of the plant. Pull off the smaller crowns at the base to leave 3 or 4 crowns per plant. This will concentrate the plant's energies into producing good-sized fruits.

The developing fruits will also need protection. To protect the crop from birds, drape a fruit net on posts about 1.2m (4ft) high over the crop. Use wire netting if squirrels are a problem. You also need to keep individual fruits clean of soil. Sheet mulches will prevent soil splash on raised beds. Crops on the flat need to be protected by a mulch of straw or bracken, or a strawberry mat (*see below*). Straw can be a source of botrytis (*see p.252*) and home to slugs when wet, and should therefore be removed in the autumn.

Covering some strawberry plants in late winter with a 20–30cm (8–12in) deep layer of straw (secured with netting if exposed), or an opaque white plastic sheet, will delay flowering by seven days by trapping cold in the soil. This slightly extends the fruiting season. Remove the covering in late spring so the plants resume normal growth.

### CONTAINER-GROWN STRAWBERRIES

To extend the fruiting season further, move plants in containers into a frost-free greenhouse or conservatory in late winter. Heating it to a minimum of 10°C (50°F) will bring forward the time of flowering, but air temperatures should not exceed 16°C (61°F) until flowering to avoid flower blindness (when flowers do not form). Increase the temperature to 16°C (61°F) at flowering to enhance the flowers' ability to pollinate and set fruit. If pollinating insects are in short supply, use hatching fishing maggots to provide flies for pollination. You may prefer to hand-pollinate, using a paintbrush or a hair dryer to redistribute the pollen between the flowers. After fruit set, maintain a temperature of 17°C (63°F) and ventilate at 20°C (68°F) until harvest.

To enhance growth of new leaves and of flower buds for the following year, continue watering and feeding

## Protecting the fruits

**Using a straw mulch**
*Tuck clean straw under developing fruits to protect them from soil splash. On black plastic sheet mulches, this also prevents the fruits from being scorched.*

**Using strawberry mats**
*These fibre mats are often easier to buy and use than straw, and last longer. Put a mat around each plant. Use in early autumn to protect late fruits from rain and cold weather.*

until early autumn and, for perpetuals, until the end of harvest. Allow all plants to experience the winter cold; most need a spell at cold temperatures to break plant dormancy and stimulate flowers and growth in the new season.

## PROPAGATION

Strawberries are fairly easy to propagate by transplanting rooted runner into pots. Choose only those from the previous year's certified plants that are free from aphids (which carry viruses). If you use runners from an older crop, there is no guarantee they will be free from disease, especially viruses.

## HARVESTING AND STORING STRAWBERRIES

Bare-root runners, if planted in late summer, and runners propagated in pots and planted in early spring, will fruit in the new season. Expect to pick 450g (1lb) or more of fruit per plant from healthy plants. Picking when daytime temperatures are high

---

### RECOMMENDED STRAWBERRY CULTIVARS

**Summer bearers**

**'Alice'** ♀ *Mid-late season, good flavour and yield. Good resistance to verticilium wilt.*
**'Cambridge Favourite'** ♀ *Mid-season. Excellent flavour.*
**'Hapil'** ♀ *Mid-season. Orange-red fruits. Ideal for dry soils. Heavy yields.*
**'Honeoye'** ♀ *Early. Firm, dark red fruits.*
**'Pegasus'** ♀ *Mid-season. Good tolerance of pests and diseases.*
**'Symphony'** ♀ *Late season. Firm, regular-shaped fruits. Resistant to red core and vine weevil; prone to powdery mildew.*

**Perpetuals**

**'Aromel'** ♀ *Fruits twice a year. Remove flowers in May for good autumn crop. Superb flavour.*
**'Baron Solemacher'** *Neat clump with no runners. Alpine strawberry flavour.*
**'Bolero'** *Moderate resistance to verticillium wilt. Regular conical shape. Excellent taste.*
*Fragaria vesca* **'Mara des Bois'** *Alpine strawberry flavour and good-sized fruit. Resistant to powdery mildew.*
**'Viva Rosa'** *Large pink flowers and fruit up to the first autumn frosts.*

---

gives juicy, sweet-flavoured fruits. Harvest fruits when they are fully coloured and eat them as soon as possible, otherwise they may continue to ripen after picking.

To store strawberries, pick them when the fruit has a white tip and is slightly unripe, cool them quickly, and keep for a few days at 2–4°C (36–39°F). Strawberries can be frozen but not

many cultivars remain intact and look appetizing after they have been thawed out; an exception is 'Totem'.

## COMMON PROBLEMS

Monitor for pests and diseases all year round, especially in the greenhouse. Particular problems that may affect strawberries are viruses and botrytis. Strawberry viruses (*see p.263*) can be minimized by planting only plants that have been certified virus-free and by controlling aphids (*see p.251*). To avoid botrytis (*see p.252*), maintain dry foliage and good ventilation around the plants. Remove any overripe or mouldy fruits.

Other likely problems include birds (*see p.209 and p.252*), squirrels (*see p.262*), verticillium wilt (*see p.263*), strawberry seed beetle (*see p.263*) and red core (*see p.261*). If red spider mite (including the glasshouse species) is a problem, buy in natural predators (*see p.261*). Avoid wet mulches if slugs and snails (*p.262*) are present, and encourage natural predators. Plastic sheet mulches can harbour vine weevil (*p.263*). To avoid powdery mildew (*p.260*), which affects protected crops and perpetuals, maintain good ventilation and watering.

Strawberry blossom weevil may affect late-summer fruiting cultivars. The weevils nip off individual flowers, reducing the crop. If the problem is not serious, beneficial insects may be able to control the weevils. Otherwise, use an insecticide spray, before flowers open and avoiding pollinating insects. The capsid bug (*p.253*) may cause fruit malformation on perpetuals. Pick off any insects as you see them.

---

### ALPINE STRAWBERRIES

These attractive and fragrant miniature strawberries are best grown from seed and replanted every two years or so. Once the seeds have germinated, prick them out. Harden off both autumn and spring sowings

to plant out in late spring. Allow 30cm (12in) between plants and 75cm (30in) between rows. Harvest the ripe fruits in the evening, crush them, add sugar, and leave overnight to develop their full flavour.

▶ **Dainty crop**
*Alpine strawberries are quite hardy and will happily seed themselves around the garden. The tiny fruits are not as sweet as those of garden cultivars, but nonetheless a useful crop. The plants also make a good ground cover in a potager garden.*

◀ **Raising from seed**
*Collect seeds from dried alpine strawberries, removing them by rolling the fruits between thumb and fingers (see left). Keep in a paper packet in a cool, dry place. Sow the seed in autumn or spring in seed compost, covered with sharp sand. Keep shaded at 18–24°C (65–75°F).*

# Raspberry, blackberry, and hybrid berries

Cane fruits are so called because they flower and fruit on sideshoots of long, vigorous canes. These fruits include raspberries (*Rubus idaeus*), blackberries (*R. fruticosus*), and many hybrid berries. The hybrids include loganberries, boysenberries, and tayberries, among others, and result from crosses between species within the *Rubus* genus. Some are less vigorous than blackberries, while others are thornless – both qualities making them ideal for the fruit or ornamental garden. They have the same cultivation needs as blackberries.

Raspberries have a life expectancy of up to ten years, while blackberries may remain productive for 15 years. Most cane fruits flower and fruit on canes produced in the previous year; autumn-fruiting cultivars fruit on canes grown in the same year. Raspberries produce upright growth – with the exception of the Artic raspberry, which has trailing canes ideal for ground cover. Hybrid berries and blackberries have longer growth, requiring more attention to training and support to keep it off the soil. Cane fruits are a useful addition to the fruit garden since they flower later than most other fruits and so usually avoid frost damage. Fruiting is from

## Types of cane fruit berry

Raspberry · Blackberry · Loganberry · Boysenberry · Tayberry

midsummer to early autumn. With some protection from frosts and cold, autumn-fruiting raspberries can fruit into early winter, and when summer-fruiting cane fruits are potted up and brought under protection in midwinter they can be forced, with gentle heat, to produce fruit by mid-spring (*see below*). It is feasible for the amateur to produce these succulent fruits for eight or nine months of the year. The fruits also store well when frozen.

Cane fruits like full sun but blackberries tolerate partial shade, particularly where the summer temperatures are high. Shelter from wind (*see pp.12–13*) is important to reduce damage to fruiting canes.

### PREPARING THE SITE

Plant quality, good soil drainage, and depth of planting are critical for the success of cane fruits. To prepare the soil, start by digging the whole area (*see pp.37–40*) and removing weeds. Incorporate organic matter such as well-rotted manure or compost. A soil analysis (*see p.17*) will indicate whether more fertilizer, particularly phosphate and potash, needs to be added.

Raspberries in particular require good drainage (*see p.16*). On heavy soils, cane fruits can be planted in a raised bed to improve drainage, soil warming, and rooting depth. Autumn-fruiting raspberries need a warm, sunny position to ripen before the first frosts.

Think at this stage about what kind of support structure you would like to use (*see p.216*), although erection of the support systems can wait until the autumn following planting. Cane fruits are traditionally planted in rows with freestanding supports to prevent wind damage; it is also possible to train them on horizontal wires against a wall or fence. Raspberries are usually planted to form continuous rows of canes, while, for ease of training, blackberries and hybrids are planted and maintained as individual plants.

Planting and training in a spiral around a single, stout post (less vigorous cultivars, for example the thornless loganberry are best for this) or vertically up an arch (*see p.216*) are other space-saving options that add an interesting feature to the garden, making the most of the plants' decorative features. For example, the blackberry 'Veronique' has

## Potting early raspberry canes

**1** **In midwinter**, lift unpruned canes and trim off any dead or damaged wood. Check that each plant has at least 1 good bud on the roots and a good root system. Pot 2 or 3 canes into a 10 litre (10in) pot, using a light, free-draining potting compost. Fill around the roots with compost, ensuring the rootball is about 5–8cm (2–3in) below soil level, firm well, and water in.

**2** **Cut the canes** to a bud at about 1.2m (4ft). Grow under protection for a crop in mid-spring. For pollination and fruit set, either introduce insects or use a hair dryer on a cool setting to redistribute pollen at flowering.

pink-purple flowers, while blackberry 'Oregon Thornless' has attractively cut leaves with good autumn colour.

## CHOOSING PLANTS

Choose plants from a certified source so that they are vigorous, free of pests and diseases, and of a named cultivar. Each new plant should have a stem of pencil thickness, or 7–10mm (¼–½in), with a fibrous root system showing at least one white bud. This bud should produce a new cane soon after planting.

Raspberries may be bought bare-root or container-grown; blackberries and hybrid berries are usually bought as container-grown plants. Plant bare-root raspberry canes in late autumn or early in winter. If soil conditions are poor, with freezing or waterlogging, delay planting to late winter or early spring. Container-grown plants can be planted at any time of the year.

## PLANTING RASPBERRIES

When planting, space raspberry plants 35–45cm (14–18in) apart along the row. The space between rows depends on the vigour of the cultivar; allow 1.5–2m (5–6ft) for summer-fruiting cultivars. A row of autumn-fruiting raspberries needs to be at least 2m (6ft) away from other fruits; the wider row is to produce enough fruit at each picking since autumn-fruiting raspberries crop less abundantly than others.

To encourage new canes to emerge and grow to their optimum height, plant raspberries no deeper than 5–8cm (2–3in); use the soil mark on the stem as a guide. On bare-root plants, cut any long roots back to 20cm (8in) before planting to promote new root growth, and spread the roots horizontally. After firming in, cut the cane to 30cm (12in) from soil level; leave the cane unpruned

on container-grown plants since the root system is already well-established.

Raspberries can also be planted in containers for early fruits (see p.215), or to overcome poor soil conditions, such as drainage. The pots can be brought in from the risk of frost when in flower.

## PLANTING BLACKBERRIES AND HYBRID BERRIES

Prepare the ground (see pp.37–40). It is simplest to erect the supports before planting since the canes will require support in their first summer. Spacing for blackberries and hybrid berries varies widely. A moderately vigorous cultivar needs 2.5–3.5m (8–11ft) between plants. A particularly vigorous blackberry cultivar may need up to 4.5m (13ft) to allow enough space to train the much longer canes. Plant the canes so that the rootball is covered with about 8cm (3in) of soil.

---

## Supports for summer-fruiting raspberries, blackberries, and hybrids

These systems are all ideal for summer-fruiting raspberries, while the stool system is best for blackberries and hybrid berries. All cane fruits can be grown over an arch to form a compact and decorative feature. Of the row systems, the hedgerow system takes the least space and produces the highest yield. The stool system is the easiest to manage, with good light and air and access for weed control. For supports, use preservative-treated posts 75mm (3in) in diameter and 2.5m (8ft) long (75cm/30in driven into the soil) at the ends of rows, plus intermediate posts up to 10m (30ft) apart if needed. Use galvanized 12 gauge or 3.5mm (⅛in) thick wires.

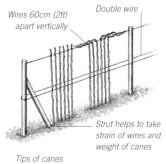

Wires 60cm (2ft) apart vertically
Double wire

### Hedgerow system

After fruiting, cut out unwanted canes and tie in new canes 10cm (4in) apart to the 2 sets of wires. Prune the tops of the canes to 15cm (6in) above the top wire in early spring or, for a higher yield, twist them in.

Strut helps to take strain of wires and weight of canes

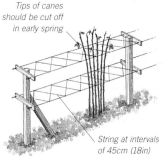

Tips of canes should be cut off in early spring

### Double post-and-wire system

Tie strings between 2 wires to create a support "net" for new canes. Use a second tier of wires and string for strong cultivars. The fruit canes are not tied in, so this method is not suitable for windy sites.

String at intervals of 45cm (18in)

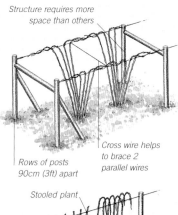

Structure requires more space than others

Cross wire helps to brace 2 parallel wires

Rows of posts 90cm (3ft) apart

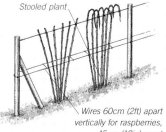

Stooled plant

Wires 60cm (2ft) apart vertically for raspberries, 45cm (18in) apart for blackberries

Canes firmly tied to support with string

### Scandinavian system

Wrap new canes around 1 of the 2 parallel wires and tie them in to form a V-shaped row. The following year's canes will grow up through the centre of the fruiting canes, allowing you clear access for picking the fruit.

### Stool system

Remove all but 6 or 7 canes per plant, and tie these to the wires in a fan shape to give improved ventilation and light levels. Prune the tops of canes to 15cm (6in) above the top wire or loop them over and tie in (see also p.210).

### Training over an arch

Train new canes over the arch and tie them in with garden twine. There should be no need to trim the cane tops. With this system, it may be difficult to separate fruiting and non-fruiting canes, so picking may be less easy.

**Looping canes over wires**

*When training in the new raspberry canes that remain after the fruited canes have been removed, loop over the long, pliable canes and tie them in with a figure-of-eight knot to the top wire. This keeps them secure against winter winds. Tip prune any weaker canes.*

## TRAINING CANE FRUITS

Careful training is essential for healthy, productive cane fruits. It helps to protect the canes from wind damage, and separates the new from the fruiting canes, making harvesting and pruning easier and decreasing the risk of diseases passing from old to new canes. Training also allows sufficient light and air to circulate around the canes, discouraging pests and diseases.

There are several training systems from which to choose (*see facing page*); you need to consider the space available and vigour of the cultivar.

Since blackberries and hybrid berries tend to be more vigorous than raspberries, they require more training. There are several training systems that leave room for new canes that will bear next year's crop to grow upwards and be kept separate from currently fruiting canes. A basic fan shape (*see p.210*) is good for less vigorous cultivars; new canes grow up through the centre. Fruiting canes can also be trained in one direction along the wires to leave space for training the new canes in the opposite direction. Vigorous cultivars with pliable canes can be woven in horizontal wave shapes and attached to the wires to save space; again, the new canes grow up through the middle. Wear gloves to handle cultivars with thorns. Thornless cultivars are more amenable to work with and safer when grown over a structure such as an arch.

Raspberries can also be woven, or looped over (*see above*) for the winter. Tip prune the canes in spring to about 15cm (6in) above the topmost wire. Autumn-fruiting raspberries do not need such elaborate supports because their canes are cut down over the winter. A post and single string system along either side of the row should support canes with ripening fruit and stop them flopping over.

## PRUNING CANE FRUITS

Pruning is important to remove fruited canes and promote new cane growth from the roots. If left, the old canes can be a source of pests and diseases; also, they can suffer from windrock, where the wind causes the rocking cane to create a hole at soil level that fills with water, causing the roots to die.

Canes of summer-fruiting raspberries flower and fruit in their second year. Cut off those that have fruited at soil level in early to mid-autumn. Select new canes of pencil thickness and thicker and tie or train them into the supports. Remove thin canes and any that do not reach the lowest support wire or are growing more than 20cm (8in) away from the centre of the row.

To reduce the egg-laying activity of the raspberry cane midge, which causes raspberry cane blight (*see p.260*), cut off new canes of summer raspberries when they are 20cm (8in) tall. New growth will emerge about two weeks later; the delay will be enough to allow fruit to be picked from the previous year's wood, while the new shoot tips will often emerge after the egg-laying period of the raspberry cane midge.

Since autumn-fruiting raspberries flower and fruit on canes produced in the same season, all the canes need to be cut off at soil level in late winter. To extend the fruiting period into early winter, immediately remove fruited canes to encourage replacements. Alternatively, for an extra, late spring crop of fruit in the new year, cut off the fruited tips of the canes in late winter.

Prune blackberries and hybrids as for summer-fruiting raspberries, but leave new canes tied together with soft string attached to the wires over winter for frost protection. Untie them and retrain them to replace the old canes in spring just before they start into growth.

**Cutting back canes after fruiting**

*Prune fruited canes to ground level after fruiting, leaving no stubs to harbour rot. With summer-fruiting raspberries, blackberries, and hybrid berries, take care to avoid damaging the new season's canes. Select the best of these to keep and train in, and prune out the others. For autumn-fruiting raspberries, prune out all of the canes.*

## ROUTINE CARE

Watering is particularly beneficial as the fruit starts to change colour, and will markedly improve the size and weight of fruit. Water the soil to avoid wetting the fruit and new canes which could provide a possible site for diseases.

Hoeing off weeds may damage surface roots, so use mulches instead. Apply organic mulches in early spring. A black sheet mulch (*see p.208*) will smother weeds and emerging new canes, allowing only stronger and better quality growth through the planting holes. Top-dress annually in spring with a balanced compound fertilizer (*see p.20*) from the second year onwards.

Control numbers of new canes in the growing season to keep the crop within bounds and to produce fewer but better quality canes for the following year. Summer-fruiting raspberries grown as rows need ten canes per metre (3ft) of row, and stool systems seven to ten canes per stool. The more vigorous blackberries and hybrids can retain up to 24 canes per stool and still fruit well. Remove unwanted new canes by pulling them or digging them out, or cut them off at soil level. Autumn-fruiting canes do not need thinning.

To protect flowers and the soft new cane from frost, drape hessian or fleece over a support structure. Ventilate well during the day. When fruits start to change colour, exclude birds (*see p.209*).

## PROPAGATION

Cane fruits can be propagated by lifting new canes along with their rootballs, cutting them away from the main row of canes, and replanting. Shoot tips of blackberries and hybrid berries root naturally when in contact with the soil. They can be cut away once rooted and replanted. If necessary, pin down shoot ends to encourage rooting. Choose only newly planted, disease-free stock from which to propagate.

## HARVESTING AND STORING CANE FRUITS

Summer cultivars will ripen for picking by midsummer, yielding between 2–3kg (4lb 8oz–6lb 12oz) per metre (3ft) of row. Autumn-fruiting raspberries, yield up to 1kg (2lb 4oz) per metre (3ft) of

row and ripen from late summer to the first frosts. Rain causes fruits to rot and shortens the fruiting period, so a raincover (*see p.209*) will ensure good fruit and may extend fruiting into early winter. Yields from blackberries and hybrids can reach 6.75–9kg per 3m (15–20lb per 10ft) row.

The best time to eat the berries is freshly picked on a warm evening. Pick the fruit every two or three days to prevent any overripe fruit rotting and spreading disease. Fruit can be bagged to avoid desiccation and kept in a fridge for two or three days. It can be frozen for eating and processing when thawed.

### Picking cane fruits

*Pick blackberries* (left) *and hybrid berries complete with core, or plug, and stalk; the core is edible and helps the fruit to keep its shape. Raspberries for show exhibits need to be picked with core and stalk. Pick raspberries for eating and storing by gripping each fruit between the fingertips and, with a gentle squeeze, pulling it from the core. Always inspect fruits for raspberry beetle larvae before eating.*

*Raspberry without core*

*Blackberry with core*

## COMMON PROBLEMS

Cane spot (*see p.253*) and fungal leaf spots (*see p.257*) may affect raspberries; resistant cultivars are available. Raspberries may also suffer from raspberry cane blight (*p.217 and p.260*), raspberry leaf and bud mite (*see pp.261*), birds (*see p.252*) on early raspberries, and raspberry viruses (*see p.261*). Other problems on cane fruits are: raspberry beetle (*see p.260*), raspberry spur blight (*see p.261*), botrytis (*see p.252*), and chlorosis (*see p.254*). Rusts (*pp.261–262*) are unlikely to be serious. Red spider mite (*see p.261*) may affect plants in warm, sheltered sites. Bushy dwarf virus, spread by aphids (*see p.251*), reduces the height and vigour of cane fruits.

---

### RECOMMENDED CANE FRUIT CULTIVARS

**Summer-fruiting raspberry**

**'Glen Ample'** ♀ *Mid-season. Spine-free with long laterals. Heavy yields and good disease resistance.*

**'Leo'** ♀ *Late. Vigorous. Firm, aromatic fruits.*

**'Malling Admiral'** ♀ *Mid-season. Vigorous canes and good-quality, heavy yields.*

**'Malling Jewel'** ♀ *Early. Well-established with compact growth and reasonable yields.*

**'Tulameen'** ♀ *Mid- to late season. Good flavour and yields.*

**Autumn-fruiting raspberry**

**'Autumn Bliss'** ♀ *Heavy crops of large fruits with firm texture and good flavour. Canes need minimum support.*

**'Polka'** ♀ *Heavy crops of good flavour and texture.*

**Blackberry**

**'Karaka Black'** *Moderate vigour. Canes have small thorns. Long, good flavoured fruits.*

**'Loch Ness'** ♀ *Erect, thornless canes. Compact habit.*

**'Oregon Thornless'** *Parsley-shaped leaves with good autumn colour.*

**'Sylvan'** *Good tolerance of heavy soil, wind, and drought. Large fruit. Thorns.*

**'Waldo'** *Thornless with good resistance to cane and leaf spot. Brittle canes. Large fruit.*

**Hybrid berries**

**Boysenberry** *Thornless. Large purplish fruit.*

**Japanese wineberry (Chinese blackberry)** *Canes 2m (6ft) long, covered with soft, red bristles. Fruits golden yellow ripening to red, with a sweet, juicy, and refreshing taste.*

**Loganberry 'LY 59'** ♀ *Thorns. Medium vigour. Long, acidic fruit.*

**Loganberry 'LY 654'** ♀ *Thornless.*

**Tayberry** ♀ *Early, heavy crops. Thorns.*

**Tayberry 'Buckingham'** *Thornless. Sweet-tasting fruit excellent for jam.*

# Gooseberry

Up to 3,000 gooseberry cultivars (*Ribes uva-crispa*) have been recorded since the 1700s and there are currently up to 150 in cultivation. New cultivars overcome some of the hazards of growing gooseberries, such as mildew and leaf spot, and the fierce spines. The berries are the earliest soft fruits of the year, and may be red, green, or yellow and suitable for both cooking and eating fresh as a dessert. The natural growth habit varies from upright to pendent (weeping), depending on the cultivar.

Gooseberries are amenable to various forms of training. A gooseberry is most often grown as a bush on a short "leg" that raises the level of the branches to make fruit picking and care easier. It can also be grown as a standard on a longer leg, or trained on a freestanding support or against a wall as a single-stemmed or multi-stemmed cordon, or fan. On posts and wires in the open, cordons and fans are dramatic features when the sun shines through them.

A standard plant allows the site to be used more efficiently since strawberries, bedding plants, and vegetables can be planted underneath. For a standard, choose a vigorous cultivar, or, if you want to grow a less vigorous one, buy it grafted onto a rootstock of *Ribes aureum*.

## Planting gooseberries

**1** **Dig a hole** large enough for the rootball. Position it so that the soil mark on the stem is level with the surface.
**2** **Fill with soil**, firm, and water. Make sure there is 10–20cm (4–8in) of leg clear below the branches. If planting in autumn or winter, do not prune until spring. If planting in early spring, as here, select 5 main stems; prune to 15–23cm (6–8in). Remove surplus stems.

Gooseberries need good drainage; they tolerate slightly alkaline soils and some shade. Since they flower very early in the year, do not plant them in a frost pocket (*see p.11*). Shelter (*see pp.12–13*) is also needed to protect the brittle new shoots from wind. Gooseberries flourish in containers, a good option where garden soil is poorly drained. Plants in containers brought under cover in late winter will start into growth earlier and crop in the late spring.

One-year-old, fruiting wood

Two-year-old wood

Current season's growth, which will fruit in following year

**The fruiting habit of gooseberries**
*Gooseberries fruit on one-year-old wood and older spurs. Spur pruning encourages fruiting spurs. Renewal pruning (see p.220) removes older wood for a balanced shape.*

### PREPARING THE SITE
Prepare soil by digging in a 2.5–5cm (1–2in) layer of well-rotted organic matter. Double-dig heavy, poorly drained soils (*see p.39*). Before planting, take a soil sample to check pH and nutrient levels (*see p.17*). Incorporate compound granular fertilizer into the top 15–20cm (4–8in) where required.

### PLANTING
Gooseberry bushes can be bought as bare-root or container-grown plants. Choose plants with 10–20cm (4–8in) of clear stem (leg) above the roots, and at least four or five young branches. Bushes grown as standards are also available to purchase ready trained and, where necessary, pre-grafted.

Plant bare-root bushes between autumn and early spring. Container-grown plants can be planted all year round, but need plentiful watering to help the bushes establish. For improved weed control and moisture retention, lay a plastic sheet mulch and plant the gooseberries through slits in the plastic (*see p.208*). Since gooseberries are a long-term crop, lasting up to ten years, the plastic needs to be thick or covered with a layer of bark chippings or gravel.

Plant bushes 1.2–1.5m (4–5ft) apart. Space single-stemmed cordons 30–40cm (12–16in) apart; for a multi-stemmed cordon, allow an extra 30cm (12in) for each additional arm. Space plants to be fan-trained 1.5m (5ft) apart. For standards, stake at planting with a sturdy stake tall

## Renewal pruning an established bush

The primary aim of renewal pruning an established bush is to maintain eight to ten well-spaced branches. The balanced shape allows light and air to penetrate, especially during summer, to encourage new growth and prevent the onset of diseases such as botrytis (*see p.252*) and American gooseberry mildew (*see p.251*). It also makes it easier to pick the fruit.

Prune in early spring to allow the identification and removal of wood that may not have any buds or is dead due to disease. Remove also shoots where the buds look wispy and have not fully closed over winter due to mildew. Additional pruning in summer improves the air circulation, reducing the risk of fungus disease, and produces fewer but larger fruits. Cut back new stems arising from the main stems by half in midsummer. If you wish, you can cut the same stems back to two healthy buds in early spring.

▲ **Removing old branches**
*Use loppers to remove a proportion of old, unproductive branches, cutting them back to their base.*

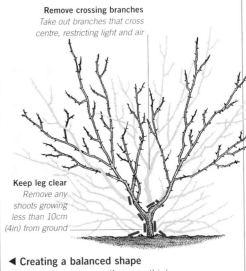

**Remove crossing branches**
*Take out branches that cross centre, restricting light and air*

**Keep leg clear**
*Remove any shoots growing less than 10cm (4in) from ground*

◀ **Creating a balanced shape**
*Aim to remove no more than one-third of branches, including crowded, crossing, weak, and damaged ones.*

---

enough to reach the top of the stem at its final height. For details about how to prepare a container, *see p.208.*

### PRUNING AND TRAINING GOOSEBERRIES
Tailor your pruning cuts to the habit of the cultivar. Cut to an outward-facing bud on an upright cultivar, and to an upward-facing bud on a pendent one.

When pruning a bush after planting (*see p.219*), aim to obtain a vase-shaped bush of four or five evenly spaced branches. Leaving pruning until spring enables the removal of any winter damage, and ensures the good healing of cuts. Prune a two-year-old bush in spring, cutting back the new growth at the end of each branch by half. Cut out any new shoots that are surplus to the permanent framework, and those that are crowding or crossing the centre.

Once the bush is established you can prune it in one of two ways. Renewal pruning (*see above*) aims to encourage new, well-spaced shoot growth, while spur pruning (*see p.210*) is a much more detailed method concentrating on the production of fruiting spurs.

To train a standard, take the strongest vertical stem and tie it to the planting stake. Shorten other shoots to one bud. When the main stem is 60cm–1.2m (2–4ft) tall, cut off the tip. Next year,

select 4–5 evenly spaced shoots near the top of the stem, remove all others, then train as for a bush. Train cordons and fans as for redcurrants (*see pp.221–222*).

### ROUTINE CARE AND PROPAGATION
Water in dry periods, especially as fruits swell, using 25–50 litres/sq m (5.5–11 gallons/sq yd) each time. Gooseberries are prone to potassium deficiency. Add sulphate of potash at 15g/sq m (½oz/ sq yd) in late winter, with a balanced fertilizer. Mulch against weeds in early to mid-spring with a well-rotted manure or compost. A healthy bush will produce fewer suckers – shoots at ground level – than one under stress. Pull off any suckers with a gloved hand; cutting them off will encourage more suckers to grow the following year.

Bring container-grown plants in flower under cover for frost protection. Outside, use fleece or plastic sheeting draped over the plants to protect them from frost or, from winter onwards, to advance the crop. All gooseberries need netting (*see p.209*) against bullfinches, which feed on dormant flower buds in late autumn to mid-spring, and black-birds, which feed on ripening fruit.

To propagate gooseberries, take hardwood cuttings from healthy wood as for blackcurrants (*see p.224*), making the cuttings about 30cm (12in) long.

### HARVESTING GOOSEBERRIES
A mature bush should yield 3.5–4.5kg (7–10lb). A single cordon bears up to 1kg (2lb 4oz). Protected plants ripen fruit by late spring and fruit until early summer. For early fruits for cooking on outdoor plants, thin alternate fruits when they are 12mm (½in) long in early summer. Leave the others to ripen for harvesting later in the summer. Pick fruit with a short stalk, otherwise the skin may tear when pulled off its stalk.

### COMMON PROBLEMS
Problems include gooseberry sawfly (*see p.256*), capsid bug (*see p.253*), American gooseberry mildew (*see p.251*), botrytis (*see p.252*), fungal leaf spot (*see p.257*), aphids (*see p.251*), birds (*see p.252*), squirrels (*see p.262*), caterpillars (*p.253*), and gooseberry dieback (*see p.256*).

---

### RECOMMENDED CULTIVARS

**'Careless'** ♀ *Green culinary cultivar with earliest fruits. Reliable cropping.*

**'Greenfinch'** ♀ *Green culinary cultivar. Resistant to mildew and leaf spot.*

**'Invicta'** ♀ – *Green culinary cultivar. Heavy cropping and mildew-resistant.*

**'Leveller'** ♀ – *Yellow dessert cultivar with excellent flavour. Needs good soil.*

**'Whinham's Industry'** ♀ – *Red culinary or dessert cultivar. Tolerates heavy soils.*

# Redcurrant and whitecurrant

These deciduous shrubs (*Ribes rubrum*) form attractive ornamental plants, especially when the fruits are ripening. Redcurrant cultivars, old and new, display incredible shades of scarlet as the fruit ripens, while whitecurrants are pure white through cream to almost yellow when ripe. The fruits are borne in dense trusses, known as "strigs". The strigs show considerable differences in length and fruit size, and can be used for table decoration as well as in summer puddings, jellies, and sauces.

Red- and whitecurrants fruit at the base of the previous year's shoots, and on spurs on older wood. They can be grown in bush form on a leg, or as single- or multi-stemmed cordons and fans where space is restricted or for their interesting shapes. Growing under cover results in fruits about two weeks earlier than unprotected bushes.

Choose a sunny site with shelter (*see pp.12–13*) from strong winds. Avoid frost pockets (*see p.11*). Partial shade is tolerated and plants can be trained against a north-facing fence or wall; the fruits will be later and have less flavour than those from plants in the sun. A well-drained, fertile soil is needed, with a slightly acid or neutral pH (*see p.18*).

## PREPARING THE SITE AND PLANTING

Soil preparation, planting, and spacing, is as for gooseberries (*see pp.219–220*). Improve poor drainage (*see p.16*) in particular, since red- and whitecurrants do not tolerate waterlogging.

Buy healthy bushes from a reliable source. A one-year-old plant is the least expensive option; two- and three-year-old trained bushes are also available.

Cordons and fans require a support system of horizontal wires, attached to freestanding posts or to a wall or fence. Position the first wire at 60cm (2ft) above soil level, and fix subsequent ones at 60cm (2ft) intervals. On planting, tie the stems and required branches to canes attached to the support wires. For preparing a container, *see p.208*.

## PRUNING AND TRAINING

Pruning of red- and whitecurrants mainly takes place in early spring. Always cut carefully to a healthy bud to promote quick healing, because these plants are particularly prone to botrytis (*see p.252*) and the subsequent coral spot (*see p.254*). In summer it is possible to snap off the new season's growth, and this seems to cause fewer dieback problems than cutting them off. Prune bushes as for gooseberries (*see p.220*).

## PRUNING A REDCURRANT OR A WHITECURRANT CORDON

For pruning and training a single cordon, *see below*. A double cordon has two vertical main shoots in a "U" shape. To start training a double cordon, look for two strong shoots that are nearly opposite each other. Cut back the central shoot to just above the higher of these

---

## Pruning redcurrant cordons

**1** **In early spring** following planting a one-year-old plant, cut the main vertical stem back by half of the previous year's growth. Cut other shoots back to 1 bud.

**2** **In the summer** after planting, shorten the new growth on the shoots. This concentrates the plant's growth on strengthening the main stem rather than on extending the shoots. If the shoots have developed sideshoots, cut or pinch these to 1 leaf. Repeat this pruning each summer.

**3** **In early spring** in subsequent years, keep pruning the new growth on the main vertical stem by a quarter of the previous year's growth, or by half if growth is weak. Cut to a bud on the opposite side to the previous year's cut to keep the growth straight. Once the cordon is at the desired height, cut to 1 bud of new growth each year in early summer. Prune the shoots from the main stem and any other sideshoots to build up fruiting spur systems.

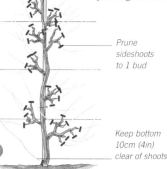

**Pruning spurs**
*Each year cut back the shoots pruned the previous summer to 1 bud. As spur systems build up, thin any unproductive sections by cutting them out.*

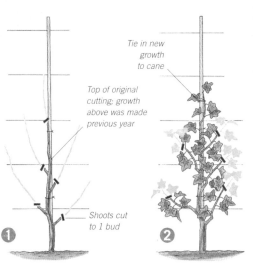

*Tie in new growth to cane*

*Top of original cutting; growth above was made previous year*

*Shoots cut to 1 bud*

① ② ③

**Shorten new shoots**
*When the shoots pruned the previous winter have about 8 leaves, shorten them to 5 leaves, either by breaking them off or pruning the shoots.*

*Prune sideshoots to 1 bud*

*Keep bottom 10cm (4in) clear of shoots*

two. Trim to two leaves any shoots below the chosen two, and remove them altogether in summer. Tie the two shoots to canes fixed to the wires at an angle of 30°. When each shoot tip is 30cm (12in) from the main leg, train the new growth vertically up canes attached to the wires. From then on, treat each vertical arm as a single cordon (*see p.221*). Keep each arm cut to the same height to avoid one growing more dominant than the other.

For a triple cordon, which has a central vertical stem plus one on either side, start by selecting three well-positioned shoots. Train the central one as for a single cordon (*see p.221*), and the shoots on either side as for a double cordon. Keep the middle vertical shoot cut to the same height as the other two so that it does not become dominant. As the three vertical arms develop, prune each as for a single cordon.

## PRUNING AND TRAINING A RED- OR A WHITECURRANT FAN

To train a fan, select up to five strong lateral shoots after planting. Prune out the central vertical stem above the topmost lateral. Train the laterals on either side of the main stem on canes at 45° attached to support wires. Cut each back by half. In summer, select several well-spaced sideshoots on each shoot and train in to form permanent ribs to the fan. Keep the shape balanced, and remove over-vigorous shoots.

In the second spring, shorten shoots and ribs by half and sideshoots to one bud. Fill in gaps by training in more shoots in the following summer for an even framework of shoots of the same

**Fan-trained redcurrant**
*With a fan you are aiming for several well-spaced shoots with permanent sideshoots to fill the available space and provide an even covering. Five main shoots are usually trained, but the number is often determined by the vigour of the new growth, with extra shoots trained to divert excessive vigour. A wall or fence will provide extra shelter for the fan, so that pollination and netting are easier, and the fruit should ripen more quickly.*

length. Prune each permanent shoot as for a cordon (*see p.221*), ensuring that the tips of the main shoots are cut to the same height to stop the middle, vertical stems becoming dominant.

## ROUTINE CARE AND PROPAGATION

In late winter apply 15g/sq m (½oz/ sq yd) of sulphate of potash or bonfire ash. On light sandy or poor soils, apply a balanced compound fertilizer (*see p.20*) at the same time. In early to mid-spring, as the soil starts to warm up, put down a 2.5–5cm (1–2in) thick organic mulch (*see p.41*). In dry conditions, water the soil beforehand, using 25–50 litres/ sq m (5.5–11 gallons/sq yd). Mulch under the plant as far as the furthest tips of the branches. Water with similar amounts of water in summer as fruits start to swell and ripen.

Fork out perennial weeds when the soil is moist or treat them with a systemic chemical weedkiller directed away from the crop. Pull off any suckers by hand. Net the bushes against birds (*see p.209*) as the fruits change colour.

To propagate red- and whitecurrants, take hardwood cuttings about 30cm (12in) long from healthy wood, as for blackcurrants (*see p.224*).

## HARVESTING RED- OR WHITECURRANTS

Plants grown under protection can be ready for picking in early summer. Those grown outside will be ready from mid- to late summer. A mature bush may yield 4–5kg (9–11lb) and a single cordon up to 1kg (2lb 4oz) of fruit. Most cultivars are thin-skinned and it is difficult to pick individual fruits without squashing and tearing them. Instead, use scissors to sever the entire strig from the bush.

## COMMON PROBLEMS

Aphid infestation (*p.251*) is seen as red blistered foliage on young shoots. Other problems include birds (*p.252*), capsid bug (*p.253*), gooseberry sawfly (*p.256*), botrytis (*p.252*), mostly on fruits, coral spot (*p.254*), fungal leaf spots (*p.257*).

**Redcurrant in flower**
*The flowers on this redcurrant are displayed to their best advantage since the plant is trained as a fan. The contrast between the boldly shaped leaves and delicate flowers is one of the more ornamental features of this plant.*

### RECOMMENDED CULTIVARS

**'Blanka'** *Late season. Very long strigs.*
**'Jonkheer van Tets'** ♀ *Very heavy, early crop of large, red berries.*
**'Junifer'** *Earliest ripening with long trusses of high-quality redcurrants. High yielding and good disease resistance.*
**'Red Lake'** ♀ *Heavy crops of long, easy-to-pick strigs of red berries.*
**'Stanza'** ♀ *Mid- to late season berries with good flavour and yields.*
**'Versailles Blanche'** *Large, light yellow, sweet-tasting fruit. Upright growth.*
**'White Grape'** ♀ *Strong, upright growth. Good flavour.*

# Blackcurrant

Easy to grow and very productive, blackcurrants (*Ribes nigrum*) produce delicious clusters, or "strigs", of fruits that are full of vitamin C. They form large, rather straggly bushes that can reach up to 2m (6ft) in height and spread. Their flowers are insignificant but, particularly after rain, the foliage of these deciduous shrubs has a wonderful scent. New cultivars developed in Scotland, known as the Ben Series, possess increased resistance to cold temperatures and, because they flower later than the traditional cultivars such as 'Baldwin' and 'Wellington XXX', the flowers and fruits are likely to survive the spring frosts. Jostaberries, hybrids of blackcurrants and gooseberries, are cultivated as for blackcurrants.

Blackcurrants fruit best on strong, young shoots produced the previous summer and, to a lesser extent, on two-year-old and older wood. They are usually grown as stooled, or multi-stemmed, bushes with plenty of new growth from soil level being stimulated by annual hard pruning. Very vigorous cultivars, such as 'Wellington XXX'

Young wood has smooth, brown bark, and fruits in following year

Two-year-old and older wood has grey, peeling bark

Stalks that carried strigs of fruit may be visible on two-year-old wood

**Stages of growth**
*Aim to keep as much of the smooth, young wood as you can when pruning. Some of the older, peeling wood is cut out, although it will fruit a second time and may bear new shoots.*

## Planting depth for blackcurrants

**▲ Judging the planting depth**
*Use a length of wood across the planting hole to check the planting level. This container-grown bush is being planted 5cm (2in) deeper than it was in its pot.*

**▶ Planting a bare-root bush**
*Make a hole large enough to spread the roots and deep enough to cover the stems to 5cm (2in) above the nursery soil mark, to encourage the basal buds to shoot.*

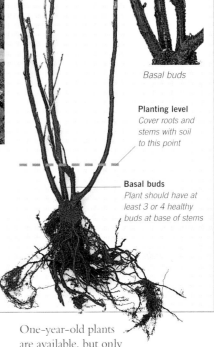

Basal buds

**Planting level**
Cover roots and stems with soil to this point

**Basal buds**
Plant should have at least 3 or 4 healthy buds at base of stems

and 'Ben Nevis', can be grown on a short leg, as for gooseberries (*see p.220*) and redcurrants, to control their growth in restricted spaces, and to provide an attractive, goblet-shaped bush.

Blackcurrants tolerate a wide range of soils, including slightly alkaline ones, but the soil needs to be highly fertile and moisture-retentive. Being heavy feeders, they demand plenty of organic matter to give sufficient nutrients and to hold an adequate supply of water. Slightly impeded drainage is tolerated, but they prefer a site that is free from frost and sheltered from cold, damaging winds (*see pp.12–13*).

An alternative growing method is to plant blackcurrants in containers so that they can be brought under cover to protect them against cold winds at flowering, ensuring good pollination and fruit set. They can also be kept under cover from winter to early summer to bring forward cropping.

### PLANTING
Prepare the soil well by removing perennial weeds (*see p.49*) and digging in a 5cm (2in) layer of well-rotted compost or farmyard manure.

One-year-old plants are available, but only two-year-olds are certified disease-free and of the named cultivar. It is advisable to buy a certified plant to avoid viruses, to which blackcurrants are particularly prone. Plant bare-root plants from autumn to spring, preferably in autumn. Container-grown plants can be planted at any time, but need copious watering to aid establishment in summer.

It is crucial to plant both bare-root and container-grown blackcurrants at about 5cm (2in) lower than the nursery soil mark. This stimulates the plant's natural habit of producing vigorous new shoots from the base; these young shoots are vital to ensure a productive, stooled bush (*see above*). Space plants 1.5–2m (5–6ft) apart, except the dwarf cultivar 'Ben Sarek', which needs only 1.2m (4ft) between plants. For planting in containers, *see p.208*.

### PRUNING AND TRAINING BLACKCURRANTS
When planting a bare-root blackcurrant in winter or spring, cut all shoots back to two buds 2.5cm (1in) above soil level to help the roots establish. If the bush

## Pruning a blackcurrant bush in winter

**◀ Cutting to the base**
*Remove a quarter of stems to within 2.5cm (1in) of soil level to generate young growth. Cut out weak and crowded branches and those drooping towards the soil. Retain a mixture of one-year-old and older wood, both of which can be recognized by their colour (see p.223).*

**◀ Before pruning**
*The centre of this bush is crowded, allowing little light and air to circulate between the stems, and so encouraging disease and making ripening slower.*

**▶ After pruning**
*This pruned bush has a balanced shape, with unproductive older wood removed, and the remaining stems thinned.*

is planted earlier, in autumn, the roots should establish before winter and you can leave half of the shoots unpruned to yield a small crop in the following summer. In general, do not prune container-grown plants after planting; however, if they are planted in the summer and regular watering cannot be guaranteed, prune them as for autumn bare-root plantings so that new growth is initially concentrated in the roots.

Prune established blackcurrant bushes in winter, as shown above. Overgrown and neglected bushes can be renovated by cutting down all of the branches to soil level in autumn, and applying a mulch (*see below*) to provide nutrients for the roots. The subsequent new growth should be thinned to leave 8 to 12 vigorous, young shoots.

### ROUTINE CARE

Apply a balanced compound fertilizer in early spring, plus extra nitrogen at a rate of 25g/sq m (¾oz/sq yd). Spread a thick mulch of mushroom or garden compost, or well-rotted manure, around the plant every spring to provide the required nutrients and suppress weeds.

Blackcurrants need a minimum of 50 litres/sq m (11 gallons/sq yd) at each watering. Frequency of watering will depend on the weather conditions and temperature, but it is particularly essential during dry spells and as the fruits start to swell and colour. To avoid disease infections, attempt to keep the base of the bush dry by watering carefully onto the soil or laying down a low-pressure

watering system (*see p.54*). Birds like to feed on ripe fruit, so it is essential to net blackcurrants (*see p.209*) as fruits ripen.

Repot blackcurrant bushes planted in containers every two or three years. As the plant grows larger and heavier, it may be worth putting the pot on a base with castors so that it is easy to move under cover for protection against frost or for protected cropping.

### PROPAGATION

Prunings from newly planted certified plants can be used to propagate more blackcurrants; avoid using long-established plants that may carry disease. Make each cutting 20cm (8in) long, using a straight cut below a bud at the base, and an angled cut above a bud at the top, removing the soft tip of the shoot. Push the hardwood cutting into the soil or into cuttings compost in a container. The cuttings should root readily and produce several shoots to make a stooled bush.

### HARVESTING

Fruit will ripen from midsummer through to early autumn. Protected crops will ripen about two weeks earlier than those grown outside. Expect to pick at least 4.5kg (10lb) of fruit per bush when established.

Older cultivars have fruits that ripen at different times along the strig. Pick these fruits individually, taking care not to damage them, or they will not store well. The newer Ben Series cultivars are bred to ripen all their fruits together

along the strig. They can therefore be picked as complete strigs, using scissors. Whole strigs are required for showing at competitions.

### COMMON PROBLEMS

Possible problems include aphids (*see p.251*), big bud mite (*see p.252*), American gooseberry mildew (*see p.251*), birds (*see p.252*), blackcurrant gall midge (*see p.252*), capsid bug (*see p.253*), botrytis (*see p.252*), which mostly affects the fruits, and reversion disease (*see p.261*), transmitted by big bud mites. Fungal leaf spots (*see p.257*) may occur but are seldom serious.

### RECOMMENDED CULTIVARS

**'Ben Connan'** ⚥ *Resists blackcurrant gall midge, American gooseberry mildew, and frost. Early to ripen; very large berries of excellent flavour. Compact growth habit.*

**'Ben Gairn'** *Early, compact bush with resistance to reversion virus.*

**'Ben Hope'** *Vigorous, upright bush, resistant to big bud mite.*

**'Ben Lomond'** ⚥ *Susceptible to mildew. Late-flowering and resistant to frost.*

**'Ben Sarek'** ⚥ *Small, compact bush that is resistant to mildew and frost. Spreading branches may need support when fruiting due to large size of fruit.*

**'Ebony'** *Early, open habit, fruits are low in acid and so good for eating fresh.*

**Jostaberry** *This hybrid between a blackcurrant and a gooseberry is resistant to mildew, leaf spots, and big bud mites; has blackcurrant-type fruits, but twice the size. Thornless and very vigorous.*

# Blueberry

American highbush blueberries
(*Vaccinium corymbosum*) are branching,
deciduous shrubs that provide interest
for much of the year, with their white
bell-shaped flowers, dusty blue fruits,
and spectacular autumn colour. Some
cultivars reach 2m (6ft). Blueberries
need a light, free-draining, acid soil
of pH 4–5.5. They prefer sun or partial
shade and are relatively frost-hardy.
Provide shelter (*see pp.12–13*) from cold
winds. For regular, heavier crops, plant
more than one cultivar because they
are only partially self-fertile. Blueberries
may be planted as freestanding bushes,
as part of a hedge, or in a container.

### PLANTING
Soil pH (*see p.18*) is critical, so prepare
for planting well in advance. Neutral
to alkaline soil can be acidified, but this
is laborious and hard to maintain. To
lower the pH of alkaline soil, add peat,
sulphur (as flowers of sulphur), and
sawdust individually or as a mix. Peat
can be added to the planting hole prior
to planting; dig in the other additives
a year before planting. Application rates
depend on soil type and pH. Sawdust
needs nitrogen to decompose, so reduces
the amount in the soil. Add sulphate
of ammonia at 15g/sq m (½oz/sq yd)
annually to counteract this.

Alternatives to acidifying soil are
to use a raised bed or container. A
raised bed, 15–20cm (6–8in) high
and 1.5m (5ft) wide, aids drainage
on badly drained soils and can be
filled with peat-based compost.
Peat substitute may have a high pH,
so add flowers of sulphur to lower
it. In pots, use an ericaceous
compost with grit added.

Container-grown
blueberries often establish
more quickly than bare-root ones. Plant
from autumn to spring (*see p.208*). Space
bushes 1.5m (5ft) apart. If planting in a
container, start with a 2 litre (3½ pint)
pot and pot on in later years.

### PRUNING AND TRAINING BLUEBERRIES
Prune after leaf drop. Follow
the method for blackcurrants (*see
pp.223–224*), pruning at soil level
to encourage strong, new shoots.

Cut one or two unproductive branches
to soil level each year, ideally in early
spring when flower buds are obvious.

### ROUTINE CARE
After pruning, apply a balanced
compound fertilizer plus extra nitrogen
(sulphate of ammonia) at 15g/sq m
(½oz/sq yd). To maintain a low pH and
suppress weeds, mulch (*see p.41*) in mid-
spring with a 8–15cm (3–6in) layer of
acidic material, such as bark, old pine
needles, or peat. If chlorosis (*see p.254*)
shows in the leaves, top-dress soil with
flowers of sulphur to lower the pH.

Blueberries need copious amounts
of water, preferably rainwater, which is
acidic. Apply 50 litres/sq m (11 gallons/
sq yd) at each watering. If you have to
use alkaline tap water, monitor its effect
on the soil, adjusting the sulphur top-
dressing as needed. Raised beds demand
more water. During flowering, either
provide frost and wind protection in
the form of fleece or plastic sheeting,
or bring plants in containers under cover.

Repot blueberries in containers every
two years in autumn. The largest size
you should need is a 50 litre (11 gallon)
pot for a bush about 1.5m (5ft) tall.

#### ▼ Maximizing the crop
*Fruit buds are considerably
fatter than growth buds. When
pruning, learn to recognize and
retain branches bearing more
fruit buds since they are likely
to crop more heavily. Prune
out branches with a larger
proportion of growth buds so
that the plant's energies go
into producing fruit, not foliage.*

*Growth bud*

*Fruit bud*

### PROPAGATION
Take 10–15cm (4–6in) cuttings of soft,
healthy growth in midsummer. Trim
off the lower leaves. Insert the cuttings
into pots of one part peat and three parts
coarse sand and place in a propagator.
Once they have rooted, transplant into
pots, harden them off, and give a high-
potash feed every ten days. Plant in their
final positions after about a year.

### HARVESTING BLUEBERRIES
Harvest from late summer to early
autumn. A bush will yield 2.25–5kg
(5–11lb). Pick berries by gentle pulling.

### COMMON PROBLEMS
Birds (*see p.252*), botrytis (*p.252*), and
chlorosis (*p.254*) may cause problems.

---

**RECOMMENDED CULTIVARS**

**'Berkeley'** *Large, firm fruits with a sweet
flavour. Golden stems in winter.*
**'Bluecrop'** *Best all-round cultivar with
large, mid-season fruit of good flavour.*
**'Coville'** *Medium yields of very large fruit
on large, spreading bush.*
**'Herbert'** *Very large, late fruit. High yields
from a large, spreading bush.*

---

#### ▲ Blueberry with heavy crop
*Borne on large, attractive bushes, blueberry fruits are rather
bland to eat fresh, but keep well even in the freezer. When
cooked, they make deliciously aromatic muffins and jam.*

# Cranberry

An evergreen, straggling, low-growing shrub, the cranberry (*Vaccinium macrocarpon*) likes boggy soil conditions and so is well suited to poorly drained gardens. Its wiry stems root along the ground, enabling the plant to spread readily. It needs soil with a low pH to grow and fruit well, and prefers a sunny, fairly cool site. In addition to the red fruits, widely used for cranberry sauce, the bush provides good autumn colour.

**Fruiting cranberry**
*Wild cranberries naturally grow in moorland and boggy areas and those under cultivation require similarly acidic and moist growing conditions in order to fruit well.*

### PLANTING
Cranberries are usually grown in a sunken bed to maintain moist conditions, and a soil with a pH of 4–5.5 (*see below*). Only container-grown plants are available for planting. Plant at any time of year after saturating the bed with water, or prepare the bed before winter and plant in the spring.

### PRUNING AND TRAINING CRANBERRIES
Cranberries need pruning to thin the stems and keep plants within bounds. Start once a plant covers the surface of the bed. In autumn after harvesting, trim the bed edges to remove straggly stems. In early spring, prune to prevent overcrowding. Cut out excess stems at soil level to leave a single layer across the ground. Hedging shears can be used to trim top-growth, but a more detailed pruning is needed every three years.

### ROUTINE CARE AND PROPAGATION
Maintain the moisture content of the bed with copious amounts of water in early to midsummer, using rainwater if possible to keep pH low. Apply a 2.5cm (1in) layer of coarse, lime-free sand every three years after pruning to the bed surface to encourage the stems to root, promoting plant vigour and fruit yield. Maintain a low soil pH as for blueberries (*see p.225*). Cranberries can be propagated by layering: shoots will root naturally and can then be detached from the parent plant and replanted.

### HARVESTING CRANBERRIES
The first cranberries will be ready to pick in early autumn, but it is easier to wait until the majority of the fruit is ripe. The yield may be as much as 0.5–0.75kg/sq m (1lb–1lb 8oz/sq yd). Either pick individual fruits by hand or, with fingers spread, gently "comb" the fruits off the stems. Store cranberries dry for up to three weeks at room temperature or three months in a refrigerator at 2–4°C (36–39°F). Fruit will freeze for longer storage.

### COMMON PROBLEMS
No problems affect cranberries except possibly chlorosis (*see p.254*) on alkaline soils, and birds (*see p.252*).

## Making a cranberry bed

Dig out the soil to a spade blade's depth and about 1m (3ft) square. Line the pit with a sheet of fine proprietary plastic mesh to maintain water to a high level, but allow drainage of excess moisture. If the soil is particularly heavy and poor-draining, dig the pit to 30cm (12in) deep, and lay a drainage pipe leading to a sump or ditch. Cover the pipe with a 8–10cm (3–4in) deep layer of coarse, lime-free aggregate and place a sheet of fine plastic mesh over the aggregate to prevent the topsoil from blocking the drainage of excess water. Fill the remaining hole with a mix of two parts peat-free ericaceous compost and one part soil, avoiding heavy garden soil (which will not mix well) and alkaline soil. Alternatively, use 100 per cent peat-free ericaceous compost or a suitable light, low pH soil. Finally cover with a 2.5cm (1in) layer of coarse, lime-free sand to act as a mulch and so reduce the drying out of the bed and control weeds. The mulch also encourages the rooting of the stems as they grow. Water the bed regularly with rainwater.

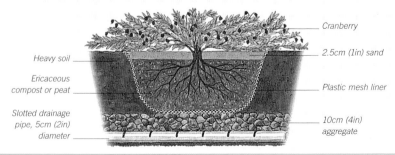

Heavy soil
Ericaceous compost or peat
Slotted drainage pipe, 5cm (2in) diameter
Cranberry
2.5cm (1in) sand
Plastic mesh liner
10cm (4in) aggregate

### RECOMMENDED CULTIVARS
**'CN'** *Large fruits. Branching, vigorous growth.*
**'Early Black'** *Early, dark red-black fruits.*
**'McFarlin'** *Large, dark red fruits covered with a thick, waxy bloom.*

# GRAPE VINES

## Planning

Grape vines have been cultivated for thousands of years both for their sweet fruits, known as dessert grapes, and for wine-making. They probably arose in Asia Minor and the Caucasus region, and spread to Mediterranean countries and North Africa. In cooler climates than these, their outdoor cultivation is less reliable, but provided that cultivars are carefully chosen and conditions are suitable they may be grown successfully (*see pp.231–232*). Grape vines grow and crop best in regions with warm, frost-free and fairly dry conditions in spring, late summer, and autumn. If you are doubtful of providing the necessary conditions outside, it is best to grow vines under cover (*see pp.228–230*).

Vines may easily be propagated from hardwood cuttings and grown on their own root systems; however, in countries where the root pest *Daktulosphaira vitifolii* is present, it is necessary to grow them on resistant rootstocks (*see below*).

**Grapes grown under cover**
*Many greenhouses and conservatories are suitable for growing grape vines, provided that they are well-ventilated. In a small conservatory, you can grow the vines as a cordon along the central ridge; in large greenhouses, it is possible to train them up one or both sides towards the ridge. Both methods require a system of stakes and wires in order to support the fruiting sideshoots (see pp.228–229).*

### GRAPE VINES IN THE GARDEN

The grape vine is a vigorous climbing plant that produces fruit on one-year-old shoots, and therefore needs careful annual pruning. Because of its vigour it will bleed sap profusely if pruned when in active growth, so it is essential to complete all major pruning of vines while they are dormant in late winter. There are several good methods of training vines for optimum cropping, of which the cordon, guyot, and standard forms are the most suitable for garden or greenhouse cultivation.

### SINGLE AND MULTIPLE CORDONS

The cordon, sometimes known as the rod-and-spur system, is one of the most versatile forms of training grape vines, and is widely used under cover; it is also suitable for growing vines on walls, fences, and pergolas, or in rows on freestanding posts and wires.

A single cordon (*see p.228*) consists of one permanent stem that produces

a series of fruiting sideshoots, or laterals, spaced about 23–30cm (9–12in) apart along it, and supported on horizontal wires. The main stem can be as long as can be accommodated in the space, but 2–3.6m (6–12ft) is usual. Single cordons may be grown vertically or at an angle if under cover, or vertically and then horizontally on an outdoor pergola. Multiple cordons (*see p.229*) consist of two rods – a double cordon – or several vertical rods, 1–1.2m (3–4ft) apart, produced from two horizontal stems. Horizontal branches can also be developed, about 60cm (2ft) apart, from the rods. These are suitable for a range of outdoor situations, such as house walls, pergolas, and arches.

### THE GUYOT SYSTEM

Widely used in vineyards, this system (*see p.232*) creates fruiting arms that are replaced each year. A single guyot has one arm, and a double guyot has two. Single guyots should be spaced about 1m (3ft) apart and double guyots about 1.5m (5ft) apart. They are trained on support systems of posts and wires.

### STANDARD VINES

Standard vines have a clear, tall main stem, which must be well staked, with a group of spurs at the top (*see p.230*). They are suitable for container-grown vines, and for those grown under cover in areas that are too small for a cordon.

### ROOTSTOCKS

In the world's great wine regions, the European vine, *Vitis vinifera*, is grafted onto rootstocks of American vines such as *V. labrusca*, which are resistant to the devastating insect pest, *Daktulosphaira vitifolii* (*see p.233*). Only in countries such as Chile, where it is absent, or where there is no major wine industry, as in the UK, is *V. vinifera* grown on its own roots. If you want a vine grafted onto a rootstock, choose one for your soil type. On deep, fertile, non-chalky soils, suitable rootstocks are 125AA, 5C, and S04; on deep, fertile, chalky soils, 5BB, 125AA, 5C, and S04; on shallow, poor, stony, dry soils, 5BB and 125AA; on heavy clays, 5BB, 125AA, and S04; on heavy, chalky clays or on chalk, S04.

# GRAPE VINES UNDER COVER

In cool climates, the large-berried table, or dessert, grapes must be grown under cover, in a greenhouse, conservatory, or even a porch. In particularly cool areas, and for late-ripening cultivars, some additional heat (*see p.44*) in spring and sometimes autumn may be required. Vines under cover are usually grown as cordons, but they can also be grown as standards in containers if space is tight. To fruit successfully, grape vines need a cool period in winter: if they are grown

in a greenhouse or conservatory that is heated throughout winter, they must be container-grown so that they can be moved outside for a few weeks.

## PLANTING GRAPES UNDER COVER

Vines to be grown in a greenhouse can be planted from early autumn to early spring. Planting them outside and training the rod inside the greenhouse makes watering and feeding easier. Those planted inside in a border,

however, have the advantage of starting earlier into growth, as the soil warms up earlier, but need good preparation of the border soil, with plenty of added manure, and regular watering. Over time, the roots will spread outside.

## CREATING A SINGLE CORDON

Single cordons require a support system of tautly stretched horizontal wires (*see p.162, p.231*) that are 23–30cm (9–12in) apart. Formative pruning (*see below*) will

---

## Formative pruning of a single cordon vine

Pinch back laterals between finger and thumb

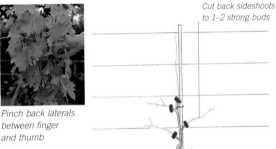

Cut back sideshoots to 1–2 strong buds

**1 Year 1, early winter:** after planting a strong, healthy vine, whether indoors or outdoors, use a pair of sharp secateurs to cut down the leading shoot to a strong bud on well-ripened wood, about 30cm (12in) above the level of the soil.

**2 Year 1, summer:** tie in the new leading shoot to a cane, and allow it to grow unhindered. Pinch back the main sideshoots, or laterals, to 5–6 leaves. Pinch any sideshoots that the laterals themselves have produced back to 1 leaf.

**3 Year 2, winter:** after the leaves have fallen, cut back the new growth of the leading shoot by a half to two-thirds of its length, leaving only brown, ripened wood. Prune back all the laterals and sideshoots to 1 or 2 strong-looking buds.

Tie in leading shoot

Reduce laterals to 5–6 leaves

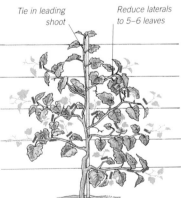

Carefully prune back all laterals to 1–2 strong, healthy buds

**4 Year 2, summer:** tie in the leading shoot, and pinch back the laterals to 5–6 leaves and any sublaterals to 1 leaf. Remove any flower trusses, unless the vine is growing very well, in which case allow just 1 to develop into a bunch of grapes.

**5 Year 3, winter:** as in the previous winter, prune back the leading shoot to well-ripened wood, and the laterals to 1 or 2 strong-looking buds. On the leading shoot, the bud should face in the opposite direction to the one chosen a year earlier.

**6 Year 3, spring:** from each spur, the point where the laterals join the main stem, 3–4 shoots will have formed. Thin these out at the base to 1–2 strong shoots. A second one may be useful as a replacement if the first fails to develop.

take several years, but is well worth the effort. After the third year, repeat the pruning cycle for the established cordon until the grape vine has reached the required length (*see below*). Then, gradually increase the number of flower trusses allowed to develop into bunches of grapes on the established cordon until one bunch per spur is obtained.

### CREATING A MULTIPLE CORDON
In the first summer, train a strong, healthy vine as a single stem, as for a single cordon (*see facing page*). Early in the first winter, prune the stem back

to a bud about 38–45cm (15–18in) above the ground. In the following summer, select one shoot on each side and tie it to a cane angled at 45°. In early winter, lower these to the horizontal and prune back to a bud at about 60cm (2ft) from the central stem. If you want only a double cordon, in the following summer train the endmost shoots up to a cane in the same way as for a single cordon. Prune back the laterals along the horizontal stem to five leaves, in order to develop fruiting laterals. To obtain a larger multiple cordon, train the endmost shoot at a 45-degree angle

to continue it, and train the adjacent shoot vertically. Repeat this process until the required number of arms has been started. The arms themselves are extended in the same way as described for a single cordon (*see facing page*).

### CARE OF MATURE MULTIPLE CORDONS
Prune established multiple cordons as for a single cordon (*see below*), with the rods 1–1.2m (3–4ft) apart. Horizontal arms to be developed from the rods should be spaced 50–60cm (20–24in) apart. To encourage new shoots, bend the stems over (*see bottom*).

## Pruning an established single cordon vine

Established single cordon grape vines require regular attention to pruning and training in order to keep them producing healthy new growth and cropping well.

**1** **In summer,** select 1 lateral from each spur, and also a reserve shoot, and remove all the other shoots. Prune the laterals at 5–6 leaves past a flower truss, allowing 1 bunch of grapes to develop per lateral, and cut sublaterals back to 1 leaf. Pinch out all other flower trusses.

**2** **In winter,** shorten the laterals to 2 buds. If spurs are becoming over-long, shorten to the replacement lateral; the spurs should be 23–30cm (9–12in) apart. Thin out congested, over-large spurs, using a pruning saw for a clean cut.

In early spring, cut back the leading shoot to a bud below the top wire, untie it, and bend it down to the horizontal carefully. Tie it into a wire. This encourages shoots to break along the lower part of the main stem. When the buds start to break, retie the leader in a vertical position.

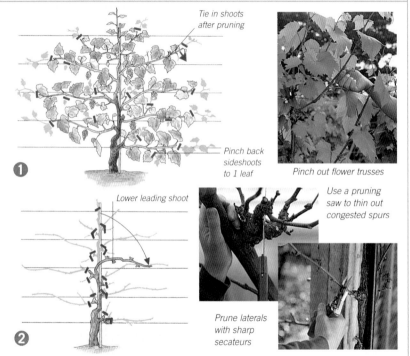

*Tie in shoots after pruning*

*Pinch back sideshoots to 1 leaf*

*Pinch out flower trusses*

*Lower leading shoot*

*Use a pruning saw to thin out congested spurs*

*Prune laterals with sharp secateurs*

## Training an established multiple cordon vine

**1** **To encourage production** of new shoots all along the multiple cordon stems, untie them from their supports in early spring. Carefully bend the stems over to the horizontal so that the top is arched downwards, and tie them into the wires. Buds will break at regular intervals along the stems (*see inset*).

**2** **Once the buds have opened** all along the stems, and started to grow out strongly, untie the stems and gently ease them back into a vertical position.

## Creating a standard vine

Standard vines have a stem 1–1.2m (3–4ft) tall with spurs at the top. For the first 1–2 years, allow laterals to develop on the stem. In the third winter, remove these to leave just the top spurs. Tie the stem to a cane so that the laterals can be supported with string when carrying grapes. Let 5–6 laterals develop at the top; prune these to 5 leaves and sublaterals to 1 leaf. In the first cropping year, allow 1 bunch only; thereafter allow 1 bunch per lateral. In early winter, prune the laterals to 2 buds.

*Thin out old spurs on mature plants if they are congested*

**Thinning grapes**
*Once bunches of berries have formed, thinning the grapes will enable the others to grow large and juicy. Prop the bunch with a forked twig, and use sharp, fine scissors to snip out about one-third of the berries evenly throughout the bunch. Start at the top sprig or shoulder, and work your way down the bunch.*

### ROUTINE CARE OF INDOOR VINES
Grape vines rooted under cover and in containers need additional nutrients and will benefit from liquid feeds of a high-potash fertilizer (*see pp.20–23*) from about one month after growth starts until the fruits start to ripen. If they are making poor growth, use a more balanced or high-nitrogen liquid feed.

Vines grown in the greenhouse border or in containers require regular watering during the growing season. Those that have their roots outside the greenhouse, however, will need little or no additional water.

Apply a 5–8cm (2–3in) layer of mulch, such as well-rotted manure, garden compost, or bark (*see pp.41–42*), to a radius of 45cm (18in) around each vine each year in late winter. Do not let the mulch touch the stem.

In early to midwinter, carefully remove any loose bark (*see below*) to expose any pests. If there are any present, such as mealybug (*see p.257*) or brown scale (*see p.253*), spray the vine with a winter wash.

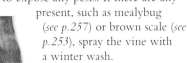

**Scraping off old bark**
*To reduce problems with pests such as mealybugs, which shelter in crevices, after winter pruning remove most of the outer layers of old, loose bark from the vine stems. Use a sharp knife. This will expose any lurking pests, which can then be easily eradicated.*

### TEMPERATURE REQUIREMENTS
Most vines will grow well in unheated greenhouses or conservatories, but in areas with a short growing season, or where late-ripening vines are being grown, it may be necessary to provide extra heat. A good time to start is in late winter, when a minimum night temperature of 4–7°C (39–45°F) is beneficial. It is very important to ventilate the plants, however, if daytime temperatures reach about 19°C (66°F).

Container-grown grape vines in greenhouses or conservatories that are constantly heated in winter should be moved outside into temperatures below 5°C (40°F) for 4–6 weeks in order for them to experience the period of chilling necessary to initiate flowering.

### POLLINATION OF GRAPE VINES
Some vines will set fruit under cover without any additional pollination. Most benefit, however, if you tap the rods around midday on warm days during flowering. If they do not set well, then gently stroking the bunches with cupped hands will transfer pollen from the stamens to the stigmas and so assist pollination. Keep the atmosphere fairly dry during flowering, and do not water from above.

### THINNING DESSERT GRAPES
This is necessary in order to produce berries of a good size and to allow air movement between the berries and so prevent the development of grey mould, or botrytis. Thin with scissors when the berries are small (*see above*), using a small forked stick to support the bunch:

touching grapes with fingers damages the bloom on the surface of the berries and can lead to infection. First remove any berries that are crowding the centre of the bunch, and then thin those on the outside. Avoid over-thinning the top sprigs, or shoulders, of the bunches; aim for a balanced shape.

### HARVESTING DESSERT GRAPES
Dessert grapes should be harvested when fully ripe (*see below*). To avoid touching them with your fingers, which might cause damage, cut the bunch off together with a piece of the lateral stem above it, to use as a handle. It is best to harvest just one bunch at a time, as they ripen, since the grapes will only keep for a few days once harvested.

**Harvesting dessert grapes**
*The grapes are ripe when the skin of the fruits becomes translucent. To avoid damaging the bloom of the grapes, hold the stem above the bunch, and cut it 4–5cm (1½–2in) either side of the bunch to form a handle (see inset).*

# GRAPE VINES OUTDOORS

A warm, sunny slope, wall, or fence, preferably below an altitude of about 120m (400ft), is best for growing grape vines outdoors. Vines are tolerant of a wide range of soils, provided that they are at least 30cm (12in) deep and well-drained. They have deep and extensive root systems, and are therefore capable of withstanding drought. The ideal pH is 6.5–7 (*see p.18*). They may suffer lime-induced chlorosis on thin soils over chalk (*see* Iron deficiency, *p.256*); a high-potash feed can remedy this. It is vital to choose cultivars that are suitable for cultivation in the open; these will usually be white wine grapes (*see p.233*).

Vines can be planted outdoors in the dormant season between late autumn and early spring. However, container-grown vines, are best purchased and planted in late spring when they have started to grow and all danger of air frosts has passed. Vines outdoors may be grown as cordons (*see pp.228–229*) or on the guyot system.

## THE GUYOT SYSTEM

This is the most widely used vineyard form of training vines, and it is also an excellent form for garden cultivation, particularly for wine grapes. The vines are pruned on a replacement system (*see p.232*) as either single or double guyots (with one or two fruiting arms). This usually results in good-quality fruit buds each year, and a fine crop of grapes. Vines should be planted 1m (3ft) apart for a single guyot and, for a double guyot, 1.5m (4ft) apart. If you intend to grow more than one row of vines, orient the rows north–south and space them 1.5–2m (5–6ft) apart.

## CREATING A SUPPORT SYSTEM

Guyot vines require a support system of posts and wires, using 2mm-gauge (¹⁄₁₆in) galvanized wire. This should consist of treated posts spaced 4–5m (12–15ft) apart, depending on the spacing of the plants, with two single lower wires at 40cm (16in) and 55cm (22in) from the ground. There should also be three sets of double wires at 90cm (3ft), 1.2m (4ft), and 1.5m (5ft). Use straining bolts to attach the wires to the end posts, running them

through cup-hooks on the intermediate posts so that they can be easily removed for winter pruning. The end posts require support struts, as described for tree fruit supports (*see pp.162–163*). Guyot vines grown against walls or fences need only single rather than double wires, since the shoots will be trained between the wires and the wall or fence.

## GUYOT TRAINING

To create a double guyot vine, follow the formative pruning steps outlined on *p.232*. For a single guyot, the training is the same except that only two shoots are used, and then one arm only is selected. In the first cropping year – the first year that the arms are tied in place – retain only one or two bunches on each arm to avoid overly stressing the vine. In the second cropping year, retain two or three bunches per arm. In the third cropping year, if the grape vine is growing strongly, retain all the bunches.

Established guyot vines should be pruned every year (*see p.232*). As the use of a three-bud "stub" leads to the framework gradually getting higher, occasionally select a lower-placed shoot as a stub, so that the vine can be cut back to this in the following year.

## ROUTINE CARE OF OUTDOOR VINES

In late winter, feed with a general compound fertilizer (*see pp.20–23*) at a rate of approximately 70g/sq m (2½oz/sq yd) and sulphate of potash at about 15g/sq m (½oz/sq yd). Mulch with a 5–8cm (2–3in) layer of well-rotted manure, garden compost, or of bark mulch, spread over a radius of 45cm (18in) for the first 4–5 years, and every year for wall-trained vines. The mulch should not touch the stem.

Established vines require little or no watering, but newly planted vines need irrigation during dry periods in spring and summer. Foliage should be thinned out in late summer (*see below*).

## HARVESTING VINE GRAPES

For wine-making, grapes must contain the maximum amount of sugar; the sugar levels can be determined using specialist instruments, but a good guide is to taste the grapes as they approach ripeness and harvest when they are very sweet. Green grapes usually turn more translucent and slightly yellow when ripe. Cut them off where the stalk joins the cropping lateral. Grapes are best eaten fresh, but should keep for a little while if stored in a cool place.

**Thinning the foliage of outdoor grape vines**
*In late summer, as the fruits (here of the black wine grape 'Rondo') are ripening, thin out the foliage to allow the sun to reach the fruits.*

*Using sharp secateurs, cut out at the base any leaves that are shading the fruits. Try to avoid touching the grapes while you are working.*

## Formative pruning of a double guyot vine

**1** **On planting in winter,** insert a stake and tie it into the horizontal wires. Prune the vine back to 15cm (6in) above the soil, with at least 2 strong buds.

**2** **Year 1, summer:** tie the leading shoot to the stake with soft twine. Cut sideshoots back to 5 leaves, and remove strong, upright shoots and low shoots.

**3** **Year 2, winter:** cut the leading shoot back to just above 3 strong buds that are below the lowest set of wires.

**4** **Year 2, spring and summer:** as the vine grows, choose 3 strong shoots, pruning back any others, and train them upwards, tying them into the central support (*see right*). Tuck the sideshoots from the 3 main shoots into the parallel wires to grow horizontally; their leaves will feed and strengthen the vine. Throughout the summer, rub or pull off any other shoots at the base of the vine (*see inset*).

**5** **Year 3, winter:** tie 2 of the 3 side-shoots to the bottom wires on each side in a shallow arc to form the guyot's arms. If either breaks off, use the third unpruned shoot to replace it. If not, prune this shoot to 3–4 good buds (*see far right*).

**6** **Year 3, summer:** guide shoots from each arm vertically through the pairs of wires. Pinch out their tips when they reach the top; pinch any sideshoots they produce back to 1 leaf. Let 3 shoots grow from the central stub, also pinching back their sideshoots. These 3 shoots are reserved to form next year's fruiting arms.

**7** **Year 4, winter:** untie and cut off the guyot's arms completely. As in step 5, bend 2 of the central, reserved shoots to the horizontal and tie them into the 2 bottom wires. If the third is not needed as a reserve, prune it back to 3–4 buds.

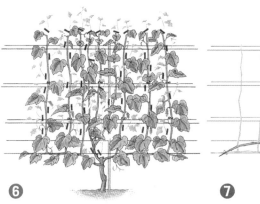

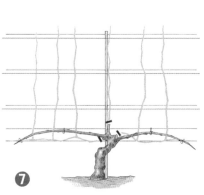

## Pruning an established guyot vine

In summer, as in step 6 above, train evenly spaced sideshoots upwards from the guyot's arms, tucking them between the double wires. These shoots will flower and fruit. Tie in and reserve three strong shoots from the central "stubs" as before. Remove any flowers produced by these shoots. Prune all vertically trained shoots back to 10–15cm (4–6in) above the top wire when necessary, and pinch or cut back any sideshoots they produce to one leaf. Remove any shoots on the clear trunk. In early winter, as in step 7 above, cut back the fruited arms and tie in the replacement shoots.

*Pinching sublaterals on the three reserved shoots*

*Summer pruning of shoot tips and sideshoots*

## RECOMMENDED GRAPE VINE CULTIVARS

### Dessert grapes for under cover

Dessert grapes are the only ones suitable for growing under cover, and they are classified in three groups: sweetwater, muscat, and vinous. Sweetwater are the earliest to mature and are easiest to grow in an unheated greenhouse. Muscat grapes have the finest flavour and ripen later. They can be grown in an unheated greenhouse in milder areas, but usually benefit from some additional heat. Vinous grapes are difficult to grow, so are not recommended.

**'Buckland Sweetwater'** ♀ *Early-cropping, white, sweetwater grape.*

**'Chasselas'** ♀ *Early, small, white, sweetwater grape; it can also be grown outside in warmer areas.*

**'Foster's Seedling'** ♀ *Early-cropping, white sweetwater grape.*

**'Muscat Hamburg'** ♀ *Earliest to crop of the muscats, a good-flavoured, black grape.*

**'Muscat of Alexandria'** ♀ *Late-ripening, white, muscat grape, one of the best-flavoured, but often needs additional heat in spring and autumn to ripen well.*

**'Schiava Grossa' (syn. 'Black Hamburgh')** ♀ *Well-known, mid-season, black sweetwater grape.*

### Outdoor cultivars

Generally, white wine grapes are the most successful for growing outside, but there are also suitable black wine grapes and some dessert grapes, although berries will be small.

### Wine grapes

**'Bacchus'** ♀ *Mid-autumn, white grape.*

**'Léon Millot'** ♀ *Mid-autumn, heavy-cropping black grape with good mildew resistance.*

**'Madeleine Angevine'** ♀ *Early to mid-autumn, very vigorous, heavy-cropping, white grape.*

**'Orion'** ♀ *Promising new white grape with good disease resistance.*

**'Rondo'** ♀ *Promising new black grape.*

**'Schönburger'** ♀ *Mid-autumn, good-quality white grape.*

**'Seibel 13.153' (syn. 'Cascade')** *Mid-autumn, black grape, with some mildew resistance.*

**'Seyval Blanc'** *Mid-autumn, white grape, not the highest-quality flavour but can be relied on to crop well, good mildew resistance.*

**'Siegerrebe'** ♀ *Early autumn, white grape, good flavour for both dessert use and wine.*

**'Triomphe d'Alsace'** *Early autumn, heavy-cropping black grape, with good mildew resistance.*

### Outdoor dessert grapes

**'Boskoop Glory'** *Mid-autumn, black grape with good flavour.*

**'Brant'** *Mid- to late autumn, small, tight bunches of black grapes, useful for growing on pergolas, good autumn foliage colour, some resistance to mildew.*

**'Himrod'** *Mid-autumn, seedless, white grape, grows best against a warm, sunny wall or a fence.*

**'New York Muscat'** ♀ *Mid-autumn, excellent outdoor white grape, needing a warm, sunny wall or fence in order to crop well.*

**'Tereshkova'** *Early autumn black grape, with good autumn foliage colour.*

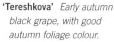
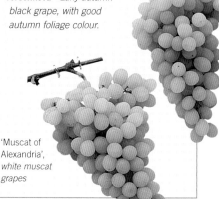

'Muscat of Alexandria', white muscat grapes

## COMMON PROBLEMS OF GRAPE VINES

In warm climates, where vines are widely grown outdoors, they may succumb to a number of common problems. In cooler areas, vines grown outside suffer from few pests other than birds taking the fruits, but they can be affected by certain diseases and disorders. Vines grown under cover are more susceptible to all types of problem. For more details, *see* Plant Problems, *pp.246–262*.

### Pests

**Birds** *As fruits ripen, net vines both outside and across the doors and ventilators of greenhouses, to protect them from birds.*

**Brown scale** *Usually only a problem under cover, but sometimes also for wall-trained vines (see p.262).*

**Daktulosphaira vitifolii (syn. Phylloxera vastatrix)** *This pest can cause serious problems in certain countries, although not in the UK. A voracious root feeder, it causes severe stunting; leaf galls may form and the vine may die. This pest multiplies rapidly and is impossible to eradicate using conventional pesticides. The solution in is*

grafting onto resistant rootstocks (see p.227).

**Mealybug** *Only a serious problem for vines under cover (see p.257).*

**Red spider mite** *Often a problem under cover, but rarely outside (see p.261).*

**Vine weevil** *Adults attack the foliage, but it is the grubs in the soil that can seriously harm a vine (see p.264).*

**Wasps** *May affect early-ripening cultivars. Use traps, or protect fruits with muslin bags or sections of nylon tights (see p.264).*

### Diseases

**Downy mildew** *Seldom affects vines in cooler areas (see p.255).*

**Botrytis** *Also known as grey mould, this is a common problem both outside and under cover, but regular pruning and fruit thinning reduces the risk (see p.252).*

**Powdery mildew** *Affects leaves and fruits, and can be a problem both outside and under cover (see p.260). Resistant cultivars are available (see above).*

**Root rots** *Caused by honey fungus (see p.256) and* Phytophthora *(see p.259).*

### Cultural disorders

**Magnesium deficiency** *May occur both outside and under cover, but is easily controlled (see p.257).*

**Oedema** *May occur on vines under cover when conditions are too moist, usually through lack of ventilation. Do not remove the affected parts as this will exacerbate the problem (see p.258).*

**Scald and scorch** *Can be a problem with vines under cover, when grapes and leaves near glass suffer as a result of lack of ventilation. Remove affected parts and improve air circulation (see p.262).*

**Shanking** *Can affect vines under cover. The cause is damage to the root system due to waterlogging, drought, reduction of the rooting area, or overcropping. If spotted early, reduce the number of bunches and correct any root problem (see p.262).*

**Spray damage** *Vines are very susceptible to damage from hormonal weedkillers, causing twisted and distorted growth. Do not spray near vines or store chemicals near them.*

# GROWING TENDER FRUITS

This section includes a selection of tender fruits that make fascinating specimens to grow under glass in cool temperate zones. Since most need warmth and many hours of summer sunshine to crop heavily and ripen well, they are highly productive as crop plants only in warmer parts of the world. But with careful cultivation, most will bear and ripen fruit in a conservatory or greenhouse in cooler climates. Although not economic crops in these conditions, they are nevertheless very satisfying to grow, and several, especially citrus and passion fruits, make splendid and productive ornamentals. Following the advice in this section will produce the best possible harvests of tender fruits in cool temperate regions.

## Citrus

### *Citrus* species

Many citrus species are grown for their fruits, including oranges, grapefruits, lemons, and limes. Calamondins (x *Citrofortunella microcarpa*), and kumquats (*Fortunella japonica* and *F. margarita*), are also classified as citrus fruits.

Citrus trees are evergreen and can reach 3–10m (10–30ft) tall, with a spread of 5–8m (15–25ft); they require restrictive pruning under glass. In warm climates, flowers and fruits are borne year-round, often appearing on the tree at the same time.

It is usual to grow grafted citrus trees, and the chosen rootstock will affect the degree of pruning needed. As a general rule, choose a plant grown on a dwarfing rootstock if it is to be grown under glass; take specialist advice from the supplier.

Most citrus will survive brief spells at 0°C (32°F), but will fruit freely only in frost-free climates that have hot summers and an average winter minimum of 15°C (59°F). In cool temperate climates, grow them in a frost-free greenhouse or conservatory. Citrus become dormant at 13°C (55°F) and to bear ripe fruit, need a minimum of 14°C

(55°F) for six months after flowering. Fruit ripens 9–11 months after pollination. Most are self-fertile, so no pollinator is required.

■ **Site and planting** Citrus tolerate a range of soils, but prefer fertile, well-drained, slightly acid conditions (pH 6–6.5). Plant in spring into prepared beds, or containers at least 60cm (2ft) in diameter, filled with a fertile, loam-based compost. Keep almost dry during winter dormancy and, as temperatures rise in spring, resume watering to initiate flowering. Provide full light and excellent ventilation and maintain a temperature of at least 14°C (55°F) after flowering; allow it to rise to 20–25°C (68–75°F) with a humidity of 75 per cent or more in summer. The higher the temperature, the better is the flavour of the fruit. Cold and draughts will cause fruit drop.

■ **Pruning and training** Citrus may be trained as a standard (*see below*), which is an ideal form when grown in a container.

Prune between late winter and early spring. To train citrus as a bush, once the trunk has reached about 50cm (20in), select three or four shoots above the clear stem to form the permanent framework. Prune these by one-third to encourage branching. Continue over the next 3–4 years to shorten these shoots and any strong sideshoots to

achieve an even, bushy shape. Thin the fruits during training and, once the tree is established, keep pruning to a minimum; shorten overlong or cold-damaged shoots and remove dead, diseased, and crossing branches to maintain productive growth and a compact, open habit.

■ **Routine care** Water well and give a high-nitrogen, medium-potassium liquid feed monthly during the growing season; use a fertilizer that includes trace elements (*see p.20*). Do not allow citrus to dry out, since drought causes fruit drop.

Remove any suckers from the rootstock, cutting them back to their points of origin. Repot citrus in containers every third or fourth year in early spring.

■ **Harvesting and storage** Expect perhaps a dozen fruits per year on each tree. Harvest the fruits when ripe, using secateurs to cut them with a short stem. Undamaged fruits can be stored for several weeks at 4–6°C (38–42°F) in well-ventilated conditions.

■ **Propagation** For named cultivars, T-budding is the usual propagation method. This is similar to chip-budding (*see p.154*), but instead of grafting a "chip" onto the rootstock, a bud is grafted. Make a T-shaped cut through the bark of the rootstock about 23cm (9in) above ground

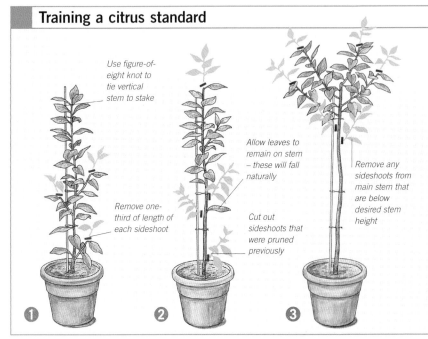

## Training a citrus standard

Use figure-of-eight knot to tie vertical stem to stake

Remove one-third of length of each sideshoot

Allow leaves to remain on stem – these will fall naturally

Cut out sideshoots that were pruned previously

Remove any sideshoots from main stem that are below desired stem height

**1** **When planting,** tie in the main vertical stem, or leader, to a stake, and shorten any sideshoots by one-third.

**2** **Once the main stem** has grown to more than the final required height of the trunk, prune it back to a healthy bud. Do not prune any new sideshoots, since these will help to thicken the trunk, but remove any sideshoots that were shortened in the previous year.

**3** **When 3 or 4 well-spaced sideshoots** have developed above the desired trunk height, remove all shoots below these to leave a clear trunk and the beginnings of the permanent head of the standard. Prune the 3 or 4 remaining shoots by 3–5 leaves. In subsequent seasons, prune as for a bush tree (*see above*) to gain a rounded, balanced shape.

**1** **2** **3**

level. Prepare a bud of the cultivar to be grafted by choosing a section of ripe, new growth and slicing out a bud with a gentle scooping cut. Insert the bud into the T-shaped cut, and bind the area with plastic tape so the graft cannot dry out. Remove the tape after 4–6 weeks. When the budded shoot is 2.5cm (1in) long, cut off the rootstock top-growth just above it.

Citrus can also be raised from seed. Although many citrus do produce offspring that are similar to the parent, seed-raised plants can take six years or more to begin fruiting, and there is always a risk of inferior quality fruit. It is better to buy in named cultivars from a reputable supplier.

■ **Common problems** Citrus may be affected by mealybugs (*p.257*), red spider mite (*p.261*), scale insect (*p.261*), and whitefly (*p.264*). Crown rot (*p.254*), root-knot eelworm (*p.261*), fruit fly (*p.256*), and thrips (*p.263*) are sometimes troublesome. Viruses (*p.264*), spread by aphids, cause loss of vigour, smaller fruits, and pitting on fruits. Spray against aphids when seen.

■ **Recommended citrus cultivars**
x *Citrofortunella microcarpa* ♀ – calamondin; small, ornamental fruit, good for preserves.
*C. aurantiifolia* 'Tahiti', *syn.* 'Persian' – lime; the most cold-tolerant, with fairly sweet fruit.
*C. aurantium* 'Chinotto' – sour orange; compact, free-flowering, bitter flavour.
*C. limon* 'Garey's Eureka' – lemon; few-seeded, very acid, medium-sized fruit.
*C.* x *meyeri* 'Meyer' – the hardiest and most compact lemon; small, rounded, acid fruit.
*C.* x *paradisi* 'Marsh' – grapefruit; free-flowering with seedless, white-fleshed fruit.
*C. reticulata* 'Dancy' – mandarin orange; compact with small, sweet, juicy fruit.
*C. sinensis* 'Washington' – sweet orange; sweet, juicy, seedless navel orange.
*C.* x *tangelo* 'Minneola' – tangelo; aromatic, with sweet, tangy flesh.

# Kiwi fruit

## *Actinidia deliciosa*

Kiwi fruits, or Chinese gooseberries, are rampant, twining, deciduous plants that grow up to 9m (28ft) in length; they require sturdy, permanent supports and a great deal of space.

Kiwi fruits need temperatures of 5–25°C (40–77°F) to fruit well, although they will survive temperatures down to –8°C (18°F) when dormant. Protection from wind is vital (*see pp.12–13*). They should be grown against a south- or west-facing wall in cool temperate areas. It is rarely practicable to grow them in a conservatory, but a dedicated polytunnel or plastic screening may be used for extra protection in cold areas.

■ **Site and planting** Choose deep, well-aerated soil rich in organic matter and with a pH of 6–7. Add a general-purpose fertilizer at a rate of 50–110g (2–4oz) per plant. Erect post-and-wire support with horizontal wires

## Summer pruning kiwi fruit

In early to midsummer, look for sideshoots that have developed fruitlets at the base. Use secateurs to cut back each shoot to 5 leaves above the fruitlets, making the cut just above a leaf. This will divert energy from producing foliage to the swelling fruits. After fruiting, cut the sideshoots back to 2 buds beyond the last fruit. This method of pruning will build up a productive system of fruiting spurs.

at 30cm (12in) intervals. Plant in winter, allowing 4–5m (12–15ft) between plants.

For successful pollination, plant both male (non-fruiting) and female plants; one male will pollinate up to eight or nine females.

■ **Pruning and training** The most practical way to grow a kiwi fruit in domestic gardens is as an espalier (*see p.152*).

After planting, tie in the leading shoot as it grows to a cane attached vertically to the wires. Train in a pair of shoots along each horizontal wire, pinching out the tips when they fill the allotted space; these will form the permanent fruiting framework. The fruits are borne on one-year-old wood.

Allow sideshoots to develop at 50cm (20in) intervals, pinching them out to leave five leaves. These should bear fruit the following year; for summer pruning, *see above*. Every three years or so, cut the sideshoots back to dormant buds near the main horizontal shoot to encourage new sideshoots.

■ **Routine care** Apply a thick mulch in spring (*see pp.41–42*) and a general-purpose fertilizer rich in phosphate and potassium. Water well to keep moist throughout the growing season.

■ **Harvesting and storage** About three or four years after planting, the vines should start to bear fruit. Harvest the fruits as they start to soften. Store laid out in trays in single layers. Wrapped in kitchen film at near-freezing temperatures, they keep for four to six weeks.

■ **Propagation** Take softwood cuttings, about 10–15cm (4–6in) long, in spring, selecting healthy, unripened wood. Trim the leaves off the lower third of each cutting and insert in a pot of cuttings compost with bottom heat (*see p.62*). Once rooted, pot up into larger pots before hardening off and planting out. Alternatively, take some hardwood cuttings in winter. Trim to 20–30cm (8–12in) long, and insert them in sandy compost. Once rooted, transplant to their final positions.

Selected cultivars may be grafted by means of T-budding (*see* Citrus, *left*) or whip-and-tongue grafting (*see p.155*).

■ **Common problems** Kiwi fruit are seldom prone to significant pest or disease attack.

■ **Recommended cultivars**
'Bruno' – female; large, elongated, dark brown fruits, with bristly hairs and sweet flavour.
'Hayward' – female; large, oval, pale brown fruits, softly hairy with good, sweet flavour.
'Tomuri' – male; good pollinator.

# Passion fruit

## *Passiflora* species

Vigorous climbers, passion fruit bear yellow or purple fruits on the current year's growth. The species usually grown for their fruit are the yellow-fruited *P. edulis* f. *flavicarpa* and the purple-fruited *P. edulis*. Both require a winter minimum temperature of 10°C (50°F). When in growth, purple-fruited variants do best above 20°C (68°F), while those with yellow fruits need temperatures above 24°C (75°F). Both need moderate humidity to fruit well.

**Purple passion fruit**
*Once a shoot has produced fruit, like this purple-fruiting* Passiflora edulis, *it will not fruit again, so it should be pruned back after fruiting to 2 healthy buds.*

■ **Site and planting** Passion fruits thrive in full sun, and grow well in beds against the back wall of a greenhouse or conservatory. They tolerate a range of soil types as long as there is good drainage – add well-rotted organic matter and sharp sand to the planting hole, along with a general-purpose fertilizer. For containers (*see pp.35–36*), use a fertile compost with a high organic content and add a general-purpose fertilizer; choose a container over 35cm (14in) in diameter.

Prepare a support in the form of a trellis or wires on a wall (*see p.162*). Plant in spring, and space the plants about 3m (10ft) apart.

You may need to pollinate by hand (*see p.157*) and fruit set will be poor where temperatures fall below 16°C (61°F). For good health and productivity, replace the plants every five or six years.

■ **Pruning and training** Select and train two main stems up and then along the top of the support. These stems will produce sideshoots every year that hang down and bear fruit. Tip prune these to keep them clear of the ground. If the main stems are reluctant to flower, pinch out the tips.

Every year after fruiting, prune back the hanging sideshoots to about 20cm (8in) or two buds; fruited shoots will not fruit again.

■ **Routine care** For plants grown in beds, apply a general-purpose fertilizer with a medium- to high-nitrogen content every three or four months, from spring onwards. Keep plants mulched (*see pp.41–42*) and well-watered. In pots, use a liquid feed or general-purpose fertilizer (*see pp.20–23*) every four weeks during the growing season.

■ **Harvesting and storage** The best quality fruits are obtained when left on the plant until fully coloured and slightly shrivelled. They can, however, be ripened off the plant if picked as they begin to change colour.

Fruits may be stored for up to 21 days at a temperature of 6–7°C (43–45°F) and 85–90 per cent humidity.

■ **Propagation** To grow passion fruit from seed, extract the seeds from ripe fruits and allow them to ferment in their own pulp for a few days, then wash and dry them. Sow into a proprietary seed compost and cover lightly. Germinate at a temperature of 20–25°C (68–77°F). When the seedlings are 20–35cm (8–14in) tall, transplant to their final position.

To propagate by cuttings, take 15–20cm (6–8in) lengths of softwood or semi-ripe stems between spring and late summer and insert in cuttings compost. Root with bottom heat (*see p.62*) on a mist bench, or mist them regularly until the cuttings have rooted.

Chip-budding (*see p.154*) can also be used to propagate passion fruit.

■ **Common problems** Passion fruit may be affected by aphids (*see p.251*), fruit fly (*p.256*), red spider mite (*p.261*), and scale insect (*p.261*). Cucumber mosaic virus (*see p.254*), transmitted by aphids, can cause woodiness.

■ **Recommended cultivars**
'Crackerjack' – free-flowering, with large, aromatic, deep purple to black fruits.
'Golden Nuggett' – free-flowering, with sweet, golden yellow fruit.

# Pineapple

*Ananas comosus*

Pineapples are succulent perennials, of the bromeliad family, that originate in tropical climates. To produce fruit, pineapples need high levels of light, moderately high humidity, and temperatures of 18–30°C (64–86°F). Plants usually fruit at about three years of age. Pineapples grown in containers are more easily managed, but will produce smaller fruits than those grown in beds.

■ **Site and planting** Pineapples prefer a sandy medium loam with a pH of 5–6.5 (*see p.18*), although they will tolerate a range of soil conditions. In spring, plant suckers or "slips" in prepared beds, about 30cm (12in) apart, with 60cm (24in) between rows, or at 50cm (20in) apart each way. Alternatively, use 30cm (12in) diameter pots filled with compost with a high organic content. Provide maximum light, a temperature of at least 20°C (68°F) and humidity of about 70 per cent. Bottom heat improves growth.

**Propagating from a crown shoot**
*Increase your stock by removing the crown shoot of a ripe pineapple with 1cm (½in) of the fruit attached; do not cut through the base of the shoot. Insert into a pot of cuttings compost.*

Pineapples are very sensitive to draughts, so avoid exposure to them at all times. You could create a microclimate around the plants in the greenhouse using a film plastic "tent".

■ **Routine care** Water regularly, particularly when young, and provide a thick organic mulch (*see pp.41–42*) on beds to help retain moisture. Apply a high-nitrogen, medium-potassium liquid feed every three or four weeks during the growing season.

■ **Harvesting and storage** Each plant will produce a single fruit. When fruits begin to turn yellow, cut through the stem below each fruit, leaving a small stalk attached. The fruits can be stored at 8°C (46°F) with 90 per cent humidity for about three weeks.

■ **Propagation** Suckers grow from the leaf axils, stem bases, or below the fruit. Cut off the sucker with a sharp knife, dip the cut surfaces in fungicide, and leave to dry for several days. Trim off the lower leaves and insert into sandy compost to root.

Take crown shoots as cuttings (*see below*), keeping them at a temperature of 18–21°C (64–70°F). Once the suckers or crown roots have rooted, pot them into 15cm (6in) pots.

■ **Common problems** Mealybugs (*see p.257*), root-knot eelworm (*p.261*), scale insect (*p.261*), red spider mite (*p.254*), and thrips (*p.254*) may affect pineapples. In overly wet conditions, *Phytophthora* heart-rot (*see p.259*) may become a problem.

■ **Recommended cultivars**
Cultivars are seldom offered in the UK, but if propagating from the crowns of shop-bought pineapples, 'Queen', imported from Kenya or Malaysia, is sweet, well-flavoured and ripens quickly. 'Smooth Cayenne', grown in Hawaii and the Azores, has smooth, spineless leaves and very juicy, highly flavoured fruit.

# Olive

*Olea europea*

Olives are slow-growing, evergreen trees, reaching a height of 9–12m (28–40ft) and a spread of 7–9m (22–28ft) in optimum conditions. They thrive in Mediterranean regions with an ideal temperature range of 5–25°C (41–77°F). Trees remain productive for decades, developing gnarled bark and a twisted habit. To set and ripen fruits, trees need long, hot summers followed by cool winters. Although moderately cold-hardy, even mature trees will sustain damage if temperatures fall below –10°C (14°F).

In cool climates, olives can be grown in pots (*see pp.35–36*) and brought under cover during the winter months. They may be grown outdoors in very sheltered town gardens and here, and in exceptionally warm years, they may produce some fruit.

■ **Site and planting** Select a well-drained site with soil of medium to low fertility. Alkaline soils (*see p.18*), up to pH 8.5, are

suitable. Provide shelter (*see pp.12–13*) from wind. A warm site against or near a sunny wall is essential in cool temperate climates.

Choose either rooted cuttings or budded plants, and stake firmly on planting. Space them 7–12m (22–40ft) apart. Under glass, use pots at least 30–35cm (12–14in) in diameter; fill with a fertile, loam-based compost and incorporate a slow-release fertilizer.

Olives are wind-pollinated and most cultivars are self-fertile, but you may need to plant two or more plants in cooler climates to improve pollination and fruiting.

■ **Pruning and training** Prune olives in early spring. Take out the main vertical shoot when it is about 1.5m (5ft) tall, selecting three or four strong branches below the shoot to form a permanent framework. Keep the stem clear of shoots below the framework shoots. Routine pruning consists of removing older branches to promote new growth (fruits are borne on one-year-old wood) and to maintain an open centre to the tree.

To restrict the size of a pot-grown olive, tip prune the main branches, cutting back to a good replacement shoot each year.

■ **Routine care** Apply a general-purpose fertilizer with medium to high nitrogen levels two or three times a year. Water regularly while the tree establishes and mulch with organic material. Keep plants in containers moist during the growing season and apply a liquid feed every three or four weeks.

Do not move pot-grown plants outside for the summer until all danger of frost has passed. Aim to maintain a temperature above 21°C (70°F) in summer. Keep dry in a cold greenhouse during winter, but protect the roots from frost. Olives need a period of winter chilling to initiate flowers.

■ **Harvesting and storage** An olive in the open may start to fruit three or four years after planting. Timing of harvesting depends on what the olives are to be used for.

Olives to be used for fermenting are picked when they are ripe but green; these fruits

**Mature olive tree**
*Olive trees are very long-lived; the pretty creamy white flowers appear in midsummer, followed by fruits in autumn.*

## Propagating prickly pears from stem sections

**1** **Cut a stem segment** away from the parent plant with secateurs or a sharp knife, dividing it into 2 or 3 if it is very large. Wear thick gloves and use paper or card "sleeves" when handling the segment to protect you from the spines.

**2** **Leave the segments** in a warm, dry place for several days to allow calluses to form. Insert each piece into a pot of sandy compost topped with grit. Transfer the rooted cuttings into 15–20cm (6–8in) pots, or into position in a border.

are processed to remove their bitterness. Those that are used as table olives are picked when they are black and firm, then packed in salt until dehydrated, and subsequently stored in olive oil or brine.

■ **Propagation** Olives are usually propagated by stem cuttings. Take hardwood cuttings in winter, removing sections of one- or two-year-old wood about 30cm (12in) long. Treat the base with a hormone rooting product, then insert the cutting to half its depth in a pot of cutting compost. Rooting should take about 30 days at a temperature between 13–21°C (55–70°F).

Transplant into larger pots to grow on. Semi-ripe cuttings, 10–15cm (4–6in) long, can be taken in summer.

T-budding (*see* Citrus, *p.235*) can be used to graft cultivars onto vigorous olive seedling rootstocks or, for a dwarfing influence, onto *Osmanthus* stock.

■ **Common problems** Fruit fly (*see p.256*), olive scab (*see p.251*), root-knot eelworm (*see p.261*), scale insect (*p.261*), and verticillium wilt (*p.263*) may all affect olives grown in the open. Under cover, common problems may include red spider mite (*p.261*), thrips (*p.263*), and whitefly (*p.264*).

■ **Recommended cultivars**
'El Greco' – large fruit with small stones.
'Mission' – free-fruiting and cold-resistant.

# Prickly pear

*Opuntia ficus-indica*

Occurring largely in the dry and arid subtropics, the prickly pear belongs to the cactus family. They need a temperature range of 18–25°C

(64–77°F) to fruit well, although they tolerate temperatures as low as 10°C (50°F). Ripe fruits are purple or red and are borne on the top of stem sections, or "pads". Wear gloves or use paper sleeves for handling the plants since the tiny, barbed spines cause severe skin irritation. Commercially cultivated variants are often almost spineless.

■ **Site and planting** Prickly pears prefer sandy, well-aerated soil with a pH of 5.5–7 (*see p.18*). Plant rooted pads in beds or pots of sandy compost in a greenhouse or in a conservatory. Add a little slow-release fertilizer (*see p.20*) and, if necessary, add grit or sharp sand to ensure good drainage (*see p.16*). Keep temperatures at 18–25°C (64–77°F) with a humidity of no more than 60 per cent to discourage diseases.

■ **Routine care** Prickly pears thrive in dry conditions and require little watering once they are established. They rarely require applications of additional fertilizer unless the soil is exceptionally poor.

■ **Harvesting and storage** The first fruits should appear three or four years after planting. Cut the fruits away from the stem segments with a sharp knife. They are best eaten within a few days of harvesting, although storage is possible for short periods of time in cool conditions.

■ **Propagation** Prickly pears are usually propagated from stem sections (*see above*); they should take two or three months to root.

■ **Common problems** Prickly pears may be affected by mealybugs (*see p.257*). Damping off (*see p.254*) may also be a problem in humid conditions.

■ **Recommended cultivars**
Cultivars are seldom available to the amateur gardener in cool temperate climates.

# Crop planner

Good planning is the key to running a productive kitchen garden. This quick reference chart draws together all the information given throughout the text on sowing, planting and harvesting vegetables, strawberries and annual herbs, so that you can plan how to use your plot most effectively throughout the year. Perennial herbs and fruit are not included here because they will occupy a permanent and specific place in the garden.

Time spent on planning what crop to grow, and where to do so, will pay dividends in the following year. You may find it helpful to use this chart in conjunction with the crop rotation diagram (*see p.31*). Decide on your priorities: to grow as much produce as possible, you will need to plant a variety of crops to ensure a year-round supply. Alternatively, you may be interested in growing only vegetables that are not readily available in the shops.

For each crop, the chart indicates up to three ways of managing sowing and planting: starting indoors, under cover, or outdoors. Sometimes this decision will be dictated by the particular climatic conditions in your area and the hardiness of each crop. You may wish to extend the season of a crop by using more than one method. Where relevant, two outdoor management lines are used to show the effects of planting at different times of the year for long-term crops, and for perennial vegetables, such as asparagus.

The chart also indicates how long approximately each crop will occupy space in the ground, so that you can calculate how many plants you can fit into your plot at any one time. Allocate space first for the crops that you are keenest to grow and then you can work out how to fill the remaining space, and time, with more crops for an efficient and bountiful garden.

## How to use crop planner

This chart will help you establish whether any crop listed will need protection in the greenhouse or under cover, or if it is hardy enough to flourish in the open ground in cool, temperate climates. The chart is divided into the four seasons, with a sub-division for early (E), mid- (M), and late (L) part of the season. The shaded part-seasons will help you to identify the crops that hog the ground, and those that can be grown as short-term crops.

For instance, carrots sown in early spring will be out of the ground by early summer, allowing you to replant the row for an autumn crop of peas, as well as refreshing the soil by rotating the crops.

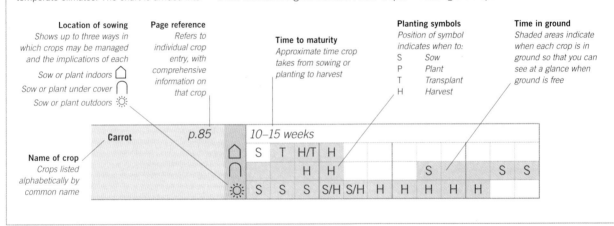

**Location of sowing**
*Shows up to three ways in which crops may be managed and the implications of each*

Sow or plant indoors ⌂
Sow or plant under cover ⋒
Sow or plant outdoors ☼

**Page reference**
*Refers to individual crop entry, with comprehensive information on that crop*

**Time to maturity**
*Approximate time crop takes from sowing or planting to harvest*

**Planting symbols**
*Position of symbol indicates when to:*
S    Sow
P    Plant
T    Transplant
H    Harvest

**Time in ground**
*Shaded areas indicate when each crop is in ground so that you can see at a glance when ground is free*

**Name of crop**
*Crops listed alphabetically by common name*

| Carrot | p.85 | 10–15 weeks | | | | | | | | | | |

| Crop | Season | | | | | | | | | | | |
|---|---|---|---|---|---|---|---|---|---|---|---|---|
| | | SPRING | | | SUMMER | | | AUTUMN | | | WINTER | |
| | | E | M | L | E | M | L | E | M | L | E | M | L |
| **Amaranth** p.125 | | 10–12 weeks | | | | | | | | | | |
| ⌂ | | | S | | T/H | H | H | H | H | | | |
| ☼ | | | | S | | H | H | H | H | | | |
| **Asparagus** p.133 | | 2–3 years | | | | | | | | | | |
| ⌂ | | S | H | H | T | | | | | | | |
| ☼ | | S/P | H | H | T | | | | | | | P |
| **Asparagus pea** p.98 | | 9–14 weeks | | | | | | | | | | |
| ⌂ | | | S | T | H | H | H | | | | | |
| ☼ | | | | S | | H | H | | | | | |
| **Aubergine** p.111 | | 16–24 weeks | | | | | | | | | | |
| *or* eggplant ⌂ | | S | S | T | T | H | H | H | H | | | |
| **Basil** p.142 | | 6–8 weeks | | | | | | | | | | |
| ⌂ | | S | S | T | H | H | H | H | | | | |

| Crop | Season | | | | | | | | | | | |
|---|---|---|---|---|---|---|---|---|---|---|---|---|
| | | SPRING | | | SUMMER | | | AUTUMN | | | WINTER | |
| | | E | M | L | E | M | L | E | M | L | E | M | L |
| **Bean, broad** p.98 | | 14–32 weeks | | | | | | | | | | |
| *or* fava ⌂ | | T | T | H | H | | | | | | S | S |
| ⋒ | | | | H | H | H | | | S | S | | S | S |
| ☼ | | S | S | | H | H | H | | S | S | | | S |
| **Bean, French** p.99 | | 9–14 weeks | | | | | | | | | | |
| *or* kidney ⌂ | | | S | S | T/H | H | H | | | | | |
| ⋒ | | | | S | | H | H | H | H | | | |
| ☼ | | | | | S | S/H | H | H | H | H | | |
| **Bean, Lima,** p.99 | | 14–23 weeks | | | | | | | | | | |
| *and* yard long ⌂ | | | S | S | T | | H | H | | | | |
| ⋒ | | | | S | S | | | H | H | | | |
| **Bean, runner** p.100 | | 14 weeks | | | | | | | | | | |
| ⌂ | | | S | S | T | H | H | H | | | | |
| ⋒ | | | | | S | S | S | H | H | H | | |

| Crop | | | | SPRING | | | SUMMER | | | AUTUMN | | | WINTER | | |
|---|---|---|---|---|---|---|---|---|---|---|---|---|---|---|---|
| | | | | E | M | L | E | M | L | E | M | L | E | M | L |
| Beetroot | p.85 | 8–12 weeks | | | | | | | | | | | | | |
| | | | ∩ | S | S | S | H | H | H | | | | | | |
| | | | ☼ | | | | S | S | | H | H | | | | |
| Brussels sprouts | p.78 | 20–40 weeks | | | | | | | | | | | | | |
| | | | ⌂ | | T | T | | | H | H | H | | | | S |
| | | | ☼ | | S | S | T | T | | | H | H | H | H | H |
| Cabbage, Chinese | p.126 | 9–10 weeks | | | | | | | | | | | | | |
| | | | ⌂ | | S | S | T | T/H | T/H | H | | | | | |
| | | | ☼ | | | | S | S | S/H | H | H | H | | | |
| Cabbage, red | p.78 | 12–16 weeks | | | | | | | | | | | | | |
| | | | ⌂ | S | S | T | T | H | H | | | H | | | |
| | | | ☼ | S | S | T | T | H | H | | | H | | | |
| Cabbage, spring | p.78 | 31–33 weeks | | | | | | | | | | | | | |
| | | | ⌂ | | H | H | | | S | T | T | | | | |
| | | | ☼ | | H | H | | | S | T | T | | | | |
| Cabbage, early summer | p.78 | 12–14 weeks | | | | | | | | | | | | | |
| | | | ⌂ | S | T | T | H | H | | | | | | | S |
| | | | ☼ | S | T | T | H | H | | | | | | | |
| Cabbage, summer, autumn | p.78 | 10–14 weeks | | | | | | | | | | | | | |
| | | | ⌂ | | S | T/S | T/S | T/S | H/T | H | H | H | H | | |
| | | | ☼ | | S | T/S | T/S | T/S | H/T | H | H | H | H | | |
| Cabbage, winter | p.78 | 22–36 weeks | | | | | | | | | | | | | |
| | | | ⌂ | H | | S | T/S | T | | | | H | H | H | H |
| | | | ☼ | H | | S | T/S | T | | | | H | H | H | H |
| Calabrese | p.79 | 10–14 weeks | | | | | | | | | | | | | |
| | | | ⌂ | | H | H | | | | | S | | T | | |
| | | | ☼ | S | S | S | H/S | H/S | H | H | H | | | | |
| Cardoon | p.133 | 36–38 weeks | | | | | | | | | | | | | |
| | | | ⌂ | S | S | T | T | | | H | H | H | | | |
| Carrot | p.85 | 10–15 weeks | | | | | | | | | | | | | |
| | | | ⌂ | S | T | H/T | H | | | | | | | | |
| | | | ∩ | S | | H | H | | | | S | | | S | S |
| | | | ☼ | | S | S | S/H | S/H | H | H | H | H | H | | |
| Cauliflower, early summer | p.79 | 16–30 weeks | | | | | | | | | | | | | |
| | | | ⌂ | T | | | H | | | | | | | S | |
| | | | ∩ | T | | | H | | | | S | | | | |
| Cauliflower, summer | p.79 | 16 weeks | | | | | | | | | | | | | |
| | | | ⌂ | | S | | T | | H | H | | | | | |
| | | | ☼ | S | S | T | | | H | H | | | | | |
| Cauliflower, autumn | p.79 | 16–18 weeks | | | | | | | | | | | | | |
| | | | ⌂ | | S | S | T | T | | H | H | H | | | |
| Cauliflower, winter heading | p.79 | 32–44 weeks | | | | | | | | | | | | | |
| | | | ☼ | H | | S | | | T | | | | H | H | H |
| Cauliflower, spring heading | p.79 | 40–44 weeks | | | | | | | | | | | | | |
| | | | ☼ | H | H | H/S | H | | T | | | | | | |
| Cauliflower, mini | p.79 | 13–18 weeks | | | | | | | | | | | | | |
| | | | ☼ | | S | S | T/S | T/S | H | H | H | H | | | |
| Celeriac | p.121 | 24–28 weeks | | | | | | | | | | | | | |
| | | | ⌂ | HS | H/T/S | T | T | | | H | H | H | H | H | H |
| Celery, leaf | p.121 | 12–15 weeks | | | | | | | | | | | | | |
| | | | ⌂ | HS | H/T/S | T | T | | H/S | H/T | H | H | H | H | H |
| Celery, self-blanching | p.121 | 20–24 weeks | | | | | | | | | | | | | |
| | | | ⌂ | S | ST | T | T | H | H | H | H | | | | |
| Celery, trench | p.121 | 34–38 weeks | | | | | | | | | | | | | |
| | | | ⌂ | S | S | T | T | | | | | H | H | | |
| Ceylon *or* Malabar spinach | p.125 | 10–12 weeks | | | | | | | | | | | | | |
| | | | ⌂ | | | S | S/T/H | T/H | H | H | | | | | |
| Chicory, red | p.103 | 9–14 weeks | | | | | | | | | | | | | |
| | | | ⌂ | | S | S | T | H | H | H | | | | | |
| | | | ☼ | | | | S | | H/S | H | H | | | | |
| Chicory, sugarloaf | p.103 | 9–14 weeks | | | | | | | | | | | | | |
| | | | ⌂ | | S | S | T | H | H | H | | | | | |
| | | | ☼ | | | | S | S | S/H | H | H | | | | |

| Crop | | | | SPRING | | | SUMMER | | | AUTUMN | | | WINTER | | |
|---|---|---|---|---|---|---|---|---|---|---|---|---|---|---|---|
| | | | | E | M | L | E | M | L | E | M | L | E | M | L |
| Chicory, Witloof | p.103 | 23–27 weeks | | | | | | | | | | | | | |
| | | | ☼ | | | S | S | | | | H | H | H | | |
| Chilli pepper | p.111 | 18–23 weeks | | | | | | | | | | | | | |
| | | | ⌂ | S | S | T | T | H | H | H | H | | | | |
| Chinese, artichoke | p.134 | 40–50 weeks | | | | | | | | | | | | | |
| | | | ☼ | P | | | | | | | | | H | H | H |
| Chinese broccoli | p.126 | 10 weeks | | | | | | | | | | | | | |
| | | | ⌂ | | S | S | T | H | H | H | | | | | |
| | | | ☼ | | | | S | S | H | H | H | H | | | |
| Corn salad *or* lamb's lettuce | p.103 | 4–12 weeks | | | | | | | | | | | | | |
| | | | ∩ | H | H/S | H/S | H | H | H | S | | | | H | H |
| | | | ☼ | | | | S | S | S | H | H | H | H | H | |
| Courgette | p.117 | 9–14 weeks | | | | | | | | | | | | | |
| | | | ⌂ | | S | T/S | T | H | H | | | | | | |
| | | | ☼ | | | | S | | | H | H | | | | |
| Cucumber | p.117 | 14–18 weeks | | | | | | | | | | | | | |
| | | | ⌂ | S | S | T | T | H | H | | | | | | |
| | | | ∩ | S | | | | | H | H | H | | | | |
| | | | ☼ | | | | S | | H | H | H | | | | |
| Endive | p.104 | 12–14 weeks | | | | | | | | | | | | | |
| | | | ⌂ | | S | S | T | H/T | H | | | | | | |
| | | | ∩ | | | | S | S | | H | H | H | H | | |
| Florence fennel | p.122 | 15–18 weeks | | | | | | | | | | | | | |
| | | | ⌂ | S | ST | T | H | H | | | | | | | |
| | | | ☼ | | | | S | S | S | H | H | H | | | |
| Flowering greens *or* choy sum | p.126 | 10 weeks | | | | | | | | | | | | | |
| | | | ⌂ | | S | S | T/S | T/H | T/H | H | | | | | |
| | | | ☼ | | | | | | S | | H | H | | | |
| Garlic | p.92 | 22–32 weeks | | | | | | | | | | | | | |
| | | | ☼ | P | | H | H | H | H | H | P | P | P | P | P |
| Gherkin | p.117 | 14–18 weeks | | | | | | | | | | | | | |
| | | | ⌂ | | S | S | T | T | H | H | | | | | |
| | | | ☼ | | | | S | | | | H | H | | | |
| Globe artichoke | p.134 | 60–64 weeks | | | | | | | | | | | | | |
| | | | ⌂ | | | H | H/T | | | | | | | | S |
| | | | ☼ | P | P | H | H | | | | | | | | |
| Hamburg parsley | p.86 | 28–36 weeks | | | | | | | | | | | | | |
| | | | ☼ | H | H | S | S | S | H | H | H | H | H | H | H |
| Ice plant | p.104 | 4–12 weeks | | | | | | | | | | | | | |
| | | | ⌂ | | S | | T/H | H | H | H | H | | | | |
| Jerusalem artichoke | p.135 | 40–45 weeks | | | | | | | | | | | | | |
| | | | ☼ | P | P | P | | | | | | | H | H | H/P |
| Kale *or* curly kale | p.80 | 28–42 weeks | | | | | | | | | | | | | |
| | | | ⌂ | H | HS | S | T/S | T/S | T | | | H | H | H | H |
| | | | ☼ | H | HS | S | T/S | T/S | T | | | H | H | H | H |
| Kohlrabi | p.80 | 12–16 weeks | | | | | | | | | | | | | |
| | | | ⌂ | S | S/T | T/H | H | | | | | | | | S |
| | | | ☼ | | S | S | S | H/S | H/S | H | H | H | H | | |
| Komatsuna | p.104 | 4–12 weeks | | | | | | | | | | | | | |
| | | | ⌂ | | | | | | S | T | | | H | H | H |
| | | | ☼ | | | | | S | S | H | H | H | | | |
| Landcress | p.105 | 4–12 weeks | | | | | | | | | | | | | |
| | | | ⌂ | H | H | | | S | S | T | T | H | H | H | H |
| | | | ☼ | | S | S | S | H | H | H | H | H | H | H | |
| Leek | p.93 | 18–40 weeks | | | | | | | | | | | | | |
| | | | ⌂ | | T | T | | | H | H | H | | | S | S |
| | | | ☼ | H/S | H/S | | T | T | T | H | H | H | H | H | H |
| Lettuce, all types | p.105 | Mini: 8–10 weeks<br>Butterhead: 10–12 weeks<br>Crisphead and cos: 12–13 weeks<br>Iceberg: 14 weeks | | | | | | | | | | | | | |
| | | | ⌂ | ST | T | T | H | H | | | | | | S | S |
| | | | ∩ | H | H | H | | | | S | | | | | S |
| | | | ☼ | S | S | S | S | H/S | H/S | H/S | H | H | | | |

Season key columns: SPRING (E, M, L), SUMMER (E, M, L), AUTUMN (E, M, L), WINTER (E, M, L). The "Env" column indicates the row symbol: **house** = under cover, **tunnel** = cloche/tunnel, **sun** = open ground.

| Crop | Page | Duration | Env | Sp E | Sp M | Sp L | Su E | Su M | Su L | Au E | Au M | Au L | Wi E | Wi M | Wi L |
|---|---|---|---|---|---|---|---|---|---|---|---|---|---|---|---|
| Mibuna and Mizuna greens | p.106 | 4–12 weeks | house | S | S | T | H | H | H | | | | | | |
| | | | tunnel | | | | S | S | | H | H | H | | | |
| | | | sun | | | S | S | H | H | H | H | | | | |
| Mustard and cress | p.106 | 2 weeks | sun | S/H | S/H | S/H | S/H | S/H | S/H | S/H | S/H | S/H | S/H | S/H | |
| Mustard greens and spinach cress | p.127 | 6–8 weeks | house | | S | S | T/H | T/H | H | | | | | | |
| | | | sun | | | S | S | S/H | H | H | H | | | | |
| New Zealand spinach | p.127 | 6 weeks | house | | S | T | H | | | | | | | | |
| | | | sun | | | S | S | H | H | H | | | | | |
| Okra | p.112 | 18–23 weeks | house | S | S | T | T | H | H | H | | | | | |
| Onion, bulb | p.92 | from seed: 24–40 weeks; sets: 24–36 weeks | house | S | T | T | | | | H | H | | | | S |
| | | | sun | P | S/P | | H | H | H | H/S | S/P | S/P | | P | P |
| Onion, Japanese bunching | p.93 | 10–14 weeks | house | T | T | T | | | | H/S | H/S | H/S | H/S | H/S | H/S |
| | | | sun | | | S | S | S | S | H | H | H | H | H | H |
| Onion, pickling | p.93 | 20–22 weeks | sun | S | S | S | | | H | | | | | | |
| Onion, spring | p.94 | 10–14 weeks | sun | H/S | H/S | S | H/S | H/S | H/S | H/S | H | | | | |
| Onion, tree or Egyptian | p.94 | 36–40 weeks | sun | P | P | P | | | | H | P | P | P | | |
| Onion, Welsh | p.94 | 24–30 weeks | sun | H/S/P | H/S/P | H/S/P | H | H | S/H | H | H | H | H | H | |
| Pak choi | p.127 | 10 weeks | house | | S | S | T | T/H | T/H | | | | | | |
| | | | sun | | | S | S | H | H | H | | | | | |
| Parsley | p.144 | 12–20 weeks | house | S | T/S | S/T | T/H | T/H | H | H | H | | S | S | |
| | | | tunnel | | | S | S | | | H | H | | | | |
| | | | sun | | | | S | S | S | S | H | H | | | |
| Parsnip | p.86 | 16–18 weeks | sun | H | H/S | S | | | H | H | H | H | H | H | H |
| Pea | p.99 | 12–14 weeks | house | T | T | T | H | | | | S | | | S | S |
| | | | tunnel | | | | H | | | | S | | | | S |
| | | | sun | S | S | S | S/H | S/H | H | H | H | | | | |
| Potato, early | p.86 | 14–20 weeks | tunnel | P | P | | H | H | H | | | | | | |
| Potato, maincrop | p.86 | 20 weeks | sun | | P | P | | H | H | H | H | | | | |
| Pumpkin | p.118 | 23–27 weeks | house | | S | ST | T | | | H | H | | | | |
| | | | sun | | | | S | | | H | H | | | | |
| Radish, summer | p.106 | 2–8 weeks | house | | | T | H | | | | | | S | S | |
| | | | tunnel | S | | | H | H | | | | | | | |
| | | | sun | | | S | S | H/S | H/S | H/S | H/S | H | H | H | |
| Radish, winter | p.106 | 12–20 weeks | sun | | | | | | S | S | H | H | H | H | |
| Rhubarb | p.135 | 2 years | house | | | T | H | H | H | | | | | | S |
| | | | sun | P | | | H | H | H | H | P | P | P | P | P |
| Rocket or erugula | p.107 | 4–12 weeks | tunnel | H | H | S | H | | | S | | | H | H | |
| | | | sun | | H/S | S | H/S | H/S | H | H | H | H | H | | |
| Salsify | p.87 | 27–45 weeks | sun | H/S | S | S | | | | H | H | H | H | H | |
| Scorzonera | p.87 | 27 weeks | sun | H/S | S | S | | | S | | H | H | H | H | |

| Crop | Page | Duration | Env | Sp E | Sp M | Sp L | Su E | Su M | Su L | Au E | Au M | Au L | Wi E | Wi M | Wi L |
|---|---|---|---|---|---|---|---|---|---|---|---|---|---|---|---|
| Seakale | p.135 | 2 years, 18 weeks | house | H | H | H | T | | | | | | | | S |
| | | | sun | H/P | H/S | H | | | | | | | | | |
| Shallot | p.94 | 16–32 weeks | house | | T | | H | H | | | | | | | S |
| | | | sun | P | S/P | S | H | H | | | | | P | P | P |
| Spinach | p.128 | 10–12 weeks | house | T/H | H | | | | | | | | | S | S |
| | | | sun | S/H | S/H | S/H | S/H | S/H | S/H | S/H | H | H | | S | S |
| Sprouting broccoli | p.81 | 15–20 weeks or 46–50 weeks | house | H/T/S | H/T/S | H/T/S | H/T | H/T | T/H | H | H | H | | | H/S |
| | | | sun | H/S | H/S | H/S | S/T/H | S/T/H | T/H | H | H | H | | | H |
| Strawberry, alpine | p.211 | 10–20 weeks | tunnel | S | S/P/T | P/T/H | | H | H | H/S | T/S | T/S | | | |
| | | | sun | | | P | H | H | H | H | | | | | |
| Strawberry, perpetual | p.211 | 36–52 weeks | house | | | | P/H | P/H | P/H | H | H | P | P | | |
| | | | sun | | | P | P | P/H | H/P | H/P | H/P | H/P | H/P | P | |
| Strawberry, summer bearing | p.211 | 40–52 weeks | house | | | | | H/P | H/P | P | | | P | P | |
| | | | sun | | | | P | P | P/H | H/P | H/P | P | P | P | P |
| Summer purslane | p.107 | 4–12 weeks | tunnel | | | | S | | H | | | | | | |
| | | | sun | | | | S | S | S/H | H | H | H | | | |
| Summer squash | p.117 | 14–18 weeks | house | | | | S | ST | T | H | H | | | | |
| | | | sun | | | | | S | | H | H | | | | |
| Swede | p.88 | 20–26 weeks | sun | | | | | S | S | | H | H | H | H | |
| Sweet melon | p.118 | 18–23 weeks | house | | | | S | | T | H | H | | | | |
| | | | tunnel | | | | S | S | | H | H | | | | |
| Sweet pepper | p.111 | 18–23 weeks | house | S | S | T | T | H | H | H | H | | | | |
| Sweet potato | p.88 | 27 weeks | house | S | S | T | T | | | H | | | | | |
| Sweetcorn | p.112 | 18 weeks | house | | S | | T | | | H | H | | | | |
| | | | sun | | | | S | | | H | H | H | | | |
| Swiss chard or spinach beet | p.128 | 8–12 weeks | sun | | S | S/T | H/S | H | H | H | | | | | |
| | | | sun | H | H | H | | S | S | | | | | | |
| Texsel greens | p.81 | 5–8 weeks | sun | S | | S | H/S | H/S | H/S | H/S | H/S | H | H | | |
| Tomatillo | p.113 | 18–23 weeks | house | S | S | T | T | H | H | H | | | | | |
| Tomato | p.113 | 18–23 weeks | house | S | S | T | T | H | H | H | H | | | | S |
| Turnip | p.88 | 6–10 weeks | tunnel | S | S | H | H | H | | | | | | | S |
| | | | sun | | | S | S/H | S/H | S/H | H | H | H | H | | |
| Turnip tops | p.88 | 4–6 weeks | sun | S | H | | | | | S | S | H | H | | |
| Vegetable marrow | p.119 | 14–18 weeks | house | | | | S | ST | T | H | H | | | | |
| | | | sun | | | | | S | | H | H | | | | |
| Watermelon | p.119 | 18–23 weeks | house | | | | S | T | T | | H | H | | | |
| Winter purslane | p.107 | 12 weeks | house | | | | | S | S | T | H | H | | | |
| | | | sun | | | | S | S | S | S | H | H | H | H | |
| Winter squash | p.118 | 23–27 weeks | house | | | | S | ST | T | H | H | | | | |
| | | | sun | | | | | S | | H | H | | | | |

# Average crop yields

Use this chart to help plan your crops. All quantities are approximate, and will vary from year to year, depending on season, spacing, stage of harvesting, age of fruit trees and bushes, and specific growing conditions of vegetables. They are provided here as a quick-reference guide when deciding how much of each crop to plant. For more detail, *see individual crop entries, pp.74–135 and 174–237.* Culinary herbs are harvested continuously, so are not included here.

## AVERAGE VEGETABLE YIELDS

| Crop | Yield | Crop | Yield |
|---|---|---|---|
| Amaranth | 7.25kg per 3m (16lb per 10ft) row | Lettuce, butterhead | 9–12 heads per 3m (10ft) row |
| Asparagus | 9–12 spears per crown | Lettuce, cos | 9–12 heads per 3m (10ft) row |
| Asparagus pea | 450g per 3m (1lb per 10ft) row | Lettuce, crisphead | 8–9 heads per 3m (10ft) row |
| Aubergine or eggplant | 3–4.5kg per 3m (6½–10lb per 10ft) row | Lettuce, iceberg | 8–9 heads per 3m (10ft) row |
| Bean, asparagus or yard long | 560g per 3m (1¼lb per 10ft) row | Lettuce, mini | 18–20 heads per 3m (10ft) row |
| | | Mibuna and Mizuna greens | 6–9 heads per 3m (10ft) row |
| Bean, broad | 3kg per 3m (6½lb per 10ft) row | Mustard greens | 1.5kg per sq m (3–4lb per sq yd) |
| Bean, French or kidney | 4.5kg per 3m (10lb per 10ft) row | New Zealand spinach | 6kg per 3m (13lb per 10ft) row |
| Bean, lima or butter | 560g per 3m (1¼lb per 10ft) row | Okra | 1.5kg per 3m (3¼lb per 10ft) row |
| Bean, runner | 6kg per 3m (13lb per 10ft) row | Onion, bulb | 60 small, 30 large, or 15 very large onions, approx 1–3kg (2¼–6½lb) per 3m (10ft) row |
| Beetroot | 30 450g–1kg beetroot per 3m (1–2lb per 10ft) row | | |
| | | Onion, Japanese bunching | 250–300, or 40–50 large, per 3m (10ft) row |
| Brussels sprout | 60–70 sprouts per plant | | |
| Cabbage, Chinese | 9–12 heads per 3m (10ft) row | Onion, pickling | 1–1.5kg per 3m (2¼–3lb per 10ft) row |
| Cabbage, spring | 12 110–225g (4–8oz) heads per 3m (10ft) row | Onion, spring | 250–300 per 3m (10ft) row |
| | | Pak choi | 9–12 heads per 3m (10ft) row |
| Cabbage, summer or autumn | 6–8 cabbages, 450–900g (1–2lb) each, per 3m (10ft) row | Parsnip | 4kg per 3m (9lb per 10ft) row |
| | | Pea (all types) | 3kg per 3m (6½lb per 10ft) row |
| Calabrese | 110–225g (4–8oz) per plant | Potato | early: 4.5kg per 3m (10lb per 10ft) row; maincrop: 10kg per 3m (22lb per 10ft) row |
| Cardoon | 3–6 heads per 3m (10ft) row | | |
| Carrot | 3kg per 3m (6lb per 10ft) row | Pumpkin | 1 large or 4–6 small fruits per plant |
| Cauliflower | 5–6 (or up to 20 mini) curds per 3m (10ft) row | Radish, summer | 100–120 per 3m (10ft) row |
| | | Radish, winter | 10 per 3m (10ft) row |
| Celeriac | 10 heads, 225–400g (8–12oz) each, per 3m (10ft) row | Rhubarb | 4.5–13.5kg per 3m (10–30lb per 10ft) row |
| | | Rocket or erugala | 9–12 bunches per 3m (10ft) row |
| Celery | 12 heads, 450g (1lb) each, per 3m (10ft) row | Salsify | 1.5kg per 3m (3lb per 10ft) row |
| | | Scorzonera | 1.5kg per 3m (3lb per 10ft) row |
| Ceylon or Malabar spinach | 3kg per 3m (6½lb per 10ft) row | Seakale | 8–10 stems per plant |
| Chicory | 8–9 heads per 3m (10ft) row | Shallot | 60–180 shallots per 3m (10ft) row |
| Chilli pepper | 3–4.5kg per 3m (6½–10lb per 10ft) row | Spinach | 6kg per 3m (13lb per 10ft) row |
| Chinese artichoke | 20–30 tubers per plant | Sprouting broccoli | 1.5kg per 3m (3–4lb per 10ft) row |
| Chinese broccoli | 9–12 bunches per 3m (10ft) row | Summer purslane | 20–24 bunches per 3m (10ft) row |
| Corn salad or lamb's lettuce | 18–20 heads per 3m (10ft) row | Summer squash | 6–8 small fruits per plant |
| Courgette or zucchini | 6–12 fruits per plant; 4.5kg per 3m (10lb per 10ft) row | Swede | 6kg per 3m (13lb per 10ft) row |
| | | Sweet melon | 2–4 fruits per plant |
| Cucumber | 15 fruits per plant | Sweet pepper | 2.75–4.5kg per 3m (6–10lb per 10ft) row |
| Endive | 9–12 heads per 3m (10ft) row | Sweet potato | 1.5kg per 3m (3lb per 10ft) row |
| Florence fennel | 1.4–2.25kg per 3m (3–5lb per 10ft) row | Sweetcorn | 6–9 cobs per sq m (sq yd) |
| Flowering greens or choy sum | 9–12 bunches per 3m (10ft) row | Swiss chard or spinach beet | 6kg per 3m (13lb per 10ft) row |
| | | Texsel greens (salad crop) | 6–9kg per 3m (13–20lb per 10ft) row |
| Garlic | 17 bulbs per 3m (10ft) row | Tomatillo | 1–2kg (2¼–4½lb) per plant |
| Gherkin | 30 fruits per plant | Tomato, bush outdoors | 4kg (9lb) per plant |
| Globe artichoke | 6–15 large, 24–60 small, per 3m (10ft) row | Tomato, vine outdoors | 1.8–4kg (4–9lb) per plant |
| Hamburg parsley | 3kg per 3m (6½lb per 10ft) row | Tomato, vine greenhouse, unheated | 2.75–5kg (6–11lb) per plant |
| Ice plant | 4.5kg per 3m (10lb per 10ft) row | | |
| Jerusalem artichoke | 10–12 tubers per plant | Turnip | 30 500–750g (1–1½lb) turnips, or 48 multiblock (baby) turnips, per 3m (10ft) row |
| Kale or curly kale | 1.8–2.25kg per 3m (4–5lb per 10ft) row | | |
| Kohlrabi | 2.5kg per 3m (4–6lb per 10ft) row | Turnip tops | 500g (1lb) per 3m (10ft) row |
| Komatsuna | 6–9 heads per 3m (10ft) row | Vegetable marrow | 2 large or 6–8 small fruits per plant |
| Land cress | 18–20 heads per 3m (10ft) row | Watermelon | 1–2 fruits per plant |
| Leaf celery | 15–20 heads per 3m (10ft) row | Winter purslane | 20–24 bunches per 3m (10ft) row |
| Leek | early: 4–6kg per 3m (8½–13lb per 10ft) row; late: 3–5kg per 3m (6½–11lb per 10ft) row | Winter squash | 1 large or 4–6 small fruits per plant |

## AVERAGE FRUIT YIELDS

| Crop | Yield | Crop | Yield |
|---|---|---|---|
| Acid or sour cherry, bush | 13.5kg–18kg (30–40lb) per tree | Nectarine, fan | 5.5–11.25kg (12–25lb) per tree |
| Acid or sour cherry, fan | 5.5–15.75kg (12–35lb) per tree | Peach, bush | 13.5–27kg (30–60lb) per tree |
| Almond | Erratic cropping | Peach, fan | 5.5–11.25k (12–25lb) per tree |
| Apple, bush | 27–55kg (60–120lb) per tree | Pear, bush | 18–45.5kg (40–100lb) per tree |
| Apple, dwarf/spindle/ pyramid | 13.5–22.5kg (30–50lb) per tree | Pear, dwarf/spindle/ pyramid | 9–18kg (20–40lb) per tree |
| Apple, espalier | 13.5–18kg (30–40lb) per tree | Pear, espalier | 9–13.5kg (20–30lb) per tree |
| Apple, fan | 5.5–13.5kg (12–30lb) per tree | Pear, fan | 5.5–13.5kg (12–30lb) per tree |
| Apple, single cordon | 2.25–4.5kg (5–10lb) per tree | Pear, single cordon | 1.75–3.5kg (4–8lb) per tree |
| Apricot, bush | 13.5–45.5kg (30–100lb) per tree | Plum, bush | 13.5–27kg (30–60lb) per tree |
| Apricot, fan | 5.5–15.75kg (12–35lb) per tree | Plum, fan | 6.75–11.25kg (15–25lb) per tree |
| Blackberry | 6.75–9kg per 3m (15–20lb per 10ft) row | Plum, pyramid | 13.5–22.5kg (30–50lb) per tree |
| Blackcurrant | 4.5kg (10lb) per bush | Plum, single cordon | 3.5–6.75kg (8–15lb) per tree |
| Blueberry | 2.25–5kg (5–11lb) per bush | Quince, bush | 25–45.5kg (55–100lb) from a mature tree |
| Cobnut and filbert | 5–15.75kg (11–35lb) from a mature bush | Raspberry | 6.75–9kg per 3m (15–20lb per 10ft) row |
| Cranberry | 0.5–0.75kg per sq m (1–1.5lb per sq yd) | Redcurrant | 4–5kg (9–11lb) per bush |
| Fig | 2.25–9kg (5–20lb) from a mature fan | Strawberry | 450g (1lb) per plant |
| Gooseberry | 3.5–4.5 kg (7–10lb) per bush | Sweet or duke cherry, bush | 13.5–45.5kg (30–100lb) per tree |
| Grape | 2.25–3.5kg (5–8lb) or 8–10 bunches from a mature single cordon or single guyot | Sweet or duke cherry, fan | 5.5–15.75kg (12–35lb) per tree |
| Medlar | 13.5–27kg (30–60lb) from a mature standard | Sweet or duke cherry, pyramid | 13.5–27kg (30–60lb) per tree |
| Mulberry | Erratic cropping | Walnut | Erratic cropping |
| Nectarine, bush | 13.5–27kg (30–60lb) per tree | Whitecurrant | 4–5kg (9–11lb) per bush |

# Seasonal tasks

Use this chart as a handy reminder of seasonal tasks to do in the kitchen garden. As a distillation of advice from text throughout the book, it aims to aid forward planning, but bear in mind that timings of operations vary considerably because climatic conditions differ from region to region. Sowing dates, for example, will be later at more northerly latitudes and higher altitudes. Make allowances also for seasonal fluctuations, such as cold springs or mild winters.

## SEASONAL TASKS PLANNER

| Vegetables and herbs | Fruit |
|---|---|
| **Early spring** | **Early spring** |

### Vegetables and herbs — Early spring

- **Sow broad beans,** Brussels sprouts, calabrese, leeks, lettuce, onions, parsley, parsnips, peas, radishes, red cabbage, rocket, salsify, scorzonera, spinach, spring onions, summer cauliflowers, Texsel greens, turnips, and hardy annual herbs, for example dill and chervil, when conditions are favourable.
- **Protect newly sown crops** with cloches in very cold areas.
- **Sow asparagus peas,** aubergines, beetroot, cardoons, carrots (Amsterdam, Nantes, and Round), celeriac, celery, cucumbers, Florence fennel, leeks, lettuce, parsley, peppers, sweet potatoes, tomatoes, tomatillos, and half-hardy herbs, such as basil, under glass or in frames, as appropriate.
- **Plant asparagus,** early summer cauliflowers, Jerusalem and globe artichokes, garlic, onion sets and seedlings, early potatoes, rhubarb, shallots and seakale.
- **Harvest** last of winter brassicas under cloches.
- **Cut back old growth** on perennial herbs, and divide clump-forming herbs, if not done in autumn.
- **Lift invasive herbs** planted in sunken containers, divide, and replant.
- **Discard or plant out** herbs that were potted up for winter use.
- **Hoe regularly between** crops to keep down weeds.
- **Mulch around plants** to suppress weeds and conserve moisture in soil.
- **Fork over soil,** weed, and apply fertilizer in preparation for later sowings and plantings.
- **Sow green manures** on vacant plots.

### Fruit — Early spring

- **Finish planting** and pruning fruit trees and bushes.
- **Prune flowering cobnuts** and filberts if pollen is being shed.
- **Mulch young trees,** fruit bushes, raspberries, and other cane fruits, and apply fertilizers that are appropriate to the fruit in question.
- **Control weeds** in all fruit beds, preferably by hand pulling – to avoid potential root damage by hoeing.
- **Prune fan-trained peaches,** nectarines, and apricots.
- **Where mildew has been a problem,** spray gooseberries just before the flowers open and continue at fortnightly intervals. Check integrity of netting covers to ensure continued protection against bullfinches, which eat the buds.
- **Hand-pollinate** wall-trained fruit if insects are not on the wing. Protect flowers from frost.
- **Aid pollination** on vines under protection (glass).
- **Check blackberries,** loganberries, and tayberries, and tie canes into wires as necessary.
- **Plant strawberry runners** in prepared ground, and mulch.
- **Tidy up** strawberry beds, removing dead, damaged, and diseased leaves and old runners.
- **Cover established flowering strawberries** with cloches or fleece for earlier fruits; lift during the day for pollinating insects to do their work.

## SEASONAL TASKS PLANNER

| Vegetables and herbs | Fruit |
|---|---|

### Mid-spring

- **Outdoors, sow** beetroot, broccoli, Brussels sprouts, cabbages, calabrese, carrots, cauliflowers, corn salad, kohlrabi, leeks, lettuce, peas, radish, rocket, salsify, scorzonera, spinach, Swiss chard, turnips. Begin successional sowing of regularly used herbs.
- **Sow asparagus peas,** celeriac, celery, French, broad, Lima and runner beans, okra, sweetcorn, and sweet melons under glass.
- **Plant out** Jerusalem and globe artichokes, onion sets, and potatoes, and transplant cabbages, leeks, Japanese onions, and seakale.
- **Water and continue weeding** newly planted vegetables and herbs.
- **Erect supports** for peas and climbing beans.
- **Continue earthing up** potatoes; pull up Brussels sprouts' stumps.
- **Repot or top-dress** plants in containers.

### Late spring

- **Sow under glass** courgettes, marrows, pumpkins, and summer squash.
- **Outdoors, sow** autumn, winter and spring cauliflowers, carrots, chicory, endive, French and runner beans, Hamburg parsley, lettuces, parsnips, peas, purslane, radish, rocket, salsify, scorzonera, spinach, sweetcorn and Swiss chard.
- **Begin to transplant** or pot on aubergines, cucumbers, peppers, indoor tomatoes and tomatillos under glass.
- **Harden off and transplant** well-developed seedlings of cauliflowers, cabbages, and other brassicas, cardoons, celeriac, celery, courgettes and marrows, Florence fennel, leeks. Provide cloche or fleece protection as needed.
- **Stake peas;** finish earthing up potatoes; weed and mulch vegetables.
- **Sow seed outdoors** of hardy and half-hardy annual herbs.
- **Water and feed** container-grown plants.
- **Harvest asparagus,** broad beans, kohlrabi, radish, rhubarb, texsel greens and early salad leaves.
- **Prepare the soil** for summer planting of moisture-loving herbs.

### Early summer

- **Sow beetroot,** calabrese, carrots, chard, chicory, courgettes, outdoor cucumbers, endive, Florence fennel, French and runner beans, kohlrabi, lettuce, parsley, peas, radishes, rocket, spring onions, squash, and swedes.
- **Finish transplanting** aubergines, cucumbers, peppers, indoor tomatoes, and tomatillos grown under glass.
- **Transplant broccoli,** Brussels sprouts, cabbages, cauliflowers, celeriac, celery, courgettes, French, Lima and runner beans, kale, leeks, pumpkins, sweetcorn, outdoor tomatoes, and winter squash.
- **Water, feed, and weed** outdoor crops as necessary.
- **Continue sowing** annual and biennial herbs, such as coriander, fennel, dill, and parsley, outdoors every 2–4 weeks. Pick and deadhead regularly.
- **Plant** container-grown herbs, and mulch moisture-loving herbs.
- **Harvest beetroot,** cabbage, carrots, cauliflower, radish and salad onions.

### Midsummer

- **Watch for blight** on maincrop potatoes and spray if necessary.
- **Earth up Brussels sprouts** and other brassicas on exposed, windy sites.
- **Nip out sideshoots** and the tops of outdoor cordon tomatoes when 4 or 5 trusses have set fruit.
- **Lift garlic** and dry off the bulbs.
- **Train in climbing vegetables** to their supports.
- **Top-dress Brussels sprouts,** weed, feed, and water other vegetable crops as appropriate. Feed and water herbs in containers.
- **Deadhead herbs** unless seed is needed.
- **Harvest summer vegetables,** salad leaves, and herbs.
- **Take semi-ripe,** softwood and stem cuttings of perennial and shrubby herbs.
- **Gather seed** from annual and biennial herbs as soon as it is ripe. Clean the seed and store in paper packets in a cool, dry, dark place.
- **Sow beetroot,** calabrese, kohlrabi, oriental greens, and salad onions.

### Late summer

- **Lift onions and shallots** and dry them off before storing them.
- **Cut off and burn** the top-growth of maincrop potatoes if it is blighted.
- **Sow endive,** kohlrabi, oriental and winter salad leaves, radishes, scorzonera, spinach, spring cabbage, turnips, and winter radish.
- **Continue to harvest** summer vegetables, salad leaves, and herbs.
- **Begin to harvest** early Brussels sprouts, autumn cabbage, Hamburg parsley, baby leeks, Lima beans, mini-cauliflowers, early parsnips, and sweetcorn.
- **Pick leaves or sprigs** regularly of all herbs to keep the plants productive.

### Mid-spring

- **Pick flowers** off new young strawberry plants, which should not be allowed to flower in their first year.
- **Finish planting raspberries,** if not done in late autumn.
- **Prune and tie** in new growth on fig trees if necessary.
- **Hand-pollinate** wall-trained fruit with a soft brush, if necessary.
- **Check nets,** stakes, and ties.
- **Prune young** stone fruit trees, and branch leaders on trained trees and plum pyramids.
- **Protect almond** and plum flowers and those of wall-trained sweet cherries from late frosts.
- **Pick off** sawfly caterpillars if they attack gooseberry and currant bushes.

### Late spring

- **Pick off** sawfly caterpillars if they attack gooseberry bushes.
- **Start to pick gooseberries** that have been grown under protection.
- **Pull out** any new young raspberry canes that emerge a long way from the original rows.
- **Water** as necessary, especially wall-trained trees.
- **Continue to weed** strawberries, and put straw around the plants, together with a sprinkling of slug pellets if slugs are known to be a problem.
- **Put netting** over developing soft fruit.
- **Begin to tie** in selected shoots to extend framework of wall-trained peaches, nectarines, apricots, and plums, and thin out badly placed new shoots.
- **Prune fan-trained** acid cherries.
- **Begin to pinch out** and disbud new vine shoots, to leave two laterals at each spur.
- **Remove blossom** from newly planted fruit trees.

### Early summer

- **Check and water** all fruit trees and bushes in dry periods.
- **Pick strawberries,** raspberries, currants, and gooseberries regularly.
- **Begin to train** and tie in new shoots of blackberries and hybrid berries.
- **Remove strawberry runners** unless needed to make new plants.
- **Begin routine thinning** of tree and wall-trained fruits.
- **Tie in framework shoots** on wall-trained plums and sweet cherries, shorten the remainder, and pinch or prune out any going in the wrong direction.
- **Tie in selected shoots** of wall-trained peaches and nectarines, and thin the fruit if necessary.
- **Pinch out** shoot tips on figs.
- **Protect ripening fruits** of wall-trained cherries from rain and birds.
- **Put up pheromone traps** for codling and plum moths.

### Midsummer

- **Continue to train in** the canes of blackberries and hybrid berries.
- **After fruiting,** cut the leaves off strawberry plants, remove the straw, and weed between the rows. Water if dry.
- **Finish thinning tree fruits** that have not thinned themselves naturally.
- **Continue to train** and tie in tree fruit growing against walls.
- **Support branches** of plum trees that are very heavily laden, if necessary.
- **Protect cane fruits** against raspberry beetle.

### Late summer

- **Begin summer pruning** of restricted forms of apples and pears.
- **Plant out** well-rooted runners in new strawberry beds.
- **After summer-fruiting raspberries** fruit, cut out old canes; tie in new ones.
- **Prune damsons and plums,** if necessary, when they have fruited and cut out any damaged branches.
- **Summer prune** peaches and nectarines after fruiting.
- **Prune fan-trained acid cherries,** cut out wood which has borne fruit, after fruiting, and secure new shoots by tying in.

## SEASONAL TASKS PLANNER

| Vegetables and herbs | Fruit |
|---|---|

### Late summer *(cont.)*

- **Deadhead shrubby herbs** as the flowers fade and start cutting them back.
- **Dig in** any earlier sowings of green manures before they flower.
- **Regularly pick and deadhead** second-year biennial herbs.

### Early autumn

- **Cut down dying haulms** of maincrop potatoes prior to lifting them.
- **Ripen pumpkins** and winter squash before storing them.
- **Harvest autumn brassicas** and continue to earth up winter brassicas.
- **Transplant** spring cabbages.
- **Sow** oriental salad leaves, Japanese onions, and spinach.
- **Lift Witloof chicory** for forcing and red and sugarloaf chicory for late crops in cold greenhouse.
- **Sow seed outdoors** of hardy annual herbs for early crops next year.
- **Lift, divide, and pot up** mature herb plants for winter use indoors.
- **Take hardwood or semi-ripe cuttings** and finish cutting back shrubby herbs.
- **Divide clump-forming** and rhizomatous herbs after flowering, if not done in early spring. Transplant rooted shoots of mound-layered shrubby herbs.
- **Begin planting out** seedlings of biennial herbs into their final positions.

### Early autumn

- **After fruiting,** cut out at base old canes of blackberries and other hybrid berries, and tie in new canes.
- **Weed thoroughly** around fruit trees growing in grass.
- **Cut off and burn** any mildewed top-growth on gooseberries.
- **Order new** fruit trees and bushes.
- **Finish summer pruning** of restricted forms of apples and pears, if not done already.
- **Shorten shoots and cut out** wood which has borne fruit on wall-trained acid cherries, after fruiting, if not done already, and secure new shoots by tying in.

### Mid-autumn

- **Store root vegetables** such as beetroot, cabbage hispi, carrots, swedes, and turnips as you lift them. Keep them in a cool, frost-free place.
- **Plant garlic;** sow broad beans, calabrese, carrots, early summer cauliflowers, peas. Protect seedlings over winter with cloches.
- **Continue to harvest** autumn brassicas, and lift and store root crops.
- **Clear away** bean sticks, tomato stakes, and rotting vegetation.
- **Cut down stems** of asparagus and Jerusalem artichokes.
- **Manure and dig** ground once it has been cleared of crops.
- **Continue planting out** seedlings of biennial herbs to their final positions.
- **Sow seed outdoors** of hardy annual herbs for early crops next year.

### Mid-autumn

- **Harvest and store** good fruit in cool, frost-free place.
- **Take cuttings,** if necessary, from gooseberry and currant bushes.
- **Prepare ground** for planting new fruit trees and bushes.
- **Tidy up** alpine strawberry plants, removing dead leaves.
- **Apply grease bands** to fruit trees to protect against winter moths.

### Late autumn

- **In cold areas,** protect globe artichoke crowns with straw or bracken.
- **Plant** rhubarb.
- **Sow broad beans** and hardy lettuce and sow Japanese onions under cover.
- **Continue to plant** garlic.
- **Continue lifting** and storing root crops and net and hang autumn cabbages.
- **Burn or dispose of** off-site any brassica material affected by clubroot.
- **Move tender** and container-grown herbs under cover for winter before frosts.
- **Finish planting out** biennial herb seedlings to their final positions.
- **Finish sowing seed** outdoors of hardy annual herbs, for an early flush of growth next year. In cold regions, protect seedlings over winter with cloches.
- **Collect fallen leaves** and stack to make leaf mould.
- **Manure and dig** ground once it has been cleared of crops.

### Late autumn

- **Finish picking** apples and pears and store sound fruit.
- **Begin planting new fruit trees,** bushes, and raspberry canes as soon as possible after leaf fall.
- **Check tree ties** and rabbit guards on fruit trees.
- **Net apples, pears,** and plums against bullfinches, which attack fruit buds.

### Early winter

- **Continue to harvest** winter vegetables.
- **Plant cabbage 'Hispi'** in frames or greenhouse.
- **Check stored vegetables** and remove any that show signs of rot.
- **Prepare ground** for spring planting; apply lime as necessary.
- **Order vegetable seeds** and seed potatoes.

### Early winter

- **Prepare ground** for spring planting.
- **Inspect stored apples** and pears regularly, and take out any fruit that is starting to go rotten.

### Midwinter

- **Force rhubarb** from midwinter onwards.
- **Sow broad beans,** early summer cauliflowers, Amsterdam, Round and Nantes carrots, leeks, lettuce, and onions and shallots under cover.
- **Plant onion** and shallot sets and garlic under cover.
- **Set out seed potatoes** in boxes to "chit".
- **Continue to prepare ground** for spring planting; apply lime as necessary.

### Midwinter

- **Inspect stored apples** and pears regularly, and take out any fruit that is starting to go rotten.
- **Prune apples and pears** if frosts are not too hard.
- **Continue to plant** fruit trees and bushes if weather permits.
- **Insulate pots** of container-grown fruits in severe weather.
- **Begin spraying** peaches and nectarines against peach leaf curl.

### Late winter

- **Finish digging** and manuring ground, and prepare it for spring planting.
- **Prepare seedbeds** for early sowings.
- **Apply sheet mulches** or cloches to warm up prepared soil prior to sowing.
- **Sow tomatoes,** flowering greens, globe artichokes, and lettuce in warmth.
- **Sow broad beans,** Brussels sprouts, early summer cabbages, leeks, onions, peas, radishes, shallots, seakale, spinach, and turnips under cover. Sow peas and hardy lettuce in mild areas.
- **Plant** rhubarb.
- **Plant Jerusalem artichokes** under cloches.

### Late winter

- **Cover strawberry plants** with cloches for an early crop.
- **Prune cobnuts** and filberts when the catkins are shedding pollen.
- **Continue to plant** fruit trees and bushes, if weather permits.
- **Check tree ties** and rabbit guards on fruit trees.

# Plant problems

The first lines of defence against plant problems in the kitchen garden are to use sound cultivation techniques, sustain a fertile soil, and practise good hygiene (*see pp.51–52*). This ensures strong crops with natural resistance to pests, diseases, and cultural disorders. But even a well-managed garden may suffer infestations.

This section forms a handy reference to the most common problems that you may encounter. Unusual problems have been omitted – to include them would be to imply that plants are always beset by legions of pests and diseases, which is seldom the case. Some crops, such as brassicas, attract many problems, while others, like medlars, suffer relatively few.

For ease of reference, pests, diseases, and cultural disorders are listed together alphabetically in the following "A–Z of plant problems" (*pp. 251–264*). Solutions can be accessed in several ways.

A list of the most usual problems is found under the heading "Common problems" in each individual crop

entry throughout the book; these direct you to the relevant information in the "A–Z of plant problems". Or you may prefer to use the quick-reference charts (*see pp.247–249*) to identify a possible problem from signs visible on the plant. For example, if you observe deformed roots on your sea kale, look up the "Roots and tubers" column; you will find the most likely culprit, clubroot, listed. A third option – for experienced gardeners – is simply to confirm your suspicions by looking up details directly.

The controls described in the "A–Z of plant problems" include chemical and organic methods, as well as cultural ones that reduce or avoid infection or infestation. The importance of prompt action cannot be underestimated – the earlier you control a problem, the less damage will be sustained by the crop. Untreated disorders may also spread to other crops or become established in the soil, leading to recurring troubles with crops in following years.

## How to use this section

▼ **Symptom identification chart**

*Charts on the following pages list each crop by common name. The most likely problems* *for each crop are in columns that indicate the part of the plant in which symptoms appear.*

| Crop | Symptoms | | |
|---|---|---|---|
| | Roots | Leaves and stems | Fruits and flowers |
| Strawberry | Honey fungus<br>Red core<br>Verticillium wilt<br>Vine weevil | Aphids<br>Powdery mildew<br>Red spider mite<br>Strawberry viruses | Birds<br>Botrytis<br>Powdery mildew<br>Slugs & Snails<br>Squirrels<br>Strawberry seed beetle |

**Site of plant symptoms**
*In strawberries, powdery mildew affects leaves, stems, and fruits*

▶ **A-Z listings**
*The "A–Z of plant problems" forms a directory of the pests, diseases, and cultural disorders affecting crops covered in this book. The directory lists all problems in alphabetical order. Each entry discusses crops affected, symptoms, causes, and controls – biological or cultural remedies are given as the preferred option.*

### Black bean aphid

■ **Crops affected** Beans, beetroot, cardoon, and globe artichoke.
■ **Symptoms** Clusters of black insects, to 2mm (¹⁄₁₂in) long, congregate at stem tips and beneath leaves. Plants are weakened and bean pods fail to develop.
■ **Cause** A sap-feeding aphid, *Aphis fabae*.
■ **Control** Inspect plants regularly; if beans have reached almost full size, pinch out infested shoot tips and destroy them. The organic insecticides pyrethrum, and fatty acids are effective if used before heavy infestations develop. Use deltamethrin or lambda-cyhalothrin on bean crops.

**Blackberry cane spot:** *see* Cane spot.

**Crops affected**
*Plants listed here include those most affected, as detailed on charts, as well as plants that may act as hosts or suffer little real damage.*

**Cross-reference**
*Alternative names cross-referenced to relevant entry*

## COMMON VEGETABLE PROBLEMS

| Crop | Symptoms | | | Crop | Symptoms | | |
|---|---|---|---|---|---|---|---|
| | Roots and tubers | Leaves and stems | Fruits, pods, and seeds | | Roots and tubers | Leaves and stems | Fruits, pods, and seeds |
| Amaranth | — | Aphids<br>Powdery mildew | — | Cucumber | Foot & root rots<br>Bean seed fly | Cucumber mosaic virus<br>Powdery mildew<br>Red spider mite<br>Slugs & Snails<br>Whitefly | Bitter fruits<br>Poorly formed fruits |
| Asparagus | Foot & root rots<br>Violet root rot<br>Fusarium wilt | Asparagus beetle<br>Foot & root rots<br>Slugs & Snails | — | Endive | | As for Chicory | |
| Aubergine | — | Aphids<br>Red spider mite<br>Verticillium wilt<br>Whitefly | Botrytis | Florence fennel | Rhizoctonia | Slugs | — |
| | | | | Flowering greens | | As for Brassicas | |
| Bean, broad | — | Black bean aphid<br>Chocolate spot<br>Pea & bean weevil<br>Rusts | Bean seed beetle<br>Birds<br>Mice<br>Rusts | Garlic | | As for Onion | |
| | | | | Globe artichoke | Honey fungus<br>Root aphid | Black bean aphid<br>Slugs & Snails | Artichoke bud rot |
| | | | | Hamburg parsley | | As for Parsnip | |
| Bean, French, runner, and Lima | Bean seed fly<br>Foot & root rots<br>Root aphid | Anthracnose<br>Black bean aphid<br>Halo blight<br>Red spider mite<br>Rusts<br>Slugs & Snails | Anthracnose<br>Birds<br>Mice<br>Rusts | Ice plant | — | Slugs | — |
| | | | | Jerusalem artichoke | Root aphid<br>Slugs | Sclerotinia<br>Slugs & Snails | |
| | | | | Kale | | As for Brassicas | |
| | | | | Kohlrabi | | As for Brassicas | |
| Beetroot | Cutworm | Black bean aphid<br>Boron deficiency<br>Damping off<br>Leaf spot (fungal)<br>Manganese deficiency | — | Komatsuna | | As for Brassicas | |
| | | | | Land cress | | No major problems | |
| | | | | Leek | Cutworm<br>Onion fly | As for Onion<br>Leek rust | — |
| Brassicas | Cabbage root fly<br>Clubroot<br>Cutworm<br>Leatherjacket | Birds (pigeons)<br>Boron deficiency<br>Caterpillars<br>Downy mildew<br>Flea beetle<br>Leaf spot (bacterial)<br>Mealy cabbage aphid<br>Molybdenum deficiency<br>Powdery mildew<br>Slugs & Snails<br>Whitefly<br>White blister | Bolting | Lettuce | Cutworm<br>Leatherjackets<br>Lettuce root aphid<br>Wireworm | Aphids<br>Botrytis<br>Downy mildew<br>Sclerotinia<br>Slugs & Snails<br>Tip burn | — |
| | | | | Malabar spinach | | No major problems | |
| | | | | Marrow, vegetable | | As for Courgette | |
| Broccoli | | As for Brassicas | | Melon, sweet | Foot & root rots<br>Bean seed fly | Aphids<br>Cucumber mosaic virus<br>Powdery mildew<br>Red spider mite<br>Slugs & Snails<br>Whitefly | — |
| Brussels sprouts | | As for Brassicas | | | | | |
| Cabbage | | As for Brassicas | | | | | |
| Calabrese | | As for Brassicas | | | | | |
| Cardoon | Root aphid | Black bean aphid<br>Slugs & Snails | Artichoke bud rot | | | | |
| | | | | Mibuna and Mizuna greens | | As for Brassicas | |
| Carrot | Carrot fly<br>Root aphid<br>Violet root rot | Aphids<br>Powdery mildew | — | Mint | — | Mint rust | — |
| | | | | Mustard and Cress | — | Botrytis<br>Damping off | — |
| Cauliflower | | As for Brassicas | | Mustard greens | | As for Brassicas | |
| Celeriac | | As for Celery | | New Zealand spinach | | As for Spinach | |
| Celery, leaf celery | Carrot fly<br>Foot & root rots<br>Violet root rot | Celery leaf miner<br>Leaf spot (fungal)<br>Slugs & Snails | — | Okra | — | Aphids<br>Red spider mite<br>Whitefly | Botrytis |
| Ceylon spinach | | No major problems | | Onion, bulb, Japanese bunching, spring, tree or Egyptian, Welsh, and shallot | Fusarium<br>Onion fly<br>Onion neck rot<br>Onion white rot | Birds<br>Downy mildew<br>Onion thrips<br>Stem & bulb eelworm<br>Viruses | Bolting |
| Chicory | Lettuce root aphid<br>Slugs | Slugs & Snails<br>Tip burn | — | | | | |
| Chinese artichoke | Root aphid | Slugs & Snails | — | | | | |
| Chinese broccoli | | As for Brassicas | | Pak choi | | As for Brassicas | |
| Chinese cabbage | | As for Brassicas | | Parsnip | Parsnip canker<br>Carrot fly<br>Violet root rot | Celery leaf miner<br>Downy mildew<br>Powdery mildew | — |
| Corn salad | — | Aphids<br>Slugs | — | | | | |
| Courgette | Bean seed fly<br>Foot & root rots | Cucumber mosaic virus<br>Powdery mildew<br>Red spider mite<br>Slugs & Snails<br>Whitefly | Bitter fruits<br>Poorly formed fruits<br>Slugs | Pea, all types<br><br>(continued over) | Foot & root rots | Birds (Pigeon)<br>Downy mildew<br>Mice<br>Pea aphid<br>Powdery mildew<br>Pea thrips | Birds<br>Downy mildew<br>Pea leaf and pod spot<br>Pea moth<br>Pea seed beetle |

## COMMON VEGETABLE PROBLEMS

| Crop | Symptoms | | | Crop | Symptoms | | |
|------|----------|--|--|------|----------|--|--|
| | Roots and tubers | Leaves and stems | Fruits, pods, and seeds | | Roots and tubers | Leaves and stems | Fruits, pods, and seeds |
| Pea, all types (*cont.*) | | Pea & bean weevil | Pea thrips | Summer purslane | — | Slugs & Snails | — |
| | | | | Sunflower | — | Slugs & Snails | — |
| Pepper, chilli and sweet | — | Aphids Botrytis Red spider mite Viruses Whitefly | Blossom end rot | Swede | Cabbage root fly Clubroot Turnip gall weevil | Boron deficiency Downy mildew Flea beetle Mealy cabbage aphid Powdery mildew | — |
| Potato | Cutworm Potato blight Potato common scab Potato cyst eelworm Potato powdery scab Slugs Wireworm | Black leg Colorado beetle Frost damage Potato blight Potato viruses Slugs & Snails | — | Sweetcorn | — | Birds Frit fly Mice | Badgers Squirrels Sweetcorn smut |
| | | | | Sweet potato | — | Aphids Red spider mite Whitefly | |
| Pumpkin | Foot & root rots | Cucumber mosaic virus Powdery mildew Slugs & Snails | — | Swiss chard, spinach beet | — | Leaf spot (fungal) | |
| | | | | Texsel greens | | As for Brassicas | |
| Radish | Cabbage root fly Clubroot | Flea beetle Slugs & Snails | — | Tomatillo | | No major problems | |
| Rhubarb | Honey fungus | Crown rot Leaf spots Slugs & Snails Viruses | — | Tomato | Foot & root rots Potato cyst eelworm | Caterpillars Magnesium deficiency Potato blight Red spider mite Viruses Whitefly | Blossom end rot Caterpillars Potato blight Tomato blotchy ripening Tomato ghost spot |
| Rocket | — | Flea beetle Slugs & Snails | — | Turnip, turnip tops | Cabbage root fly Clubroot Cutworm Turnip gall weevil Wireworm | Downy mildew Flea beetle Powdery mildew | — |
| Salsify | — | White blister | — | | | | |
| Scorzonera | — | White blister | — | Watermelon | | As for melon, sweet | |
| Sea kale | Clubroot | Flea beetle | — | Winter purslane | — | Aphids Slugs | — |
| Spinach | — | Birds Downy mildew Rusts | Bolting | | | | |
| Spinach mustard | | As for Brassicas | | | | | |
| Sprouting broccoli | | As for Brassicas | | | | | |
| Squash, summer | | As for Courgette | | | | | |
| Squash, winter | | As for Pumpkin | | | | | |

## COMMON FRUIT PROBLEMS

| Crop | Symptoms | | | Crop | Symptoms | | |
|------|----------|--|--|------|----------|--|--|
| | Roots | Leaves and stems | Fruits, and flowers | | Roots | Leaves and stems | Fruits, and flowers |
| Almond | Honey fungus Phytophthora | Aphids Canker (bacterial) Peach leaf curl Red spider mite Scale insect | Frost damage Split stone | Blackberry | Honey fungus Phytophthora | Aphids Cane spot Chlorosis Leaf spot (fungal) Raspberry spur blight Viruses | Botrytis Raspberry beetle |
| Apple | Honey fungus Phytophthora | Apple scab Apple powdery mildew Blossom wilt Canker (fungal) Capsid bug Caterpillars Fireblight Iron deficiency Red spider mite Replant disease Rosy apple aphid Woolly aphid Winter moth | Apple scab Apple sawfly Apple sucker Birds Bitter pit Blossom wilt Brown rot Capsid bug Codling moth Fireblight Frost damage | Blackcurrant (*see also* Red- & whitecurrant) | Honey fungus Phytophthora | American gooseberry mildew Aphids Big bud mite Blackcurrant gall midge Capsid bug Leaf spot (fungal) Reversion disease Viruses | Birds Botrytis |
| | | | | Blueberry | Phytophthora | Botrytis Chlorosis | Birds |
| Apricot | Honey fungus Phytophthora | Brown scale Canker (bacterial) Dieback Silver leaf | Birds | Cherry, acid and sweet (*continued over*) | Honey fungus Phytophthora | Aphids Brown rot Canker (bacterial) Magnesium deficiency | Birds Blossom wilt Brown rot Frost damage |

## COMMON FRUIT PROBLEMS

| Crop | Symptoms | | | Crop | Symptoms | | |
|---|---|---|---|---|---|---|---|
| | Roots | Leaves and stems | Fruits and flowers | | Roots | Leaves and stems | Fruits and flowers |
| Cherry, acid and sweet (*cont.*) | | Pear & cherry slugworm<br>Scorch<br>Silver leaf<br>Winter moth | Fruit fly | Pineapple | Phytophthora<br>Root knot eelworm | Mealybugs<br>Scale insect<br>Red spider mite<br>Thrips | — |
| Citrus fruit | Crown rot | Mealybugs<br>Red spider mite<br>Scale insect<br>Thrips<br>Whitefly | Fruit fly<br>Viruses | Plum | Honey fungus<br>Phytophthora | Birds<br>Canker (bacterial)<br>Caterpillars<br>Plum leaf-curling, mealy plum aphid<br>Red spider mite<br>Silver leaf<br>Winter moth | Birds<br>Brown rot<br>Frost damage<br>Plum fruit moth |
| Cobnut and filbert | Honey fungus<br>Phytophthora | Aphids<br>Powdery mildew | Nut weevil<br>Squirrels | Prickly pear | — | Mealybugs | — |
| Cranberry | | Chlorosis<br>Rusts | Birds | Quince | Honey fungus | Fireblight<br>Frost damage<br>Monilinia blight<br>Powdery mildew<br>Quince leaf blight<br>Verticillium wilt | Blossom wilt<br>Brown rot<br>Frost damage<br>Monilinia blight<br>Quince leaf blight |
| Fig | Honey fungus | Brown scale<br>Coral spot<br>Frost damage<br>Red spider mite | Birds<br>Frost damage | | | | |
| Gooseberry | Honey fungus<br>Phytophthora | American gooseberry mildew<br>Aphids<br>Birds<br>Botrytis<br>Capsid bug<br>Caterpillars<br>Gooseberry dieback<br>Gooseberry sawfly<br>Leaf spot (fungal) | American gooseberry mildew<br>Birds<br>Squirrels | Raspberry | Honey fungus<br>Phytophthora | Aphids<br>Cane spot<br>Chlorosis<br>Leaf spot (fungal)<br>Raspberry cane blight<br>Raspberry leaf and bud mite<br>Raspberry spur blight<br>Raspberry viruses<br>Rusts | Birds<br>Botrytis<br>Raspberry beetle |
| Grape vine | Honey fungus<br>Phytophthora<br>Vine weevil | Brown scale<br>Downy mildew<br>Magnesium deficiency<br>Mealybugs<br>Oedema<br>Powdery mildew<br>Red spider mite<br>Scorching<br>Vine weevil | Birds<br>Botrytis<br>Shanking of grapes<br>Wasps | Red- and whitecurrant | Honey fungus<br>Phytophthora | Aphids<br>Coral spot<br>Leaf spot (fungal)<br>Capsid bug<br>Gooseberry sawfly<br>Rusts | Birds<br>Botrytis |
| Hybrid berries | | As for Blackberry | | Strawberry | Honey fungus<br>Red core<br>Verticillium wilt<br>Vine weevil | Aphids<br>Powdery mildew<br>Red spider mite<br>Strawberry viruses | Birds<br>Botrytis<br>Powdery mildew<br>Slugs & Snails<br>Strawberry seed beetle |
| Kiwi fruit | | No major problems | | | | | |
| Medlar | Honey fungus | Leaf spot<br>Monilinia blight | Monilinia blight | Walnut | Honey fungus<br>Phytophthora | Walnut blotch<br>Walnut leaf blight | Birds<br>Squirrels |
| Mulberry | Honey fungus | Mulberry canker | Birds | | | | |
| Olive | Honey fungus<br>Phytophthora<br>Root knot eelworm | Olive scab<br>Red spider mite<br>Scale insect<br>Thrips<br>Verticillium wilt<br>Whitefly | Fruit fly | | | | |
| Passion fruit | Honey fungus | Aphids<br>Mealybug<br>Red spider mite<br>Scale insect | Cucumber mosaic virus<br>Fruit fly | | | | |
| Peach and nectarine | Honey fungus<br>Phytophthora | Aphids<br>Brown scale<br>Canker (bacterial)<br>Peach leaf curl<br>Red spider mite<br>Silver leaf | Brown rot<br>Frost damage<br>Split stone<br>Squirrels | | | | |
| Pear | Honey fungus<br>Phytophthora | Aphids<br>Pear scab<br>Birds<br>Canker (fungal)<br>Caterpillars<br>Fireblight<br>Pear leaf blister mite<br>Pear & cherry slugworm<br>Pear rust<br>Replant disease<br>Winter moth | Birds<br>Blossom wilt<br>Boron deficiency<br>Brown rot<br>Codling moth<br>Fireblight<br>Frost damage<br>Pear midge<br>Pear rust<br>Pear scab | | | | |

**Blackfly on globe artichoke**
*There are some pests and diseases that can afflict virtually any crop in the garden, such as these blackfly, as well as other types of aphid, slugs and snails, honey fungus, and damping off. Such problems are listed in the charts above only if they are a particular nuisance.*

# Most common problems

## Use this index to locate details of the most common problems.

*Aleyrodes proletella* p.264
**Cabbage whitefly**

*Botrytis cinerea* p.252
**Botrytis** *damage*

*Brachycaudus helichrysi* p.259
**Plum leaf-curling aphid** *damage*

*Bremia lactucae* p.255
**Downy mildew** *on lettuce*

*Byturus tomentosus* p.260
**Raspberry beetle** *damage on fruits*

*Cydia nigricana* p.258
**Pea moth caterpillar**

*Cydia pomonella* p.254
**Codling moth** *damage on apple*

*Milax species* p.262
**Keeled slug** *damage on potato*

*Nematus ribesii* p.256
**Gooseberry sawfly larvae**

*Otiorhynchus sulcatus* p.263
**Vine weevil larvae**

*Phyllotreta species* p.255
**Flea beetle** *damage on baby turnip*

*Phytophthora infestans* p.260
**Potato blight** *on tomato*

*Plasmodiophora brassicae* p.254
**Clubroot**

*Podosphaera leucotricha* p.251
**Apple powdery mildew**

*Psila rosae* p.253
**Carrot fly** *damage*

*Puccinia allii* p.257
**Leek rust**

*Sclerotinia sclerotiorum* p.262
**Sclerotinia** *on lettuce*

*Sclerotium cepivorum* p.258
**Onion white rot**

*Streptomyces scabies* p.260
**Potato common scab**

*Taphrina deformans* p.258
**Peach leaf curl**

*Tetranychus urticae* p.261
**Red spider mite** *damage on cucumber leaf*

*Venturia inaequalis* p.251
**Apple scab**

p.254
**Cucumber mosaic virus** *on courgette*

p.252
**Bitter pit** *on apple*

p.257
**Magnesium deficiency** *on grape vine*

# A–Z OF PLANT PROBLEMS

## American gooseberry mildew

■ **Crops affected** Blackcurrant and gooseberry.
■ **Symptoms** Powdery, grey-white fungal growth appears on upper leaf surfaces, stems, and fruits. Young growth may become distorted and die off. Mildew on the skin of fruits turns buff as it ages and can be scraped off. Fruits are unsightly but edible, although they turn brown when cooked.
■ **Cause** The fungus *Podosphaera mors-uvae*, which is encouraged by stagnant air around the branches and by excessive use of nitrogen fertilizers. It overwinters on the branches and in the buds.
■ **Control** Prune out affected branches as seen; prune to thin growth and improve air circulation. Use a general fertilizer rather than a high-nitrogen one. Grow cultivars with some resistance, such as 'Invicta' ♀ or 'Greenfinch' ♀. Spray with a fungicide containing myclobutanil.

## Anthracnose

■ **Crops affected** Various, especially French, dwarf, and runner bean, and cucumber.
■ **Symptoms** Various fungi cause spots or patches of discoloration on leaves, stems, and on bean pods. Affected tissue may die; in severe cases, the whole plant dies back. On bean crops, longitudinal, sunken brown marks appear on stems. Leaf veins may develop red colouration and leaves may brown and die off. Red-brown spots appear on pods, followed in wet weather by pink slimy growths.
■ **Causes** *Colletotrichum* species are the most common agents; the bean anthracnose fungus, *Colletotrichum lindemuthianum*, is seed-borne. Spores are spread by rain or water splash from infected seedlings to nearby plants.
■ **Control** Remove infected plants as soon as seen; do not save their seed. Use resistant cultivars of beans, such as 'Aramis' or 'Rido Kenyan'. There are currently no fungicides available to gardeners to control this disease.

## Aphids

■ **Crops affected** Few plants are unaffected by aphids; some are host-plant specific.
■ **Symptoms** Affected plants show varying degrees of reduced growth and leaf distortion. Upper leaf surfaces are often sticky with the honeydew excreted by aphids and this often becomes infested by black sooty mould. The nymphs shed their whitish skins as they grow, which accumulate on leaves below those on which aphids are feeding. Viruses are often spread from one plant to another on aphid mouthparts.
■ **Cause** Sap-sucking insects, about 2mm (1/12in) long, may be green, grey, pink, black, yellow, or brown, depending on species.
■ **Control** Organic treatments include pyrethrum, fatty acids and plant oils. Control overwintering eggs in winter on deciduous fruit trees or bushes with a plant oil wash. Deltamethrin, lambda-cyhalothrin, or thiacloprid can be used on vegetables and fruits listed in pesticide manufacturers' instructions. Details of control on specific plants are listed in individual entries.
*See also* Black bean aphid, Lettuce root aphid, Mealy cabbage aphid, Pea aphid, Plum leaf-curling aphid, Root aphid, Rosy apple aphid, Woolly aphid.

**Apple canker:** *see* Canker (fungal).
**Apple and pear canker:** *see* Canker (fungal).

## Apple powdery mildew

■ **Crops affected** Apple, and less seriously, pear, quince, and medlar.
■ **Symptoms** Leaves are covered in powdery white fungal growth (*see p.250*); young leaves may be badly infected from spores that overwintered from the previous year. They become distorted, fail to develop fully, and die prematurely. Stems may show silvery white patches in winter.
■ **Cause** The fungus *Podosphaera leucotricha* overwinters on apple buds or on stems. Spread and development is rapid in hot summers, especially when dews are heavy. Dry soils also encourage development.
■ **Control** Keep apples well watered and well mulched to conserve water. Prune out badly affected growth. Keep the crowns of trees open to permit good air circulation. Spray with a fungicide that contains difenoconazole or myclobutanil.

## Apple sawfly

■ **Crops affected** Apple.
■ **Symptoms** Fruitlets fall off in early to midsummer and have maggot holes in the side. This exit hole is filled with frass (excrement) produced by a caterpillar-like, brown-headed white larva. Mature fruits may be misshapen and marked with a ribbon-like scar, usually from the bottom to the middle of the fruit.
■ **Cause** The sawfly, *Hoplocampa testudinea*, lays its eggs in the fruitlets at flowering time. After hatching, the larva tunnels into the fruit, first beneath the skin, then to the core. Badly damaged fruitlets fall, but if the larva dies before it reaches the core, the fruit will mature (although it will be scarred and misshapen). The larvae leave the fruit to pupate in the soil.
■ **Control** Pick off and destroy damaged fruitlets before the larvae can escape and pupate. If the crop has been significantly affected in previous years, spray with deltamethrin within seven days of petal fall.

## Apple, pear, *and* olive scabs

■ **Crops affected** Apple, pear, and olive.
■ **Symptoms** Black or brown scabby areas on the surface of young fruits (*see p.250*). In severe cases, it may be widespread and cause misshapen, cracked fruits. Brown or olive-green spots appear on the leaves, which may appear blistered. Early leaf fall can occur, reducing the crop the following year. Young shoots are also attacked.
■ **Causes** The fungus *Venturia inaequalis* on apples and pears, *Venturia pirina* on pears, and *Spilocaea oleagina* on olives. The fungi overwinter on young stems and fallen leaves. Scabs are most prevalent in damp seasons and on trees with crowded branches.
■ **Control** Gather up and destroy fallen leaves. Prune out cracked or scabby shoots to limit overwintering. Prune regularly to ensure good air flow, and to reduce conditions favourable to fungal growth. Seek cultivars showing resistance, such as dessert apples 'Ashmead's Kernel' ♀, 'Discovery' ♀, 'Sunset' ♀, and 'Laxton's Fortune' ♀, and culinary apples 'Edward VII' ♀ and 'Grenadier' ♀. The pears 'Jargonelle' and 'Catillac' ♀ similarly show resistance. Difenoconazole or myclobutanil may be used to control these diseases.

## Apple sucker

■ **Crops affected** Apple.
■ **Symptoms** Pale green, flattened insects, to 2mm (1/12in) long, infest flower trusses in spring, turning the petals brown and killing the blossom if infestation is heavy.
■ **Cause** Sap-sucking, aphid-like insects, *Psylla mali*, hatch from overwintering eggs as the tree comes into leaf. Damage is caused by immature nymphs (described above) at flowering time. The adult, which looks like a winged aphid, is present on the foliage after petal fall.
■ **Control** Use a plant oil winter wash to control overwintering eggs. Spray nymphs with deltamethrin or pyrethrum at the green bud stage, before flowering.

## Artichoke bud rot

■ **Crops affected** Cardoon and globe artichoke.
■ **Symptoms** The flowerheads develop pale brown spots and later the entire head becomes shrivelled and infected by fluffy grey fungal growth. Sometimes, pinprick-sized, black fruiting bodies (sclerotia) are seen on the fungal mass. If infection is extensive, the whole crop may be lost.
■ **Cause** The grey mould fungus, *Botrytis cinerea*. Spores are spread readily by water splash and air currents, and they persist from year to year in the soil, or on plant debris, as sclerotia.
■ **Control** Good cultural practice and hygiene are the first lines of defence, since control of such a widespread fungus is difficult. Avoid damp or shaded sites. Keep plants growing well and in good health by regular feeding and watering. Remove any dying buds or flowerheads promptly as soon as seen; the fungus will rapidly invade dying or damaged tissues and will spread to previously unaffected ones. Cut back to clean, healthy stems. Clear away all plant debris promptly. *See also* Botrytis.

## Asparagus beetle

■ **Crops affected** Asparagus.
■ **Symptoms** Asparagus plants defoliated as beetle adults and larvae strip the outer bark and leaves from the stem. Damaged areas become yellow-brown and desiccated.
■ **Cause** Adults and larvae of the leaf beetle *Crioceris asparagi*. Adults are 6–8mm (1/4–3/8in) long, black with a red thorax, and with six yellow blotches on the wing cases. In late spring, they emerge from the soil to lay eggs on stems and leaves. The grey-black, hump-backed larvae, to 1cm (1/2in) long, have three pairs of legs. They appear in late spring or early autumn; there are two generations each year.
■ **Control** Destroy overwintering beetles by burning old stems at the end of the season. From late spring, search for and destroy adults and larvae by hand. On larger plots, this is impracticable, so spray with pyrethrum at dusk, so as not to harm day-flying bees and other beneficial insects.

**Bacterial canker:** *see* Canker.

## Badger

■ **Crops affected** Cobnut, carrots, raspberry, strawberry, and sweetcorn.
■ **Symptoms** Cobs, nuts, and fruits are taken; plants are often severely trampled by these heavy, burly, and determined mammals. The long forepaws with prominent claws leave characteristic prints and their droppings usually have a muddy consistency. There may also be evidence of digging, and coarse, grey and white hairs remain on fences where they gain entry.
■ **Cause** Badgers, *Meles meles*, are omnivores, but they, and especially their cubs, appear to prefer vegetable food sources in late summer and autumn. They are nocturnal and emerge at dusk, although the cubs will forage in daylight if food is scarce in summer. Badgers are usually a denizen of rural habitats, but they are now increasingly seen in suburban gardens.
■ **Control** Regularly maintained, stout fencing is the only option; they are great and persistent diggers. Badgers and their setts are protected in Britain.

**Bean aphid:** *see* Black bean aphid.
**Bean beetle:** *see* Bean seed beetle.
**Bean halo blight:** *see* Halo blight.
**Bean root aphid:** *see* Root aphid.
**Bean rust:** *see* Rusts.

## Bean seed beetle

■ **Crops affected** Broad bean and pea.
■ **Symptoms** Holes in dry bean and pea seeds, which are the exit holes of adult beetles. In fresh beans, small, pale, circular patches on the seed coat indicate the presence of the beetle grub within.
■ **Causes** Several seed beetles affect beans and peas. *Bruchus rufimanus* is usually the culprit in broad beans. It lays its eggs in the pods as the seeds are forming. The grubs are usually unnoticed in cooked beans, but they develop during storage and emerge as adults the following year.
■ **Control** Check for exit holes before sowing seeds and discard badly damaged seeds. The grub eats only part of the cotyledons rather than the seed embryo, so the seed can still germinate. There is no chemical control currently available for garden use.

## Bean seed fly

■ **Crops affected** French and runner bean, cucurbits.
■ **Symptoms** Ragged leaves and damaged stems are seen on newly germinated seedlings; sometimes, seedlings fail to emerge, having been eaten below soil level. Provided that the growing point has not been destroyed, plants will survive although growth will be slow at first and sideshoots may develop.
■ **Cause** The maggots of *Delia platura*. The adults look like house flies.
■ **Control** Slow-germinating seed is most vulnerable, so avoid sowing when the soil is cold or wet. Instead, sow in pots or trays and set out after the first true leaves have unfolded. The adult fly is attracted to fresh organic matter, so apply manures in autumn rather than spring. There are no approved insecticides to control this pest.

**Bean weevil:** *see* Pea and bean weevil.

## Big bud mite

■ **Crops affected** Blackcurrant.
■ **Symptoms** Winter buds are abnormally large and rounded and do not develop into leaves or stems. Each bud contains hundreds of microscopic white mites. The buds become swollen in winter, but desiccated big buds can be found at any time of year. Infestation causes loss of vigour, but, more seriously, the mite can spread reversion disease (*see p. 261*).
■ **Cause** A mite, *Cecidophyopsis ribis*. The mites breed in summer and autumn and feed inside the buds during winter. At bud burst in early spring, they move on to infest previously healthy buds.
■ **Control** Removing big buds by hand from lightly infested bushes in winter, well before bud burst, provides a measure of control. Dig up and burn badly affected plants after fruiting and replace in autumn. The cultivar 'Ben Hope' is resistant. Chemicals available to gardeners do not control the mites.

## Birds

■ **Crops affected** Most soft and tree fruits, onion sets, pea, bean, brassicas, spinaches, and sweetcorn.
■ **Symptoms** Birds may eat flower buds, peck or eat whole fruits, strip leaves off brassicas and peas, eat pea and bean seeds and lettuce seedlings, or pull up newly planted brassicas and onion sets.
■ **Causes** Bullfinches are the prime suspect if fruit tree flower buds are eaten; the brown bud scales are discarded and are easily visible in winter if snow or frost are on the ground. Since they flock and are voracious, damage can be severe. The terminal buds are often left intact, and in spring, barren shoots with flowers only at the tips confirm the culprits. Blackbirds, starlings, and other birds peck holes in fruits and eat whole small fruits, such as raspberries. Blackbirds are the main culprits in pulling up onion sets, and pigeons will damage the foliage of brassicas and peas.
■ **Control** Small trees and soft fruits can be netted or grown in a fruit cage; on larger trees, protect best fruit trusses with bags of muslin or old tights. For other crops, fine-gauge netting is the only certain way of deterring birds. Scarecrows, humming lines, glitter strips, and model cats or predator birds work

only for a while; birds quickly get used to them, especially if they are hungry and other food sources are scarce. Shooting pigeons is not an option in suburban and urban areas.

## Bitter fruits

■ **Crops affected** Cucumber and gherkin.
■ **Symptoms** Fruits have a bitter flavour.
■ **Causes** Pollination of fruit-bearing, female flowers by male flowers, or an excess of nitrogen in the soil.
■ **Control** Remove all male flowers as they appear (female flowers have tiny, nascent fruit immediately behind the flower) or grow all-female cultivars. Use a balanced rather than a high-nitrogen fertilizer.

## Bitter pit

■ **Crops affected** Apple.
■ **Symptoms** Apple skins speckled with slightly sunken brown spots, usually 1–3mm (¹⁄₁₆–¹⁄₈in) in diameter (*see p.250*). The flesh tastes slightly bitter. The marks sometimes develop while the fruits are on the tree; more often they develop in storage. Large fruits and those from heavy cropping trees are most susceptible.
■ **Causes** Calcium deficiency in the fruits. Soil calcium levels may be adequate, but in dry weather the tree cannot take up sufficient calcium – hence the greater susceptibility of large fruits and heavy-cropping trees. The condition may also be caused by excessive levels of calcium and magnesium in the fruit.
■ **Control** Use a mulch to retain soil moisture and keep trees well watered. Avoid excessive use of high-nitrogen fertilizers; use balanced fertilizers instead. Spray developing fruits with calcium nitrate solution between early summer and early autumn. 'Bramley's Seedling', 'Discovery' ♀, and Crispin ('Mutsu') fruits may be damaged by this treatment, so use it with care on these cultivars.

## Black bean aphid

■ **Crops affected** Beans, beetroot, cardoon, and globe artichoke.
■ **Symptoms** Clusters of black insects, to 2mm (¹⁄₁₂in) long, congregate at stem tips and beneath leaves. Plants are weakened and bean pods fail to develop.
■ **Cause** A sap-feeding aphid, *Aphis fabae*.
■ **Control** Inspect plants regularly; if broad beans are almost full size, pinch out infested shoot tips and destroy them. The organic insecticides pyrethrum and fatty acids, are effective if used before heavy infestations develop. Use deltamethrin or lambda-cyhalothrin on bean crops.

**Blackberry cane spot:** *see* Cane spot.

## Blackcurrant gall midge

■ **Crops affected** Blackcurrant.
■ **Symptoms** Leaves are crumpled and fail to develop to their full size; they may become desiccated and die. Shoot tips may also be killed, causing branching.
■ **Causes** White maggots, up to 2mm (¹⁄₁₂in) long, feed on leaves at the shoot tips. They are larvae of the midge *Dasineura tetensi*, which produce

chemicals that cause the characteristic leaf crumpling. There are three generations each summer; the first symptoms appear with the flowers in late spring. While the maggots pupate in the soil, several normal leaves may appear before the next generation becomes active.
■ **Control** Choose resistant cultivars, such as 'Ben Connan' or 'Ben Sarek' ♀. The first generation is potentially the most harmful, since it can limit normal shoot extension. There are no chemical controls approved for garden use.

**Blackcurrant gall mite:** *see* Big bud mite.
**Blackcurrant reversion:** *see* Reversion disease.
**Blackfly:** *see* Black bean aphid.
**Black leg:** *see* Potato black leg.

## Blossom end rot

■ **Crops affected** Tomato and sweet pepper.
■ **Symptoms** A sunken patch occurs at the blossom end of developing fruits; the skin at the base becomes leathery, then turns brown or black. Not all fruits in a truss will be affected, nor will all trusses on the same plant necessarily suffer.
■ **Causes** Calcium deficiency due to dry conditions at the plant roots inhibiting its uptake. Lack of calcium causes cells to collapse and discolour. A very acidic growing medium increases the problem.
■ **Control** Ensure an adequate and regular water supply. If rot does develop, remove affected fruits and improve irrigation. Small-fruited cultivars and plants grown in open ground or large containers are less susceptible.

## Blossom wilt

■ **Crops affected** Apple, apricot, cherry, plum, peach, and pear.
■ **Symptoms** Flower trusses wither shortly after emergence. Dead trusses remain on the tree, forming a source of infection for leaves. which wilt, turn brown, and die, remaining on the branch. Raised, buff-coloured, pinprick-sized fungal pustules appear on infected areas. Localized dieback of stems may occur.
■ **Causes** The fungus *Monilinia laxa* or, on apple crops, *M. laxa* f. *laxa*. It may overwinter as cankers on affected stems, or as pustules on flowers and foliage. Wind-borne spores spread most rapidly in damp weather.
■ **Control** Prune out infected flower trusses before infection spreads to the leaves or into the spur. Difenoconazole is labelled to control blossom wilt on cherries, plums, gages, damsons, and ornamental trees.

**Blotchy ripening:** *see* Tomato blotchy ripening.

## Bolting

■ **Crops affected** Various, including brassicas, the onion family, and spinach.
■ **Symptoms** Premature production of flowers and seeds, before full development of the crop, or before harvest is complete.
■ **Causes** Various factors. The most common include exposure to low temperatures at a critical growth stage, often accompanying a cold, late onset of spring, and excessively dry soil

conditions during early growth stages.
■ **Control** Avoid growing early varieties of susceptible vegetables, as these are more prone to bolting. Choose cultivars that are listed as having bolt-resistance.

## Boron deficiency

■ **Crops affected** Listed below.
■ **Symptoms** The symptoms vary with the crop affected.
■ **Beetroot:** Rough, cankered patches on roots, often with secondary rotting at the heart, revealed as the development of brown rings in the inner root tissue and crown. Leaves are small and necrotic.
■ **Cabbage:** Distorted leaves and hollow areas in the stems.
■ **Carrot:** Splitting of root, often exposing a greyish central core, and splitting of stems. Yellow and pink discoloration of leaves.
■ **Cauliflower:** Poor curd development and browning of curds. Roughening of main stems, leaf stalks, and midribs.
■ **Celery:** Transverse cracks in the outer leaf stalk, followed by reddening of inner tissues, sometimes with leaf distortion.
■ **Pear:** Fruits are distorted, with hard brown flecks in the flesh. This may be accompanied by slight shoot dieback.
■ **Radish:** Dull, split skin with woody flesh.
■ **Strawberry:** General stunting. Small leaves are puckered and yellowed at tips. Berries are small and pale, typically forming a "waist" close to the calyx. Not a common affliction.
■ **Swede and turnip:** "Brown heart", which is revealed when the roots are cut across as grey or brown, discoloured areas. These may appear in concentric rings in the lower parts of the root.
■ **Causes** Boron deficiency often occurs on light soils because this element is readily leached out by high rainfall; it also occurs if soil is limed excessively or when soil is allowed to become very dry.
■ **Control** For vegetable and strawberry crops, apply 35g of borax per 20sq m (1oz per 175sq ft) of ground before sowing or planting. Mix the borax with fine horticultural sand to make even distribution easier. For pear crops, spray at petal fall with 70g borax in 22 litres of water (2½oz in 5 gallons) together with a wetting agent. Take care when applying borax; it is easy to overdo it.

## Botrytis

■ **Crops affected** Various.
■ **Symptoms** Fuzzy, grey, off-white, or grey-brown fungal growth (*see p.250*) on infected areas (hence the common name, grey mould). This ubiquitous, air-borne fungus lives on dead or living plant material, and can attack most above-ground tissues. It usually gains entry through wounds.
Fruits may be infected through open flowers; the fungus remains dormant until fruit ripens. Prior to development of the fungal fruiting stage, plant tissue becomes discoloured, often turning brown and soft. Growth above the site of infection may deteriorate, leaves may yellow and wilt, and flowers and fruit may die. Infection of petals or fruit can cause colour changes without rotting; petals appear bleached or form pale brown spots (ghost spotting). The fungal resting bodies – small, black sclerotia – resist a wide range of adverse conditions, staying dormant until conditions are suitable for their growth.
■ **Causes** The fungus *Botrytis cinerea*;

spores are spread readily by water splash and air currents, and persist from year to year in the soil, or on plant debris, as sclerotia.

■ **Control** Good hygiene is the first line of defence as control of such a widespread fungus is difficult. Clear away all plant debris promptly. Remove dead and injured plant parts before infection sets in. Remove infected tissues from live plants as soon as seen, cutting back into clean, healthy growth. There are no fungicides currently available to gardeners to control this disease.

## Brown rot

■ **Crops affected** Tree fruits.
■ **Symptoms** Soft brown areas develop on skins of fruits, the flesh deteriorates, and the rot spreads rapidly to the whole fruit. Raised, creamy white pustules appear on infected areas, and are apparent as concentric rings. Fruits may become mummified, remaining on the tree, or may fall; in both cases, they will form a source of re-infection.
■ **Causes** The fungus *Monilinia fructigena* on most types of fruit. *M. laxa* mainly on plums. The fungus gains entry via wounds, such as bird pecks, frost cracks, codling moth exit holes, and scab infections; any wound will predispose plants to infection. Spores are spread by birds, insects, rain splash or by direct contact with a source of infection.
■ **Control** Take all precautions against possible injuries. Control insect pests, net against birds, remove infected and fallen fruits promptly, and prune out mummified fruits, along with a short section of their spur, and destroy by burning. Spray with difenoconazole on cherries, plums, gages, and damsons.

## Brown scale

■ **Crops affected** Many tree and bush fruits, including fig, grape vines, peach, nectarine, apricot, and plum.
■ **Symptoms** Shell-like, convex, brown scales, up to 5mm (¼in), appear on stems of infested plants. Sooty moulds grow on leaves that are sticky with honeydew. Infestations are most common in warm, sheltered sites; on plants that are trained against warm walls or grown in greenhouses, for example.
■ **Cause** *Parthenolecanium corni*, a sap-feeding insect, which lays its eggs beneath the scale. There is one generation a year.
■ **Control** Spray deciduous fruit trees and bushes with a plant oil winter wash to target overwintering nymphs. Deltamethrin or lambda-cyhalothrin are approved for summer treatment of scale insect on some fruits.
*See also* Scale insect.

**Bud drop:** *see* Drought.
**Bulbous or blown fruits:** *see* Poorly formed fruits.

## Cabbage root fly

■ **Crops affected** Brassicas, including swede, turnip, and radish.
■ **Symptoms** Plants wilt readily on sunny days and growth is slow. Seedlings die shortly after transplanting. Legless white maggots, to 9mm (½in) long, eat the finer roots, leaving a rotting stump. Maggots may also bore into swollen roots of radishes, turnips, and swedes.
■ **Cause** The maggots of a fly, *Delia*

*radicum*, which has three generations between mid-spring and early autumn. The eggs are laid in the soil near the base of the host plant.
■ **Control** Established plants usually tolerate infestations, but transplanted seedlings are especially vulnerable. There are no insecticides approved for the amateur gardener to control this pest, but covering seed rows and transplants with horticultural fleece will exclude egg-laying flies. Alternatively, for transplanted seedlings, prevent the flies from laying their eggs by positioning a collar or disc of carpet underlay, cardboard, or roofing felt, approximately 10cm (4in) in diameter, around the plant base at transplanting time. The females deposit eggs on the disc, rather than in the soil, and they perish before hatching.

**Cabbage whitefly:** *see* Whitefly.

## Calcium deficiency

■ **Crops affected** Various.
■ **Symptoms** Shoots and young leaves often grow poorly, curl, and they generally deteriorate. Symptoms are various, depending on plant and plant part affected.
■ **Brassicas:** Internal browning of Brussels sprout buttons and cabbage hearts.
■ **Carrots:** Root cavities.
■ **Celery:** Blackening of central leaves.
■ **Lettuce:** Tip burn (*see p.263*).
■ **Potato:** Rolled leaves and spindly shoots.
■ **Causes** Calcium may be deficient in the soil or compost, or be unavailable for uptake if very dry or acidic conditions in the growing medium.
■ **Control** Keep plants well watered and mulch to retain soil moisture. If possible, lime acid soils to raise the pH.
*See also* Bitter pit, Blossom end rot.

## Cane spot

■ **Crops affected** Blackberry, raspberry, and hybrid berries.
■ **Symptoms** Lens-shaped, purple or brown-purple spots that have silver-grey centres appear on the canes, sometimes spreading to leaves and flower stalks. As spots enlarge, canes may split and die.
■ **Cause** The fungus *Elsinoë veneta*, which is most active in early summer.
■ **Control** Prune out infected canes as soon as seen. Avoid growing susceptible cultivars, such as raspberry 'Lloyd George' and 'Norfolk Giant'. Spray affected loganberry and raspberry plants with copper oxychloride.

## Canker

■ **Crops affected** Tree fruits.
■ **Symptoms: bacterial canker** affects cherry, plum, apricot, peach, and nectarine crops. Clearly defined areas of bark flatten and sink inwards, and amber-coloured resin may ooze from the bark, especially when injured. Buds at the branch tips fail to open and leaves may wither and die back. Leaves on affected limbs may be small and yellowed, and often have holes in them.
■ **Symptoms: fungal canker** affects apple, pear, and mulberry crops. Areas of bark sink inwards, usually starting near a bud or wound. Bark becomes discoloured then shrinks and cracks, forming concentric rings of flaky bark, and there may be swelling around the

infected site. As the canker enlarges, it may girdle the shoot, causing dieback of growth above it. Any infected fruits rot before maturity. In summer, the canker may host raised white pustules, and in winter, red fruiting bodies appear.
■ **Causes** The bacterium *Pseudomonas mors-prunorum* (on plum and sweet cherry) and *P. syringae* (on peach, apricot, cherry, and plum). The fungi *Neonectria galligena* (on apple and pear) or *Gibberella baccata* (on mulberry), infect mainly in spring. (*See also* Mulberry canker, *p.258*.)

Bacterial infections occur most commonly in wet, windy weather in autumn, or in damp conditions in spring, when soft young growth is most vulnerable. Spring infections usually begin on the leaves and spread to the bark. Most bark infections enter through wounds caused by pruning, frost crack, or leaf fall. Summer infection is rare.

Fungal spores are wind-borne and enter through leaf scars, pruning or insect wounds, frost crack, or scab infections (*see also* Apple and pear scab, *p.251*).
■ **Control** Prune out areas affected by bacterial canker during the summer. Spray infected cherries and plums with copper oxychloride or Bordeaux mixture, once at the end of summer, and once in early and mid-autumn. There are no preparations for bacterial canker on other stone fruits, but copper-based fungicide for control of peach leaf curl gives some protection.

The cherries 'Merton Glory', 'Merton Premier', 'Merla', and 'Merpet' have some resistance, as do plums 'Marjorie's Seedling' ♀ and 'Warwickshire Drooper'.

If the cankers are fungal, prune out entire infected spurs or branches where possible. On larger branch or trunk infections, carefully pare away all infected material, cutting back to clean healthy tissue. Spray with copper oxychloride or Bordeaux mixture and treat the wound with a proprietary wound dressing. Dispose of prunings carefully, preferably by burning. Improve cultural conditions, especially poor drainage; wet soils increase susceptibility. Avoid growing apple cultivars known to be vulnerable, such as 'Cox's Orange Pippin', 'James Grieve' ♀, 'Worcester Pearmain' ♀, and 'Spartan'. The apple cultivars 'Laxton's Superb', 'Newton Wonder' ♀, 'Bramley's Seedling' ♀, and 'Lane's Prince Albert' ♀ show a degree of resistance. Sprays for apple scab and apple powdery mildew give a degree of incidental control.

**Canker of parsnips:** *see* Parsnip canker.

## Capsid bug

■ **Crops affected** Apple, gooseberry, currants, pear, plum, and strawberry.
■ **Symptoms** Leaves at the shoot tip are misshapen and full of small, ragged holes; shoot tips may be killed. Growth emerging from affected buds is distorted. Developing apples may have irregular bumps on their surface and strawberry fruits may also be distorted.
■ **Cause** The common green capsid bug, *Lygocoris pabulinus*. It is pale green, about 6mm (¼in) long. Other species cause similar damage. These sap-sucking insects inject toxic saliva into the shoot tips, killing plant cells. They are active between late spring and late summer but are very elusive and fly away when disturbed.

■ **Control** Check vulnerable plants during the summer; spray apples, pears, and strawberries with deltamethrin at petal fall.

## Carrot fly

■ **Crops affected** Carrot, parsnip, parsley, and celery.
■ **Symptoms** Roots are tunnelled by slender, creamy white maggots, up to 9mm (½in) long. They leave rusty brown lines on the outside of the roots where tunnels close to the surface have collapsed (*see p.250*). Damaged roots rot in store.
■ **Cause** Larvae of the carrot fly, *Psila rosae*, which produces three generations between late spring and early autumn.
■ **Control** Fleece or ultra-fine netting barriers prevent female flies from laying their eggs. Carrots sown after late spring will miss the first generation and those harvested before late summer will miss the second. Choose cultivars with some resistance, such as 'Flyaway', 'Resistafly', or 'Sytan'. There are no approved chemical controls available for garden use.

## Caterpillars

■ **Crops affected** Various.
■ **Symptoms** Most caterpillars feed on leaves, as with cabbage white butterfly larvae. Ragged holes are left in leaves, and a black frass (excrement) may remain; the culprits are often found on or beneath the leaves. Some attack roots, while others bore into stems, feed inside leaves as leaf miners, or feed on fruits and berries.
■ **Causes** Caterpillars are the larval stage of moths and butterflies. They vary in size, colour, and hairiness, but are generally long and tubular in form with a distinct head. They have three pairs of jointed legs at the head end and two to five pairs of clasping legs on the abdomen.
■ **Control** Some caterpillars are easily removed by hand and, as most are night feeders, can be found easily by torchlight. They can be sprayed with deltamethrin, pyrethrum, or lambda-cyhalothrin as soon as the plants show signs of caterpillar feeding.
*See also* Codling moth, Cutworm, Pea moth, Plum fruit moth, Winter moth.

**Celery fly:** *see* Celery leaf miner.

## Celery leaf miner

■ **Crops affected** Celeriac, celery, parsnip, lovage, and parsley.
■ **Symptoms** Leaves develop desiccated brown patches where the interior has been consumed by one or more white maggots, each measuring up to 7mm (⅜in) long. If infestations are severe, the plants have a scorched appearance, and in celery, the stems develop an unpleasantly bitter flavour.
■ **Cause** The larvae of the leaf-mining fly, *Euleia heraclei*. There are two generations a year, causing damage between late spring and late summer.
■ **Control** If infestations are light, pick off affected leaves by hand. There are no chemical controls approved for use by amateur gardeners.

**Cherry slugworm:** *see* Pear and cherry slugworm.

## Chlorosis

■ **Crops affected** Various.
■ **Symptoms** Yellowing of leaves primarily, but also other plant tissues. Yellow, red, or orange colouration may also develop. The primary symptom is due to the loss or deterioration of chlorophyll; this green pigment usually masks other natural pigments and its loss reveals them.
■ **Causes** Most commonly deficiencies of iron and manganese (so-called lime-induced chlorosis), nitrogen, or magnesium. It can also be caused by viruses and unfavourable cultural conditions, such as waterlogging, low temperatures, or weedkiller contamination.
■ **Control** Take appropriate action to remedy nutrient deficiencies, remove sources of viral contamination, and ameliorate poor cultural conditions. *See also* Iron deficiency, Magnesium deficiency, Manganese deficiency.

## Chocolate spot

■ **Crops affected** Broad bean.
■ **Symptoms** Chocolate-brown spots on upper leaf surfaces, and brown streaks on stems, pods, and flowers. The seed coats may also be affected. Severe infections may kill plants and even mild cases can reduce yield.
■ **Causes** The fungus *Botrytis fabae*. It is most prevalent when the air is damp and humid. The fungus overwinters on plant remains and may be seed-borne.
■ **Control** Grow beans in well-drained soil. Space the plants more widely than at the usual recommended spacings – more than 23cm (9in) apart – to permit thorough air circulation around the plants. Maintain good weed control between rows to minimize local humidity and any damp air around plants. Avoid the use of high-nitrogen fertilizers, which will encourage soft, infection-prone growth; sulphate of potash will help to harden the plant tissues slightly.

## Clubroot

■ **Crops affected** Brassicas, including radish, sea kale, swede, and turnip.
■ **Symptoms** Swollen roots and a distorted root system (*see p.250*) with pale, chlorotic foliage. Plants wilt readily especially in hot weather, even if the soil is moist. Crops are reduced and plants may die.
■ **Cause** A soil-borne slime mould, *Plasmodiophora brassicae*. It can live in soil for 20 years or more, even without a host. Infection enters through the root hairs, and when the roots disintegrate, they release spores into the soil. The pathogen can be introduced to gardens in soil that adheres to boots, tools, and wheelbarrows, in garden compost or manure, and directly on infected plants. It is most common on acid and waterlogged soils.
■ **Control** Improve drainage and lime the soil. Burn all infected plants promptly, before roots disintegrate. Raise your own rather than buy plants, in 5cm (2in) pots or larger, so their root systems are well established before setting out. Otherwise, buy from a trusted source and check plants thoroughly before planting. Choose resistant cultivars, like calabrese 'Trixie', Chinese cabbage 'Harmony', kale 'Tall Green Curled', and swede 'Marian'. Maintain good weed control; weeds such as charlock, shepherd's purse, and wild radish are alternative hosts for clubroot. Avoid spreading spores around the garden on boots and tools, and do not transfer potentially infected soil to other parts of the garden.

## Codling moth

■ **Crops affected** Apple and pear.
■ **Symptoms** In mid- to late summer, fruits are tunnelled by small, brown-headed white caterpillars. By ripening time, the caterpillars have tunnelled to the core and the fruits are inedible; exit holes may be seen at the eye end (opposite stalk) of the fruit (*see p.250*) or elsewhere on the fruit surface. Damage is similar to – but less extensive than – apple sawfly (*see p. 251*), but codling moth is more common.
■ **Cause** The larvae of the codling moth, *Cydia pomonella*. Females lay their eggs on fruits on warm nights in early to midsummer. Larvae hatch two weeks later and tunnel into the fruit at the eye end, leaving no visible entry holes. After feeding, they leave to spin cocoons under flakes of bark; most overwinter, but some pupate in late summer to produce a second adult generation in early autumn.
■ **Control** Pheromone traps attract males, reducing the mating success of females and the incidence of maggoty apples. Timing of chemical treatments is critical, because it is vital to destroy larvae before they enter the fruit; pheromone traps indicate when adults are active and likely to be laying eggs. Spray with deltamethrin or lambda-cyhalothrin in early summer, with a second treatment three weeks later.

## Colorado beetle

■ **Crops affected** Aubergine, potato, pepper, and tomato.
■ **Symptoms** Foliage is eaten by pale yellow-orange beetles, up to 1cm (½in) long, with five black stripes on each wing case. Rotund, orange-red grubs, with black heads and two rows of black spots along the sides of their bodies, also eat the foliage, causing extensive defoliation.
■ **Causes** Adults and larvae of the Colorado beetle, *Leptinotarsa decemlineata*. It originated in North America but can now be found throughout Europe, except in Britain and Ireland.
■ **Control** Insecticide-resistant strains of this beetle occur. If found in Britain or Ireland, gardeners are required by law to notify the authorities, who will organize the necessary eradication measures. Elsewhere, infested plants can be sprayed with an approved pesticide when adults or larvae are seen.

## Copper deficiency

■ **Crops affected** Various.
■ **Symptoms** Yellowing of leaves or blue-green discoloration is occasionally followed by dieback (*see below*). Symptoms are rather vague and difficult to distinguish from many other problems.
■ **Cause** Copper deficiency is uncommon but most likely to occur on acid soils.
■ **Control** Treatment with a general compound fertilizer (*see p.20*) may help.

## Coral spot

■ **Crops affected** Currant and fig crops are most susceptible, but many different woody plants can be affected.
■ **Symptoms** Bright coral-pink or orange raised pustules appear on dead woody stems or branches. They may not arise until the tissue has been dead for several weeks. Dieback occurs, and if the infection spreads down into the crown, the whole plant may die.
■ **Cause** The fungus *Nectria cinnabarina*. It lives on dead twigs, old pea sticks, logs, and other woody debris, and it produces spores throughout the year. They are spread in water splash. Infection gains entry through wounds or dead snags left after pruning and may then colonize living tissue, causing dieback. If left unchecked, the whole plant may die.
■ **Control** Prune out infected tissue promptly, cutting back to healthy, living wood. Remove and burn infected tissue. Maintain good hygiene to remove all potential sources of infection.

## Crown rot

■ **Crops affected** Rhubarb, apple, strawberry, and citrus fruits.
■ **Symptoms** Rotting of tissues at the plant crown, the junction between stem and roots. Rot may spread to stems and foliage and the plant can die.
■ **Causes** Various soil- and water-borne fungi and bacteria, often in combination (rhubarb). *Phytophthora* species affect many plants.
■ **Control** Prompt action may save the plant. Remove affected areas by cutting well back into healthy tissue. *See also* Phytophthora.

## Cucumber mosaic virus

■ **Crops affected** Various, including aubergine, but especially cucurbits.
■ **Symptoms** Plants and leaves are stunted and deformed, and leaves show distinctive yellow mosaic patterning (*see p.250*). Flowering is reduced or non-existent, and plants may die completely. In cucumbers, courgettes, and marrows, the fruits, if produced at all, are small, pitted, and unusually dark green with bright yellow patches; they are also hard and inedible.
■ **Causes** The cucumber mosaic virus has a very wide host range and can be spread to crop plants on the mouthparts of aphids and other sap-sucking insects.
■ **Control** Destroy infected plants; there are no chemical controls available. Reduce risk of infection by controlling aphids and clearing weeds, which may be alternative hosts. Do not handle healthy plants after touching infected material without washing hands first. Resistant cultivars include aubergine 'Bonica'; courgettes 'Defender', 'Supremo', and 'Tarmino'; cucumbers 'Bush Champion', 'Crispy Salad', 'Jazzer', 'Petita', and 'Pioneer'; marrows 'Badger Cross' and 'Tiger Cross'.

**Currant reversion:** *see* Reversion disease.

## Cutworm

■ **Crops affected** Root vegetables, brassicas, lettuce, and leek.
■ **Symptoms** Young plants wilt and die. Examination of the roots reveals that they have been severed just below soil level. Root vegetables may have cavities eaten into them. Creamy brown or greenish-brown caterpillars, up to 4cm (1½in) long, may be found in the soil near affected plants. They may also feed on foliage above soil level at night.
■ **Causes** Soil-dwelling caterpillars of several moths, including the large yellow underwing (*Noctua pronuba*), lesser yellow underwing (*N. comes*), turnip moth (*Agrotis segetum*), heart and dart (*A. exclamationis*), and garden dart (*Euxoa nigricans*).
■ **Control** Cutworms will work their way along seed rows. Sifting the soil near a damaged plant may reveal the culprit. Good weed control reduces the incidence of these pests. Insecticides for use against these pests are no longer available to the amateur gardener.

## Damping off

■ **Crops affected** All seedlings are vulnerable, including mustard and cress.
■ **Symptoms** Seedlings flop over, often showing dark discoloration at the stem base, which may appear water-soaked. The infection spreads rapidly and clumps of seedlings die off; whole trays of seedlings can be killed within a few days. Any ungerminated seeds may also fail to appear. A fuzzy, white fungal growth appears on the surface of dead and dying seedlings.
■ **Causes** Several soil-borne fungi, in particular, *Pythium*, *Phytophthora*, and *Rhizoctonia* species. They proliferate in over-wet compost and in prolonged high temperatures. The most common reason for damping off is sowing seed too thickly, causing overcrowding, and inadequate light. It is also encouraged by poor hygiene. Unsterilized compost, pots, trays, and implements, and non-mains water (from a water butt) may all be contaminated with fungal spores.
■ **Control** Observe strict hygiene; scrub all pots, trays, and implements before use and use only proprietary, sterilized seed composts. Use only tap water for watering. Sow seedlings thinly and make sure that they have good light and are not exposed to high temperatures for longer than is needed for germination. Drench the compost with a copper-based fungicide before sowing. Treat seedlings with the same fungicide during their early development.

## Deer

■ **Crops affected** A wide range.
■ **Symptoms** Whole shoots and flowers are eaten; on woody stems the damage is very characteristic. Since deer have no front teeth in their upper jaw, they cut off stems by biting and tugging. This gives a clean-edged cut part way through the stem, and a ragged edge on the remainder where the shoot has been tugged away. Tree trunks and side-branches may also be damaged by fraying – the habit that male deer have of rubbing their antlers against the bark to remove the velvet.
■ **Causes** Several species of deer cause problems in gardens: roe deer (*Capreolus capreolus*), fallow deer (*Dama dama*), muntjac (*Muntiacus muntjak*), and red deer (*Cervus elaphus*).
■ **Control** These agile creatures can be very difficult to exclude from gardens since they are incorrigible leapers of fences. A fence of at least 2m (6ft) in height is needed to keep out roe deer. They are also inquisitive feeders and new plantings are particularly attractive

to them. It is worthwhile giving newly planted trees the protection of individual cages. Proprietary repellents usually give disappointing results; their effects tend to be short-lived and frequently have the unwanted effect of encouraging feeding in other areas of the garden.

## Dieback

■ **Crops affected** Woody-stemmed crops, such as tree and bush fruits.
■ **Symptoms** Plant stems die back, usually from the tip, but often from the base, or sometimes part-way up the stem. Dieback rarely affects all stems simultaneously. Dark blotches or sunken patches may develop at the initial point of infection. Leaves wilt, turn yellow, and die. If unchecked, the symptoms spread down the stem, finally to the base or crown, causing death of the whole plant.
■ **Causes** Various fungi, some of which are wound-invading pathogens, while others can affect formerly healthy stems. Root infection by soil-dwelling pathogens, such as honey fungus (*see p.256*) or phytophthora (*see p.259*), can also cause stem dieback in woody plants. It may be also be caused by unfavourable cultural conditions, especially where dieback occurs from the stem tip downwards. These include drought, waterlogging, and poor establishment of newly planted trees and bushes – if watering has been neglected, for example.
■ **Control** Prune out affected stems back to healthy growth. Improve cultural conditions to increase plant vigour and ensure plenty of replacement shoots.

## Downy mildew

■ **Crops affected** A wide range.
■ **Symptoms** Discoloured or yellowed areas appear on upper leaf surfaces, with corresponding slightly fuzzy, pale grey or purplish fungal growth beneath each patch (*see p.250*). As the infection spreads, large areas or even entire leaves die. Downy mildew is most commonly found on young plants and on those growing in damp environments. It can be difficult to distinguish from powdery mildew (*see p.260*), which is more prevalent in dry conditions.
■ **Causes** A range of fungi, mostly *Peronospora*, *Bremia*, and *Plasmopara* species. Some are specific to their host: *Peronospora parasitica* on brassicas, *P. destructor* on onion, *P. farinosa* f. *spinaceae* on spinach, *Bremia lactucae* on lettuce, and *Plasmopara viticola* on grape vines.
■ **Control** Remove infected leaves as soon as seen. Improve air circulation around plants by maintaining good weed control and planting at wider than usual spacings. Keep greenhouses well ventilated. Avoid overhead watering. There are no fungicides available to amateur gardeners for the control of downy mildew.

## Drought

■ **Crops affected** Various.
■ **Symptoms** Symptoms vary according to crop and whether the drought is recurrent, continuous, or occasional. Poor growth and stunting occurs if drought is recurrent or continuous; foliage wilting is the first sign of dry conditions. If prolonged, drought may cause poor flowering, bud or fruit drop, and the formation of small, poor quality

fruits. Drought followed by high rainfall or sudden watering may cause splitting of fruits and stems.
■ **Causes** Inadequate rainfall or watering is the most obvious cause. Occasionally, it results from root damage that prevents uptake of sufficient water. Plants in containers or with restricted root runs are especially vulnerable, as are those on light, freely draining, sandy or chalky soils.
■ **Control** Water consistently and regularly to prevent soil from becoming completely dry. Take all steps to improve the soil's moisture retention by incorporating plentiful organic matter and by mulching. Protect container-grown plants from the desiccating effects of direct sunlight and consider using water-retaining gels or granules in the growing medium.

## Eelworms

■ **Crops affected** Various.
■ **Symptoms** Generally, eelworms cause distortion, discoloration, and death of plants. Many are specific plant parasites, which cause characteristic symptoms in their host plants.
■ **Causes** Eelworms, or nematodes, are mostly microscopic, worm-like creatures. Not all are pests, many feed on dead tissue, bacteria, fungi, and on other microscopic creatures. Some eelworms are parasitic on garden pests. Slugs and vine weevils, for example, can be controlled in gardens by beneficial eelworms. Pest species may feed internally on their hosts, or are soil-dwelling, attacking root hairs. They are sap-suckers and so may spread virus diseases from plant to plant on their mouthparts.
■ **Control** Parts of the garden from which virus-infected plants have been removed should not be replanted with the same type of plant, otherwise they may quickly become infected by the eelworms. The normal life cycle needs soil moisture to develop, but dormant larvae and eggs protected in cysts can survive adverse soil conditions for many years.

Eelworms and their associated viruses are most often spread in gardens on infected plant debris, or in soil on boots, tools, and plant rootballs – maintain good hygiene. There is no effective chemical control available to gardeners for eelworms. *See also* Potato cyst eelworm, Root knot eelworm, Stem and bulb eelworm, Virus vectors.

## Fireblight

■ **Crops affected** Pome (apple-like) fruit crops of the family Rosaceae, including apple, pear, quince, and medlar. Many ornamental plants are affected, notably amelanchiers, cotoneasters, hawthorns, photinias, pyracanthas, and sorbus; these plants may be a source of infection.
■ **Symptoms** Flowers wilt, wither, and die back, followed shortly by adjacent leaves and stems. Plants may show extensive dieback and are killed within a few seasons. Infection occurs most commonly at flowering time and is usually scattered throughout the crown; healthy stems may coexist with infected ones. The bark sinks inwards on young stems, and if pared back, a foxy-red discoloration is seen on the wood. Bacterial ooze may exude from affected areas. The symptoms are similar to those of blossom wilt (*see p.252*).

■ **Cause** The bacterium *Erwinia amylovora*. It is most prevalent in warm, wet weather. It usually enters through open blossoms, but it can also gain entry through stem injuries. It may be carried in water splash and spread on pruning tools. In certain areas – Northern Ireland, the Isle of Man, and the Channel Islands, for example, but not mainland Great Britain – fireblight is a notifiable disease; it must be reported to the local authorities.
■ **Control** Prune out affected stems to at least 60cm (2ft) into healthy wood. Dispose of all prunings by burning, and sterilize all tools after use. If the infection is widespread, or the tree is small, it may be best to remove it entirely. If planting ornamental plants near susceptible crops, avoid those that might be a source of infection (*see above*). The risk of fireblight is low in most years, so gardeners with hawthorn hedges should keep them. There is no effective chemical control.

## Flea beetle

■ **Crops affected** Potato, brassicas, swede, turnip, sea kale, radish, and rocket.
■ **Symptoms** Small, shiny black beetles, sometimes with yellow-striped wing cases and usually about 2mm (¹⁄₁₂in) long, leap from affected foliage when disturbed. Some species are larger, to 4mm (¹⁄₈in), and are metallic blue or yellow-brown in colour. They eat small round holes in the upper leaf surfaces (*see p.250*), seldom penetrating the leaf entirely. Damaged tissues desiccate and turn pale brown. Heavy attacks may kill seedlings and check the growth of established plants.
■ **Causes** There are many species of flea beetle. Brassicas are most usually affected by *Phyllotreta* species; potatoes suffer most often from *Psylliodes affinis*. Adults damage the foliage while the soil-dwelling larvae feed on roots. Adults are active in mid-spring and late summer.
■ **Control** Sow when growing conditions are good, so that seedlings can germinate and grow rapidly through the vulnerable seedling stage. Protect seedlings and young plants with horticultural fleece or similar barriers. If necessary, spray seedlings with deltamethrin or lambda-cyhalothrin.

## Foot and root rots

■ **Crops affected** Asparagus, celery, tomato, cucurbits, melon, pea, bean, and greenhouse and soft fruits.
■ **Symptoms** Infections at the stem base cause tissues to darken, atrophy, and soften. The upper parts respond by wilting, discolouring, and dying back. Root rotting may occur at the same time.
■ **Causes** Various fungi, often those responsible for damping off (*see facing page*). Other fungi, including fusarium and verticillium (*see pp.256, 263*) may cause both wilting and foot rot symptoms.
■ **Control** There is no cure for infected plants. Prevent the spread of the disease by immediate removal of affected plants, along with the soil or compost at their roots. Maintain impeccable hygiene, washing pots, trays, and implements thoroughly before use. Use only sterilized composts and mains water for irrigation.

## Frit fly

■ **Crops affected** Sweetcorn.
■ **Symptoms** Longitudinal yellow stripes appear on young leaves, which later deteriorate, fraying into strips. Plants fail to grow and crops are diminished. In severe infestations, growing points are killed, and plants may die. Small white larvae, 5mm (¹⁄₄in) long, may be found feeding in the stems and at the base of leaves in midsummer.
■ **Cause** Larvae of the fly *Oscinella frit*. Adults lay eggs in early summer, at or near the base of the plant. Larvae hatch two or three weeks later, entering the stems to feed. There may be three generations between early summer and autumn; the last overwinters as larvae in grasses and cereal crops.
■ **Control** Maintain good weed control, especially of grasses. Provide good growing conditions so that plants establish rapidly; well-established plants are less vulnerable to attack. Raise seedlings singly in pots under glass and plant them out after the early summer egg-laying period to avoid this pest. There are no approved chemical controls available to amateur gardeners for frit fly.

## Frost damage (buds and flowers)

■ **Crops affected** Various, especially bush and tree fruits.
■ **Symptoms** Buds, whether tightly closed or partially open, become discoloured. They turn brown and often become soft and squidgy to the touch. Buds on more exposed areas of the plant are the worst affected. Damage may only occur at certain developmental stages of the bud or flower, so on any given plant, some will escape damage. Nevertheless, there will be a subsequent loss of the fruit crop to a greater or lesser degree.
■ **Causes** Freezing causes extensive cell damage; cells are ruptured as the frozen cell contents expand. This is exacerbated when thawing is rapid. Slightly tender plants and early flowering cultivars are most vulnerable, but late frosts, which often occur unpredictably after the flower buds have opened, can be particularly damaging.
■ **Control** Choose planting sites with care. Avoid known frost pockets and sites where plants will receive direct early morning sun, if possible. Protect more tender plants, such as peaches and nectarines, by growing against a warm, sheltered wall and cover with fleece or similar when frost threatens. In cold areas, choose later flowering cultivars.

Seek out local cultivars of tree and bush fruits; these are generally older cultivars that have been selected to suit prevailing climatic conditions and are most likely to be available from specialist local nurseries.

## Frost damage (foliage and stems)

■ **Crops affected** Various leafy crops, including early potato crops.
■ **Symptoms** Leaves, usually towards the shoot tips, and on other exposed parts of the plant, appear scorched and turn brown or black. Affected parts may wilt, wither, and die, and young stem growth adjacent to frosted leaves may also die back. Occasionally, isolated patches of damage occurs on otherwise sound stems.

■ **Causes** Freezing causes extensive cell damage in plant tissue; cells are ruptured as the frozen cell contents expand. This is exacerbated when thawing is rapid, as it is when crops are exposed to direct early morning sun. Slightly tender plants, overwintering and early crops are most vulnerable, but late spring frosts, which often occur unpredictably, can be particularly damaging.
■ **Control** Choose planting sites carefully, especially for crops known to be easily frost-damaged. Avoid known frost pockets and sites that receive direct morning sun when possible. Protect vulnerable crops, such as early potatoes, with horticultural fleece or similar. With potatoes, earthing up helps to reduce damage. An autumn dressing of sulphate of potash helps to harden stem growth and may minimize damage to overwintering crops, such as sprouting broccoli.

## Fruit fly

■ **Crops affected** Apple, cherry, citrus, passion fruit, peach, plum, olive, melon.
■ **Symptoms** Fruit flesh is infested with small white maggots, which sometimes cause galls. Adult insects, up to 6mm (¼in) long, have red-orange heads, black bodies marked yellow and white, and mottled wings. They resemble tiny house flies and may be seen on or flying around plants.
■ **Cause** Many species, including *Ceratitis capitata*. They are native to Mediterranean and subtropical regions, but they do not occur in some cooler climates such as the UK. The flies breed throughout the year where temperatures permit and are serious fruit pests in warmer parts of the world, but not in cool-temperate climates, such as northern Europe.
■ **Control** Yellow sticky traps and pheromone traps help reduce populations, the latter by foiling the reproductive success of females by attracting and trapping male flies. Food lure traps attract both sexes of the fly. Chemical treatments should be targeted at adult flies, since once inside fruits, larvae are difficult to reach with sprays. Prevent adult flies from laying eggs by spraying with an approved insecticide at times when the adults are seen to be active.

**Fruit splitting:** *see* Drought, Splitting.
**Fruit tree red spider mite:** *see* Red spider mite.

## Fusarium basal rot

■ **Crops affected** Bulb onion, Welsh onion, and garlic.
■ **Symptoms** Decay spreads up through the bulbs from the basal plate. Once infected, the plant is effectively dead.
■ **Cause** Several *Fusarium* species including the fungus *Fusarium oxysporum* f. sp. *cepae* on onions. Unlike most other strains of *F. oxysporum* (*see below*), this one does not cause wilting. It is more prevalent in warm-temperate climates.
■ **Control** Remove and burn infected plants promptly to minimize spread. Do not put them on the compost heap. Practise crop rotation (*see p.31*).

## Fusarium wilt

■ **Crops affected** Various, both woody- and soft-stemmed. Pea crops are commonly affected.
■ **Symptoms** Soft stems wilt, in part or

in their entirety, while woody-stemmed plants may retain their overall shape, but leaves on affected parts wilt and wither. The decisive symptom is brown or black staining on the internal vascular tissue, which is apparent beneath the bark or at the root core. Plant death is almost inevitable. In cool, damp conditions, fluffy, pale pink, or white fungal growth may be visible on infected tissues.
■ **Causes** Various strains of the fungus *Fusarium*, most commonly *F. oxysporum*, cause fusarium wilt. The fungi are often host-specific, but all are responsible for blocking the vascular tissues with gum-like substances, which cause wilting in much the same manner as drought. Unlike plants suffering from drought, however, those affected by fusarium wilt do not recover when watered. The fungus persists in plant debris and is also capable of surviving in the soil, in the absence of a host, for several years.
■ **Control** Remove infected plants promptly to minimize spread and destroy, preferably by burning. Do not put them on the compost heap. Where practicable, remove soil or compost from the immediate vicinity of the roots. Do not grow the same or closely related plants on the same site again, or for a minimum of five years. There is no chemical cure.

**Gall mites:** on blackcurrant, *see* Big bud mite; on pears, *see* Pear leaf blister mite.
**Ghost spotting:** *see* Tomato ghost spot.

## Gooseberry dieback

■ **Crops affected** Gooseberry and, less commonly, blackcurrant.
■ **Symptoms** Dieback of stems. Usually only some of the stems are affected, but the infection occasionally spreads; if the main stem or base of the plant is affected, the entire bush will die back. In damp weather, fuzzy, grey fungal growth is seen around damaged areas. Leaves on infected stems yellow, turn brown, and fall prematurely. Any developing fruits may shrivel and die.
■ **Cause** The fungus *Botrytis cinerea* (*see also* Botrytis, *p.252*). Spores are spread in air currents and in water splash.
■ **Control** Prune out infected shoots promptly, removing all wood that shows staining or discoloration; cut back to a bud on healthy wood. Remove any infected fruits, which form a source of further infection.

## Gooseberry sawfly

■ **Crops affected** Gooseberry, redcurrant, and whitecurrant.
■ **Symptoms** Rapid and severe defoliation occurs, the bush often being reduced to bare stems by harvest time. Pale green, caterpillar-like larvae (*see p.250*), up to 2cm (¾in) long, often heavily marked with black spots, eat the leaves. Damage starts in mid- to late spring, but there can be three generations a year, so it may continue through the summer.
■ **Causes** Sawfly larvae. Three species attack gooseberry crops: common gooseberry sawfly (*Nematus ribesii*), lesser gooseberry sawfly (*N. leucotrochus*), and pale gooseberry sawfly (*Pristiphora appendiculata*).
■ **Control** Inspect gooseberry and currant bushes carefully from mid-spring onwards; examine leaf undersides, especially in the centre of the bush. Infestations commonly begin at the

heart of the bush and the pest defoliates upwards and outwards, causing considerable damage before being noticed. Spray affected plants with pyrethrum or lambda-cyhalothrin as soon as the larvae are discovered.

**Grey mould:** *see* Botrytis.

## Halo blight

■ **Crops affected** Dwarf French and runner bean.
■ **Symptoms** Small, angular spots appear on the foliage, at first appearing water-soaked and then darkening in colour; each spot is surrounded by a bright yellow "halo". The leaves begin to turn yellow between the veins and eventually the entire leaf is affected and dies. Growth and yields can be seriously affected. If stems or pods are infected, they develop grey patches, again with a water-soaked appearance.
■ **Cause** The bacterium *Pseudomonas syringae* pv. *phaseolicola*, which is spread by water splash and is carried by seeds – usually the initial source of infection.
■ **Control** Pick off infected leaves as soon as seen and avoid overhead watering. Remove and burn all affected plants at the end of the season and do not store the seed. The dwarf French bean cultivars 'Forum' and 'Red Rum' show some resistance to this infection.

## Honey fungus

■ **Crops affected** Tree and bush fruits, strawberry, rhubarb, and globe artichoke. Most woody plants are susceptible.
■ **Symptoms** Affected plants begin to die back, leaves may discolour and wilt, or trees may fail to leaf up in spring. Death can be rapid or drawn out over several seasons. Fruit trees may set an unusually good crop before dying. The roots and stem or trunk bases develop a white fungal sheet, with a decidedly mushroom-like aroma, between the bark and the woody tissues beneath. Around the root system in the soil, there may be "rhizomorphs", which resemble black or brown bootlaces, or old tree roots. They can be branched and flattened or may be plump and more rounded, varying in diameter from less than a millimetre to several millimetres across. If the black outer rind is stripped off, it may be lined with pink or white fungal growth. The rhizomorphs feed on dead woody material, but may grow through the soil to latch onto living tissues. Rhizomorphs may also be found beneath the bark at the base of the stem or trunk of infected plants. In late summer or autumn, clumps of honey-coloured toadstools may appear. They cluster at the base of the plant, or may form colonies that follow the line of the roots. They are commonly seen infesting old, dead tree stumps. The stipe or stem of the toadstools usually bears a distinctive creamy white ruff or collar.
■ **Causes** Various species of the fungus *Armillaria*. These show varying degrees of ability to cause disease, with some being less virulent than others. Less virulent species tend only to infect plants that have root wounds or are otherwise stressed. Without laboratory identification, it can be difficult to differentiate between the species, except on the basis of the damage they cause. Spread occurs either by direct root contact or by rhizomorphs, which can grow at a rate of up to 1m (3ft) per year.

■ **Control** Keep plants in good health by good cultivation, keeping them well fed, mulched, and watered. Avoid root damage when cultivating the soil around plants. Honey fungus will infect more readily plants that are stressed, for example by drought, excessive pruning, or severe pest infestations. Remove all dead trees from the garden, including their roots, regardless of their cause of death, since dead woody tissues are a prime food source for honey fungus. It is imperative to remove as much of the root system of infected plants as possible; hire a stump grinder if necessary.

## Iron deficiency

■ **Crops affected** Many, including apple, pear, blueberry, raspberry, and blackberry.
■ **Symptoms** Leaf yellowing, or chlorosis (*see p.254*), between the leaf veins, often in combination with brown discoloration that starts at the leaf margins and moves in towards the veins. Young growth is affected earlier and more severely than older growth.
■ **Causes** Iron deficiency is usually seen in combination with manganese deficiency (*see facing page*). It is most common in acid-loving plants, such as blueberries, when grown on limy (alkaline) soils; hence the term lime-induced chlorosis. It can also affect other plants that are not noted as being acid-lovers. A shortage of soil iron is rare, but iron (and manganese) can be rendered unavailable to plants if soils are too alkaline; the mechanism is complex but, in brief, the excess calcium "locks up" the iron in the soil, so that plants cannot absorb it.
■ **Control** Do not grow acid-loving plants on soils that are not sufficiently acidic. Treat affected tree, bush, and soft fruits with a chelated compound containing iron, manganese, and other trace elements; these will be in a form that does not become locked up by calcium, and they will be available to plant roots.
   Restrict liming on soils that are already alkaline. If soils are very alkaline, consider acidifying the soil by using sulphur or aluminium sulphate and ferrous sulphate before planting. For acid-loving plants, use an acidic mulch of pine needles or chopped conifer bark; incorporate some in the planting hole before planting. Feed with a fertilizer formulated for use on acid-loving plants.

**Leaf blight:** of walnuts, *see* Walnut leaf blight.
**Leaf blotch:** of walnuts, *see* Walnut blotch.
**Leaf-curling aphid:** *see* Plum leaf-curling aphid.
**Leaf-curling midge:** *see* Blackcurrant gall midge.
**Leaf miner:** *see* Celery leaf miner.

## Leaf spots (bacterial)

■ **Crops affected** Various, including brassicas, cucumber, and mulberry.
■ **Symptoms** Grey or brown, usually angular or circular necrotic spots appear on leaves, often with a yellow "halo" around them. There are no minute, raised fungal bodies visible, as there are in fungal leaf spots.
■ **Causes** Various bacteria may be involved. Examples include *Pseudomonas syringae* pv. *maculicola* on brassicas,

*P. syringae* pv. *lachrymans* on cucumber, and *P. syringae* pv. *mori* on mulberry. They are most often spread by water splash, or occasionally from stem lesions to leaves (as with bacterial canker, which can cause leaf spots on *Prunus* species). In most cases, the damage is cosmetic, but it can indicate a plant is under stress or suffering from another, more serious problem.

■ **Control** Remove infected leaves promptly and avoid overhead watering. There is no chemical treatment.

## Leaf spots (fungal)

■ **Crops affected** Beetroot, blackberry, celery, currants, Swiss chard, gooseberry, and raspberry.
■ **Symptoms** Grey or brown, circular necrotic spots appear on leaves; they may join together so that large areas of leaves die. The spots often have concentric rings of discoloured tissue around them and often bear tiny, raised, black or brown fungal fruiting bodies.
■ **Causes** A wide range of fungi, some of which are host-specific, for example, *Ramularia beticola* and *Cercospora beticola* on beet leaves. Although entire leaves may die, fungal spots are not very serious, but they may indicate that the plant is suffering from some other, more fundamental problem.
■ **Control** Remove affected leaves if needed. At the end of each season, rake up fallen leaves to minimize the numbers of overwintering spores. Difenoconazole can be used to control fungal leaf spots on brassicas, celeriac, celery, rhubarb and asparagus.

## Leatherjackets

■ **Crops affected** Many, including young brassicas, lettuce, and strawberry. Seedlings are very vulnerable to attack.
■ **Symptoms** Plants turn yellow, wilt, and may die. The symptoms are similar to those seen in cutworm damage (*see p.254*) and in some foot and root rots (*see p.255*). The roots are eaten, and sifting the soil around the site of damage may reveal legless, grey-brown larvae, up to 4.5cm (1¾in) long; they have no obvious heads. Most damage is seen in spring and it is particularly common on newly cultivated ground that was previously grassed over.
■ **Causes** The larvae of crane flies, or daddy-long-legs. The most common species are *Tipula paludosa*, *T. oleracea*, and *Nephrotoma maculata*. The adults lay their eggs in the soil in late summer and larvae hatch two weeks later. They feed during the autumn and again in the following spring and summer. There is usually only one generation a year, but there may be huge populations following a warm, damp summer and autumn.
■ **Control** By the time leatherjackets are large enough to cause noticeable damage, they have become fairly resistant to insecticides. Biological control, using the pathogenic nematode *Steinernema feltiae*, is possible, but the soil must be moist and warm (at least 12°C/54°F). The larvae are a favourite food of starlings, thrushes, and blackbirds; turning over the soil in autumn can expose the larvae to birds. If converting grassland to a vegetable plot, consider laying a sheet of black plastic over the area following heavy rain or irrigation. The larvae will come to the surface and can be collected up and removed as the plastic is rolled back.

There are no chemical controls approved for use by amateur gardeners.

## Leek rust

■ **Crops affected** Leeks, onions, shallots, garlic and chives.
■ **Symptoms** Outer leaves develop lens-shaped, bright orange, raised fungal pustules, 1–2mm (¹⁄₁₆–¹⁄₁₂in) long. When these erupt, they release conspicuous masses of bright orange spores. Affected leaves turn yellow and die back. Inner leaves are seldom badly affected.
■ **Causes** Strains of the fungus *Puccinia allii*. The strains that attack leeks do not attack onions or chives. They are most prevalent in damp conditions and in wet weather.
■ **Control** Remove and destroy all affected leaves at harvest. Dispose of all debris thoroughly at the end of the season and grow leeks and other onion family members on a fresh site each year. Avoid the use of high-nitrogen fertilizers, which encourage soft, disease-prone growth. At planting time, apply a dressing of sulphate of potash at a rate of 15–20g per sq m (½–¾oz per sq yd); this helps harden tissues and improves resistance. Space plants more widely than usual to improve air circulation and maintain good weed control. Choose leek cultivars with known resistance, such as 'Walton Mammoth', 'Titan', 'Poristo', 'Poribleu', and 'Splendid'.

## Lettuce root aphid

■ **Crops affected** Lettuce, chicory, and endive.
■ **Symptoms** Lettuce plants wilt and make slow growth in sunny weather, even in moist soils. If plants are dug up, the roots and surrounding soil will be seen to be coated with a waxy white powder. Closer examination reveals creamy yellow aphids, up to 2mm (¹⁄₁₂in) long, on the roots.
■ **Cause** The lettuce root aphid, *Pemphigus bursarius*. This sap-sucking aphid feeds on outdoor lettuce roots during mid- to late summer.
■ **Control** Keep lettuces well watered and grow them on a different site each year. Choose cultivars with some resistance, such as lettuce 'Avoncrisp', 'Avondefiance', 'Debby', 'Lakeland', and 'Sigmaball'. Insecticides do not give good control of root aphids.

**Lime-induced chlorosis:** *see* Chlorosis, Iron Deficiency.

## Magnesium deficiency

■ **Crops affected** Apple, some brassicas, cherry, grape vine, lettuce, potato, and tomato.
■ **Symptoms** Yellowing develops between the leaf veins (interveinal chlorosis) and around the leaf margins, leaving clear green bands immediately adjacent to the veins (*see p.250*). As the green colour is lost, other pigments may be revealed, so instead of yellowing, red, purple, or brown discoloration may occur. Apple crops may be so severely affected as to defoliate. Symptoms are most pronounced towards the end of the season, and the older leaves always show deficiency symptoms first (compare with iron deficiency, *see facing page*). Magnesium is very mobile in the plant and when in short supply it is

transferred from older lower leaves to new ones nearer the stem tips.
■ **Causes** Magnesium deficiency is most common in very acid soils or potting composts, and after heavy rain or watering, especially on light, sandy soils. When water levels are high, magnesium is readily leached from the soil. The excessive use of high-potash fertilizers or sulphate of potash may exacerbate this deficiency, because high levels of potassium in the soil can render magnesium unavailable to plant roots.
■ **Control** When liming, consider using magnesian limestone. For more rapid amelioration, apply magnesium as a foliar spray. Apply Epsom salts at a rate of 200g in 10 litres of water (8oz in 2 gallons), adding a wetting agent. Alternatively, apply Epsom salts to the soil at a rate 40g per sq m (1½oz per sq yd) or Kieserite at 70–140g per sq m (2½–5oz per sq yd).

## Manganese deficiency

■ **Crops affected** Various, including pea, bean, brassicas, beetroot, parsnip, spinach, and bush and tree fruits.
■ **Symptoms** Yellowing develops between the leaf veins (interveinal chlorosis) of older leaves, and necrotic brown patches often appear on the yellowed areas. In potato crops, the young foliage may be pale and rolled upwards at leaf margins. Pea and bean seeds may exhibit almost circular brown spots that become visible when the cotyledons are pulled apart.
■ **Causes** Manganese deficiency, which is most common in acid, peaty soils and on poorly drained, sandy soils. It can be induced by an excess of iron in the soil, but may also occur in tandem with an iron deficiency.
■ **Control** Avoid overliming susceptible soils. Spray affected plants with a solution of manganese sulphate at the manufacturer's recommended rate. *See also* Chlorosis, Iron deficiency.

## Mealybugs

■ **Crops affected** Most greenhouse plants, including citrus fruits, grape vine, pineapple, and prickly pear.
■ **Symptoms** Soft-bodied, pale grey or pink insects, up to 4mm (¼in) long, infest stems, usually in inaccessible places like leaf axils. A fluffy white wax is secreted by the insect and this also conceals their eggs. Excretions of honeydew are host to black sooty mould.
■ **Causes** There are several species of mealybugs that occur in greenhouses; the most common are *Pseudococcus* and *Planococcus* species.
**Control** A thorough spray with fatty acids or plant oils can be effective, as can hand-picking if done frequently. Where daytime temperatures are 24°C (75°F) or more, a biological control – the ladybird predator *Cryptolaemus montrouzieri* – can reduce infestations.

## Mealy cabbage aphid

■ **Crops affected** Brassicas and swede.
■ **Symptoms** Yellow patches appear on the foliage between mid-spring and mid-autumn. Beneath the leaves, there are dense colonies of grey-white aphids, which are covered with a mealy white wax. During early summer, the aphids infest the shoot tips. The new leaves are distorted when they emerge and they have a pale mottled appearance. If infestations

are severe, the shoot tip may be killed and multiple branching occurs as a result.
■ **Causes** The sap-sucking aphid *Brevicoryne brassicae*.
■ **Control** Treat with fatty acids, deltamethrin, pyrethrum, lambda-cyhalothrin, or thiacloprid.

## Mice

■ **Crops affected** Stored fruits, vegetables, and seeds; and in the garden, pea, bean, and sweetcorn are especially vulnerable to nibbling by mice.
■ **Symptoms** Pea, bean, and sweetcorn seeds and seedlings are removed and eaten. Stored produce is also eaten during autumn and winter, when mice migrate indoors, or raid sheds and outhouses.
■ **Causes** *Mus* and *Apodemus* species, (house, wood, and field mice) are the usual suspects.
■ **Control** Set mouse traps in places where mice have caused damage. In the garden, put traps under the cover of logs or bricks, away from birds or pets.

Humane mouse traps, which trap live animals, are only humane if checked at least twice daily, because these small creatures are killed easily by starvation, stress, dehydration, or heatstroke. The culprits should be released at least 300m (330yds) away from the capture site.

## Mint rust

■ **Crops affected** Mint, marjoram, and savory.
■ **Symptoms** Leaves and stems are distorted and flecked with yellow; in mint, the stems may be conspicuously contorted as they emerge from the ground in spring. Cupped, orange fungal fruiting bodies develop on the stems and leaves, later turning yellow-orange, then dark brown.
■ **Cause** The fungus *Puccinia menthae*. This overwinters as resting spores in the soil and within infected rhizomes.
■ **Control** The easiest means of control is simply to dig up and burn plants, and to replace them with new ones in spring. Obtain stock from a reliable source and plant in a completely new site. It is possible to kill the fungus with a flame weeder; burn off the top-growth at the end of the season and scorch the soil. It is difficult to do this safely and reliably and there is a risk of overdoing it and killing the plant entirely.

## Molybdenum deficiency

■ **Crops affected** Broccoli and cauliflower.
■ **Symptoms** Leaves are mottled yellow and stunted, and they may die off. Growing tips are often distorted; this is a typical symptom of molybdenum deficiency, sometimes known as whiptail of brassicas.
■ **Causes** It is rare that soils are deficient in molybdenum, but acid soils or composts may render this element unavailable. It is needed for the assimilation of nitrogen by the plant, hence abnormal cell formation and subsequent check to growth.
■ **Control** Increase pH of acid soils by liming. Alternatively, drench soil of affected plots with ammonium or sodium molybdate; dissolve 2.5g (¹⁄₁₆oz) in 0.5 litre (1 pint) of water to treat 1 sq m (1 sq yd).

## Mulberry canker

■ **Crops affected** Mulberry.
■ **Symptoms** Small cankers girdle the stem causing shoot dieback. Tiny, reddish-brown pustules arise around the cankers and are most noticeable in summer.
■ **Cause** The fungus *Gibberella baccata*.
■ **Control** Prune out affected shoots and areas of dieback to limit its spread. *See also* Canker.

**Nectria canker:** *see* Canker, fungal.
**Nematodes:** *see* Eelworms.

## Nitrogen deficiency

■ **Crops affected** Various.
■ **Symptoms** Growth is reduced and leaves are small and yellowed (chlorotic). In some plants, red or purple discoloration of the leaves may occur as chlorophyll levels drop. The oldest, lower leaves are affected first, but if the deficiency is not corrected, all parts of the plant may be affected. Flowering, fruiting, and root or tuber formation are impaired.
■ **Causes** Most soils can develop nitrogen deficiency, but it is more prevalent on light soils and those with a low organic matter content. Plots that have been heavily cropped are also susceptible. In cool springs, nitrogen deficiency may occur temporarily, but this is usually self-righting as the soil warms up and soil bacteria become active. Soils that have been heavily mulched with wood chips may suffer deficiency because nitrogen is removed from the soil as the lignin in the wood is broken down.
■ **Control** Make regular applications of composts and well-rotted or matured mulch materials, and apply nitrogen-rich fertilizers. Grow legumes (for example, peas and beans), which are capable of fixing nitrogen by means of bacteria in their root nodules. Leguminous green manures, such as crimson clover (*Trifolium incarnatum*) and winter tares (*Vicia sativa*), will also fix nitrogen in the soil.

## Nut weevil

■ **Crops affected** Cobnut and filbert.
■ **Symptoms** In late summer, nuts develop round holes, 1–2mm (¹⁄₁₆–¹⁄₁₂in) across, in their shells; these are the exit holes of the weevil grubs, which bore their way out of the nut to pupate in the soil. The nut kernel is eaten by a white maggot with a pale brown head.
■ **Cause** The grubs of a weevil, *Curculio nucum*. The adult is about 1cm (½in) long, with a long slender snout that is more than half its body length.
■ **Control** In most cases, only a small proportion of the crop is affected, so routine control measures are unnecessary. There are no pesticides approved for use by amateur gardeners against this pest.

## Oedema

■ **Crops affected** Various, but grape vines are particularly vulnerable.
■ **Symptoms** Raised, wart-like growths appear, most often on lower leaf surfaces, but sometimes on grapes. They are leaf-coloured at first, but may become brown and corky. Affected leaves may become distorted, but death is not inevitable.
■ **Causes** A cultural condition whereby leaves take up more water than is lost by

transpiration. Small groups of cells become waterlogged, swelling to form blister-like, pale green warty growths. If conditions do not improve, the cells rupture and die, turning brown and corky. The condition is most common when humidity is high and water levels at the roots are excessive.
■ **Control** Avoid overwatering, improve drainage, and ventilate crops under glass. Space plants more widely than the recommended distances to permit good air circulation. Do not remove affected leaves – this exacerbates the problem.

**Olive scab:** *see* Apple, pear, and olive scabs.
**Onion eelworm:** *see* Stem and bulb eelworm.

## Onion fly

■ **Crops affected** Onion family: mostly onion, but also leek, shallot, and garlic.
■ **Symptoms** Young plants collapse in early summer, with the roots eaten by white maggots, up to 8mm (¹⁄₃in) long.
■ **Causes** The maggots are the larval stage of the fly *Delia antiqua*, which resembles a house fly. There is one generation in early summer and a second in late summer; the latter feeds on roots and burrows into the bulbs, causing secondary rots to set in.
■ **Control** Grow onions from sets; they are less vulnerable than seedlings to attack by first-generation maggots. Growing the plants under horticultural fleece will keep out egg-laying females. Lift infested plants and destroy them before the maggots move into the soil to pupate. There are no chemical controls available to amateur gardeners, and maggots inside the bulbs would be inaccessible anyway.

## Onion neck rot

■ **Crops affected** Onion family.
■ **Symptoms** The bulb scales of infected onions become semi-transparent, pale brown, and soft. The affected areas develop a dense grey fungal growth and begin to dry out, taking on a mummified appearance. Black tiny fruiting bodies (sclerotia), which may be several millimetres long, arise on affected parts and are often clustered around the neck end of the bulb. The rot is often first noticed on stored bulbs.
■ **Cause** The fungus *Botrytis allii*. It is the commonest cause of rot in stored onions. The sclerotia can persist in the soil or on onion debris, as a source of re-infection.
■ **Control** Do not grow onions on the same site for more than three years in succession. Buy seed and sets only from a reputable supplier, as the fungus may be brought in on infected seed or sets. Do not apply fertilizers after midsummer, and avoid the use of high-nitrogen fertilizers, since they induce soft, infection-prone growth. Keep crops well watered and improve cultural conditions so that firm, well-ripened bulbs are produced. At harvest time, allow onion necks to flop naturally rather than bending them over to terminate growth; bending can cause wounds that form entry points for disease. When they are drying off prior to storage, protect onions from rainfall in a covered, open, well-ventilated place. Red- or yellow-bulbed, rather than white onions, are more resistant to infection, as is the cultivar 'Norstar'.

## Onion thrips

■ **Crops affected** Onion family, including leek.
■ **Symptoms** A fine, white mottling develops on onion or leek leaves during the summer. Black or pale yellow, narrow-bodied insects, up to 2mm (¹⁄₁₂in) long, are found on the leaves.
■ **Causes** The adults and nymphs of a sap-sucking insect, *Thrips tabaci*. Many ornamental plants are alternative hosts. Thrips are most troublesome in hot, dry summers and, while light infestations are tolerable, heavy ones cause a significant check to growth. Heavy infestations are characterized by the loss of much of the green colour in leaves before late summer.
■ **Control** Effective treatments include deltamethrin (on leek) or pyrethrum.

## Onion white rot

■ **Crops affected** Onion family.
■ **Symptoms** The foliage turns yellow and wilts. The base of the bulb and roots develop fluffy white fungal growth (*see p.250*), which later produces tiny black fruiting bodies (sclerotia). The sclerotia fall off into the soil, where they can persist for seven years or more.
■ **Cause** A fungus, *Sclerotium cepivorum*.
■ **Control** Remove and burn infected plants as soon as seen and do not grow members of the onion family on the same site for at least eight years. The onion cultivar 'Norstar' is known to exhibit a degree of resistance. There is no chemical treatment available.

## Parsnip canker

■ **Crops affected** Parsnip.
■ **Symptoms** Roughened cankers appear on the root, especially at the shoulder. They are usually red-brown, orange-brown, or black.
■ **Causes** The fungus *Itersonilia pastinacae* or, less commonly, *Mycocentospora acerina*. It may spread to the soil from infected leaf spots and often enters through damaged root hairs. Carrot fly damage (*see p.250*) is also a significant point of entry.
■ **Control** No control is available. Grow resistant cultivars, such as 'Avonresister'. Improve soil drainage and avoid or remove all potential sources of root injury. Late sowing at closer than normal spacings produces smaller roots, which appear to be less susceptible to canker.

## Pea and bean weevil

■ **Crops affected** Pea and broad bean.
■ **Symptoms** The margins of pea and bean leaves have U-shaped notches at their margins, producing a typically scalloped effect. They are caused by grey-brown weevils, 3–4mm (¹⁄₈–¹⁄₆in) long. They may be observed in action, but are elusive, dropping off the plant when disturbed.
■ **Causes** The adult weevil *Sitona lineatus*, which overwinters in plant debris and feeds from early spring. The larval stage feeds on the nitrogen-fixing root nodules of peas and beans.
■ **Control** Plants can withstand the small amount of damage usually caused. If infestations are severe, or small plants are heavily attacked, spray with deltamethrin or lambda-cyhalothrin. Avoid spraying plants in flower to protect bees.

## Pea aphid

■ **Crops affected** Pea.
■ **Symptoms** Young growths are infested by large, pale green, pink, or yellow aphids, which cause a check to growth.
■ **Cause** The pea aphid, *Acyrthosiphon pisum*. This species is a significant carrier of a range of viral diseases that have the potential to affect legumes.
■ **Control** Treat with deltamethrin, pyrethrum, or lambda-cyhalothrin in early summer if aphids are present. *See also* Aphids.

## Pea leaf and pod spot

■ **Crops affected** Pea.
■ **Symptoms** Sunken brown or yellow spots appear on leaves, stems, flower stems, and pods. These lesions may also bear small, pinprick-sized, fungal fruiting bodies.
■ **Causes** Various fungi, including *Ascochyta pisi* and *A. pinodes*. They usually attack fully grown peas, but occasionally attack seedlings, usually fatally. It persists from year to year on plant debris and, if seeds are collected from infected pods, the resultant seedlings will succumb too.
■ **Control** Clear up and burn infected plant material at the end of the season. Do not save seed from infected plants. Sow fresh seed in a new site in spring.

## Pea moth

■ **Crops affected** Pea.
■ **Symptoms** Caterpillars, to 6mm (¹⁄₄in) long, with dark-dotted, creamy white bodies and black heads, feed within the pods on developing peas (*see p.250*). They occur in greatest numbers during mid- to late summer.
■ **Cause** Caterpillars of the pea moth, *Cydia nigricana*. Eggs are laid when peas are in flower; the adult moths are active between early and late summer. Early- or late-sown peas, which flower outside this period, usually escape infestation.
■ **Control** Early and late sowings avoid the egg-laying period. Spray other sowings with deltamethrin or lambda-cyhalothrin about a week after the onset of flowering to kill the hatching caterpillars.

**Pea seed beetle:** *see* Bean seed beetle.

## Pea thrips

■ **Crops affected** Pea and broad bean.
■ **Symptoms** Foliage and pods are distorted and discoloured with a silvery sheen or brownish scarring. Pea pods contain only a few peas at the stalk end of the pod. The adult thrips are black, 2mm (¹⁄₁₂in) long, with narrow, elongated bodies. The nymphs are similar, but pale yellow.
■ **Causes** The pea thrips, *Kakothrips pisivorus*. The adults emerge in late spring and early summer. Populations peak between mid- to late summer and are especially troublesome in hot, dry summers.
■ **Control** Look out for thrips activity as the pods develop and, if necessary, spray with deltamethrin, pyrethrum, or lambda-cyhalothrin.

## Peach leaf curl

■ **Crops affected** Peach, nectarine, and almond.
■ **Symptoms** Leaves develop pale green puckering and blistering that later turns

bright red or purple (*see p.250*); they are affected when or soon after they unfurl in spring. A white powdery layer of spores develops on the leaf surfaces, and affected leaves fall prematurely. When a second flush of leaves appears later in summer, they are usually healthy. In nectarine crops, the infection may spread to the fruits, causing rough, slightly raised patches; peach fruits are usually unaffected.

■ **Cause** The fungus *Taphrina deformans*. Growth and cropping is usually only seriously compromised if repeated infections occur over several successive years. The fungus overwinters as spores that lodge in bark cracks and crevices, or in bud scales. They are spread by wind and in water splash.

■ **Control** Remove affected leaves as soon as seen. Keep trees well fed and watered to promote healthy new growth. Plants grown under glass are seldom affected as spore dispersal is limited by the protection of the glass. It is worth providing outdoor, wall-grown fruits with the protection of open-sided, clear plastic covers; to be effective, this needs to be in place from midwinter to late spring. If trees cannot be protected, spray with a copper-based fungicide several times between mid- to late winter, but ensure that spraying is complete before blossom burst. Repeat the spraying in autumn before leaf fall.

*Pear and apple canker: see* Canker.

## Pear and cherry slugworm

■ **Crops affected** Pear, plum, cherry, and almond.

■ **Symptoms** Foliage is eaten by club-shaped, pale yellow, caterpillar-like larvae, up to 1cm (½in) long, between late spring and mid-autumn. They are covered with black mucilage, giving them a slug-like appearance. They feed by grazing off the upper leaf surfaces, skeletonizing them and causing damaged parts to become brown and desiccated.

■ **Cause** The larvae of a sawfly, *Caliroa cerasi*, which produces two or three generations during the summer. The larvae overwinter in cocoons in the soil.

■ **Control** Contact insecticides offer good control on trees small enough to spray. Spray when larvae are seen with deltamethrin, pyrethrum, or lambda-cyhalothrin.

## Pear leaf blister mite

■ **Crops affected** Pear; apple crops are also affected, but less frequently.

■ **Symptoms** Young pear leaves develop pink or yellowish-green blisters, or raised blotches that superficially resemble the damage caused by peach leaf curl (*see facing page*). On expanded leaves, the damage forms broad bands on either side of the midrib; by midsummer, the blisters have turned black. Less than 3mm (⅛in) across, these lesions should not be confused with the larger ones caused by apple and pear scab (*see p.251*).

■ **Causes** A microscopic mite, *Eriophyes pyri* lives within the leaves. The blisters are the plant's response to chemicals that are secreted by the mites as they feed.

■ **Control** Although the unsightly lesions give the appearance of ill health, the damage is largely cosmetic and does not seriously affect cropping. None of the insecticides available to amateur gardeners gives control. On lightly infested small trees, affected leaves can be picked off. If done thoroughly, this will reduce populations in subsequent years.

## Pear midge

■ **Crops affected** Pear.

■ **Symptoms** After apparently making good initial growth, shortly after petal fall, pear fruitlets begin to turn black at the eye end (opposite the stalk). Affected fruitlets become distorted and extensively blackened before falling prematurely in early summer. If infestation is severe, the entire crop may be lost. Inside the fruitlets are small, pale orange-yellow maggots, 2mm (¹⁄₁₂in) long. The infestation causes fruitlets to swell abnormally, and it is this that gives the impression of rapid initial growth.

■ **Cause** The larvae of a small gall midge, *Contarinia pyrivora*. As the fruitlets drop, the larvae enter the soil and pupate in silken cocoons. They emerge as adults the following spring. This midge is one of two that commonly affect pears. The other, the aptly named pear leaf-curling midge does not cause serious damage.

■ **Control** Early- or late-flowering pears often escape pear midge, so choose these cultivars if possible. On small trees, pick off and destroy affected fruitlets before the larvae finish feeding and certainly before the fruitlets fall. Prevent the adults laying eggs by spraying with deltamethrin or lambda-cyhalothrin when blossom buds show colour, but before flowers open.

*Pear scab: see* Apple, pear, and olive scabs.

## Phytophthora

■ **Crops affected** Various, including pineapple, apple, and other tree fruits, raspberry, and strawberry.

■ **Symptoms** Plants begin rotting at the collar around the roots and the stem base. Foliage may be sparse, discoloured, and show signs of dieback. Roots are blackened and finer roots are killed. Stems may show signs of dieback and the whole plant may be killed. Bark under the main stem or trunk is reddish- or blackish-brown.

■ **Causes** Various soil- or water-borne fungi of the genus *Phytophthora*; *P. cinnamomi* is common and can cause root rot of tree fruits. *P. cactorum* causes fruit rot of apples and collar rot of apples and other fruit trees; *P. syringae* also affects several tree fruits in a similar way. *Phytophthora* is also one of the causal agents of damping off (*see p.254*).

■ **Control** Maintain good hygiene and water only with mains water. Improve drainage and ventilation. Unfortunately, this fungus thrives in exactly the damp and humid conditions in which pineapple crops are grown. Remove infected plants, along with the soil in the vicinity of the roots. There is no chemical control available to gardeners.
*See also* Foot and root rots, Potato blight, Red core.

**Pigeons:** *see* Birds.

## Plum fruit moth

■ **Crops affected** Plum, damson, and gage.

■ **Symptoms** Brown-headed, pale pink caterpillars, to 12mm (½in) long, feed inside ripening fruits around the stone, and the damaged area is filled with brown frass (excrement). Damaged fruits ripen early and may have one or more depressions at the surface, where the larva has eaten its way out.

■ **Cause** Caterpillars of *Grapholita funebrana*. There is usually only one generation a year, but there may be two if summers are long and hot. When fully fed, the larvae leave the fruits to overwinter beneath flakes of bark.

■ **Control** Collect and destroy affected fruits in midsummer before the larvae have left. Pheromone traps attract male moths, reducing the mating success of females and so the incidence of maggoty plums. More importantly, pheromone traps indicate when adults are active and likely to be laying eggs; timing of chemical treatments is critical in destroying the larvae before they enter the fruit. Use deltamethrin or lambda-cyhalothrin in early summer.

**Pod spot:** of peas, *see* Pea leaf and pod spot.

## Plum leaf-curling aphid

■ **Crops affected** Plum, damson, and gage.

■ **Symptoms** The leaves become tightly curled and crumpled shortly after they emerge in spring (*see p.250*). On the undersides of the leaves, small, pale yellow-green insects, up to 2mm (¹⁄₁₂in) long, are found, along with their cast skins.

■ **Cause** A sap-sucking aphid, *Brachycaudus helichrysi*. During late spring and early summer, winged adults migrate to their alternate hosts – a wide range of herbaceous plants. After this period, new leaves grow normally. The aphids return in autumn to lay overwintering eggs at the base of twigs and buds. This generation hatches in late winter and infests the breaking buds.

■ **Control** Reduce overwintering eggs by using a plant oil winter wash on dry, mild days between early and midwinter. Small trees may be sprayed with thiacloprid when the leaves emerge.

## Poor fruit setting

■ **Crops affected** Many fruit crops: raspberry, strawberry, apple, pear, and other tree fruits.

■ **Symptoms** On tree fruits, flowers appear as normal but fail to set fruit. On raspberry and strawberry crops, some fruits form incompletely or are distorted. On raspberries, individual drupelets on the berry may be dried and brown, while other adjacent berries are perfect.

■ **Causes** There can be several causes. On fruit trees, poor pollination may result from a lack of a compatible pollinator or frost damage (*see p.255*) at flowering time. With all fruits, poor pollination may also be a result of a lack of pollinating insects, usually bees, either because there are none in the vicinity, or because cold, wet or windy weather prevents them from flying.

■ **Control** When planting fruit trees, check on their pollination requirements and plant accordingly; choose self-pollinating cultivars if available. Choose sheltered spots to avoid frost damage; this will also be beneficial for bees. Plant plenty of other flowering plant species to attract pollinating insects. Use any chemical sprays with care, selecting specific pesticides where possible; try to spray at dusk when bees have ceased flying.
*See also* Potassium deficiency.

## Poorly formed fruits

■ **Crops affected** Cucurbits.

■ **Symptoms** Fruits are small, pitted, and unusually dark green with bright yellow patches; they are also hard and inedible.

■ **Cause** Cucumber mosaic virus (*see p.254*). The virus has a wide host range and can be spread on the mouthparts of aphids and other sap-sucking insects.

■ **Control** Destroy infected plants; there are no chemical controls available. Reduce risks of infection by controlling aphids and clearing weeds, which may form alternative hosts. Do not handle healthy plants after touching infected material without washing hands thoroughly first. Resistant cultivars include courgettes 'Defender', 'Supremo', and 'Tarmino'; cucumbers 'Bush Champion', 'Crispy Salad', 'Jazzer', 'Petita', and 'Pioneer'; and marrows 'Badger Cross' and 'Tiger Cross'.

## Potassium deficiency

■ **Crops affected** Various.

■ **Symptoms** The most frequent symptom is poor flowering, often with undersized flowers and a correspondingly poor fruit set. On tomato crops, this is often a factor in blotchy ripening (*see* Tomato blotchy ripening, *p.263*). Leaves may appear scorched at the tip or margins, and show purple-brown spotting beneath.

■ **Causes** A deficiency of potassium in the soil. It is most common on light, sandy soils and those with a low clay content.

■ **Control** Apply rock potash or sulphate of potash in spring and autumn.

## Potato black leg

■ **Crops affected** Potato.

■ **Symptoms** Leaves are stunted and yellowed with slightly incurled leaf margins, most noticeably on the uppermost leaves. The stem base is blackened, slimy, and rotten at ground level. If the stem is cut across, it reveals distinct, discoloured, or black spotting. The parent tuber is completely rotted and plants may die before a crop is produced.

■ **Causes** The bacterium *Pectobacterium atrosepticum*. It is most prevalent in wet soils and may be introduced on symptomless, but nevertheless infected, seed tubers. When these are planted, affected plants may be seen scattered throughout a crop of healthy, apparently unaffected plants. The bacterium infects via wounds made while plants are in the soil, or when seed tubers are lifted.

■ **Control** Do not lift potato crops in wet weather, and lift carefully to avoid causing any damage; both factors make infection more likely. Clear away all crop debris, and do not allow heaps of discarded potatoes to stand; they may form a source of infection. Store only perfectly healthy, undamaged potatoes; infected ones rot in store and the rot will spread to healthy tubers. Avoid growing cultivars known to be susceptible: 'Arran Pilot', 'Majestic', 'Maris Bard', 'Desirée', and 'Estima'.

## Potato blight

■ **Crops affected** Potato and tomato.
■ **Symptoms** Necrotic brown patches appear on the leaves and fruits or tubers (*see p.250*), mainly at the tips and at the margins. As they enlarge, the leaf withers and dies. Slightly fluffy, white fungal growth may appear around the spots, usually beneath the leaves, in humid conditions or in wet weather. Haulms of infected potatoes develop dark brown patches and collapse. Skins of infected tubers have sunken dark patches with red-brown colouration on the flesh beneath. These are dry at first, but often become foul-smelling and slimy due to secondary infections, which usually rot the entire tuber.
■ **Cause** The fungus *Phytophthora infestans*. The same organism causes blight on tomatoes. Spores produced by the leaf lesions are spread by rain splash and air currents, and they may wash down to the tubers in rainfall or irrigation water. The fungus becomes active only when there are two consecutive 24-hour periods with a minimum temperature of 10°C (50°F) and a relative humidity of 89 per cent or more for 11 hours in each of the 24-hour periods.
■ **Control** Reduce the risk of infection spreading to the tubers by earthing up deeply. If haulms show symptoms of infection, remove them as soon as they begin to die down. The genetic population of the fungus is ever-changing. The resistance of old cultivars, such as 'Cara', 'Kondor', 'Orla' 'Markies', and 'Valor', has been overcome by one dominant new strain. Spray the foliage with a copper-based fungicide such as Bordeaux mixture or copper oxychloride. If weather conditions are favourable for fungal growth, or a "Blight Infection Period" warning is given on local radio or farming programmes, spray as a precaution.

## Potato common scab

■ **Crops affected** Potato, swede, turnip, radish, and beetroot.
■ **Symptoms** The tuber develops rough, raised, corky patches on the skin (*see p.250*). The skin ruptures leaving the scabs with ragged edges. Damage may be superficial or may result in cracking or pitting. The flesh is usually undamaged, although there may be some discoloration beneath the scabs.
■ **Causes** *Streptomyces scabies*, an organism that is related to both fungi and bacteria. It is particularly common on sandy soils that are deficient in organic matter, but it occurs naturally as part of the microflora in most soils. Potatoes planted in plots that were formerly grassland are especially prone to attack. The organism thrives in soils that have been limed, and it is less common on acid soils.
■ **Control** Do not lime the soil prior to planting potatoes. Improve the organic content of the soil and keep it well watered in dry weather; there is a link between dry soil conditions and the proliferation of this organism. Use acidic materials, such as sulphate of ammonia or superphosphate, to reduce scabbing. Although crops are seldom badly reduced and tubers remain edible, they usually have to be peeled deeply to become palatable. The following potato cultivars show some resistance: 'Arran Pilot', 'Golden Wonder', and 'King Edward'. There is no chemical treatment available.

## Potato cyst eelworm

■ **Crops affected** Potato and tomato.
■ **Symptoms** Leaves become progressively more yellowed and dried up from the base of the stem upwards. Potato plants die prematurely, usually by mid- to late summer, and so produce a reduced crop of small potatoes. When potato cyst eelworm first appears in a garden, small clumps of potatoes within the rows show symptoms. Each time potatoes are grown on the same site, the area of affected plants enlarges, until it finally becomes impossible to obtain a worthwhile crop. Tomatoes are also affected. If plants are carefully dug up, spherical cysts, up to 1mm (1/16in) across, can be seen on the roots. Each is the body of a female eelworm and may contain up to 600 eggs.
■ **Causes** There are two species of cyst eelworm that affect tomato and potato crops. Golden cyst eelworm, *Globodera rostochiensis*, has cysts that are white at first, passing through a yellow phase before turning brown at maturity. Cysts of white cyst eelworm, *G. pallida*, turn from white to brown without an intermediate yellow stage. Both develop within the roots and when mature, the females swell and burst out through the root wall. Poor growth is due to disrupted uptake of nutrients and water inflicted by the eelworms.
■ **Control** There is no chemical control available to amateur gardeners. Potato cyst eelworm eggs can remain encysted and viable in the soil for many years. The eggs are stimulated to hatch by chemicals that are secreted into the soil by the host plants' roots. Adopting a rotation system may delay the build-up of damaging pest levels, but the normal three- or four-year rotation is not sufficient to eliminate them. Once a serious eelworm problem has developed, the problem is intractable.

There are some potato cultivars with a measure of resistance, such as the earlies 'Accent', 'Nadine', 'Pentland Javelin', 'Rocket', and 'Swift', and the maincrops 'Alhambra', 'Cara', 'Harmony', 'Kingston', 'Maris Piper', 'Maxine', 'Sante', and 'Stemster'.

## Potato powdery scab

■ **Crops affected** Potato and tomato.
■ **Symptoms** Small, scabby patches develop on potato tubers. They are almost circular with a slightly raised margin. When the scabs mature, they burst open to release spores into the soil. There may be cyst-like growths on roots and stolons. In rare instances, a canker form of powdery scab develops causing marked deformations of the tuber, which resemble symptoms of the notifiable, but now very uncommon, potato wart disease. In powdery scab, the tuber protuberances are smooth, not warty, and wart disease never affects the roots.
■ **Cause** The fungus *Spongospora subterranea*. It is most common in wet seasons and on heavy soils, especially on sites that have grown crops of potatoes for many seasons.
■ **Control** Dispose of all infected tubers; do not put them on the compost heap because they will spread the disease. Do not grow potatoes for at least three years following an outbreak. Improve soil aeration before planting. 'Desiree', 'Hermes', 'King Edward', 'Pixie', and 'Sante' show some resistance to powdery scab.

## Potato viruses

■ **Crops affected** Potato.
■ **Symptoms** Various, depending on the potato variety, the growing conditions, and the virus or combination of viruses involved. Leaf symptoms include yellow flecking, streaking or mosaicing, dark spotting and leaf distortion, and stiffening and upward rolling of the leaflets. If home-saved seed potatoes are grown for many years in succession, expect a gradual decline in vigour and crop quality due to a build-up of viruses.
■ **Causes** Several different viruses including potato leaf-rolling virus, tobacco rattle, and potato viruses X and Y.
■ **Control** None is available. Always grow potatoes on a fresh site, do not save tubers for seed, and buy in certified, virus-free seed potatoes.

## Powdery mildew

■ **Crops affected** Various.
■ **Symptoms** Powdery white fungal growth occurs, first on upper leaf surfaces, later often spreading to lower surfaces. Mildew may also affect all other above-ground plant parts, but its location depends on the mildew and plant species involved. Affected leaves and other parts may yellow and become distorted; distortion is particularly common when young growth is affected. Affected fruits may split or crack because they cannot expand normally. On leaves, mildew may kill small areas of tissue, which will die and fall away, giving a shot-hole effect. Growth may be poor and, in extreme cases, dieback or even death may follow premature leaf fall.
■ **Causes** Various fungi, including species of *Erysiphe*, *Golovinomyces*, *Neoerysiphe*, and *Podosphaera*. These fungi are most prevalent where soils are dry, but the air around the plants is humid and stagnant.
■ **Control** Keep plants adequately watered but avoid overhead watering. Remove affected leaves promptly. Seek out resistant cultivars. Some crops may be sprayed with a suitable fungicide, for example difenoconazole, myclobutanil or triticonazole.

**Premature seeding:** *see* Bolting.

## Quince leaf blight

■ **Crops affected** Quince.
■ **Symptoms** Many small, irregular red spots appear on the leaves; the spots later turn turn black and may join together. The leaves turn yellow before falling prematurely. Sometimes, similar spots occur on the fruits, which may also become distorted. Affected shoot tips may develop dieback.
■ **Cause** The fungus *Diplocarpon mespili*, which overwinters on infected shoots.
■ **Control** Remove and burn fallen leaves, and prune out infected stems. Difenoconazole applications for powdery mildew may give incidental control.

## Rabbits

■ **Crops affected** A wide range.
■ **Symptoms** Grazing occurs on all parts of leafy plants, to a height of about 50cm (20in). Tree bark may be gnawed, and if the damage girdles the stem or trunk, the tree dies. Bark feeding occurs at any time of year, but trees are especially at risk when snow is on the ground and other food sources are scarce. New plantings may also receive special attention; like deer, rabbits are inquisitive feeders.
■ **Cause** Rabbits, *Oryctolagus cuniculus*.
■ **Control** Trapping, shooting, and gassing are generally unsuitable techniques in a garden situation. The only reliable way of excluding rabbits is to erect fencing. This must be 1.2–1.4m (4–4½ft) tall, with 30cm (12in) of the netting buried below ground, angled outwards, to deter them from digging through or burrowing beneath. The mesh size must be a maximum of 25mm (1in), otherwise young rabbits can squeeze through. Do not forget to net gates as well, and keep them closed when not in use. Protect trees with individual guards, either netting or spiral tree guards around the base of the trunks. Animal repellent products are generally not reliable, but domestic cats can be very efficient hunters of rabbits.

## Raspberry beetle

■ **Crops affected** All cane fruits, including raspberry, blackberry, and hybrid berries.
■ **Symptoms** Ripe fruits exhibit desiccated patches at the stalk end of the berries (*see p.250*). Creamy white grubs, up to 8mm (⅜in) long, feed at the base of the berries initially, then move into the inner core or plug. They are most readily seen after picking, when they leave the fruit and crawl around the bowl.
■ **Cause** The larvae of a small grey-brown beetle, *Byturus tomentosus*, which lays its eggs on the flowers during early and midsummer.
■ **Control** Timing of controls is critical in preventing newly hatched grubs. On raspberry crops, spray when the first fruits turn pink; on blackberry crops when the flowers first open; and on loganberry and other hybrid berry crops, spray at 80 per cent petal fall. Spray with deltamethrin at dusk to minimize the danger to any pollinating insects.

## Raspberry cane blight

■ **Crops affected** Raspberry.
■ **Symptoms** Areas of bark peel away from the canes in summer and autumn and the stems die back, becoming very brittle. Minute, black, fungal fruiting bodies form on dead stems and eject spores.
■ **Causes** This is a fungal infection, caused by *Leptosphaeria coniothyrium* which enters wounds in the canes. The wounds can result from pruning, late spring frosts, or the cane midge larvae, *Resseliella theobaldii*, feeding beneath the bark. The larvae are small, red, or pink and 4mm (⅙in) long.
■ **Control** Prune carefully to avoid creating ragged cuts and protect from frost where possible. If cane midge is present, cultivate the soil around the bases of the canes in winter to expose overwintering larvae to bird predators and bad weather; spray canes with deltamethrin in late spring and repeat two weeks later. If blight does occur, cut out affected canes and any discoloured wood from the crown. Spray plant crowns and any new growth with copper oxychloride.

**Raspberry cane spot:** *see* Cane spot.

## Raspberry leaf and bud mite

■ **Crops affected** Raspberry.
■ **Symptoms** Rounded, pale yellow blotches appear on upper leaf surfaces from late spring onwards, with slightly darker, corresponding patches beneath. By midsummer, the leaves may be extensively discoloured and those at the shoot tips may be distorted. Fortunately, damage is largely cosmetic. Affected canes grow to their normal height and usually produce an adequate crop. The symptoms can be mistaken for viral infection, but with viruses, the crop and vigour are both adversely affected.
■ **Cause** Microscopic mites, *Phyllocoptes gracilis*, suck sap from the leaf undersides. In autumn, they hide in or near buds, but cause no damage in winter.
■ **Control** Cultivars vary in their susceptibility: 'Malling Jewel' ♀ is often attacked, while 'Malling Promise' shows some resistance. Plants grown in warm, sheltered spots are more likely to suffer heavy infestations. No chemical control is available.

## Raspberry spur blight

■ **Crops affected** Raspberry, loganberry, blackberry, and hybrid berry crops.
■ **Symptoms** Buds of new canes develop dark pink-purple patches around them, which enlarge and spread down the canes causing widespread discoloration. In autumn, canes develop a greyish silver colour and are covered in many pinprick-sized, black fruiting bodies. Infected canes bear very few viable buds in the following spring and, if they survive, produce very few fruits.
■ **Cause** The fungus *Didymella applanata*. It occurs in most seasons but is especially prevalent in wet weather.
■ **Control** Avoid high-nitrogen fertilizers, which induce soft, more disease-prone growth. Avoid overcrowding, which encourages rapid spread, by selecting only the strongest canes when pruning. Prune out affected canes. No fungicides are sold to gardeners for this problem, but copper oxychloride applications for cane spot (*see p.253*) may give incidental control.

## Raspberry viruses

■ **Crops affected** Raspberry.
■ **Symptoms** Leaves develop yellow patterning, usually in mosaic form, and this is accompanied by various distortions, down-curling of the leaves, stunting, and general failure to thrive. Cropping is often reduced.
■ **Causes** Various viruses. The most common are raspberry mosaic, curly dwarf, and raspberry yellow dwarf; they may occur alone or in combination.
■ **Control** Remove and dispose of affected plants promptly. Choose a new site for replacement canes, and do not use the same site again for raspberries. Control insect vectors, such as aphids; some viruses are also spread by soil-dwelling eelworms.

## Red core

■ **Crops affected** Strawberry.
■ **Symptoms** Clumps of stunted plants, with stiff, red-brown leaves, are noticed in late spring. Roots are discoloured with a red inner core.
■ **Cause** The fungus *Phytophthora*

*fragariae*. It proliferates in wet, heavy soils and produces resistant spore stages from the deteriorating roots. These are released into the soil and may persist for more than ten years. The fungus is easily introduced on boots and tools, or contaminated plants.
■ **Control** None is available. Remove and burn infected plants promptly, together with the soil from the root vicinity. Do not grow strawberries on the same site again and avoid moving soil from the infected site elsewhere in the garden.

## Red spider mites

■ **Crops affected** Many, including tree fruits and greenhouse crops.
■ **Symptoms** Foliage loses its healthy green colour and develops a silvery sheen, becoming increasingly dull and chlorotic. On fruit trees, a fine pale mottling may be seen on the upper leaf surfaces (*see p.250*). Large numbers of tiny, dark red mites, 1mm (¹⁄₁₆in) long, and their spherical eggs can be seen beneath the leaves. Severe infestations cause premature leaf fall. Under glass, plant leaves exhibit similar dullness and loss of colour. Close examination of the lower leaf surface, preferably with a ×10 hand lens, will reveal spherical eggs and tiny, yellow-green mites with two large dark marks on the back near the head end (sometimes known as two-spotted mites). In autumn and winter, they turn orange-red. In heavy infestations, silky white webbing covers the leaves and stems. Leaves dry up and fall prematurely, and only young leaves remain at the stem tips.
■ **Causes** There are two common species of red spider mite. The sap-feeding fruit tree red spider mite, *Panonychus ulmi*, occurs outdoors. The heaviest infestations occur in hot, dry summers. Under glass, the glasshouse red spider mite, *Tetranychus urticae*, is the culprit. In hot, dry summers, it moves outdoors to attack a wide range of crops.
■ **Control** The fruit tree red spider mite is not generally a problem on unsprayed trees since predatory mites and other predators provide a degree of natural control. Sprays are often indiscriminate and kill many beneficial insects. Where trees have been routinely sprayed, mite populations build to problem proportions and their overwintering eggs, laid in bark crevices, may be so numerous as to give the bark a distinct red hue. If red spider mite becomes a problem, spray with fatty acids, or plant oils.

Glasshouse red spider mites breed rapidly in warm conditions and strains have developed that are resistant to pesticides. Biological control with the predatory mite *Phytoseiulus persimilis* gives good results if introduced before heavy infestations develop. It needs warm daytime conditions in the absence of pesticides to become established. It can also be used on outdoor plants in summer. Misting indoor plants with water twice daily provides high humidity, which will suppress mite activity. Alternatively, use sprays as for fruit tree red spider mite; several applications will be necessary.

## Replant diseases

■ **Crops affected** Soft fruits, tree fruits.
■ **Symptoms** Newly planted trees and bushes fail to thrive and may show signs of dieback. There are no obvious cultural

problems, such as drought, waterlogging, or poor planting technique. This occurs where new trees are planted on a site previously occupied by the same species.
■ **Causes** The exact mechanism of replant problems is unclear, but it may involve eelworms, viruses, soil-borne fungi, and nutritional depletion. The last may be a result of infection of roots that renders them incapable of taking up nutrients properly. There is also evidence that some plants' roots exude chemicals to deter growth of plants of the same species too near to them; a mechanism that, under natural circumstances, would prevent competition.
■ **Control** Affected plants may recover if moved to a fresh site. The problem is best avoided by not planting on a site where the same species has been grown previously. There is no reliable control. If absolutely necessary, the soil may be removed and replaced with virgin soil. A "cube" of soil, that has a minimum dimension of approximately 45 x 45 x 45cm (18 x 18 x 18in), must be replaced, so this is not a task to be undertaken lightly if many plants are to be replaced. Planting well-established, container-grown plants with a good root system, feeding with a high-nitrogen fertilizer, and watering well can help minimize the problem. It is essential also to keep the soil in good health by incorporating plenty of well-rotted organic matter.

## Reversion disease

■ **Crops affected** Blackcurrant.
■ **Symptoms** Leaves are produced that are slightly yellow, with unusually small main veins. Leaves are small with fewer lobes than normal. Flowering and cropping are reduced.
■ **Causes** A graft-transmissible virus that is most usually spread by big bud mite (*see p.252*). Big buds are also often present.
■ **Control** Remove infected plants promptly; the disease is untreatable and plants become infectious, spreading the disease to healthy plants nearby. Always buy plants that are certified as virus-free.

## Root aphids

■ **Crops affected** Various, including cardoon, Chinese artichoke, Jerusalem artichoke, globe artichoke, French bean, runner bean, lettuce, carrot, and parsnip.
■ **Symptoms** Infested plants show poor growth and will readily in warm weather, even when the soil is moist. Dirty-cream aphids, sometimes blue-green, up to 2–3mm (¹⁄₁₂–¹⁄₈in) long, are seen on the roots and on stem bases. Root aphids often secrete a protective, waxy white powder or fluff and this will be seen on soil particles around the site of infestation.
■ **Causes** Several species occur in gardens and they are frequently host-specific: *Smynthurodes betae* on French and runner bean crops, *Trama troglodytes* on Jerusalem artichoke, *Dysaphis crataegi* on carrot and parsnip, and *Pemphigus bursarius* on lettuce.
■ **Control** Root aphids are more difficult to control than leaf feeders. Crop rotation helps avoid infestation by aphids that have overwintered in the soil on the remains of last year's crop. Insecticides do not give good control of root aphids.
*See also* Lettuce root aphid.

## Root knot eelworms

■ **Crops affected** A wide range.
■ **Symptoms** Plants fail to thrive, display poor foliage colour, and knobbly swellings form on the roots.
■ **Causes** Microscopic eelworms that live within the roots and cause knobbly swellings (not to be confused with nitrogen-fixing nodules normally found on the roots of legumes).The tissue distortion they cause disrupts the intake of water and nutrients. There are several species, most in the genus *Meloidogyne*. It is not a common problem in Britain.
■ **Control** Remove affected plants along with the soil around their roots. There is no effective chemical control available to gardeners.

**Root rots:** *see* Foot and root rots.

## Rosy apple aphid

■ **Crops affected** Apple.
■ **Symptoms** Young foliage is infested in spring by pinkish-grey insects, up to 2mm (¹⁄₁₂in) long. Their feeding causes curling of the leaf tips and yellowing of the leaves. They may also feed on fruitlets, which may fail to grow and have a pinched appearance at the eye end (opposite stalk). Not all fruits will be affected, and some will continue to develop normally.
■ **Cause** The rosy apple aphid, *Dyaphis plantaginea*. It overwinters on the tree as eggs, which hatch at bud burst; the aphids are active on the tree until early or midsummer. They then migrate to their summer wildflower host, plantains.
■ **Control** Control the overwintering eggs with a plant oil wash in winter or spray at bud burst with deltamethrin, lambda-cyhalothrin, or thiacloprid.

## Rusts

■ **Crops affected** Various.
■ **Symptoms** Foliage and stems may be affected, depending on the host plant and the rust involved. Spore masses or pustules are usually bright orange or dark brown, but their colour may vary at different times of the year and they frequently begin yellow or orange and turn brown later. They often have several distinct spore stages, commonly known as winter, spring, and summer spores. Affected areas usually discolour and may wither and die.
■ **Causes** Various fungi, the most common of which are species of *Puccinia* (*see p.250*), *Uromyces*, *Phragmidium*, *Melampsora*, and *Gymnosporangium*. Some need an alternate host to complete their life cycle, while others are monospecific. All need a moist environment to become infectious, so they are generally more troublesome in damp weather conditions.
■ **Control** Remove affected leaves. Improve air circulation, and where possible, choose resistant cultivars. Currant and gooseberry crops may be sprayed with copper-based fungicides. and difenoconazole can be used to control rusts on certain fruit and vegetables.
*See also* Leek rust, Mint rust.

## Scale insects

■ **Crops affected** Various.
■ **Symptoms** The stems and foliage of many garden and greenhouse plants can be affected. The insects secrete a waxy

shell or scale over their bodies. They are mobile when young, but once they have found a suitable niche, they settle down and are fixed in place for the rest of their lives. The scales may be grey or brown in colour, and flat or domed in shape. The size, which varies according to species, is 1–6mm ($\frac{1}{16}$–$\frac{1}{4}$in). Some scale insects excrete honeydew, which hosts black sooty moulds. Most outdoor species hatch in midsummer, but under glass, breeding may occur through the year.

■ **Causes** Scale insects, many species.

■ **Control** Most scale insects conceal their eggs beneath their own bodies. Newly hatched nymphs are more vulnerable to insecticides, like fatty acids or plant oils.
*See also* Brown scale.

## Sclerotinia

■ **Crops affected** Various.

■ **Symptoms** Fruit and stem base infections are the most common, but the majority of above-ground tissues can be affected, becoming brown and slimy as they rot (*see p.250*). Large quantities of fluffy, cotton-wool-like fungal growth develops, which is scattered with black fruiting bodies (sclerotia). Fruits and tubers may be affected when in store.

■ **Cause** The fungus *Sclerotinia sclerotiorum*. It is most prevalent in cool, damp conditions and overwinters in the soil. It then produces cup-shaped fungal growths known as apothecia, which contain the spores that are responsible for the following season's infections.

■ **Control** Remove and burn all affected plants promptly. At the end of each season, dispose of all plant debris. Do not grow susceptible plants on the same site for at least four years following an outbreak of the disease.

## Scorch

■ **Crops affected** Various, but greenhouse plant crops, such as grape vines, are usually more susceptible.

■ **Symptoms** Scorched tissue, usually of softer parts like petals or leaves, turns pale brown or bleached. Damaged areas dry out and become crispy. Stems are occasionally scorched, with the area of damage appearing on the exposed side.

■ **Causes** Hot or bright sun is the most common cause, but cold, dry winds can also be very damaging. With sun scorch, the problem is exacerbated by droplets of moisture on the leaf surfaces, which magnify the sun's rays. Sun scorch of bark is most likely on young, thin-barked trees. Water droplets may also increase low temperature damage if they remain on the leaf surfaces during cold nights, especially in spring and autumn. Accidental contact with weedkillers, either directly or from drifting spray, may also produce similar symptoms, as can the use of inappropriate pesticides. Some plants are very sensitive to certain chemical sprays.

■ **Control** Water in the early evening so that leaves have chance to dry off before nightfall and are not exposed to bright sunlight immediately afterwards. In greenhouses, provide adequate shading. Check label recommendations for pesticides to ensure that they are suitable for use on the plant in question.

## Shanking of grapes

■ **Crops affected** Grape vines under cover.

■ **Symptoms** Individual berries in a truss fail to colour up normally. Black grapes remain red and white (green) grapes become translucent. The berries wrinkle and begin to resemble raisins, and they develop a watery or unpleasant flavour.

■ **Causes** Cultural problems, including under- or overwatering, under-feeding, overcropping, and stagnant soil conditions.

■ **Control** Cut out affected berries and spray the foliage with a foliar feed. Make sure that drainage around the roots is unimpeded and water carefully and thoroughly, but not excessively.

## Silver leaf

■ **Crops affected** Stone fruits, particularly plum and cherry, and also peach, nectarine, almond, apple, and pear.

■ **Symptoms** Single or several branches develop leaves with a silvery sheen. If affected stems of 2.5cm (1in) diameter or greater are cut across, the inner tissues reveal central brown staining. Other apparently normal limbs may show symptoms at a later date. Affected limbs may die off and fall, or fail to leaf up the following spring. Fruiting bodies, often clustered together and adhering closely to the bark, may form on dead wood. Their exposed surface is dark purple-grey. These symptoms may be mimicked by other causes, such as bad weather damage, drought, malnutrition, or insect attack.

■ **Cause** The fungus *Chondrostereum purpureum*. This is a fresh-wound parasite of deciduous trees and shrubs, and pruning cuts or pest attack are the most frequent wounding agents. Spores are produced from fruiting bodies on limbs of infected trees or on fallen timber. It is spread on air currents, in water splash, and on pruning tools. The fungus produces a toxin that causes the upper leaf surface to become detached from the main leaf blade, and air that accumulates between the two layers deflects light, giving a silvered appearance to the leaf. The infection is not carried by the leaves themselves.

■ **Control** None is available. Mildly affected trees sometimes recover spontaneously. In general, however, the infection spreads through the tree unless affected branches are removed. Cut them off at least 15cm (6in) beyond the point where staining is apparent, cutting back to clean white wood. Infection is least likely to occur during the summer months, so all pruning of susceptible trees should be undertaken in summer. Although it is no longer generally recommended to use wound paints, it is certainly recommended in trees that are susceptible to silver leaf and should be done straight after pruning. Locate any sources of infection, such as fallen timber, and remove and burn them.

Plum and cherry crops are especially prone to infection and 'Victoria' ♀ plums are the most susceptible. The rootstock also influences susceptibility, with 'Brompton' being very vulnerable. Other cultivars, such as 'Pixie', have a marked degree of resistance.

## Slugs

■ **Crops affected** Various.

■ **Symptoms** A wide range of plants are damaged by slugs; soft parts of plants are most susceptible. Irregular holes are eaten in flowers, leaves, and stems. Some slugs are soil-dwelling and eat tubers of potatoes (*see p.250*) and Jerusalem artichokes. Slugs secrete a slimy, silvery mucilage from their bodies; these silvery deposits, left as trails on affected plants, are a key sign of slug and snail damage.

■ **Causes** Several species of slugs occur in gardens: the grey field slug (*Deroceras reticulatum*), the large black slug (*Arion ater*), the garden slug (*A. hortensis*), and keeled slugs (*Milax* species). They are ubiquitous and present through the year, continuing to feed whenever temperatures remain above 5°C (40°F). Most are night feeders.

■ **Control** Slugs can never be completely eliminated from gardens, so control measures should be concentrated on protecting vulnerable plants, especially seedlings and soft-leaved plants, such as lettuce. Non-chemical means of control include hunting by torchlight on mild, damp nights. Slug traps consisting of a jar half-filled with beer sunk into the ground invite slugs to death by drowning. Grapefruit skins, placed open end down, are also attractive traps; the victims can be collected and disposed of in the morning. Plants in containers may be protected by applying copper tape around the pots just below the rims.

The parasitic nematode *Phasmarhabditis hermaphrodita* is used as a biological control that can be applied where soils are moist but well-drained, and above a temperature of 5°C (40°F). It is most effective in spring and autumn. The microscopic nematodes penetrate the slugs' bodies when they enter the soil to seek shelter during the day and release a bacterium that causes a fatal disease in infected slugs. It is extremely useful for controlling soil-dwelling slugs that damage potato tubers. Under suitable conditions, it gives effective reduction in numbers for up to six weeks.

Damage to tubers is also reduced if crops are lifted as soon as they have matured. Some potato cultivars are less susceptible than others to slug damage: 'Pentland Ivory', 'Pentland Dell', 'Wilja', 'Stemster', 'Charlotte', and 'Estima' have some resistance. The following are especially vulnerable to attack: 'Maris Piper', 'Maris Bard', 'Cara', 'Golden Wonder', and 'Kondor'.

Poisoned baits in the form of slug pellets can harm cats, dogs, and birds, which may consume poisoned slugs, so use with great care. Scatter them thinly among vulnerable plants according to the manufacturer's instructions, to reduce risks to pets and wildlife. Slug pellets containing metaldehyde cause slugs to secrete an excess of slime and they die of dehydration, but slugs may recover in wet conditions. Ferric phosphate pellets are less toxic to pets and wildlife.

**Smut:** *see* Sweetcorn smut.

## Snails

■ **Crops affected** Various.

■ **Symptoms** A wide range of plants are damaged between spring and autumn; soft parts are most susceptible. Flowers, leaves, fruits, and stems are eaten, with irregular holes rasped away. Often their surfaces are grazed off and the tissue beneath becomes desiccated and browned or bleached. This is apparent on the stems of cardoons. Silvery slime trails are left behind. Snails are most active after dark and in wet weather. They are less common on acid soils, which lack the calcium necessary to form their shells.

■ **Causes** The most common pest is the garden snail, *Cornu aspersum*. Banded *Cepaea* species are much less damaging.

■ **Control** As for slugs. Biological control is less effective because snails live mainly above the soil and are less likely to be infected by bacteria-carrying nematodes. Since snails often hibernate communally, significant numbers can be trapped by strategic placement of hibernation shelters such as old drainage pipes, planks of wood, or upturned flowerpots. Collect congregating snails *en masse* during the winter months and dispose of them.

**Split stone:** *see* Splitting.

## Splitting

■ **Crops affected** Various.

■ **Symptoms** Fruits or stems split, usually longitudinally, sometimes only around the fruit stalk, while the rest of the plant appears perfectly healthy. Earwigs may enter at the wounds. Cracks may dry and heal over, but dieback and rotting may follow due to secondary infections entering the wounds. Fruits may have an impaired flavour.

■ **Causes** An erratic supply of water and nutrients, such as calcium deficiency, are the most common causes, along with poor pollination and great fluctuations in temperature, as in frost crack.

■ **Control** Mulch to conserve soil moisture and keep plants well fed and watered. Hand pollinate fruit crops. Observe damaged areas for signs of secondary infections and treat as appropriate. Remove damaged fruits – they will rot and form a source of further infection.

**Spur blight:** *see* Raspberry spur blight.

## Squirrels

■ **Crops affected** Cobnut, filbert, tree and bush fruits, strawberry, and sweet corn.

■ **Symptoms** Squirrels eat shoot tips, flower buds, nuts, and tree and soft fruits, and they are generally very destructive. They will even remove plant labels and use them to sharpen their teeth.

■ **Cause** The grey squirrel, *Sciurus carolinensis*.

■ **Control** Shooting, traps, and poisoned baits are used in forestry or large public gardens, but these methods are impractical and undesirable in domestic gardens. Squirrels are very mobile, and others will quickly move into a territory to replace any that have been removed. Use netting to protect fruits during periods that squirrels are taking an interest in them. Permanent wire-mesh fruit cages are best; squirrels will chew through plastic.

## Stem and bulb eelworm

■ **Crops affected** Onion family.

■ **Symptoms** Young onion plants are abnormally swollen and distorted. The tissues become soft and mealy, and they are readily infected with secondary rots.

Plants usually die before reaching maturity; onions may produce bulbs if infested late in the season, but they will rot in store.
■ **Causes** The microscopic nematode, *Ditylenchus dipsaci*.
■ **Control** There is no effective chemical control available to gardeners. Remove infested plants as soon as seen. Eelworms are spread in gardens on infested plant debris, or in soil on boots, tools, and plant rootballs, so maintain good hygiene. Buy onion seeds and sets from reputable suppliers to reduce the risk of bringing eelworms into the garden. Crop rotation may reduce infestations; grow crops that are not affected, such as lettuce, swede, turnip, and any of the brassicas.

## Strawberry seed beetle

■ **Crops affected** Strawberry.
■ **Symptoms** Seeds are taken from the surface of ripening strawberries, leaving small, desiccated brown patches. The fruits are sometimes eaten into and this often looks like slug damage.
■ **Causes** Fast-moving black carabid or ground beetles, 15mm (⅝in) long; they are *Pterostichus* species or *Harpalus rufipes*, both of which are active at night.
■ **Control** Keep the strawberry bed clear of weeds to discourage a build-up of seed beetles (at other times of year, they feed on weed seeds). You can use pit-fall traps (a jam jar sunk into the soil), but these may also trap beneficial predatory beetles. Chemical controls are not desirable because the fruits are thin-skinned, and chemicals used so near to harvest may persist. If absolutely necessary, treat plants with unripe fruits with deltamethrin at dusk.

## Strawberry viruses

■ **Crops affected** Strawberry.
■ **Symptoms** Stunting and distortion of the whole plant, with the same symptoms accompanying yellowing in the leaves. Various patterns of discoloration are seen: streak, ring-spot, and mosaic or yellowing of leaf margins. Plants fail to thrive and may not flower or fruit well.
■ **Causes** Various viruses, the most common being strawberry yellow edge or little leaf virus, arabis mosaic, strawberry ring spot, and tomato black ring, which is spread by eelworms.
■ **Control** None available. Remove and burn affected plants as soon as symptoms are seen. Control aphids (*see p.251*), which are important virus vectors. Do not grow strawberries on the site again. Do not propagate from infected plants; runners carry infection without always showing symptoms. Always buy certified stocks of strawberry plants; they are guaranteed to be virus-free when purchased.

## Sweetcorn smut

■ **Crops affected** Sweetcorn.
■ **Symptoms** Individual kernels on the cob become greatly enlarged and deformed. Each kernel turns pale grey and ruptures to release large quantities of powdery black spores. In wet weather, these may be carried in rainwater, forming a black liquid that run down the plant. Leaves and stems are only occasionally affected; the fungus is not systemic, so healthy and infected cobs may develop on the same plant.
■ **Cause** The fungus *Ustilago maydis*. Spores are carried on air currents and in rain splash, and they may infect the plants directly or persist in the soil. It is most prevalent during hot summers.
■ **Control** None available. Remove affected cobs before the swollen kernels rupture. Remove and burn all infected plant debris at the end of the season. Do not grow sweetcorn on the same site for at least five years.

## Thrips

■ **Crops affected** Many, including onion, leek, and pea.
■ **Symptoms** A fine, silvery white discoloration appears on upper leaf surfaces. Plant growth is checked. Adult thrips may be visible on the leaves; unlike most sap-sucking pests, they feed readily on upper leaf surfaces instead of concealing themselves beneath.
■ **Causes** Most thrips are narrow-bodied black insects, up to 2mm (1⁄12in) long, with two pairs of heavily fringed wings. The wings are folded when not in flight so the hairy fringing may not be apparent. Immature nymphs are wingless and creamy yellow. Some thrips are virus vectors. The most common type on vegetable crops is the onion thrips, *Thrips tabaci*, and on peas, *Kakothrips pisivorus*.
■ **Control** As for pea thrips (*see p.258*) and onion thrips (*see p.258*).

## Tip burn

■ **Crops affected** Chicory, lettuce.
■ **Symptoms** Leaf margins are scorched and brown.
■ **Causes** Calcium deficiency, botrytis, or bacterial infection. Of these calcium deficiency is the most usual cause.
■ **Control** As for calcium deficiency (*see p.253*) and botrytis (*see p.252*).

## Tomato blotchy ripening

■ **Crops affected** Tomato.
■ **Symptoms** Randomly scattered patches of hard, green or yellow flesh remain unripened. Damage is visible only on mature fruits, and those on the lower trusses are the most often affected.
■ **Causes** The disorder is usually associated with some form of malnutrition. A deficiency of potassium (*see p.259*) is the most frequent cause, but dry soil or potting compost, or a poorly functioning root system, may also play a part. High greenhouse temperatures will exacerbate the damage.
■ **Control** Keep plants well fed. In particular, ensure that a high-potash feed (*see p.20*) is used. Keep the greenhouse well ventilated and the plants well watered.

## Tomato ghost spot

■ **Crops affected** Tomato.
■ **Symptoms** Unripe fruits display rings of pale green or yellow discoloration. As the fruits ripen, the rings turn yellow or pale orange.
■ **Cause** The fungus *Botrytis cinerea*. The fruit are edible; the discoloration is a hypersensitive reaction to fungal spores. Spores are spread by rain or water splash and on air currents, and the fungus is widespread.
■ **Control** As the fruits remain edible, and rarely deteriorate further, there is no need to treat or remove them. Good hygiene helps to eliminate sources of infection. *See also* Botrytis.

## Turnip gall weevil

■ **Crops affected** Brassicas, including swede and turnip.
■ **Symptoms** Plant roots produce rounded swellings that enclose legless white grubs, up to 4mm (⅙in) long. Symptoms are similar to those caused by clubroot (*see p.254*). They are distinguished by cutting galls open; turnip weevil galls are hollow and may contain grubs, or have circular exit holes in them where the grubs have left to pupate in the soil. Clubroot galls are solid and less regularly rounded.
■ **Cause** Larvae of the beetle *Ceutorhynchus pleurostigma*. The adult lays its eggs on the roots of turnips, swedes, and leafy brassicas. The growth of leafy brassicas is seldom impeded, but the pest is more troublesome if it develops on the edible roots of turnips and swedes.
■ **Control** There are no effective chemical controls available to amateur gardeners.

**Two-spotted mite:** *see* Red spider mite.

## Verticillium wilt

■ **Crops affected** Many, including aubergine, olive, strawberry, apple, pear, plum, cherry, and quince.
■ **Symptoms** Plant foliage wilts. All or nearly all of the leaves on affected branches or stems show symptoms, but the whole plant is seldom affected simultaneously. Leaves may turn yellow or brown between the veins and then die. Stem death follows shortly after, but it may take several years for large woody plants to succumb totally. Smaller bushes or herbaceous plants, such as strawberries, may be killed within a single season.

If the bark is removed from an affected stem, staining can be seen on the vascular tissues beneath; purple-brown or brown streaks run the length of the stem but are more apparent at the stem base. Roots also develop a central core of discoloured tissue.
■ **Causes** The fungi *Verticillium albo-atrum* and *V. dahliae*. Both are common in plant debris, plant tissues, and soil; the latter species forms fungal resting bodies that persist in the soil. They have a wide host range and many garden weeds can harbour the infections.
■ **Control** None available. Remove affected plants promptly, along with the soil in the immediate vicinity of the roots. The infection may be spread on pruning tools, so always clean them thoroughly when they have been used on an infected plant. Do not introduce the same species of plant on sites that have previously supported infected plants.

## Vine weevil

■ **Crops affected** Mainly strawberry.
■ **Symptoms** Both adults and larvae cause damage. Adults eat irregular notches from the leaf margins between spring and autumn, and although this damage is largely cosmetic, it should alert the gardener to the far greater potential damage caused by the fat, creamy white larvae under the soil. Plants make slow growth, followed by wilting and eventual death. The larvae (*see p.250*) eat plant roots and may sever them completely; they also remove the outer bark from woody stem bases. Plants grown in containers are particularly at risk of attack by the grubs.
■ **Causes** The adults and larvae of the vine weevil, *Otiorhynchus sulcatus*. The adults are active at night between spring and autumn. They are slow-moving, dull black weevils, to 1cm (½in) long, with pear-shaped bodies and and antennae that are bent at an angle about half-way along their length. They are capable of laying many hundreds of eggs over a period of several months. The legless, soil-dwelling larvae are up to 1cm (½in) long, with slightly curved bodies.
■ **Control** Adult vine weevils can be seen by torchlight at night and disposed of. The biological control for the grubs is a pathogenic nematode, *Steinernema kraussei*. Water the nematodes into the potting mix in late summer, while it is warm and moist, but before the grubs are large enough to cause serious damage. Pathogenic nematodes are ineffective in dry, heavy, or cold soils (less than 5°C/41°F). There are no suitable insecticides available for use on edible plants.

## Violet root rot

■ **Crops affected** Asparagus, celery and other leafy vegetables, carrot, potato, beetroot, and parsnip.
■ **Symptoms** Plants are yellowed and stunted, but the most characteristic symptom is seen on affected roots, tubers, and rhizomes. Their surfaces are covered in dark purple fungal strands, and this felty mass often has considerable quantities of soil adhering to it. These closely packed threads bear large, velvety black fruiting bodies (sclerotia), which fall off into the soil where they persist. The tissue beneath the fungal mycelium may turn brown and rot; this, in turn, may play host to secondary bacterial rots.
■ **Cause** The fungus *Helicobasidium brebissonii* (syn. *H. purpureum*).This is most prevalent in wet, acid soils, in warm conditions. The velvety black sclerotia persist in the soil for many years.
■ **Control** No effective chemical treatments are available. Lift and burn affected plants, if possible, before sclerotia are shed. Likewise, dispose of any remaining crop plants at the end of the season. Improve soil drainage. Do not grow susceptible plants on the soil again.

## Virus vectors

■ Many viruses that affect plants are spread by certain pests, and these are described as virus vectors. Nearly all of these are sap-feeders and have piercing mouthparts; aphids (*see p.251*) and thrips (*see above*) are common examples. When they insert their mouthparts into virus-infected plants, they pick up some virus particles and transfer them to new host plants when next they feed. Some soil-dwelling eelworms (*see p.255*) also transmit viruses as they feed on plant roots. This is one of the reasons why it is so important to control pests; some virus vectors feed on a wide range of plants and are capable of transmitting more than 100 viruses. Although they may not cause debilitating damage in themselves, the viruses that they spread often do. Moreover, there are no chemical treatments currently available to control viruses. It is best to destroy virused plants by burning, and new plants of the same type should not be grown on the soil that has harboured them.

## Viruses

■ **Crops affected** A wide range.
■ **Symptoms** The most common effects of viruses are stunting and distortion. Distortions may take the form of crinkling, crumpling, curling, or rolling. Leaves and other above-ground parts of plants show various markings, usually yellow, and they take the form of spotting, mottling, mosaic, streaking, or flecking. Virused plants generally crop poorly, if at all, and they often suffer premature death. Some viruses can infect without causing visible symptoms and this is known as latent infection. It is often the case that alternative hosts show no symptoms; cucumber mosaic virus (*see p.254*) for example, may exist in a number of common weeds that act as a source of infection for other plants, even though these plants appear to be perfectly healthy.
■ **Causes** There are many virus species, the majority of which are sole agents of disease. Some, however, infect plants in combination, and plants that are stressed, for whatever reason, may fall prey to several viruses at once. There are several means of transmission, the most common being sap-sucking insect vectors. Whitefly, aphids, thrips, and leafhoppers are a few examples. Eelworms and fungi can also be virus vectors.
In most cases, viral infection is non-persistent, meaning that the virus cannot survive for long outside its host. An insect can acquire a virus after feeding on a plant, but the virus has a window of only a few seconds or minutes during which it must be passed on to another host, otherwise it dies. Other viruses, however, are persistent. The insect may pass it on for hours after feeding and may even carry the virus for rest of its life.
■ Viruses can also be transmitted by handling plants; by grafting (so-called graft-transmissible viruses); by handling tubers, bulbs, and corms; and during routine operations such as pruning, disbudding, or pinching out.
■ **Control** None available. Remove and dispose of affected plants promptly. Wash hands and tools thoroughly after handling infected plants. Do not introduce plants of a similar type onto sites that have previously supported infected plants. Control vectors, and control weeds, which may be alternative hosts. Do not propagate from infected plants. Where possible, choose resistant cultivars and buy plants that are certified as virus-free.

## Walnut blotch

■ **Crops affected** Walnut.
■ **Symptoms** Leaves develop necrotic brown blotches and fall prematurely. Similar blotches appear on the fruits, turning them brown to black.
■ **Cause** The fungus *Gnomonia leptostyla*. It overwinters on fallen leaves.
■ **Control** Gather up and dispose of affected fallen leaves. There are no chemical controls available

## Walnut leaf blight

■ **Crops affected** Walnut.
■ **Symptoms** Small, angular black spots on leaves and leaf stalks. It also similarly affects the fruit.
■ **Cause** The bacterium *xanthomonas arboricola* pv. *juglandis*.
■ **Control** Remove affected leaves as soon as they are detected. There are no chemical controls available.

## Wasps

■ **Crops affected** Ripe, sugar-rich fruits.
■ **Symptoms** Soft inner tissues of fruits are eaten out, eventually creating large hollow cavities. On relatively soft-skinned fruits, wasps are capable of initiating damage; on tougher-skinned ones, such as apples and pears, wasps usually enlarge existing damage caused by bird pecks.
■ **Causes** Various species of social wasp are significant fruit pests: *Vespula germanica* and *V. vulgaris*, and tree-nesting species *Dolichovespula media* and *D. sylvestris*.
■ **Control** Protect ripening fruits by enclosing selected fruit trusses inside muslin bags or old nylon tights. If wasp nests can be located, they can be controlled by using a phenothrin and tetramethrin aerosol spray, or by placing an insecticidal dust, such as bendiocarb, in the nest entrance at dusk when the wasps have stopped flying for the night.

## Waterlogging

■ **Crops affected** Any.
■ **Symptoms** Foliage wilts and yellows; in extreme cases flowers may also wilt. Yellowed leaves fall prematurely. Inspection of the roots may reveal deterioration; the outer skin may peel and can often be stripped easily from the root core.
■ **Causes** Overwatering, excessive rainfall, or poor drainage may all be implicated, singly or together.
■ **Control** Attempt to improve soil conditions and avoid overwatering. On heavy soils, make sure that a large area of soil is lightened by the incorporation of large quantities of grit and bulky, well-rotted organic matter before planting. The application of a foliar feed can help to counteract the effects of slight or temporary waterlogging; it stimulates root production to replace those lost.

**Whiptail of brassicas:** *see* Molybdenum deficiency.
**White rot:** *see* Onion white rot.

## Whiteflies

■ **Crops affected** Brassicas, okra, pepper, sweet potato, tomato, cucurbits, and many other glasshouse fruits and vegetables.
■ **Symptoms** Small insects, about 2mm (1/12in) long, fly up when disturbed from beneath the leaves (*see p.250*). Adults have white wings. They lay their eggs beneath the leaves and these hatch into flat, oval, scale-like nymphs. The final nymphal stage is sometimes called a pupa, and is plumper, often with hairs or waxy white secretions on the upper surface. Both nymphs and adults excrete sticky honeydew, which drops onto the leaves and is host to sooty moulds.
■ **Causes** There are two important pest species: the cabbage whitefly, *Aleyrodes proletella*, and the glasshouse whitefly, *Trialeurodes vaporariorum*, which may infest outdoor plants in warm summers. The cabbage whitefly has several generations over the summer, and overwinters as an adult. The glasshouse whitefly breeds continuously throughout the year under glass, but it will not survive winters in cold areas outdoors.
■ **Control** On brassicas, light infestations can be tolerated. Treat heavy infestations

on brassicas with deltamethrin, lambda-cyhalothrin, fatty acids, or pyrethrum. Several treatments at weekly intervals may be necessary with organic sprays.
Pesticide resistance is a problem with glasshouse whitefly; biological control with a tiny parasitic wasp, *Encarsia formosa*, is often the best remedy under glass. It must be introduced between mid-spring and late summer, when temperatures will be high enough for it. Release the wasp when pest populations are still low; it needs time to breed before it can control whitefly. Sticky yellow traps are effective and useful indicators of rising whitefly populations. Sooty moulds can be wiped off tomato and cucumber fruits with a damp cloth.
*Encarsia* can be used along with fatty acids, which do not affect it. Other pesticides, such as those used for cabbage whitefly (*see above*), are harmful to *Encarsia* and, in any case, may give poor control if a resistant strain is present. Several applications at five-day intervals are needed even for susceptible strains. Thiacloprid can be used on greenhouse aubergines, peppers, and tomatoes.

## White blister

■ **Crops affected** Brassicas, salsify, and scorzonera.
■ **Symptoms** Plants develop white, chalky, blister-like pustules, usually on lower leaf surfaces, with corresponding sunken, yellowish areas above. Tissues distort.
■ **Causes** The fungi *Albugo candida* on brassicas, and *Pustula tragopogonis* on salsify and scorzonera. *A. candida* can persist on hosts such as wallflowers (*Erysimum*), honesty (*Lunaria*), and shepherd's purse (*Capsella bursa-pastoris*), while *P. tragopogonis* affects some members of the daisy family.
■ **Control** Remove all affected plants promptly. Avoid overcrowding and the associated stagnant, humid air around the plants, which encourages fungi to proliferate. When watering, direct water onto the soil, not the plants, to avoid washing spores into the soil. Do not grow alternative host plants nearby. Brussels sprout 'Bridge F1' shows a degree of resistance. There are no chemical controls available for use by the amateur gardener.

## Wind damage

■ **Crops affected** Any.
■ **Symptoms** Leaves appear scorched, and one side of a plant is often more severely affected than the other. Most damage occurs on the side of the prevailing wind. If winds are salt-laden, the damage is exacerbated and the plant may die back or die completely. Where strong winds are persistent, as they often are in coastal areas, for example, trees may develop a lop-sided growth habit; this is known as "krumholtz" or wind-training, where they grow away from the prevailing wind.
■ **Cause** Wind. The effects of wind are made worse if wind tunnels are present (where wind speeds up when funnelled between two walls, for example) or if windbreaks are removed.
■ **Control** Construct a shelter or plant or erect windbreaks (*see pp.12–13*) to filter the wind. Prune out dead stems to prevent secondary infections setting in.

## Winter moth

■ **Crops affected** Tree fruits.
■ **Symptoms** Leaves are bound together with silken threads to form a nest for yellow-green caterpillars with pale lines along their bodies. The caterpillars, up to 25mm (1in) long, eat foliage between bud burst and late spring. They also eat fruit blossoms and make holes in apple fruitlets, which become misshapen as they develop.
■ **Causes** The larvae of the winter moth, *Operophtera brumata*. Adult moths emerge between late autumn and midwinter. Only males are winged; the females have swollen bodies and tiny wings incapable of flight. When the females emerge from pupae in the soil, they crawl up tree trunks to lay eggs on the branches.
■ **Control** Sticky grease bands (*see p.52*), placed around the trunk in mid-autumn, will prevent females from climbing the tree. Newly hatched caterpillars can be controlled by spraying with deltamethrin or lambda-cyhalothrin at bud burst.

## Wireworm

■ **Crops affected** Root vegetables and seedlings, lettuce.
■ **Symptoms** Seedlings are killed and stems are severed just below soil level. Potato tubers and carrots are extensively tunnelled in late summer. Slender, orange-brown, worm-like larvae, up to 25mm (1in) long, with three pairs of short legs near the head end may be found in the soil or in the tubers. They have a small but distinctive protuberance at the rear end of the abdomen.
■ **Causes** The larval stage of click beetles. There are several species, including *Agriotes lineatus*, *A. obscurus*, *A. sputator*, and *Athous haemorrhoidalis*. They occur most commonly in plots that have been newly converted from grassland. If the ground is kept in cultivation, they will decline steadily over a three- or four-year period.
■ **Control** Dig up potato tubers as soon as they mature to reduce damage. There are no chemical controls available to amateur gardeners for the control of wireworms.

## Woolly aphid

■ **Crops affected** Apple.
■ **Symptoms** A woolly, white waxy growth occurs on the bark of apple trees in late spring and summer. It is secreted by blackish-brown aphids. They often cluster around old pruning wounds and cracks or splits in the bark. Later in the summer, they migrate to young branches and cause knobbly swellings to develop. If these galls split in frosty weather, they can form an entry point for canker (*see p.253*).
■ **Cause** A sap-sucking aphid, *Eriosoma lanigerum*. It overwinters as immature nymphs beneath loose bark.
■ **Control** Spray as soon as seen with deltamethrin, lambda-cyhalothrin, or thiacloprid. Heavy infestations are difficult to control.

# INDEX

Page numbers in **bold** indicate main references; *italic* numbers refer to the illustrations

# ACKNOWLEDGMENTS

**Consultants: Plant Problems**
Andrew Halstead (pests)
Beatrice Henricot; Chris Prior (diseases)

**Illustrations** Karen Gavin, artworks
Gill Tomblin, garden plans, page 30

**Index** Hilary Bird

**PUBLISHER'S ACKNOWLEDGMENTS**
**First edition, 2002**
Dorling Kindersley would like to thank all staff at
the RHS for their time and assistance, in particular:
At Vincent Square, Susanne Mitchell, Barbara Haynes
and Karen Wilson.
At Wisley, Jim Arbury and Jim England for their
invaluable guidance during photography; the
ever-patient staff in the garden, including Jonathan
Keyte, Dean Peckett, Anna Stankiewicz-Davies,
Alessandra Valsecchi, and Richard White; Paul
Alexander and Mike Grant for their expert advice.
  Thanks also for the loan of equipment and plants
to: Defenders Ltd; S.E. Marshall & Co. Ltd; Suttons
Seeds; and for horticultural advice to Amanda Denis
at the Citrus Centre, R. Boskovic, T. Sonneveld,
and K.R. Tobutt.

**Photographic models** Jim Arbury, Paul Atkinson,
Murdo Culver, Jim England, Ron Gilkerson,
Jonathan Keyte, Hannah Reid, Anna Stankiewicz-
Davies, Kit Strange, Alessandra Valsecchi

**Editors** Louise Abbott, Alison Copland,
Helen Fewster, Candida Frith-Macdonald, Linden
Hawthorne, Jane Simmonds
**Editorial assistance** Joanna Chisholm; Victoria
Heyworth-Dunne; Letitia Luff; Simon Maughan;
Frank Ritter; Diana Vowles; Fiona Wild
**Designer** Alison Donovan
**Design assistance** Thomas Keene; Antonio Toma
**Managing editor** Anna Kruger
**Managing art editor** Lee Griffiths
**DTP design** Louise Waller
**Media resources** Romaine Werblow
**Picture research** Samantha Nunn

**Revised edition, 2012**
**Picture research** Susie Peachey
**DK Images** Lucy Claxton; Rose Horridge;
Romaine Werblow
**Proof reader** Ella James

**PHOTOGRAPHIC CREDITS**
The publisher would like to thank the following for
their kind permission to reproduce their photographs:
(Key: t=top, b=bottom, r=right, l=left, c=centre,
a=above, f=far)

Defenders Ltd: 52b (all).
DK/Alan Buckingham: 4b, 98, 141 (*Anthriscus;
Satureja*), 148 (*Mespilus; Morus; Prunus armenica*),
250 (*Psila rosae;* bitter pit; magnesium deficiency).

DK/Elaine Hewson: 141(*Foeniculum; Salvia*).
GAP Photos: Elke Borkowski 2c.
Garden Picture Library: Mayer/Le Scanff 11tl;
Mel Watson 205t.
John Glover: 7t, 36bl, 43tc, 46bcr, 46t, 181,
196tc, 204t.
Holt Studios International: 45br, 236b; Nigel
Cattlin 17, 250tr, 250cra, 250cr, 250bc, 250cbl;
Inga Spence 206t.
Hozelock Ltd: 53bl, 54bc.
Andrew Lawson: 151.
Joy Michaud/Sea Spring Photos: 44b, 75c.
Oxford Scientific Films: Bob Gibbons 185.
Photolibrary: Lynn Keddie 29clb; Gary K. Smith
35ftr; Juliette Wade 132ftr.
Photos Horticultural: 32bl, 32bc, 41b, 42br, 48bl,
211b, 226t, 235b, 250tl.
Michael Pollock: 13bc, 13br, 23tl, 39tc, 250bcl,
250bfr.
Harry Smith Collection: 120bl, 177.

All other images © Dorling Kindersley.
For further information see:
**www.dkimages.com**

# VEGETABLE & FRUIT GARDENING